BOOKS BY JOHN O'HARA

Appointment in Samarra
The Doctor's Son and Other Stories
Butterfield 8
Hope of Heaven
Files on Parade
Pal Joey
Pipe Night
Hellbox
A Rage to Live
The Farmers Hotel
Sweet and Sour
Ten North Frederick
A Family Party
Selected Short Stories
From the Terrace
Ourselves to Know
Sermons and Soda Water / A Trilogy
The Girl on the Baggage Truck
Imagine Kissing Pete
We're Friends Again
Five Plays
The Farmers Hotel
The Searching Sun
The Champagne Pool
Veronique
The Way It Was
Assembly
The Big Laugh
The Cape Cod Lighter
Elizabeth Appleton
The Hat on the Bed
The Horse Knows the Way
The Lockwood Concern
My Turn
Waiting for Winter
The Instrument
And Other Stories
The O'Hara Generation

BOOKS BY JOHN O'HARA

Appointment in Samarra
The Doctor's Son and Other Stories
Butterfield 8
Hope of Heaven
Files on Parade
Pal Joey
Pipe Night
Hellbox
A Rage to Live
The Farmers Hotel
Sweet and Sour
Ten North Frederick
A Family Party
Selected Short Stories
From the Terrace
Ourselves to Know
Sermons and Soda-Water: A Trilogy
    The Girl on the Baggage Truck
    Imagine Kissing Pete
    We're Friends Again
Five Plays:
    The Farmers Hotel
    The Searching Sun
    The Champagne Pool
    Veronique
    The Way It Was
Assembly
The Big Laugh
The Cape Cod Lighter
Elizabeth Appleton
The Hat on the Bed
The Horse Knows the Way
The Lockwood Concern
My Turn
Waiting for Winter
The Instrument
And Other Stories
The O'Hara Generation

THE O'HARA GENERATION

THE O'HARA GENERATION

JOHN O'HARA

RANDOM HOUSE / NEW YORK

CONTENTS

CONTENTS

INTRODUCTION

These twenty-two stories were chosen from the nine volumes of John O'Hara's short stories that were published in the thirty-two years from 1935 through 1966. A number of persons had a hand in choosing from the 251 available stories, and the author has approved their selection. It is, I believe, a good well-rounded sampling of the great variety of Mr. O'Hara's talents and an excellent introduction to the imposing body of work of which it represents, by necessity, only a very small fraction.

What would further embellish this book, of course, would be some prefatory remarks by the author, who more than once has been known to make some—to the delight of many readers, but producing in others, especially certain reviewers, foam at the mouth. This time there is no O'Hara foreword, and since part of the editorial plight is doing things the author prefers not to, readers of this book are faced with taking or leaving an introduction, which Mr. O'Hara does not need, by his editor. But I intend to make liberal use of his own forewords to other volumes, and he will thereby make his contribution.

In 1946 *Here's O'Hara*, an omnibus selection from previously published books, was issued, and among its contents were twenty short stories from his first three story volumes. The author consented to do a foreword, and it begins like this:

The contents of this book came out of the author's typewriters (*zip-zip!* just like that) over a period of about fourteen years. . . . Obviously it was too much of a chore, or a word that rhymes with it, for me to go back over those years and pick up the pieces which I would care to put in a book to be called, shyly, Here's O'Hara. The title is not mine, and so I allowed the publishers also to select the stories.

Change the title and extend the period, and it works equally well for the volume before you.

But let no one be misled by that *zip-zip*. That is how they came out of the typewriter, but not the way they went into it. I believe that by the time Mr. O'Hara starts to put a story on paper, it already exists as a fully formed, nearly finished work in his mind, which is where, *zip-zip*, the real work never stops. An example: about five years ago Mr. O'Hara went off to Bermuda for a two-week vacation; it was to be, he said, all rest and relaxation and no work; he wasn't taking along a typewriter. Even so, while he was down there in repose, *The New Yorker* received from Bermuda a new short story, and their letter of acceptance was in his mail when he came back home to work. Later I heard how it had happened: he went to bed one night but couldn't sleep because a story that had been taking shape in his head was suddenly all there, and he had to get up and borrow a typewriter from the hotel office. The next morning the story was sent off. Soon after that, when the manuscript of *The Horse Knows the Way* was delivered to Random House, I had no trouble in identifying the story because it was the only one that was not on the sleazy yellow paper he insists on using under normal circumstances.

The table of contents of *The O'Hara Generation* lists the volume in which each of the stories originally appeared; the dates of these books, also given, are interesting to look at. Four volumes containing 129 stories were published in the thirteen years from 1935 through 1947; none for the next fourteen years. That big gap between *Hellbox* (1947) and *Assembly* (1961) does not reflect, however, a period of complete idleness for Mr. O'Hara, since during those years he published five novels (including his four longest), four novellas, five plays and a book of essays.

Assembly has, besides its twenty-six stories, a brief foreword by the author, which begins:

> All but three or four of these stories were written during the summer of 1960. I wrote most of them in two sittings of about three hours apiece, and it was some of the most joyful writing I have ever done. The pleasure was in finding that after eleven years of not writing short stories, I could begin again and do it better; and the joy was in discovering that at fifty-five, and in spite of aches in spine and tendons, I had an apparently inexhaustible urge to express an unlimited supply of short story ideas.

In the next five years four additional volumes with ninety-six more stories gave a convincing demonstration that Mr. O'Hara had not overestimated either his urge or his supply.

It is equally clear that he was correct in his feeling that he could now "do it better." The value of the earlier stories is not diminished by insisting that the later ones are even better. They tend, on average, to be much longer than the earlier; and while it would be absurd to say that they are better because they are longer, I feel no hesitation in saying that many of them are longer because they are better, that they require their length because of their greater substance and deeper purpose, which the laconic earlier style would not fully convey.

Since the time of Mr. O'Hara's fiftieth birthday in 1955, there has been evident a growing sense of urgency that drove him to produce more in his fifties than he did in the preceding two decades; he has referred to this in a number of his forewords to various volumes, as in the following (*Sermons and Soda-Water*, 1960):

> I want to get it all down on paper while I can. I am now fifty-five years old and I have lived with as well as in the Twentieth Century from its earliest days. The United States in this Century is what I know, and it is my business to write

about it to the best of my ability, with the sometimes special knowledge I have. The Twenties, the Thirties, and the Forties are already history, but I cannot be content to leave their story in the hands of the historians and the editors of picture books. I want to record the way people talked and thought and felt, and to do it with complete honesty and variety. I have done that in these three novellas, within, of course, the limits of my own observations.

This description underestimates his achievement; he has done all that is stipulated here and done it probably better than anybody else, and he has been honored for it, though not enough. Too much of the critical discussion of his work, when favorable, has stressed O'Hara the novelist of manners, the social historian, with the tape-recorder ear for dialogue and the camera eye for detail; this is a true and important part of the picture, but it is not enough. His "special knowledge" is part of his raw material, and his famous dialogue is evidence of his craft, but his power to captivate and to move us is the product of his teeming imagination and broad human understanding.

Though popular approval came to him early and has continued to increase, the kind of recognition his work deserves has been slow in coming, but it is on its way. He is, and has been for a long time, eligible to receive every literary honor that exists for prose fiction, though some are still withheld. He has been ignored or disdained by members of the academic community who should know better, but there are many signs that light is penetrating this darkness and that his work will be studied more and more widely in the universities (if we still have universities). Reviewers will continue to be sharply divided, with a clear majority in the author's favor but with a significant number being clever at what they think is his expense. All serious writers must somehow live with the knowledge that on every publication day an unpredictable number of reviewers will be out there eagerly waiting in the bushes, reshuffling their witticisms. Having more publication days than anyone else, Mr. O'Hara has more experiences of this than most.

I must relate, for the record, one fine episode in the history of literary mugging. *The Horse Knows the Way*, published Thanksgiving Day, 1964, has a short foreword by the author which, admittedly, displays no overfriendly attitude toward critics and reviewers. The last paragraph of the foreword is a single short sentence that was quoted in reviews all across the nation. Here is how two of the most influential took note of it:

> In his Foreword he warns us that this may be his last book of stories for a while, assures us that he makes a nice income from stories, reminds us (reviewers particularly?) that he has the Award of Merit from the American Academy of Arts and Letters, avers that he will push on. "I have work to do, and I am not afraid to do it."
> —*The New York Review of Books*, December 17, 1964

> John O'Hara's foreword . . . is a statement compounded of gratitude and resentment, and culminating in a deceptively simple remark: "I have work to do, and I am not afraid to do it."
> —*New York Times Book Review*, November 29, 1964

What Mr. O'Hara had said, of course, was:

> I have work to do, and I am afraid not to do it.

While I am absolutely certain that the misquotation was not deliberate, the inadvertency does not excuse the act. Both reviewers saw what they wanted to see, what fitted their view of John O'Hara, and each used his misreading to prove his point, completely blind to the fact that the words bear a close familial resemblance to a more famous line: "When I have fears that I may cease to be. . . ."

They are impressive words and deserve to be quoted correctly.

ALBERT ERSKINE

THE O'HARA GENERATION

THE O'HARA GENERATION

THE DOCTOR'S SON

My father came home at four o'clock one morning in the fall of 1918, and plumped down on a couch in the living room. He did not get awake until he heard the noise of us getting breakfast and getting ready to go to school, which had not yet closed down. When he got awake he went out front and shut off the engine of the car, which had been running while he slept, and then he went to bed and stayed, sleeping for nearly two days. Up to that morning he had been going for nearly three days with no more than two hours' sleep at a stretch.

There were two ways to get sleep. At first he would get it by going to his office, locking the rear office door, and stretching out on the floor or on the operating table. He would put a revolver on the floor beside him or in the tray that was bracketed to the operating table. He had to have the revolver, because here and there among the people who would come to his office, there would be a wild man or woman, threatening him, shouting that they would not leave until he left with them, and that if their baby died they would come back and kill him. The revolver, lying on the desk, kept the more violent patients from becoming

3

too violent, but it really did no good so far as my father's sleep was concerned; not even a doctor who had kept going for days on coffee and quinine would use a revolver on an Italian who had just come from a bedroom where the last of five children was being strangled by influenza. So my father, with a great deal of profanity, would make it plain to the Italian that he was not being intimidated, but would go, and go without sleep.

There was one other way of getting sleep. We owned the building in which he had his office, so my father made an arrangement with one of the tenants, a painter and paperhanger, so he could sleep in the room where the man stored rolls of wallpaper. This was a good arrangement, but by the time he had thought of it, my father's strength temporarily gave out and he had to come home and go to bed.

Meanwhile there was his practice, which normally was about forty patients a day, including office calls and operations, but which he had lost count of since the epidemic had become really bad. Ordinarily if he had been ill his practice would have been taken over by one of the young physicians; but now every young doctor was as busy as the older men. Italians who knew me would even ask me to prescribe for their children, simply because I was the son of Mister Doctor Malloy. Young general practitioners, who would have had to depend upon friends of their families and fraternal orders and accidents and gonorrhea for their start, were seeing—hardly more than seeing—more patients in a day than in normal times they could have hoped to see in a month.

The mines closed down almost with the first whiff of influenza. Men who for years had been drilling rock and had chronic miner's asthma never had a chance against the mysterious new disease; and even younger men were keeling over, so the coal companies had to shut down the mines, leaving only maintenance men, such as pump men, in charge. Then the Commonwealth of Pennsylvania closed down the schools and churches, and forbade all congregating. If you wanted an ice cream soda you had to have it put in a cardboard container; you couldn't have it at the fountain in a glass. We were glad when school closed, because it meant a holiday, and the epidemic had touched very few of us. We lived in Gibbsville; it was in the tiny mining villages—"patches"—that the epidemic was felt immediately.

The State stepped in, and when a doctor got sick or exhausted so he literally couldn't hold his head up any longer, they would send a young man from the graduating class of one of the Philadelphia medical schools to take over the older man's practice. This was how Doctor Myers came to our town. I was looking at the pictures of the war in the *Review of Reviews*, my father's favorite magazine, when the doorbell rang and I answered it. The young man looked like the young men who came to our door during the summer selling magazines. He was wearing a short coat with a sheepskin collar, which I recognized as an S. A. T. C. issue coat.

"Is this Doctor Malloy's residence?" he said.

"Yes."

"Well, I'm Mr. Myers from the University."

"Oh," I said. "My father's expecting you." I told my father, and he said: "Well, why didn't you bring him right up?"

Doctor Myers went to my father's bedroom and they talked, and then the maid told me my father wanted to speak to me. When I went to the bedroom I could see my father and Doctor Myers were getting along nicely. That was natural: my father and Doctor Myers were University men, which meant the University of Pennsylvania; and University men shared a contempt for men who had studied at Hahnemann or Jefferson or Medico-Chi. Myers was not an M.D., but my father called him Doctor, and as I had been brought up to tip my hat to a doctor as I did to a priest, I called him Doctor too, although Doctor Myers made me feel like a lumberjack; I was so much bigger and obviously stronger than he. I was fifteen years old.

"Doctor Myers, this is my boy James," my father said, and without waiting for either of us to acknowledge the introduction, he went on: "Doctor Myers will be taking over my practice for the time being and you're to help him. Take him down to Hendricks' drugstore and introduce him to Mr. Hendricks. Go over the names of our patients and help him arrange some kind of a schedule. Doctor Myers doesn't drive a car, you'll drive for him. Now your mother and I think the rest of the children ought to be on the farm, so you take them there in the big Buick and then bring it back and have it overhauled. Leave the little Buick where it is, and you use the Ford. You'll understand, Doctor, when you see our roads. If you want any money your mother'll give it to you. And no cigarettes, d'you understand?" Then he handed Doctor Myers a batch of prescription blanks, upon which were lists of patients to be seen, and said good-bye and lay back on his pillow for more sleep.

Doctor Myers was almost tiny, and that was the reason I could forgive him for not being in the Army. His hair was so light that you could hardly see his little mustache. In conversation between sentences his nostrils would twitch and like all doctors he had acquired a posed gesture which was becoming habitual. His was to stroke the skin in front of his right ear with his forefinger. He did that now downstairs in the hall. "Well . . . I'll just take a walk back to the hotel and wait till you get back from the farm. That suit you, James?" It did, and he left and I performed the various chores my father had ordered, and then I went to the hotel in the Ford and picked up Doctor Myers.

He was catlike and dignified when he jumped in the car. "Well, here's a list of names. Where do you think we ought to go first? Here's a couple of prescription blanks with only four names apiece. Let's clean them up first."

"Well, I don't know about that, Doctor. Each one of those names means at least twenty patients. For instance, Kelly's. That's a saloon, and there'll be a lot of people waiting. They all meet there and wait for my father. Maybe we'd better go to some single calls first."

"O.K., James. Here's a list." He handed it to me. "Oh, your father said something about going to Collieryville to see a family named Evans."

I laughed. "Which Evans? There's seventy-five thousand Evanses in Collieryville. Evan Evans. William W. Evans. Davis W. Evans. Davis W. Evans, Junior. David Evans?"

"David Evans sounds like it. The way your father spoke they were particular friends of his."

6

"David Evans," I said. "Well—he didn't say who's sick there, did he?"

"No. I don't think anybody. He just suggested we drop in to see if they're all well."

I was relieved, because I was in love with Edith Evans. She was nearly two years older than I, but I liked girls a little older. I looked at his list and said: "I think the best idea is to go there first and then go around and see some of the single cases in Collieryville." He was ready to do anything I suggested. He was affable and trying to make me feel that we were pals, but I could tell he was nervous, and I had sense enough to know that he had better look at some flu before tackling one of those groups at the saloons.

We drove to Collieryville to the David Evans home. Mr. Evans was district superintendent of one of the largest mining corporations, and therefore Collieryville's third citizen. He would not be there all the time, because he was a good man and due for promotion to a bigger district, but so long as he was there he was ranked with the leading doctor and the leading lawyer. After him came the Irish priest, the cashier of the larger bank (of which the doctor or the lawyer or the superintendent of the mines is president), the brewer, and the leading merchant. David Evans had been born in Collieryville, the son of a superintendent, and was popular, a thirty-second degree Mason, a graduate of Lehigh, and a friend of my father's. They would see each other less than ten times a year, but they would go hunting rabbit and quail and pheasant together every autumn and always exchanged expensive Christmas gifts. When my mother had large parties she would invite Mrs. Evans, but the two women were not close friends. Mrs. Evans was a Collieryville girl, half Polish, and my mother had gone to an expensive school and spoke French, and played bridge long before Mrs. Evans had learned to play "500." The Evanses had two children: Edith, my girl, and Rebecca, who was about five.

The Evans Cadillac, which was owned by the coal company, was standing in front of the Evans house, which also was owned by the coal company. I called to the driver, who was sitting behind the steering wheel, hunched up in a sheepskin coat and with a checkered cap pulled down over his eyes. "What's the matter, Pete?" I called. "Can't the company get rid of that old Caddy?"

"Go on wid you," said Pete. "What's the wrong wid the doctorin' business? I notice Mike Malloy ain't got nothin' better than Buicks."

"I'll have you fired, you round-headed son of a so and so," I said. "Where's the big lad?"

"Up Mike's. Where'd you t'ink he is?"

I parked the Ford and Doctor Myers and I went to the door and were let in by the pretty Polish maid. Mr. Evans came out of his den, wearing a raccoon coat and carrying his hat. I introduced Doctor Myers. "How do you do, sir," he said. "Doctor Malloy just asked me to stop in and see if everything was all right with your family."

"Oh, fine," said Mr. Evans. "Tell the dad that was very thoughtful, James, and thank you too, Doctor. We're all O.K. here, thank the Lord, but while you're here I'd like to have you meet Mrs. Evans. Adele!"

Mrs. Evans called from upstairs that she would be right down. While we waited in the den Mr. Evans offered Doctor Myers a cigar, which was declined. Doctor Myers, I could see, preferred to sit, because Mr. Evans was so large that he had to look up to him. While Mr. Evans questioned him about his knowledge of the anthracite region, Doctor Myers spoke with a barely discernible pleasant hostility which was lost on Mr. Evans, the simplest of men. Mrs. Evans appeared in a housedress. She looked at me shyly, as she always did. She always embarrassed me, because when I went in a room where she was sitting she would rise to shake hands, and I would feel like telling her to sit down. She was in her middle thirties and still pretty, with rosy cheeks and pale blue eyes and nothing "foreign"-looking about her except her high cheekbones and the lines of her eyebrows, which looked as though they had been drawn with crayon. She shook hands with Doctor Myers and then clasped her hands in front of her and looked at Mr. Evans when he spoke, and then at Doctor Myers and then at me, smiling and hanging on Mr. Evans' words. He was used to that. He gave her a half-smile without looking at her and suggested we come back for dinner, which in Collieryville was at noon. Doctor Myers asked me if we would be in Collieryville at that time, and I said we would, so we accepted his invitation. Mr. Evans said: "That's fine. Sorry I won't be here, but I have to go to Wilkes-Barre right away." He looked at his watch. "By George! By now I ought to be halfway there." He grabbed his hat and kissed his wife and left.

When he had gone Mrs. Evans glanced at me and smiled and then said: "Edith will be glad to see you, James."

"Oh, I'll bet she will," I said. "Where's she been keeping herself anyway?"

"Oh, around the house. She's my eldest," she said to Doctor Myers. "Seventeen."

"Seventeen?" he repeated. "You have a daughter seventeen? I can hardly believe it, Mrs. Evans. Nobody would ever think you had a daughter seventeen." His voice was a polite protest, but there was nothing protesting in what he saw in Mrs. Evans. I looked at her myself now, thinking of her for the first time as something besides Edith's mother . . . No, I couldn't see her. We left to make some calls, promising to be back at twelve-thirty.

Our first call was on a family named Loughran, who lived in a neat two-story house near the Collieryville railroad station. Doctor Myers went in. He came out in less than two minutes, followed by Mr. Loughran. Loughran walked over to me. "You," he said. "Ain't we good enough for your dad no more? What for kind of a thing is this he does be sending us?"

"My father is sick in bed, just like everybody else, Mr. Loughran. This is the doctor that is taking all his calls till he gets better."

"It is, is it? So that's what we get, and doctorin' with Mike Malloy sincet he come from college, and always paid the day after payday. Well, young man, take this back to Mike Malloy. You tell him for me if my woman pulls through it'll be no thanks to him. And if she don't pull through, and dies, I'll come right down to your old man's office and kill him wid a rock. Now you and this one get the hell outa here before I lose me patience."

9

We drove away. The other calls we made were less difficult, although I noticed that when he was leaving one or two houses the people, who were accustomed to my father's quick, brusque calls, would stare at Doctor Myers' back. He stayed too long, and probably was too sympathetic. We returned to the Evans home.

Mrs. Evans had changed her dress to one that I thought was a little too dressy for the occasion. She asked us if we wanted "a little wine," which we didn't, and Doctor Myers was walking around with his hands in his trousers pockets, telling Mrs. Evans what a comfortable place this was, when Edith appeared. I loved Edith, but the only times I ever saw her were at dancing school, to which she would come every Saturday afternoon. She was quite small, but long since her legs had begun to take shape and she had breasts. It was her father, I guess, who would not let her put her hair up; she often told me he was very strict and I knew that he was making her stay in Collieryville High School a year longer than was necessary because he thought her too young to go away. Edith called me Jimmy—one of the few who did. When we danced together at dancing school she scarcely spoke at all. I suspected her of regarding me as very young. All the little kids at dancing school called me James, and the oldest girls called me sarcastic. "James Malloy," they would say, "you think you're sarcastic. You think you're clever, but you're not. I consider the source of that remark." The remark might be that I had heard that Wallace Reid was waiting for that girl to grow up—and so was I. But I never said things like that to Edith. I would say: "How's everything out in the metropolis of Collieryville?" and she would say they were all right. It was no use trying to be sarcastic or clever with Edith, and no use trying to be romantic. One time I offered her the carnation that we had to wear at dancing school, and she refused it because the pin might tear her dress. It was useless to try to be dirty with her; there was no novelty in it for a girl who had gone to Collieryville High. I told her one story, and she said her grandmother fell out of the cradle laughing at that one.

When Edith came in she took a quick look at Doctor Myers, which made me slightly jealous. He turned and smiled at her, and his nostrils began to twitch. Mrs. Evans rubbed her hands together nervously, and it was plain to see that she was not sure how to introduce Doctor Myers. Before she had a chance to make any mistakes I shook hands with Edith and she said, "Oh, hello, Jimmy," in a very offhand way, and I said; "Edith, this is Doctor Myers."

"How do you do?" said Edith.

"How are you?" said the doctor.

"Oh, very well, thank you," Edith said, and realized that it wasn't quite the thing to say.

"Well," said Mrs. Evans. "I don't know if you gentlemen want to wash up. Jimmy, you know where the bathroom is." It was the first time she had called me Jimmy. I glanced at her curiously and then the doctor and I went to wash our hands. Upstairs he said: "That your girl, James?"

"Oh, no," I said. "We're good friends. She isn't that kind."

"What kind? I didn't mean anything." He was amused.

"Well, I didn't know what you meant."

"Edith certainly looks like her mother," he said.

"Oh, I don't think so," I said, not really giving it a thought, but I was annoyed by the idea of talking about Edith in the bathroom. We came downstairs.

Dinner was a typical meal of that part of the country: sauerkraut and pork and some stuff called nep, which was nothing but dough, and mashed potatoes and lima beans, coffee, tea, and two kinds of pie, and you were expected to take both kinds. It was a meal I liked, and I ate a lot. Mrs. Evans got some courage from somewhere and was now talkative, now quiet, addressing most of her remarks to Doctor Myers and then turning to me. Edith kept looking at her and then turning to the doctor. She paid no attention to me except when I had something to say. Rebecca, whose table manners were being neglected, had nothing to contribute except to stick out her plate and say: "More mash potatoes with butter on."

"Say please," said Edith, but Rebecca only looked at her with the scornful blankness of five.

After dinner we went to the den and Doctor Myers and I smoked. I noticed he did not sit down; he was actually a little taller than Edith, and just about the same height as her mother.

He walked around the room, standing in front of enlarged snap-shots of long-deceased setter dogs, one of which my father had given Mr. Evans. Edith watched him and her mother and said nothing, but just before we were getting ready to leave, Mrs. Evans caught Edith staring at her and they exchanged mysterious glances. Edith looked defiant and Mrs. Evans seemed puzzled and somehow alarmed. I could not figure it out.

In the afternoon Doctor Myers decided he would like to go to one of the patches where the practice of medicine was wholesale, so I suggested Kelly's. Kelly's was the only saloon in a patch of about one hundred families, mostly Irish, and all except one family were Catholics. In the spring they have processions in honor of the Blessed Virgin at Kelly's patch, and a priest carries the Blessed Sacrament the length of the patch, in the open air, to the public school grounds, where they hold Benediction. The houses are older and stauncher than in most patches, and they look like pictures of Ireland, except that there are no thatched roofs. Most patches were simply unbroken rows of company houses, made of slatty wood, but Kelly's had more ground between the houses and grass for the goats and cows to feed on, and the houses had plastered walls. Kelly's saloon was frequented by the whole patch because it was the postoffice substation, and it had a good reputation. For many years it had the only telephone in the patch.

Mr. Kelly was standing on the stoop in front of the saloon when I swung the Ford around. He took his pipe out of his mouth when he recognized the Ford, and then frowned slightly when he saw that my father was not with me. He came to my side of the car. "Where's the dad? Does he be down wid it now himself?"

"No," I said. "He's just all tired out and is getting some sleep. This is Doctor Myers that's taking his place till he gets better."

Mr. Kelly spat some tobacco juice on the ground and took a wad of tobacco out of his mouth. He was a white-haired, sickly man of middle age. "I'm glad to make your acquaintance," he said.

"How do you do, sir?" said Doctor Myers.

"I guess James here told you what to be expecting?"

"Well, more or less," said Doctor Myers. "Nice country out here. This is the nicest I've seen."

"Yes, all right I guess, but there does be a lot of sickness now. I guess you better wait a minute here till I have a few words with them inside there. I have to keep them orderly, y'understand."

He went in and we could hear his loud voice: ". . . young Malloy said his dad is seriously ill . . . great expense out of his own pocket secured a famous young specialist from Philadelphee so as to not have the people of the patch without a medical man . . . And any lug of a lunkhead that don't stay in line will have me to answer to . . ." Mr. Kelly then made the people line up and he came to the door and asked Doctor Myers to step in.

There were about thirty women in the saloon as Mr. Kelly guided Doctor Myers to an oilcloth-covered table. One Irishman took a contemptuous look at Doctor Myers and said, "Jesus, Mary and Joseph," and walked out, sneering at me before he closed the door. The others probably doubted that the doctor was a famous specialist, but they had not had a doctor in two or three days. Two others left quietly but the rest remained. "I guess we're ready, Mr. Kelly," said Doctor Myers.

Most of the people were Irish, but there were a few Hunkies in the patch, although not enough to warrant Mr. Kelly's learning any of their languages as the Irish had had to do in certain other patches. It was easy enough to deal with the Irish: a woman would come to the table and describe for Doctor Myers the symptoms of her sick man and kids in language that was painfully polite. My father had trained them to use terms like "bowel movement" instead of those that came more quickly to mind. After a few such encounters and wasting a lot of time, Doctor Myers more or less got the swing of prescribing for absent patients. I stood leaning against the bar, taking down the names of patients I didn't know by sight, and wishing I could have a cigarette, but that was out of the question because Mr. Kelly did not approve of cigarettes and might have told my father. I was standing there when the first of the Hunkie women had her turn. She was a worried-looking woman who even I could see was pregnant and had been many times before, judging by her body. She had on a white knitted cap and a black silk shirtwaist—noth-

13

ing underneath—and a nondescript skirt. She was wearing a man's overcoat and a pair of Pacs, which are short rubber boots that men wear in the mines. When Doctor Myers spoke to her she became voluble in her own tongue. Mr. Kelly interrupted: "Wait a minute, wait a minute," he said. "You sick?"

"No, no. No me sick. Man sick." She lapsed again into her own language.

"She has a kid can speak English," said Mr. Kelly. "Hey, you. Leetle girl Mary, you daughter, her sick?" He made so-high with his hand. The woman caught on.

"Mary. Sick. Yah, Mary sick." She beamed.

Mr. Kelly looked at the line of patients and spoke to a woman. "Mame," he said. "You live near this lady. How many has she got sick?"

Mame said: "Well, there's the man for one. Dyin' from the way they was carryin' on yesterday and the day before. I ain't seen none of the kids. There's four little girls and they ain't been out of the house for a couple of days. And no wonder they're sick, runnin' around wild widout no—"

"Never mind about that, now," said Mr. Kelly. "I guess, Doctor, the only thing for you to do is go to this woman's house and take a look at them."

The woman Mame said: "To be sure, and ain't that nice? Dya hear that, everybody! Payin' a personal visit to the likes of that but the decent people take what they get. A fine how-do-ya-do."

"You'll take what you get in the shape of a puck in the nose," said Mr. Kelly. "A fine way you do be talkin' wid the poor dumb Hunkie not knowing how to talk good enough to say what's the matter wid her gang. So keep your two cents out of this, Mamie Brannigan, and get back into line."

Mamie made a noise with her mouth, but she got back into line. Doctor Myers got through the rest pretty well, except for another Hunkie who spoke some English but knew no euphemisms. Mr. Kelly finally told her to use monosyllables, which embarrassed Doctor Myers because there were some Irishwomen still in line. But "We can't be wasting no time on politeness," said Mr. Kelly. "This here's a doctor's office now." Finally all the patients except the Hunkie woman were seen to.

Mr. Kelly said: "Well, Doctor, bein's this is your first visit here you gotta take a little something on the house. Would you care for a brandy?"

"Why, yes, that'd be fine," said the doctor.

"James, what about you? A sass?"

"Yes, thank you," I said. A sass was a sarsaparilla.

Mr. Kelly opened a closet at the back of the bar and brought out a bottle. He set it on the bar and told the doctor to help himself. The doctor poured himself a drink and Mr. Kelly poured one and handed it to the Hunkie woman. "There y'are, Mary," he said. "Put hair on your chest." He winked at the doctor.

"Not joining us, Mr. Kelly?" said the doctor.

Mr. Kelly smiled. "Ask James there. No, I never drink a drop. Handle too much of it. Why, if I took a short beer every time I was asked to, I'd be drunk three-quarters of the time. And another advantage is when this here Pro'bition goes into effect I won't miss it. Except financially. Well, I'll take a bottle of temperance just to be sociable." He opened a bottle of ginger ale and took half a glassful. The Hunkie woman raised her glass and said something that sounded more like a prayer than a toast, and put her mouth around the mouth of the glass and drank. She was happy and grateful. Doctor Myers wanted to buy another round, but Mr. Kelly said his money was no good there that day; if he wanted another drink he was to help himself. The doctor did not want another, but he said he would like to buy one for the Hunkie woman, and Mr. Kelly permitted him to pay for it, then we said good-bye to Mr. Kelly and departed, the Hunkie woman getting in the car timidly, but once in the car her bottom was so large that the doctor had to stand on the running board until we reached the house.

A herd of goats in various stages of parturition gave us the razz when we stopped at the house. The ground around the house had a goaty odor because the wire which was supposed to keep them out was torn in several places. The yard was full of old wash boilers and rubber boots, tin cans and the framework of an abandoned baby carriage. The house was a one-and-a-half story building. We walked around to the back door, as the front door is reserved for the use of the priest when he comes on sick calls.

The Hunkie woman seemed happier and encouraged, and prattled away as we followed her into the house, the doctor carefully picking his way through stuff in the yard.

The woman hung up her coat and hat on a couple of pegs on the kitchen wall, from which also hung a lunch can and a tin coffee bottle, the can suspended on a thick black strap, and the bottle on a braided black cord. A miner's cap with a safety lamp and a dozen buttons of the United Mine Workers of America was on another peg, and in a pile on the floor were dirty overalls and jumper and shirt. The woman sat down on a backless kitchen chair and hurriedly removed her boots, which left her barefoot. There was an awful stink of cabbage and dirty feet in the house, and I began to feel nauseated as I watched the woman flopping around, putting a kettle on the stove and starting the fire, which she indicated she wanted to do before going to look at the sick. Her bosom swung to and fro and her large hips jounced up and down, and the doctor smirked at these things, knowing that I was watching, but not knowing that I was trying to think of the skinniest girl I knew, and in the presence of so much woman I was sorry for all past thoughts or desires. Finally the woman led the way to the front of the house. In one of the two front rooms was an old-fashioned bed. The windows were curtained, but when our eyes became accustomed to the darkness we could see four children lying on the bed. The youngest and the oldest were lying together. The oldest, a girl about five years old, was only half covered by the torn quilt that covered the others. The baby coughed as we came in. The other two were sound asleep. The half-covered little girl got awake, or opened her eyes and looked at the ceiling. She had a half-sneering look about her nose and mouth, and her eyes were expressionless. Doctor Myers leaned over her and so did her mother, speaking to the girl, but the girl apparently made no sense even in the Hunkie language. She sounded as though she were trying to clear her throat of phlegm. The doctor turned to me and said dramatically: "James, take this woman out and get her to boil more water, and go out to the car and get your father's instrument case." I grabbed the woman's arm and pulled her to the kitchen and made signs for her to boil the water, then I went out to the Ford and wrestled with the lid of the rear compartment, wondering what the hell Myers wanted with the instrument case, wondering whether he himself knew what he wanted with it. At last I yanked the lid open and was walking back with the leather case in my hand when I heard a loud scream. It sounded more deliberate than wild, it started so low and suddenly went so high. I hurried back to the bedroom and saw Doctor Myers trying to pull the heavy woman away from her daughter. He was not strong enough for her, but he kept pulling and there were tears in his eyes: "Come away, God damn it! Come away from her, you God-damn fool!" He turned to me for help and said: "Oh, Jesus, James, this is awful. The little girl just died. Keep away from her. She has diphtheria!"

"I couldn't open the back of the car," I said.

"Oh, it wasn't your fault. Even a tracheotomy wouldn't have saved her, the poor little thing. But we've got to do something for these others. The baby has plenty of spots, and I haven't even looked at the other two." The other two had been awakened by their mother's screams and were sitting up and crying, not very loud. The woman had the dead girl in her arms. She did not need the English language to know that the child was dead. She was rocking her back and forth and kissing her and looking up at us with fat streams of tears running from her eyes. She would stop crying for a second, but would start again, crying with her mouth open and the tears, unheeded, sliding in over her upper lip.

Doctor Myers took some coins from his pocket and tried to make friends with the in-between kids, but they did not know what money was, so I left him to go in to see how the man was. I walked across the hall to the other bedroom and pulled up the curtains. The man was lying in his underwear; gaunt, bearded, and dead.

I knew he was dead, but I said: "Hyuh, John, hyuh." The sound of my voice made me feel silly, then sacrilegious, and then I had to vomit. I had seen men brought in from railroad wrecks and mine explosions and other violent-accident cases, but I had been prepared for them if only by the sound of an ambulance bell. This was different. Doctor Myers heard me being sick and came in. I was crying. He took a few seconds to see that the man was dead and then he took me by the arm and said: "That's all right, kid. Come out in the air." He led me outside into the cold afternoon and I felt better and hungry.

He let go of my arm. "Listen," he said. "As soon as you feel well enough, take the car and go to the hospital. The first thing you do there is to get them to give you twenty thousand units of antitoxin, and while you're doing that tell them to send an ambulance out here right away. Don't go near anybody if you can help it except a doctor." He paused. "You'd better find out about an undertaker."

"You'll need more than twenty thousand units of antitoxin," I said. I had had that much in my own back when I was eight years old.

"Oh, no. You didn't understand me. The antitoxin's for you. You tell whoever's in charge at the hospital how many are sick out here, and they'll know what to send."

"What about you?"

"Oh, I'll stay here and go back in the ambulance. Don't worry about me. I want to stay here and do what I can for these kids." I suddenly had a lot of respect for him. I got into the Ford and drove away. Doctors' cars carried cardboard signs which said By Order State Department of Health, which gave them the right to break speed laws, and I broke them on my way to the hospital. I pulled in at the porte-cochère and met Doctor Kleiber, a friend of my father's, and told him everything. He gave me antitoxin. He smiled when I mentioned getting an undertaker. "Lucky if they get a wooden rough box, even, James. These people aren't patients of Daddy's, are they, James?"

"No."

"Well then, I guess maybe we have to send an Army doctor. I'm full up so I haven't a minute except for Daddy's patients. Now go home and I'll take care of everything. You'll be stiff in the back and you want to rest. Good-bye now." So I drove home and went to bed.

I was stiff the next morning from the antitoxin, but it had not been so bad as the other time I had taken it, and I was able to pick up Doctor Myers at the hotel. "I feel pretty damn useless, not being able to drive a car," he said. "But I never had much chance to learn. My mother never had enough money to get one. You know that joke: we can't afford a Ford."

"Oh, well," I said, "in Philadelphia you don't need one. They're a nuisance in the city."

"All the same I'd like to have one. I guess I'll have to when I start practicing. Well, where to first?" We outlined a schedule, and for the next couple of days we were on the go almost continually. We hardly noticed how the character of the region was changed. There was little traffic in the streets, but the few cars tore madly. Most of them were Cadillacs: black, company-owned Cadillacs which were at the disposal of young men like Doctor Myers and the two drunken Gibbsville doctors who did not own cars; and gray Cadillacs from the USAAC base in Allentown, which took officers of the Army Medical Corps around to the emergency hospitals. At night the officers would use the cars for their fun, and there were a few scandals. One of my friends, a Boy Scout who was acting as errand boy—"courier," he called himself—at one of the hospitals, swore he witnessed an entire assignation between an Army major and a local girl who was a clerk in the hospital office. One officer was rumored to be psychopathic and had to be sent elsewhere. Opinion among us boys was divided: some said he was taken away and shot, some said he was sent to Leavenworth, others said he was dishonorably discharged. The ambulances were being driven by members of the militia, who wore uniforms resembling those of the marine corps. The militia was made up of young men who were exempt from active service. They had to make one ambulance driver give up his job, because he would drive as fast as the ambulance would go even when he was only going to a drugstore for a carton of soap. Another volunteer driver made so much noise with the ambulance bell that the sick persons inside would be worse off than if they had walked. The women of wealth who could drive their own cars drove them, fetching and carrying blankets and cots, towels and cotton, but their husbands made some of the women stop because of the dangers of influenza and Army medical officers. Mrs. Barlow, the leader of society, did not stop, and her husband knew better than to try to insist. She was charming and stylish and looked very English in her Red Cross canteen division uniform. She assumed charge of the emergency hospital in the armory and bossed the Catholic sisters and the graduate nurses around and made them like it. Her husband gave money and continued to ride a sorrel hunter about the country-side. The rector of the Second Presbyterian Church appeared before the Board of Health and demanded that the nuns be taken out of the hospitals on the ground that they were baptizing men and women who were about to die, without ascertaining whether they were Catholics or Protestants. The *Standard* had a story on the front page which accused unnamed undertakers of profiteering on "rough boxes," charging as much for pine board boxes as they had for mahogany caskets before the epidemic.

Doctor Myers at first wore a mask over his nose and mouth when making calls, and so did I, but the gauze stuck to my lips and I stopped wearing it and so did the doctor. It was too much of a nuisance to put them on and take them off every time we would go to a place like Kelly's, and also it was rather insulting to walk in on a group of people with a mask on your face when nobody in the group was wearing one. I was very healthy and was always glad to go in with the doctor because it gave me something to do. Of course I could have cleaned spark plugs or shot some air into the tires while waiting for the doctor, but I hated to monkey around the car almost as much as I liked to drive it.

In a few days Doctor Myers had begun to acquire some standing among the patients, and he became more confident. One time after coming from my father's bedroom he got in the car with some prescriptions and we started out. To himself he said, looking up from a prescription: "Digitalis . . . now I wonder?" I turned suddenly, because it was the first time in my life I had heard anyone criticize a prescription of my father's. "Oh, I'm sorry, Jimmy," he said.

"You better not ever let him hear you say anything about his prescriptions."

"Yes, I know. He doesn't want anyone to argue with him. He doesn't think I'm seeing as many people as I should."

"What does he expect?" I said.

"Oh, he isn't unreasonable, but he doesn't want his patients to think he's neglecting them. By the way, he wants us to stop in at the Evanses in Collieryville. The David Evanses. Mrs. Evans phoned and said their maid is sick."

"That's O.K. with me," I said.

"I thought it would be," he said.

Collieryville seemed strange with the streets so deserted as on some new kind of holiday. The mines did not work on holy days of obligation, and the miners would get dressed and stand around in front of poolrooms and saloons, but now they were not standing around, and there was none of the activity of a working day, when coal wagons and trucks rumble through the town, and ten-horse teams, guided by the shouted "gee" and "haw" of the driver, would pull loads of timber through the streets on the way to the mines. Collieryville, a town of about four thousand persons, was quiet as though the people were afraid to come out in the cold November gray.

We were driving along the main street when I saw Edith. She was coming out of the P. O. S. of A. Hall, which was a poolroom on the first floor and had lodge rooms on the two upper stories. It was being used as an emergency hospital. I pulled up at the curb and called to Edith. "Come on, I'll give you a ride home," I said.

"Can't. I have to get some things at the drugstore," she said.

"Well, we're going to your house anyway. I'll see you there," I said.

We drove to the Evans house and I told the doctor I would wait outside until Edith came. She appeared in about five minutes and I told her to sit in the car and talk to me. She said she would.

"Well, I'm a nurse, Jimmy," she said.

"Yes, you are," I said scornfully. "That's probably how your maid got sick."

"What!"

"Why, you hanging around at the P. O. S. of A. Hall is probably the way your maid got sick. You probably brought home the flu—"

21

"Oh, my God!" she said. She was nervous and pale. She suddenly jumped out of the car and I followed her. She swung open the front door and ran toward the kitchen, and I was glad she did; for although I followed her to the kitchen, I caught a glimpse of Mrs. Evans and Doctor Myers in Mr. Evans' den. Through the half-closed doors I could see they were kissing.

I didn't stop, I know, although I felt that I had slowed up. I followed Edith into the kitchen and saw that she was half crying, shaking her hands up and down. I couldn't tell whether she had seen what I had seen, but something was wrong that she knew about. I blurted out, "Don't go in your father's den," and was immediately sorry I had said it; but then I saw that she had guessed. She looked weak and took hold of my arms; not looking at me, not even speaking to me, she said: "Oh, my God, now it's him. Oh, why didn't I come home with you? Sarah isn't sick at all. That was just an excuse to get that Myers to come here." She bit her lip and squeezed my arms. "Jimmy, you mustn't ever let on. Promise me."

"I give you my word of honor," I said. "God can strike me dead if I ever say anything."

Edith kissed me, then she called out: "Hey, where is everybody?" She whispered to me: "Pretend you're chasing me like as if I pulled your necktie."

"Let go!" I yelled, as loud as I could. Then we left the kitchen, and Edith would pull my necktie at every step.

Mrs. Evans came out of the den. "Here, what's going on here?"

"I'm after your daughter for pulling my tie," I said.

"Now, Edith, be a good girl and don't fight with James. I don't understand what's the matter with you two. You usedn't to ever fight, and now you fight like cats and dogs. You oughtn't to. It's not nice."

"Oh—" Edith said, and then she burst into tears and went upstairs.

I was genuinely surprised, and said: "I'm sorry, Mrs. Evans, we were only fooling."

"Oh, it's not your fault, James. She feels nervous anyhow and I guess the running was too much for her." She looked at the doctor as if to imply that it was something he would understand.

"I guess I'll go out and sit in the car," I said.

"I'll be right out," said the doctor.

I sat in the car and smoked, now and then looking at the second floor window where I knew Edith's room was, but Edith did not come to the window and in about twenty minutes the doctor came out.

"The maid wasn't sick after all," he said. "It was Mrs. Evans. She had a slight cold but she didn't want to worry your father. I guess she thought if she said she was sick, your father'd come out himself."

"Uh-huh," I said. "Where to now?"

"Oh, that Polish saloon out near the big coal banks."

"You mean Wisniewski's," I said.

Doctor Myers must have known I suspected him, and he might even have suspected that I had seen him kissing Mrs. Evans. I was not very good at hiding my likes and dislikes, and I began to dislike him, but I tried not to show it. I didn't care, for he might have told my father I was unsatisfactory, and my father would have given me hell. Or if I had told my father what I'd seen, he'd have given Doctor Myers a terrible beating. My father never drank or smoked, and he was a good, savage amateur boxer, with no scruples against punching anyone smaller than himself. Less than a year before all this took place my father had been stopped by a traffic policeman while he was hurrying to an "OBS." The policeman knew my father's car, and could have guessed why he was in a hurry, but he stopped him. My father got out of the car, walked to the front of it, and in the middle of a fairly busy intersection he took a crack at the policeman and broke his jaw. Then he got back and drove around the unconscious policeman and on to the confinement case. It cost my father nearly a thousand dollars, and the policeman's friends and my father's enemies said: "God damn Mike Malloy, he ought to be put in jail." But my father was a staunch Republican and he got away with it.

I thought of this now and I thought of what my father would have done to Doctor Myers if he found out. Not only would he have beaten him up, but I am sure he would have used his influence at the University to keep Myers from getting his degree.

So I hid, as well as I could, my dislike for Doctor Myers, and the next day, when we stopped at my home, I was glad I did. My father had invented a signal system to save time. Whenever there was a white slip stuck in the window at home or at the office, that meant he was to stop and pick up a message. This day the message in the window read: "Mrs. David Evans, Collieryville."

Doctor Myers looked at it and showed it to me. "Well, on to Collieryville," he said.

"O.K., but would you mind waiting a second? I want to see my mother."

He was slightly suspicious. "You don't need any money, do you? I have some."

"No, just wanted to see if she would get my father to let me have the car tonight." So I went in and telephoned to the Evanses. I got Edith on the phone and told her that her mother had sent for Doctor Myers.

"I know," she said. "I knew she would. She didn't get up this morning, and she's faking sick."

"Well, when we get there you go upstairs with the doctor, and if he wants you to leave the bedroom, you'll have to leave, but tell your mother you'll be right outside, see?"

"O.K.," said Edith.

I returned to the car. "How'd you make out?" said Doctor Myers.

"She thinks she can get him to let me have it," I said, meaning that my father would let me have the car.

When we arrived at the Evans house I had an inspiration. I didn't want him to suspect that we had any plan in regard to him, so I told him I was going in with him to apologize to Edith for our fight of the day before. There was the chance that Edith would fail to follow my advice and would come downstairs, but there was the equally good chance that she would stay upstairs.

The plan worked. In some respects Edith was dumb, but not in this. Doctor Myers stayed upstairs scarcely five minutes, but it was another five before Edith came down. Doctor Myers had gone out to wait in the Ford.

Edith appeared. "Oh, Jimmy, you're so nice to me, and I'm often mean to you. Why is that?"

"Because I love you." I kissed her and she kissed me.

"Listen, if my dad ever finds this out he'll kill her. It's funny, you and me. I mean if you ever told me a dirty story, like about you know—people—"

"I did once."

"Did you? I mustn't have been listening. Anyhow it's funny to think of you and me, and I'm older than you, but we know something that fellows and girls our age, they only guess at."

"Oh, I've known about it a long time, ever since I went to sisters' school."

"And I guess from your father's doctor books. But this isn't the same when it's your own mother, and I bet this isn't the first time. My dad must have suspicions, because why didn't he send me away to boarding school this year? I graduated from high last year. I bet he wanted me to be here to keep an eye on her."

"Who was the other man."

"Oh, I can't tell you. Nobody you know. Anyhow, I'm not sure, so I wouldn't tell you. Listen, Jimmy, promise to telephone me every time before he comes here. If I'm not here I'll be at the Bordelmans' or at the Haltensteins', or if not there, the Callaways'. I'll stay home as much as I can, though. How long is he going to be around here, that doctor?"

"Lord knows," I said.

"Oh, I hope he goes. Now give me a good-bye kiss, Jimmy, and then you have to go." I kissed her. "I'm worse than she is," she said.

"No, you're not," I said. "You're the most darling girl there is. Good-bye, Ede," I said.

Doctor Myers was rubbing the skin in front of his ear when I came out. "Well, did you kiss and make up?"

"Oh, we don't go in for that mushy stuff," I said.

"Well, you will," he said. "Well . . . on to Wizziski's."

"It's a good thing you're not going to be around here long," I said.

"Why? Why do you say that?"

"Because you couldn't be in business or practice medicine without learning Hunkie names. If you stayed around here you'd have to be able to pronounce them and spell them." I started the car. I was glad to talk. "But I tell you where you'd have trouble. That's in the patches where they're all Irish with twenty or thirty cousins living in the same patch and all with the same name."

"Oh, come on."

"Well, it isn't as bad as it used to be," I said. "But my father told me about one time he went to Mass at Forganville, about fifteen miles from here, where they used to be all Irish. Now it's half Polack. Anyhow my father said the priest read the list of those that gave to the monthly collection, and the list was like this: John J. Coyle, $5; Jack Coyle, $2; Johnny Coyle, $2; J. J. Coyle, $5; Big John Coyle, $5; Mrs. John Coyle the saloonkeeper's widow, $10; the Widow Coyle, $2. And then a lot of other Coyles."

He did not quite believe this, but he thought it was a good story, and we talked about college—my father had told me I could go to Oxford or Trinity College, Dublin, if I promised to study medicine—until we reached Wisniewski's.

This was a saloon in a newer patch than Kelly's. It was entirely surrounded by mine shafts and breakers and railroads and mule yards, a flat area broken only by culm banks until half a mile away there was a steep, partly wooded hill which was not safe to walk on because it was all undermined and cave-ins occurred so frequently that they did not bother to build fences around them. The houses were the same height as in Kelly's patch, but they were built in blocks of four and six houses each. Technically Wisniewski's saloon was not in the patch; that is, it was not on company ground, but at a crossroad at one end of the rows of houses. It was an old stone house which had been a tavern in the days of the King's Highway. Now it was a beery-smelling place with a tall bar and no tables or chairs. It was crowded, but still it had a deserted appearance. The reason was that there was no one behind the bar, and no cigars or cartons of chewing tobacco on the back bar. The only decorations were a calendar from which the October leaf had not been torn, depicting a voluptuous woman stretched out on a divan, and an Old Overholt sign, hanging askew on the toilet door.

The men and women recognized Doctor Myers and me, and made a lane for us to pass through. Wisniewski himself was sick in bed, and everybody understood that the doctor would see him first, before prescribing for the mob in the barroom.

Doctor Myers and I went to Wisniewski's room, which was on the first floor. Wisniewski was an affable man, between forty and fifty, with a Teutonic haircut that never needed brushing. His body under the covers made big lumps. He was shaking hands with another Polack whose name was Stiney. He said to us: "Oh, hyuh, Cheem, hyuh, Cheem. Hyuh, Doc."

"Hyuh, Steve," I said. "Yoksheemosh?"

"Oh, fine dandy. How's yaself? How's Poppa? You tell Poppa what he needs is lay off this here booze." He roared at this joke. "Ya, you tell him I said so, lay off this booze." He looked around at the others in the room, and they all laughed, because my father used to pretend that he was going to have Steve's saloon closed by the County. "You wanna drink, Cheem?" he asked, and reached under the bed and pulled out a bottle. I reached for it, and he pulled the bottle away. "Na na na na na. Poppa close up my place wit' the County, I give you a drink. Ya know, miners drink here, but no minors under eighteen, hey?" He passed the bottle around, and all the other men in the room took swigs.

Doctor Myers was horrified. "You oughtn't to do that. You'll give the others the flu."

"Too late now, Doc," he said. "T'ree bottle now already."

"You'll lose all your customers, Steve," I said.

"How ya figure dat out?" said Steve. "Dis flu make me die, dis bottle make dem die. Fwit! Me and my customers all together in hell, so I open a place in hell. Fwit!"

"Well, anyhow, how are you feeling?" said the doctor. He placed a thermometer under Steve's arm. The others and Steve were silent until the temperature had been taken. "Hm," said Doctor Myers. He frowned at the thermometer.

" 'M gonna die, huh, Doc?" said Steve.

"Well, maybe not, but you—" he stopped talking. The door opened and there was a blast of sweaty air from the barroom, and Mr. Evans stood in the doorway, his hand on the knob. I felt weak.

"Doctor Myers, I'd like to see you a minute please," said Mr. Evans.

"Hyuh, Meester Ivvins," called Steve. Evans is one name which is consistently pronounced the same by the Irish, Slavs, Germans, and even the Portuguese and Negroes in the anthracite.

"Hello, Steve, I see you're drunk," said Mr. Evans.

"Not yet, Meester Ivvins. Wanna drink?"

"No, thanks. Doctor, will you step outside with me?"

Doctor Myers stalled. "I haven't prescribed for this man, Mr. Evans. If you'll wait?"

"My God, man! I can't wait. It's about my wife. I want to know about her."

"What about her?" asked the doctor.

"For God's sake," cried Mr. Evans. "She's sick, isn't she? Aren't you attending her, or don't you remember your patients?"

I sighed, and Doctor Myers sighed louder. "Oh," he said. "You certainly—frightened me, Mr. Evans. I was afraid something had happened. Why, you have no need to worry, sir. She has hardly any temperature. A very slight cold, and she did just the sensible thing by going to bed. Probably be up in a day or two."

"Well, why didn't you say so?" Mr. Evans sat down. "Go ahead, then, finish with Steve. I'll wait till you get through. I'm sorry if I seemed rude, but I was worried. You see I just heard from my timber boss that he saw Doctor Malloy's car in front of my house, and I called up and found out that Mrs. Evans was sick in bed, and my daughter sounded so excited I thought it must be serious. I'll take a drink now, Steve."

"Better not drink out of that bottle, Mr. Evans," said the doctor, who was sitting on the edge of the bed, writing a prescription.

"Oh, hell, it won't hurt me. So anyhow, where was I? Oh, yes. Well, I went home and found Mrs. Evans in bed and she seemed very pale, so I wanted to be sure it wasn't flu. I found out you were headed this way so I came right out to ask you if you wouldn't come back and take another look. That's good liquor, Steve. I'll buy a case of that." He raised the bottle to his lips again.

"I give you a case, Meester Ivvins. Glad to give you a case any time," said Steve.

"All right, we'll call it a Christmas present," said Mr. Evans. "Thanks very much." He was sweating, and he opened his raccoon coat. He took another drink, then he handed the bottle to Stiney. "Well, James, I hear you and Edith were at it again."

"Oh, it was just in fun. You know. Pulling my tie," I said.

"Well, don't let her get fresh with you," he said. "You have to keep these women in their place." He punched me playfully. "Doctor, I wonder if you could come to the house now and make sure everything's all right."

"I would gladly, Mr. Evans, but there's all that crowd in the barroom, and frankly, Mrs. Evans isn't what you'd call a sick woman, so my duty as a—physician is right here. I'll be only too glad to come if you'd like to wait."

The Hunkies, hearing the Super talked to in this manner, probably expected Meester Ivvins to get up and belt the doctor across the face, but he only said: "Well, if you're sure an hour couldn't make any difference."

"Couldn't possibly, Mr. Evans," said Doctor Myers.

He finished with Steve and told him to stop drinking and take his medicine, then he turned to leave. Steve reached under the pillow and drew out a bundle of money. He peeled off a fifty-dollar bill and handed it to the doctor.

"Oh, no, thanks," said Doctor Myers. "Doctor Malloy will send you a bill."

"Aw, don't worry about him, eh, Cheem? I always pay him firs' the mont', eh, Cheem? Naw, Doc, dis for you. Go have a good time. Get twenty-five woman, maybe get drunk wit' boilo." I could imagine Doctor Myers drinking boilo, which is hot moonshine. I nudged him, and he took the money and we went to the barroom.

I carried the chair and table and set them in place, and the Hunkies lined up docilely. Mr. Evans waited in Steve's room, taking a swig out of the bottle now and then until Doctor Myers had finished with the crowd. It was the same as usual. It was impractical to get detailed descriptions from each patient, so the flu doctor would ask each person three or four questions and then pretend to prescribe for each case individually. Actually they gave the same prescription to almost all of the patients, not only to save time, but because drug supplies in the village and city pharmacies were inadequate, and it was physically impossible for druggists to meet the demand. They would make up large batches of each doctor's standard prescription and dole out boxes and bottles as the patrons presented the prescriptions.

It took about two hours to dispose of the crowd at Steve's. Mr. Evans told Doctor Myers to come in the Cadillac because it was faster than the Ford—which I denied. I followed in the Ford and got to the Evans house about three minutes after the Cadillac. Edith met me at the door. "Oh, what a scare!" she said.

"If you think you were scared, what about me?" I said. I told her how I had felt when her father appeared at Steve's.

"Your father phoned and wants you to take that Myers home," she said, when I had finished.

"Did he say why?" I asked.

"No, he just said you weren't to make any more calls this afternoon."

"I wonder why."

"I hope it hasn't anything to do with him and my mother," she said.

"How could it? Only four people know about it. He couldn't guess it, and nobody would tell him. Maybe he's got up and wants me to drive for him."

"Maybe . . . I can't think. I'm afraid of them up there. Oh, I hope he goes away." I kissed her, and she pushed me away. "You're a bad actor, James Malloy. You're bad enough now, but wait till you grow up."

"What do you mean grow up? I'm almost six feet."

"But you're only a kid. I'm seventeen, and you're only fifteen."

"I'll be in my seventeenth year soon." We heard footsteps on the stairs, and Doctor Myers' voice: ". . . absolutely nothing to worry about. I'll come in again tomorrow. Good-bye, Mr. Evans. Good-bye, Edith. Ready, Jim?"

I gave him my father's message and we drove home fast. When we got there one of the Buicks was in front of the house, and we went in the living room.

"Well, Doctor Myers," my father said. "Back in harness again. Fit as a fiddle, and I want to thank you for the splendid attention you've given my practice. I don't know what my patients would have done without you."

"Oh, it's been a privilege, Doctor. I'd like to be able to tell you how much I've appreciated working for you. I wouldn't have missed it for the world. I think I'd like to serve my interneship in a place like this."

"Well, I'm glad to hear it. I'm chief of staff at our hospital, and I'm sorry I can't offer you anything here, but you ought to try some place like Scranton General. Get the benefit of these mining cases. God-damn interesting fractures, by the way. I trephined a man, forty-eight years old—all right, James, I'll call you when I need you." I left the room and they talked for half an hour, and then my father called me. "Doctor Myers wants to say good-bye."

"I couldn't leave without saying good-bye to my partner," said the doctor. "And by the way, Doctor Malloy, I think I ought to give part of this cheque to James. He did half the work."

"If he did I'll see that he gets his share. James knows that. He wants one of these God-damn raccoon coats. When I was a boy the only people that wore them drove hearses. Well—" My father indicated that it was time for the doctor and me to shake hands.

"Quite a grip James has," said the doctor.

"Perfect hands for a surgeon. Wasted, though," my father said. "Probably send him to some God-damn agricultural school and make a farmer out of him. I want him to go to Dublin, then Vienna. That's where the surgeons are. Dublin and Vienna. Well, if you ever meet Doctor Deaver tell him I won't be able to come down for the Wednesday clinics till this damn thing is over. Good luck, Doctor."

"Thank you, many thanks, Doctor Malloy."

"James will drive you to the hotel."

I took him to the hotel and we shook hands. "If you ever want a place to stay in Philadelphia you're always welcome at my house." He gave me the address of a fraternity house. "Say good-bye to the Evanses for me, will you, Jim?"

"Sure," I said and left.

My father was standing on the porch, waiting impatiently. "We'll use the Buick," he said. "That Ford probably isn't worth the powder to blow it to hell after you've been using it. Do you really want one of those livery stable coats?"

"Sure I do."

"All right. Now, ah, drive to Kelly's." We drove to Kelly's, where there was an ovation, not too loud, because there were one or two in the crowd on whom my father was liable to turn and say: "You, ya son of a bitch, you haven't paid me a cent since last February. What are you cheering for?" We paid a few personal visits in the patch. At one of them my father slapped a pretty Irish girl's bottom; at another he gave a little boy a dollar and told him to stop picking his nose; at another he sent me for the priest, and when I came back he had gone on foot to two other houses, and was waiting for me at the second. "What the hell kept you? Go to Terry Loughran's, unless the skunk got another doctor."

"He probably did," I said jovially. "He probably got Lucas."

"*Doctor* Lucas. Doctor Lucashinsky. Ivan the Terrible. Well, if he got Lucas it serves him right. Go to Hartenstein's."

We drove until one o'clock the next morning, taking coffee now and then, and once we stopped for a fried-egg sandwich. Twice I very nearly fell asleep while driving. The second time I awoke to hear my father saying: ". . . And my God! To think that a son of mine would rather rot in a dirty stinking newspaper office than do this. Why, I do more good and make more money in twenty minutes in the operating room than you'll be able to make the first three years you're out of college. If you *go* to college. Don't drive so fast!"

It was like this for the next two days. I slept when he allowed me to. We were out late at night and out again early in the morning. We drove fast, and a couple of times I bounded along corduroy roads with tanks of oxygen (my father was one of the first, if not the first, to use oxygen in pneumonia) ready to blow me to hell. I developed a fine cigarette cough, but my father kept quiet about it, because I was not taking quinine, and he was. We got on each other's nerves and had one terrible scene. He became angered by my driving and punched me on the shoulder. I stopped the car and took a tire iron from the floor of the car.

"Now just try that again," I said.

He did not move from the back seat. "Get back in this car." And I got back. But that night we got home fairly early and the next morning, when he had to go out at four o'clock, he drove the car himself and let me sleep. I was beginning to miss Doctor Myers. It was about eight o'clock when I came down for breakfast, and I saw my father sitting in the living room, looking very tired, staring straight ahead, his arms lying on the arms of the chair. I said hello, but he did not answer.

My mother brought me my breakfast. "Did you speak to your father?"

"Oh, I said hello, but he's in a stupor or something. I'm getting sick of all this."

"Hold your tongue. Your father has good reason to be unhappy this morning. He just lost one of the dearest friends he had in the world. Mr. Evans."

"Mr. Evans!" I said. "When'd he die?"

"At about four o'clock this morning. They called your father but he died before he got there. Poor Mrs. Evans—"

"What he die of? The flu?"

"Yes." I thought of the bottle that he had shared with Steve and the other Hunkies, and Mrs. Evans' illness, and Doctor Myers. It was all mixed up in my mind. "Now you be careful how you behave with your father today," my mother said.

I called up Edith, but she would not come to the phone. I wrote her a note, and drove to Collieryville with some flowers, but she would not see me.

Even after the epidemic died down and the schools were

reopened she would not see me. Then she went away to school and did not come home for the Easter holidays, and in May or June I fell in love with another girl and was surprised, but only surprised, when Edith eloped. Now I never can remember her married name.

OVER THE RIVER
AND THROUGH THE WOOD

Mr. Winfield's hat and coat and bag were in the hall of his flat, and when the man downstairs phoned to tell him the car was waiting, he was all ready. He went downstairs and said hello to Robert, the giant Negro chauffeur, and handed Robert the bag, and followed him out to the car. For the first time he knew that he and his granddaughter were not to make the trip alone, for there were two girls with Sheila, and she introduced them: "Grandfather, I'd like to have you meet my friends. This is Helen Wales, and this is Kay Farnsworth. My grandfather, Mr. Winfield." The names meant nothing to Mr. Winfield. What did mean something was that he was going to have to sit on the strapontin, or else sit outside with Robert, which was no good. Not that Robert wasn't all right, as chauffeurs go, but Robert was wearing a raccoon coat, and Mr. Winfield had no raccoon coat. So it was sit outside and freeze or sit on the little seat inside.

Apparently it made no difference to Sheila. He got inside, and when he closed the door behind him, she said, "I wonder what's keeping Robert?"

"He's strapping my bag on that thing in the back," said Mr. Winfield. Sheila obviously was not pleased by the delay, but in a minute or two they got under way, and Mr. Winfield rather admired the way Sheila carried on her conversation with her two friends and at the same time routed and rerouted Robert so that they were out of the city in no time. To Mr. Winfield it was pleasant and a little like old times to have the direction and the driving done for you. Not that he ever drove himself any more, but when he hired a car, he always had to tell the driver just where to turn and where to go straight. Sheila knew.

The girls were of an age, and the people they talked about were referred to by first names only. Ted, Bob, Gwen, Jean, Mary, Liz. Listening with some care, Mr. Winfield discovered that school acquaintances and boys whom they knew slightly were mentioned by their last names.

Sitting where he was, he could not watch the girls' faces, but he formed his opinions of the Misses Wales and Fransworth. Miss Wales supplied every other word when Sheila was talking. She was smallest of the three girls, and the peppy kind. Miss Farnsworth looked out of the window most of the time, and said hardly anything. Mr. Winfield could see more of her face, and he found himself asking, "I wonder if that child really likes anybody." Well, that was one way to be. Make the world show *you*. You could get away with it, too, if you were as attractive as Miss Farnsworth. The miles streamed by and the weather got colder, and Mr. Winfield listened and soon understood that he was not expected to contribute to the conversation.

"We stop here," said Sheila. It was Danbury, and they came to a halt in front of the old hotel. "Wouldn't you like to stop here, Grandfather?" He understood then that his daughter had told Sheila to stop here; obediently and with no dignity he got out. When he returned to the car, the three girls were finishing their cigarettes, and as he climbed back in the car, he noticed how Miss Farnsworth had been looking at him and continued to look at him, almost as though she were making a point of not helping him—although he wanted no help. He wasn't really an *old* man, an *old* man. Sixty-five.

The interior of the car was filled with cigarette smoke, and

Miss Farnsworth asked Mr. Winfield if he'd mind opening a window. He opened it. Then Sheila said one window didn't make any difference; open both windows, just long enough to let the smoke get out. "My! That air feels good," said Miss Wales. Then: "But what about you, Mr. Winfield? You're in a terrible draught there." He replied, for the first use of his voice thus far, that he did not mind. And at that moment the girls thought they saw a car belonging to a boy they knew, and they were in Sheffield, just over the Massachusetts line, before Miss Farnsworth realized that the windows were open and creating a terrible draught. She realized it when the robe slipped off her leg, and she asked Mr. Winfield if he would mind closing the window. But he was unable to get the crank started; his hands were so cold there was no strength in them. "We'll be there soon," said Sheila. Nevertheless, she closed the windows, not even acknowledging Mr. Winfield's shamed apologies.

He had to be first out of the car when they arrived at the house in Lenox, and it was then that he regretted having chosen the strapontin. He started to get out of the car, but when his feet touched the ground, the hard-packed frozen cinders of the driveway flew up at him. His knees had no strength in them, and he stayed there on the ground for a second or two, trying to smile it off. Helpful Robert—almost too helpful; Mr. Winfield wasn't that old—jumped out of the car and put his hands in Mr. Winfield's armpits. The girls were frightened, but it seemed to Mr. Winfield that they kept looking toward the library window, as though they were afraid Sheila's mother would be there and blaming them for his fall. If they only knew . . .

"You go on in, Grandfather, if you're sure you're all right," said Sheila. "I have to tell Robert about the bags."

"I'm all right," said Mr. Winfield. He went in, and hung up his coat and hat in the clothes closet under the stairs. A telephone was there, and in front of the telephone a yellow card of numbers frequently called. Mr. Winfield recognized only a few of the names, but he guessed there was an altogether different crowd of people coming up here these days. Fifteen years make a difference, even in a place like Lenox. Yes, it was fifteen years since he had been up here in the summertime. These trips, these annual trips for Thanksgiving, you couldn't tell anything about the character of the place from these trips. You never saw anybody but your own family and, like today, their guests.

He went out to the darkened hall and Ula, the maid, jumped in fright. "Ugh. Oh. It's you, Mr. Winfield. You like to scare me."

"Hello, Ula. Glad to see you're still holding the fort. Where's Mrs. Day?"

"Upstairs, I think . . . Here she is now," said Ula.

His daughter came down the steps; her hand on the banister was all he could see at first. "Is that you, Father? I thought I heard the car."

"Hello, Mary," he said. At the foot of the stairs they went through the travesty of a kiss that both knew so well. He leaned forward so that his head was above her shoulder. To Ula, a good Catholic, it must have looked like the kiss of peace. *"Pax tibi,"* Mr. Winfield felt like saying, but he said, "Where have you—"

"Father! You're freezing!" Mrs. Day tried very hard to keep the vexation out of her tone.

"It was a cold ride," he said. "This time of year. We had snow flurries between Danbury and Sheffield, but the girls enjoyed it."

"You go right upstairs and have a bath, and I'll send up—what would you like? Tea? Chocolate? Coffee?"

He was amused. The obvious thing would be to offer him a drink, and it was so apparent that she was talking fast to avoid that. "I think cocoa would be fine, but you'd better have a real drink for Sheila and her friends."

"Now, why do you take that tone, Father? You could have a drink if you wanted it, but you're on the wagon, aren't you?"

"Still on it. Up there with the driver."

"Well, and besides, liquor doesn't warm you up the same way something hot does. I'll send up some chocolate. I've put you in your old room, of course. You'll have to share the bathroom with one of Sheila's friends, but that's the best I could do. Sheila wasn't even sure she was coming till the very last minute."

"I'll be all right. It sounds like—I didn't bring evening clothes."

"We're not dressing."

He went upstairs. His room, the room itself, was just about the same; but the furniture was rearranged, his favorite chair not where he liked it best, but it was a good house; you could tell it was being lived in, *this year*, today, tomorrow. Little touches, ashtrays, flowers. It seemed young and white, cool with a warm breath, comfortable—and absolutely strange to him and, more especially, he to it. Whatever of the past this house had held, it was gone now. He sat in the chair and lit a cigarette. In a wave, in a lump, in a gust, the old thoughts came to him. Most of the year they were in the back of his mind, but up here Mr. Winfield held a sort of annual review of far-off, but never-out-of-sight regrets. This house, it used to be his until Mary's husband bought it. A good price, and in 1921 he certainly needed the money. He needed everything, and today he had an income from the money he got for this house, and that was about all. He remembered the day Mary's husband came to him and said, "Mr. Winfield, I hate to have to be the one to do this, but Mary— Mary doesn't—well, she thinks you weren't very nice to Mrs. Winfield. I don't know anything about it myself, of course, but that's what Mary thinks. I expected, naturally, I thought you'd come and live with us now that Mrs. Winfield has died, but— well, the point is, I know you've lost a lot of money, and also I happen to know about Mrs. Winfield's will. So I'm prepared to make you a pretty good offer, strictly legitimate based on current values, for the house in Lenox. I'll pay the delinquent taxes myself and give you a hundred and fifty thousand dollars for the house and grounds. That ought to be enough to pay off your debts and give you a fairly decent income. And, uh, I happen to have a friend who knows Mr. Harding quite well. Fact, he sees the President informally one night a week, and I know he'd be only too glad, if you were interested . . ."

He remembered how that had tempted him. Harding might have fixed it so he could go to London, where Enid Walter was. But even then it was too late. Enid had gone back to London because he didn't have the guts to divorce his wife, and the reason he wouldn't divorce his wife was that he wanted to "protect" Mary, and Mary's standing, and Mary's husband's standing, and Mary's little daughter's standing; and now he was "protecting" them all over again, by selling his house so that he would not become a family charge—protecting the very same people from the embarrassment of a poor relation. "You can have the house," he told Day. "It's worth that much, but no more, and I'm grateful to you for not offering me more. About a political job, I think I might like to go to California this winter. I have some friends out there I haven't seen in years." He had known that that was exactly what Mary and her husband wanted, so he'd gone.

There was a knock on the door. It was Ula with a tray. "Why two cups, Ula?" he said.

"Oh. Di put two cups? So I did. I'm just so used to putting two cups." She had left the door open behind her, and as she arranged the things on the marble-topped table he saw Sheila and the two girls, standing and moving in the hall.

"This is your room, Farnie," said Sheila. "You're down this way, Helen. Remember what I told you, Farnie. Come on, Helen."

"Thank you, Ula," he said. She went out and closed the door, and he stood for a moment, contemplating the chocolate, then poured out a cup and drank it. It made him a little thirsty, but it was good and warming, and Mary as right; it was better than a drink. He poured out another cup and nibbled on a biscuit. He had an idea: Miss Farnsworth might like some. He admired that girl. She had spunk. He bet she knew what she wanted, or seemed to, and no matter how unimportant were the things she wanted, they were the things she wanted, and not someone else. She could damn well thank the Lord, too, that she was young enough to have a whack at whatever she wanted, and not have to wait the way he had. That girl would make up her mind about a man or a fortune or a career, and by God she would attain whatever it was. If she found, as she surely would find, that nothing ever was enough, she'd at least find it out in time; and early disillusionment carried a compensatory philosophical atti- tude, which in a hard girl like this one would take nothing from her charm. Mr. Winfield felt her charm, and began regarding her as the most interesting person he had met in many dull years. It would be fun to talk to her, to sound her out and see how far she had progressed toward, say, ambition or disillusionment. It would be fun to do, and it would be just plain nice of him, as former master of this house, to invite her to have a cup of cocoa with him. Good cocoa.

He made his choice between going out in the hall and knocking on her door, and knocking on her door to the bathroom. He decided on the second procedure because he didn't want anyone to see him knocking on her door. So he entered the bathroom and tapped on the door that led to her room. "In a minute," he thought he heard her say. But then he knew he must have been wrong. It sounded more like "Come in." He hated people who knocked on doors and had to be told two or three times to come in, and it would make a bad impression if he started the friendship that way.

He opened the door, and immediately he saw how right he had been in thinking she had said "In a minute." For Miss Farnsworth was standing in the middle of the room, standing there all but nude. Mr. Winfield instantly knew that this was the end of any worthwhile life he had left. There was cold murder in the girl's eyes, and loathing and contempt and the promise of the thought his name forever would evoke. She spoke to him: "Get out of here, you dirty old man."

He returned to his room and his chair. Slowly he took a cigarette out of his case, and did not light it. He did everything slowly. There was all the time in the world, too much of it, for him. He knew it would be hours before he would begin to hate himself. For a while he would just sit there and plan his own terror.

DO YOU LIKE IT HERE?

The door was open. The door had to be kept open during study period, so there was no knock, and Roberts was startled when a voice he knew and hated said, "Hey, Roberts. Wanted in Van Ness's office." The voice was Hughes'.

"What for?" said Roberts.

"Why don't you go and find out what for, Dopey?" said Hughes.

"Phooey on you," said Roberts.

"Phooey on *you*," said Hughes, and left.

Roberts got up from the desk. He took off his eyeshade and put on a tie and coat. He left the light burning.

Van Ness's office, which was *en suite* with his bedroom, was on the ground floor of the dormitory, and on the way down Roberts wondered what he had done. It got so after a while, after going to so many schools, that you recognized the difference between being "wanted in Somebody's office" and "Somebody wants to see you." If a master wanted to see you on some minor matter, it didn't always mean that you had to go to his office, but if it was serious, they always said, "You're wanted in Somebody's office."

That meant Somebody would be in his office, waiting for you, waiting specially for you. Roberts didn't know why this difference existed, but it did, all right. Well, all he could think of was that he had been smoking in the shower room, but Van Ness never paid much attention to that. Everybody smoked in the shower room, and Van Ness never did anything about it unless he just happened to catch you.

For minor offenses Van Ness would speak to you when he made his rounds of the rooms during study period. He would walk slowly down the corridor, looking in at each room to see that the proper occupant, and no one else, was there; and when he had something to bawl you out about, something unimportant, he would consult a list he carried, and he would stop in and bawl you out about it and tell you what punishment went with it. That was another detail that made the summons to the office a little scary.

Roberts knocked on Van Ness's half-open door and a voice said, "Come in."

Van Ness was sitting at his typewriter, which was on a small desk beside the large desk. He was in a swivel chair and when he saw Roberts he swung around, putting himself behind the large desk, like a damn judge.

He had his pipe in his mouth and he seemd to look over the steel rims of his spectacles. The light caught his Phi Beta Kappa key, which momentarily gleamed as though it had diamonds in it.

"Hughes said you wanted me to report here," said Roberts.

"I did," said Van Ness. He took his pipe out of his mouth and began slowly to knock the bowl empty as he repeated, "I did." He finished emptying his pipe before he again spoke. He took a long time about it, and Roberts, from his years of experience, recognized that as torture tactics. They always made you wait to scare you. It was sort of like the third degree. The horrible damn thing was that it always did scare you a little, even when you were used to it.

Van Ness leaned back in his chair and stared through his glasses at Roberts. He cleared his throat. "You can sit down," he said.

"Yes, sir," said Roberts. He sat down and again Van Ness made him wait.

"Roberts, you've been here now how long—five weeks?"

"A little over. About six."

"About six weeks," said Van Ness. "Since the seventh of January. Six weeks. Strange. Strange. Six weeks, and I really don't know a thing about you. Not much, at any rate. Roberts, tell me a little about yourself."

"How do you mean, Mister?"

"How do I mean? Well—about your life, before you decided to honor us with your presence. Where you came from, what you did, why you went to so many schools, so on."

"Well, I don't know."

"Oh, now. Now, Roberts. Don't let your natural modesty overcome the autobiographical urge. Shut the door."

Roberts got up and closed the door.

"Good," said Van Ness. "Now, proceed with this—uh—dossier. Give me the—huh—huh—*lowdown* on Roberts, Humphrey, Second Form, McAllister Memorial Hall, et cetera."

Roberts, Humphrey, sat down and felt the knot of his tie. "Well, I don't know. I was born at West Point, New York. My father was a first lieutenant then and he's a major now. My father and mother and I lived in a lot of places because he was in the Army and they transferred him. Is that the kind of stuff you want, Mister?"

"Proceed, proceed. I'll tell you when I want you to—uh—halt." Van Ness seemed to think that was funny, that "halt."

"Well, I didn't go to a regular school till I was ten. My mother got a divorce from my father and I went to school in San Francisco. I only stayed there a year because my mother got married again and we moved to Chicago, Illinois."

"Chicago, Illinois! Well, a little geography thrown in, eh, Roberts? Gratuitously. Thank you. Proceed."

"Well, so then we stayed there about two years and then we moved back East, and my stepfather is a certified public accountant and we moved around a lot."

"Peripatetic, eh, Roberts?"

44

"I guess so. I don't exactly know what that means." Roberts paused.

"Go on, go on."

"Well, so I just went to a lot of schools, some day and some boarding. All that's written down on my application blank here. I had to put it all down on account of my credits."

"Correct. A very imposing list it is, too, Roberts, a very imposing list. Ah, to travel as you have. Switzerland. How I've regretted not having gone to school in Switzerland. Did you like it there?"

"I was only there about three months. I liked it all right, I guess."

"And do you like it here, Roberts?"

"Sure."

"You do? You're sure of that? You wouldn't want to change anything?"

"Oh, I wouldn't say that, not about any school."

"Indeed," said Van Ness. "With your vast experience, naturally you would be quite an authority on matters educational. I suppose you have many theories as to the strength and weaknesses inherent in the modern educational systems."

"I don't know. I just—I don't know. Some schools are better than others. At least I like some better than others."

"Of course. Of course." Van Ness seemed to be thinking about something. He leaned back in his swivel chair and gazed at the ceiling. He put his hands in his pants pockets and then suddenly he leaned forward. The chair came down and Van Ness's belly was hard against the desk and his arm was stretched out on the desk, full length, fist closed.

"Roberts! Did you ever see this before? Answer me!" Van Ness's voice was hard. He opened his fist, and in it was a wristwatch.

Robert looked down at the watch. "No, I don't think so," he said. He was glad to be able to say it truthfully.

Van Ness continued to hold out his hand, with the wristwatch lying in the palm. He held out his hand a long time, fifteen seconds at least, without saying anything. Then he turned his

45

hand over and allowed the watch to slip onto the desk. He resumed his normal position in the chair. He picked up his pipe, slowly filled it, and lit it. He shook the match back and forth long after the flame had gone. He swung around a little in his chair and looked at the wall, away from Roberts. "As a boy I spent six years at this school. My brothers, my two brothers, went to this school. My *father* went to this school. I have a deep and abiding and lasting affection for this school. I have been a member of the faculty of this school for more than a decade. I like to think that I am part of this school, that in some small measure I have assisted in its progress. I like to think of it as more than a mere steppingstone to higher education. At this very moment there are in this school the sons of men who were my classmates. I have not been without my opportunities to take a post at this and that college or university, but I choose to remain here. Why? Why? Because I love this place. I love this place, Roberts. I cherish its traditions. I cherish its good name." He paused, and turned to Roberts. "Roberts, there is no room here for a thief!"

Roberts did not speak.

"There is no room here for a thief, I said!"

"Yes, sir."

Van Ness picked up the watch without looking at it. He held it a few inches above the desk. "This miserable watch was stolen last Friday afternoon, more than likely during the basketball game. As soon as the theft was reported to me I immediately instituted a search for it. My search was unsuccessful. Sometime Monday afternoon the watch was put here, here in my rooms. When I returned here after classes Monday afternoon, this watch was lying on my desk. Why? Because the contemptible rat who stole it knew that I had instituted the search, and like the rat he is, he turned yellow and returned the watch to me. Whoever it is, he kept an entire dormitory under a loathsome suspicion. I say to you, I do not know who stole this watch or who returned it to my rooms. But by God, Roberts, I'm going to find out, if it's the last thing I do. If it's the last thing I do. That's all, Roberts. You may go." Van Ness sat back, almost breathless.

Roberts stood up. "I give you my word of honor, I—"

"I said you may go!" said Van Ness.

Roberts was not sure whether to leave the door open or to close it, but he did not ask. He left it open.

He went up the stairs to his room. He went in and took off his coat and tie, and sat on the bed. Over and over again, first violently, then weakly, he said it, "The bastard, the dirty bastard."

SUMMER'S DAY

There were not very many people at the beach when Mr. and Mrs. Attrell arrived. On this particular day, a Wednesday, possibly a little more than half the morning swimming crowd had come out of the water and gone home for lunch, some on their bicycles, some on the bus which stopped almost anywhere you asked to stop, and a still rather large number driving their cars and station wagons. The comparatively few persons who stayed at the club for lunch sat about in their bathing suits in groups of anywhere from two to seven.

Mrs. Attrell got out of the car—a shiny black 1932 Buick with fairly good rubber and only about thirty thousand miles on it—at the clubhouse steps and waited while Mr. Attrell parked it at the space marked "A. T. Attrell." Mr. Attrell then joined his wife, took her by the arm, and adapted his pace to her slightly shorter steps. Together they made their way to their bench. The bench, seating six, had a sign with "A. T. Attrell" on it nailed to the back, and it was placed a few feet from the boardwalk. On this day, however, it was occupied by four young persons, and so Mr. and Mrs. Attrell altered their course and went to a bench just a bit lower on the dune than their own. Mrs. Attrell placed her blue tweed bag and her book, which was in its lending-library jacket, in her lap. She folded her hands and looked out at the sea. Mr. Attrell seated himself on her left, with his right arm resting on the back of the bench. In this way he was not sitting too close to her, but he had only to raise his hand and he could touch her shoulder. From time to time he did this, as they both looked out at the sea.

It was a beautiful, beautiful day and some of the hungry youngsters of teen age forgot about lunch and continued to swim and splash. Among them was Bryce Cartwright, twelve, grandson of Mr. and Mrs. Attrell's friend T. K. Cartwright, whose bench they now occupied.

"Bryce," said Mr. Attrell.

"Mm-hmm," said Mrs. Attrell, nodding twice.

They filled their lungs with the wonderful air and did not speak for a little while. Then Mr. Attrell looked up the beach to his left. "Mr. O'Donnell," he said.

"Oh, yes. Mr. O'Donnell."

"Got some of his boys with him. Not all, though."

"I think the two oldest ones are at war," said Mrs. Attrell.

"Yes, I believe so. I think one's in the Army and the other's in, I *think*, the Navy."

Mr. O'Donnell was a powerfully built man who had played guard on an obscure Yale team before the last war. With him today, on parade, were his sons Gerald, Norton, Dwight, and Arthur Twining Hadley O'Donnell, who were sixteen, fourteen, twelve, and nine. Mrs. O'Donnell was at home with the baby which no one believed she was going to have until she actually had it. Mr. O'Donnell and the boys had been for a walk along the beach and now the proud father and his skinny brown sons were coming up the boardwalk on their way to lunch. A few yards away from the Cartwright bench Mr. O'Donnell began his big grin for the Attrells, looking at Mrs. Attrell, then at Mr. Attrell, then by compulsion at Mr. Attrell's hatband, that of a Yale society, which Mr. O'Donnell had nothing against, although he had not made it or any other.

"Mr. and Mrs. Attrell," he said, bowing.

"How do you do, Mr. O'Donnell?" said Mr. Attrell.

"How do you do, Mr. O'Donnell?" said Mrs. Attrell.

"You don't want to miss that ocean today, Mr. Attrell," said Mr. O'Donnell. "Magnificent." He passed on, and Mr. Attrell laughed politely. Mr. O'Donnell's greetings had, of course, done for the boys as well. They did not speak, nor did they even, like their father, slow down on their way to the bathhouse.

"He's an agreeable fellow, Henry O'Donnell," said Mr. Attrell.

"Yes, they're a nice big family," said his wife. Then she removed the rubber band which marked her page in her book and took out her spectacles. Mr. Attrell filled his pipe but made no move to light it. At that moment a vastly pregnant and pretty young woman—no one he knew—went down the boardwalk in her bathing suit. He turned to his wife, but she was already reading. He put his elbow on the back of the bench and he was about to touch his wife's shoulder again when a shadow fell across his leg.

"Hello, Mrs. Attrell, Mr. Attrell. I just came over to say hello." It was a tall young man in a white uniform with the shoulder-board stripe-and-a-half of a lieutenant junior grade.

"Why, it's Frank," said Mrs. Attrell. "How are you?"

"Why, hello," said Mr. Attrell, rising.

"Just fine," said Frank. "Please don't get up. I was on my way home and I saw your car in the parking space so I thought I'd come and say hello."

"Well, I should think so," said Mr. Attrell. "Sit down? Sit down and tell us all about yourself."

"Yes, we're using your bench. I suppose you noticed," said Mrs. Attrell.

"Father'll send you a bill for it, as you well know," said Frank. "You know Father."

They all had a good laugh on that.

"Where are you now?" said Mr. Attrell.

"I'm at a place called Quonset."

"Oh, yes," said Mrs. Attrell.

"Rhode Island," said Frank.

"Oh, I see," said Mrs. Attrell.

"Yes, I think I know where it is," said Mr. Attrell. "Then do you go on a ship?"

"I hope to. You both look extremely well," said Frank.

"Well, you know," said Mr. Attrell.

"When you get our age you have nothing much else to do," said Mrs. Attrell.

"Well, you do it beautifully. I'm sorry I've got to hurry away like this but I have some people waiting in the car, but I had to say hello. I'm going back this afternoon."

"Well, thank you for coming over. It was very nice of you. Is your wife down?" said Mrs. Attrell.

"No, she's with her family in Hyannis Port."

"Well, remember us to her when you see her," said Mrs. Attrell.

"Yes," said Mr. Attrell. They shook hands with Frank and he departed.

Mr. Attrell sat down. "Frank's a fine boy. That just shows how considerate, seeing our car. How old is Frank, about?"

"He'll be thirty-four in September," said Mrs. Attrell.

Mr. Attrell nodded slowly. "Yes, that's right," he said. He began tamping down the tobacco in his pipe. "You know, I think that water—would you mind if I had a dip?"

"No, dear, but I think you ought to do it soon, before it begins to get chilly."

"Remember we're on daylight saving, so it's an hour earlier by the sun." He stood up. "I think I'll just put on my suit and get wet, and if it's too cold I'll come right out."

"That's a good idea," she said.

In the bathhouse Mr. Attrell accepted two towels from the Negro attendant and went to his booth, which was open and marked "A. T. Attrell," to undress. From the voices there could not have been more than half a dozen persons in the men's side. At first he paid no attention to the voices, but after he had untied the double knot in his shoelaces he let the words come to him.

"And who is T. K. Cartwright?" a young voice was saying.

"He's dead," said the second young voice.

"No, he isn't," said the first young voice. "That's the old buzzard that's sitting in front of us."

"And what makes you think *he* isn't dead, he and the old biddy?"

"You're both wrong," said a third young voice. "That isn't Mr. Cartwright sitting there. That's Mr. Attrell."

"So what?" said the first young voice.

"All right, so what, if you don't want to hear about them, old Attrell and his wife. They're the local tragedy. Ask your mother; she used to come here. They had a daughter or, I don't know, maybe it was a son. Anyway, whichever it was, he or she hung himself."

"Or herself," said the first young voice.

"I think it was a girl. They came home and found her hanging in the stable. It was an unfortunate love affair. I don't see why—"

"Just a minute, there." Mr. Attrell recognized the voice of Henry O'Donnell.

"Yes, sir?" asked one young voice.

"You sound to me like a pack of goddam pansies. You oughta be over on the girls' side," said Mr. O'Donnell.

"I'd like to know what business of—" a young voice said, then there was a loud smack.

"Because I made it my business. Get dressed and get outa here," said O'Donnell. "I don't give a damn whose kids you are."

Mr. Attrell heard the deep breathing of Henry O'Donnell, who waited a moment for his command to be obeyed, then walked past Mr. Attrell's booth with his head in the other direction. Mr. Attrell sat there, many minutes probably, wondering how he could ever again face Henry O'Donnell, worrying about how he could face his wife. But then of course he realized that there was really nothing to face, really nothing.

THE DECISION

The home of Francis Townsend could have been taken for the birthplace of a nineteenth-century American poet, one of those little white houses by the side of the road that are regarded by the interested as national shrines. In front of the house there was a mounting block and a hitching post, iron, with the head of a horse holding an iron ring, instead of a bit, in its mouth. These, of course, had not been used in the last thirty years, but use did not govern the removal of many objects about the Townsend place. Things were added, after due consideration, but very little was ever taken away.

The Townsend place was on the outskirts of the seacoast village, out of the zone where the sidewalks were paved. In the fall of the year and in the spring, the sidewalk was liable to be rather muddy, and Francis Townsend several times had considered bricking the path—not that he minded the mud, but out of consideration for the female pedestrians. This project he had dismissed after studying the situation every afternoon for a week. He sat by the window in the front room and came to the conclusion that (a) there were not really many pedestrians during the muddy seasons, since there were few summer people around in spring or fall, and (b) the few natives who did use the sidewalk in front of his place were people who had sense enough to be properly shod in muddy weather. Another and very satisfying discovery that Francis Townsend made was that few people—men, women, or children—came near his house at all. For a long, long time he had entertained the belief that the street outside was a busy thoroughfare, more or less choked with foot and vehicular traffic. "I am really quite alone out here," he remarked to himself. This allowed for the fact that he had made his study of the muddy-sidewalk problem in the afternoon, when traffic was presumably lighter than in the morning, when, for instance, housewives would be doing their shopping. The housewives and others could not have made *that* much difference; even if the morning traffic were double that of the afternoon, it still was not considerable. It was, of course, impossible for Francis Townsend to make his study in the morning, except Sunday morning, for Francis Townsend's mornings were, in a manner of speaking, spoken for.

Every morning, Francis Townsend would rise at six-thirty, shave and have his bath, and himself prepare first breakfast, which consisted of two cups of coffee and a doughnut. In the winter he would have this meal in the kitchen, cheerful with its many windows and warm because of the huge range. In the summer he would take the coffee and doughnut to the front room, where it was dark and cool all day. He would run water into the dirty cup and saucer and put them in the sink for the further attention of Mrs. Dayton, his housekeeper, who usually made her appearance at eight-thirty. By the time she arrived, Francis Townsend would have changed from his sneakers and khaki pants and cardigan to a more suitable costume—his black suit, high black kid shoes, starched collar, and black four-in-hand-tie. He would smoke a cigarette while he listened to Mrs. Dayton stirring about in the kitchen, and pretty soon would come the sound of the knocker and he would go to the front door. That would be Jerry Bradford, the letter carrier.

"Good morning, Jerry."

"Good morning, Francis. Three letters an-n-nd the New York paper."

"Three letters and the paper, thank you."

"Fresh this morning. Wind's from the east. Might have a little rain later in the day."

"Oh, you think *so?*"

"Well, I might be wrong. See you tomorrow, in all likelihood."

Jerry would go away and Francis would stand at the open doorway until Jerry had passed the Townsend property line. Then sometimes Francis would look at the brass nameplate, with its smooth patina and barely distinguishable name: "F. T. Townsend, M.D." The plate was small, hardly any larger than the plate for a man's calling card, not a proper physician's shingle at all, but there it was and had been from the day of his return from medical school.

He would go back to his chair in the front room and wait for Mrs. Dayton to announce breakfast, which she did in her own way. She would say, "Morning," as greeting, and nod slowly, indicating that breakfast was on the table. Francis then would take his paper and letters to the dining room and partake of second breakfast—oatmeal, ham and eggs, toast that was toasted over a flame, and a pot of coffee. Mrs. Dayton appeared only once during breakfast, when she brought in the eggs and took away the cereal dishes.

Francis Townsend's mail rarely was worth the pleasure of anticipation. That did not keep him from anticipating Jerry Bradford's knock on the door or from continuing to hope for some surprise when he slit the envelopes with his butter knife. The reading of his mail did, in fact, give him pleasure, even though it might be no more than an alumni-association plea, a list of candidates for membership in his New York club, or an advertisement from a drug or instrument company. Francis Townsend would read them all, all the way through, propping them against the tall silver salt-cellar, and then he would take them with him to the front room, so that Mrs. Dayton could not see them, and there he would toss them in the fire or, in warm weather, put a match to them.

Then, every day but Sunday, Francis Townsend would take his walk. For the first thirty of the last forty years, Francis Townsend had had a companion on his walk. The companion always had been a collie; not always the same collie, but always a collie. But about ten years ago, when the last Dollie (all of Francis Townsend's dogs had been called Dollie) died, Francis Townsend read somewhere or heard somewhere that it took too much out of you to have dogs; you no sooner grew to love them, and they you, than they died and you had to start all over again with a new one. This bit of dog lore came at a time when Francis Townsend had just lost a Dollie and was suffering a slight nosebleed. It was not a proper hemorrhage, but it was not exactly reassuring as to Francis Townsend's life expectancy, and he did not want to take on the responsibility of another Dollie if Dollie were to be left without anyone to take care of her, any more than he wanted to go through the pain of losing another dog. Therefore, for the last ten years or so, Francis Townsend had taken his walk alone.

Although he would not have known it, Francis Townsend's daily—except Sunday—walk was as much a part of the life of the village as it was of his own life. The older merchants and their older children and older employees took for granted that around a certain hour every morning Francis Townsend would be along. Harris, the clothing-store man; McFetridge, the hardware-store man; Blanchard, the jeweler; Bradford, brother of Jerry Bradford, who had the Ford-Lincoln-Mercury agency—among others—took for granted that Francis Townsend would be along around a certain hour every morning. He had to pass their places on his way to the bank, and when they saw him, they would say, "Hello, Francis," and would usually say something about the weather, and Francis would nod and smile, and, without coming to a full stop, he would indicate that the comment or the prediction was acceptable to him.

His first full stop always was the bank. There he would go to Eben Townsend's desk and Eben would push toward him a filled-in check. "Morning, Francis," "Good morning, Eben," they would say, and Francis would put "F. T. Townsend, M.D." on the check, and his cousin would give Francis three five-dollar bills. Francis would thank him and resume his walk.

At his next stop, Francis would sometimes have to wait longer than at the bank. Eventually, though, the barkeep would come to wait on Francis. "Hyuh, Francis," he would say, and place a quart of rye whiskey and a pitcher of water on the bar.

"Hyuh, Jimmy," Francis would say, and pour himself a rye-and-water. "Well, well, well."

"Ixcuse me, Francis, I got a salesman here," Jimmy might say. "Be with you in two shakes of a ram's tail."

"That's all right, Jimmy. Take your time. I'll be here for a while."

This conversational opening, or something very like it, had been fairly constant for forty years, inasmuch as the barkeep's name always had been Jimmy, since a father and a son had owned the business, or at least tended bar, during the forty mature years of Francis Townsend's life. Jimmy the father had discovered long, long ago that, as he put it, Francis was good for the entire bloody morning and didn't take offense if you left him a minute to transact your business. Francis was indeed good for the entire morning. If it happened to be one of Jimmy's busy days, he would remember to put four toofers—two-for-a-quarter cigars—on the bar in front of Francis before he left him, and Francis would smoke them slowly, holding them in his tiny, even teeth, looking up at the ceiling with one of them in his mouth, as though William Howard Taft or Harry Truman had just asked his advice on whom to appoint to the Court of St. James's. Francis never bothered anybody, not even during the years of two World Wars. He never tried to buy drinks for the Coast Guard or the Army Air Forces, and he was not a man whose appearance welcomed invitations on the part of strangers. Among the villagers—the few who would drink in the morning out of habit or temporary necessity—none would bother Francis or expect to be bothered by him. Francis had his place at the bar, at the far corner, and it was his so long as he was present. First-generation Jimmy and second-generation Jimmy had seen to that.

Each day, Monday through Saturday, January through December, Francis Townsend would sip his drinks and smoke his cigars until the noon Angelus from St. Joseph's Church. If he happened to be the only customer in the bar, Francis would say to Jimmy, "Ahem. The angel of the Lord declared, if I may say so."

"Correct, Francis."

Francis would take two of the three five-dollar bills from a lower vest pocket, and Jimmy would size up the rye bottle and pick up the money and return the estimated and invariably honest change. The tradition then was for Jimmy to say, "Now the house breaks down and turns Cath'lic."

"A rye, then," would be Francis Townsend's answer, in Francis Townsend's weak attempt at brogue. Whereupon Jimmy would hand Francis Townsend a wrapped bottle of rye and Francis would go home and eat the nice lunch Mrs. Dayton had prepared and take a good nap till time for supper, and after supper, when Mrs. Dayton had gone home, he would sit and read some of the fine books, like *Dombey and Son*, the Waverley Novels, Bacon's *Essays*—the fine books in the front room—till it was time to bank the kitchen fire for the next morning and finish off the last of the wrapped bottle of rye.

That was about the way it had been with Francis Townsend from the time he finished medical school. That year, soon after his graduation, his uncle, who had raised him, said to him one day, "What are your plans, France?"

"First, I thought I'd interne at a hospital in Pittsburgh. A great many mines and factories out there and a man can learn a lot. Then, of course, I'll come back here and hang out my shingle. And I have an understanding with a girl in Philadelphia, Uncle. We're not engaged, but—we have an understanding."

His uncle got up and filled his pipe from the humidor on the mantelpiece in the front room. "No, boy," he said. "I'm sorry to say you can't have any of those things. You can never practice medicine, and you can't marry."

"Why, I can do both. I'm accepted at the hospital out in Pittsburgh, and the girl said she'd wait."

"Not when I tell you what I have to tell you. Do you know that both your father and your mother died in an institution? No, of course you don't know. There aren't many people in this village know. Most of the people my age think your father and mother died of consumption, but it wasn't consumption, France. It was mental."

"I see," said Francis. He stood up and filled his own pipe, with his class numerals in silver on the bowl. "Well, then, of course you're right." He took his time lighting up. "I guess there's no way out of that, is there, Uncle?"

"I don't know. I don't know enough about such things, putting to one side that I do know you shouldn't marry or you shouldn't doctor people."

"Oh, I agree with you, Uncle. I agree with you." Francis sat down again, trying to assume the manner of one Deke talking to another Deke in the fraternity house. "I wonder what I ought to do? I don't think I ought to just sit here and wait till I begin to get loony myself. There ought to be some kind of work where I couldn't do anybody any harm."

"You won't have to worry about money. I've fixed that at the bank. Give yourself plenty of time to pick and choose. You'll decide on something."

"Oh, very likely I will," Francis said. "I won't just stay on here in the village." But that, it turned out, was what he did decide to do.

DRAWING ROOM B

Nobody big had taken Leda Pentleigh to the train, and the young man from the publicity department who had taken her was not authorized to hire the Rolls or Packard that used to be provided for her New York visits. Nor had they taken their brief ride from the Waldorf to Grand Central. This time, she was riding west on the Broadway and not the Century, had come to the station in an ordinary taxicab, from a good but unspectacular hotel north of Sixtieth Street. Mr. Egan, it is true, was dead, but his successor at Penn Station, if any, did not personally escort Leda to the train. She just went along with the pleasant young hundred-and-fifty-a-week man from the publicity department, her eyes cast down in the manner which, after eighteen years, was second nature to her in railroad stations and hotel lobbies, at tennis matches and football games. Nobody stopped her for her autograph, or to swipe the corsage which the publicity young man's boss had sent instead of attending her himself. Pounding her Delman heels on the Penn Station floor, she recalled a remark which she was almost sure she had originated, something about the autograph hounds not bothering her: it was when they didn't bother you that they bothered you. Of course, it was Will Rogers or John Boles or Bill Powell or somebody who first uttered the thought, but Leda preferred her way of putting it. The thought, after all, had been thought by thousands of people, but she noticed it was the way *she* expressed it that was popular among the recent johnny-come-latelies when they were interviewed by the fan magazines. Well, whoever had said it first could have it; she wouldn't quarrel over it. At the moment of marching across Penn Station, there seemed to be mighty few travellers who would take sides for or against her in a controversy over the origin of one of her routine wisecracks; far from saying, "There goes Leda Pentleigh, who first said . . ." the travellers were not even saying, "There goes Leda Pentleigh—period." The few times she permitted her gaze to rise to the height of her fellow-man were unsatisfactory; one of the older porters raised his hat and smiled and bowed; two or three nice-appearing men recognized her—but they probably were Philadelphians in their thirties or forties, who would go home and tell their wives that they had seen Leda Pentleigh in Penn Station, and their wives would say, "Oh, yes. I remember her," or "Oh, yes. She was in Katie Hepburn's picture. She played the society bitch, and I'll bet she's qualified." Katie Hepburn, indeed! It wasn't as if Katie Hepburn hadn't been in pictures fifteen years. But no use getting sore at Katie Hepburn because Katie was a few years younger and still a star. At this thought, Leda permitted herself a glance at a Philadelphia-type man, a man who had that look of just about getting into or out of riding togs, as Leda called them. He frowned a little, then raised his hat, and because he was so obviously baffled, she gave him almost the complete Pentleigh smile. Even then he was baffled, had not the faintest idea who she was. A real huntin'-shootin' dope, and she knew what he was thinking—that here was a woman either from Philadelphia or going to Philadelphia and therefore someone he must know. The gate was opened, and Leda and Publicity went down to her car. Publicity saw that she was, as he said, all squared away, and she thanked him and he left, assuring her that "somebody" from the Chicago office would meet her at Chicago, in case she needed anything. Her car was one of the through cars, which meant she did not have to change trains at Chicago, but just in case she needed anything. (Like what, she said to herself. Like getting up at seven-thirty in the morning to be ready to pose for photographs in the station? Oh, yes? And let every son of a bitch in the Pump Room know that Leda Pentleigh no longer rated the star treatment?)

In her drawing room, Leda decided to leave the door open. There might, after all, be a Coast friend on the train. If she wanted to play gin with him—or her—she could do it, or if she wanted to give her—or him—the brush, she knew how to do that, too. Her window was on the wrong side of the car to watch people on the platform, and she sat in a corner where she could get a good look at the passengers going by her door. She opened a high-class book and watched the public (no longer so completely hers) going by. They all had that beaten look of people trying to find their space; bent over—surely not from the weight of their jewelry boxes and briefcases—and then peering up at the initial on her drawing room, although they could plainly see that the room was occupied by a striking, stunning, chic, glamorous, sophisticated woman, who had spent most of the past week in New York City, wishing she were dead.

She drove that little thought out of her mind. It would do no good now to dwell on that visit, ending now as the train began to pull out—her first visit to New York in four years, and the unhappiest in all her life. What the hell was the use of thinking back to the young punk from one of the dailies who had got her confused with Renée Adoré? What difference the wrong tables in restaurants and the inconveniently timed appointments at hairdressers and the night of sitting alone in her hotel room while a forty-dollar pair of theatre tickets went to waste? The benefit in Union City, New Jersey. The standup by Ken Englander, the aging architect, who had been glad enough in other days to get once around the floor with her at the Mayfair dances. The being made to wait on the telephone by the New York office of her agent, her own agent. The ruined Sophie dress and the lost earring at that South American's apartment. Why think of those things? Why not think of the pleasanter details of her visit?

Think, for instance, of the nice things that had been said about her on that morning radio program. Her appearance had been for free, but the publicity was said to be valuable, covering the entire metropolitan area and sometimes heard in Pennsylvania. Then there was the swell chat with Ike Bord, publicity man for a company she had once been under contract to. "*Whenner you coming back to us, Leda?* . . . Anything I can do for you while you're in town, only too glad, you know. I didn't even know you were here. Those bums where you are now, they never get anything in the papers." And it was comforting to know she could still charge things at Hattie's, where she had not bought anything in four years. And the amusing taxidriver: "Lady, I made you right away. I siss, 'Lydia Penley. Gay me an autograft fa Harry.' Harry's my kid was killed in the U.S. Marines. Guadalcanal. *Sure, I remember you.*" And, of course, her brother, who had come down all the way from Bridgeport with his wife, bringing Leda *a pair of nylons and a bona-fide cash offer* in case she had a clean car she wasn't using. The telephone service at her hotel had been something extra special because one of the operators formerly had been president of Leda's Brooklyn fan club. Through it all was the knowledge that her train fare and hotel bill were paid for by the company because she obligingly posed for fashion stills for the young-matron departments of the women's magazines, so the whole trip was not costing her more than eight or nine hundred dollars, including the visit to Hattie's. There were some nice things to remember, and she remembered them.

The train rolled through Lancaster County, and it was new country to Leda. It reminded her of the English countryside and of American primitives.

She got up and closed her door once, before washing her hands, but reopened it when she was comfortable. Traffic in the passageway had become light. The train conductor and the Pullman conductor came to collect her tickets and asked for her last name. "Leda Pentleigh," she said. This signified nothing to the representative of the Pennsylvania Railroad, but the Pullman conductor said, "Oh, yes, Miss Pentleigh. Hope you have an enjoyable trip," and Leda thanked him and said she was sure she would, lying in her beautiful teeth. She was thinking about sending the porter for a menu when the huntin'-shootin' type stood himself in her doorway and knocked.

"Yes?" she said.

"Could a member of Actors' Equity speak to you for a moment, Miss Pentleigh?" he said. He didn't so much say the line as read it. She knew that much—that rehearsal was behind the words and the way he spoke them.

"To be sure," she said. "Sit down, won't you?"

"Let me introduce myself. My name is Kenyon Littlejohn, which of course doesn't mean anything to you, unless you've *seen* me?"

"I confess I did see you in the station, Mr. Littlejohn. In fact, I almost spoke to you. I thought I recognized you."

He smiled, showing teeth that were a challenge to her own. He took a long gold case out of his inside coat pocket and she took a cigarette. "That can mean two things," he said. "Either you've seen me—I've been around a rather long time, never any terribly good parts. I've usually got the sort of part where I come on and say, 'Hullo, thuh, what's for tea? Oh, crom-pits! How jolly!' " She laughed and he laughed "Or else you know my almost-double. Man called Crosby? Very Back Bay-Louisburg Square chap from Boston. Whenever I've played Boston, people are always coming up to me and saying, 'Hello, Francis.' "

"Oh, I've met Francis Crosby. He used to come to Santa Barbara and Midwick for the polo."

"That's the chap," said Kenyon Littlejohn, in his gray flannel Brooks suit, Brooks shirt, Peal shoes, Players Club tie, and signet ring. "No wonder you thought you knew me, although I'm a bit disappointed it was Crosby you knew and not me."

"Perhaps I did know you, though. Let me see—"

"No. Please don't. On second thought, the things I've been in —well, the things I've been in have been all right, mostly, but as I said before, the parts I've had weren't anything I particularly care to remember. Please let me start our acquaintance from scratch."

"All right," she said.

He took a long drag of his cigarette before going on. "I hope you don't think I'm pushy or anything of that sort, Miss Pentleigh, but the fact is I came to ask your advice."

"You mean about acting?" She spoke coldly, so that this insipid hambo wouldn't think he was pulling any age stuff on her.

"Well, hardly that," he said. He spoke as coldly as he dared. "I've very seldom been without work and I've lived quite nicely. My simple needs and wants. No, you see, I've just signed my first picture contract—or, rather, it's almost signed. I'm going out to California to make tests for the older-brother part in 'Strange Virgin.' "

"Oh, yes. David's doing that, isn't he?"

"Uh—yes. They're paying my expenses and a flat sum to make the test, and, if they like me, a contract. I was wondering, do you think I ought to have an agent out there? I've never had one, you know. Gilbert and Vinton and Brock and the other managers, they usually engage me themselves, a season ahead of time, and I've never *needed* an agent, but everybody tells me out there I ought to have one. Do you agree that that's true?"

"Well, of course, to some extent that depends on how good you are at reading contracts."

"I had a year at law school, Miss Pentleigh. That part doesn't bother me. It's the haggling over money that goes on out there, and I understand none of the important people deal directly with the producers."

"Oh, you're planning on staying?"

"Well . . ."

"New York actors come out just for one picture, or, at least, that's what they say. Of course, they have to protect themselves in case they're floperoos in Hollywood. Then they can always say they never planned to stay out there, and come back to New York and pan pictures till the next offer comes along, if it ever does."

"Yes, that's true," said Mr. Littlejohn.

" 'That place,' they say. 'They put caps on your teeth and some fat Czechoslovakian that can't speak English tries to tell you how to act in a horse opera,' forgetting that the fat Czechoslovakian knows more about acting in his little finger than half the hamboes in New York. Nothing *personal*, of course, Mr. Little."

"Thank you," said Mr. Littlejohn.

"But I've got a bellyful of two-hundred-dollar-a-week Warfields coming out and trying to high-hat us, trying to steal scenes and finding themselves on the cutting-room floor because they don't know the first thing about picture technique, and it serves them right when they find themselves out on their duffs and on the way back to their Algonquins and their truck-garden patches in Jackson Heights or wherever they live. God damn it to hell, making pictures is work!"

"I realize—"

"Don't give me any of that I-realize. Wait'll you've got up at five and sweated out a scene all day and gone to the desert on location and had to chase rattlesnakes before you could go to bed. Find out what it's like and then go back and tell the boys at the Lambs Club. Do that for twenty or fifteen years." She stopped, partly for breath and partly because she didn't know what was making her go on like this.

"But we're not all like that, Miss Pentleigh," said Littlejohn when she did not go on.

His talking reminded her that she had been talking to a human being and not merely voicing her hatred of New York. His being there to hear it all (and to repeat it later, first chance he got) made her angry at him in particular. "I happen to think you are, eef you don't mind. I don't care if you're Lunt and Fontanne or Helen Hayes or Joe Blow from Kokomo—if you don't click in Hollywood, it's because you're not good enough. And, oh, boy, don't those managers come out begging for us people that can't act to do a part in their new show. When they want a name, they want a movie name. Why, in less than a week, I had chances to do a half a dozen plays, including a piece of the shows. What good can New York do me, I ask you."

"The satisfaction of a live audience," he said, answering what was not a question. "Playing before a—"

"A live audience! On a big set you play to as many people as some of the turkeys on Broadway. Live audience! Go to a première at Graumann's Chinese or the Cathay Circle and you have people, thousands, waiting there since two o'clock in the afternoon just to get a look at you and hear you say a few words into the microphone. In New York, they think if they have three hundred people and two cops on horses, they have a crowd. On the Coast, we have better than that at a preview. A *sneak* preview! But of course you wouldn't know what that is."

"Really, Miss Pentleigh, I'm very glad to be going to Hollywood. I didn't have to go if I didn't want to."

"That wasn't your attitude. You sat down here as if you were patronizing me, *me!* And started in talking about agents and producers as if Hollywood people were pinheads from Mars. Take a good gander at some of the swishes and chisellers on Broadway."

"Oh, I know a lot about them."

"Well, then, what are you asking me for advice for?"

"I'm terribly sorry," he said, and got up and left.

"Yes, and I think you're a bit of a swish yourself," said Leda to the closed door. She got a bottle of Bourbon out of her bag and poured herself a few drinks into doubled paper cups and rang for the porter.

Presently, a waiter brought a menu, and by that time Leda was feeling fine, with New York a couple of hundred miles and a week and a lifetime behind her. Dinner was served, and she ate everything put before her. She had a few more shots and agreed with her conscience that perhaps she had been a little rough on the actor, but she had to take it out on somebody. He wasn't really too bad, and she forgave him and decided to go out of her way to be nice to him the next time she saw him. She thereupon rang for the porter.

"Yes, Ma'am?" said the porter.

"There's a Mr. Entwhistle—no, that's not his name. Littlefield. That's it. Littlefield. Mr. Littlefield is on the train. He's going to California. Do you think you could find 'im and ask 'im that I'd tell 'im I'd like to speak to him, please?"

"The gentleman just in here before you had your dinner, Ma'am?"

"Yes, that's the one."

"Mr. Littlejohn. He's in this same car, PA29. I'll give him your message, Ma'am."

"Do that," she said, handing the waiter a ten-dollar bill.

She straightened her hair, which needed just a little straightening, and assumed her position—languor with dignity—on the Pullman seat, gazed with something between approval and enchantment at the darkening Pennsylvania countryside, and looked forward to home, California, and the friends she loved. She could be a help to Mr. Littlejohn (*that* name would have to be changed). She *would* be a help to Mr. Littlejohn. "That I will, that I will," she said.

MRS. STRATTON OF OAK KNOLL

As was their nightly custom, Evan Reese and his wife Georgia finished their small chores and took their seats to watch the eleven o'clock news program on the television. Evan Reese's chore was to put the backgammon men in place for the next night's game; Georgia's was to remove the coffee tray to the kitchen. Evan Reese now lit his pipe, Georgia lit a cigarette, and they sat patiently through the preliminary commercial announcements. "And now the news," said the announcer.

"Do tell," said Georgia, stroking the head of their Airedale.

Evan Reese smiled. His wife had given up her letters of protest to the newspaper editorial pages against the length and number of commercials, but she always made some small audible comment when the man said, "And now the news."

"Quiet, please," said Evan Reese.

"A four-engine bomber on a routine training flight over the Rocky—" the announcer began. At that moment the dog growled and the Reeses' doorbell rang.

Evan Reese frowned and looked at his wife, and they said, together: "Who could that be?" and Georgia Reese added, "At this hour?"

"You pay attention to the news, I'll see who it is," said Evan Reese. He switched on the carriage lamps at the front door and the floodlight that illuminated the driveway. He peeked through the draperies and saw, in the driveway, a large black limousine. He held the dog by the collar and opened the door.

A middle-aged man in chauffeur's livery raised his hand in a semi-military salute. "Stratton residence?" he said.

"No, this isn't the Stratton residence. You have the wrong house."

"This is Ridge Road and West Branch Lane, isn't it?" said the chauffeur.

"Yes it is, but if you'll notice there's a driveway across the road, with a sign that says Oak Knoll. That's the entrance to Mrs. Stratton's place."

"Sorry, I didn't see no sign."

"It's there in plain sight," said Evan Reese.

"What the hell's the delay?" The voice came from inside the limousine, and Evan Reese could make out a man's hatless head but little more. The Airedale barked once.

"I'll leave the floodlight on and you can turn around—and you can tell your employer to mind his manners."

"I'll tell him a lot more when I get my tip," said the chauffeur. "I don't work for him, I work for the rental company. He only hired this car, and believe me, I'll never drive him again."

"Is he drunk? He sounds it."

"Drunk? He was drunk when I called for him. The Racquet Club."

"New York, or Philadelphia?"

"New York. Well, sorry to trouble you, Mister."

"That's all right. Hope you get a big tip. Goodnight."

"Goodnight, sir, and thanks again." The chauffeur saluted, and Evan Reese closed the door, watching through the draperies until the limousine was out of his driveway.

"A drunken man calling on Mrs. Stratton. Obviously with the intention of spending the night, since it's a hired car. Now we have something on her."

"I guess it must be that son."

"No, I'd rather think it was some gigolo she sent for."

"She's a little old for that. Did you get a look at him?"

"I can give you a perfect description. Black patent leather hair, waxed moustache, and a gold bracelet . . . No, I didn't really see him. Would her son belong to the Racquet Club?"

"Oh, at least. You can look him up in the Social Register."

"Where is it?"

"It's in my sewing-room, by the telephone."

"Too much trouble," said Evan Reese. "Anything in the news?"

"I wasn't listening very carefully, I was overcome with curiosity about who'd call on us at eleven o'clock at night."

"Mrs. Stratton's drunken son, I guess. Now the next time she writes us one of her neighborly notes about our dog, we can come back at her."

"Oh, Ev, that was ten years ago."

"Well, it's still the only time we ever heard from her. Ten years and she never came to call on you. I think I *will* look up the son. By the telephone?"

"On the lower shelf of the little table."

Evan Reese obtained the book and returned to the library. "Now then," he said. "Stratton, there *she* is. Mrs. Francis, Oak Knoll, High Ridge, New Jersey. Phone number 7-1415. Ah, yes, here he is. Francis A., Junior, 640 East Eighty-third. R for Racquet, B for Brook, K for Knickerbocker, H-37. Harvard, '37. That would make him about forty-five years old. Oh, and here's one. Stratton, Mrs. Virginia C., Virginia Daniels, and under her name another Virginia, at Foxcroft, and another Francis, at St. Mark's. There we have the whole story, the whole tragic story of the drunken mama's-boy, coming home to see mama because the boys at the club were mean to him."

"It may not be that at all."

"I'll bet it's close to it. Now let's see if he's in *Who's Who?*" said Evan Reese. He took down a volume and opened it. "Nope. I didn't think he would be. I formed my impression of him when he barked at the driver of that car. Driver was a polite, decent-looking fellow. Probably very efficient, too, except for not seeing the Oak Knoll sign. *Say*, that's interesting."

"Why?"

"Wouldn't you think that Stratton would know where his mother lived? Maybe he was asleep, or so drunk—no, he wasn't that drunk. And he wasn't asleep. Maybe it isn't her son after all. But I think it is. Do you know what I think, Georgia?"

"What?"

"I think we have a mystery on our hands."

"Well, you puzzle it out, I'm retiring. I have all sorts of things to do tomorrow, and don't forget. We have Bob and Jennie for dinner tomorrow night."

"God, is tomorrow Wednesday? Well, at least they're coming here. We don't have to go out."

"If you stay up reading, don't fall asleep in your chair or your arm'll get stiff again and you won't be able to work."

This was a bit of caution she gave him about once a week. He was miserable when his arm hurt and he could not paint, especially when he was painting well, and more especially when he was finishing the last of his pictures for a one-man show in the spring. It was not only his habit of falling asleep in his chair that made his arm sore, nor was he telling the truth when he blamed the weather. He had bursitis, he knew it and she knew it, but they pretended he was in perfect health. He—they—would not admit that he was sixty years old and already a victim of the painter's occupational disease. He refused to see a doctor, to confirm what he had long suspected, to submit to treatment that was never wholly successful. "The minute I hear myself snoring, I'll come to bed," he said.

"Goodnight, dear," she said.

"Goodnight, Pussycat," he said. He put her hand to his cheek and kissed it, and she left him. The dog stretched out on the rug and dozed.

Evan Reese turned the television to a different channel and for an hour or so watched a lovely British movie that he knew by heart, having seen it at least ten times. He did not have to follow the plot, which was nothing much to begin with and concerned the refusal of some Scotsmen in a remote village to pay their taxes until the government promised them a new road. Evan Reese could share the Scotsmen's feelings toward London; he could sing "Men of Harlech" in the Welsh, although he had never been to the land of his fathers; but he knew the movie so well that he could pick up the story anywhere along the way, and there was no suspense in it for him. The charm of it was in the characters and the acting and in the verisimilitude of the exteriors and interiors—the laird had a forty-year-old Rolls-Royce station wagon instead of the 1960 Cadillac that Hollywood would have considered suitable for a laird. The house in which the laird lived was not too unlike Evan Reese's; built to last, furnished for comfort, a warm shelter whether the winds came down from Canada or from the North Sea.

The movie came to its happy ending and Evan Reese turned off the television. At the cessation of the sound, Mike, the Airedale, raised his head, expecting to be let out. "Just you hold it now till I finish my pipe," said Evan Reese. The dog wagged his tail to indicate that he knew he was being addressed, and Evan Reese reached down and scratched the animal's head. "I think you must be getting old, too," said Evan Reese. "You're not the watchdog you used to be. You never heard Mr. Stratton's car."

The dog again wagged his tail.

"Well, you're twelve years old," said Evan Reese. "And that's supposed to be the equivalent of eighty-four human years. You're a good boy."

At the words "good boy" the dog got to his feet and began to back out of the room, keeping his eyes on the master.

"All right," said Evan Reese, and opened the front door and let the dog run into the darkness. It was not his custom to turn on the floodlights for Mike, and in the moonless, starless night he noticed that Mrs. Stratton's house was lit up on two stories. The shades were drawn, but there was light behind them, and he could not recall ever having seen light in the house at such a late hour. It was past midnight. As his eyes became accustomed to the darkness he began to see smoke issuing forth from one of the chimneys on the Stratton roof, and he wondered what could be going on, what scene was taking place between the widow and her son. A happy reunion? He thought not.

Evan Reese whistled softly for his dog, which responded to the signal, and man and dog returned to the warm house. "Snow tomorrow, for sure," said Evan Reese. "I can feel it in my bones." He saw that the dog was curling up on his piece of carpet in the library, and he now retired for his own rest.

Bob and Jennie Hewitt were fourth-generation residents of High Ridge. She as an amateur painter and he as president of the local bank had been the Reeses' first acquaintances in the town and the friendship between the two couples had become a pleasant one. The men were the same age, the women were only two years apart, and when Bob Hewitt got over the first shock of discovering that he was somewhat less conservative than a man who earned a good living as a painter, the weekly dinner-and-bridge was instituted and had continued. A running score was kept, and at the end of their October-through-May season never more than $50 changed hands.

"Bob, get Evan to tell you about the visitor he had last night," said Jennie Hewitt. "Go on, Evan. He'd be interested. I think it's fascinating."

"Well, with that build-up, who was it, Ev? Brigitte Bardot?" said Bob Hewitt.

"Not quite," said Evan Reese, and related the events of the previous night.

Bob Hewitt was a good listener, and at the end of Evan's report he said: "Well, you have him pegged about right. Frank Stratton is a mama's-boy and a heavy drinker. Did you see him around today?"

"No. I looked for him, but there was no sign of him."

"The last time he did this, came home to mama, was before you moved to High Ridge. It was when his wife left him. He came home then, under almost the same circumstances. Drunk, and in a hired car. But the next day the old lady sent him packing. Banished him. She didn't want him around, or that was the story. Jennie, you tell that part."

"I'm dying to," said Jennie Hewitt. "And I'm dying to know if she lets him stay this time. What happened before was that Mrs. Stratton was furious because Frank did what everybody always said he'd do. Come home to mother at the first sign of trouble. And there *was* trouble. It even got in the papers, a little bit. You see, Frank is—well it was *in* the *papers*, so I might as well say it. Frank is a fairy."

"Well, don't say it that positively, Jennie. After all, he did marry and he had two children." Bob Hewitt spoke sardonically.

"But what was he arrested for?"

"*He* wasn't arrested. The other fellow was arrested for beating him up and stealing money and stuff. You've got it all mixed up."

"Well then you tell it," said Jennie Hewitt.

"There isn't much else to tell. He was beaten up by a young serviceman that he met in a bar, and the police found Frank's wallet and cigarette case on him. Stupid. You'd think he'd have got rid of such incriminating evidence, but as I recall it the soldier tried to sell the cigarette case in some bar on Eighth Avenue and the bartender tipped off the military police. Then the New York cops went to Frank's apartment and found him lying in a pool of blood, and that was how the story got out. You had to read between the lines—"

"Oh, Bob. Between the lines. They couldn't have been more explicit."

"No, maybe not, but there was no charge preferred against Frank. That's where you're giving the Reeses the wrong impression."

"I was trying to give them the right impression. Ev, Georgia, what would you think if you read that story in the newspapers?"

"I'd be inclined to think that Mr. Stratton was very indiscreet, not to say impulsive," said Evan Reese.

"I'd say he got what was coming to him," said Georgia Reese. "Picking up soldiers in a bar."

"And you'd be right, and his mother was furious," said Jennie Hewitt. "She told him to go right back to New York and face it out. Brazen it out, I'd call it. But she was right, as it turned out. He did go back to New York, and went right on seeing people and of course nobody could come up and say to him point-blank, 'Were you a fairy with that soldier?' And after a while people began to say well maybe the soldier *did* follow him to his apartment and try to rob him. In other words, people sort of gave him the benefit of the doubt. That was his version to the police."

"Maybe it was true," said Evan Reese. "When I was a young man living in Greenwich Village there were certain reprehensible characters who made a living by blackmailing older men. They'd see a man getting drunk in a speakeasy and they'd get in a taxi with him or follow him home, and then threaten to expose him if he didn't shell out. Some of those men were certainly guilty, or at least vulnerable, but I wonder how many were innocent. I knew a sculptor who paid blackmail for years because he got drunk with a male model and he could never actually remember whether he'd made passes at him or not. My friend, the sculptor, was of course vulnerable. He was bisexual. He said to me more than once, 'Reese, I honestly don't know. Maybe I did.'"

"What ever happened to him?" said Jennie Hewitt.

"My friend? He gave up. He became very successful, made a lot of money, and one day when the young bum came around for his cheque, my friend told him to go to hell. 'You can't black-mail me any more,' he said. 'I've stopped denying it or pretend-ing I'm anything else, so get out.'"

"How delightful," said Jennie Hewitt.

"Not really," said Georgia Reese. "He later hanged himself. He was genuinely in love with a girl, and she wouldn't have him."

"I guess the old Greenwich Village must have been quite a place, Ev?" said Bob Hewitt.

"It doesn't sound much different today, only worse," said Georgia.

"We had some gifted people," said Evan Reese. "Real talent. Once in a while a genius, or very close to it. Anyway, real artists. First-rate writers, some of the best. But now all I ever hear about is an occasional saxophone player. You see, we worked. We did a lot of talking, and a great deal of drinking and sleeping around, but we also worked. Now we don't hear much about work down there. Talk, yes. Drinking and sleeping around, and dope. But they don't seem to know how to paint or write."

"I never liked the Village," said Georgia. "You never did anything really good till you got out of it."

"Oh, yes, I did some good things, but I never did anything first-rate till I was past forty anyhow, so the Village did me no harm. And I did work."

"Well, this isn't very interesting to the Hewitts. We were talking about this Stratton man."

"And I wouldn't waste any pity on him," said Jennie. "Unfortunately, Bob and I weren't surprised when that happened, the beating and so on."

"No, it's one of those small-town secrets that only a few people think they're in on, but it was pretty generally known, I guess," said Bob Hewitt. "When did we first hear about it?"

"When did we first hear about it? Why, that time—"

"That time he had that friend home from college. You're right. The maid quit because Frank brought a friend home from college and—"

"Lorna. Lorna Parton."

"Lorna walked in to clean the drawing-room and there was the friend sitting at the piano, stark naked at nine o'clock in the morning. Went right on playing, too."

"Where was Stratton?" said Evan Reese.

"Oh, I don't know where he was, probably upstairs sleeping off a hangover," said Bob Hewitt. "But the friend went right on playing, even when Mrs. Stratton came in to remonstrate with him. What was it he said to her?"

"He was the boldest thing I ever heard of. He finished playing whatever it was, regardless of her saying *Mister* Jones, or whatever his name was. He came to the end of the piece and then he turned to her and said: 'Do you play?' You know, as though he expected her to join him in a duet."

"No more friends home from Harvard," said Bob Hewitt.

"What do you *mean?* No more *Frank.* She told him she didn't want him to come home at all," said Jennie Hewitt.

"That's right," said her husband. "She wouldn't have him in the house, not even at Christmas."

"Till he announced his engagement. And even then she wouldn't go to the wedding. She stayed home on some pretext or other. She never actually met Frank's wife till the first grandchild was born, and then she couldn't do enough for them. She adored the grandchildren, and they used to all four of them come visit her."

"The money," said Bob Hewitt.

"Oh, yes. She gave Frank's wife a hundred thousand dollars when each grandchild was born, *and* a trust fund for the children."

"And changed her will."

"And changed her will so that Frank gets nothing, not a penny. He gets what is it?"

"A thousand a month while she's alive. Twelve thousand a year. Then when she dies, nothing. It all goes into a trust fund for the grandchildren."

"And the ex-wife gets the income as long as she doesn't remarry. If she remarries, it all goes into the children's trusts."

"And that's our neighbor?" said Evan Reese. "I had no idea she was so rich."

"*Rich?* At one time she owned this whole mountain, or her husband did. You've never been in that house, have you?" said Bob Hewitt.

"I've never even had a good look at it from the outside. The trees and the hedges," said Evan Reese.

"Tell them about the downstairs," said Bob Hewitt.

"Tell us about the whole house," said Georgia Reese.

"Well, you knew that Frank had an older sister," said Jennie. "Bernice. She was my age."

"No, we never heard about a sister," said Georgia Reese.

"Oh, yes. Bernice, about twelve years older than Frank. I went there a lot when we were children and until Bernice eloped, at seventeen. Mrs. Stratton would send the car to my house—"

"A Rolls, needless to say," said Bob Hewitt. "Limousine when the weather was bad, and a touring car when it was good."

"I was one of the girls that Bernice was allowed to play with, but she never came to my house except to things like birthday parties. I always had to go to her house, but of course I didn't mind."

"The house, the house," said Bob Hewitt.

"But later I want to know about the daughter," said Georgia Reese.

"So do I," said her husband.

"First let her describe the house," said Bob Hewitt.

"Well, it's so long since I've been inside it that now it's almost unbelievable, although I'm told it hasn't been changed much. The main hall was two stories high, with at one end stained glass windows, imported from Italy, and they went all the way up to the second floor. On the right as you went in, a small reception room, then next to that, the drawing-room, where Frank's friend played the piano, and off that the music-room, as it was called. That was all done in white and gold and those two rooms were where we danced when they had their big parties. On the other side of the hall, the big dining room, easily room enough for, oh, sixty people. The library, lined with books all the way up to the ceiling with one of those ladders on a track like the old-time shoe stores. Two huge fireplaces. When I was little I could stand erect in the fireplaces. And a smaller room that had been Mr. Stratton's office, although they called it a study. I remember he had a stock ticker in that room, although I didn't know what it was then. They changed it after he died. On that side of the house was an enclosed porch, and on the other side, opening off the drawing-room, the conservatory. And I wouldn't attempt to describe the furniture. The dining-room chairs, high-back armchairs, brocaded, of course, and I'll bet the table weighed a ton. The paintings, you *must* have a look at them somehow, Ev. There's a Gainsborough in the main hall. A Van Dyke, a Rubens—"

"Yes, yes," said Bob Hewitt. "But don't start telling all about the paintings. Just give them the general idea. For instance, the pipe organ."

"They had a pipe organ, that was in the main hall, with the console on the first landing. They used to have an organist from Philadelphia with the wonderful name of Thunder, he'd come and give recitals once a year. Henry Thunder, a famous organist he was. And on Easter they always had a big crowd for lunch and then they'd have one of the local organists play."

"The only house in this part of the State with a pipe organ.

And I'll bet no other house had something else they had. A barber chair. A real barber chair in Mr. Stratton's dressing-room."

"Sunken bathtubs?" said Georgia Reese.

"No, I guess the house was built too early for that. The tubs were iron, but had wood all around them. Encased in wood with mother-of-pearl inlaid. I remember when they added an elevator. We were absolutely forbidden to ride in it, probably because of several experiences when we got stuck in the dumb-waiter."

"Ev, this will impress you," said Bob Hewitt. "They had their own road-roller. A steam road-roller, with a little whistle. They used to lend it to the township, but it belonged to them. I suppose at one time they had around eight hundred acres. Now it's dwindled down to, oh, I think she has no more than twenty acres now, but I think I remember the figure eight hundred. This house that you're in, this used to be occupied by a cousin of Old Man Stratton's."

"Yes, I heard that when I bought it," said Evan Reese.

"They owned all these houses on Ridge Road and rented them out to relatives and retired couples for practically nothing. I don't think there was a house within a mile of the Strattons' that they didn't own. Not that there were so many houses in those days. This section wasn't started to be built up till the Thirties," said Bob Hewitt.

"Where did Stratton's money come from?" said Evan Reese.

"In two words, Wall Street. Railroad stocks, land out west, coal mines in Pennsylvania and West Virginia. He didn't make it all himself, by any means. His father was in with Jim Fisk and Dan Drew and Gould, that crowd, but not as a very big operator. Enough to leave old Frank Senior a nice fortune, and Frank had brains. He may not have been the most honest man in the world, by present-day standards, but he stayed out of trouble. He married late in life. The present Mrs. Stratton, the old lady, was about nineteen or twenty and he was in his forties when they got married. He was well in his fifties when the present Frank was born."

"Who was she?" said Georgia Reese.

"She was a High Ridge girl, born here. She was a Crowder. The Crowders weren't immensely wealthy, but they were well fixed and got around in New York society. Oh, she had plenty to offer. She was a good-looking girl."

"She was a handsome young woman," said Jennie Hewitt. "I can remember her very well. Beautiful bone structure and quite sexy-looking."

"When did he die?" said Evan Reese.

"Let me see now, in the late Twenties. He was eighty or close to it when he died," said Bob Hewitt.

"And that was when she became a recluse?" said Georgia Reese.

"Before that. Mr. Stratton was paralyzed and they practically never left Oak Knoll after that."

"Just lived there in solitary splendor?" said Evan Reese.

"Solitary splendor!" said Jennie Hewitt. "Splendor, but not solitary. They had Phillips, the majordomo. Pierre, the chauffeur. Tripp, the coachman, and a colored groom. A head gardener whose name I forget, and as many as five or six other gardeners. Mrs. Phillips, the cook. A full-time waitress. Three or four chambermaids. Mrs. Stratton's personal maid, Alice. A tweeny."

"What's a tweeny?" said Georgia Reese.

"A tweeny is a sort of a cook's helper and not quite a regular maid. In-between."

"I never heard of it," said Georgia Reese.

"It's English, and I understand that the butler has certain privileges there. *Droit de seigneur,* you know, although I don't think Phillips claimed his. How many is that?"

"About seventeen or eighteen," said Bob Hewitt. "And you didn't include the handyman-carpenter, the night watchman, or people like the old boy's secretary, O'Neill, or nurses for the children."

"Well, twenty or so. So it was splendor, Ev, but not solitary," said Jennie Hewitt.

"No, and you left out Madigan, the superintendent, and a lot of these people had husbands and wives living on the place, but not what you might call staff," said Bob Hewitt.

"Where did they put them all?" said Georgia Reese.

"Oh, some lived in the big house, some over the garage and the carriage-house," said Jennie Hewitt.

"I had no idea we were so close to such grandeur," said Evan Reese.

"Grandeur is right," said Bob Hewitt. "They even had their own buttons for the servants' livery. An oak, of course, and if you looked carefully, the letter 'S' in the foliage."

"No coat of arms?" said Georgia Reese.

"I never saw one," said Bob Hewitt. "In spite of everything we've told you, the old boy wasn't much for show. He had the very best of everything, mind you. Cars and horses, and paintings by famous artists. But when he took the train to New York, he rode in the day coach. He had a pass, of course. And when he got to Jersey City, his private car was probably sitting there on a siding. For a man as rich as he was, he lived very inconspicuously. Take for instance, living here. This was never like Tuxedo or one of your Long Island communities. Nothing fashionable about High Ridge."

"That's true," said his wife. "And they never had a yacht or a racing stable or any of those things."

"Don't disillusion me," said Evan Reese. "I was beginning to feel that some of the grandeur would rub off on me."

"I'm afraid there isn't much of it left," said Bob Hewitt. "My father told me one time how much it cost Stratton to whitewash all the post-and-rail at Oak Knoll. You know, my father was in the building supply business. Brick and lumber, cement and paint. So he knew pretty well what Stratton spent. Stratton was my Dad's best customer, year in, year out. We—my Dad, that is —supplied the trap rock for Stratton's roads. Stratton put me through college, if you want to look at it that way. But I'll tell you one thing. Madigan, the superintendent, never had any chance to knock down a little graft. You'd always see that 'S' on the upper right-hand corner of every bill, which meant that Stratton had seen it before okaying payment. If Stratton caught a man stealing or even cheating a little bit, the fellow'd be on the next train out of here, bag and baggage, with orders to never return to High Ridge."

"The result was there was very little cheating," said Jennie Hewitt. "And they all knew they had a good thing. They were well paid, and they didn't have to eat slop or live in broken-down shacks."

"Yes, the Strattons paid their help a little more than the going rate because this was such an out-of-the-way place," said Bob Hewitt. "And he was a great believer in education. For instance, Phillips's son graduated from Johns Hopkins with an M.D. degree, and practices medicine out in California somewhere. Quite a few of the kids on the place went to college with Stratton's help."

"Anybody that wanted to, if his mother or father had been with the Strattons long enough. Ten years, I think it was," said Jennie Hewitt.

"The boy that wanted to go to Harvard," said Bob Hewitt.

"Oh, yes. Pierre, the chauffeur, had a son that was the same age as Frank Stratton, and the boy decided he wanted to go to Harvard. So Pierre told Mrs. Stratton his son wanted to go to college and would she lend him—"

"Four thousand dollars," said Bob Hewitt.

"Four thousand dollars," said his wife. "Pierre didn't want to touch his savings account, and Mrs. Stratton could take the money out of his salary. 'Why of course,' she said. She'd be *glad* to help. And what college was Joseph going to? 'Harvard,' said Pierre."

"That cooked it," said Bob Hewitt.

"She said no. 'But Madame is sending her own son to Harvard,' said Pierre. 'Precisely,' said Madame. Then of course Pierre, being a Frenchman, caught on. So Joseph went to Dartmouth."

"She was no fool," said Bob Hewitt. "Frank and his naked piano-players, classmates of her chauffeur's son."

"I'm dying to know about Bernice, the sister," said Georgia Reese.

"Shall we forget about bridge tonight?" said Evan Reese. "I'd rather hear about my neighbors. Ten years. Might as well have been living in an apartment house in New York. There you don't expect to know your neighbors."

"I'm perfectly willing, if you'd care to hear about them," said Jennie Hewitt. "You never heard of Bunnie Stratton?"

"I don't think so," said Georgia Reese.

"Madcap Bunnie Stratton? That's what she was called by the newspapers. Madcap Bunnie Stratton."

"She made up for all the publicity her father didn't get," said Bob Hewitt.

"Notoriety, you mean. Not just publicity. She was a regular F. Scott Fitzgerald heroine," said Jennie Hewitt.

"Which one?" said Evan Reese.

"Which one?" said Jennie Hewitt. "Why—I don't know which *one*."

"The reason I asked, Fitzgerald's heroines weren't madcaps," said Evan Reese.

"Well, I always thought they were," said Jennie Hewitt.

"No. Here's another example of the picture versus the printed word. People tend to think of John Held's girls when they hear Fitzgerald's name. But Fitzgerald's heroines, at least the ones I remember, were totally unlike the Held girls. Do you remember Daisy, in *The Great Gatsby*? She wasn't a Held girl. And Nicole, in *Tender Is the Night*. The very thought of John Held doing a picture of that tragic figure is repellent to me."

"Ev, I'm afraid you're a little too literal-minded. When I said an F. Scott Fitzgerald heroine I might as well admit I never read a word he wrote. And I *was* thinking of the John Held Junior drawings."

"Then call her a John Held Junior girl, but don't call her a Fitzgerald heroine. Give the artist his due, and don't distort what the author wrote."

"Oh, come on, Ev," said Bob Hewitt.

"No, now don't you protest before you think," said Evan Reese. "If I came into your bank and tried to tell you that a share of stock was a bond, you'd correct me damn quickly. Well, this happens to be something *I* know about. For years I've been hearing and reading people talking about John Held's girls and Fitzgerald's, as though they were one and the same thing. They just simply weren't. From the literary point of view, one of the worst things that ever happened to Fitzgerald was the simultaneous popularity of John Held's drawings. Those damn editorial writers were largely to blame. Who would want to take Fitzgerald seriously if all they ever knew about him was that he wrote about those John Held girls? Held was a very good satirist, and he didn't *want* his girls to be taken seriously. Of course Fitzgerald was partly to blame. He called one book *Flappers and Philosophers*, and in the public mind the flapper was the John Held girl. Actually, of course, Fitzgerald and Held and the editorial writers were all misusing the word flapper. A flapper was English slang, and it meant a society girl who had made her debut and hadn't found a husband. On the shelf, they used to say. It wasn't an eighteen-year-old girl with flopping galoshes."

"Well, according to your definition, Ev, Bernice was never a flapper, but according to mine she was," said Jennie Hewitt. "She was a sort of a John Held girl. One of the first to bob her hair and smoke in public and all the rest of it. And she didn't even make her debut."

"And *that* was a party we were looking forward to," said Bob Hewitt. "The plans."

"They started planning that party I don't know how many years ahead," said Jennie. "She was to have a New York party, but her real party was going to be here, June 1921, it was supposed to be. A thousand invitations. Mrs. Stratton hired a secretary just for that party, and she came to work over a year ahead of time. Special trains were going to leave Jersey City and Philadelphia."

"Art Hickman," said her husband.

"Art Hickman, Ted Lewis, and Markel's orchestra."

"The club," said Bob Hewitt.

"They engaged the whole club for the weekend, a year in advance, and every available hotel room for miles around. Not including families like my family and Bob's that offered to put up guests."

"Sherry. Louis Sherry."

"You can imagine the preparations Sherry's would have had to make. A thousand guests, extra servants and musicians. Supper and breakfast. Dinner before the party and luncheon at the club the next day."

"What about liquor?" said Evan Reese. "We had Prohibition by that time."

"I don't know what they were going to do about liquor. We had Prohibition, but not much enforcement then. They wouldn't have had any trouble. The stuff was coming in from Rum Row and Canada, and you can be sure Stratton would have had the best, not just Jersey Lightning."

"What was Jersey Lightning?" said Georgia Reese.

"Applejack. What we drank instead of corn liquor. They served it over the bar in every country hotel, and it wasn't bad. It had the desired effect."

"But they never had this party?" said Georgia Reese.

"No," said Jennie Hewitt. "Bunnie eloped. Don't either of you remember that? Bunnie Stratton and Jack Boyle?"

"Oh, hell," said Evan Reese. "Of course I remember now. Jack Boyle, the baseball player. Played first base for the New York Giants, and one of the first All-Americans Fordham ever had. But I'd forgotten *her* name. How did they ever get together?"

"They weren't together very long," said Jennie Hewitt. "Less than a year. Jack was a lifeguard at Belmar."

"Belmar?" said Georgia Reese.

"Belmar-by-the-Sea. A summer resort we used to go to in those days. Bob's family went there and so did mine, and quite a few of the *nicer* Irish."

"Which didn't include Jack's family. Jack was a hell of a good athlete and a handsome son of a gun, but let's face it, they weren't the lace-curtain Irish. Jack was from Jersey City, and his father was a watch repairman for the Jersey Central. White-collar, but not lace-curtain."

"We'll come to that," said Jennie Hewitt. "Anyway, Bunnie was allowed to spend a whole week with me at Belmar, the summer of 1919. She'd never swam in the ocean before, in spite of all their money, and I can't give you any better proof of how strictly *I* was brought up than by telling you that the Strattons allowed Bunnie to visit me. And a whole *week*. Six days too long."

"She took one look at Jack Boyle," said Bob Hewitt.

"And he at her. One day was too long. Love at first sight if there ever was a case of it," said Jennie Hewitt.

"Your father," said her husband.

"My father told Jack that if he didn't stop hanging around our house he'd have him fired, and Jack told my father to go straight to hell and he *was* fired. So then he had nothing to lose, and he saw Bunnie every day and every night."

"She was sixteen then?" said Georgia Reese.

"Sixteen. Jack was about twenty-one."

"Older than that, Jennie," said Bob Hewitt. "He'd been overseas in the war. He was a good twenty-three or four."

"Well, whatever. My parents were afraid to tell Mr. and Mrs. Stratton, and hoped it would blow over, but Jack went back to Fordham and that year Bunnie was at Spence and they managed to see each other."

"Then Boyle quit Fordham and went with the Giants," said Bob Hewitt.

"Now I remember. Sure. Boyle eloped, and McGraw fired him," said Evan Reese.

"But *I* don't know any of this, so go on, Jennie," said Georgia Reese.

"Well, her family of course were outraged, but so were his. They were Catholic and Bunnie and Jack had been married by a justice of the peace, in Greenwich, Connecticut. So the Boyles wouldn't have anything to do with Jack. Wouldn't let him in the house. And the only thing Jack could do was play baseball."

"But as I remember it, he did," said Evan Reese. "He played for some team in the International League, Binghamton or one of those teams."

"It *was* Binghamton," said Bob Hewitt.

"But they didn't pay him much, and Bunnie was pregnant. Mr. Stratton sent a lawyer to talk to Bunnie, but Jack wouldn't let him see her."

"Wouldn't let him *see* her?" said Bob Hewitt. "He was arrested for giving the lawyer a punch in the nose, and he told him that was what Mr. Stratton could expect, too, if he ever came around."

"Bunnie adored her father," said Jennie Hewitt. "And he did come to see her in Binghamton, while Jack was away, and he persuaded her to come home with him, knowing that Jack would follow her."

"*Thinking* that Jack would follow her. Mr. Stratton *wanted* Jack to follow her. I know that. And he wanted to give Jack a job. But he didn't know Jack Boyle. That fierce Irish pride, I guess. When Boyle got back to Binghamton and read Bunnie's letter, he quit baseball and Bunnie never heard from him again. Never. Not a word, not a line."

"What happened to him?" said Georgia Reese.

"He drifted around for a while, and then joined the Army. He'd been a lieutenant, but he enlisted as a private. I think you had to enlist for seven years then. Anyway, when he got out he became a bootlegger with some of his old friends in Jersey City. He's still alive. Frank Hague got him a job on the Hudson County payroll. Inspector of something or other. The last I heard he was a sort of an organizer for one of the labor unions."

"And what happened to her?" said Georgia Reese.

"Oh, plenty," said Jennie Hewitt. "She didn't have the baby. Whether she lost it or they got her an abortion, I don't know. The latter, I suspect, because after she divorced Jack and married the Englishman she had two children, one of which the Englishman refused to take credit for."

"When you say the Englishman, you mean the first Englishman," said Bob Hewitt. "She married two Englishmen. The Army officer, and the writer."

"Yes, but the writer was an Australian, and if he was a writer, nobody ever heard of anything he wrote," said Jennie Hewitt. "Except bad cheques. I always understood that the first Englishman, the *English*man, was quite attractive and very much in love with Bunnie. He resigned from the Army to marry her, and I guess he took all he could stand."

"What happened to her two children?" said Georgia Reese.

"The first was killed in the war, North Africa. The second was a girl," said Jennie Hewitt. "I heard that she got married during the war, but what's happened to her since I have no idea."

"And where is Bunnie herself?" said Georgia Reese.

"Majorca, surrounded by pansies and Lesbians of all nationalities. She has enough to live on and supply wine and gin for her hangers-on. She's a countess. She picked up an Italian along the way. There's some doubt about the title, or not so much about the title as her right to it. She married her Italian on a steamship, or so she says. But if she wants to call herself countess, none of her present friends are going to object. The count is over seventy and feeble-minded. I haven't seen or heard from Bunnie in over twenty years. We saw her once, briefly, in London before the war. But a friend of ours looked her up in Majorca and she said Bunnie refuses to speak English because all her little boys and girls are Italian or Spanish or French. When we saw her in London we could hardly understand her, she was so English. But not any more. She's had her face lifted a couple of times and she wears oversize sunglasses and big floppy hats, never goes out in the daylight, and her house is lit by candles. I wonder what she thinks."

"Yes," said Georgia Reese.

"You know. People like you and I, Georgia. Let's face it, we live a lot on our memories. We love our grandchildren and these two nice old things that we're stuck with—"

"Oh, thanks," said Bob Hewitt.

"But my life would be very empty without my memories, the good times we had, *and* the bad, and the old sentimental recollections. Think of what our life would be like without them. And yet I don't suppose Bunnie ever gives a thought to Jack Boyle and those days."

"Probably not," said Georgia Reese.

"Or the Englishman, or the Australian. Or the dear-knows how many lovers she had. I imagine she shuts all that out and just goes on from day to day, as though one part of her brain had been removed."

"Let me give you the other side of the coin," said Evan Reese.

"All right, Ev," said Jennie Hewitt.

"What about Mrs. Stratton, who has nothing *but* memories?"

Jennie Hewitt nodded. "Yes, that's a pretty horrible thought, too."

They were all silent for a moment, then Georgia Reese spoke. "They must suffocate her, her memories."

"Yes, who has it worse? The mother remembering everything, or the daughter remembering nothing?" said Bob Hewitt.

"Why, Robert Morris Hewitt, you're almost poetic tonight," said his wife.

"I have my moments," said Bob Hewitt. "I get in the same rut everybody gets in, and I take the old lady for granted. But every once in a while I have to talk to her on the phone, about bank business, and when she calls me Robert, I feel as though I were just starting out and she was old Queen Mary. The most personal she ever gets is to say 'Good morning, Robert,' and 'Thank you, Robert.' She never asks about Jennie or our children or grandchildren. These are business calls. But she's quite an old gal, to be able to make me feel like a fumbling assistant paying teller at my age. I don't really give a damn what Bunnie thinks, if she thinks anything. But I often wonder about the old lady in that house, the money going, the place shrinking a little every year. From eight hundred acres to twenty in a little over one generation. And the God damn futile mess that her two children have made of their lives. That was a beautiful woman once, Mrs. Stratton. I remember one time twenty-five or thirty years ago, I happened to be walking up Fifth Avenue and she was twenty or thirty feet ahead of me. She was alone. But as I followed her I couldn't help noticing how the people coming in her direction would automatically fall out of the way. Just looking at her, they'd make way for her. I never forgot that."

"I wish she hadn't written that letter about the dog," said Evan Reese. "The only communication we ever had from her."

"What did the letter say?" said Jennie Hewitt.

"Well, it was ten years ago, and I can't quote it verbatim, but to the effect that Airedales were known as one-man dogs and ours had snapped at somebody on her place."

"I know why she sent that letter," said Jennie Hewitt. "Ten

years ago? Ten years ago her grandchildren used to come here a lot."

"Then why didn't she say so?" said Evan Reese.

"Oh, that wasn't her way," said Jennie Hewitt. "Nothing dramatic or appealing to your better nature. Or sentimental about children. She was simply stating the facts about Airedales, impersonally. She wouldn't dream of mentioning her grandchildren. That would be a show of weakness on her part, inviting familiarity."

"That's true, Ev," said Bob Hewitt. "She approved of you, or you never would have got this house. She probably knew your work, and for all I know, she may even own one of your paintings."

"No, I know where all my paintings are."

"In any event, you were okayed as a purchaser and a neighbor, but that's as far as she'd ever go. Like she wouldn't call on Georgia, not because she wanted to be rude to Georgia, but because she didn't want Georgia to return the call. I see her household bills, you know, and as far as I know, she hasn't had anyone for dinner in at least ten years. At least. She buys a lot of books, and she has four television sets in the house. But for instance, she hasn't bought a bottle of liquor or wine since before Pearl Harbor. She smokes a lot of cigarettes. Camels. That was the only thing she asked for during the war, was a regular supply of Camels. And I got them for her because she never cheated on gas rationing, or shoe coupons or any of those things, and it would have been easy for her to. Technically, Oak Knoll was a farm, and there was a lot of funny business by so-called farmers then."

"I'm going to have to see this woman. That's all there is to it," said Evan Reese.

"Make it accidental," said Bob Hewitt. "Don't let her see you coming up the driveway, or she'll hide in the closet."

"Not hide," said Jennie Hewitt. "She just won't be at home."

"Well, that's what I meant. Ev knows that. And it's nothing personal. I've known her all my life, and I handle a lot of her business and talk to her over the phone, but I never go to her house, even when there are papers to sign. I send my secretary, who happens to be a notary public."

"Oh, I'll make it accidental," said Evan Reese.

"And make it soon," said Jennie Hewitt. "She's over eighty."

"Yes, and *I'm* over sixty," said Evan Reese.

The Hewitt's car was covered with snow when the time came for them to depart. "I missed the weather report," said Bob Hewitt. "Was this expected?"

"Ev expected it," said Georgia Reese.

"Look at Mike," said Bob Hewitt. "He doesn't want to go out in it. Come on, Jen. Goodnight, Reeses, thanks for a pleasant evening. And I didn't lose any money."

"Have you got snow tires?" said Georgia Reese.

"We'll be all right. Bob's careful."

"I'd feel better if you'd call us when you get home," said Georgia Reese.

"All right, as soon as we get home, but don't worry. It hasn't had a chance to freeze," said Jennie Hewitt.

For a little while Evan Reese stood at the window, looking out at the new winter scene under the floodlight. "I can think of three men that I'd like to see do that. Maxfield Parrish, George Luks, and Charles Sheeler. And Salvador Dali, that makes four. Each of them had his own special blue, and none of them would see it the way I do."

"How are you going to do it?" said his wife.

"I'm not going to attempt it. When I finish this picture I'm not going to paint anything for at least six months."

"I wasn't talking about your painting. How are you going about meeting Mrs. Stratton?"

"Is that what I was thinking about, Georgie?"

"That's my guess. Whenever you're really thinking about painting, you don't talk about it."

"It must be fun to guess. Well, you're right, this time. I'm not always thinking about something else when I talk about painting, but this time I was. With that son staying there she's not going to be very receptive, less so than usual. But then isn't that just the time to make a sortie, when she's least prepared for it?"

"Sounds mean."

"I am above meanness. However, I'm not above curiosity, and believe me, I'm damn curious. Instead of a rather dull, cranky, faceless old woman, our neighbor turns out to be—well, Jack Boyle's first mother-in-law. Boyle to me was one of the really interesting baseball players. Much more interesting really than if he'd stayed in the game and been as good as your fellow Georgian, Mr. Tyrus Raymond Cobb. And he might have been almost as good as Cobb. Potentially he was, they all said. Maybe he'd have been better. But I've always been interested in the near-misses. Understandably. I'm one myself."

"Now, now," said his wife.

"Well, you know how I feel about my work, so the hell with that. But Boyle was a near-miss, and in her way, so is Mrs. Stratton. She was never one of the famous hostesses, or mistresses, or philanthropists, and yet she could have been any of those things. Or all three. Or any two. I never even heard of her as a great beauty."

"You never heard of her husband, either."

"Yes, I did. He was a well-known millionaire, but I forgot all about him many years ago, and never connected him with the woman we bought this house from. When I was young and living in Paris and the Village, I knew the names of the millionaires. If a millionaire bought one of our pictures our prices went way up, overnight. If one of us sold a picture to Jules Bache for a thousand dollars, that was ever so much better than getting a thousand dollars from someone with less money. The inconspicuous fellow, the art-lover that happened to like your picture, and happened to have a thousand dollars—that was nice. But that kind of a sale was usually considered a lucky accident. On the other hand, if someone like Bache shelled out a thousand bucks, we never sold another picture for that little. We didn't have to. Writers have the same experience. I'm sure that William Faulkner and Ernest Hemingway got big prices for pieces that they would have sold for fifty dollars when they first wrote them. And that's as it should be. Faulkner is a great artist, and all his work is extremely valuable, whether it's his best work or his worst. The mere fact that he wrote it makes it valuable, because there is only one Faulkner. Fortunately, people believe that about painters. Look at Pablo Picasso."

"Look at Evan Reese," said his wife.

"Yes. You'll never starve, as long as you have enough of my pictures lying around," he said. "A snowscape! Tomorrow morning. I shall take my little camp stool and some of the tools of my trade, and do some sketches."

"No."

"I'll bundle up good and warm. I'll go up West Branch Road, where I can be seen from the big house. We'll *try* that anyway."

"So that's what you were thinking?" said Georgia Reese.

"Well—yes," said her husband. Bob Hewitt telephoned, and the Reeses retired for the night.

In the morning Evan Reese put on hunting socks, heavy shoes and six-buckle arctics; tweed suit and sweaters; sheep-skin reefer and cap with earlaps. He carried his camp stool, large sketch pad, and a vacuum bottle of coffee, and established a vantage point in the middle of the West Branch Road, which had not yet been visited by the township snow-plow. He made several quick sketches of the valley, then paused to take a few sips of the coffee. He screwed the cap back on the bottle and resumed sketching, aware that he was about to have company.

"Do you mind if I watch?" said his visitor. Evan Reese recognized the voice from the limousine, the same harshness but now without petulance. The harshness was of the kind that is usually attributed to whiskey-drinking.

"Why, no," said Evan Reese. "If you'd like to see what effect cold weather has on fingers. My name is Reese."

"Oh, I know. My name is Frank Stratton. My mother's a neighbor of yours."

"Of course."

"I won't talk any more. Don't let me interrupt."

Evan Reese quickly finished the sketch he had begun, turned over the page and started another. "Do you know anything about this kind of work?"

"Not a thing."

"Well, then I'll explain what I'm doing. This is what I call my shorthand. My notes. As you see, I didn't try to do that barn or that farmhouse in any detail. The silo. The pigpen. I've lived here ten years and I know all that. But as I sketch—now here for instance, I'll do this clump of trees. Ten years from now, twenty years from now, if I'm alive, I'll be able to look at this sketch and remember what I don't want to forget, which is the metallic white of the snowdrifts over there to the right, as it looks at half past ten, Eastern Standard Time. There. That's enough. My fingers are getting clumsy with the cold. Would you like a spot of coffee?"

"I was going to suggest that you come back to the house and have a cup with me."

"Thank you very much, but I think I've done enough walking. I'm headed for home. But you're obviously out for exercise. Would you like to come down with me and have a cup of coffee at my house? Do you like hot cinnamon buns? That's what I'm going to have."

"I haven't had one since I was ten years old. Sure, if it's all right?"

"Of course it is. Here, you're a young fellow. I'll give you this stool to carry, and you'll feel as if you earned your cinnamon bun."

"Fine."

"I'm not going to do this again, till I get one of those electric hand-warmers. You know the ones I mean, in the Abercrombie catalog?"

"Let me send you one when I go back to New York."

"All right. I'll trade you. One of these sketches for a hand-warmer."

"Oh, no, Mr. Reese. I get much too much the best of that deal."

"I suggested it, so it's satisfactory to me."

"Well—okay. But if you're going to be generous, will you put your initials on it?"

"When we get to my house," said Evan Reese. "You know, it's God damn cold up here. That kitchen's going to feel good."

They entered the house through the kitchen door, unbuckling

their arctics and leaving them inside the storm door. "Georgia, I have a customer for a hot cinnamon bun. This is Mr. Stratton, our neighbor's son. Mr. Stratton, my wife."

"How do you do, Mr. Stratton. Come in and get warm. Just put your things any old place. It's nice to have a visitor. You take coffee?"

"I'd love some coffee."

"And I dunk," said Evan Reese. "The molasses sticks to my teeth if I don't dunk. A good cold slice of butter, dunk just a little so the butter doesn't melt, and then enjoy yourself. And don't count the calories."

"I never count the calories," said Stratton. "I'm glad to see you've kept this kitchen just the way it used to be. I used to come here when I was a boy. My cousins lived in this house, and they had a cook that made apple butter."

"Apple butter," said Evan Reese. "Let's get some, Georgia?"

"All right. I'll put it down."

"Did you ever eat apple butter on fried scrapple?" said Stratton.

"Never heard of it, but I don't know why it wouldn't be delicious," said Evan Reese. "But scrapple is no good any more. We tried it, and it isn't the same. I'm a Pennsylvanian, and I got some to introduce it to my wife, but it just wasn't right."

"No, I didn't care for it," said Georgia Reese.

"It's a long time since I've had scrapple. Or fried mush with molasses."

"I had that for breakfast every morning before I went to school," said Evan Reese. "Or mush-milk. Corn meal mush in a soup dish, with milk and sugar."

"That's why children are so nervous these days. They go to school without breakfast, half the time," said Georgia Reese. "They might as well start the day with a cigarette and a Coke, the kind of breakfasts they eat nowadays. Have you got children, Mr. Stratton?"

"I have two. A boy and a girl, and I know what you mean." Stratton looked about him. "You *have* made some changes. Do you use the big range at all?"

"Hardly ever from about the first of April to November," said

Georgia Reese. "But beginning around Thanksgiving I use it. I like to cook on it, and there's nothing like it for heating the kitchen."

"Please don't ever get rid of it. You have bottled gas, I suppose? Oh, now I see. You have all the new things in what used to be the laundry. Your electric icebox. This is the dishwasher? Electric iron. *That's* how you did it. You have the old kitchen, but you have the modern conveniences. You see, we didn't have bottled gas in my day, and I can remember when we had our own electricity. We had a Delco plant, for Oak Knoll and the nearest houses like this one." He got up and went to a cabinet and opened a drawer. "Oh, look. You still have it." He took from the drawer a removable hand-grip for the laundry irons. "Where are the irons? Have you still got them?"

"Where they always were. Keep looking," said Georgia Reese.

"They should be—*there* they are." On a brick ledge beside the coal range were half a dozen laundry irons. He clamped the grip on one of them. "See, I remember how it works. My sister used to love to iron. I have an older sister. She lives abroad now, but I can remember coming down here with her when I was just a small boy, and she loved to help my cousin in the kitchen. Have you ever been to Majorca, Mr. Reese?"

"No."

"That's where my sister lives. She's a good deal older than I am. But she loved this house. She was very domestic, considering. I mean she's been married a lot and lives an odd sort of life. Oh, well . . . You have all those wonderful canisters. The spices and coffee and sugar. This table used to be covered with blue-and-white checkered oilcloth. I see you like it better without the cover."

He asked to see the rest of the house, and they showed him around. He enjoyed himself in simple fashion, admiring the Reeses' possessions, exclaiming delightedly on recognizing items that had been in the house when he knew it. His delight was strange, coming from a man of middle age who carried the scars of dissipation in face and figure. His sweater and tweed jacket fitted him tightly; the jacket sleeves were a little short, indicating that he had put on weight in shoulders and arms since the jacket was made. The fat sloped down from his temples and his original features were hidden in the puffy veined cheeks. He was just under six feet tall, the same height as Evan Reese, but beside Reese he appeared chubby. Reese, mentally carving away the excess flesh, saw a sensitive man enlarded in the person Stratton had made of himself. And yet as Stratton's visit extended to an hour, Evan Reese found that he was liking the man, pitying him, and hoping that he would remain as he now saw him. No matter what his intelligence told him—which was that Frank Stratton was a committed voluptuary, beyond redemption—Evan Reese wanted to postpone the reversion, and to do so he prolonged Stratton's visit.

"I'm having an exhibition in February," said Evan Reese. "How would you like to have a preview?"

"I'd be delighted, on condition that you won't hold it against me if I say anything stupid," said Stratton. "Where do you work?"

"You remember the potting-shed your cousin used to have? I turned it into a studio. It looks small, but it has as much space as some studios I've had in New York. I'm very pleased with it. I put in skylights and a linoleum floor, and that's about all I had to do. We won't be there very long, however. The only heat is from two electric heaters, and they're so murderously expensive, I never turn them on except when I'm working. So put your coat on."

Evan Reese put on his reefer, Stratton put on his trench coat and they went to the studio. It was a strictly utilitarian one-room house, containing canvases of various sizes in profusion; easels and paint tubes, brushes, knives and palettes and paint-stained rags; one damaged leather chair, several camp chairs and stools, and a bridge table on which lay a couple of large metal ash trays and a half-filled pipe rack. There were two naked electric bulbs hanging from the ceiling. "You see what I mean by cold," said Evan Reese. He turned one of the two spigots of a kitchen sink, and water came forth. "Not frozen," said Evan Reese. "But I'm going to have to get that snow shoveled off the skylight."

"Maybe I can do it. Have you got a ladder?"

"Thanks, but there'll be a fellow along some time today. A sort of a handy man. He'll be out to put the chains on my tires and maybe he might even clear the driveway, if he's in the mood. One of those local characters. I don't like to make suggestions to him, because he always says, 'Mr. Reese, I got it all planned out, now you just let me do it my way.' And he's usually right. He wants to make sure that I understand, you see, that he knows this property better than I do."

"Oh, I guess that's Charley Cooper."

"That's who it is, all right. But he's Mr. Cooper to me. Well, here are thirty-nine pictures, and on the big easel is the fortieth. All sizes. They're the ones I'm going to show in February. My last exhibition was six years ago, and these are all pictures I've done since about—well, since I chose the ones for my 1954 show. These aren't all I've done, of course. I often have three going at a time, and always two. Now for instance, here is a house in Rhode Island, Saunderstown. While I was painting this I was also painting—where is it, now? Here it is, this young lady. Pretty, isn't she?"

"Lovely."

"She talked a blue streak and smoked one cigarette after another. She was very stimulating company, and a very relaxing change from the job of doing that house. This is Spithead, Bermuda. This is a still life done right here in two days, actually in about six hours. But this son of a bitch, this took me three months before I got it right. Same size picture, and apparently just another still life. Same number of objects, just about. But why do you suppose this one took six hours, and this one three months?"

"Just answering for myself, you probably felt like painting when you did the quick one, and were getting fed up when you did the other."

"You've hit it on the nose. My wife and I'd been abroad and I hadn't had a brush in my hand for over two weeks, and we got home and I came right here and started painting without even taking my hat off. Literally. But this one, the one that took me three months, it wasn't because I was fed up with painting. No. You see, I'd seen a picture I didn't like, in Dublin. Had a quick glance at it and dismissed it from my mind, or so I thought.

99

Then one day I arranged some fruit in a bowl and set a table for two. Plates, knives and forks, and began to paint. I worked on that damn thing, I thought about it, I had dreams about it. And then one morning, just before I woke up, I had a dream that I was painting this picture and someone kept getting in my way, standing in front of the table and obstructing my view. And do you know what I decided it was? It was the artist who had painted that picture in Dublin. I didn't know the artist's name or whether it was a man or a woman, but I was unconsciously plagiarizing him, or her. So I went right on and deliberately plagiarized, as much as I could remember of that ugly picture in Dublin, and when I finished it it was about as unlike the original as a picture could be. If you look on the back, I don't always give names to my pictures, but this is one called Plagiarism."

"Fascinating," said Stratton. "And they're not at all alike?"

"Yes, they are alike. A layman would say right away that the two pictures had been painted by the same man, but an expert, another painter or a first-rate dealer or an art historian, would know right away that the two pictures couldn't possibly have been painted by the same man. If I get a good price for this picture I'm going to track down the Dublin picture and buy it. It was a terrible, terrible picture, but it was that artist's masterpiece. The son of a bitch got something in there, in his picture, that offended and irritated me, and it was good. And *he* wouldn't be able to tell me what it was. He wouldn't know it was there. I'm sure of that, because he was such a bad, mediocre painter for the rest of the picture, that he couldn't possibly know what was good. Now that, of course, poses a problem in ethics."

"How so?"

"Well, I could buy his picture, pay a good price for it if he still owns it, which I don't doubt. But then what do I do? Do I tell him that I, a pretty well-known painter, have bought his picture and thereby encourage him? Or do I keep quiet? Or do I buy it and tell him the truth, that he's a bad painter and try to discourage him? Tell him to quit while he's ahead?"

"I really don't know."

"There's still another alternative. I can destroy *my* picture. But I can't, because I know it's good."

"Maybe you ought to find out all about the painter before you decide."

"That's the humanitarian approach, and I've rejected it. I don't want to know about this painter. If it's a he or a she, a dilettante, a half-taught amateur, a poor struggling bog-trotter. Art is cruel, and in this problem I represent art. This painter will never do anything good. Never."

"He did once, Mr. Reese."

Evan Reese laughed. "Damn it, Stratton, you've touched me where I'm vulnerable. I can't *be* art, with a capital A. A genius would be ruthless. A genius would do what it's only my inclination to do."

"A man that makes a mistake usually gets a second chance. I think a man that does something good ought to, too."

"Well, apparently that's what I've decided. I had all this out with myself a dozen times, and never done a thing. So I probably won't do anything."

"And the Dublin artist did inspire a good picture."

"Oh, naturally I keep telling myself that," said Evan Reese. "Hello, dear?" Georgia Reese entered the studio.

"Mr. Stratton is wanted on the telephone," said Georgia Reese.

"Wanted on the telephone?" said Stratton.

"I'll show you," said Georgia Reese. "And you come in, Ev. You've been out here long enough."

Evan and Georgia Reese waited in noncommittal silence in the kitchen while Stratton was answering the telephone in the library. He returned shortly, smiling. "That was my mother. She was afraid I might have fallen in the snow and broken my leg."

"How did she know you were here?" said Georgia Reese.

"That's funny. How did she? I never thought to ask her."

"I imagine she was going to try every house in the neighborhood before sending out a scouting expedition," said Evan Reese.

"That's probably it. Well, it's been a very interesting morning, at least for me," said Stratton. "Thank you very much for the coffee and the cinnamon buns, Mrs. Reese. And, Mr. Reese, may I remind you that we made a deal?" He obviously was about to leave.

"Here's your sketch. I'll expect the hand-warmer any day now." Evan Reese had written: "To Frank Stratton, Oak Knoll, November 1960. Faithfully, Evan Reese."

"I'll have it framed. Maybe I'll become an art collector."

"I'm all for that, if you have the money," said Evan Reese.

"That's very dubious, but many thanks. Goodbye."

"Nice to've seen you," said Evan Reese.

The Reeses watched him trudging up the hill in the snow.

"That's going to take it out of him," said Evan Reese. "He's in terrible physical condition."

"His manners aren't any too good, either," said Georgia Reese. "Not even a mention of our coming to his mother's."

"How did she seem over the phone?"

"She didn't ask for him. It was a maid with an Irish brogue."

"We'll be invited, don't think we won't," he said.

"Why are you so sure all of a sudden?"

"Why am I so sure? Because he's going to want to come back here, and he can't very well do that without inviting us to his house *sometime*."

"And why is he going to be so anxious to come back here? Were you at your most fascinating?"

"Yes, I was at my most fascinating, and you were nice to him, and he likes this house. He isn't very bright, and he isn't much of a man. But he isn't the pig I thought he was. He *has* good manners, and when I told him about the Dublin still life I liked his reactions. Decent. Honorable. Also, he isn't an art-phony. People with a bit of pansy in them are apt to be art-phonies. One thing you've got to say for the Zuleika Dobson school, they aren't art-phonies."

"That's my school."

"I know it is. Someone brought up as rich as Stratton was shouldn't have to be phony about anything, but unfortunately you get just as much bullshit about art from the rich as you do from everybody else. I wish I knew something about the ballet. I'd try this fellow out on the ballet and see if he goes phony there. Why don't *you* know something about the ballet?"

"Because for thirty-one years I've been your cook and mistress, and nursemaid and mother of your children, and haven't had time to get culture."

"Well, I'll accept that excuse. But don't let it happen again. *Telephone.* Probably Joel Channing wanting to know when he can see the pictures. Tell him I've gone skiing." He followed her slowly to the library and listened to her side of the conversation.

"Yes it is," she said, "Oh, yes . . . This afternoon? Well, I'd have to ask my husband and call you back. He's working and I can't disturb him, but he'll be in for lunch any minute . . . I hope so, too. And thank you for calling."

"The old lady?" said Evan Reese.

"Could we come in for tea this afternoon about five. So bland. You might think we'd moved here yesterday."

"Maybe from her viewpoint it *was* yesterday."

"Do you want me to say we'll go?"

"Yes, what's the use of pretending? She'd see through that," said Evan Reese. "And as Jennie pointed out, the time is getting short."

A few minutes before five that afternoon the Reeses' doorbell rang. Evan Reese recognized the man at the door, Elwood Blawen, who had a farm on West Branch Road. "Hello, Mr. Blawen. Come in."

"No thanks. I came to fetch you to Mrs. Stratton's," said Blawen. He pointed to an old jeep with a winter top.

"How did that happen?"

"How did that happen? Why, she just called me up and said I was to go fetch you at five o'clock in my jeep. Wasn't any more to it than that. But I *imagine* she figured'd take a jeep to get you there, and she's pretty near right. You'd never get up the hill in your car, 'specially without chains. No Charley Cooper, I see."

"No, he must be counting on all this to melt away."

"Charley's all right once he gets working, but I never saw such a man for putting things off. Deliberating, he always calls it. But there's other names for it, too. Good afternoon, Mizz Reese."

"Mr. Blawen. You going to be our transportation?"

"Looks that way. She's all cleaned out inside," said Blawen. "I even got a heater in there for you."

"Not just for us, I hope," said Georgia Reese.

"Oh, no. If you mean did I put it in special." He smiled. "Oh, no. Those days are gone forever. But mind you, I seen the day when the Stratton family *would* do a thing like that. Why, they tell me she used to have a man come all the way from Philadelphia just to play a few tunes on the organ." He lowered his voice. "Paid him five—hundred—dollars." They got in the jeep. "Five hundred dollars, just to play a few tunes on the pipe organ. One time they had Woodrow Wilson here for Sunday dinner. The President of the United States. And old Stratton wasn't even a Democrat. But him and Wilson were acquainted with one another outside of politics. Oh, yes, there was always something going on around here in those days. Twenty-eight people on the payroll, sometimes more."

"You don't work for Mrs. Stratton, do you?" said Evan Reese.

"Only when she has something special and I can spare the time. Like today, she knows I have my jeep, so she phoned and said would I call for you and Mizz Reese. I always try to accommodate her if I can. Never been here before, have you?"

"No, but how did you know that?" said Evan Reese.

"How did I know that? Just took a good guess. She don't have many visitors. She only got twenty acres left out of what used to be eight hundred, and I guess she feels hemmed in. Here we are."

"Thank you very much," said Evan Reese.

"Oh, I'll be here when you come out," said Blawen.

"How long will *we* be here?" said Evan Reese.

"Well, maybe that's not for me to say, but not more'n a half an hour."

Frank Stratton came out to greet them. "I heard the jeep," he said. "I'm so glad you could come."

A maid took their things and Frank Stratton showed the way to the library. Mrs. Stratton turned from gazing into the fireplace, but she did not rise. Her left hand clutched the silver mounting of a highly polished walnut walking stick. She was obviously very feeble.

"Mother, this is Mr. and Mrs. Reese."

"Good afternoon. I'm glad you could come," said Mrs. Stratton. "Did you have a nice ride in Elwood Blawen's hideous conveyance? But it does do the trick, doesn't it?"

"My first ride in a jeep," said Georgia Reese.

"And you, Mr. Reese? Your first ride in a jeep too?" said the old lady.

"Oh, no. I did some painting for the Navy during the war, and I rode in a lot of jeeps."

"What kind of painting? Camouflage?" said Mrs. Stratton.

"No. I did some pictures of the landings at Iwo Jima, in 1945."

"Photography?"

"No. Paintings."

"*Painting?*" she said. "But wouldn't photography be much more accurate? I don't understand."

"There's no lens wide enough to take in the whole scene, so we did some sketches and the painting came later."

"And weren't you frightened?"

"I was on a big ship. It was noisy, but you don't mind it so much if you have something to do."

"How far away were you?"

"Three or four miles, most of the time."

"But that's close enough to be dangerous, isn't it?"

"Yes. But not much more dangerous than it is around here during the deer season."

"Oh, come now, Mr. Reese," said the old lady. "Did you approve of this undertaking, Mrs. Reese?"

"Yes. My husband wanted to do it very much," said Georgia Reese.

"Frank, will you ring, please?" said the old lady. "And you believe in supporting your husband in such matters? Well, I must say so do I. Division of authority only leads to confusion." She pronounced her words so slowly that they seemed to be shaking during utterance, but plainly her speech was not keeping up with her thought. "My son tells me you are preparing for an exhibition. February, did he say?"

"The last week in February," said Evan Reese.

"We'll have some tea and then Frank can show you some of my husband's purchases. They should all be in museums, but I can't bear to part with them. Not because I appreciate their merit. I don't. But I'd miss them. They're all spoken for, or I'd give one or two of them to private people. I'm not at all sure that a museum is the right place for a painting. How do you feel about that, Mr. Reese?"

"Most good pictures should be in museums," said Evan Reese.

"Then we don't agree. Do you paint to have your pictures in museums?"

"No one ever asked me that before. In fact, I never asked myself. Do I paint to have my pictures in museums? No. I paint to satisfy my need to paint, and in the hope that one person will see a picture and like it well enough to buy it. Preferably someone who can afford to pay a lot."

"I got an original Evan Reese for the price of a hand-warmer."

"What's that about a hand-warmer, my dear?"

"Mr. Reese and I made a trade. He gave me a sketch, and I'm giving him an electric hand-warmer."

"That isn't why I'm giving you the sketch, Mr. Stratton. I'm giving you the sketch because you impulsively offered to give me the hand-warmer."

"Mrs. Reese, would you with your steady young hands . . ." The old lady directed the maid with the tea things to place them in front of Georgia Reese. "Not very strong for me, please. One lump. No cream or lemon. Frank, will you take Mr. Reese on a very brief tour, but don't be gone long, as I have to leave our guests."

Evan Reese followed Stratton into the great hall and inspected the Gainsborough, the Van Dyke, and the Rubens, devoting about one minute to each picture, but making no comment. After each picture he looked at Stratton, and after the Rubens he said: "Very interesting. Now I think we ought to go back."

"Yes. You can come again and have a longer look," said Stratton.

In the library the old lady looked at Evan Reese. "Very interesting, don't you think, Mr. Reese?" she said.

"Very."

"I thought you'd find them so. Now I'm afraid you'll have to excuse me." She got to her feet. "Thank you for coming, and now you understand why I haven't been more hospitable before. Mr. Reese, I'm sure *you* understand?"

"I do indeed, Madam," said Evan Reese. "Perfectly."

The old lady took the maid's arm and left them.

"Would you have time to see some more of the house?" said Stratton.

"Oh, I'd—" Georgia Reese began.

"Not today, thanks," said Evan Reese, quickly and emphatically. "But ask us again, will you? Or come in for a cup of coffee tomorrow. I'll have some heat in the studio, and we can have our coffee there."

The Reeses were returned to their house, and Evan Reese, taking his accustomed chair in the library, lit his pipe and stretched out his legs.

"Why did you rush us away? I wanted to see the rest of the house."

"We'll be seeing the rest of the house. And why am I sure? Well, I was sure before and I'm just as sure now. I also know why the old lady never invited us before."

"Obviously because she's so helpless and didn't want to be seen," said Georgia Reese.

Evan Reese shook his head. "You didn't get that little by-play between her and me, at the end."

"No. I thought she was being old-lady flirtatious. A by-play?"

"Yes. She and I understood each other. Do you know why we were never invited to her house? I'll tell you. Because I'm a painter. And there isn't a painter in the world over twenty-five years old that wouldn't know right away that the Rubens, the Van Dyke and the Gainsborough are all fakes. And the son doesn't know it. The Gainsborough is in Pasadena, California. The Rubens is owned by a man named Lee, in Chicago. And the Van Dyke is owned by the Spencer family, in Newport. Mrs. Stratton hasn't owned either of the originals since long before the war. I wonder if she has any jewelry that her heirs presumptive are counting on. If so, I'll bet it's all paste."

"But how do you get rid of three old masters without any publicity?"

"You do it through a dealer, who arranges a private sale, and you make sure that the picture isn't bought for a museum. You sell to people who have the money and want the pictures, but don't want the publicity. There are still a few people in this country who can pay a hundred and fifty thousand for a picture for their own private enjoyment. I imagine that a condition of the sales was that there should be no public announcement, and a reputable dealer would keep quiet."

"But Bob Hewitt knows all about her financial condition."

"No he doesn't. He talks big, but Bob only knows about her account in his bank. She probably deals with some firm like the United States Trust, in New York. Bob handles the grocery bills, but I'll bet you he's never had anything to do with her securities."

"I wonder what made her change her mind, and let you in the house?"

"Well, she knows what we're like after ten years, and I think she trusts us. But of course it also has something to do with her son's visit. We'll know when she gets ready to tell us."

"She's very feeble."

"But she's a fighter."

In the morning Evan Reese was in his studio, intent on his painting, and he was irritated when Stratton knocked on the door. "Come—in," said Evan Reese. He had his pipe in his clenched teeth and he knew he sounded fierce, but Stratton's interruption was unwelcome.

"Is it too early for a cinnamon bun?" said Stratton. "I can come back, or maybe you'd like to be left alone."

"Oh, that's all right," said Evan Reese. Stratton was almost pathetic in his desire for company. "Have a seat and I'll be with you in about two minutes."

"I'll be perfectly quiet."

"You can talk. I don't mind, if you don't mind getting delayed answers."

"You've got it nice and warm in here today."

"Yes, the electric heaters."

"With the heat on it's a very pleasant room. Cozy," said Stratton. "You must like it here."

"I do," said Evan Reese. "I can work any place, but I've done more work in this little shack than anywhere else. And I've become attached to it. Probably in more ways than one."

Stratton was silent for a moment, and Evan Reese glanced at him quickly.

"What was I thinking?" said Stratton. "I was thinking about how you can hold the pipe in your mouth and go on talking and painting. The English do that. You see them riding along on bicycles, both hands on the handlebars and never taking their pipes out of their mouths."

"But I'm not English. I'm Welsh."

"Of course. Of course," said Stratton apologetically. Then, as though to make up for his mistake, he said: "You made a great hit with my mother."

"She made a great hit with me."

"You know, Mother knows a lot more about you than you might think."

"There isn't a hell of a lot to know," said Evan Reese. "Unless you want to argue that there's a hell of a lot to know about everybody. But there's nothing very spectacular about me. I've never had much personal publicity."

"That isn't the kind of thing I meant anyway. Mother doesn't care for that sort of thing, either. But she's studied you."

"Has she? I don't see how. I never met her before yesterday."

"I'll show you how," said Stratton. He stood up and went to a window. "Would you like to see how?"

"Just one second," said Evan Reese. He pressed his thumb on the canvas, put down his brush and palette, wiped his hands with a rag, and took his pipe out of his mouth. "Okay. Through for the morning."

"Well, you see the bay window on the second floor of Mother's house?"

"Indeed I do. I've often envied her that view."

"That's where she sits. And do you know what she has there? A telescope."

"I would too, if I had that bay window. And that's how she studies me?"

Stratton nodded. "You, and Mrs. Reese, and God knows how many others. People think of Mother as an old lady all alone in her mountain fastness. Actually she's an old busybody."

"In Pennsylvania a busybody is an arrangement of mirrors. You see them on second-story window-sills. You can see who's walking on the sidewalk to the right or left of your house, or ringing the doorbell, without opening the window."

"I've heard of them. At least I've seen them mentioned in novels without quite knowing what they were. But Mother's the other kind. The human kind."

"Oh, indeed she is. Very human. That's why I like her."

"Oh, you like her? I'm glad you like her. She's had a very tough life, at least the second half of it. My father was ill, and between me and my sister, we didn't give her much to be thankful for. I suppose you may have read about my sister, or heard about her."

"A little."

"A little is enough, and that goes for me, too, if you know anything about me, and I'm sure you do. People talk. People gossip."

"Yes. They do," said Evan Reese. "Shall we go over to the kitchen?"

"You'd rather I didn't talk about myself?"

"Oh, you're wrong. But there's coffee in the kitchen, and a place to sit."

"You don't *mind* if I talk?"

"Not a bit. I just thought we'd be more comfortable in the house."

"Oh, fine. You see, Mr. Reese, I know what people say about me, and they have every right to. But I always think that artistic people and writers take a different point of view. More tolerant, if you know what I mean."

"I don't know that they're really more tolerant, but they have to pretend to be."

"Well, that's almost as good. It's better than being avoided. I'm not going to be a pest, honestly I'm not. But I felt right away that you were someone I could talk to. I could tell that you'd heard about me. I always can. But you didn't try to get rid of me first thing, the way so many do."

"Let's have some coffee, and a cinnamon bun."

110

Stratton's face was transformed, from middle-aged voluptuary's to trusting boy's. "Yes, let's," he said.

Georgia and Evan Reese, jointly present, restrained Stratton from further candor, if that had been his inclination; but he stayed an hour and the conversation was easy and obviously enjoyable to him. "I hate to leave you two," he said. "But Mother likes me to be prompt. By the way, Mr. Reese, it's perfectly all right to tell Mrs. Reese about the telescope."

"Oh, I'd have told her without your permission."

"I know you would. I was just kidding," said Stratton. "Thank you both, I had *such* a good time."

Georgia Reese said to her husband: "Watch out, Ev. You may be taking on a responsibility that you didn't ask for."

"I've thought of that," said Evan Reese. "But the poor son of a bitch."

"Yes," said Georgia Reese. "We were lucky with ours."

"It wasn't all luck."

"No, it wasn't."

"Any more than what's happened to this fellow was all bad luck. Or what's happened to his sister. That old lady with her telescope, and her fake paintings. I must find out more about her. And the father, her husband."

"Well, you'll find out more from people like Elwood Blawen and Charley Cooper. Bob and Jennie Hewitt want us to think they knew the Strattons better than they really did."

"Frank Stratton? You mean the old man?" said Charley Cooper. "I don't know's I could tell you anything about him, beyond that he loved the almighty dollar. I aint saying he was a stingy man, not by any manner or means. He got rid of it, but he knew where every penny went and he made sure he always got value received. Take for instance when we voted to get rid of the horses and buy motorized equipment down't the hose company. We went to Mr. Stratton and asked how much we could count on from him. And he said, and I remember because I was there, he said if we went about it the usual way, not a penny. He said he wasn't going to give any money for a fire truck, knowing that some slick salesman would arrange to take care of certain parties

111

on the committee. Well, now how did Francis A. Stratton, a mul-tie-millionaire, know that that was the usual way? But he knew it, and that's the way it was going to be done, till he spoke up. Embarrassed hell out of the committee, and I was tickled pink, because I didn't figure to get a red cent out of it. So what Francis A. Stratton did, he bought the fire truck through one of the big corporations he was interested in. Through a regular purchasing agent. And then he *do*nated it to the borough. But he wouldn't let a few fellows have their little graft.

"Same thing with other opportunities for a bit of hanky-panky. Like one time he bought fifty dollars' worth of chances for some prize the Legion was auctioning off. By golly, the night they had the drawing, there was Francis A. Stratton, with all his stubs, in case one of his numbers won. That was kind of embarrassing, too. Because some of the Legion boys had it all arranged that one of their wives was going to get the prize. But when Francis A. Stratton showed up they had to quick dump a lot of his tickets in the bowl, and of course he won. A Victrola, I think it was. Yes. A Vic. And as soon as he won, he said he was donating it to the children's ward at the hospital. Made a certain friend of mine's wife sore as all hell. But that's the way he was, old Stratton. He you might say kept us honest. On the other hand, like donating land for a playground, he done that without the least hesitation. I guess you'd say, about honesty, he carried it to an extreme."

"Tell me about his appearance. What did he look like?"

"What did he look like? Oh-ho. If you was a stranger in town and you saw Francis A. Stratton, you'd know right away who was the big noise around these parts. If he wasn't riding in one of his Rolls-Royce English cars, if you happened to see him before he took sick, he was a regular country squire. Derby hat, checkered riding pants and polished-up boots, one of them there white collar-and-tie affairs only the tie and the collar are the same piece of cloth. They had a name for them."

"Stock."

"Stock is right. Stocks and bonds. I ought to be able to remember that, talking about Francis A. Stratton. Well, once in a while he'd take a notion to come down to town on horseback.

He usually rode a white horse, although he had every color of horse there was, and every kind of carriage and buggy. But he'd ride down and leave the horse at the livery stable and do his errands, carrying one of them riding whips. And if he didn't look like he owned the town, nobody did. Polite and all. But he was Francis A. Stratton and nobody knew it better than he did. The time he fell off his horse, he lay there because nobody had the nerve to touch him. They didn't. They stood around and looked at him lying there, unconscious, till somebody had sense enough to send for Doc Frelinghuysen."

"He fell off his horse? Was he drunk?"

"Well now that's where you won't get any two agreeing, on whether he was drunk or sober. If he was drunk, it was the only time any town people ever seen him in that condition, and some didn't believe he was a drinker. But for others it was a pretty well-known fact that Francis A. Stratton sometimes would come home from New York and more or less lock himself up with a bottle and stay out of sight for a week at a time. He had a stock ticker in his house. You know, one of those stock tickers? And he had a fellow worked for him as secretary, O'Neill, that they used to say knew as much about Stratton's business as Stratton did. And maybe more than business. Never liked that O'Neill. He was honest, but the people in town never trusted him. Everybody always shut up when O'Neill was around, for fear he'd carry tales back to Stratton. But he was faithful to Stratton, no doubt about that, and I always heard that O'Neill was a bitterly disappointed man when Stratton didn't leave him anything in his will. Must of been some reason, but I never knew what it was."

"So Stratton was a secret drinker?"

"Well, I don't know's you'd call him secret. The way he lived, as far as the town people knew, he was a secret eater. By that I mean, he didn't drink with town people, but he didn't eat with them neither."

"How old was he when he fell off the horse?"

"Along. Fifties. Maybe more. I understand he got some kind of a clot in the brain from it, but maybe that was just talk. It didn't stop him from working. Or riding horseback. He was out again in a couple months."

"He was quite a handsome man, wasn't he? Or was he?"

"Well, yes. Yes, he was handsome, for a man. Bald-headed, and he had a little black moustache. Not as big a moustache as most men wore in those days. I don't know whether you'd call him handsome or not. If you're thinking of a movie actor's looks, no. Had a nice set of teeth, I remember. In fact, you could have taken him for an Eye-talian, in the summer. Sunburned from being outdoors so much. She used to play tennis with him. They had two tennis courts, one inside and one outside, and they were the first ones around here to have a swimming pool. That was considered the height of luxury then, to have a swimming pool. But I considered the height of luxury having an inside tennis court. It's the ways they think of to spend their money that makes one rich man different than another. I used to think, who would want to play tennis in the winter? Who'd ever think of it? Would you? Maybe now you would, but not that long ago. Tennis wouldn't of been my game in the middle of the summer, let alone spend a wad of money to play it inside in the winter. But Francis A. Stratton wanted to play tennis, so he built himself a house for it, and a lot of famous players used to come there and practice."

"Who, for instance?"

"Oh, don't ask me. I never cared for tennis that much. My sport was cycling. Frank Kramer was my man, the *Iron* Man, they used to call him. I used to go over to Newark, to the Velodrome, just to watch him. If I could of been anybody else I'd have been Frank Kramer. The Iron Man."

"I don't think I ever heard of him."

"Well, that's the same way I was with your tennis players."

"To each his own, as they say."

"Yes, as far as I know, Francis A. Stratton never rode a wheel, so we didn't have much to talk about, him and I."

"What was he like, to talk to?"

"Well, as I said before, polite. There was men in town that he could buy and sell, that they wouldn't treat you as polite as Mr. Stratton. The help all liked him, too. I only ever heard of one quitting on their own accord, but she didn't quit on account of

114

Mr. Stratton." Charley Cooper giggled. "That was a funny one, but it happened long after Francis A. Stratton passed on. You know Lorna Disney, works in the post office?"

"Know her to say hello to," said Evan Reese.

Cooper giggled again. "A fine hello she got one day. Lorna was Lorna Parton then, a hired girl working for Mrs. Stratton, and one day young Frank was home from school and had a friend visiting him. Lorna walks in to do her dusting and there sat Frank's friend in his bare skin, not a thing on him, and playing the piano. Must of been quite a shock to Lorna. She quit then and there. Did her some good, though. She got married soon after. Left an impression, you might say. Oh, there was always something to talk about going on up at the Strattons', but they had so many foreigners working for them and they didn't mix. Lorna could tell you a thing or two, but don't ask her about the piano player. She don't like to have that brought up. *I* can joke with her about it, but she wouldn't like *you* to."

"No, I guess not."

"Everybody has some story about the Strattons, everybody that was living here forty-fifty years ago, what you might call their heyday. Since then you don't hear so much about them. Young Frank—well, I don't know. And Bunnie, now that she's an Italian princess. But they're a different generation, gone to pot. And they moved away. Just as well they did move away. Young Frank, he liked the boys. And Bunnie, she liked the boys, too. If they'd of stayed around here there'd have been trouble, for certain. The old lady was right in kicking them out."

"She kicked them out?"

"As good as. Wouldn't let them hang around here. If they were gonna make damn fools of themselves and get into scrapes, she didn't want it to happen here. And don't forget, it wasn't as easy to buy their way out of trouble. Mrs. Stratton, the widow, didn't carry as much weight as Francis A. when he was alive. I doubt if she's worth a tenth as much as when Mister passed on."

"Where did it all go?"

"You tell me. A fellow like myself, an ordinary working man, I been making money and saving it all these years. But I don't know what happens to a big fortune. Taxes, but that don't explain it. I think she must of got hold of some bad advice in the stock market. I don't know *where* it went. But it's a shame and a disgrace to let a big fortune like that get all pissed away. They could of done a lot for this town if they'd of held on to it, but I'll bet you when she dies there won't be enough to pay the inheritance taxes, and nowadays you can't *give* away a house like that. They used to have thirty people working up there, but the last couple years she only has me there two days a week, and two women in the house, and Elwood Blawen helps out. You know, when she married Francis A. Stratton and got him to build that house and all, it looked like High Ridge was safe and sound. But the last twenty-five-thirty years she's been selling land, and school taxes went up four or five times and this town, I'm predicting, this town inside of another couple years will be so changed nobody will recognize it. I don't want to be living here when *that* happens, and my folks have lived here since the 1700's. No matter what you say about Francis A. Stratton, he was pretty fond of this town. And I guess when you come right down to it, we were pretty fond of him."

"That's what I wanted to hear you say."

"Well, I never would of thought to say it if it wasn't for getting started talking this way. But it's a fair statement. He didn't suck up to nobody. He wasn't natured that way. But he was polite to people, and he didn't infringe on anybody's rights. He wasn't so different from any the rest of us, except richer, and nobody minded him marching around in his riding pants. What the hell? We wouldn't of trusted a man that rich that went around wearing overhalls."

"All in all, you liked Mr. Stratton, then?" said Evan Reese.

"That's what I been trying to tell you, Mr. Reese. You wanted to know some facts, and I's willing to give them to you. You're entitled to any facts I have—"

"Why? How am I?" said Evan Reese, vaguely complimented.

"How are you entitled? Well, facts is the truth, and the truth will out, and everybody's entitled to the truth. But there's different ways of telling facts, so one person telling the same facts could give a different impression. 'S far as we know, you're a reliable man and that entitles you to the facts the way I see them."

"What if I hadn't been a reliable man, Mr. Cooper?"

Cooper smiled. "You'd be surprised how little you'd find out."

"Oh."

"Newspaper reporters been around here two-three times. Once when Bunnie run away and got married. Once when Francis A. Stratton died. And a scandal sheet when Frank Junior got into trouble. They all went back and wrote up High Ridge people like we was afraid to talk about the Strattons. Afraid? Not afraid, Mr. Reese. One thing we never was was afraid. There was Coopers buried here two hundred years before any Stratton ever set foot in High Ridge. And plenty of Crowders in the same churchyard. She was a Crowder."

"Ah, now I see. She belongs to High Ridge, too."

"Sure does."

"So it wasn't so much that you liked Mr. Stratton that made you protect him, as much as her being a Crowder?"

"I thought you knew that, Mr. Reese."

"Well, it's a little hard to follow, unless you bear in mind that Mrs. Stratton was a Crowder."

"That's the whole thing. If she was just some stranger."

"But your real loyalty was to her, to Mrs. Stratton."

"To High Ridge, put it that way. Take Lorna Disney, for instance. Lorna wouldn't have no difficulty proving kinship to Mrs. Stratton. She might not be as close as the Coopers, but the Partons go back, and Lorna was a Parton."

"What about the Hewitts, for instance?"

Charley Cooper shook his head. "Not High Ridge. They come up from South Jersey, an altogether different breed of cat, you might say. There was some Coopers and some Hewitts got together in New York, but these weren't the same Hewitts. These here in town came from South Jersey."

"Then I take it Mrs. Stratton is a cousin of yours?"

"Yes indeed. The Crowders and the Coopers married over and over again. You take a walk through the churchyard and you'll wonder if they ever married anybody else. Didn't always draw the line at first cousins, either. Back in those days, I guess they didn't always know for sure, when it was mostly farms. Twenty miles away'd be a good strong young woman, and a young farmer had to have a wife. A young fellow tried to run a farm without a wife, he couldn't *do* it. You had to have a wife. And not only for the work, either, if you know what I mean. Come a certain age, and a young fellow had to have a *woman*."

"To go to bed with?" said Evan Reese.

"To, right, go to bed with. It was that or start buggerin' the sheep. Or one another. And when that happened it wasn't long before everybody'd know it. A farmer that didn't have a woman, first he'd go to pot. Usually he'd stink so that nobody'd want to go near him. And pretty soon the farm would go to hell."

"Was this in your lifetime?"

"Sure was in my lifetime. I remember one Crowder had a piece of land he tried to farm without a woman. Him and his brother, the two of them. Jack'd never bring the brother to town with him, just come by himself. Stink? That fellow you could smell him a hundred yards off, and he grew his hair long and a beard. He couldn't read or write and to tell the truth, his vocabulary was pretty small. Just enough to ask for what he wanted in the store, like salt, molasses, shells for his gun. Children used to yell at him and he'd throw stones at them. Hit them, too. But he never run after them. He was the slowest-moving white man I ever saw."

"And what happened to *him*?"

"The brother run away one day, and Jack shot himself with the shotgun."

"And what happened to the brother?"

"They found him living in a cave, couple of miles from the farm. They put him away, he was an idiot. And he died of some sickness a couple months after they locked him up. The sheriff accidentally on purpose set fire to the shack they lived in. He told my father no self-respecting pig would live in it. Slaughtered the stock, a couple of cows, and the court awarded the land to the next of kin. That was an uncle, and the uncle was a cousin of Mrs. Stratton's father. So you see?"

"Mm-hmm." Evan Reese nodded. He was not sure whether he

was supposed to see that a farm could not be run without a wife, or that Mrs. Stratton had some odd relatives.

"We had just as bad among the Coopers, I guess. They hung a Cooper when I was a young boy, and the sheriff that sprung the trap was a Cooper. How's that for family relations?"

"Well, where I come from in Pennsylvania there were over a dozen Evan Reeses in the same town, and five Reese Evanses. Originally r, h, y, s, but pronounced Reese. And Billy Williamses and Tommy Thomases and Johnny Johnses."

"Then you ought to know," said Charley Cooper. "But here it's been like that for close to three hundred years."

"I guess it was a good thing Mrs. Stratton married a stranger."

"Why?"

"New blood," said Evan Reese.

"New blood? Take a look at Frank Junior. Take a look at Bunnie. If that's all new blood can do for you, you're no better off than as if you married your first cousin. You can't go by that with people."

"You have a point," said Evan Reese. "But maybe Frank's grandchildren will be all right, or Bunnie's."

"Well, I doubt if I'll be around to see it, so I don't intend to let it worry me. I got one of my own grandchildren the brightest boy in his class at Rutgers, and another, his sister, in a mental institution. They had new blood, too. You figure it out, Mr. Reese."

"All right, Mr. Cooper, and if I do I'll call you up."

Cooper smiled. "No hurry, Mr. Reese. They're gonna make babies no matter what you tell them. That we won't be able to stop. Nobody could of stopped *me* when *I* was the right age." He jabbed a thumb in Reese's rib. "Didn't wait till it was legal, either."

"I'll bet you didn't."

"There's a few extra Coopers in addition to them that have the name. Know what I mean?"

"A few extra Coopers, eh?"

"One or two, must be. And I often think to myself, I wasn't the only one after nooky. Consequently, if I's getting mine, other

119

parties were getting theirs, and the old saying, it's a wise child that knows his own father."

"True the world over, I suppose," said Evan Reese.

"I don't know about the world over, Mr. Reese. I only know about High Ridge, but I sure know my High Ridge. An education in itself."

The conversation was taking place in Evan Reese's studio, to which Cooper had gone to report on some trees that had been overburdened in the snowfall. In cold weather it was never difficult to get Charley Cooper to talk, if the studio was warm. "Well, if you let me have your saw, I think I'll trim off some of them limbs," said Cooper, reluctantly.

"Hanging in the closet," said Evan Reese.

"Always used to rub a little ham fat on a saw," said Cooper. "As good as anything I know to keep the rust out. I never put a saw away without rubbing a little ham fat, but I guess oil's all right if it does the trick. How you coming along with your picture-painting?"

"Slow but sure," said Evan Reese.

"These here pictures, they look as good to me as some the Strattons paid thousands of dollars for."

"Thank you. They bought some very valuable paintings," said Evan Reese.

"So they did," said Cooper.

Evan Reese waited. He knew that Cooper was on the verge of saying something about the Stratton pictures.

"That puts me in mind of a question I wanted to ask you, Mr. Reese. What do they do when they *clean* a picture? Supposing you had an expensive picture. Would you send it away to have it cleaned?"

"I might, yes."

"Oh, you would?"

"Oh, yes. To have an expert job done."

"Put it in a crate and send it off to New York, eh?"

"Yes, that's done all the time, with valuable paintings. Why?"

"Costs a lot of money, I'll bet."

"It's not cheap, but it's worth it for a good picture."

120

"Mrs. Stratton used to do it. Anyway, she did it some years ago and I wondered why anybody'd want to go to all that trouble. She had me up there building crates for two or three pictures, oh, back before the war. That is, a fellow came from New York and told me how he wanted the crates built. That was carpentry, so I had to charge her extra, but she didn't complain. I made her a price of $15 a crate, labor and materials. Well, that's one of the ways the rich have of spending their money."

"In this case, protecting an investment."

"Very likely," said Cooper, unsatisfied. "Fifteen dollars apiece to me, and then whatever the cleaner charged. What would he charge?"

"That depends on the value of the painting."

"Say a painting by Van Dyke?"

"Oh, probably a thousand dollars. I don't know. Maybe more."

"Then I didn't overcharge her for my crates."

"I think that was a fair price."

"I wondered. 'S far as I know, she never sent any more away, and I wondered if she thought I overcharged her."

"The Van Dyke is the one that's hanging in the hall?" said Evan Reese.

Cooper nodded. "I wouldn't of remembered Van Dyke, except there's a whole family of Van Dykes living around here."

"Did they do a good cleaning job?"

"I don't know. I didn't unpack it for her, and I don't get in the hall very often. My work don't take me but to the cellar and the kitchen, generally speaking." He paused. "Supposing she wanted to sell a picture like that. What would she get for it?"

"Oh, Lord. Fifty, a hundred, a hundred and fifty thousand. Possibly more. The market changes, and some paintings are worth much more than others by the same man."

"What if, supposing a fellow come to you with a picture and wanted to sell it to you. Would you know right away if it was genuine?"

"That depends. If I knew the painter's work very well I think I could tell. And of course you realize that some individual paintings are famous. The Mona Lisa, for instance. Everybody knows where that is."

"I don't. I heard of it, but I don't know where it is."

"It's in the Louvre, in Paris. And to a certain extent that's true of a great many famous paintings."

"Then if you took a look at a painting by Van Dyke, you'd know right away if it was genuine?"

"If I had occasion to study it, probably. Why? Have you been wondering about Mrs. Stratton's Van Dyke?"

"Oh, I wouldn't want you to say that," said Cooper. "No, sir, I wouldn't want that at all, Mr. Reese. Don't put words in my mouth."

"I wouldn't think of doing that, Mr. Cooper."

"Hope not," said Cooper. "Well, this aint getting my work done, much as I enjoyed talking with you."

"I enjoyed it too. Come in any time."

"And everything I said this morning—?"

"Oh, absolutely between the two of us."

"She never liked anybody talking about her. Starting with marrying a man twice her age."

"I imagine."

The expected call from Mrs. Stratton came later in the day. "I'd like your advice on something, if you have five minutes," she said. It was an invitation that unmistakably excluded Georgia Reese. "My son's gone over to Princeton for lunch, so it'll be just you and I."

Evan Reese was led by the maid to the study-office.

"Some coffee, Mr. Reese?" said Mrs. Stratton.

"No thanks."

"Do have some? It's here, and it's hot, and I always feel more like a hostess if my guests take *something*. Sugar?"

"One lump, please." He accepted the demitasse and took a chair facing hers.

"Mrs. Reese isn't going to say anything about those frauds, is she?"

"Of course not."

"No. She's a lady. I knew that. I sold the pictures quite a long while ago. It was the only way I knew to provide for my grandchildren. Even so, I didn't get a very good price for them. The dealer took a larger commission than usual. *He* said because he wasn't getting any publicity, but what he meant was that *I* wasn't getting any publicity. In other *words*, he'd keep his mouth shut for a price. Well, I had no choice but to pay him."

"I think I ought to warn you that Charley Cooper is suspicious." He reported some of his conversation with Cooper, and she listened in silence until he finished.

"Yes," she said. "Charley Cooper would like somehow to collect a little money from me for *his* silence. But first he has to have someone to back up his suspicions. He'll try you, later, when he's decided you can be trusted. Not that that will be a very high compliment, Mr. Reese."

"No, it won't be, will it?"

"I know Charley so well because he's my cousin, or has he told you that?"

"Yes, he's told me that."

"The question on Charley's mind would be whether to risk losing the few dollars I pay him fifty-two weeks a year. When he was younger he was more trustworthy. Not more honest, but more trustworthy. He was satisfied with ten or twenty dollars a week. But he's old now, and why is it that the old like money so much? Is it because that's all there is? As a young man Charley was quite dashing. The girls in High Ridge swooned over him, if that doesn't tax your imagination. He was a handsome young man, scorching about on his bicycle. My husband used to give him a lot of his clothes, and Charley cut quite a figure. But then he married and settled down. His wife made him refuse my husband's old suits, and he became very straitlaced. Always had two or three jobs at the same time and brought up his children with an iron hand. Isn't it always that way with reformed rakes? Were you a rake when you were a younger man, Mr. Reese?"

"I did some raking, but I don't think I was a rake."

"Charley was a rake, by High Bridge standards. He's supposed to have been the father of at least two children by other men's wives. Luckily for him, though, the mothers were the kind that couldn't be sure. There was more of that here than we like to admit."

"There is, no matter where you go."

"I daresay. But I didn't ask you here to discuss my cousin Charley Cooper. I want to know what you think of my son. Is there any hope for him?"

"In what way?"

"In any way. You may not think it's fair of me to ask you such a question. You don't know me very well, and I haven't been very cordial to you and Mrs. Reese. But I'm a very old woman, and we haven't got time to get acquainted by easy stages. The nice thing about being old is that I can dispense with those easy stages, dinner twice a year for ten years, tea four times a year, and so forth. You and I can make up our minds about each other much more quickly. And I knew from the way you acted after you saw those fake pictures that I could tell you anything and ask you anything. If I had known you all my life I couldn't be surer."

"Thank you."

"You're welcome. And so—what about my son? I'd hoped that when he was divorced he'd be able to face his problem squarely. In plain language, stop torturing himself with this pretense of being like other men. He never has been. He loved the girl he married, and he loves his children. But he forced that girl to marry him by convincing her that she would be his salvation. Salvation! He very nearly ruined her life as well as his own. And he knew what a dreadful thing he was doing to her, and that was what made him take to drinking. As to the children—they're exactly like dolls, animated dolls. When he speaks of them that's the way he sounds, as though he were talking about dolls. And he loved dolls when he was a little boy. But only too well I remember that for no reason at all he would smash a doll, and I sided with his wife on the question of custody of the children."

"Well, aside from his drinking, what's the matter with him now?"

"You say *aside* from his drinking? There is nothing *aside* from his drinking, Mr. Reese."

"But he hasn't been drinking since's he's been here."

124

"He doesn't drink here because I won't have it. But in New York he drinks all day long, every day."

"What do you mean when you say you won't have it? Do you lock up the whiskey supply?"

"Nothing as easy as that. He simply knows that if he takes more than a few cocktails before meals, I'll send him away. I won't have him in my house. And he understands that."

"So he complies?"

"He has no alternative," she said.

Evan Reese stood up and went to the window.

"You seem to me to want to light your pipe," said Mrs. Stratton. "Go right ahead."

"How sensitive you are. That's exactly what I want to do," said Evan Reese.

"I like the smell of pipe tobacco. I don't like the smell of pipes, but the tobacco burning is very pleasant."

"Well, I'll light up as quickly as I can," said Evan Reese. He filled his pipe and lit it, and remained standing. "Mrs. Stratton, I agree with you that we can dispense with the early stages."

"That's good."

"But even if I'd known you, we'd known each other, all our lives, that wouldn't necessarily mean that complete candor existed between us."

"No, that's true. What are you getting at, Mr. Reese?"

"This. Whether we've known each other a couple of days, or forty or fifty years, the question is how well do we know each other? In other words, what things can we say, and what things must we not say?"

"There's nothing we can't say, when I've asked you such a terribly inside-of-me, intimate question about my son. I should think that such a question would make you feel free to answer me with complete candor. In fact, Mr. Reese, as a gentleman you *have* to reply to my question with the same candor. That's the only courteous thing you can do."

"I wonder."

"Oh, don't *wonder*. It *is*. It costs me something in pride and humility to be so frank with you."

"But I don't want to be equally frank with you. It won't cost me any humility or pride, but it might cost me your friendship. I have that, haven't I?"

"You have indeed. In fact, you may be my only friend. I can't think of any other, so I guess you are."

"Madam, I *am* your friend," said Evan Reese. "Will you believe that?"

"Yes. I promise."

"Then I'll say what I think, but I hope you'll forgive me."

"Please go on."

Evan Reese emptied his pipe in the fireplace and again seated himself, facing her. "First of all, I'm what I am, a painter, and not a psychiatrist."

"I don't want a psychiatrist."

"Your son has made a failure of his marriage. He has affection and I suppose admiration for his wife. He has a great fondness for his children, his dolls. He got out of his marriage, with its heterosexual obligations. But getting out of his marriage didn't make him happy, or give him any release. You tell me that he drinks heavily all the time."

"Morning, noon and night," she said.

"*Except!* Except when he comes here, Mrs. Stratton. Except when he's here with you. The only time he's at all happy, the only time he doesn't need to drink—"

"He knows I won't have it in my house—"

"Mrs. Stratton, he doesn't drink here because he doesn't *want* to drink here. This is where he wants to be, with you."

"Do you know what you're saying?" she said.

"Of course I do. Of course I know what I'm saying."

"Then stop saying it. You know it isn't true."

"What isn't true, Mrs. Stratton?"

"What you're thinking. It was never true, never in my life."

"I believe you."

"Then why must you say these things?"

"I believe *you*, Mrs. Stratton. *You*. But I don't disbelieve what your son feels."

"He feels nothing. He's past all feeling."

"Then let him be happy, here with you."

She shook her head. "I'm too old. I don't want him here," she said.

"My dear lady, you sent him away once before. Twice before. What happens when you send him away?"

"Oh, you know these things?"

"Yes," said Evan Reese. "And now you're old, Mrs. Stratton, but even so you'll probably outlive him."

"I'm sure I will."

"Then let him stay, the more reason."

"I *am* old, you know. But he is my son. The poor, bloated, miserable boy. I hardly know him any more. Tell me, Mr. Reese, so wise and kind you are, why does *this* last?" She held her hand to her bosom.

"Something must," he said.

MARY AND NORMA

There was a pie, a deep-dish apple pie, sitting on top of the light blue bread box, and though a wax-paper sheet covered the pie, Mary Kneely could see that a good-sized wedge had been cut out of it, a slab not quite a quarter of the whole pie. In the sink was a coffee cup and saucer, rinsed out but not washed, and she knew without looking that there would be a dozen cigarette butts in the garbage can. He had waited up for her, smoking, drinking coffee, and finally getting at the pie instead of the whiskey. She wished he had got at the whiskey instead. He had never been able to drink much whiskey; it made him sick or put him to sleep, sometimes both. But now he would be lying awake from the coffee, probably smoking in bed in violation of his own strict rule, and thinking up some sarcastic remark to greet her with.

She covered the pie more securely and put the cup and saucer and knife and fork and spoon on the right side of the sink, where they would be joined in the morning by the breakfast dishes. He had forgotten to clean the percolator, and she dumped out the coffee grounds and cleaned it herself and made it ready for the morning. She ran the cold water over her own cigarette and dropped it in the garbage can with his butts. Then she switched off the kitchen light and made her way to their room.

He was lying in bed, pretending to be reading an old *Field & Stream*, an issue that featured the firearms and fishing tackle that he would never buy. Every year he bought that special issue, if not of *Field & Stream*, of its competitors, and all winter long he would look at the pictures and read the descriptions of the guns and rods and reels and lines; just as in the spring of the year he would pay a dollar for a magazine that contained pictures of boats: big cruisers, yachts for charter, the newest in outboards, and the latest thing in houseboats for the rivers of Florida. Once he had sent away for the plans for building one of those boats, paid around fifteen dollars for the plans; but he did not know the first thing about carpentry, and the boat that had seemed so attractive in the photographs became less so in blueprints. One day he just threw the blueprints away, when she was out of the house.

He looked up at her, then back at his magazine. "You're home early," he said.

"Am I?"

"Yeah, it'll be two-three hours before daylight."

"Oh," she said.

"Who brought you home? I didn't hear any car."

"Came home in a taxi," she said.

"Frank Walen's?"

"No. The Italian fellow, Joe's."

"Why didn't you call Frank?"

"I did, but he was busy."

"Yeah, and he knows me better than the Italian fellow. He ask you a lot of questions, the Italian fellow?"

"Didn't ask me *any* questions. I didn't have any conversation with him at all. Just told him the address."

"Why did you have to tell him the address? He knows who you are by this time."

"Maybe he does, but I told him the address anyway."

"Did you sit up front with him?"

"I sat in his lap!"

"It wouldn't surprise me."

"Oh, *nothing'd* surprise *you*, Ed. You know all the answers to everything."

She hung up her dress and stood behind the opened closet door to finish her undressing and get into her nightgown and bathrobe. She took a long time in the bathroom, but he was still looking at the magazine when she came out. "Is it all right if I put the light out?" she said.

"Go ahead," he said.

She pressed the button in the base of the lamp. "Goodnight," she said.

"Goodnight, hell," he said, and in the darkness got into her bed. When he returned to his own bed he quickly fell asleep, making the whistling sound that was almost as bad as snoring. She got up and went to the living-room and smoked a cigarette in the dark, unwilling to let the neighbors see a light on. When she began to feel sleepy she went back to bed.

"Where are you going today?" she said, as she gave him his breakfast.

"This morning I gotta go over to Huntington," he said. "Al Proser. I get finished up with Al and then I gotta go see a new fellow in Riverhead. A new fellow just starting out. And if I have time I was thinking while I was over that direction I'd drop in on some of the guys in Southampton."

"And home by way of Center Moriches?"

"Yeah. Why?"

"A few beers with the Kneely family. I won't start dinner till seven o'clock."

"There won't be any beers with the Kneely family. Buddy's in New York for a convention, and Vince and I had an argument."

"Oh, how could anybody ever have an argument with dear sweet Vince? Why he has the disposition of a saint."

"You and your sarcastic remarks."

"That's what your mother says. Vince has the disposition of a saint. She must know some different saints than the ones I ever heard of."

"You can say that again. Any saints *you* know about, my mother wouldn't know them. What are *you* gonna do today?"

"The same thing I did yesterday. Help your sister with the moving."

"Where you were till two o'clock this morning?"

"Why didn't you call her up if you thought I was some place else?"

"Because the two of you are both alike, birds of a feather. I wouldn't believe Norma any more than I'd believe you."

"You're afraid to be right and afraid to be wrong, that's your trouble," she said.

"You're birds of a feather, you and Norma. It's a terrible thing to have to be ashamed of your own sister, but believe me, when the time comes I'm not gonna stand by her."

"When what time comes?"

"The time. When Harry walks in on her some night. Her and one of her boy friends. My own sister. And you stay out of it, too. If Harry starts shooting, and I wouldn't blame him, maybe you'll stop a slug yourself."

"I thought cops were supposed to be able to shoot."

"Harry can shoot all right."

"Well then he won't hit me."

"You just stay out of it."

"All right, I'll stay out of it. If I see Harry coming in with a gun in his hand I'll ask to be excused."

"You know what I mean. You know damn well."

"Maybe it would solve your problems if he did hit me.

"I don't need Harry to solve my problems."

"Well, maybe it would solve *my* problems."

"Aw, go to hell. If I didn't have any more problems than you have I'd consider myself lucky."

"You don't have any problems. The only problems you have are is dinner ready on time, and what's on TV."

"Sure. You heard of competition in business, I suppose."

"All you do is go to a contractor and ask him how many cubic yards he needs. Or tons. Or truckloads."

"That shows how much you know about sand and gravel. Nine years, and you think all I am is an order-taker. Huh. If that's all I was you'd starve to death."

"I wouldn't mind starving as much as you would."

131

"Cracks about my appetite don't have the slightest effect, not the slightest. When I lived home, before I was married, the only one of six children that didn't have a good appetite was Norma, your pal."

"Your sister."

"Don't remind me of it. She had to be made to eat her meals, and look at her. A skinny, temperamental, neurotic pushover. My own sister."

"She has two children, and they're healthy. And that stupid cop she's married to, he's not underweight."

"She's a neurotic pushover. I don't know what any guy would see in her. And they wouldn't if she wasn't a pushover. Harry's the one I feel sorry for, but he'll get wise to himself."

"And when he does, bang-bang, huh?"

"It'll be her own fault. Her own damn fault. I won't stand by her. I told her plenty of times."

"Oh, I know you did."

"Well, she can't say I didn't warn her. That much I did, and if she don't wanta take my advice, I did all I could."

"Yeah. You and Buddy and Vince."

"*And Paul.* Even her brother a priest didn't have any effect on her."

"He wouldn't have any effect on me, either."

"Oh, hell, you're a Protestant."

"Whatever I am, Paul Kneely wouldn't have any influence over me, Protestant, Catholic, Jew, Holy Roller."

"You let him marry us."

"As a favor to you, that's all. I didn't pick him."

"You be careful what you say about Paul. He isn't only my brother. He's an ordained priest."

"I'm always careful what I say about him. The only one's not afraid of him is Norma. All the rest of you're afraid of him."

"It isn't fear. It's respect."

"Well don't ask me to respect him."

"Not asking you. I'm *telling* you."

"For the one thousandth time," she said. "If you see any place selling beach plum jelly, stop and get some. It goes good at breakfast."

"I'll see you when I see you," he said, and departed.

She did her morning chores until Norma came to fetch her to Norma's house. "It's as much trouble to move from one end of town to the other as if we were moving to California," said Norma. "More. Nowadays the movers pack everything in barrels, all labeled. The woman I'm moving next door to came all the way from Seattle, Washington, and she says they take care of everything. If you tell them what room to put the stuff in, they'll do that. She and her husband came by car and had a three weeks' vacation driving all over and stopping at places, and the movers got here the day after *they* did."

"That's not my idea of a vacation, three weeks in a car with your husband."

"You'd have different ideas if you saw the husband. He looks like William Holden. They say that about a lot of men, but this one really does."

"Be careful, Norma," said Mary.

"Oh, I only said hello to him a couple of times. But I saw him first, so don't *you* get ideas. Duane Jensen. Nice name."

"Duane Jensen. It's all right."

"He's a major in the Air Force, and he has something to do at Grumman. They have three children. I think she was ready to get snooty when I told her Harry was a cop, but she acted different when I told her Harry was a major fifteen years ago."

"*Was* he?"

"In the Military Police. He sure was. So you could see her doing a little mental arithmetic and figuring if Harry was a major fifteen years ago, he'd be a lot higher than major now. So she stopped acting snooty."

"I know you, Norma, and you better be careful. You get to be friends with the wife first. Then the next thing is it's you and the husband."

"Not always," said Norma.

"Well, pretty often. Don't you ever get afraid of Harry?"

"Harry's a lunkhead or I'd of been dead by now," said Norma. "It isn't Harry I'm afraid of. He's a lunkhead. But those brothers of mine. Especially Ed. He's liable to say something sometime in front of Harry, and that's what I'm afraid of. A lunkhead like

Harry, they aren't the ones that make the trouble, but it's when they hear it from a third party. If I ever get in any trouble it'll be Ed that caused it."

"You're so right."

"Oh, sure. I know that. You know what Ed's trouble is—or maybe you don't. No, maybe you don't."

"He eats too much."

"That, and something else."

"He'll eat a whole chocolate cake. I've seen him do it when he gets upset about something, where another man would get drunk."

"Oh, he did that from a kid. Encouraged by my mother. Any time anything happened to one of us, but Ed in particular, Mom would stuff us full of something to eat. But that isn't Ed's basic trouble."

"What is?"

"Well, if you want to know, Ed wanted to be a priest. He was the one that *wanted* to be the priest in the family, but Mom decided that Paul had the true vocation. Therefore, Ed was the one that they always made jokes about girls. Mom used to say 'Our Ed, the girls won't leave him alone,' till he got to believing it himself. But I guess you know plenty about Ed in that department."

"Yeah."

"Vince and Bud, out every night raising hell but Ed was the one Mom called the ladies' man."

"Why didn't she want Ed to be a priest?"

"The only reason I can think of is because Paul was the youngest and that way she could hold on to him longer. She didn't really care what happened to the other brothers, just as long as she could have her Paul. Well, it's a good thing in a way, because God help any girl that would of married Paul after Mom got through with him."

"Did he ever fall for any girl?"

"What chance did he have? She would never of let Ed marry a Protestant if she cared what happened to him. You must of been surprised when she didn't put up more objections. I know Ed was in fear and trembling because you weren't a Catholic, but he didn't have anything to worry about." Norma chuckled. "She almost outsmarted herself, though."

"How?"

"Paul. From the time he was ten years old he got a brain-washing, that the only life for him was the priesthood. And he believed it, absolutely. He was an altar boy and served Mass practically every morning, weekdays and Sundays, and he had holy pictures in his room and all that. Then one day he dropped a bombshell, a real blockbuster. He told Mom he wanted to be a missionary. He wanted to go to China or some place and be a missionary. Oh, was that a catastrophe! I don't know how she talked him out of that, but she did. But believe me, that had her worried. So now he's just a parish priest and doesn't even get to go overseas and travel. His vacation he comes home to Center Moriches and tries to sermonize me. What the hell does he know about me? I think Ed puts him up to it. That's what Vince thinks. Vince had an argument with Ed over me. Did Ed say anything to you?"

"I knew they had some kind of an argument. I didn't know what about," said Mary.

"It was over me. Vince told Ed that what I did was Harry's business, not Ed's business or Paul's business or anybody else's. Vince, you know Vince, he's a holy terror. He'd have an argument with the Pope if he felt like it. You ought to hear him on the subject of Harry. 'That lunkhead,' he calls him. He hates cops, and I think he hates *priests*. He'll say anything in front of Paul, just to shock him. He goes too far sometimes. Vince doesn't realize that Paul never had a chance."

"I never thought of it that way, but I guess it's true. To me Paul is just a big fat nothing."

"They all are. And if we lived in Center Moriches, Mom would have Harry, because don't think Vince is all that independent, because he's not. Mom still holds on to the pursestrings, and Vince isn't a very good businessman. He owes Mom over four thousand dollars. And if we lived there she'd figure some way to have Harry obligated to her. And he'd go for it. Sometimes I think Harry's more like one of my own brothers."

They got out of the car and entered Norma's house, their

footsteps starting small echoes on the now bare floors. Norma offered her sister-in-law a cigarette, lit it and lit her own. She rested one arm across her waist, giving support to the elbow of the other arm, and holding her cigarette high in the air. She contemplated her next move. "I could do the rest of it myself," she said. "But I'm glad to have your company. I was just thinking, I lived in this house over fifteen years, the only house I ever lived in since I was married. You'd think I'd have some pangs about moving, but I don't. The children don't, either. Harry's the only one that tried to get sentimental about it. God! It's a good thing these walls can't talk."

"I'll say," said Mary.

"I didn't mean you, Mary. I was just thinking about myself."

"Oh, I know."

"The closest I ever came to getting caught, it wasn't Harry. It was my brother Vince. This friend of mine just left by the kitchen door, and two minutes later Vince barged in the front way. He had made quite a load on his way home from the harness races, and suddenly decided to pay a call on his sister."

"Why do you take such chances?"

"Why do you?"

"Yeah, I guess you're right, but I don't have any children, and Ed isn't liable to kill me. Harry would kill you, Norma."

"Maybe, if he caught me. But did you ever stop to think of how many times I thought of killing him? He comes home at five or six o'clock in the morning when he's on night duty. He takes off his uniform and hangs up his gun belt in the closet, and gets into bed with me. The usual thing, then rolls over and goes to sleep, and it's time for me to get up and get the kids' breakfast. How many times, I wonder, have I looked at that gun and thought, 'You lunkhead, what do you think I am? Some kind of a cow?' No consideration, nothing nice about it. Wakes me up out of a sound sleep just so I can be some kind of a cow. If that's all there is to it for him, it isn't enough for me. Oh, I'd never shoot him, but if he knew how many times I thought about it, he wouldn't bring his gun home."

"Ed is always looking at pictures of guns."

"Oh, I know. He always did. He even asked Harry—maybe I

shouldn't tell you this. But I will. He asked Harry one time last winter how to go about buying a gun. It's against the law in this State. A revolver. Harry told him it was practically impossible in New York. Possession is illegal without a license, and you had to go through a lot of red tape to get a license."

"I'm not afraid of Ed."

"No, I wouldn't think you would be. But I'll bet there'd be times when you'd be afraid of yourself if you had a gun in the house."

Mary stood in the middle of the emptiness, not thinking of what Norma was saying. "You lived here fifteen years," she said. "I remember when you papered this room. I guess the people that bought the house, the first thing she'll want to do is re-paper it."

"I wouldn't blame her. I was beginning to get sick of it," said Norma.

"And then there won't be anything left of fifteen years you lived here."

"Yes there will. She bought the icebox and the washer and the dryer."

"But nothing personal. Wallpaper I consider personal. Like appliances, I don't."

"Oh, yes. I see. No, I guess there won't be much of that left. It could have been anybody lived here."

"Nine years I've been married to Ed, but we lived in four different places. You lived here fifteen years."

"Mom's in the same house over thirty-five. They put additions on it, but it's the same house. Now it's too big for her, but she won't let go of it. She could save money if she did, but then she couldn't have the whole tribe around at Christmas, queening it over everybody. Making everybody eat too much. You've been there, you've seen her."

"Sure have. I sure have. 'Mary's lucky. She won't have to get up and go to early Mass.' Every Christmas Eve for nine Christmases. 'Mary can sleep late.' "

"I know."

"The funny thing is, I went and got myself mixed up with another Catholic."

"You don't have to tell me unless you feel like it."

"Joe Angelo."

"That has the new taxi business?"

"Yes."

"He's married, Mary. You know that."

"Sure, I know it."

"I guess he's all right. It takes money to get started in the taxi business, and he doesn't have a criminal record. Harry seems to think he's all right, and he'd know if anybody did. But don't let Harry find out about this, or he'll make it tough for Joe."

"That's what Joe's afraid of. He's more afraid of Harry finding out than Ed."

"I was wondering who it was," said Norma. "I knew you had somebody, but I didn't want to say anything till you told me yourself."

"Yes, since last spring."

"Well, all I can say is good luck and be careful."

"If it isn't me telling you to be careful, it's you telling me."

"Yes, but I had more experiences in that line, Mary. I'm married to a real lunkhead, but Ed Kneely's no lunkhead. He's shrewd, mean and shrewd. And one of these days he's going to be a rich man."

"Ed?"

"He's like my father. My father didn't start making any money till he was well up in his thirties, and Ed's branching out. He's getting known over in Suffolk. You know, five years ago Ed wouldn't have had an argument with Vince. Vince was always kind of the big shot, the one that made the most noise. But like now Vince owes Mom over four thousand dollars, and she doesn't figure to get that back. It'll be taken out of Vince's share when she dies. Ed'll get his full share, and if she hangs on another five years he'll come into it just about when he needs it in the business. Ed Kneely's going to be a rich man, so don't spoil it for yourself. You're entitled to reap the benefit."

"The benefit of what?"

"Sticking with the son of a bitch all these years. The only thing that'll stop Ed is if he eats himself to death. Which he'll do if you worry him too much. Keep him off the pies and cakes till he makes his fortune."

Mary smiled. "Then what?"

"Then let him enjoy himself. Give him waffles for breakfast and pie à la mode every night. He'll eat it, and you'll be a rich widow when you're still in your forties. I wish it was as easy as that with Harry, but Harry didn't gain ten pounds since he got out of the Army."

"I wonder if they hate us as much," said Mary.

"If they didn't, we wouldn't be talking this way."

"I guess not."

"I got the look from Duane Jensen. He knows. But I'm 'way ahead of him. I'm thinking of when he begins to wish he never saw me, when he wishes he was back in Seattle."

"Yes. Joe said last night I ought to use Frank Whalen once in a while, just to throw people off."

"That's one of the first signs," said Norma. "He wouldn't have told you that last spring. *I* hate *them*. It isn't only them hating us. But what are you gonna do?"

YOU CAN
ALWAYS TELL NEWARK

Not many people ever see the game and not all those who see it can follow the scoring, and among those who can score it fewer still can play it, and, finally, in the entire world there are probably fewer than fifty men who play it well. It is a beautiful game to watch, requiring a quick eye, a strong wrist, and a dancer's agility of its players; but as is the case with another exciting game, high goal polo, it can become a bore. Too much skill, too much beauty, too much excitement, too much excellence, and the spectator's attention will wander, in polo, at a symphony concert, in court tennis, as in life itself.

The girl had been applauding good shots during the first set, and applauding them in a way that indicated she had some knowledge of the game. She was sitting in the first row of spectators, and from time to time one of the players, when it was his turn to serve, would address some remark to her, apparently not seeing her, but speaking her name. "How'd you like that one, Nance? Who you betting on, Nance?" he would mutter, and she would smile, and the young people sitting near her would turn and smile at her, with what they deliberately intended to be a knowing smile. There was some small joke between her and them, some special knowledge.

There were three rows of benches for the spectators, benches without backs, but the men and women in the third row could rest their backs against the wall. It was cold on the court, and not warm where the spectators sat, and at the end of the second set, when the two players stopped to sip iced soft drinks, all the spectators rose to stretch. It was then that Williams saw that the girl was pregnant, probably in her seventh month. When play resumed the girl sat down, but now she knew how tired she was, and she sat with her back against the second-row seats, and the young couple behind her, in the second row, made room for her, but it was an uncomfortable position. Williams watched her; she was tired, and once she hunched her shoulders in an involuntary reaction to the cold. Williams, from his seat in the third row, tapped her arm, and she turned and looked up at him, a stranger and an elderly stranger at that.

"Wouldn't you like to sit up here? Support your back? We can make room for you," said Williams.

"Oh, no thanks. I'm all right, thank you." She smiled with her mouth only. Now she sat up straight and lit a cigarette, and there was exasperation in the forceful blowing out of smoke and in her stiff manner of sitting. Plainly she was annoyed that a stranger had noticed her pregnancy and tiredness, and she did not look at Williams again. She wanted no help from anyone. When the match was over and the winner and loser were photographed receiving their silver bowls she did not applaud.

"What's the matter, Nance?" said one of her young companions. "Just because your man lost?"

"Oh, shut up," she said. "And stop *saying* that. Let's get out of here."

"There's free booze," said one of the young men.

"Oh, all right," said the girl. "But let's not stay forever? I'm cold."

"Have a couple of scoops and it'll warm you up," said the young man.

The picture-taking over, the player who had been speaking *sotto voce* to Nancy crossed the court to the place where she had been sitting. "Hey, Joe, where's Nancy?" he said. "Isn't she staying? She go?"

"She's staying. Hard luck, by the way."

"No, he beat me. Listen, tell her to be sure and wait, will you? I have to take a shower, I stink. But I won't be more than ten or fifteen minutes. Will you tell her?"

"Okay, Rex. See you," said Joe.

"Be sure and tell her, Joe. Now don't let her go home without my seeing her. I'll be fifteen minutes at the most," he said, then, in a lower voice: "Is Bud here?"

Joe laughed. "Bud come to see you, especially when you had a chance of winning? Get *with* it, boy."

"Well, I wanted to be sure. I have to go back to New York on the seven o'clock train."

They were all young enough so that what was overheard by someone as old as Williams did not matter. He was fifty, and they were their own world.

"Well, Ned, shall we go have some of that free booze?" said Williams's host and companion.

"Sure," said Williams. The two men smiled.

"Aren't you glad we have all that behind us?" said Smith.

"Sometimes I am," said Williams. "Who is she?"

"I'm all prepared," said Smith. "Her name is Nancy Phillips, married to Bud Phillips. They live in Chestnut Hill. Her name *was* Nancy Standish. That ought to help you."

"*Oh*. That *does* help. The daughter of Bob Standish and Evie Jeffcott."

"Uh-huh."

"No wonder I was drawn to her, so to speak."

"I was terribly amused, you know," said Smith. "I thought God damn it, here is history repeating itself right before my very eyes."

"Is that what you thought?"

"That's what I thought. Don't you think she looks a lot like Evie?"

"Well now I do, but it never occurred to me before," said Williams. "And it isn't actually that she looks so much like Evie."

"No, not terribly much, but at least you're consistent."

"Yes, I guess you could say that. So is the girl, for that matter. Her mother didn't like me the first time she saw me, either."

"She made up for it," said Smith. "We go down this way."

"Why didn't she say hello to you? Where are her manners?"

"What manners? None of them have any manners any more. No manners, no style, no ambition. They're a bunch of self-centered little pigs."

"I wonder what we were?" said Williams.

"Self-centered little pigs, no doubt, but we damn well had our manners drilled into us. These little bastards blame our generation for the state of the world. I think they're taught that in school and college. So they hate us. Really hate us, Ned. I don't think there's a God damn one of them that ever stops to think that we weren't responsible for 1929. We were the victims of it. And World War Two, we get blamed for that. What the hell did we have to do with it? We went, that's all. We had to go, so we went. But these little pricks blame us for the whole damn shooting-match. They don't even know their history. Or Social Studies, as they call it. Jesus Christ! You're lucky you have no children."

"You make me think I am."

"Well, as you know, I have four, and after they're ten years old they start taking pot-shots, and by the time they're fifteen—oh, brother. 'Daddy, you just don't *know*.' That's their stock answer for everything. I just don't know about segregation, or about war. I have one snot-nose about to go in the Army and *he's* telling *me* how awful war is. And if I *told* him about Guadal he'd accuse me of wallowing in it, so I've never told him. I've learned to keep my mouth shut, the only way to avoid having a scene. 'Daddy, you just don't *know*.' If I'd said that to my father I'd have been clouted over the head. And if one of my sisters had said it to my father, my mother would have taken good care of her. Actually they loved my father, in a way that my daughters have never loved me. They still think he was a great and wonderful man, and all he was was an honest, decent, strict father. The whole purpose of my existence is when I get through paying for their education, to come through with an Austin-Healey for graduation. As a matter of fact I couldn't have paid for their education without help from their various grandparents. Betty and I just get by, and you know how much I make. This booze is free, so drink it up, boy. Would you like to meet Nancy?"

"Is she like the others?"

"I think so, but you can find out for yourself. She pretended not to see me before, but we'll just go right up to her. Come on. Be brave."

The men pushed through to where Nancy Phillips was leaning against a table. "Hello there, Nancy."

"Oh, hello, Mr. Smith. Have you been here all the time?" She had a drink in her hand and she smiled agreeably enough.

"Sitting right behind you. I want you to meet a friend of your mother's. *And* father's. This is Mr. Williams, Mr. Ned Williams."

"Oh, hello, Mr. Williams. *You* were there, I saw *you*. At least —weren't you the one that . . . ?"

"I'm the one that."

"Did you ever sit on anything as uncomfortable as those benches? Mr. Smith, *can't* this club afford something more *comfortable?*"

"You better take that up with your father. He's on the board. Where was he today, by the way?"

"Oh, hunting, I guess. Saturday, this time of year. Are you over from New York, Mr. Williams?"

"Just for the day."

"Just to see the match?"

"More or less. Partly business with Mr. Smith. How's your mother?"

"Mummy's fine, or I guess she is. I haven't seen her for a couple of weeks. We live in Chestnut Hill, and Mummy and Daddy are still in Ardmore. Do you know Philadelphia, Mr. Williams?"

"I used to."

"Before your mother married your father, he means," said Smith.

"Oh, you were a *beau* of Mummy's? What was she like then?"

"I don't know that she was any different then from now. I saw her about a year ago. Nowadays I seem to see her and your father at weddings, for the most part."

"I meant as a—what did they call them—flapper? Was she a flapper, my mother?"

"I wouldn't think so, would you?" Williams asked Smith.

"Definitely not. But definitely," said Smith.

"Well, you, Mr. Williams. Were you a—playboy? I guess that would be the opposite of flapper."

"George? Was I?"

"I don't know why you say 'Was I?' As far as I know, you still are."

"Oh, are you, Mr. Williams?"

"You sound incredulous. No, I was never one of the outstanding playboys. As we used to say, I got around."

"Then how did you and Mummy get together, if Mr. Smith is right." She did not wait for an answer but said, largely to herself, "Still—Bud and I."

"Well of course we *didn't* get together or you'd be my daughter instead of Bob Standish's."

"I didn't necessarily mean that close together, Mr. Williams."

"Well, now the conversion is taking a decided turn for the better," said Smith.

"It's taken a turn, all right," said the girl. "So let's turn back."

"Any direction you say," said Williams.

Now, before any more could be said, they were joined by the tennis player, whose hair was wet. "Hello, Nance," he said.

"Hello, Rex. I'd like you to know Mr. Smith, and Mr. Williams. This is Rex Ivers, who played such spec*ta*cular tennis this afternoon. Spec*ta*cular."

"Mr. Smith. Mr. Williams. Oh, hello, Mr. Williams. I've met Mr. Williams."

"I thought you played extremely well," said Williams. "Your only trouble was that you missed the easy ones."

"Four straight. But he beat me. He played better."

"Oh, you're such a good, good sport, Rex," said Nancy.

"Well, what's wrong with that? Anyway, I'm not such a good, good sport. I wish I were."

"Yes you are, that's why you missed the easy ones, as Mr. Williams said. You were playing like a good sport instead of to win, and I consider that insulting to my opponent."

"*He* doesn't feel insulted. He got the hardware, and some of my cash."

"Oh, you actually bet on yourself?" said Nancy. "You had money going on this match?"

"Yes. We bet a hundred dollars apiece. I think you put the whammy on me. Every one of those easy shots I missed, I just happened to be facing in your direction."

"Oh, of course. And I waved my handkerchief to distract you."

"I didn't say that. I meant it as a compliment, what I did say. Where's Bud?"

"He sent his regrets," said the girl.

"I think we'll leave you two," said Smith.

"Say hello to your mother, and your father," said Williams.

"I will, thank you. Nice to've seen you," said the girl.

Smith and Williams rode the elevator in silence and went to the bar, seated themselves, ordered drinks. "Well, that was a happy thought," said Smith.

"Oh, I wanted to meet her."

"I didn't mean that. I was thinking about how she could have been your daughter."

"Oh, I see. Well, is this her first child?"

"It's no excuse. At this moment she's probably raking him over the coals, and he's so much in love with her that it's coming out of his eyes."

"That's very poetic."

"Entirely accidental. Tell me about Ivers. I didn't know you knew him."

"I don't. I just see him at the club and I guess I've met him there a few times. I was surprised he remembered me. Now *he* has good manners."

"Yes, but where does it get him in his own crowd? They not only don't appreciate good manners. Did you happen to notice during the match, he'd say something to her. Nice. And those others with her, they'd all look wise, as if they knew the whole story."

146

"I did notice that, yes. What's her husband like?"

"He's still in medical school, out at the University. I think he has another year to go."

"Bob Standish has plenty of money."

"Oh, the Phillipses are loaded too. No money problem there. The problem is going to be when she finds out what it's like to be the wife of a doctor. It's tough enough now, of course, while Bud's in medical school, but just wait till she finds out what the first few years are going to be like."

"She seems to be having a very hard time of it."

"For God's sake, why?"

"Oh, well there you've got me."

"Hell of an attractive mother, father's a nice guy, husband working his ass off trying to be something. Plenty of money. A nice young guy in love with her, obviously. And she's having a baby. I don't know what else a young girl could want."

"Is there any chance that this baby belongs to Ivers?"

"Oh, there's always that chance, but she didn't greet him like the father of her child. Is Ivers married, do you happen to know?"

"I happen to know he's not."

"And she's a good-looking little bitch, too. Add that to the rest of her complaints. Quite a shape, when her belly's flat."

"I could see that it would be."

"Ned?"

"What?"

"She *isn't* your daughter, by any chance?"

"Well, you know, George. She could be. Evie never said so, and I was hoping you wouldn't ask, but I was just figuring it out. She could be, mathematically."

"I sort of thought so. At least as a possibility."

"As you said, there was always that chance, but you'd think Evie would have told me."

"I wouldn't think anything of the kind."

"No, I guess not. Evie was a hard one to figure sometimes."

"Why didn't you and Evie get married?"

"Before she married Bob?"

"Yes."

"Because she wasn't in love with me."

"Oh, come."

"She wasn't. She said so."

"She gave you enough proof to the contrary."

"She didn't consider that proof of anything, except of course that she considered me safe to go to bed with. But her family were against it, and God knows I wasn't very reliable in those days, and Bob had been hanging around for years."

"But then after she married Bob?"

"Well—then she discovered she was in love with me. All right, I'll give it to you straight. She wanted to divorce Bob and I was the one that prevented it. Plus the fact that I was leaving for Quantico. It was just before Pearl. Maybe I was running away from marriage, I don't know. But that's why we didn't get married. Mathematically, this girl could be the result of the summer of '41. My daughter. George, I think she is."

"I think so too."

"Something. Even before I knew her name, who she was. I felt protective. You know, when I offered her a seat with us?"

"Sure, sure."

"And it was more than her resemblance to Evie. Maybe not more. Different from. Apart from. She didn't feel anything, though."

"Yes she did."

"Yes, I guess she did."

"Something bothered her. She looked at you, and maybe she saw something without any idea of what it was. Some resemblance to herself, maybe. Not only the color of your eyes, but the shape of them."

"Maybe that's what *I* saw."

"And maybe she did too. That can be very baffling, to see resemblances to yourself in your children. Elusive. And if you didn't know of the relationship, God knows how disturbing it might be. I imagine it must be especially true for girls, who spend a lot more time looking at themselves than we do. You didn't get any feeling that she resented you because you were on the make, did you?"

"No."

"Neither did I. She was annoyed, but that wasn't what annoyed her. Well, we've got it all figured out." Smith raised his glass. "Congratulations, Papa."

"Thank you."

"Now you're one of us. The rejected generation."

"Are we rejected, George? I'd hate to think that."

"Two hours ago I certainly didn't. But I'll never be the same as I was two hours ago."

"No, you won't. Are you going to say anything to Evie?"

"I don't know. I don't know whether she'd tell me the truth."

"Do you need to have her tell you?"

"A little bit. Yes."

"Why don't you depend on your instinct, and to hell with what Evie says or doesn't say? Don't even ask her."

"Maybe I won't. I wish I could talk to the girl again."

"That can be arranged. My daughter sees her fairly frequently. That's comparatively easy."

"Before she has her baby?"

"Ned, nobody dies in childbirth any more, if that's worrying you."

"No, but it was cold up there today."

"Nobody dies of pneumonia, either."

"Well then what the hell *do* all these people die of?"

"Worry, so stop it," said Smith. "I don't want to rush you, Ned, but if you're counting on making the seven o'clock train . . ."

The seven o'clock to New York was a train that originated in Washington and it was late, with the result that the train crew wanted no time wasted at the Thirtieth Street station. Passengers were hurried off, passengers were hurried on, and the confusion was worse than usual. An Air Force second lieutenant with a flight kit and a guitar was blocked by passengers trying to board the train, and he in turn refused to budge for them. In the disorder the train was held up for six minutes, and the delay was fortunate for Rex Ivers, who came running down the steps, taking them two or three at a leap. He had a small suitcase and an old pigskin tennis bag of a vintage that had not been manufactured in more than twenty years. He stowed the luggage on

149

the shelf at the end of the car, and considered where to sit. There were vacant seats, but most of them had coats or hats that belonged to passengers who were in the dining-car. "Taken? Taken? Taken?" said Ivers, walking down the aisle. "Hello, Mr. Williams? Is this taken?"

"Probably, but so's the one I'm sitting in," said Williams. "They can eat or they can sit, but they can't do both."

"There'll be a row," said Ivers.

"What if there is? I'm not budging. Have a seat till they come —and I'll bet they stay in the diner till Newark."

"All right. I'm with you," said Ivers. He seemed to be a little bit tight. His hair, now dry, fell down over his forehead. His club tie was crooked, the knot somewhere under the collar. And there was lipstick on his chin.

"I see someone saw you off, affectionately," said Williams.

"Why? Oh, have I got telltale traces?"

"On your chin."

Ivers moistened his handkerchief and rubbed the lipstick off. "All gone?"

"All gone," said Williams.

"Listen, go ahead and read your paper, sir. I don't want to bother you."

"Oh, that's all right. Light's not very good. But I may doze off."

"Yes, I might too."

"I should think you would."

"I had a couple of scoops. If I'd won I'd be high, but I lost, so the only effect is to make me sleepy."

"Have you got your ticket? Give it to me and I'll give it to the conductor."

"Sir, but you want to take a nap."

"After North Philadelphia. Push that gadget and the seat goes back. Get yourself a nap."

"Well—thanks very much. Just a nap's all I want." He handed his ticket to Williams, altered the angle of the seat, stretched out and was asleep in three minutes, heavily, deeply, helplessly, rather sadly asleep.

"Teeks for North Philadelphia. North Philadelphia teeks please," said the trainman.

Williams read his *Evening Bulletin*, saw that the sleeping young man at his right—according to this edition of the newspaper—was one of the finalists in the court tennis tournament. It was strange to come upon this item after the outcome had been decided, like having a look into the future with the certainty that what one saw would take place. Williams read the item again, then turned to the Evening Chat column, which contained society news. At this moment some people he knew in Wynnewood were getting ready to receive guests for dinner: Mr. and Mrs. John Arthur Kersley will entertain at dinner this evening in honor of their daughter Willela Kersley, whose engagement, etc. What if he knew the score of that dinner party, as he now knew the score of Ivers's tennis match? What if he could call up Jack Kersley and tell him for God's sake not to let John Jones sit next to Mary Brown, that before the night was over John Jones would say something to Mary Brown that would wreck their lives? What if he could call Mary Brown and tell her not to listen to anything John Jones said? And what if he had been able to speak to Rex Ivers and persuade him to default, so that he would not have gone to Philadelphia and seen Nancy. "My daughter."

"I beg your pardon?"

"Oh—I must have dozed off," said Williams.

Young Ivers grinned. "Like somebody hit you with a croquet mallet."

"Where are we?" said Williams. He looked out the window but could not identify landmarks.

"We just passed through New Brunswick," said Ivers.

"New Brunswick? How long have you been awake?"

"Oh, I guess I only slept about ten minutes. I woke up just after North Philadelphia. Here's your paper, sir, I borrowed it. Gave me a funny feeling to read about my match before it happened. You know, when this was printed, I was on equal terms with my worthy opponent. Now I'm second banana."

"Do you know Jack Kersley?" said Williams.

"Kersley? No, I don't think so. Should I?"

"No, I just happened to think of him. Lives in Philadelphia."

"I might have met him this week. I met a lot of guys during the tournament. Oh, I did meet an older man named Kersley. Has he got a daughter, Wilhelmina or something like that?"

"Yes he has."

"Then I did meet him. What made you mention him?"

"I don't really know," said Williams. "I guess I'm still in a bit of a fog."

"Why don't you go back to sleep?"

"No, no. A nap was all I wanted."

"You know, when you said Jack Kersley, that didn't register. But the daughter is a friend of a friend of mine. In fact, my girl. My girl is going to a dinner party at the Kersleys' tonight. The girl that saw me off at the station."

"Oh, you have a girl in Philadelphia?"

"Yes. Not the way that sounds, though. A girl in Philadelphia. A girl in Boston. A girl in Chicago."

"This is the real thing? The one and only, we used to say."

"Yes. Married, though."

"Have to watch out for that," said Williams.

"Telling *me*. Do you remember my father? Was killed in World War Two?"

"Sure, I knew him. A fine man."

"That's what everybody says, without fail. But I never knew him. I was three years old when he joined the Navy, and honestly I have no recollection of him except what I hear from my mother and his friends. And I couldn't possibly live up to his reputation. Not possibly. God, at school they had his name on a tablet and every time I got into trouble, sure as hell some master would take me for a walk and steer me in the direction of the memorial. You know. Illustrating the lecture. What I'm getting at is I guess I have some kind of a guilt complex because my father was this idol, and here I am, the original mixed-up kid. It's not something you go to the head-shrinker for, and yet I don't know any minister I'd feel like talking to. That's what it is, too. More of a religious problem."

"Ethical."

"Ethical, right. This girl would marry me. She wants to divorce her husband and marry me."

"Well, if you love her. And you say she's your girl."

"It isn't all that easy. The husband hates me, and he has good reason to. He knows I was there first, she told him. But he's—he's doing something constructive. He's doing something, a line of work, that takes up all his time and energy, and it's worthwhile work. If she left him, it wouldn't only be their marriage. Well, I don't think you know the people, so I'll tell you. The husband is studying to be a doctor and they say he's brilliant. Brilliant. But I know he's dependent on her. Not financially, but for moral support. She's dependent on me—for immoral support. Or was. I hadn't seen her till today, she turned up at the tennis match with her crowd. And she came with me to the station. God, she wants me to get a job in Philadelphia, and she'll get a divorce, and we'll get married, and the hell with her husband. There's a certain reason why she wants me to be in Philadelphia now. Sort of a crisis going on."

"Well, as I see it, Rex, the thing that's holding you back is this ethical problem. Your girl's husband and his career. But where does that leave her and the child?"

"The child? Do you know who it is?"

"I think I sat two rows behind your girl at the match. The crisis is she's having a baby, isn't it?"

"Jesus, yes. Then you know who the girl is."

"Yes, I know who the girl is."

"I know you were talking to her afterward but I didn't figure you'd guess anything. Well, sir, what would you do? As an unprejudiced observer."

"Well, I have an ethical problem, too. My ethical problem is whether to advise you one way or the other. As a matter of fact, Rex, my problem is really more difficult than yours."

"Yes, I suppose it is," said Ivers. "Why should you get into the act, eh? It isn't your responsibility." The young man chewed his lip thoughtfully. "Mr. Williams, I hope you don't think I go around blabbing stuff this way all the time."

"Of course I don't, Rex."

"Well, I *don't*. If you knew me better you'd know that. I don't know whether it was because I had a couple of drinks or what. I wish I could convince you of that."

"Don't let it bother you."

"The thing is, it does bother me. I hope everything I told you is in the strictest confidence."

"It will be."

"Have I got your word on that?"

"You have my word. I promise you I won't repeat any of this conversation to anybody."

"I wish you could forget everything I told you."

"That I can't promise."

The young man was still very uneasy. "You see, Mr. Williams, this girl's had everything she ever wanted."

"Except marriage to you."

"Yes, but it wouldn't work out now. It never will work out. She thinks she wants to be married to me, but it wouldn't last a year before she was discontented. And meanwhile she'd have broken up her marriage and possibly ruined her husband's career, and the kid wouldn't have a father. In other words, this is the time for somebody to make sense, and it's up to me to be the one."

"Probably."

"So—what I'm getting at, the importance of keeping this confidential. Nancy will get over this and stay with her husband, and in two years it'll all be a thing of the past."

"And you don't think you're being tough on her."

"No tougher on her than I am on myself. She's my girl, Mr. Williams. Make no mistake about that."

"Rex, I'm going to ask you a question you may not like."

"You're entitled to ask anything you please."

"What if this baby she's having is yours?"

"If it was, I think she would have told me."

"Would that have made a difference, to you?"

The boy—for now he looked about seventeen—shook his head. "No. It would make things tougher for me, but as long as she didn't tell Bud, her husband, she and the baby are better off."

"Thank you."

"Why do you say that?"

"Oh—thank you for trusting me with your confidences."

"Hell, I ought to be thanking you. And I do. You know, her father and mother, they're your generation, but they don't seem to know what it's all about. I could never talk to them the way I've talked to you. Of course that may be Philadelphia."

"It may be Philadelphia."

"Nancy does a big production of laughing at the whole thing, but you'd never get her out of Philadelphia."

"I guess not. Well, here's Newark. I can always tell Newark, can't you?"

"Yes, you can always tell Newark."

PAT COLLINS

Now they are both getting close to seventy, and when they see each other on the street Whit Hofman and Pat Collins bid each other the time of day and pass on without stopping for conversation. It may be that in Whit Hofman's greeting there is a little more hearty cordiality than in Pat Collins's greeting to him; it may be that in Pat Collins's words and smile there is a wistfulness that is all he has left of thirty years of a dwindling hope.

The town is full of young people who never knew that for about three years—1925, 1926, 1927—Whit Hofman's favorite companion was none other than Pat Collins. Not only do they not know of the once close relationship; today they would not believe it. But then it is hard to believe, with only the present evidence to go on. Today Pat Collins still has his own garage, but it is hardly more than a filling station and tire repair business on the edge of town, patronized by the people of the neighborhood and not situated on a traffic artery of any importance. He always has some young man helping out, but he does most of the work himself. Hard work it is, too. He hires young men out of high school—out of prison, sometimes—but the young men don't stay. They never stay. They like Pat Collins, and they say so, but they don't want to work at night, and Pat Collins's twenty-four-hour service is what keeps him going. Twenty-four hours, seven days a week, the only garage in town that says it and means it. A man stuck for gas, a man with a flat and no spare, a man skidded into a ditch—they all know that if they phone Pat Collins he will get there in his truck and if necessary tow them away. Some of the motorists are embarrassed: people who never patronize Pat Collins except in emergencies; people who knew him back in the days when he was Whit Hofman's favorite companion. They embarrass themselves; he does not say or do anything to embarrass them except one thing: he charges them fair prices when he could hold them up, and to some of those people who knew him long ago that is the most embarrassing thing he could do. "Twelve dollars, Pat? You could have charged me more than that."

"Twelve dollars," he says. And there were plenty of times when he could have asked fifty dollars for twelve dollars' worth of service—when the woman in the stalled car was not the wife of the driver.

Now, to the younger ones, he has become a local symbol of misfortune ("All I could do was call Pat Collins") and at the same time a symbol of dependability ("Luckily I thought of Pat Collins"). It is mean work; the interrupted sleep, the frequently bad weather, the drunks and the shocked and the guilty-minded. But it is the one service he offers that makes the difference between a profit and breaking even.

"Hello, Pat," Whit Hofman will say, when they meet on Main Street.

"Hyuh, Whit," Pat Collins will say.

Never more than that, but never less . . .

Aloysius Aquinas Collins came to town in 1923 because he had heard it was a good place to be, a rich town for its size. Big coal interests to start with, but good diversification as well: a steel mill, a couple of iron foundries, the railway car shops, shoe factories, silk mills, half a dozen breweries, four meat packing plants and, to the south, prosperous farmers. Among the rich there were two Rolls-Royces, a dozen or more Pierce-Arrows, a couple of dozen Cadillacs, and maybe a dozen each of Lincolns, Marmons, Packards. It was a spending town; the Pierce-Arrow families bought small roadsters for their children and the women were beginning to drive their own cars. The Rolls-Royces and Pierce-Arrows were in Philadelphia territory, and the franchises for the other big cars were already spoken for, but Pat Collins was willing to start as a dealer for one of the many makes in the large field between Ford-Dodge and Cadillac-Packard, one of the newer, lesser known makes. It was easy to get a franchise for one of those makes, and he decided to take his time.

Of professional experience in the automobile game he had none. He was not yet thirty, and he had behind him two years at Villanova, fifteen months as a shore duty ensign, four years as a salesman of men's hats at which he made pretty good money but from which he got nothing else but stretches of boredom between days of remorse following salesmen's parties in hotels. His wife Madge had lost her early illusions, but she loved him and partly blamed life on the road for what was happening to him. "Get into something else," she would say, "or honest to God, Pat, I'm going to take the children and pull out."

"It's easy enough to talk about getting another job," he would say.

"I don't care what it is, just as long as you're not away five days a week. Drive a taxi, if you have to."

When she happened to mention driving a taxi she touched upon the only major interest he had outside the routine of his life: from the early days of Dario Resta and the brothers Chevrolet he had been crazy about automobiles, all automobiles and everything about them. He would walk or take the "L" from home in West Philadelphia to the area near City Hall, and wander about, stopping in front of the hotels and clubs and private residences and theaters and the Academy of Music, staring at the limousines and town cars, engaging in conversation with the chauffeurs; and then he would walk up North Broad Street, Automobile Row, and because he was a nice-looking kid, the floor salesmen would sometimes let him sit in the cars on display. He collected all the manufacturers' brochures and read all the advertisements in the newspapers. Closer to home he

would stand for hours, studying the sporty roadsters and phae-
tons outside the Penn fraternity houses; big Simplexes with
searchlights on the running-boards, Fiats and Renaults and His-
panos and Blitzen-Benzes. He was nice-looking and he had nice
manners, and when he would hold the door open for one of the
fraternity men they would sometimes give him a nickel and say,
"Will you keep your eye on my car, sonny?"

"Can I sit in it, please?"

"Well, if you promise not to blow the horn."

He passed the horn-blowing stage quickly. Sometimes the
fraternity men would come out to put up the top when there was
a sudden shower, and find that Aloysius Aquinas Collins had
somehow done it alone. For this service he wanted no reward but
a ride home, on the front seat. On his side of the room he shared
with his older brother he had magazine and rotogravure pictures
of fine cars pinned to the walls. The nuns at school complained
that instead of paying attention, he was continually drawing
pictures of automobiles, automobiles. The nuns did not know
how good the drawings were; they only cared that one so bright
could waste so much time, and their complaints to his parents
made it impossible for Aloysius to convince Mr. and Mrs. Collins
that after he got his high school diploma, he wanted to get a job
on Automobile Row. The parents sent him to Villanova, and
after sophomore year took him out because the priests told them
they were wasting their money, but out of spite his father refused
to let him take a job in the auto business. Collins got him a job
in the shipyards, and when the country entered the war, Aloysius
joined the Navy and eventually was commissioned. He married
Madge Ruddy, became a hat salesman, and rented half of a
two-family house in Upper Darby.

Gibbsville was on his sales route, and it first came to his special
notice because his Gibbsville customer bought more hats in his
high-priced line than any other store of comparable size. He thus
discovered that it was a spending town, and that the actual
population figures were deceptive; it was surrounded by a lot of
much smaller towns whose citizens shopped in Gibbsville. He
began to add a day to his normal visits to Gibbsville, to make a
study of the automobile business there, and when he came into a

small legacy from his aunt, he easily persuaded Madge to put in her own five thousand dollars, and he bought Cunningham's Garage, on Railroad Avenue, Gibbsville.

Cunningham's was badly run down and had lost money for its previous two owners, but it was the oldest garage in town. The established automobile men were not afraid of competition from the newcomer, Collins, who knew nobody to speak of and did not even have a dealer's franchise. They thought he was out of his mind when he began spending money in sprucing up the place. They also thought, and said, that he was getting pretty big for his britches in choosing to rent a house on Lantenengo Street. The proprietor of Cunningham's old garage then proceeded to outrage the established dealers by stealing Walt Michaels' best mechanic, Joe Ricci. Regardless of what the dealers might do to each other in the competition to clinch a sale, one thing you did not do was entice away a man's best mechanic. Walt Michaels, who had the Oldsmobile franchise, paid a call on the new fellow.

A. A. Collins, owner and proprietor, as his sign said, of Collins Motor Company, was in his office when he saw Michaels get out of his car. He went out to greet Michaels, his hand outstretched. "Hello, Mr. Michaels, I'm Pat Collins," he said.

"I know who you are. I just came down to tell you what I think of you."

"Not much, I guess, judging by—"

"Not much is right."

"Smoke a cigar?" said Pat Collins.

Michaels slapped at the cigar and knocked it to the ground. Pat Collins picked it up and looked at it. "I guess that's why they wrap them in tinfoil." He rubbed the dirt off the cigar and put it back in his pocket.

"Don't you want to fight?" said Michaels.

"What for? You have a right to be sore at me, in a way. But when you have a good mechanic like Joe, you ought to be willing to pay him what he's worth."

"Well, I never thought I'd see an Irishman back out of a fight. But with you I guess that's typical. A sneaky Irish son of a bitch."

"Now just a minute, Michaels. Go easy."

"I said it. A sneaky Irish son of a bitch."

"Yeah, I was right the first time," said Collins. He hit Michaels in the stomach with his left hand, and as Michaels crumpled, Collins hit him on the chin with his right hand. Michaels went down, and Collins stood over him, waiting for him to get up. Michaels started to raise himself with both hands on the ground, calling obscene names, but while his hands were still on the ground Collins stuck the foil-wrapped cigar deep in his mouth. Three or four men who stopped to look at the fight burst into laughter, and Michaels, his breath shut off, fell back on the ground.

"Change your mind about the cigar, Michaels?" said Collins.

"I'll send my son down to see you," said Michaels, getting to his feet.

"All right. What does *he* smoke?"

"He's as big as you are."

"Then I'll use a tire iron on him. Now get out of here, and quick."

Michaels, dusting himself off, saw Joe Ricci among the spectators. He pointed at him with his hat. "You, you ginny bastard, you stole tools off of me."

Ricci, who had a screwdriver in his hand, rushed at Michaels and might have stabbed him, but Collins swung him away.

"Calling me a thief, the son of a bitch, I'll kill him," said Ricci. "I'll *kill* him."

"Go on, Michaels. Beat it," said Collins.

Michaels got in his car and put it in gear, and as he was about to drive away Collins called to him: "Hey, Michaels, shall I fill her up?"

The episode, the kind that men liked to embellish in the retelling, made Pat Collins universally unpopular among the dealers, but it made him known to a wider public. It brought him an important visitor.

The Mercer phaeton pulled up at Pat Collins's gas pump and Collins, in his office, jumped up from his desk, and without putting on his coat, went out to the curb. "Can I help you?" he said.

"Fill her up, will you, please?" said the driver. He was a

161

handsome man, about Collins's age, wearing a brown Homburg and a coonskin coat. Pat Collins knew who he was—Whit Hofman, probably the richest young man in the town—because he knew the car. He was conscious of Hofman's curiosity, but he went on pumping the gasoline. He hung up the hose and said, "You didn't need much. That'll cost you thirty-six cents, Mr. Hofman. Wouldn't you rather I sent you a bill?"

"Well, all right. But don't I get a cigar, a new customer? At least that's what I hear."

The two men laughed. "Sure, have a cigar," said Collins, handing him one. Hofman looked at it.

"Tinfoil, all right. You sure this isn't the same one you gave Walt Michaels?"

"It might be. See if it has any teeth marks on it," said Collins.

"Well, I guess Walt had it coming to him. He's a kind of a sorehead."

"You know him?"

"Of course. Known him all my life, he's always lived here. He's not a bad fellow, Mr. Collins, but you took Joe away from him, and Joe's a hell of a good mechanic. I'd be sore, too, I guess."

"Well, when you come looking for a fight, you ought to be more sure of what you're up against. Either that, or be ready to take a beating. I only hit him twice."

"When I was a boy you wouldn't have knocked him down that easily. When I was a kid, Walt Michaels was a good athlete, but he's put away a lot of beer since then." Hofman looked at Collins. "Do you like beer?"

"I like the beer you get around here. It's better than we get in Philly."

"Put on your coat and let's drink some beer," said Hofman. "Or are you busy?"

"Not that busy," said Collins.

They drove to a saloon in one of the neighboring towns, and Collins was surprised to see that no one was surprised to see the young millionaire, with his Mercer and his coonskin coat. The men drinking at the bar—workingmen taking a day off, they appeared to be—were neither cordial nor hostile to Hofman. "Hello, Paul," said Hofman. "Brought you a new customer."

"I need all I can get," said the proprietor. "Where will you want to sit? In the back room?"

"I guess so. This is Mr. Collins, just opened a new garage. Mr. Collins, Mr. Paul Unitas, sometimes called Unitas States of America."

"Pleased to meet you," said Paul, shaking hands.

"Same here," said Collins.

"How's the beer?" said Hofman.

Paul shook his head. "They're around. They stopped two truckloads this morning."

"Who stopped them? The state police?" said Hofman.

"No, this time it was enforcement agents. New ones."

Hofman laughed. "You don't have to worry about Mr. Collins. I'll vouch for him."

"Well, if you say so, Whit. What'll you have?"

"The beer's no good?"

"Slop. Have rye. It's pretty good. I cut it myself."

"Well, if you say rye, that's what we'll have. Okay, Collins?"

"Sure."

Hofman was an affable man, an interested listener and a hearty laugher. It was dark when they left the saloon; Collins had told Hofman a great deal about himself, and Hofman drove Collins home in the Mercer. "I can offer you some Canadian Club," said Collins.

"Thanks just the same, but we're going out to dinner and I have to change. Ask me again sometime. Nice to've seen you, Pat."

"Same to you, Whit. Enjoyable afternoon," said Collins.

In the house Collins kissed Madge's cheek. "Whew! Out drinking with college boys?" she said.

"I'll drink with that college boy any time. That's Whit Hofman."

"How on earth—"

She listened with increasing eagerness while he told her the events of the afternoon. "Maybe you could sell him a car, if you had a good franchise," she said.

"I'm not going to try to sell him anything but Aloysius Aquinas Collins, Esquire. And anyway, I like him."

"You can like people and still sell them a car."

"Well, I'm never going to try to make a sale there. He came to see me out of curiosity, but we hit it off right away. He's a swell fellow."

"Pat?"

"What?"

"Remember why we moved here."

"Listen, it's only ha' past six and I'm home. This guy came to see me, Madge."

"A rich fellow with nothing better to do," she said.

"Oh, for God's sake. You say remember why we moved here. To have a home. But *you* remember why I wanted to live on this street. To meet people like Whit Hofman."

"But not to spend the whole afternoon in some hunky saloon. Were there any women there?"

"A dozen of them, all walking around naked. What have you got for supper?"

"For *dinner*, we have veal cutlets. But Pat, remember what we are. We're not society people. What's she like, his wife?"

"How would I know? I wouldn't know her if I saw her. Unless she was driving that car."

They had a two weeks' wait before Whit Hofman again had the urge for Pat Collins's company. This time Hofman took him to the country club, and they sat in the smoking-room with a bottle of Scotch on the table. "Do you play squash?" said Hofman.

"Play it? I thought you ate it. No, I used to play handball."

"Well, it's kind of handball with a racquet. It's damn near the only exercise I get in the winter, at least until we go South. If you were a good handball player, you'd learn squash in no time."

"Where?" At the U.N.?"

"Here. We have a court here," said Hofman. He got up and pointed through the French window. "See that little house down there, to the right of the first fairway? That's the squash court."

"I was a caddy one summer."

"Oh, you play golf?"

"I've never had a club in my hand since then."

"How would you like to join here? I'll be glad to put you up

164

and we'll find somebody to second you. Does your wife play tennis or golf?"

"No, she's not an athlete. How much would it cost to join?"

"Uh, family membership, you and your wife and children under twenty-one. They just raised it. Initiation, seventy-five dollars. Annual dues, thirty-five for a family membership."

"Do you think I could get in? We don't know many people that belong."

"Well, Walt Michaels doesn't belong. Can you think of anyone else that might blackball you? Because if you can't, I think I could probably get you in at the next meeting. Technically, I'm not supposed to put you up, because I'm on the admissions committee, but that's no problem."

Any hesitancy Pat Collins might have had immediately vanished at mention of the name Walt Michaels. "Well, I'd sure like to belong."

"I'll take care of it. Let's have a drink on it," said Whit Hofman.

"We're Catholics, you know."

"That's all right. We take Catholics. Not all, but some. And those we don't take wouldn't get in if they were Presbyterian or anything else."

"Jews?"

"We have two. One is a doctor, married to a Gentile. He claims he isn't a Jew, but he is. The other is the wife of a Gentile. Otherwise, no. I understand they're starting their own club, I'm not sure where it'll be."

"Well, as long as you know we're Catholics."

"I knew that, Pat," said Hofman. "But I respect you for bringing it up."

Madge Collins was upset about the country club. "It isn't only what you have to pay to get in. It's meals, and spending money on clothes. I haven't bought anything new since we moved here."

"As the Dodge people say, 'It isn't the initial cost, it's the upkeep.' But Madge, I told you before, those are the kind of people that're gonna be worth our while. I'll make a lot of connections at the country club, and in the meantime, I'll get a franchise. So far I didn't spend a nickel on advertising. Well, this is gonna be the best kind of advertising. The Cadillac dealer is the only other dealer in the country club, and I won't compete with him."

"Everything going out, very little coming in," she said.

"Stop worrying, everything's gonna be hunky-dory."

On the morning after the next meeting of the club admissions committee Whit Hofman telephoned Pat Collins. "Congratulations to the newest member of the Lantenengo Country Club. It was a cinch. You'll get a notice and a bill, and as soon as you send your cheque you and Mrs. Collins can start using the club, although there's no golf or tennis now. However, there's a dance next Friday, and we'd like you and your wife to have dinner with us. Wear your Tuck. My wife is going to phone Mrs. Collins some time today."

In her two years as stock girl and saleslady at Oppenheim, Collins—"my cousins," Pat called them—Madge had learned a thing or two about values, and she had style sense. The evening dress she bought for the Hofman dinner and club dance was severely simple, black, and Pat thought it looked too old for her. "Wait till you see it on," she said. She changed the shoulder straps and substituted thin black cord, making her shoulders, chest, and back completely bare and giving an illusion of a deeper décolletage than was actually the case. She had a good figure and a lovely complexion, and when he saw her ready to leave for the party, he was startled. "It's not too old for you any more. Maybe it's too young."

"I wish I had some jewelry," she said.

"You have. I can see them."

"Oh—oh, stop. It's not immodest. You can't see anything unless you stoop over and look down."

"Unless you happen to be over five foot five, and most men are."

"Do you want me to wear a shawl? I have a nice old shawl of Grandma's. As soon as we start making money the one thing I want is a good fur coat. That's all I want, and I can get one wholesale."

"Get one for me, while you're at it. But for now, let's get a move on. Dinner is eight-thirty and we're the guests of honor."

"Guests of honor! Just think of it, Pat. I haven't been so excited since our wedding. I hope I don't do anything wrong."

"Just watch Mrs. Hofman. I don't even know who else'll be there, but it's time we were finding out."

"Per-*fume!* I didn't put on any per*fume.* I'll be right down."

She was excited and she had youth and health, but she also had a squarish face with a strong jawline that gave her a look of maturity and dignity. Her hair was reddish brown, her eyes grey-green. It was a face full of contrasts, especially from repose to animation, and with the men—beginning with Whit Hofman —she was an instant success.

The Hofmans had invited three other couples besides the Collinses. Custom forbade having liquor bottles or cocktail shakers on the table at club dances, and Whit Hofman kept a shaker and a bottle on the floor beside him. The men were drinking straight whiskey, the women drank orange blossoms. There was no bar, and the Hofman party sat at the table and had their drinks until nine o'clock, when Hofman's wife signalled the steward to start serving. Chincoteagues were served first, and before the soup, Whit Hofman asked Madge Collins to dance. He was feeling good, and here he was king. His fortune was respected by men twice his age, and among the men and women who were more nearly his contemporaries he was genuinely well liked for a number of reasons: his unfailingly good manners, no matter how far in drink he might get; his affability, which drew upon his good manners when bores and toadies and the envious and the weak made their assaults; his emanations of strength, which were physically and tangibly demonstrated in his expertness at games as well as in the slightly more subtle self-reminders of his friends that he *was* Whit Hofman and *did have* all that money. He had a good war record, beginning with enlistment as a private in the National Guard for Mexican Border service, and including a field commission, a wound chevron, and a Croix de Guerre with palm during his A.E.F. service. He was overweight, but he could afford bespoke tailors and he cared about clothes; tonight he was wearing a dinner jacket with a white waistcoat and a satin butterfly tie. Madge Ruddy Collins had never known anyone quite like him, and her first mistake was to believe that

167

his high spirits had something special to do with her. At this stage she had no way of knowing that later on, when he danced with his fat old second cousin, he would be just as much fun.

"Well, how do you like your club?" he said.

"My club? Oh—*this* club. Oh, it's beautiful. Pat and I certainly do thank you."

"Very glad to do it. I hope you're going to take up golf. More and more women are. Girl I just spoke to, Mrs. Dick Richards, she won the second flight this year, and she only started playing last spring."

"Does your wife play?"

"She plays pretty well, and could be a lot better. She's going to have a lot of lessons when we go South. That's the thing to do. As soon as you develop a fault, have a lesson right away, before it becomes a habit. I'm going to have Pat playing squash before we leave."

"Oh."

"He said he was a handball player, so squash ought come easy to him. Of course it's a much more strenuous game than golf."

"It is?"

He said something in reply to a question from a man dancing by. The man laughed, and Whit Hofman laughed. "That's Johnny King," said Hofman. "You haven't met the Kings, have you?"

"No," said Madge. "She's pretty. Beautifully gowned."

"Oh, that's not his wife. She isn't here tonight. That's Mary-Louise Johnson, from Scranton. There's a whole delegation from Scranton here tonight. They all came down for Buz McKee's birthday party. That's the big table over in the corner. Well, I'm getting the high sign, I guess we'd better go back to our table. Thank you, Madge. A pleasure."

"Oh, to me, too," she said.

In due course every man in the Hofman party danced with every woman, the duty rounds. Pat Collins was the last to dance with Madge on the duty rounds. "You having a good time?" he said.

"Oh, *am* I?" she said.

"How do you like Whit?"

"He's a real gentleman, I'm crazy about him. I like him the best. Do you like her, his wife?"

"I guess so. In a way yes, and in a way no."

"Me too. She'd rather be with those people from Scranton."

"What people from Scranton?"

"At the big table. They're here to attend a birthday party for Buzzie McKee."

"Jesus, you're learning fast."

"I found that out from Whit. The blonde in the beaded white, that's Mary-Louise Johnson, dancing with Johnny King. They're dancing every dance together."

"Together is right. Take a can-opener to pry them apart."

"His wife is away," said Madge. "Where did Whit go?"

Pat turned to look at their table. "I don't know. Oh, there he is, dancing with some fat lady."

"I don't admire his taste."

"Say, you took a real shine to Whit," said Pat Collins.

"Well, he's a real gentleman, but he isn't a bit forward. Now where's he going? . . . Oh, I guess he wanted to wish Buzzie McKee a happy birthday. Well, let's sit down."

The chair at her left remained vacant while Hofman continued his visit to the McKee table. On Madge's right was a lawyer named Joe Chapin, who had something to do with the admissions committee; polite enough, but for Madge very hard to talk to. At the moment he was in conversation with the woman on his right, and Madge Collins felt completely alone. A minute passed, two minutes, and her solitude passed to uneasiness to anger. Whit Hofman made his way back to the table, and when he sat down she said, trying to keep the irritation out of her tone, "That wasn't very polite."

"I'm terribly sorry. I thought you and Joe—"

"Oh, *him*. Well, I'll forgive you if you dance this dance with me."

"Why of course," said Hofman.

They got up again, and as they danced she closed her eyes, pretending to an ecstasy she did not altogether feel. They got through eighteen bars of "Bambalina," and the music stopped. "Oh, hell," she said. "I'll let you have the next."

"Fine," he said. She took his arm, holding it so that her hand clenched his right biceps, and giving it a final squeeze as they sat down.

"Would you like some more coffee?" he said. "If not, I'm afraid we're going to have to let them take the table away."

"Why?"

"That's what they do. Ten o'clock, tables have to be cleared out, to make room for the dancing. You know, quite a few people have dinner at home, then come to the dance."

"What are they? Cheap skates?"

"Oh, I don't know about that. No, hardly that."

"But if *you* wanted to keep the table, they'd let you."

"Oh, I wouldn't do that, Madge. They really need the room."

"Then where do we go?"

"Wherever we like. Probably the smoking-room. But from now on we just sort of—circulate."

"You mean your dinner is over?"

"Yes, that's about it. We're on our own."

"I don't want to go home. I want to dance with you some more."

"Who said anything about going home? The fun is just about to begin."

"I had fun before. I'm not very good with strangers."

"You're not a stranger. You're a member of the club, duly launched. Let's go out to the smoking-room and I'll get you a drink. How would you like a Stinger?"

"What is it? Never mind telling me. I'll have one."

"If you've never had one, be careful. It could be your downfall. Very cool to the taste, but packs a wallop. Sneaks up on you."

"Good. Let's have one." She rose and quickly took his unoffered arm, and they went to the smoking-room, which was already more than half filled.

At eleven o'clock she was drunk. She would dance with no one but Whit Hofman, and when she danced with him she tried to excite him, and succeeded. "You're hot stuff, Madge," he said.

"Why what do you *mean?*"

"The question is, what do *you* mean?"

"I don't know what you're *talking* about," she said, sing-song.

170

"The hell you don't," he said. "Shall we go for a stroll?"

"Where to?"

"My car's around back of the caddyhouse."

"Do you think we ought to?"

"No, but either that or let's sit down."

"All right, let's sit down. I'm getting kind of woozy, anyhow."

"Don't drink any more Stingers. I told you they were dangerous. Maybe you ought to have some coffee. Maybe I ought to, too. Come on, we'll get some coffee." He led her to a corner of the smoking-room, where she could prop herself against the wall. He left her, and in the hallway to the kitchen he encountered Pat Collins on his way from the locker-room.

"Say, Pat, if I were you—well, Madge had a couple of Stingers and I don't think they agree with her."

"Is she sick?"

"No, but I'm afraid she's quite tight."

"I'd better take her home?"

"*You* know. Your first night here. There'll be others much worse off, but she's the one they'll talk about. The maid'll get her wrap, and you can ease her out so nobody'll notice. I'll say your goodnights for you."

"Well, gee, Whit—I'm sorry. I certainly apologize."

"Perfectly all right, Pat. No harm done, but she's ready for beddy-bye. I'll call you in a day or two."

There was no confusing suggestion with command, and Pat obeyed Hofman. He got his own coat and Madge's, and when Madge saw her coat she likewise recognized authority.

They were less than a mile from the club when she said, "I'm gonna be sick."

He stopped the car. "All right, *be* sick."

When she got back in the car she said, "Leave the windows down, I need the fresh air."

He got her to bed. His anger was so great that he did not trust himself to speak to her, and she mistook his silence for pity. She kept muttering that she was sorry, sorry, and went to sleep. Much later he fell asleep, awoke before six, dressed and left the house before he had to speak to her. He had his breakfast in an all-night restaurant, bought the morning newspapers, and opened

171

the garage. He needed to think, and not so much about punishing Madge as about restoring himself to good standing in the eyes of the Hofmans. He had caught Kitty Hofman's cold appraisal of Madge on the dance floor; he had known, too, that he had failed to make a good impression on Kitty, who was in a sour mood for having to give up the Buz McKee dinner. He rejected his first plan to send Kitty flowers and a humorous note. Tomorrow or the next day Madge could send the flowers and a thank-you note, which he would make sure contained no reference to her getting tight or any other apologetic implication. The important thing was to repair any damage to his relationship with Whit Hofman, and after a while he concluded that aside from Madge's thank-you note to both Hofmans, the wiser course was to wait for Whit to call him.

He had a long wait.

Immediately after Christmas the Hofmans went to Florida. They returned for two weeks in late March, closed their house, and took off on a trip around the world. Consequently the Collinses did not see the Hofmans for nearly a year. It was a year that was bad for the Collins marriage, but good for the Collins Motor Company. Pat Collins got the Chrysler franchise, and the car practically sold itself. Women and the young took to it from the start, and the Collins Motor Company had trouble keeping up with the orders. The bright new car and the bright new Irishman were interchangeably associated in the minds of the citizens, and Pat and Madge Collins were getting somewhere on their own, without the suspended sponsorship of Whit Hofman. But at home Pat and Madge had never quite got back to what they had been before she jeopardized his relationship with Whit Hofman. He had counted so much on Hofman's approval that the threat of losing it had given him a big scare, and it would not be far-fetched to say that the designers of the Chrysler "70" saved the Collins marriage.

Now they were busy, Pat with his golf when he could take the time off from his work—which he did frequently; and Madge with the game of bridge, which she learned adequately well. In the absence of the Whit Hofmans the social life of the country club was left without an outstanding couple to be the leaders, although several couples tried to fill the gap. In the locker-room one afternoon, drinking gin and ginger ale with the members of his foursome, Pat Collins heard one of the men say, "You know who we all miss? Whit. The club isn't the same without him." Pat looked up as at a newly discovered truth, and for the first time he realized that he liked Whit Hofman better than any man he had ever known. It had remained for someone else to put the thought into words, and casual enough words they were to express what Pat Collins had felt from the first day in Paul Unitas's saloon. Like nearly everyone else in the club the Collinses had had a postcard or two from the Hofmans; Honolulu, Shanghai, Bangkok, St. Andrew's, St. Cloud. The Hofmans' closer friends had had letters, but the Collinses were pleased to have had a postcard, signed "Kitty and Whit"—in Whit's handwriting.

"When does he get back, does anyone know?" said Pat.

"Middle of October," said the original speaker. "You know Whit. He wouldn't miss the football season, not the meat of it anyway."

"About a month away," said Pat Collins. "Well, I can thank him for the most enjoyable summer I ever had. He got me in here, you know. I was practically a stranger."

" 'A stranger in a strange land,' but not any more, Pat."

"Thank you. You fellows have been damn nice to me." He meant the sentiment, but the depth of it belonged to his affection for Whit Hofman. He had his shower and dressed, and joined Madge on the terrace. "Do you want to stay here for dinner?"

"We have nothing at home," she said.

"Then we'll eat here," he said. "Did you know the Hofmans are getting back about four weeks from now?"

"I knew it."

"Why didn't you tell me?"

"I didn't know you wanted to know, or I would have. Why, are you thinking of hiring a brass band? One postcard."

"What did you expect? As I remember, you didn't keep it any secret when we got it."

"You were the one that was more pleased than I was."

"Oh, all right. Let's go eat."

They failed to be invited to the smaller parties in honor of the returning voyagers, but they went to a Dutch Treat dinner for the Hofmans before the club dance. Two changes in the Hofmans were instantly noticeable: Whit was as brown as a Hawaiian, and Kitty was pregnant. She received the members of the dinner party sitting down. She had lost one child through miscarriage. Whit stood beside her, and when it came the Collinses' turn he greeted Pat and Madge by nickname and first name. Not so Kitty. "Oh, hello. Mrs. Collins. Nice of you to come. Hello, Mr. Collins." Then seeing the man next in line she called out: "Bob-bee! Bobby, where were you Tuesday? You were supposed to be at the Ogdens', you false friend. I thought you'd be at the boat."

The Collinses moved on, and Madge said, "We shouldn't have come."

"Why not? She doesn't have to like us."

"She didn't have to be so snooty, either."

"Bobby Hermann is one of their best friends."

"I'm damn sure we're not."

"Oh, for God's sake."

"Oh, for God's sake yourself," she said.

The year had done a lot for Madge in such matters as her poise and the widening of her acquaintance among club members. But it was not until eleven or so that Whit Hofman cut in on her. "How've you been?" he said.

"Lonely without you," she said.

"That's nice to hear. I wish you meant it."

"You're pretending to think I don't," she said. "But I thought of you every day. And every night. Especially every night."

"How many Stingers have you had?"

"That's a nasty thing to say. I haven't had any. I've never had one since that night. So we'll change the subject. Are you going to stay home a while?"

"Looks that way. Kitty's having the baby in January."

"Sooner than that, I thought."

"No, the doctor says January."

"Which do you want? A boy, or a girl?"

"Both, but not at the same time."

"Well, you always get what you want, so I'm told."

"That's a new one on me."

"Well, you can *have* anything you want, put it that way."

"No, not even that."

"What do you want that you haven't got?"

"A son, or a daughter."

"Well, you're getting that, one or the other. What else?"

"Right now, nothing else."

"I don't believe anybody's ever that contented."

"Well, what do *you* want, for instance?"

"You," she said.

"Why? You have a nice guy. Kids. And I hear Pat's the busiest car dealer in town."

"Those are things I have. You asked me what I wanted."

"You don't beat about the bush, do you, Madge? You get right to the point."

"I've been in love with you for almost a year."

"Madge, you haven't been in love with me at all. Maybe you're not in love with Pat, but you're certainly not in love with me. You couldn't be."

"About a month ago I heard you were coming home, and I had it all planned out how I was going to be when I saw you. But I was wrong. I couldn't feel this way for a whole year and then start pretending I didn't. You asked me how I was, and I came right out with it, the truth."

"Well, Madge, I'm not in love with you. You're damn attractive and all that, but I'm not in *love* with you."

"I know that. But answer me one question, as truthful as I am with you. Are you in love with your wife?"

"Of course I am."

"I'll tell you something, Whit. You're not. With her. With me. Or maybe with anybody."

"Now really, that *is* a nasty thing to say."

"People love you, Whit, but you don't love them back."

"I'm afraid I don't like this conversation. Shall we go back and have a drink?"

"Yes."

They moved toward the smoking-room. "Why did you say that, Madge? What makes you think it?"

"You really want me to tell you? Remember, the truth hurts, and I had a whole year to think about this."

"What the hell, tell me."

"It's not you, it's the town. There's nobody here bigger than you. They all love you, but you don't love them."

"I love this town and the people in it and everything about it. Don't you think I could live anywhere I wanted to? Why do you think I came back here? I can live anywhere in the God damn world. Jesus, you certainly have that one figured wrong. For a minute you almost had me worried."

He danced with her no more that night, and if he could avoid speaking to her or getting close to her, he did so. When she got home, past three o'clock, she gave Pat Collins a very good time; loveless but exceedingly pleasurable. Then she lay in her bed until morning, unable to understand herself, puzzled by forces that had never been mysterious to her.

The Hofman baby was born on schedule, a six-pound boy, but the reports from the mother's bedside were not especially happy. Kitty had had a long and difficult time, and one report, corroborated only by constant repetition, was that she had thrown a clock, or a flower vase, or a water tumbler, or all of them, at Whit at the start of her labor. It was said, and perfunctorily denied, that a group of nurses and orderlies stood outside her hospital room, listening fascinatedly to the obscene names she called him, names that the gossips would not utter but knew how to spell. Whatever the basis in fact, the rumors of hurled bric-a-brac and invective seemed to be partially confirmed when Kitty Hofman came home from the hospital. The infant was left in the care of a nurse, and Kitty went to every party, drinking steadily and chain-smoking, saying little and watching everything. She had a look of determination, as though she had just made up her mind about something, but the look and decision were not followed up by action. She would stay at the parties until she had had enough, then she would get her wrap and say goodnight to her hostess, without any word or sign to Whit, and it would be up to him to discover she was leaving and follow her out.

Their friends wondered how long Whit Hofman would take that kind of behavior, but no one—least of all Pat Collins—was so tactless, or bold, as to suggest to Whit that there *was* any behavior. It was Whit, finally, who talked.

He was now seeing Pat Collins nearly every day, and on some days more than once. He knew as much about automobiles as Pat Collins, and he was comfortable in Pat's office. He had made the garage one of his ports of call in his daytime rounds—his office every morning at ten, the barber's, the bank, the broker's, his lawyer, lunch at the Gibbsville Club, a game of pool after lunch, a visit with Pat Collins that sometimes continued with a couple of games of squash at the country club. On a day some six weeks after the birth of his son Whit dropped in on Pat, hung up his coat and hat, and took a chair.

"Don't let me interrupt you," he said.

"Just signing some time-sheets," said Pat Collins.

Whit lit a cigarette and put his feet up on the windowsill. "It's about time you had those windows washed," he said.

"I know. Miss Muldowney says if I'm trying to save money, that's the wrong way. Burns up more electricity. Well, there we are. Another day, another dollar. How's the stock market?"

"Stay out of it. Everything's too high."

"I'm not ready to go in it yet. Later. Little by little I'm paying back Madge, the money she put in the business."

"You ought to incorporate and give her stock."

"First I want to give her back her money, with interest."

"Speaking of Madge, Pat. Do you remember when your children were born?"

"Sure. That wasn't so long ago."

"What is Dennis, about six?"

"Dennis is six, and Peggy's four. I guess Dennis is the same in years that your boy is in weeks. How is he, Pop?"

"He's fine. At least I guess he's fine. I wouldn't know how to tell, this is all new to me."

"But you're not worried about him? You sound dubious."

"Not about him. The doctor says he's beginning to gain weight

177

and so forth. Kitty is something else again, and that's what I want to ask you about. You knew she didn't have a very easy time of it."

"Yes, you told me that."

"How was Madge, with her children?"

"I'll have to think back," said Pat. "Let me see. With Dennis, the first, we had a couple false alarms and had the doctor come to the house one time at four o'clock in the morning. He was sore as hell. It was only gas pains, and as soon as she got rid of the gas, okay. The real time, she was in labor about three hours, I guess. About three. Dennis weighed seven and a quarter. With Peggy, she took longer. Started having pains around eight o'clock in the morning, but the baby wasn't all the way out till three-four in the afternoon. She had a much harder time with the second, although it was a smaller baby. Six and a half, I think."

"What about her, uh, mental state? Was she depressed or anything like that?"

"No, not a bit. Anything but."

"But you haven't had any more children, and I thought Catholics didn't believe in birth control."

"Well, I'll tell you, Whit, although I wouldn't tell most Protestants. I don't agree with the Church on that, and neither does Madge. If that's the criterion, we're not very good Catholics, but I can't help that. We had two children when we could only afford one, and now I don't think we'll ever have any more. Two's enough."

"But for financial reasons, not because of the effect on Madge."

"Mainly financial reasons. Even if we could afford it, though, Madge doesn't want any more. She wants to enjoy life while she's young."

"I see," said Whit Hofman. The conversation had reached a point where utter frankness or a change of the subject was inevitable, and Whit Hofman retreated from candor. It then was up to Pat Collins to break the silence.

"It's none of my business, Whit," he began. "But—"

"No, it isn't, Pat. I don't mean to be rude, but if I said any more about Kitty, I'd sound like a crybaby. Not to mention the fact that it goes against the grain. I've said too much already."

"I know how you feel. But nothing you say gets out of this office, so don't let that worry you. I don't tell Madge everything I know. Or do. She made some pretty good guesses, and we came close to busting up. When I was on the road, peddling hats and caps, I knew a sure lay in damn near every town between Philly and Binghamton, New York. Not that I got laid every night—but I didn't miss many Thursdays. Thursday nights we knew we were going home Friday, salesmen. You don't make any calls on Friday, the clients are all busy. So, somebody'd bring out a quart."

"Did you know a sure lay in this town?"

"Did I! Did you ever know a broad named Helene Holman?"

"I should say I did."

"Well, her," said Pat Collins.

"You don't see her now, though, do you?"

"Is that ány of your business, Whit?"

"Touché. I wasn't really asking out of curiosity. More, uh, incredibility. *Incredulity.* In other words, I've always thought you behaved yourself here, since you've been living here."

"I have. And anyway, I understand the Holman dame is private property. At least I always see her riding around with the big bootlegger, Charney."

"Ed Charney. Yes, she's out of circulation for the present, so my friends tell me."

"Yes, and you couldn't get away with a God damn thing. You're too well known."

"So far I haven't tried to get away with anything," said Whit Hofman. "How would you feel about a little strenuous exercise?"

Pat Collins looked up at the clock. "I don't think any ripe prospect is coming in in the next twenty minutes. Two games?"

"Enough to get up a sweat."

They drove to the country club in two cars, obviating the continuance of conversation and giving each man the opportunity to think his own thoughts. They played squash for an hour or so, took long hot showers, and cooled out at the locker-room table with gin and ginger ale. "I could lie right down on that floor and go to sleep," said Whit. "You're getting better, or maybe I'm getting worse. Next year I'm not going to give you a handicap."

"I may get good enough to take you at golf, but not this game. You always know where the ball's going to be, and I have to lose time guessing." They were the only members in the locker-room. They could hear occasional sounds from the kitchen of the steward and his staff having supper, a few dozen feet and a whole generation of prosperity away. The walls of the room were lined with steel lockers, with two islands of lockers back-to-back in the center of the room, hempen matting in the passageways, a rather feeble ceiling lamp above the table where their drinks rested. It was an arcane atmosphere, like some goat-room in an odd lodge, with a lingering dankness traceable to their recent hot showers and to the dozens of gold shoes and plus-fours and last summer's shirts stored and forgotten in the lockers. Whit, in his shorts and shirt, and Pat, in his B.V.D.'s, pleasantly tired from their exercise and additionally numbed by the gin and ginger ales, were in that state of euphorious relaxation that a million men ten million times have called the best part of the game, any game. They were by no means drunk, nor were they exhausted, but once again they were back at the point of utter frankness or retreat from it that they had reached in Pat's office, only now the surrounding circumstances were different.

"Why don't you get it off your chest, Whit?"

Whit Hofman, without looking up, blew the ash off his cigarette. "Funny, I was just thinking the same thing," he said. He reached for the gin bottle and spiked Pat's and his own drinks. "I have too damn many cousins in this town. If I confided in any of them they'd call a family conference, which is the last thing I want." He scraped his cigarette against the ash tray, and with his eyes on the operation said, "Kitty hates me. She hates me, and I'm not sure why."

"Have you got a clear conscience?"

"No," said Whit. "That is I haven't. When we were in Siam, on our trip, Kitty got an attack of dysentery and stayed in the hotel for a couple of days. I, uh, took advantage of that to slip off with an American newspaper fellow for some of the local nookie. So I haven't got a clear conscience, but Kitty doesn't know that.

Positively. I don't think it's that. I *know* it isn't that. It's something—I don't know where it began, or when. We didn't have any fights or anything like that. Just one day it was there, and I hadn't noticed it before."

"Pregnant."

"Oh, yes. But past the stage where she was throwing up. Taking it very easy, because she didn't want to lose this baby. But a wall between us. No, not a wall. Just a way of looking at me, as if I'd changed appearance and she was fascinated, but not fascinated because she *liked* my new appearance. 'What's this strange animal?' That kind of look. No fights, though. Not even any serious arguments. Oh, I got sore at her for trying to smuggle in a ring I bought her in Cairo. I was filling out the customs declaration and I had the damn thing all filled out and signed, then I remembered the ring. I asked her what about it, and she said she wasn't going to declare it. She was going to wear it in with the stone turned around so that it'd look like a guard for her engagement ring. So pointless. The ring wasn't *that* valuable. The duty was about a hundred and fifty dollars. An amethyst, with a kind of a scarab design. Do you know that an amethyst is supposed to sober you up?"

"I never heard that."

"Yeah. The magical power, but it doesn't work, I can tell you. Anyway, I gave her hell because if you try to pull a fast one on the customs inspectors and they catch you, they make you wait, they confiscate your luggage, and I'm told that for the rest of your life, whenever you re-enter the country, they go through everything with a fine tooth comb. And incidentally, an uncle of Jimmy Malloy's was expediting our landing, and he would have got into trouble, no doubt. Dr. Malloy's brother-in-law, has something to do with the immigration people. So I had to get new forms and fill out the whole God damn thing all over again. But that was our only quarrel of any consequence. It did make me wonder a little, why she wanted to save a hundred and fifty when it wasn't even her money."

They sipped their drinks.

"The day she went to the hospital," Whit Hofman continued, "it was very cold, and I bundled her up warm. She laughed at me and said we weren't going to the North Pole. Not a nice laugh. Then when we got to the hospital the nurse helped her change into a hospital gown, but didn't put her to bed. She sat up in a chair, and I put a blanket over her feet, asked her if she wanted anything to read. She said she did. Could I get her a history of the Hofman family? Well, there *is* one, but I knew damn well she didn't want it. She was just being disagreeable, but that was understandable under the circumstances. Then I sat down, and she told me I didn't have to wait around. I said I knew I didn't have to, but was doing it because I wanted to. Then she said, 'God damn it, don't you know when I'm trying to get rid of you?' and threw her cigarette lighter at me. Unfortunately the nurse picked that exact moment to come in the room, and the lighter hit her in the teat. I don't know what came over Kitty. 'Get that son of a bitch out of here,' and a lot more on the same order. So the nurse told me I'd better go, and I did." He paused. "Kitty had an awful time, no doubt about it. I was there when they brought the baby in to show her. She looked at it, didn't register any feeling whatsoever, and then turned her face away and shut her eyes. I have never seen her look at the baby the way you'd expect a mother to. I've never seen her pick him up out of his crib just to hold him. Naturally she's never nursed him. She probably hasn't enough milk, so I have no objection to that, but along with hating me she seems to hate the baby. Dr. English says that will pass, but I know better. She has no damn use for me *or* the child." He paused again. "The Christ-awful thing is, I don't know what the hell I *did*."

"I agree with Dr. English. It'll pass," said Pat Collins. "Women today, they aren't as simple as they used to be, fifty or a hundred years ago. They drive cars and play golf. Smoke and drink, do a lot of the same things men do."

"My mother rode horseback and played tennis. She didn't smoke that I know of, but she drank. Not to excess, but wine with dinner. She died when I was eight, so I don't really know an awful lot about her. My father died while I was still in prep school. From then on I guess you'd say I was brought up by my uncle and the housekeeper and my uncle's butler. I have an older brother in the foreign service, but he's too close to me in age to have had much to do with bringing me up. He was a freshman when our father died."

"I didn't know you had a brother."

"I saw him in Rome. He's in the embassy there. Both glad to see each other, but he thinks I'm a country bumpkin, which I am. And since I don't speak French or Italian, and he has a little bit of an English accent, you might say we don't even speak the same language. He married a Boston girl and you should have seen her with Kitty. Every time the Italian men flocked around Kitty, Howard's wife would act as an interpreter, although the Italians all spoke English. But I don't think that has anything to do with why Kitty developed this hatred for me. Howard's wife disapproved of me just as heartily as she did Kitty. We were all pretty glad to see the last of each other. Howard's wife has twice as much money as he has, so he doesn't exactly rule the roost, but in every marriage one of the two has more money than the other. That's not what's eating Kitty." He sipped his drink. "I've been thinking if we moved away from here. Someone told me that this town is wrong for me."

"They're crazy."

"Well, it's bothered me ever since. This, uh, person said that my friends liked me but I didn't like them back."

"That *is* crap."

"As a matter of fact, the person didn't say like. She said love. Meaning that as long as I lived here, I wouldn't be able to love anybody. But I've always loved Kitty, and I certainly love this town. I don't know what more I can do to prove it."

"As far as Kitty's concerned, you're going to have to wait a while. Some women take longer than others getting their machinery back in place after a baby."

Whit Hofman shook his head. "Dr. English tells me Kitty's machinery is okay. And whatever it is, it started before the machinery got out of place. It's me, but what in the name of Christ is it? It's getting late, Pat. Would you have dinner with me here?"

"If you'll square me with Madge. It *is* late. I'm due home now."

"You want me to speak to her, now?"

"We both can."

There was a telephone in the hall off the locker-room and Pat put in the call.

"I knew that's where you'd be," said Madge. "You could just as easily called two hours ago."

"I'm going to put Whit on," said Pat, and did so.

"Madge, I take all the blame, but it'll be at least an hour before Pat could be home. We're still in our underwear. So could you spare him for dinner?"

"Your wish is our command," said Madge.

Whit turned to Pat. "She hung up. What do you do now?"

"We call Heinie and order up a couple of steaks," said Pat.

It was not only that the two men saw each other so frequently; it was Pat's availability, to share meals, to take little trips, that annoyed Madge. "You don't have to suck up to Whit Hofman," she would say. "Not any more."

"I'm glad I don't."

This colloquy in the Collins household resembled one in the Hofmans'. "Not that it matters to me, but how can you spend so much time with that Pat Collins person?" said Kitty.

"What's wrong with Pat? He's good company."

"Because your other friends refuse to yes you."

"That shows how little you know about Pat Collins," he said. "You don't seem to realize that he had hard going for a while, but he never asked me for any help of any kind."

"Saving you for something big, probably."

"No. I doubt if he'll ever ask me for anything. When he needed money to expand, he didn't even go to our bank, let alone ask me for help. And I would have been glad to put money in his business. Would have been a good investment."

"Oh, I don't care. Do as you please. I'm just amused to watch this beautiful friendship between you two. And by the way, maybe he never asked you for anything, but did he ever refuse anything you offered him? For instance, the club."

"He would have made it."

"Has he made the Gibbsville Club?"

"As far as I know, he's not interested."

"Try him."

"Hell, if I ask him, he'll say yes."

"Exactly my point. His way is so much cagier. He's always there when you want him, and naturally you're going to feel obligated to him. You'll want to pay him back for always being there, so he gets more out of you that way than if he'd asked for favors. He knows that."

"It's funny how *you* know things like that, Kitty."

She fell angrily silent. He had met her at a party just after the war, when he was still in uniform and with two or three other officers was having a lengthy celebration in New York. Whit, a first lieutenant in the 103d Engineers, 28th Division, met a first lieutenant in the 102d Engineers, 27th Division, who had with him a girl from New Rochelle. She was not a beauty, but Whit was immediately attracted to her, and she to him. "This man is only the 102d and I'm the 103d. He's only the 27th and I'm the 28th," said Whit. "Why don't you move up a grade?"

She laughed. "Why not? I *want* to get up in the world."

He made frequent trips to New York to see her. She was going to a commercial art school, living at home with her family but able to spend many nights in New York. Her father was a perfectly respectable layout man in an advertising agency, who commuted from New Rochelle and escaped from his wife by spending all the time he could in sailing boats. His wife was a fat and disagreeable woman who had tried but failed to dominate her husband and her daughter, and regarded her husband as a nincompoop and her daughter as a wild and wilful girl who was headed for no good. One spring day Kitty and Whit drove to Greenwich, Connecticut, and were married. They then drove to New Rochelle, the first and only time Whit Hofman ever saw his wife's parents. Two days later the newly married couple sailed for Europe, and they did not put in an appearance in Gibbsville, Pennsylvania, until the autumn. It was all very unconventional and it led to considerable speculation as to the kind of person Whit Hofman had married, especially among the mothers of nubile girls. But a *fait accompli* was a *fait accompli*, and Whit Hofman was Whit Hofman, and the girls and their mothers had to make the best of it, whatever that turned out to be.

In certain respects it turned out quite well. The town, and

indeed the entire nation, was ready to have some fun. There was a considerable amount of second-generation money around, and manners and customs would never revert to those of 1914. Kitty Hofman and the Lantenengo Country Club appeared almost simultaneously in Gibbsville; both were new and novel and had the backing of the Hofman family. Kitty made herself agreeable to Whit's men friends and made no effort in the direction of the young women. They had to make themselves agreeable to her, and since their alternative was self-inflicted ostracism, Kitty was established without getting entangled in social debts to any of the young women. A less determined, less independent young woman could not have achieved it, but Gibbsville was full of less determined, less independent young women whom Whit Hofman had not married. And at least Whit had not singled out one of their number to the exclusion of all the others, a mildly comforting and unifying thought. He had to marry somebody, so better this nobody with her invisible family in a New York suburb than a Gibbsville girl who would have to suffer as the object of harmonious envy.

Kitty did nothing deliberately to antagonize the young women —unless to outdress them could be so considered, and her taste in clothes was far too individualistic for her new acquaintances. She attended their ladies' luncheons, always leaving before the bridge game began. She played in the Tuesday golf tournaments. She precisely returned all invitations. And she made no close friendships. But she actively disliked Madge Collins.

From the beginning she knew, as women know better than men know, that she was not going to like that woman. Even before Madge got up to dance with Whit and made her extraordinary, possessive, off-in-dreamland impression with her closed eyes, Kitty Hofman abandoned herself to the luxury of loathing another woman. Madge's black dress was sound, so much so that Kitty accurately guessed that Madge had had some experience in women's wear. But from there on every judgment Kitty made was unfavorable. Madge's prettiness was literally natural: her good figure was natural, her amazing skin was natural, her reddish brown hair, her teeth, her bright eyes, her inviting mouth, were gifts of Nature. (Kitty used a great deal of makeup and dyed her blond hair a lighter shade of blond.) Kitty, in the first minutes of her first meeting with Madge, ticketed her as a pretty parlor-maid; when she got up to dance with Whit she ticketed her as a whore, and with no evidence to the contrary, Madge so remained. Kitty's judgments were not based on facts or influenced by considerations of fairness, then or ever, although she could be extremely realistic in her observations. (Her father, she early knew, was an ineffectual man, a coward who worked hard to protect his job and fled to the waters of Long Island Sound to avoid the occasions of quarrels with her mother.) Kitty, with her firmly middle-class background, had no trouble in imagining the background of Madge and Pat Collins, and the Collinses provided her with her first opportunity to assert herself as a Hofman. (She had not been wasting her first years in Gibbsville; her indifferent manner masked a shrewd study of individuals and their standing in the community.) Kitty, who had not been able comfortably to integrate herself into the established order, now rapidly assumed her position as Whit's wife because as Mrs. Whit Hofman she could look down on and crack down on Madge Collins. (By a closely related coincidence she also became a harsher judge of her husband at the very moment that she began to exercise the privileges of her marital status.) Kitty's obsessive hatred of the hick from West Philadelphia, as she called Madge Collins, was quick in its onset and showed every sign of being chronic. The other young women of the country club set did not fail to notice, and it amused them to get a rise out of Kitty Hofman merely by mentioning Madge Collins's name.

But the former Madge Ruddy was at least as intuitive as Kitty Hofman. Parlor-maid, whore, saleslady at Oppenheim, Collins—the real and imagined things she was or that Kitty Hofman chose to think she was—Madge was only a trifle slower in placing Kitty. Madge knew a lady when she saw one, and Kitty Hofman was not it. In the first days of her acquaintance with Kitty she would willingly enough have suspended her judgments if Kitty had been moderately friendly, but since that was not to be the case, Madge cheerfully collected her private store of evidence that Kitty Hofman was a phony. She was a phony aristocrat, a synthetic woman, from her dyed hair to her boyish hips to her no doubt tinted toenails. Madge, accustomed all her life to the West Philadelphia twang, had never waited on a lady who pronounced third *thade* and idea *ideer*. "Get a look at her little titties," Madge would say, when Kitty appeared in an evening dress that had two unjoined panels down the front. "She looks like she forgot to take her hair out of the curlers," said Madge of one of Kitty's coiffures. And, of Kitty's slow gait, "She walks like she was constipated." The animosity left Madge free to love Kitty's husband without the restraint that loyalty to a friend might have invoked. As for disloyalty to Pat Collins, he was aware of none, and did he not all but love Whit too?

Thus it was that behind the friendly relationship of Pat Collins and Whit Hofman a more intense, unfriendly relationship flourished between Madge Collins and Kitty Hofman. The extremes of feeling were not unlike an individual's range of capacity for love and hate, or, as Madge put it, "I hate her as much as you like him, and that's going some." Madge Collins, of course, with equal accuracy could have said: "I hate her as much as I love him, and *that's* going some." The two men arrived at a pact of silence where their wives were concerned, a working protocol that was slightly more to Whit's advantage, since in avoiding mention of Madge he was guarding against a slip that would incriminate Madge. He wanted no such slip to occur; he needed Pat's friendship, and he neither needed nor wanted Madge's love. Indeed, as time passed and the pact of silence grew stronger, Whit Hofman's feeling for Madge was sterilized. By the end of 1925 he would not have offered to take her out to his parked car, and when circumstances had them briefly alone together they either did not speak at all or their conversation was so commonplace that a suspicious eavesdropper would have convicted them of adultery on the theory that two such vital persons could not be so indifferent to each other's physical presence. One evening at a picnic-swimming party at someone's farm—this, in the summer of '26—Madge had had enough of the cold water in the dam and was on her way to the tent that was being used as the ladies' dressing-room. In the darkness she collided with a man on his way from the men's tent. "Who is it? I'm sorry," she said.

"Whit Hofman. Who is this?"

"Madge."

"Hello. You giving up?"

"That water's too cold for me."

"Did Pat get back?"

"From Philly? No. He's spending the night. It's funny talking and I can't really see you. Where are you?"

"I'm right here."

She reached out a hand and touched him. "I'm not going to throw myself at you, but here we are."

"Don't start anything, Madge."

"I said I wasn't going to throw myself at you. You have to make the next move. But you're human."

"I'm human, but you picked a lousy place, and time."

"Is that all that's stopping you? I'll go home now and wait for you if you say the word. Why don't you like me?"

"I do like you."

"Prove it. I'm all alone, the children are with Pat's mother. I have my car, and I'll leave now if you say."

"No. You know all the reasons."

"Sure I do. Sure I do."

"Can you get back to the tent all right? You can see where it is, can't you? Where the kerosene lamp is, on the pole."

"I can see it all right."

"Then you'd better go, Madge, because my good resolutions are weakening."

"Are they? Let me feel. Why, you are human!"

"Cut it out," he said, and walked away from her toward the lights and people at the dam.

She changed into her dress and rejoined the throng at the dam. It was a good-sized party, somewhat disorganized among smaller groups of swimmers, drinkers, eaters of corn on the cob, and a mixed quartet accompanied by a young man on banjo-uke. Heavy clouds hid the moon, and the only light came from a couple of small bonfires. When Madge returned to the party she moved from one group to another, eventually staying longest with the singers and the banjo-uke player. "Larry, do you know 'Ukulele Lady'?"

"Sure," he said. He began playing it, and Madge sang a solo of two choruses. Her thin true voice was just right for the sad, inconclusive little song, and when she finished singing she stood shyly smiling in the momentary total silence. But then there was a spontaneous, delayed burst of applause, and she sat down. The darkness, the fires, the previously disorganized character of the party, and Madge's voice and the words—"maybe she'll find somebody else/ bye and bye"—all contributed to a minor triumph and, quite accidentally, brought the party together in a sentimental climax. "More! More! . . . I didn't know you were a singer . . . Encore! Encore!" But Madge's instinct made her refuse to sing again.

For a minute or two the party was rather quiet, and Kitty had a whispered conversation with the ukulele player. He strummed a few introductory chords until the members of the party gave him their attention, whereupon he began to play "Yaaka hula hickey dula," and Kitty Hofman, in her bare feet and a Paisley print dress, went into the dance. It was a slow hula, done without words and with only the movements of her hips and the ritualistic language of her fingers and arms—only vaguely understood in this group—in synchronous motion with the music. The spectators put on the knowing smiles of the semi-sophisticated as Kitty moved her hips, but before the dance and the tune were halfway finished they stopped their nervous laughter and were caught by the performance. It hardly mattered that they could not understand the language of the physical gestures or that the women as much as the men were being seduced by the dance. The women could understand the movements because the movements were formal and native to themselves, but the element of seductiveness was as real for them as for the men because the men's responsiveness—taking the form of absolute quiet—was like a held breath, and throughout the group men and women felt the need to touch each other by the hand, hands reaching for the nearest hand. And apart from the physical spell produced by the circumstances and the dance, there was the comprehension by the women and by some of the men that the dance was a direct reply to Madge's small bid for popularity. As such the dance was an obliterating victory for Kitty. Madge's plaintive solo was completely forgotten. As the dance ended Kitty put her hands to her lips, kissed them and extended them to the audience as in a benediction, bowed low, and returned to the picnic bench that now became a throne. The applause was a mixture of hand clapping, of women's voices calling out "Lovely! Adorable!" and men shouting "Yowie! Some more, some more!" But Kitty, equally as well as Madge, knew when to quit. "I learned it when Whit and I were in Hawaii. Where else?" she said.

Madge Collins went to Kitty to congratulate her. "That was swell, Kitty."

"Oh, thanks. Did you think so? Of course I can't *sing*," said Kitty.

"You—don't—have—to—when—you—can—shake—that—thing," said Bobby Hermann, whose hesitant enunciation became slower when he drank. "You—got—any—more—hidden—talents —like—that—one—up—your—sleeve?"

"Not up her sleeve," said Madge, and walked away.

"Hey—that's—a—good—one. Not—up—her—sleeve. Not—up—your—sleeve—eh—Kitty?"

In the continuing murmur of admiration for the dance no one —no one but Madge Collins—noticed that Whit Hofman had not added his compliments to those of the multitude. In that respect Kitty's victory was doubled, for Madge now knew that Kitty had intended the exhibition as a private gesture of contempt for Whit as well as a less subtle chastening of Madge herself. Madge sat on a circular grass-mat cushion beside Whit.

"She's a real expert," said Madge. "I didn't know she could do the hula."

"Uh-huh. Learned it in Honolulu."

"On the beach at Waikiki."

"On the beach at Waikiki," said Whit.

"Well, she didn't forget it," said Madge. "Is it hard to learn?"

"Pretty hard, I guess. It's something like the deaf-and-dumb language. One thing means the moon, another thing means home, another means lonesome, and so forth and so on."

191

"Maybe I could get her to teach me how to say what *I* want to say."

"What's that?" said Whit.

"Madge is going home, lonesome, and wishes Whit would be there."

"When are you leaving?"

"Just about now."

"Say in an hour or so? You're all alone?"

"Yes. What will you tell *her?*"

"Whatever I tell her, she'll guess where I am. She's a bitch, but she's not a fool."

"She's a bitch, all right. But maybe you're a fool," said Madge. "No, Whit. Not tonight. Any other time, but not tonight."

"Whatever you say, but you have nothing to fear from her. You or Pat. Take my word for it, you haven't. She's watching us now, and she knows we're talking about her. All right, I'll tell you what's behind this exhibition tonight."

"You don't have to."

"Well I hope you don't think I'd let you risk it if I weren't positive about her."

"I did wonder, but I'm so crazy about you."

"When we were in Honolulu that time, I caught her with another guy. I'd been out playing golf, and I came back to the hotel in time to see this guy leaving our room. She didn't deny it, and I guessed right away who it was. A naval officer. I hadn't got a good look at him, but I let her think I had and she admitted it. The question was, what was I going to do about it? Did I want to divorce her, and ruin the naval officer's career? Did I want to come back here without her? That was where she knew she had me. I *didn't* want to come back here without her. This is my town, you know. We've been here ever since there was a town, and it's the only place I ever want to live. I've told you that." He paused. "Well, you don't know her, the hold she had on me, and I don't fully understand it myself. There are a lot of damn nice girls in town I might have married, and you'd think that feeling that way about the town, I'd marry a Gibbsville girl. But how was I ever to know that I was marrying the girl and not her mother, and in some cases her father? And that the girl wasn't marrying me but my father's money and my uncle's money. Kitty didn't know any of that when I asked her to marry me. She'd never heard of Gibbsville. In fact she wasn't very sure where Pennsylvania was. And I was a guy just out of the army, liked a good time, and presumably enjoying myself before I seriously began looking for a job. The first time Kitty really knew I didn't have to work for a living was when I gave her her engagement ring. I remember what she said. She looked at it and then looked at me and said, 'Is there more where this came from?' So give her her due. She didn't marry me for my money, and that was somewhat of a novelty. Are you listening?"

"Sure," said Madge.

"That afternoon in the hotel she said, 'Look, you can kick me out and pay me off, but I tried to have a child for you, which I didn't want, and this is the first time I've gone to bed with another man, since we've been married.' It was a good argument, but of course the real point was that I didn't want to go home without a wife, and have everybody guessing why. I allowed myself the great pleasure of giving her a slap in the face, and she said she guessed she had it coming to her, and then I was so God damned ashamed of myself—I'd never hit a woman before—that *I* ended up apologizing to *her*. Oh, I told her we were taking the next boat out of Honolulu, and if she was ever unfaithful to me again I'd make it very tough for her. But the fact of the matter is, her only punishment was a slap in the face, and that was with my open hand. We went to various places—Australia, Japan, the Philippines, China—and I got her pregnant."

"Yes. But what was behind this hula tonight?"

"I'd forgotten she knew how to do it. The whole subject of Honolulu, and ukuleles, hulas—we've never mentioned any of it, neither of us. But when she stood up there tonight, partly it was to do something better than you—"

"And she did."

"Well, she tried. And partly it was to insult me in a way that only I would understand. Things have been going very badly between us, we hardly ever speak a civil word when we're alone. She's convinced herself that you and I are having an affair—"

193

"Well, let's."

"Yes, let's. But I wish we could do it without—well, what the hell? Pat's supposed to be able to take care of himself."

"I have a few scores to settle there, too."

"Not since I've known him."

"Maybe not, but there were enough before you knew him. I used to be sick with jealousy, Monday to Friday, Monday to Friday, knowing he was probably screwing some chippy in Allentown or Wilkes-Barre. I was still jealous, even after we moved here. But not after I met you. From then on I didn't care what he did, who he screwed. Whenever I thought of him with another woman I'd think of me with you. But why isn't Kitty going to make any trouble? What have you got on her, besides the navy officer?"

"This is going to sound very cold-blooded."

"All right."

"And it's possible I could be wrong."

"Yes, but go on."

"Well—Kitty's gotten used to being Mrs. W. S. Hofman. She likes everything about it but me—and the baby. It's got her, Madge, and she can never have it anywhere else, or with anybody else."

"I could have told you that the first time I ever laid eyes on her."

"I had to find it out for myself."

There is one law for the rich, and another law for the richer. The frequent appearances of Whit Hofman with Madge Collins were treated not so much as a scandal as the exercise of a privilege of a man who was uniquely entitled to such privileges. To mollify their sense of good order the country club set could tell themselves that Whit was with Pat as often as he was with Madge, and that the three were often together as a congenial trio. The more kindly disposed made the excuse that Whit was putting up with a great deal from Kitty, and since Pat Collins obviously did not object to Whit's hours alone with Madge, what right had anyone else to complain? The excuse made by the less kindly was that if there was anything *wrong* in the Whit-

Madge friendship, Kitty Hofman would be the first to kick up a fuss; therefore there was nothing scandalous in the relationship. The thing most wrong in the relationship was the destructive effect on Madge Collins, who had been brought up in a strict Catholic atmosphere, who in nearly thirty years had had sexual intercourse with one man, and who now was having intercourse with two, often with both in the same day. The early excitement of a sexual feast continued through three or four months and a couple of narrow escapes; but the necessary lies to Pat and the secondary status of the man she preferred became inconvenient, then annoying, then irritating. She withheld nothing from Whit, she gave only what was necessary to Pat, but when she was in the company of both men—playing golf, at a movie, at a football game—she indulged in a nervous masquerade as the contented wife and the sympathetic friend, experiencing relief only when she could be alone with one of the men. Or with neither. The shame she suffered with her Catholic conscience was no greater than the shame of another sort: to be with both men and sit in self-enforced silence while the man she loved was so easily, coolly making a fool of the man to whom she was married. The amiable, totally unsuspecting fool would have had her sympathy in different circumstances, and she would have hated the character of the lover; but Pat's complacency was more hateful to her than Whit's arrogance. The complacency, she knew, was real; and Whit's arrogance vanished in the humility of his passion as soon as she would let him make love to her. There was proficiency of a selfish kind in Pat's lovemaking; he had never been so gentle or grateful as Whit. From what she could learn of Kitty Hofman it would have been neatly suitable if Pat had become Kitty's lover, but two such similar persons were never attracted to each other. They had, emotionally, everything in common; none of the essential friction of personality. Neither was equipped with the fear of losing the other.

It was this fear that helped produce the circumstances leading to the end of Madge's affair with Whit Hofman. "Every time I see you I love you again, even though I've been loving you all along," she told Whit. Only when she was alone with him—riding in his car, playing golf, sitting with him while waiting for Pat to join them, sitting with him after Pat had left them—could she forget the increasingly insistent irritation of her position. Publicly she was, as Whit told her, "carrying it off very well," but the nagging of her Catholic conscience and the rigidity of her middle-class training were with her more than she was with Whit, and when the stimulation of the early excitement had passed, she was left with that conscience, that training, and this new fear.

The affair, in terms of hours in a bed together, was a haphazard one, too dependent on Pat's unpredictable and impulsive absences. Sometimes he would telephone her from the garage late in the afternoon, and tell her he was driving to Philadelphia and would not be home until past midnight. On such occasions, if she could not get word to Whit at his office or at one of the two clubs, the free evening would be wasted. Other times they would make love on country roads, and three times they had gone to hotels in Philadelphia. It seldom happened that Whit, in a moment of urgently wanting to be with her, could be with her within the hour, and it was on just such occasions, when she was taking a foolish chance, that they had their two narrow escapes in her own house. "You can never get away when I want you to," said Whit—which was a truth and a lie.

"Be reasonable," she said, and knew that the first excitement had progressed to complaint. Any time, anywhere, anything had been exciting in the beginning; now it was a bed in a hotel and a whole night together, with a good leisurely breakfast, that he wanted. They were in a second phase, or he was; and for her, fear had begun. It told on her disposition, so that she was sometimes snappish when alone with Whit. Now it was her turn to say they could not be together when she wanted him, and again it was a truth and a lie of exaggeration. They began to have quarrels, and to Whit this was not only an annoyance but a sign that they were getting in much deeper than he intended. For he had not deceived her as to the depth or permanence of their relationship. It was true that he had permitted her to deceive herself, but she was no child. She had had to supply her own declarations of the love she wanted him to feel; they had not been forthcoming from him, and when there were opportunities that almost demanded a declaration of his love, he was silent or noncommittal. The nature of their affair—intimacy accompanied by intrigue—was such as to require extra opportunities for candor. They were closer than if they had been free and innocent, but Whit would not use their intimacy even to make casual pretense of love. "I can't even wring it out of you," she said.

"What?"

"That you love me. You never say it."

"You can't expect to *wring* it out of anyone."

"A woman wants to hear it, once in a while."

"Well, don't try to wring it out of me."

He knew—and she knew almost as soon as he—that his refusal to put their affair on a higher, romantic love plane was quite likely to force her to put an end to the affair. And now that she was becoming demanding and disagreeable, he could deliberately provoke her into final action or let his stubbornness get the same result. It could not be said that she bored him; she was too exciting for that. But the very fact that she could be exciting added to his annoyance and irritation. He began to dislike that hold she had on him, and the day arrived when he recognized in himself the same basic weakness for Madge that he had had for Kitty. And to a lesser degree the same thing had been true of all the women he had ever known. But pursuing that thought, he recalled that Madge was the only one who had ever charged him with the inability to love. Now he had the provocation that would end the affair, and he had it more or less in the words of her accusation.

"You still won't say it," she said to him one night.

"That I love you?"

"That you love me."

"No, I won't say it, and you ought to know why."

"That's plain as day. You won't say it because you don't."

"Not *don't. Can't,*" he said. "You told me yourself, a long time ago. That people love me and I can't love them. I'm beginning to think that's true."

"It's true all right. I was hoping I could get you to change, but you didn't."

197

"I used to know a guy that could take a car apart and put it together again, but he couldn't drive. He never could learn to drive."

"What's that got to do with us?"

"Don't you see? Think a minute."

"I get it."

"So when you ask me to love you, you're asking the impossible. I'm just made that way, that's all."

"This sounds like a farewell speech. You got me to go to a hotel with you, have one last thing together, and then announce that we're through. Is that it?"

"No, not as long as you don't expect something you never expected in the first place."

"That's good, that is. You'll let me go on taking all the risks, but don't ask anything in return. I guess I don't love you *that* much, Mr. Hofman." She got out of bed.

"What are you going to do?"

"I'm getting out of this dump, I promise you that. I'm going home."

"I'm sorry, Madge."

"Whit, you're not even sorry for yourself. But I can make up for it. I'm sorry for you. Do you know what I'm going to do?"

"What?"

"I'm going home and tell Pat the whole story. If he wants to kick me out, all he has to do is say so."

"Why the hell do you want to do that?"

"You wouldn't understand it."

"Is it some Catholic thing?"

"Yes! I'm surprised you guessed it. I don't have to tell him. That's not it. But I'll confess it to him instead of a priest, and whatever he wants me to do, I'll do it. Penance."

"No, I don't understand it."

"No, I guess you don't."

"You're going to take a chance of wrecking your home, your marriage?"

"I'm not very brave. I don't think it is much of a chance, but if he kicks me out, I can go back to Oppenheim, Collins. I have a charge account there now." She laughed.

"Don't do it, Madge. Don't go."

"Whit, I've been watching you and waiting for something like this to happen. I didn't know what I was going to do, but when the time came I knew right away."

"Then you really loved Pat all along, not me."

"Nope. God help me, I love you and that's the one thing I won't tell Pat. There I'll have to lie."

It was assumed, when Pat Collins began neglecting his business and spending so much time in Dick Boylan's speakeasy, that Whit Hofman would come to his rescue. But whether or not Whit had offered to help Pat Collins, nobody could long go on helping a man who refused to help himself. He lost his two salesmen and his bookkeeper, and his Chrysler franchise was taken over by Walt Michaels, who rehired Joe Ricci at decent wages. For a while Pat Collins had a fifty-dollar-a-week drawing account as a salesman at the Cadillac dealer's, but that stopped when people stopped buying Cadillacs, and Pat's next job, in charge of the hat department in a haberdashery, lasted only as long as the haberdashery. As a Cadillac salesman and head of the hat department Pat Collins paid less attention to business than to pill pool, playing a game called Harrigan from one o'clock in the afternoon till suppertime, but during those hours he was at least staying out of the speakeasy. At suppertime he would have a Western sandwich at the Greek's, then go to Dick Boylan's, a quiet back room on the second story of a business building, patronized by doctors and lawyers and merchants in the neighborhood and by recent Yale and Princeton graduates and near-graduates. It was all he saw, in those days, of his friends from the country club crowd.

Dick Boylan's speakeasy was unique in that it was the only place of its kind that sold nothing but hard liquor. When a man wanted a sandwich and beer, he had to send out for it; if he wanted beer without a sandwich, Boylan told him to go some place else for it; but such requests were made only by strangers and by them not more than once. Dick Boylan was the proprietor, and in no sense the bartender; there were tables and chairs, but no bar in his place, and Boylan wore a suit of clothes and a fedora hat at all times, and always seemed to be on the go. He would put a bottle on the table, and when the drinkers had taken what they wanted he would hold up the bottle and estimate the number of drinks that had been poured from it and announce how much was owed him. "This here table owes me eight and a half," he would say, leaving the bookkeeping to the customers. "Or I'll have one with you and make it an even nine." Sometimes he would not be around to open up for the morning customers, and they would get the key from under the stairway linoleum, unlock the door, help themselves, and leave the money where Dick would find it. They could also leave chits when they were short of cash. If a man cheated on his chits, or owed too much money, or drank badly, he was not told so in so many words; he would knock on the door, the peephole was opened, and Boylan would say, "We're closed," and the statement was intended and taken to mean that the man was forever barred, with no further discussion of the matter.

Pat Collins was at Dick Boylan's every night after Madge made her true confession. Until then he had visited the place infrequently, and then, as a rule, in the company of Whit Hofman. The shabby austerity of Dick Boylan's and Boylan's high-handed crudities did not detract from the stern respectability of the place. No woman was allowed to set foot in Boylan's, and among the brotherhood of hard drinkers it was believed—erroneously—that all conversations at Boylan's were privileged, not to be repeated outside. "What's said in here is Masonic," Boylan claimed. "I find a man blabbing what he hears—he's out." Boylan had been known to bar a customer for merely mentioning the names of fellow drinkers. "I run a san'tuary for men that need their booze," said Boylan. "If they was in that Gibbsville Club every time they needed a steam, the whole town'd know it." It was a profitable sanctuary, with almost no overhead and, because of the influence of the clientele, a minimum of police graft. Pat Collins's visits with Whit Hofman had occurred on occasions when one or the other had a hangover, and Boylan's was a quick walk from Pat's garage. At night Whit Hofman preferred to do his drinking in more elegant surroundings, and Pat Collins told himself that he was sure he would not run into

Whit at Boylan's. But he lied to himself; he *wanted* to run into Whit.

At first he wanted a fight, even though he knew he would be the loser. He would be giving twenty pounds to a man who appeared soft but was in deceptively good shape, who managed to get in some physical exercise nearly every day of his life and whose eight years of prep school and college football, three years of army service, and a lifetime of good food and medical care had given him resources that would be valuable in a real fight. Pat Collins knew he did not have a quick punch that would keep Whit down; Whit Hofman was not Walt Michaels. Whit Hofman, in fact, was Whit Hofman, with more on his side than his physical strength. Although he had never seen Whit in a fight, Pat had gone with him to many football games and observed Whit's keen and knowing interest in the niceties of line play. ("Watch that son of a bitch, the right guard for Lehigh. He's spilling two men on every play.") And Whit Hofman's way of telling about a battle during one of his rare reminiscences of the War ("They were awful damn close, but I didn't lob the God damn pineapple. I *threw* it. The hell with what they taught us back in Hancock.") was evidence that he would play for keeps, and enjoy the playing. Pat admitted that if he had really wanted a fight with Whit Hofman, he could have it for the asking. Then what *did* he want? The question had a ready answer: he wanted the impossible, to confide his perplexed anger in the one man on earth who would least like to hear it. He refused to solidify his wish into words, but he tormented himself with the hope that he could be back on the same old terms of companionship with the man who was responsible for his misery. Every night he went to Dick Boylan's, and waited with a bottle on the table.

Dick Boylan was accustomed to the company of hard drinkers, and when a man suddenly became a nightly, hours-long customer, Boylan was not surprised. He had seen the same thing happen too often for his curiosity to be aroused, and sooner or later he would be given a hint of the reason for the customer's problem. At first he dismissed the notion that in Pat Collins's case the problem was money; Collins was selling cars as fast as he could get delivery. The problem, therefore, was probably a woman, and since Collins was a nightly visitor, the woman was at home—his wife. It all came down to one of two things: money, or a woman. It never occurred to Dick Boylan—or, for that matter, to Pat Collins—that Pat's problem was the loss of a friend. Consequently Dick Boylan looked for, and found, all the evidence he needed to support his theory that Collins was having wife troubles. For example, men who were having money troubles would get phone calls from their wives, telling them to get home for supper. But the men who were having wife trouble, although they sometimes got calls from women, seldom got calls from their wives. Pat Collins's wife never called him. Never. And he never called her.

It was confusing to Dick Boylan to hear that Pat Collins's business was on the rocks. Whit Hofman did not let his friends' businesses go on the rocks. And then Boylan understood it all. A long forgotten, overheard remark about Whit Hofman and Madge Collins came back to him, and it was all as plain as day. Thereafter he watched Pat Collins more carefully; the amount he drank, the cordiality of his relations with the country clubbers, the neatness of his appearance, and the state of his mind and legs when at last he would say goodnight. He had nothing against Pat Collins, but he did not like him. Dick Boylan was more comfortable with non-Irishmen; they were neither Irish-to-Irish over-friendly, nor Irish-to-Irish condescending, and when Pat Collins turned out to be so preoccupied with his problems that he failed to be over-friendly or condescending, Dick Boylan put him down for an unsociable fellow, hardly an Irishman at all, but certainly not one of the others. Pat Collins did not fit in anywhere, although he got on well enough with the rest of the customers. Indeed, the brotherhood of hard drinkers were more inclined to welcome his company than Collins was to seek theirs. Two or three men coming in together would go to Pat's table instead of starting a table of their own and inviting him to join them. It was a distinction that Dick Boylan noticed without comprehending it, possibly because as an Irishman he was immune to what the non-Irish called Irish charm.

But it was not Irish charm that made Pat Collins welcome in the brotherhood; it was their sense of kinship with a man who was slipping faster than they were slipping, and who in a manner of speaking was taking someone else's turn in the downward line, thus postponing by months or years the next man's ultimate, inevitable arrival at the bottom. They welcomed this volunteer, and they hoped he would be with them a long while. They were an odd lot, with little in common except an inability to stand success or the lack of it. There were the medical men, Brady and Williams; Brady, who one day in his early forties stopped in the middle of an operation and had to let his assistant take over, and never performed surgery again; Williams, who at thirty-two was already a better doctor than his father, but who was opppressed by his father's reputation. Lawyer Parsons, whose wife had made him run for Congress because her father had been a congressman, and who had then fallen hopelessly in love with the wife of a congressman from Montana. Lawyer Strickland, much in demand as a high school commencement speaker, but somewhat shaky on the Rules of Evidence. Jeweler Linklighter, chess player without a worthy opponent since the death of the local rabbi. Hardware Merchant Stump, Eastern Pennsylvania trapshooting champion until an overload exploded and blinded one eye. Teddy Stokes, Princeton '25, gymnast, Triangle Club heroine and solo dancer, whose father was paying blackmail to the father of an altar boy. Sterling Agnew, Yale ex-'22, Sheff, a remittance man from New York whose father owned coal lands, and who was a part-time lover of Kitty Hofman's. George W. Shuttleworth, Yale '91, well-to-do widower and gentleman author, currently at work on a biography of Nathaniel Hawthorne which was begun in 1892. Percy Keene, music teacher specializing in band instruments, and husband of a Christian Science practitioner. Lewis M. Rutledge, former captain of the Amerst golf team and assistant manager of the local branch of a New York brokerage house, who had passed on to Agnew the information that Kitty Hofman was accommodating if you caught her at the right moment. Miles Lassiter, ex-cavalry officer, ex-lieutenant of the State Constabulary, partner in the Schneider & Lassiter Detective & Protective Company, industrial patrolmen, payroll guards, private investigators, who was on his word of honor never again to bring a loaded revolver into Boylan's. Any and at some times all these gentlemen were to be found at Boylan's on any given night, and they constituted a clientele that Dick Boylan regarded as his regulars, quite apart from the daytime regulars who came in for a quick steam, drank it, paid, and quickly departed. Half a dozen of the real regulars were also daytime regulars, but Boylan said—over and over again—that in the day-time he ran a first-aid station; the sanctuary did not open till suppertime. (The sanctuary designation originated with George Shuttleworth; the first-aid station, with Dr. Calvin K. Brady, a Presbyterian and therefore excluded from Boylan's generalities regarding the Irish.)

For nearly three years these men sustained Pat Collins in his need for companionship, increasingly so as he came to know their problems. And know them he did, for in the stunned silence that followed Madge's true confession he took on the manner of the reliable listener, and little by little, bottle by bottle, the members of the brotherhood imparted their stories even as Whit Hofman had done on the afternoon of the first meeting of Whit and Pat. In exchange the members of the brotherhood helped Pat Collins with their tacit sympathy, that avoided mention of the latest indication of cumulative disaster. With a hesitant delicacy they would wait until he chose, if he chose, to speak of the loss of his business, the loss of his jobs, the changes of home address away from the western part of town to the northeastern, where the air was always a bit polluted from the steel mill, the gas house, the abattoir, and where there was always some noise, of which the worst was the squealing of hogs in the slaughterhouse.

"I hope you won't mind if I say this, Pat," said George Shuttleworth one night. "But it seems to me you take adversity very calmly, considering the first thing I ever heard about you."

"What was that, George?"

"I believe you administered a sound thrashing to Mr. Herb Michaels, shortly after you moved to town."

"Oh, that. Yes. Well, I'm laughing on the other side of my face now. I shouldn't have done that."

"But you're glad you did. I hope. Think of how you'd feel now if you hadn't. True, he owns the business you built up, but at

least you have the memory of seeing him on the ground. And a
cigar in his mouth, wasn't it? I always enjoyed that touch. I
believe Nathaniel would have enjoyed it."

"Who?"

"Nathaniel Hawthorne. Most generally regarded as a gloomy
writer, but where you find irony you'll find a sense of humor. I
couldn't interest you in reading Hawthorne, could I?"

"Didn't he write *The Scarlet Letter?*"

"Indeed he did, indeed so."

"I think I read that in college."

"Oh, I hadn't realized you were a college man. Where?"

"Villanova."

"Oh, yes."

"It's a Catholic college near Philly."

"Yes, it must be on the Main Line."

"It is."

"Did you study for the priesthood?"

"No, just the regular college course. I flunked out sophomore
year."

"How interesting that a Catholic college should include *The
Scarlet Letter*. Did you have a good teacher? I wonder what his
name was."

"Brother Callistus, I think. Maybe it was Brother Adrian."

"I must look them up. I thought I knew all the Hawthorne
authorities. Callistus, and Adrian. No other names?"

"That's what they went by."

"I'm always on the lookout for new material on Nathaniel.
One of these days I've just got to stop revising and pack my book
off to a publisher, that's all there is to it. Stand or fall on what
I've done—and then I suppose a week after I publish, along will
come someone with conclusions that make me seem fearfully out
of date. It's a terrifying decision for me to make after nearly
thirty years. I don't see how I can face it."

"Why don't you call this Volume One?"

"Extraordinary. I thought of that very thing. In fact, in 1912 I
made a new start with just that in mind, but after three years I
went back to my earlier plan, a single volume. But perhaps I
could publish in the next year or two, and later on bring out new

editions, say every five years. Possibly ten. I'd hoped to be ready for the Hawthorne Centenary in 1904, but I got hopelessly bogged down in the allegories and I didn't dare rush into print with what I had then. It wouldn't have been fair to me or to Nathaniel, although I suppose it'd make precious little difference to him."

"You never know."

"That's just it, Pat. He's very real to me, you know, although he passed away on May eighteenth or nineteenth in 'sixty-four. There's some question as to whether it was the eighteenth or the nineteenth. But he's very real to me. Very."

This gentle fanatic, quietly drinking himself into a stupor three nights a week, driven home in a taxi with a standing order, and reappearing punctually at eight-thirty after a night's absence, became Pat Collins's favorite companion among the brotherhood. George was in his early fifties, childless, with a full head of snowy white hair brushed down tight on one side. As he spoke he moved his hand slowly across his thatch, as though still training it. Whatever he said seemed to be in answer to a question, a studied reply on which he would be marked as in an examination, and he consequently presented the manner, looking straight ahead and far away, of a conscientious student who was sure of his facts but anxious to present them with care. To Pat Collins the mystery was how had George Shuttleworth come to discover whiskey, until well along in their friendship he learned that George had begun drinking at Yale and had never stopped. Alcohol had killed his wife in her middle forties—she was the same age as George—and Boylan's brotherhood had taken the place of the drinking bouts George had previously indulged in with her. "The Gibbsville Club is no place for me in the evening," said George. "Games, games, games. If it isn't bridge in the card room, it's pool in the billiard room. Why do men feel they have to be so strenuous—and I include bridge. The veins stand out in their foreheads, and when they finish a hand there's always one of them to heave a great sigh of relief. That's what I mean by strenuous. And the worst of it is that with two or possibly three exceptions, I used to beat them all consistently, and I never had any veins stand out in *my* forehead."

As the unlikely friendship flourished, the older man, by the strength of his passivity, subtly influenced and then dominated Pat Collins's own behavior. George Shuttleworth never tried to advise or instruct his younger friend or anyone else; but he had made a life for himself that seemed attractive to the confused, disillusioned younger man. Ambition, aggressiveness seemed worthless to Pat Collins. They had got him nowhere; they had in fact tricked him as his wife and his most admired friend had tricked him, as though Madge and Whit had given him a garage to get him out of the way. He was in no condition for violent action, and George Shuttleworth, the least violent of men, became his guide in this latter-day acceptance of defeat. In spite of the friendship, George Shuttleworth remained on an impersonal basis with Pat Collins; they never discussed Madge at all, never mentioned her name, and as a consequence Pat's meetings with his friend did not become an opportunity for self-pity.

The time then came—no day, no night, no month, no dramatic moment but only a time—when George Shuttleworth had taken Whit's place in Pat Collins's need of a man to admire. And soon thereafter another time came when Pat Collins was healed, no longer harassed by the wish or the fear that he would encounter Whit. It was a small town, but the routines of lives in small towns can be restrictive. A woman can say, "I haven't been downtown since last month," although downtown may be no more than four or five blocks away. And there were dozens of men and women who had been born in the town, Pat's early acquaintances in the town, who never in their lives had seen the street in the northeastern section where Pat and Madge now lived. ("Broad Street? I never knew we had a Broad Street in Gibbsville.") There were men and women from Broad Street liberated by the cheap automobile, who would take a ride out Lantenengo Street on a Sunday afternoon, stare at the houses of the rich, but who could not say with certainty that one house belonged to a brewer and another to a coal operator. Who has to know the town as a whole? A physician. The driver of a meat-market delivery truck. A police officer. The fire chief. A newspaper reporter. A taxi driver. A town large enough to be called a town is a complex of neighborhoods, invariably within well-defined limits of economic character; and the men of the neighborhoods, freer to move outside, create or follow the boundaries of their working activities—and return to their neighborhoods for the nights of delight and anguish with their own. Nothing strange, then, but only abrupt, when Pat Collins ceased to see Whit Hofman; and nothing remarkable, either, that three years could be added to the life of Pat Collins, hiding all afternoon in a poolroom, clinging night after night to a glass.

"What did you want to tell me this for?" he had said.

"Because I thought it was right," she had said.

"Right, you say?"

"To tell you, yes," she said.

He stood up and pulled off his belt and folded it double.

"Is that what you're gonna do, Pat?"

"Something to show him the next time," he said.

"There'll be no next time. You're the only one'll see what you did to me."

"That's not what I'm doing it for."

"What for, then?"

"It's what you deserve. They used to stone women like you, stone them to death."

"Do that, then. Kill me, but not the strap. Really kill me, but don't do that, Pat. That's ugly. Have the courage to kill me, and I'll die. But don't do that with the strap, please."

"What a faker, what a bluffer you are."

"No," she said. She went to the bureau drawer and took out his revolver and handed it to him. "I made an act of contrition."

"And act of contrition."

"Yes, and there was enough talk, enough gossip. You'll get off," she said.

"Put the gun away," he said.

She dropped the revolver on a chair cushion. "You put it away. Put it in your pocket, Pat. I'll use it on you if you start beating me with the strap."

"Keep your voice down, the children'll hear," he said.

"They'll hear if you beat me."

"You and your act of contrition. Take off your clothes."

"You hit me with that strap and I'll scream."

"Take your clothes off, I said."

She removed her dress and slip, and stood in brassiere and girdle.

"Everything," he said.

She watched his eyes, took off the remaining garments, and folded her arms against her breasts.

He went to her, bent down, and spat on her belly.

"You're dirty," he said. "You're a dirty woman. Somebody spit on you, you dirty woman. The spit's rolling down your belly. No, I won't hit you."

She slowly reached down, picked up the slip and covered herself with it. "Are you through with me?"

He laughed. "Am I through with you? Am *I* through with you."

He left the house and was gone a week before she again heard from him. He stayed in town, but he ate only breakfast at home. "Is this the way it's going to be?" she said. "I have to make up a story for the children."

"You ought to be good at that."

"Just so I know," she said. "Do you want to see their report cards?"

"No."

"It's no use taking it out on them. What you do to me, I don't care, but they're not in this. They think you're cross with them."

"Don't tell me what to do. The children. You down here, with them sleeping upstairs. Don't you tell me what to do."

"All right, I won't," she said. "I'll tell them you're working nights, you can't come home for dinner. They'll see through it, but I have to give them some story."

"You'll make it a good one, of that I'm sure."

In calmer days he had maintained a balance between strict parenthood and good humor toward the children, but now he could not overcome the guilt of loathing their mother that plagued him whenever he saw the question behind their eyes. They were waiting to be told something, and all he could tell

them was that it was time for them to be off to school, to be off
to Mass, always time for them to go away and take their unan-
swerable, unphrased questions with them. Their mother told
them that he was very busy at the garage, that he had things on
his mind, but in a year he had lost them. There was more finality
to the loss than would have been so if he had always treated
them with indifference, and he hated Madge the more because
she could not and he could not absolve him of his guilt.

One night in Boylan's speakeasy George Shuttleworth, out of a
momentary silence, said: "What are you going to do now,
Pat?"

"Nothing. I have no place to go."

"Oh, you misunderstood me. I'm sorry. I meant now that
Overton's has closed."

"That was over a month ago. I don't know, George. I haven't
found anything, but I guess something will turn up. I was
thinking of going on the road again. I used to be a pretty good
hat salesman, wholesale, and when I was with Overton I told the
traveling men to let me know if they heard of anything."

"But you don't care anything about hats."

"Well, I don't, but I can't pick and choose. I can't support a
family shooting pool."

"Isn't there something in the automobile line? A man ought to
work at the job he likes best. We have only the one life, Pat. The
one time in this vale of tears."

"Right now the automobile business is a vale of tears. I hear
Herb Michaels isn't having it any too easy, and I could only
move four new Cadillacs in fourteen months."

"Suppose you had your own garage today. Could you make
money, knowing as much as you do?"

"Well, they say prosperity is just around the corner."

"I don't believe it for a minute."

"I don't either, not in the coal regions. A man to make a living
in the automobile business today, in this part of the country,
he'd be better off without a dealer's franchise. Second-hand cars,
and service and repairs. New rubber. Accessories. Batteries. All

that. The people that own cars have to get them serviced, but the people that need cars in their jobs, they're not buying new cars. Who is?"

"I don't know. I've never owned a car. Never learned to drive one."

"You ought to. Then when you go looking for material for your book, you'd save a lot of steps."

"Heavens no," said George Shuttleworth. "You're referring to trips to Salem? New England? Why it takes me two or three days of walking before I achieve the proper Nineteenth Century mood. My late lamented owned a car and employed a chauffeur. A huge, lumbering Pierce-Arrow she kept for twelve years. I got rid of it after she died. It had twelve thousand miles on the speedometer, a thousand miles for each year."

"Oh, they were lovely cars. Was it a limousine?"

"Yes, a limousine, although I believe they called it a Berliner. The driver was well protected. Windows on the front doors. I got rid of him, too. I got rid of him *first*. Good pay. Apartment over the garage. Free meals. New livery every second year. And a hundred dollars at Christmas. But my wife's gasoline bills, I happened to compare them with bills for the hospital ambulance when I was on the board. Just curiosity. Well, sir, if those bills were any indication, my wife's car used up more gasoline than the ambulance, although I don't suppose it all found its way into our tank. But she defended him. Said he always kept the car looking so nice. He did, at that. He had precious little else to occupy his time. I believe he's gone back to Belguim. He was the only Belgian in town, and my wife was very sympathetic toward the Belgians."

"Took his savings and—"

"His plunder," said George Shuttleworth. "Let's not waste any more time talking about him, Pat. You know, of course, that I'm quite rich."

"Yes, that wouldn't be hard to guess. That house and all."

"The house, yes, the house. Spotless, not a speck of dust anywhere. It's like a museum. I have a housekeeper, Mrs. Frazier. Scotch. Conscientious to a degree, but she's made a whole career

211

of keeping my house antiseptically clean, like an operating surgery. So much so, that she makes me feel that I'm in the way. So I'm getting out of the way for a while. I'm going away."

"Going down South?"

"No, I'm not going South. I'm going abroad, Pat. I haven't been since before the War, and I'm not really running away from Mrs. Frazier and her feather dusters. I have a serious purpose in taking this trip. It has to do with my book. You knew that Nathaniel spent seven years abroad. Perhaps you didn't. Seven years, from 1853 to 1860."

"You want to see what inspired him," said Pat.

"No, no! Quite the contrary. He'd done all his best work by then. I want to see how it spoiled him, living abroad. There were other distractions. The Civil War. His daughter's illness. But I must find out for myself whether European life spoiled Nathaniel *or* did he flee to Europe when he'd exhausted his talent. That may turn out to be my greatest contribution to the study of Hawthorne. I can see quite clearly how my discoveries might cause me to scrap everything I've done so far and have to start all over again. I've already written to a great many scholars, and they've expressed keen interest."

"Well, I'll be sorry to see you go, George. I'll miss our evenings. When do you leave?"

"In the *Mauretania*, the seventh of next month. Oh, when I decide to act, nothing stops me," said George Shuttleworth. "I want to give you a going-away present, Pat."

"It should be the other way around. You're the one that's leaving."

"If you wish to give me some memento, that's very kind of you. But what I have in mind, I've been thinking about it for some time. Not an impulse of the moment. How much would it cost to set you up in a business such as you describe?"

"Are you serious, George?"

"Dead serious."

"A small garage, repairing all makes. No dealership. Gas, oil, tires, accessories. There's an old stable near where I live. A neighbor of mine uses it to garage his car in. You want to go on my note, is that it?"

"No, I don't want to go on your note. I'll lend you the money myself, without interest."

"Using mostly second-hand equipment, which I know where to buy here and there, that kind of a setup would run anywhere from five to ten thousand dollars. Atlantic, Gulf, one of those companies put in the pump and help with the tank. Oil. Tools I'd have to buy myself. Air pump. Plumbing would be a big item, and I'd need a pit to work in. Anywhere between five to ten thousand. You can always pick up a light truck cheap and turn it into a tow-car."

George Shuttleworth was smiling. "That's the way I like to hear you talk, Pat. Show some enthusiasm for something. What's your bank?"

"The Citizens, it was. I don't have any at the moment."

"Tomorrow, sometime before three o'clock, I'll deposit ten thousand dollars in your name, and you can begin to draw on it immediately."

"There ought to be some papers drawn up."

"My cheque is all the papers we'll need."

"George?"

"Now, now! No speech, none of that. I spend that much every year, just to have a house with sparkling chandeliers."

"Well then, two words. Thank you."

"You're very welcome."

"George?"

"Yes, Pat."

"I'm sorry, but you'll have to excuse me. I—I can't sit here, George. You see why? Please excuse me."

"You go take a good long walk, Pat. That's what you do."

He walked through the two crowds of men and women leaving the movie houses at the end of the first show. He spoke to no one.

"You're home early," said Madge. "Are you all right?"

"I'm all right."

"You look sort of peak-ed."

"Where are the children?"

"They're out Halloweening. They finished their homework."

"I'm starting a new business."

"You are? What?"

"I'm opening a new garage."

"Where?"

"In the neighborhood."

"Well—that's good, I guess. Takes money, but it'd be a waste of time to ask you where you got it."

"It'd be a waste of time."

"Did you have your supper?"

"I ate something. I'm going to bed. I have to get up early. I have to go around and look for a lot of stuff."

"Can I do anything?"

"No. Just wake me up when the children get up."

"All right. Goodnight."

"Goodnight."

"And good luck, Pat."

"No, No, Madge. Don't, don't—"

"All right. I'm sorry," she said quietly. Then, uncontrolled, "Pat, for God's sake! Please?"

"No, Madge. I ask you."

She covered her face with her hands. "Please, please, please, please, please."

But he went upstairs without her. He could not let her spoil this, he could not let her spoil George Shuttleworth even by knowing about him.

"Hello, Pat."

"Hyuh, Whit."

Never more than that, but never less.

214

THE FIRST DAY

On Monday morning at ten minutes of eight Ray Whitehill entered the Ledger-Star Building, walked quickly through the business office and on to the news room, and came to a halt at Lester Bull's desk. "Hello, Les, here I am," said Ray Whitehill.

"Good for you, Ray. Welcome back. Let's see, I'll take you over and introduce you to the only other member of the staff that's in so far. Or do you know her? Mary McGannon."

"No, I've never met her."

At the last desk in a row of five a young woman was at a typewriter, copying from a notebook, which she peered at through heavy glasses.

"Mary, this is Ray Whitehill. Ray, Mary McGannon."

The young woman quickly removed her glasses and stood up. "Oh. Well, goodness. How do you do? Welcome back, Mr. Whitehill."

"Thank you."

"Needless to say, I've heard a lot about you, and we're all so glad you're going to be on the paper again."

"That's very nice of you. What have you got there? A P.T.A. meeting?"

"Well, just about. The League of Women Voters, but the names are almost the same."

"Get them right," said Whitehill. "And always remember that Mrs. J. Stanton Keene spells her name with three e's and the other Keens get along on two."

"Oh, Mrs. J. Stanton isn't with us any more," said the young woman. "She's been out of circulation over two years."

"You mean *more than* two years," said Whitehill. "I didn't know the old girl had cooled."

"Mary writes it *more than,* but in conversation she always says *over,*" said Bull.

"Yes, she brought down her last gavel two years ago."

"Well, don't let me interrupt you," said Whitehill.

"Will you excuse me?" said the young woman. "I've got forty names to copy before I go on my rounds. Very glad you're back, Mr. Whitehill."

"Very glad to be back, thanks."

The girl put on her glasses and sat down.

"I thought it would be nice to get you your old desk, but it's nowhere around," said Bull. "We got all these new ones in a couple of years ago. All new desks and typewriters."

"My old one would have looked out of place here."

"Yeah, I guess it would, but I asked anyway. So I've put you here, temporarily. If you want to change later I'll get one of the other boys to trade places with you, but you don't want to be over on the sports side, do you?"

"Makes no difference where I sit, Les. Although that's where I started. The sports side. When I first came on the paper I *was* the sports side. I did the whole thing myself."

"Well, we have four men doing it now. You know, every township has a high school now, with a stadium and a swimming pool, and a band. Scholastic sports really sells papers, we found. More so than the junior college."

"What junior college? You mean to say the town has a junior college?"

"Oh, since 1947. Twelve hundred students, but sportswise they don't cut as much cheese as the high school leagues."

"I've been away a long time."

"Yes, when you left I wasn't even in kindergarten."

"That was 1927."

"I'm thirty-seven. I've been here fifteen years this June. I've never worked anywhere else."

"God knows I have."

"I should say you have. I wish I had your experiences to look back on, but when you're married and three kids you think twice about making a drastic move. And I can't complain. They've treated me very well. When the two papers merged I got this promotion, and I'm in on participation. It would have been fun to get around more, but it looks like I'm here the rest of my life unless there's something drastic."

"Well, this is where I began, and this is where I end up, if that's any consolation."

"Yeah, but I never interviewed Winston Churchill, and I never palled around with Heywood Broun and Damon Runyon. Was it true that Runyon couldn't speak, that he had to write on a pad of paper?"

"Yes, the last years."

"I saw a picture of Heywood Broun, he was wearing a raccoon coat and a high silk hat. Did he really dress like that? The unmade bed, somebody called him."

"He didn't care how he looked."

"But he could write. We used to have to read old columns of his. By the way, I've arranged to have the New York papers on your desk every day. The boss said you wanted the *Trib* and the *Times*. They come in around ten o'clock, by mail. Okay?"

"Fine, fine, Thanks, Les."

"You make yourself comfortable, then. I've got to start getting out a paper. Oh, Ray, this is Bud Freedman, our assistant sports editor."

"Hello, Ray," said a young man.

"Hello, Bud." They shook hands.

"Les, I have a story you might like to run on Page One and jump to the sports page."

"What's the story?"

217

"Marty Moreno's been offered the job coaching the St. Joseph's varsity."

"Why don't you stop? You come in with that story every year."

"This time he's going to take it."

"When he does we'll run it, but never on Page One. Go to work and stop trying to win the Pulitzer prize."

"Where is Marty Moreno coaching now?" said Whitehill.

"Queen of Angels. You know Marty?" said Freedman.

"Look in the files, around 1925, and under my byline you'll find a story that says Marty Moreno has been offered the job of coaching at Villanova. I went for that in 1925, the first year Marty was coaching."

"You're kidding," said Freedman.

"Find out for yourself."

"Thirty-six years ago? Yeah, I guess he could of been coaching then."

"He was coaching, all right. Queen of Angels. Marty will be coaching with the Queen of Angels when he meets the real one."

"What was that? Let me have that again."

"It isn't all that good," said Whitehill.

"He'll be coaching the Queen of Angels when he finally meets the real one. Wait'll I see him. Will I give him that for a needle? Thanks, Ray." The young man went to his desk.

"Eager," said Les Bull.

"Young," said Whitehill. He went to the assigned desk and inspected the contents: a drawerful of *Ledger-Star* stationery in assorted sizes; typing paper and flimsies and carbons; a neatly folded clean hand towel; an area telephone directory; a box of pencils; a stapler and a package of paper clips. The neat efficiency brought back memories of a room he had once occupied in an *Essex* class carrier, even to the matching pencil and ballpoint pen set. He pulled the typewriter out of its hiding place in the desk, and the typewriter was almost new. He rolled a couple of pieces of paper into the typewriter and tapped out his byline. He saw Les Bull looking up from his work and smiling.

"Attaboy, Ray," said Bull. "That's good to hear."

218

"My byline," said Ray Whitehill. "That may be as far as I'll get, today."

"Hang in there," said Bull.

One by one the other members of the staff reported for work, all strangers to Ray Whitehill except John J. Wigmore, the county editor. The others wasted little time in the amenities, and Whitehill made no attempt to hold them in conversation, but John Wigmore was a contemporary, had started on the paper a year ahead of Whitehill. He kept his hat on and he was smoking a cigar. "Ray, it's like old times to see you back," said Wigmore. He sat on Whitehill's desk. "Do you recall the big fire of '26?"

"I sure do," said Whitehill. "That was the first time you ever let me cover a news story."

"Yes, and I guess you might say that gave you your start. Hadn't been for that you'd still be covering basketball. Not really, though. You'd have been discovered sooner or later. They couldn't keep you down, Ray. You had the old zing, the old razzmatazz, and you could write. If I'd been able to write worth a damn they wouldn't have put me on the desk."

"The boy editor," said Whitehill.

"I was the youngest city editor in this part of the State. Now I'm damn near the oldest. Where you living?"

"I took a room at the 'Y' temporarily."

Wigmore looked from right to left, lowered his voice and said, "If you're looking for a nice apartment, I can fix you up."

"What's the angle, John?" With Wigmore there was always an angle; that much had not changed.

"Oh, no angle, exactly. Strictly legitimate. You pay rent. But this new apartment building just went up at Fourth and Market."

"I noticed it."

"A little trouble with the building inspector that I happened to be instrumental in fixing up for the Roach brothers. They're the ones put up the building. So naturally I know Jerry Darby, the building inspector, and I got him together with the Roach boys. Now it's all straightened out."

"I imagine the builders are very grateful."

"Well, their apartment house could have sat there empty for

six months or a year if somebody didn't take some action. Where they made their mistake was antagonizing Jerry right at the beginning."

"Were you the bag man, John?"

Wigmore smiled. "You know, the funny thing is, no money changed hands. Not a nickel." He studied the end of his cigar. "Now just between you and I, Ray. Jerry has a daughter just got married and it wouldn't surprise me if her new house was built with surplus materials from the apartment building. It's a brick house, and so's the apartment, and I understand she got the same make of refrigerator and dishwasher you'll find in the apartments. Surplus, of course. Hard to trace. But that way everybody's happy."

"And what's your end?"

"Don't worry about me, Ray. My old motto, ask me no questions and I'll tell you no lies. But anyway, there's only two vacancies left and I can get you one for a hundred and a quarter that somebody else'd have to pay two-fifty. Do you have your own furniture?"

"In storage," said Whitehill. "New York."

"We'll send a truck for it," said Wigmore. "Like to have you meet the Roach boys. They're going to be doing a lot for this town, Ray."

"Why not? I'll be glad to meet them."

"Then I'll tell them to hold one of those apartments for you? They're both the same identical size and layout, so whichever one they hold won't make any difference. And you're more or less a prestige tenant, so don't have any hesitation."

"Just a mild payola?"

"Just a mild. Well, I gotta get to work. Where you having lunch?"

"Having lunch with the boss, at the University Club."

"Lousy food, but it's the University Club. I usually eat at the hotel. Are you going to join the University Club, Ray?"

"I don't have to. I was made an honorary member in 1943."

"Oh, that time you came back and lectured. They made you an honorary member. Does that still hold good?"

"As far as I know."

"Don't have to pay any dues, then, hey?"

"Nope."

"That makes you and the boss the only members in this shop. And you're in for free. Pretty nice, pretty nice."

"At those prices," said Whitehill.

The New York papers were delivered punctually, but in the time before their arrival he had written nothing more than his signature. The other staff members were busy at their typewriters and telephones, and when they spoke it was only to each other. They were a little in awe of him, he knew, and they could not know that that was not what he wanted now. He wanted to be made to feel at home in what had been his professional birthplace, but most of them had not been born when he was already too big for the paper and the town. He had felt more at home in bureaus in Hong Kong and Helsingfors, in tents and Quonset huts in the western hemisphere; he had been more at ease with Nehru and Ben-Gurion than with the assistant sports editor of the *Ledger-Star*. He could not concentrate on the available newspapers, the exchanges from the nearby cities in the State, and when the New York papers arrived he read them eagerly, like letters from friends, which indeed they were in at least a manner of speaking. He knew Lippmann as Walter, Alsop as Joe, Reston as Scotty, and to them he was Ray or Whitey. He read the papers and some of his confidence came back to him, and he thought of a piece he might write for the morrow's *Ledger-Star*. But now it was time to keep his date at the University Club, with the boss.

It was a three-story, red brick and white trim building, just off one of the main streets, and he could remember when it was being built, then later when he would go there to cover banquets, then—in 1943—when he went there as guest of honor. The biggest men in town had been there that night, listening respectfully to his report of the fighting against the Germans in Italy. He spared them nothing, that night. They needed to be told some hard, ugly truths after the let-down that followed Mussolini's surrender. When he sat down they were momentarily silent, but then spontaneously they rose and burst into applause and he knew he had done some good. They made him an honorary member and gave him a Revere silver bowl, and the president of the club said how appropriate the bowl was, although accidentally so. "None of us knew beforehand that Ray was going to be a modern Paul Revere," said the president. "But he sure is riding and spreading the alarm, and we'll always be grateful to him."

Ray Whitehill entered the club and started to give his name to the sixtyish attendant. "Don't you remember me, Ray? Al Redmond."

"Aloysius Patrick Xavier Redmond, for God's sake," said Whitehill. They shook hands and Redmond took his hat and coat. "Do they let you play pool here?"

"Tell you the truth I could beat most of them, even with my eyesight the way it is. You're here to stay now, Ray?"

"I think so. I hope so. Maybe we can get in a game sometime."

"Bring your money, I could always give you fifty to forty," said Redmond. "Mr. D. B. Otis would like for Mr. Whitehill to meet him in the bar. I guess that's one place you could always find your way to, Ray. Anyhow, it's to the end of the hall and down them stairs."

"Thanks, Al. See you soon," said Whitehill.

Dexter Otis was standing with his back to the bar, and as soon as he saw Whitehill he waved and pointed to a table for two against the wall. "Got wedged with a bore, and I don't even know his name," said Otis. "Will you have a drink, Ray?"

"No thanks."

"You don't drink anything at all any more?"

"Two years."

"That long, eh? Well, I seldom do during the daytime. Let's order, shall we? I'm going to have the sausage cakes and mashed potatoes. If you stick to the plain things the food here's all right, but otherwise, no. I noticed you're an honorary member, so you'll probably come here a lot, but don't expect fancy dishes."

"I'll have the sausage cakes. Yes, they made me a member in '43."

"I was in the Navy then. I guess that was when I first began to read your stuff. You were doing a lot of magazine stuff."

"Quite a lot. That, and the radio."

"And you sold one book to the movies."

"Two."

"Do you mind if I ask you a personal question?"

"No, go right ahead," said Whitehill, sensing what the question would be.

"Where did it all go, the money I mean, the dough you made?"

"Well, I sometimes wonder myself. I was married twice and divorced both times, and I had a daughter by my first wife. Her education took quite a bit, although I don't regret a nickel of that. I guess I don't regret any of it."

"But weren't you living on an expense account a lot of the time, when you were overseas?"

"Very few guys got rich that way. All that seemed to do was help us acquire expensive tastes."

"Have you any idea how much money you made?"

"All told? You mean since I left the old *Star?*"

"Yes."

"Well, I never stopped to figure it out, but thirty-four years. Over all I probably averaged twenty-five thousand a year in salary. How much would that be?"

"Uh, that would be eight hundred and fifty thousand."

"Books. Lectures. Radio. And two movie sales. And I had that television show a few years ago. I don't know, Dexter. I'd have to put it down on paper. Maybe a million. Taxes always gave me a lot of trouble."

"But you made around two million dollars."

"Yes, I guess I did."

"You make us look like chiselers at the *Ledger-Star.* I wish we could pay you more."

"I'm satisfied. I may not be worth what you are paying me. I may not work out at all."

"Well, we both agreed to try it for a year."

"A year should be plenty long enough," said Whitehill. "I just don't want you to keep me longer than a year if you're not satisfied."

"Well, frankly, we couldn't afford to, but we're hoping that by the end of a year's time you'll be syndicated. With your name, your reputation, once you get back into the swing of things—we discussed all that."

"And I'm glad to say you're more optimistic than I am."

"The way we see the picture, Ray, the paper's making money, no doubt about that. We have a monopoly, and some people will tell you that's not a good thing. But one paper that makes money is better than two that are losing money, and that's just about the way it was when my Dad bought the *Star*. The *Star* was on its last legs, and the *Ledger* hadn't shown a profit since the end of the war. So Dad merged the two papers and four years ago we began to see daylight. But what we've got we want to hold on to. It isn't only circulation-wise. It's readership-wise. We could throw the paper into every mailbox in the county and still go out of business, that's what circulation counts for. It's readership, the competition from TV. Do we pull, or don't we? It comes down to this fact, namely, do Sam Jones and his wife Minnie want to read the *Ledger-Star* six days a week? As long as they do, we stay in business. Now we have a lot of good features, syndicated stuff, but it lacks the local identification. That's why when you wrote me for a job we decided to gamble on you, to give us local identification and a well-known name. Confidentially, Ray, you're getting more than anyone else on the paper, and it's a gamble, even if it doesn't seem like much compared to what you've been accustomed to. Les Bull, our managing editor, doesn't know what you're getting. You're not on the regular editorial budget. You come out of the executive budget." At this point the sausage cakes were served.

"Well, as you say, Dexter, it's a gamble. Maybe Minnie Jones isn't going to like me."

"That we'll have to wait and see, but just go at it relaxed, as if you had all the time in the world, and I think you'll get a good response. We'll be able to tell in a month or six weeks, but you mustn't be discouraged if some of them don't know you, your reputation. Some of the younger ones don't, you know."

"A lot of them don't."

"I probably shouldn't say this, considering that you used to hobnob with F.D.R. and Hitler and Stalin, but you realize, Ray, those names are ancient history to a young housewife that wasn't born when the Japs hit Pearl."

"Yes, I realize that. My daughter isn't much older than they are. She's a young housewife."

"Then you know that. They don't even remember Korea very well."

"I didn't go to Korea. I was having booze trouble then. Booze trouble, wife trouble, income tax trouble. And I panicked whenever I looked at a typewriter."

"But you straightened yourself out. You made a lot of money after that."

"Yes, I went back to work. That was when I covered the Berlin airlift."

"When was that, Ray?"

"What I just said. When the Korean trouble started I was having trouble with my wife and I took to the bottle, but I got straightened out, and then I went over and covered the Berlin airlift."

"No. I think the Berlin airlift was before the Korean trouble. I'm pretty sure of that, Ray."

"Was it? Wait a minute. Yes, I guess it was. You're right."

"I wouldn't correct you on a thing like that, only I happen to remember wondering whether I'd have to go back in the Navy."

"It was before the Korean business, you're right."

Throughout the rest of the meal the conversation was awkward and forced. Young Dexter Otis had embarrassed himself, but it was his own fault. How could he expect a man to remember everything that had happened in those crowded years? Dexter Otis, probably a j.g., if that, at the very moments when Mitscher and Nimitz and Halsey were welcoming their friend Ray Whitehill to the Pacific Ocean Area. Would Eisenhower give a grin of recognition upon seeing Dexter Otis? Bradley? Patton? Clark? De Gaulle? Montgomery? Was he ever even sneered at by Goering, barked at by Mussolini? Of course not.

"I beg your pardon, Dexter."

"I was just asking you, in your lapel. Is that the Legion of Honor?"

"Legion of Honor, that's right. I don't often wear it, or any of them."

"How many have you got?"

"I guess about six. Purple Heart. Air Medal. Oh, I guess I have maybe six or seven." He chuckled. "Sometimes I put one on when I want to spruce up a bit, like today, my first day in the new job. Then maybe I go for two or three months without taking them out of the box. The only time I never go without this is in France. The French like you to wear it. They figure it's a courtesy to them when an American wears their decoration."

"Well, it is."

"But not many people around here know what it is, so I think I'll put them all back in the box. All that's in the past anyway, and I'm more interested in the future. As you say, Minnie Jones doesn't care what I did ten, twenty years ago."

"That's a good, healthy way to look at it, Ray."

Plainly the man was pleased to be relieved of his embarrassment. "It just occurred to me, Dexter. I have all the medals, in storage in New York. What would you think if I donated them all to Franklin High? That's where I went. Might be good promotion later on. I have the medals and in addition I have, oh, plaques and scrolls and diplomas, not to mention autographed pictures. It might have some promotional value, and I had four walls from floor to ceiling filled with the stuff. That way the stuff would have some historical value, instead of just gathering dust. And underneath, of course, a discreet little plate to remind everybody that yours truly is a staff member of the *Ledger-Star*. Oh, we'd get that in."

"Yes, Yes, I think it might be good."

"I have a very wonderful picture of me with the old man. Churchill. Completely informal, relaxed. We wouldn't want any Hollywood stuff, would we? I have any number of pictures of me with movie people. And a lot of other celebrities. Writers. Ballplayers. But I was thinking I could give the other stuff to Franklin High, and we might make use of the Hollywood and sports people somewhere in the Ledger-Star Building. You know, it does no harm to remind the old home town that a character named Ray Whitehill was on a first-name basis with the most famous people in the world, and has the pictures to prove it."

"Right. Well, we have plenty of time to talk about that, Ray. I have to go to a meeting, if you'll excuse me."

"Of course. I think I'll stay and have another cup of coffee," said Whitehill.

The younger man departed, and Ray Whitehill sat alone, he knew not how long. The waitress came to him and said, "That coffee must be cold, Mr. Whitehill. Let me give you some fresh."

"All right, thanks," he said. But it would take more than coffee, more than anything he could name, to put warmth where he felt a chill.

YOUR FAH NEEFAH NEEFACE

This woman, when she was about nineteen or twenty, had a stunt that she and her brother would play, usually in a railroad station or on a train or in a hotel lobby. I saw them work the stunt under the clock at the Biltmore in the days when that meeting-place was a C-shaped arrangement of benches, and I remember it so well because it was the first time I ever saw the stunt and the first time I ever saw her or her brother. It was more than thirty years ago.

She was sitting there, quite erect, her legs crossed, smoking a cigarette and obviously, like everyone else, waiting to meet someone. She was wearing a beret sort of hat that matched her suit, and it was easy to tell by the way she smoked her cigarette that she had handled many of them in her short life. I remember thinking that I would like to hear her talk; she was so self-possessed and good-humored in her study of the young men and young women who were keeping dates at the clock. The drag she took on her cigarette was a long one; the smoke kept coming from her nostrils long after you thought it was all gone. She was terribly pretty, with a straight little nose and lively light blue eyes.

Presently a young man came up the stairs in no great hurry. He was wearing a black topcoat with a velvet collar and carrying a derby hat. He was tall, but not outstandingly so, and he had tightly curled blond hair—a 150-pound crew type, he was. He reached the meeting-place, scanned the faces of the people who were seated there, and then turned away to face the stairs. He watched the men and women coming up the stairs, but after a minute or so he turned his head and looked back at the girl, frowned as though puzzled, then again faced the incoming people. He did that several times, and I began to think that this was a young man on a blind date who had not been given a full or accurate description of his girl. She meanwhile was paying no attention to him.

Finally he went directly to the girl, and in a firm voice that everyone under the clock could hear he said, "Are you by any chance Sallie Brown?"

"I am, but what's it to you?" she said.

"Do you know who I am?" he said.

"No."

"You don't recognize me at all?"

"Never saw you in my whole life."

"Yes you did, Sallie. Look carefully," he said.

"I'm sorry, but I'm quite positive I've never seen you before."

"Asbury Park. Think a minute."

"I've been to Asbury Park, but so've a lot of people. Why should I remember you?"

"Sallie. It's Jack. I'm *Jack*."

"Jack? Jack Who? . . . No! My brother! You—you're Jack? Oh, darling, darling!" She stood up and looked at the people near her and said to them, rather helplessly, "This is my brother. My *brother*. I haven't seen him since—oh, darling. Oh, this is so wonderful." She put her arms around him and kissed him. "Oh, where have you *been*? Where have they been keeping you? Are you all right?"

"I'm all right. What about you?"

"Oh, let's go somewhere. We have so much to talk about." She smiled at all the other young men and women, then took her brother's arm and they went down the stairs and out, leaving all of us with the happy experience to think about and to tell and re-tell. The girl I was meeting arrived ten or fifteen minutes after Sallie and Jack Brown departed, and when we were in the taxi on our way to a cocktail party I related what I had seen. The girl waited until I finished the story and then said, "Was this Sallie Brown blond? About my height? And was her brother a blond too, with curly hair cut short?"

"Exactly," I said. "Do you know them?"

"Sure. The only part of the story that's true is that they are brother and sister. The rest is an act. Her name is Sallie Collins and his name is Johnny Collins. They're from Chicago. They're very good."

"Good? I'll say they're good. They fooled me and everybody else."

"They always do. People cry, and sometimes they clap as if they were at the theater. Sallie and Johnny Collins, from Chicago. Did you ever hear of the Spitbacks?"

"No. Spitbacks?"

"It's a sort of a club in Chicago. You have to be kicked out of school to be a Spitback, and Johnny's been kicked out of at least two."

"And what about her?"

"She's eligible. She was two years behind me at Farmington."

"What was she kicked out for?"

"Oh, I don't know. Smoking, I think. She wasn't there very long. Now she's going to school in Greenwich, I think. Johnny's a runner downtown."

"What other tricks do they do?"

"Whatever comes into their heads, but they're famous for the long-lost-brother-and-sister one. They have it down pat. Did she look at the other people as much as to say, 'I can't believe it, it's like a dream'?"

"Yes."

"They can't do it as much as they used to. All their friends know about it and they've told so many people. Of course it annoys some people."

"What other *kind* of thing do they do?"

"Oh—I don't know. Nothing mean. Not practical jokes, if that's what you're thinking of."

"I'd like to meet her sometime. And him. They seem like fun," I said.

I never did meet Johnny. He was drowned somewhere in Northern Michigan a year or so after I was a member of their audience at the Biltmore, and when I finally met Sallie she was married and living in New Canaan; about thirty years old, still very pretty; but instinctively I refrained from immediately recalling to her the once famous long-lost-brother stunt. I do not mean to say that she seemed to be mourning Johnny after ten years. But fun was not a word that came quickly to mind when I was introduced to her. If I had never seen her before or known about her stunts I would have said that *her* idea of fun would be the winning of the Connecticut State Women's Gold Championship. Women who like golf and play it well do seem to move more deliberately than, for instance, women who play good tennis, and my guess that golf was her game was hardly brilliant, since I knew that her husband was a 4-handicap player.

"Where are you staying?" she said, at dinner.

"At the Randalls'."

"Oh, do you sail?"

"No, Tom and I grew up together in Pennsylvania."

"Well, you're going to have a lot to time to yourself this weekend, aren't you? Tom and Rebecca will be at Rye, won't they?"

"I don't mind," I said. "I brought along some work, and Rebecca's the kind of hostess that leaves you to your own devices."

"Work? What kind of work?"

"Textiles."

"Well, that must be a very profitable business these days, isn't it? Isn't the Army ordering millions of uniforms?"

"I don't know."

"You're not in that kind of textiles?"

"Yes, I am. But I'm not allowed to answer any questions about the Army."

"I would like to be a spy."

"You'd make a good one," I said.

"Do you think so? What makes you think I would?"

"Because the first time I ever saw you . . ." I then had been in her company for more than an hour, and felt better about recalling the incident at the Biltmore.

"How nice of you to remember that," she said, and smiled. "I wonder why you did?"

"Well, you were very pretty. Still are. But the whole performance was so expert. Professional. You could probably be a very good spy."

"No. That was all Johnny. All those things we used to do, Johnny thought them up. He was the brains of the team. I was the foil. Like the girl in tights that magicians always have. Anybody could have done it with Johnny masterminding . . . Would you like to come here for lunch Sunday? I happen to know that Rebecca's without a cook, so you're going to have to go to the club, otherwise. Unless of course you have another invitation."

I said I would love to come to lunch Sunday, and she thereupon engaged in conversation with the gentleman on her left. I was surprised to find on Sunday that she and I were lunching alone. We had cold soup, then were served crab flakes and some vegetables, and when the maid was gone Sallie took a piece of paper from the pocket of her blouse. "This is the clock at the Biltmore that day. This is where I was sitting. Here is where you were sitting. If I'm not mistaken, you were wearing a grey suit and you sat with your overcoat folded over your lap. You needed a haircut."

"By God, you're absolutely right."

"You had a watch on a chain, and you kept taking it out of your pocket, and putting it back."

"I don't remember that, but probably. The girl I was meeting was pretty late. Incidentally, went to Farmington with you. Laura Pratt."

"Oh, goodness. Laura. If she'd been on time you never would have seen the long-lost-brother-and-sister act. She hated me at Farmington, but I see her once in a while now. She lives in

Litchfield, as I suppose you know. But have I convinced you that I remembered you as well as you remembered me?"

"It's the greatest compliment I ever had in my life."

"No. You were good-looking and still are, but what I chiefly remembered was that I was hoping you'd try to pick me up. Then I was just a little bit annoyed that you didn't try. God, that was forever ago, wasn't it?"

"Just about," I said. "How come you didn't say anything at dinner the other night?"

"I'm not sure. Selfish, I guess. That was *my* evening. I wanted you to do all the remembering, and I guess I wanted to hear you talk about Johnny."

"He drowned," I said. "In Michigan."

"Yes, but *I* didn't tell you that. How did you know?"

"I saw it in the paper at the time."

"Rebecca told me you were getting a divorce. Does that upset you? Not her telling me, but breaking up with your wife."

"It isn't the pleasantest experience in the world," I said.

"I suppose not. It never is. I was married before I married my present husband, you know."

"No, I didn't know."

"It lasted a year. He was Johnny's best friend, but other than that we had nothing in common. Not that a married couple have to have too much in common, but they ought to have something else besides loving the same person, in this case my brother. Hugh, my first husband, was what Johnny used to call one of his stooges, just like me. But somehow it isn't very attractive for a *man* to be another man's stooge. It's all right for a sister to be a stooge, but not another man, and almost the minute Johnny died I suddenly realized that without Johnny, Hugh was nothing. As a threesome we had a lot of fun together, really a lot of fun. And with Hugh I could have sex. I don't think there was any of that in my feeling for Johnny, although there may have been. If there was, I certainly managed to keep it under control and never even thought about it. I didn't know much about those things, but once or twice I vaguely suspected that if either of us had any of that feeling for Johnny, it was Hugh. But I'm sure he didn't know it either."

"So you divorced Hugh and married Tatnall."

"Divorced Hugh and married Bill Tatnall. All because you were afraid to pick me up and ditch Laura Pratt."

"But I could have become one of Johnny's stooges, too," I said. "I probably would have."

"No. Johnny's stooges all had to be people he'd known all his life, like me or Hugh, or Jim Danzig."

"Who is Jim Danzig?"

"Jim Danzig was the boy in the canoe with Johnny when it overturned. I don't like to talk about poor Jim. He blamed himself for the accident and he's become a hopeless alcoholic, at thirty-two, mind you."

"Why did he blame himself? Did he have any reason to?"

"Well—he was in the canoe, and they were both a little tight. It was at night and they'd been to a party at the Danzigs' cabin and decided to row across the lake to our cabin, instead of driving eight or nine miles. A mile across the lake, eight and a half miles by car. One of those crazy ideas you get when you're tight. Johnny would have been home in fifteen minutes by car, but they started out in the canoe, heading for the lights on our landing. I guess there was some kind of horseplay and the canoe overturned, and Jim couldn't find Johnny. He kept calling him but he didn't get any answer, and he couldn't right the canoe, although Jim was almost as good a boatman as Johnny—when sober. But they'd had an awful lot to drink, and it was pitch dark. No moon. And finally Jim floated and swam ashore and then for a while was lost in the woods. It was after Labor Day and most of the cabins were boarded up for the winter, and Jim in his bare feet, all cut and bleeding by the time he got to the Danzigs' cabin, and a little out of his head in addition to all he'd had to drink. I think they had to dynamite to recover Johnny's body. I wasn't there and I'm glad I wasn't. From the reports it must have been pretty horrible, and even now I'd rather not think about it."

"Then don't," I said.

"No, let's change the subject," she said.

"All right. Then you married Tatnall."

"Married Bill Tatnall a year and a half after Hugh and I were divorced. Two children. Betty, and Johnny, ages six and four. You haven't mentioned any children. Did you have any?"

"No."

"Children hold so many marriages together," she said.

"Yours?"

"Of course mine. I wouldn't have said that otherwise, would I? How often do you see the Randalls?"

"Oh, maybe once or twice a year."

"Did they know you were coming here for lunch?"

"No," I said. "They left very early this morning, before I was up."

"That explains it, why you don't know about Bill and me. Well, when you tell them you were here today, don't be surprised if they give you that tut-tut look. Naughty-naughty. Bill and I raise a lot of eyebrows hereabouts. Next year it'll be some other couple, but at the moment it's Bill and I."

"Who's the transgressor? You, or your husband?"

"It's the marriage, more so than Bill or I individually. In a community like this, or maybe any suburban or smalltown community, they don't seem to mind adultery if they can blame one person or the other. The husband or the wife has to be the guilty party, but not both."

"I don't agree with you," I said. "I think that when a marriage is in trouble people take sides, one side or the other, and they mind a great deal."

"Yes, they want the marriage to break up and they want to be able to blame one or the other. But when the marriage doesn't break up, when people can't fix the blame on one person, they're deprived of their scandal. They feel cheated out of something, and they're outraged, horrified, that people like Bill and I go on living together. They really hate me for putting up with Bill's chasing, and they hate Bill for letting me get away with whatever I get away with. Bill and I ought to be in the divorce courts, fighting like cats and dogs. Custody fights, fights about alimony."

"But you and your husband have what is commonly called an arrangement?" I said.

"It would seem that way, although actually we haven't. At

235

least not a spoken one. You see, we don't even care that much about each other. He just goes his way, and I go mine."

"You mean to say you never had a discussion about it? The first time he found out you were unfaithful to him, or he was unfaithful to you? You didn't have any discussion at all?"

"Why is that so incredible?" she said. "Let's have our coffee out on the porch."

I followed her out to the flagstone terrace and its iron-and-glass furniture. She poured the coffee and resumed speaking. "I guessed that Bill had another girl. It wasn't hard to guess. He left me severely alone. Then I guessed he had another, and since I hadn't made a fuss about the first one I certainly wasn't going to make a fuss about the second. Or the third."

"Then I gather you began to have gentlemen friends of your own."

"I did. And I guess Bill thought I'd been so nice about his peccadillos that he decided to be just as nice about mine."

"But without any discussion. You simply tacitly agreed not to live together as man and wife?"

"You're trying to make me say what you want me to say, that somehow we did have a discussion, a quarrel, a fight ending in an arrangement. Well, I won't say it."

"Then there's something a lot deeper that I guess I'd better not go into."

"I won't deny that, not for a minute."

"Was it sexual incompatibility?"

"You can call it that. But that isn't as deep as you seem to think it was. A lot of men and women, husbands and wives, are sexually incompatible. This was deeper, and worse. Worse because Bill is a yellow coward. He never dared come out and say what he was thinking."

"Which was?"

"He got angry with me one time and said that my brother Johnny'd been a sinister influence. That's as much as he'd actually say. That Johnny'd been a sinister influence. He didn't dare accuse me—and Johnny—of what he really meant. Why didn't he dare? Because he didn't want to admit that his wife had been guilty of incest. It wasn't really so much that incest was bad as

236

that it had happened to his own wife. Someone, one of Bill's lady friends, had planted that little idea in his thick skull, and he believed it. Now he fully believes it, but I don't care."

"A question that naturally comes to my mind," I said, "is why are you telling me all this?"

"Because you saw us together without knowing us. You saw Johnny and me doing the long-lost-brother act. How did we seem to you?"

"I thought you were genuine. I fell for it."

"But then Laura Pratt told you it was an act. What did you think then?"

"I thought you were charming. Fun."

"That's what I hoped you thought. That's what *we* thought we were, Johnny and I. We thought we were absolutely charming—and fun. Maybe we weren't charming, but we *were* fun. And that's all we were. And now people have ruined that for us. For me, at least. Johnny never knew people thought he had a sinister influence over me. Or me over him, for that matter. But aren't people darling? Aren't they lovely? They've managed to ruin all the fun Johnny and I had together all those years. Just think, I was married twice and had two children before I began to grow up. I didn't really start to grow up till my own husband made me realize what people had been thinking, *and* saying, about Johnny and me. If that's growing up, you can have it."

"Not everybody thought that about you and Johnny."

"It's enough that anybody did. And it's foolish to think that only one or two thought it," she said. "We did so many things for fun, Johnny and I. Harmless jokes that hurt nobody and that we thought were uproariously funny. Some of them I don't ever think of any more because of the interpretation people put on them . . . We had one that was the opposite of the long-lost-brother. The newlyweds. Did you ever hear of our newlyweds?"

"No," I said.

"It came about by accident. We were driving East and had to spend the night in some little town in Pennsylvania. The car broke down and we went to the local hotel and when we went to register the clerk just took it for granted that we were husband and wife. Johnny caught on right away and he whispered to the clerk, loud enough for me to hear, that we were newlyweds but that I was shy and wanted separate rooms. So we got our separate rooms, and you should have seen the hotel people stare at us that night in the dining-room and the next morning at breakfast. We laughed for a whole day about that and then we used to do the same trick every time we had to drive anywhere overnight. Didn't hurt anybody."

"What else did you do?"

"Oh, lots of things. And not only tricks. We both adored Fred and Adele Astaire, and we copied their dancing. Not as good, of course, but everybody always guessed who we were imitating. We won a couple of prizes at parties. Johnny was really quite good. 'I lahv, yourfah, neeface. Your fah, neefah, neeface.'" She suddenly began to cry and I sat still.

That was twenty years ago. I don't believe that anything that happened to her since then made much difference to Sallie, but even if it did, that's the way I remember her and always will.

THE FRIENDS OF MISS JULIA

The old lady stood waiting at the receptionist's desk. It was a circular room, with niches in the wall and in each niche, under a pin-spot, was displayed one or another of Madame Olga's beauty preparations. Two or three women were seated, not together, on the curved banquette against the wall. High above and behind the receptionist's desk were the hands of a hidden clock, imbedded in the wall, with the Roman numerals signifying 12, 3 6, and 9, with brass studs substituting for 1, 2, 4, 5, 7, 8, 10, and 11. According to the hands of the clock the time was five minutes to ten.

The old lady looked at the vacant desk, and turned to the other women, but they volunteered nothing. Then a curved door opened and a chic young woman appeared. "Oh, it's Mrs. Davis," said the young woman. "And you have Miss Julia, don't you?"

"Yes, at ten o'clock," said Mrs. Davis.

The young woman looked down at a large white leather appointment book, which lay open on the desk. "Just a set, wasn't it?"

"Yes, that's all," said Mrs. Davis.

"Well—I don't know what to say," said the young woman.

"Did you give my appointment to someone else?"

"No, it isn't that," said the woman. "We're having quite a mixup here." She lowered her voice. "The trouble is—Miss Julia was taken suddenly ill."

"Oh, I'm sorry. I hope it's nothing serious."

"Well—I'm afraid it is. I'm going to have to cancel all her appointments. But I could take care of your set if you don't mind waiting. I mean I could squeeze you in, since you're already here. It just happened about fifteen or twenty minutes ago. We got a doctor from next door, he's in there now."

"Oh, it does sound serious. Is it the heart?"

"It must be," said the young woman. "They sent for the ambulance. Taking her out the back way. Miss Judith is in a real flap, worrying about Miss Julia and the customers and all."

"Well, never mind about me," said Mrs. Davis.

"Oh, I'll fit you in, but you may have to wait a little while. Have a seat, Mrs. Davis, and I don't think you'll have to wait *very* long. But don't say anything to the other ladies, please. They don't know what's going on back there, and Miss Judith gave us orders. But I know Miss Julia was always a friend of yours."

"Was?"

"They're not very hopeful," said the young woman. A light flashed on the young woman's desk and she picked up the telephone. "Yes?" she said. She listened, replaced the telephone, and now addressed the other customers. "Ladies, I'm terribly sorry, but that was Miss Judith, our manager. We're going to have to cancel all appointments for today."

"Oh, come *on*," said one of the customers. "I drove all the way in from Malibu this morning. You can't do this to me."

"What's the big idea?" said a second customer. "I've had this appointment for over a week, and I have seventy *people* coming for dinner tonight. What are you going to say about that? Damn whimsical, if you ask me."

"I'm sorry, Mrs. Polk, but *all* appointments are cancelled," said the young woman.

"Well, give us a reason, for heaven's sake," said the first woman.

"The reason is—all right, I'll give you a reason. Our Miss Julia dropped dead, if that's enough reason for you. Do you want to go in and take a look yourself?"

"You don't have to be rude," said the first woman. "Are you closing for the day?"

"Yes, we're closing for the day," said the young woman.

"Well, when you open up again I hope there'll be some changes around here," said the first woman.

"Oh, go to hell," said the young woman. By mutual instinct she went to and was embraced by Mrs. Davis, and the other women left. The young woman was weeping, and Mrs. Davis guided her to the banquette. "She was so nice, such fun, Miss Julia."

"Always very jolly," said Mrs. Davis. "Always some little jokes to tell."

"It was so *quick*," said the young woman. "I was talking to her only five minutes before."

"That's a mercy, when it's quick," said Mrs. Davis.

"I was going to have lunch with her today," said the young woman. "We always had lunch together every Wednesday. Every Wednesday since I worked here, we always went over to the Waikiki. That's a Hawaiian place over on South Beverly?"

"Yes," said Mrs. Davis. She rested a hand on the younger woman's shoulder.

"Every Wednesday, without fail. We always sat at the same booth, and she and Harry Kanoa, the bartender, they used to carry on a conversation in Hawaiian. She could speak it a little. Did you ever know she was a hairdresser on the *Lurline?*"

"The boat?" said Mrs. Davis.

"I forget how many trips she told me she made," said the young woman. "But a lot. She always wanted to go back to the Islands. She was going next October. She had me almost talked into going with her. I've never been to the Islands."

"No, neither have I."

"I'm all right now, Mrs. Davis. I just suddenly couldn't hold it in any longer."

"That's all right, dear. Do you good."

The young woman smiled. "You called me dear. You don't even know my name, do you, Mrs. Davis?"

"I guess I don't, no."

"It's Page. Page Wetterling. I always have a hard time convincing people, but it's my real name. My mother always liked the name Page. Some of the customers thought Miss Judith gave me the name because I had to page people, but that wasn't it. I have it on my birth certificate."

"It's a pretty name," said Mrs. Davis.

"Listen, I'll ask one of the other operators if they'll give you a set."

"Oh, don't do that, Page, I only have it done to occupy the time. It's something to do."

"But you have pretty hair. Let me speak to Miss Frances. Did you ever have her?"

"No, I never had anyone but Miss Julia."

"Miss Frances is really the best. She's the one all the other operators go to to do their hair, but she doesn't have the personality."

"Yes, I know which one she is," said Mrs. Davis. "But I'd just as soon go without it today."

"Well, do you want me to put you down for your usual time next Wednesday?"

"Yes, you might as well," said Mrs. Davis.

"Does it make any difference who?" said Page Wetterling.

"None. They gave me Miss Julia the first time, two years ago, and I stayed with her ever since. It's only something to do."

"I'll let you try Miss Frances."

"You better ask her first. Maybe she won't want to be bothered with an old lady."

"Oh, listen. Don't you think they all know what you gave Miss Julia for Christmas? I could tell you some big movie stars that are nowhere near as generous. She'll take you."

"All right," said Mrs. Davis.

"None of them are going to be working today, but they'd gladly give you a set before they go home. We're closing up. I'm going to type out a little notice to put on the front door."

"Then do you get the day off?"

"No. I have to be here to answer the phone, change appointments. I get my lunch hour is all. I'd rather anyway, something to do, like you say."

"I guess I didn't mean it the same way."

"Oh, I know what you meant, Mrs. Davis. A lot of the ladies only come here for something to do. Do you want me to try and get you an appointment somewhere else? I know the girl at the Lady Daphne's. Or if you wanted to try George Palermo's, but he's down there near Bullock's Wilshire."

"My hair can go without," said Mrs. Davis. "But thank you, Page. Here."

"What's this? Five dollars? You don't have to give me anything, Mrs. Davis. I wouldn't take it. Absolutely. Listen, if it wasn't for you I'd of really blown my lid. Not that I worry about my job. I have other offers any time I want to leave Madame Olga's."

"Then let me take you to lunch. Would you like to have lunch at Romanoff's?"

"I'd love to, but you don't have to do anything for me, Mrs. Davis."

"It'd be my pleasure. I guess we ought to reserve a table. Can you make an outside call on that phone? Tell them it's Mrs. Davis, Walter Becker's mother-in-law. Or Mrs. Walter Becker's mother."

"Is that so? I didn't know you were related to Walter Becker. That's the television producer Walter Becker?"

"Yes, he married my daughter. He's always trying to get me to go to Romanoff's, but I never do unless I'm with him or my daughter. I guess they know me there, but mention his name to make sure."

Page Wetterling made the telephone call and hung up. "A very nice table for two, they said," she said. "I'll meet you there at ha' past twelve. Okay?"

The old lady was tired when at last she could present herself at the restaurant. She was taken to her table—a good location, but not one of the very best—and she ordered a glass of port wine. She knew she should have ordered sherry, but she was past caring about such things. The proprietor came to her table. *"Nice* to see you, Mrs. Davis. Hope you enjoy your lunch," he said, bowed, and passed on. If he noticed her preference for port over sherry he gave no sign. He was less impassive, as were the other men at the very best tables, when Page Wetterling entered the room. She was a handsome girl in the marketplace of pretty women, but she was unknown to the men in the restaurant; a new face, no handsomer or prettier than the others, but new and unidentified.

"You want to know something? I've never been here before," said Page Wetterling. "I'll have a—oh—a Dubonnet." The waiter left to get her drink, and she did a quick survey of the room. "Some of these women are trying to place me. They can't remember where they know me from."

"I thought a girl like you would be here every day," said Mrs. Davis.

"Never was here in my life before," said Page Wetterling. "My husband could never afford it, when I was married, and since then whenever I dated a man that had the money, we always went some place else. My first visit to the famous Romanoff's and I was *born* in Southern California. Whittier. Do you know where Whittier is?"

"I've heard of it, but I've only been here a little over two years. All I know is Beverly Hills and Holmby Hills and Westwood. And Hollywood. I was there a few times to watch them televise."

"What did you do after you left the salon? Did you find something to kill the time?"

"It wasn't easy. I went to the jewelry store, but I didn't have any intention of buying. Then to the toy store and I spent some money there, on my grandchildren. Then I stopped in at the drug store and had a Coke. Mostly to sit down, though. Then I went and sat on a bench at one of the bus stops, till it was time to come here. What did you do? Were you kept busy?"

"Oh, was I? The elevens and the eleven-thirties and the

twelves started coming in, piling up one on top of the other. I could have made easily a hundred dollars on tips if I could have sneaked in a few customers. But Miss Judith sent all the operators home. Nobody paid the least attention to the sign on the door. Some of them didn't stop to read it, but others came in and tried to bribe me to sneak them in. One woman offered me fifty dollars. I wonder what *she's* doing tonight. You don't spend that kind of money for a little family party at home. They all went away mad except a few of them. Miss Julia's regulars. But even one of them acted like a perfect bitch. Pardon me for saying that, but that's what she was. You'd of thought Miss Julia was some kind of a machine, that broke down just to louse up this woman's schedule. If I didn't get away from women once in a while I'd begin to hate them all. And you know, they more or less *have* to be nice to me. I make all the appointments, and for instance if two women want to have a permanent for the same time, I can tell one of them that she can't have that time. Or I can call up and tell a woman she has to change her time, and there's nothing she can do about it. Miss Judith can't be bothered with those small details. Oh, that one that threatened to have me fired this morning. Wait till she wants a favor. Do you like women, Mrs. Davis?"

"The majority. Not all."

"Well, if you had my job you'd learn to appreciate the nice ones. But believe me, they're not in the majority. You saw two of the worst examples today. And *I* saw one of the nicest ones. You."

"Thank you," said Mrs. Davis. "I guess most of them wish they looked like you, Page."

"But those that can't, why don't they try to develop a nice disposition?"

"Why aren't you a model, with your looks and all?"

"I was, but that's for the birds. I like to eat, not starve myself to death. I eat as much as most men. I eat a steak three or four nights a week, and wait till you see what I put away for lunch. That's why most of the models I know have such lousy dispositions. They don't get enough to eat. And my doctor told me when I was still married, he said standing around like that all day, and undernourished, if you *got* pregnant, if you *could,* you were undernourishing yourself and undernourishing the baby. Well, I didn't get pregnant, thank goodness, but I quit modeling."

"Wish to order luncheon, ladies?" said the captain.

"I know what I want, Mrs. Davis," said Page Wetterling. "I want the chicken pot pie, with noodles. I was never here before, but I heard it was good here."

"I'll have that, too," said Mrs. Davis.

The girl was stimulated, and all through the meal she was entertaining. She made no pretense of a blasé indifference to the movie and television stars, and she consumed even the crust of the chicken pot pie.

"A fruit compote?" said the captain.

"I'll have that," said Page Wetterling. "You have some, too, Mrs. Davis. You didn't eat half your chicken."

"All right," said Mrs. Davis. "You'd think *I* was trying to be a model, but I never eat much."

The girl smiled at the old lady's little joke. "You know, you have a wonderful sense of humor. If more women had a sense of humor, but the women that come into the salon, and places like this, if they had a sense of humor they wouldn't be so cranky all the time. Oh-oh, we're getting a visitor. I think it's your son-in-law, from his picture."

"Hello, Mom." The speaker was a heavy-set man in a blue suit with only a hint of lapels, a very narrow blue four-in-hand, a white-on-white shirt with a tab collar. He leaned down with the heels of his hands on their table.

"Oh, hello, Walter. This is my friend Miss Wetterling, and this is my son-in-law, Mr. Becker."

"I see you finally got here under your own steam," said Walter Becker. "Or did the young lady bring you?"

"No, it was her idea," said Page Wetterling.

"Where did you two know one another, if that's a valid question?"

"I work at the beauty salon where Mrs. Davis goes."

"I see. Then you're *not* in pictures or like that? I thought I didn't recognize you. I was just saying to Rod Proskauer. Well, Mom, I just came over to say hello and pick up the tab. Nice to see you, Miss?"

"Wetterling. Page Wetterling."

"Uh-huh. Mom, I see you this evening, right?" Walter Becker returned to his table—one of the very good ones.

"He calls you Mom," said Page.

"Yes."

"What's your daughter like? She never comes in our salon."

"No. She used to, but her hairdresser opened up her own place. I went there when I moved to California, but it was twenty dollars for practically nothing. Madame Olga's isn't cheap, but I don't want to spend twenty dollars every time. Ten is bad enough, for a person my age. It's sheer waste of money. Most of my life I didn't have money to spend in a beauty parlor. I gave myself a shampoo maybe once a week, maybe not that often. With soap, too. No Madame Olga special preparations. But out here I got into the habit, and Miss Julia was nice."

"Yes. We'll all miss her. She used to come in some mornings and just hearing her describe her hangover—maybe it was hell for her, but she kept us all laughing."

"I know," said the old lady. "Well, I guess you have to get back and answer the phone. I'll take you there in a taxi, it isn't much out of my way."

"I certainly do appreciate this, Mrs. Davis. How about you being my guest next Wednesday? I'll put you down for an eleven-thirty, how would that be? Then you won't have all that time in between."

"Well, I'd like it, but are you sure you would?"

"Of course I would. I'll take you to the Waikiki. They have American food, if you don't go for the Polynesian."

"Oh, I don't much care what I eat," said Mrs. Davis.

As the next Wednesday got nearer, Mrs. Davis was tempted to cancel her hair appointment, and thus to relieve the girl of the obligation of taking her to lunch. What pleasure would one so young and pretty get out of taking an old woman to lunch? But

247

Page Wetterling was a warm and friendly girl, and if *she* wanted to get out of the engagement, there were ways of doing so, right up to the very last minute.

"When you're through with Miss Frances, I have my car. We can ride over to the Waikiki together," said Page, after greeting the old lady. "That is, if we still have our date?"

"Oh, that'll be nice," said Mrs. Davis.

The Waikiki consisted of many small rooms rather than a single large one. Bamboo was used everywhere in the furniture and the decorative scheme, and the lighting was dim. From a loudspeaker came the tune "South Sea Island Magic," insistently but quietly, and the patrons and staff all seemed to know each other—or to be about to. "Hi, Page," said the bartender.

"Aloha, Harry," said the girl. "Oooma-ooma nooka-nooka ah-poo ah ah."

The bartender laughed. "That's right. You're getting there. A little at a time. Hey, Charlie. Table Four for Page and her guest."

"Table Four? You mean Table Two," said the waiter Charlie.

"No, I mean Table Four," said Harry.

"Page sits at Table Two," said Charlie. "You're losing your grip, Mr. Harry Kanoa. Where were you last night?"

"Table Four, Table Four," said the bartender.

"I do want Table Four, Charlie," said Page.

"All right, sweetheart, Table Four you want, you can have it. Anything your heart's desire. You bring your mama today?"

"No, this is a friend of mine. Mrs. Davis. This is Charlie Baldwin."

"Of the Baldwin Locomotive Baldwins, no relation to any other Baldwins," said Charlie.

"I don't know what he means by that, but he always says it," said Page.

"Go to the Islands, sweetheart. You'll soon find out," said Charlie. "Care for native dishes or American today? Mainland, I should say. We have statehood. Goodie, goodie. Drinks, ladies? We don't make money on our food, only on drinks. Ha ha ha ha. Page? A double frozen Daiquiri? Or have a Statehood Special.

It's almost the same as a Zombie. No more than two to a customer."

"I'm a working girl."

"No profit today, huh? Mama, you want to try a Statehood Special?"

"No thank you," said Mrs. Davis.

"No sale. Well, then, what do you want to eat? Have the Charlie Baldwin Special. I recommend it. I made it up. It's roast pork with baked pineapple and an avocado with Russian dressing. You like it, Page, so why don't the both of you have it?"

"All right, Mrs. Davis?"

"Not the pork, thank you. Maybe an avocado salad?" said Mrs. Davis. "And some iced tea, please."

The old lady liked the Waikiki. The atmosphere of gay informality was just fine—so long as she could sit back and enjoy it without having to take part in it. Nearly everyone who came in knew Page Wetterling; a few stopped to express their regret at the passing of Julia. Mrs. Davis wanted to come back again, but in order to do so she would have to invite her new young friend to Romanoff's.

"Would you like to go to Romanoff's next Wednesday?" said the old lady.

"Listen, I'd like to go there any time."

It was understood that they would have lunch together every Wednesday, alternating the restaurants, and the arrangement was satisfactory to both women. In a few weeks the old lady had heard a great deal of Page's past and current history; it took a little longer for Mrs. Davis to tell much about herself. "I gabble, gabble, prattle," said Page. "I tell you more than I ever told my own mother, and that's for sure."

"I like to listen," said Mrs. Davis.

"Where does your daughter go for lunch?" said Page. "I keep thinking we'll run into her at Romanoff's."

"I guess she goes to Perino's. There, and a French place on Sunset Boulevard. She doesn't care for Romanoff's. She says the men get all the attention there. She likes to get all dressed up when she goes out."

"But a lot of women go to Romanoff's."

"I don't know. She has some reason," said Mrs. Davis.

"You give me the impression that you don't like it very much in California."

"I guess I'm still new here," said the old lady.

"Did your daughter make you move here?"

"My son-in-law. Walter Becker. He was the one. He was for years making a nice living with the radio, the TV. But then like it happened overnight he suddenly owned or part-owned three TV shows, and he sold them for a big profit and now he's in business for himself. Walter is a rich man. A Rolls-Royce car. A home in Beverly Hills on the other side of Sunset back of the hotel. Contributes to charities. It's impossible for him to go broke again. He gets a certain amount for life as a consultant with the CBS. I give him credit, he worked hard for it. But I don't know. He didn't have to make me move out here."

"Why did he, then?"

"He didn't want to have Walter Becker's mother-in-law living in a little apartment in New York City. I loved that apartment. I had a sittingroom for if I wanted to have some ladies in to play cards. A nice bedroom to sleep in. I never had to complain about the heat. They kept it warm no matter what the temperature was outside. It wasn't big, but to me it was big enough. I had two radios. One in my bedroom that I could listen to taking a bath, and one in the kitchen. And a 21-inch TV in the sittingroom. If I didn't feel like going out I could send around to the delicatessen. They delivered. Sometimes I didn't go out for two or three days. Old people are supposed to get lonely, but I wasn't. My whole life I grew up in an apartment that wasn't big enough for our family. I and my two sisters slept in the same room, my three brothers in their room. I got married and I slept in the same bed with my husband over thirty years and my two daughters they had the same bed in their room. That was supposed to be the diningroom. Then my husband passed on and my both daughters got married and I moved to a smaller apartment. Such a pleasure, a genuine luxury I had. Within easy walking distance of 149th Street, if I wanted to shop or go to a show. I was the envy of the other ladies."

"It sounds perfect," said Page.

"Uh-huh. But Walter wanted me out here. My daughter, too, but more Walter. He wanted a grandmother for his children. His mother died young, so it was me."

"You were still their grandmother, whether you lived here or back East."

The old lady shook her head. "With Walter it has to be seen. He has to show people every room in the house and everything in all the closets. 'My wife has sixty-four pairs of shoes,' he says to them, and he opens the closet door to prove it. The same way with a grandmother. A grandmother in New York isn't the same thing as a grandmother in the house!"

"But it must be nice living with your grandchildren," said Page.

"They're getting used to me," said the old lady. "They never saw me till two years ago I came here. My own daughter had to get used to me." She nodded in agreement with herself. "And *I* had to get used to *them*."

"Did you make any new friends here?"

"Here is not so easy to make new friends," said Mrs. Davis. "At my age it's too late to learn to drive a car. I have to take a taxi everywhere. The other ladies are in the same situation. My daughter would take me in her car if I asked her, but I don't like to ask her."

"You were really happier in your little apartment," said Page.

"I admit it, but I don't want to say anything to them. They think they're doing the right thing. My son-in-law took me to the TV studios, introduced me to Red Skelton and Lucille Ball and many more. Walter said I would have something to write about when I wrote to my friends. But then he asked me to show him the letter and I couldn't hurt his feelings. I wrote a letter to my friend Mrs. Kornblum, a neighbor of mine in the same building, but I couldn't show it to Walter. It was a homesick letter. I said Lucille Ball was nice, but I'll bet not as good a stuss-player as another friend of ours, Mrs. Kamm. Stuss is a game of cards we used to play. Walter asked me did I tell my friends about him owning a Rolls-Royce. I would never do that, brag about my son-in-law. One of our friends made herself obnoxious bragging so much about her son getting elected state senator. The Senator, she called him. You would of thought he was Jacob Javits instead of just a senator in Albany."

"Wouldn't it be easier if you got yourself a little apartment here?"

"I don't want a little apartment here. I just want to go home to my own apartment, East A Hundred and Fifty-third Street, The Bronx, New York. Or one just like it."

"Then go," said Page Wetterling.

"What?"

"Just go, Mrs. Davis. Just tell your daughter and your son-in-law that you're leaving next Tuesday."

"How many times I thought of that, Page. How many times."

"But did you ever say anything to them?"

"No. I wouldn't know how. They think they're doing everything for me. It would be like a slap in the face to them."

"Well, didn't you ever slap your daughter when she was little?"

"Many times. A good slap was what she needed, and I gave it to her. And her sister. And their father, too."

"You never slapped Walter Becker, though."

"No. Sometimes I felt like it, but I never did."

"But you're not afraid of him?" said Page.

"Of *him?*"

"Then slap him. I don't mean with your hand across his face. But tell him you're going back to New York. And don't let him give you a con. Don't let him argue with you. Buy your ticket on the plane and write to Mrs. Kornblum that you're coming."

"Not Mrs. Kornblum, but Mrs. Kamm would have room for me. Page, you're putting ideas in my head."

"Not me. It's all your idea. I'm just giving you a little push. Do you have the cash?"

"Plenty. They give me a hundred dollars a week spending money. Why, were you going to offer me the loan?"

"Yes."

"You're a true friend, and for such a young girl to know so much," said Mrs. Davis.

"I can't take all the credit, Mrs. Davis. Miss Julia knew you were miserable."

"That's why she was always trying to cheer me up."

"She had a big heart," said Page Wetterling.

The old lady smiled. "Don't you give *her* all the credit, either, Miss Page Wetterling."

"Why, I don't have any idea what you're talking about, Mrs. Davis."

"I'll put it in a letter," said Mrs. Davis.

THE MANAGER

The Wilburs always arrived at the Inn a little before or a little after the summer season. True, in recent years, with the popularity of skiing, the Inn enjoyed two seasons, but a very different sort patronized the place when the snow was on the ground. The Wilburs were quite definitely not of the skiing crowd.

There had been a time when the Wilburs were summer regulars, with their same room and their same table year after year, and paying the summer rates. But after thirty seasons they came only in the spring and the fall, when reduced rates were in effect, and these visits were shorter. "We don't like to let a year go by without a week or so at the Inn," said Mrs. Wilbur. "But now you have to charge almost as much for a single day as we used to pay for a week. Oh, we understand why. But it *is* a shame, isn't it?"

"It is indeed," said Mr. Greene, the proprietor. "We've lost some of our summer people on account of it. But there always seem to be others to take their places."

"Where do you suppose they get the money?" said Mrs. Wilbur. "I know that's a foolish question, but these younger people. I mean the ones in their forties. They can't possibly get away with deducting the cost as a business expense."

"Well, naturally I don't inquire into where they get it, as long as they do. But they seem to have it. Your room goes for twelve hundred for the month of August. A thousand for the month of July. And next year I don't know what it'll be. Won't be any less, that's for sure." Once, and only once, Mr. Greene had had to tell Mrs. Wilbur that much as he would like to give old patrons a special rate, the fact was that he could not make an exception for anyone. Not anyone. Not Colonel and Mrs. Broadbill. Not the Reverend and Mrs. George W. T. Magee. Not Miss Polly Woodward, whose father and mother had been the second couple to sign the registry in 1894. Mrs. Wilbur—and Mr. Greene knew it —was not so much advocating a special rate for the Broadbills and the Magees and Polly Woodward as trying to learn whether they got one. Mr. Greene was too polite to say it, but the stern fact was that even at the full rate the Inn was not making much money off the Broadbills and those others. They spent no money in the Colonial Taproom. Colonel and Mrs. Broadbill had their nip of bourbon before coming down to dinner; the others did not drink at all. And it was not only a question of the money they did not spend; there was their appearance, which was noticeably inhibiting on the younger guests, those couples in their forties who had cocktails before every meal and liqueurs in the Taproom every evening after dinner. As for the Wilburs, Mr. Wilbur was afflicted with some liver ailment that made him appear to be sunburnt in patches on his forehead and cheeks. Young children stared at him, and several young wives had asked to have their table changed so that they would not have to look at him. He was a perfectly nice man, a gentleman, well dressed and neatly groomed; but as one young woman said, very unappetizing. One child of ten had asked him, "Were you *burned?*" and Mr. Wilbur had replied, "In a manner of speaking, yes." The child's mother was infuriated, embarrassed by her daughter's forwardness, but far more annoyed that someone like Mr. Wilbur was there to provoke the child's rude curiosity. Mr. Greene heard all about that. He did nothing, since there was nothing he could do; but he was greatly relieved when the Wilburs advised him that the next year, 1959, they would not be needing their old room in August. They were going to be traveling—they did not say where —and hoped they would be able to stop at the Inn for a week or so in late September. Mr. Greene in his reply expressed regret untinged with sorrow, and advised the Wilburs that he would be unable to guarantee their getting their old room back in 1960 if they relinquished it in '59. Another couple—perhaps the Wilburs remembered them, the Lamports, from Toledo, Ohio—had applied for the Wilburs' room for '59 and subsequent years and Mr. Greene, or the Inn, was redecorating to suit Mrs. Lamport. He was sure the Wilburs would understand. They did.

But they kept coming back. In '59 they stayed two weeks in the latter half of September; in '60, a week in May; in '61 they came for the first week in October. Mr. Greene was not unhappy to see them go. He liked Mr. Wilbur, but he hoped the Wilburs would never come back, because on the Sunday evening during dinner, with the diningroom and the Taproom filled almost to capacity, Mr. Wilbur suddenly rose, with a napkin to his mouth, and hurried out of the diningroom, fighting back a vomiting spell and barely making the men's room in the lobby.

Mr. Greene, from his position behind the main desk, saw it all happen. It was distressing to see the immediate effect on the men and women in the diningroom—and not many had failed to see Mr. Wilbur, with the napkin at his mouth, staggering out toward the lobby. Nevertheless Mr. Greene obeyed the impulse to follow Mr. Wilbur, and in the men's room he found Mr. Wilbur lying on the floor, hemorrhaging from the mouth. Mr. Wilbur looked up at Mr. Greene with the eyes of a dog pleading not to be shot, then fainted away. Two young doctors, who were dining with their wives, entered the men's room. "Get him to a hospital," said one doctor. "I'll stay with him till the ambulance comes." There was nothing more Mr. Greene could do after sending for the ambulance, and he went looking for Mrs. Wilbur. In time he found her, sitting in the lobby with Colonel and Mrs. Broadbill.

"Oh, Mr. Greene, I didn't think it was right to go into the men's room. How is he?"

"There are two doctors in there with him, I guess they're doing all they can till the ambulance gets here."

"The hospital? Did they say he had to go to the hospital?"

"Now don't you worry, Edwina," said Colonel Broadbill. "I had the same thing happen to me six years ago."

"They'll want to give him transfusions, most likely," said Mrs. Broadbill. "They did with Clement."

"They sure did," said Colonel Broadbill. "Whole bunch of fellows from the Army and Navy Club volunteered, but there weren't but two had my type of blood. Mike—"

"Do you think I ought to go in there now, I mean the men's room?" said Mrs. Wilbur.

"Oh, that part'll be all right, Mrs. Wilbur. Yes, I'd go in if I were you," said Mr. Greene.

"Good Lord, Edwina, you don't have to stand on ceremony at a time like this," said the colonel. "You go right in there and pay no attention."

"Would you like me to go with you?" said Mrs. Broadbill. "Goodness me, the places I've been. I'll go in with you."

"I'd appreciate it if you would, Lillian."

"Mr. Greene and I will look out for everything," said the colonel.

Mr. Greene did not quite know what the colonel had in mind, but he was already uncomprehending of Mrs. Wilbur's ability to sit in the lobby while her husband could be bleeding to death a few feet away, behind a door marked Gentlemen.

"Hit him all of a sudden," said Colonel Broadbill. "We just finished our dinner and I was here having my cigar. Mizz Broadbill won't let me smoke one of these Castro cigars in the bedroom, she calls them. Ever since Castro we haven't been able to get any good Havana leaf, and I must say I go along with Mizz Broadbill. But I do like a cigar after dinner, good or bad. Mrs. Wilbur said he ate too much of the paté. He ate his and then he ate hers, and it was just too rich for him. You set too good a table, Mr. Greene. That hard sauce you give us with the Brown Betty, I have to order seconds on it every time. Now that I don't have to worry about my teeth any more, I eat those things like

257

your hard sauce as if I were a schoolboy. Sweets. I eat too many sweets."

Mr. Greene wanted to get in a denial that the liver paté had had anything to do with Mr. Wilbur's attack, but the colonel had raised so many points that called for denials that Mr. Greene ignored them all. "How long did they keep you in the hospital, Colonel?" he said.

"How long did they keep me in the hospital?"

"Roughly. Approximately," said Mr. Greene.

"Roughly a week."

"I suppose that means they'll keep Mr. Wilbur that long," said Mr. Greene.

As it turned out, he was wrong. By the time the ambulance arrived Mr. Wilbur was up on his feet, and he stubbornly—for him, angrily—refused to leave the Inn. The doctors said they would not be responsible; Mr. Wilbur said he would absolve them of any responsibility. The ambulance driver said there would still be a charge of thirty dollars, and Mr. Greene paid that and said he would put it on Mr. Wilbur's bill.

Mr. Greene saw the Wilburs off in the morning. They had a well-kept Dodge station wagon, six or seven years old. Mrs. Wilbur was doing the driving, as she always did nowadays, but they had a long ride ahead and Mr. Greene, taking a good look at Mr. Wilbur, was convinced he would never see him again. Mr. Wilbur was all bundled up in his old polo coat and a thick woollen scarf, and a robe over his legs; the brim of his hat turned down all around, and a large area of his face hidden by his sun glasses. He was a pitiful sight. Mrs. Wilbur, however, sitting back confidently, with her hands resting on the steering-wheel, seemed capable of driving the car as far as San Francisco.

"I'd rest easier if you phoned me when you get home," said Mr. Greene. "Reverse the charges, of course."

"Oh, now, Mr. Greene, that's very nice of you, but I'm all right. We'll be home before dark," said Mr. Wilbur.

"Not before dark, Lewis, but not long after," said Mrs. Wilbur. "It gets dark earlier now."

They lived in a place called Uniontown, Pennsylvania, and that evening, while he was having his dinner, Mr. Greene was called to the telephone. The Wilburs had had a pleasant trip, stopping for lunch at a very nice motel near Scranton, PA. Mr. Wilbur had not eaten very much for lunch; milk toast, as a matter of fact. Then they had stopped again for a cup of tea at a Howard Johnson on the Pennsylvania Turnpike. A cup of tea with lemon and a little nibble of toast was as much as he wanted. He was in bed now, and the family doctor was coming in to see him later in the evening. Mr. Wilbur had insisted on her making the call, and he wanted to thank Mr. Greene for taking an interest, and to tell him how sorry he was to have caused such a disturbance the night before. He was still weak, naturally, and Mrs. Wilbur had put him right to bed when they got home; but there was nothing to worry about. She had not even bothered to telephone their daughter, who lived in Pittsburgh, but Mr. Wilbur had insisted on her telephoning Mr. Greene. They hoped to be back in the spring, and Mr. Greene said he hoped they would be back. Mrs. Wilbur said she thought their three minutes was up, so she rung off.

Now and then, through the winter months, Mr. Greene would give a thought to the Wilburs, not of the Wilburs independently but as typical of the older crowd, who hung on and hung on in spite of the high rates (which did not affect them all), and the younger summer crowd and their children, who were now the favorite guests of the Inn. If the Wilburs and the Broadbills, people like that, ever had a good look at the skiing crowd, sitting on the floor in their stretch pants, they would not recognize the place. And Mr. Greene wished the old-timers could have a look at the ski crowd; it would tell the old-timers most effectively that the Inn was going along with the times. It would remind them that they had always been given good value at the Inn (and why else would they have come back year after year?); that he had worked hard to make them comfortable; that their steady patronage did not really entitle them to any special rights—or rates.

Mr. Greene liked the new young faces and figures of the ski crowd. They were such a welcome relief from the Wilburs and the Broadbills and the Polly Woodwards. The older ones would come back to the Inn, having been absent eight or ten months, which was just long enough for the passage of time to make those depressing changes in their countenances and in their figures and their gait. Miss Polly Woodward was almost blind, and only in 1962 had she at last begun to carry a cane. Colonel Broadbill had a breath that would knock you over, and it was not from alcohol. Mrs. Broadbill's stockings were always falling down, and when they were not falling down they clung so loosely to her skinny legs that they looked like long underwear. He could not complain about Mrs. Wilbur's appearance; too many of the other guests had been saying for years that *there* was a handsome woman, a woman who aged gracefully. But he had never liked Mrs. Wilbur. Let something, anything, go wrong, and Mrs. Wilbur noticed it, whether it was a malfunction of the plumbing or an erroneous item on the bill. And who else would have complained that the liver paté was so rich that it had made her husband sick? Mr. Greene hoped that he would never have to see Mrs. Wilbur again.

His wish was gratified.

One afternoon in May he was standing in the driveway, having a look at the newly painted shutters on the upper stories, when a station wagon drew up slowly. It came to a stop directly behind him, and as he was not expecting any arrivals that day, and as it was an expensive English car, he assumed it was bringing some drop-in trade for the Taproom.

"Hello there, Mr. Greene!"

Mr. Greene had a better look, and now he saw Mr. Wilbur on the front seat, but the woman at the wheel was not Mrs. Wilbur. "Why, it's Mr. Wilbur. This is a nice surprise."

Mr. Wilbur, in his same old polo coat but wearing a tweed cap that had a little strap in the back, got out of the car and shook hands with Mr. Greene. He looked extremely well for a man who had gone through so many ailments. "I don't see Mrs. Wilbur," said Mr. Greene.

"No, I'm afraid Mrs. Wilbur passed away during the winter. Heart. We'd never known anything about it. At least she'd never mentioned it to me. Halfway up the stairs one morning, she collapsed and that was the end."

"I'm very sorry to hear that," said Mr. Greene. "But you're looking well."

"Well, thank you. I had quite a siege myself. They took out over half of my stomach. I was just beginning to get around a bit when Mrs. Wilbur had her attack. The young lady with me is my nurse. Do you suppose you could put us up, two nice single rooms not too far apart?"

"Why yes. I can give you adjoining. Twelve and Fourteen are vacant. You know them, there on the east side where you get the morning sun."

The nurse had parked the car and now joined them. "Miss Buckley, this is Mr. Greene, our famous host. Mr. Greene, my nurse, Miss Buckley."

"I'm very pleased to meet you. Mr. Wilbur speaks very highly of you."

"Pleased to meet you," said Mr. Greene. "Mr. Wilbur's one of our most valued guests. Has been for a good many years."

"Well, the Inn has always been one of my favorite institutions in *my* life. And thanks largely to Mr. Greene, I might add."

"How long will you be with us, you and Miss Buckley?" said Mr. Greene.

"Till Monday at least, maybe a few days longer if you still have room for us."

"I may have to move you out of Twelve and Fourteen, but we'll find something."

"Miss Buckley doesn't mind sharing a bathroom with me," said Mr. Wilbur. "So if you have rooms with an adjoining bath, that'd be all right. I've been a patient of hers for so long now."

"Aaw, now, don't make it sound too long," said Miss Buckley. "He'll think you want to get rid of me."

"Now you know better than that, Miss Buckley," said Mr. Wilbur. "Well, shall we go in and register?"

"I'll send Chester out for your luggage," said Mr. Greene.

"Oh, I'm glad you still have Chester," said Mr. Wilbur. "He's in his sixties, but strong as an ox."

"Age doesn't make that much difference," said Miss Buckley. "If a man takes proper care of himself."

"That doesn't account for Chester. I have to fire him every so often, when he gets to thinking he owns what's in the cellar."

"Well, maybe if he didn't do that he'd get all tensed up," said

Miss Buckley. "This man has three ounces of bourbon every night preceding dinner, and I see that he gets it. The best thing in the world for him."

"I'd miss it, no doubt about it," said Mr. Wilbur. "I'm getting to be a drinker in my old age."

"*Stop* with that talk about old age," said Miss Buckley. "I almost wasn't going to let him come here when he started talking about the good times he had here. You'd think he wanted to come here to be buried."

"That was at first. I haven't been talking that way lately, have I?"

"No, I'll admit that, or I wouldn't have let you come," said Miss Buckley.

"Mr. Greene remembers one unfortunate episode."

"Oh, think nothing of it, Mr. Wilbur."

. . . Mr. Greene knew perfectly well what went on among the ski crowd. It would have taken an army of Pinkertons to do an hourly bed-check, and as long as order was maintained in the Taproom and the bedrooms were not occupied by more guests than were on the registry, Mr. Greene was not going to try to be everywhere at once. They were young, healthy, vigorous people, with large appetites in every sense of the word. To try to police their behavior would be like going against nature and the times. But if he was willing to overlook certain things with the ski crowd, he had never relaxed his vigilance where the summer people were concerned. Through the years the Inn had acquired a reputation for respectability that was second to none. (Some of the ski crowd had told Mr. Greene that they had heard about that respectability from their parents and grandparents, and that because of it the younger ones were felt to be in safe hands.) A newcomer to the Inn was always asked who had recommended the place, and a letter would go off to the referred-to party so that the reference would be made to feel some sense of responsibility for the newcomer. Mr. Greene had never tolerated any funny business, no matter what or who. A British lord once showed up with a young American woman who obviously was not his lady, and when Mr. Greene saw the young woman he looked the Englishman straight in the eye and told him that there had been some mixup in his reservations and that he was afraid he could not accommodate them. He suggested they try a hotel in a city fifty miles away. His lordship knew better than to risk a scene, and out he went, followed by the young woman and Chester with their luggage. In a sense they were also followed— by a sharp letter from Mr. Greene to the travel agency employed by the Englishman.

The principal stockholders of the Inn, a well-to-do group of men in the insurance business in Hartford, and women, widows, who lived in the Hartford-Springfield area, had complete confidence in Mr. Greene's discretion, integrity, and acumen, and gave him what amounted to carte-blanche. They, too, were well aware of the greater freedom accorded the ski crowd, but they relied on Mr. Greene to keep it well in hand . . .

It was not so much that Mr. Wilbur was a problem. Mr. Wilbur had been coming to the Inn too long not to be thoroughly indoctrinated in the policies maintained by Mr. Greene. And Mr. Wilbur was not a young man. Mr. Wilbur was an *old* man. But during the few minutes in the driveway Mr. Greene had formed an impression of Miss Buckley that was decidedly not in her favor. The late Mrs. Wilbur, whatever else she was, was a lady, and that much could not be said for Miss Buckley. Mr. Greene resented personally her saying "this man" has three ounces of bourbon, or whatever it was; he resented her saying that *she* was almost not going to let Mr. Wilbur come here. No doubt Mr. Wilbur had been so completely dominated by Mrs. Wilbur that her passing gave him a sense of relief; he certainly had not looked so well, so relaxed, in many years. But Mr. Greene wanted better things for Mr. Wilbur; most of all he wanted Mr. Wilbur to live out his remaining years without loss of the dignity that was perhaps his outstanding characteristic, that indeed had made the episode of the hemorrhage so distressing for Mr. Wilbur and all those who admired him. To be referred to to his face as "this man" was an affront to Mr. Wilbur's dignity, even though *he* might not yet regard it as such.

Mr. Wilbur was not a problem, and yet he was a problem for Mr. Greene. Mr. Greene usually designated as problems the men who got noisy-drunk in the Taproom, guests who antagonized the help, women who had dogs or cats. Mr. Wilbur, by appearing with this Miss Buckley, became a problem for Mr. Greene that was of a different nature from any he had dealt with as manager of the Inn. Mr. Wilbur was a good fifteen—well, a good ten—years older than Mr. Greene, and he needed protection. It came down simply to that: Mr. Wilbur needed protection.

There was a daughter living in Pittsburgh, but Mr. Greene remembered her only as a child and a young girl who was a bit of a scamp. She was not an evil girl, but she had started smoking in the lobby at a too early age, and several of the older women had spoken to Mr. Greene about the shorts she wore. The Wilburs' daughter had never appeared at the Inn after her marriage, and that was twenty years ago. In any event from what he knew of her she was not likely to concern herself much with her father's undeniable willingness to submit to a Miss Buckley, and Mr. Greene was unhappy. Long ago, as a bellhop and assistant manager, he had learned that old men and old women did not automatically become sexless when youth was gone. He had seen things that were hard to believe, but he had seen them: old women murderously jealous over an old man; lovemaking that belied all the jokes about age and impotence. Twice as a very young man with curly hair and the face of an acolyte he had been propositioned by older people, one of them not a woman. A bellhop of his acquaintance had wheedled a Packard roadster out of one old woman, and was contemptuous of the young Greene for passing up equal opportunities. Dignity therefore meant more than a dignified manner to Mr. Greene; dignity of the right kind was often the only protection the old people had. Lose your dignity, and you are putty in the hands of a Miss Buckley.

Mr. Greene was too fond of Mr. Wilbur to assign to one of the help the task of watching out for any funny business with the nurse. Saying nothing to anyone, he took on the job himself. With his reputation for attention to small details he was more or less expected to pop up here, there, and everywhere in the hotel and on the grounds, a fact which made it easier to keep an eye on Mr. Wilbur and the nurse. Rooms Twelve and Fourteen, though adjoining, were separated by a locked door, and on the morning after Mr. Wilbur's arrival Mr. Greene satisfied himself that both beds had been slept in, and not merely rumpled for show. Throughout the second day Mr. Greene kept tabs on Mr. Wilbur and the nurse. Mr. Wilbur apparently had a routine; a walk after breakfast; a nap after lunch; a game of gin rummy with Miss Buckley, followed by a perfectly legitimate massage for which Miss Buckley had requested a table. Mr. Wilbur then had his bath, dressed, and came down to the Taproom for his three ounces of bourbon before dinner. In the evening they played gin rummy again, watched the eleven o'clock news on the television set in the lobby, and went up to their rooms. In the course of the day Mr. Greene had spoken to them three or four times, not at any great length but in his offhand, casual, managerial way. Mr. Wilbur made some favorable comments on the dogwood, Miss Buckley admired the abundance of brass trinkets and wondered how they were kept so bright and shiny in these days of irresponsible help. Even in her own profession, the nurses they turned out these days . . .

Mr. Wilbur and the nurse said goodnight to Mr. Greene as they made their way to the elevator. Mr. Greene had never called a man's face beautiful, but there was a serenity in Mr. Wilbur's half-realized smile that was close to beautiful, and that in spite of the lines and discolorations. Mr. Greene mentally absolved Mr. Wilbur of all wrongdoing, and was chiding himself for suspiciousness. But just as the elevator door was closing Mr. Greene heard Mr. Wilbur laugh in a way that was different from any laugh that had ever come out of Mr. Wilbur. It had almost a cackle to it, that laugh, and Mr. Greene wondered what Miss Buckley had said to provoke it. In an instant Mr. Greene's suspicions all returned. Indeed, the laugh practically confirmed his suspicions of Miss Buckley as a woman who practiced some seductive power over Mr. Wilbur. The elevator was a self-service one, and in Mr. Greene's imagination Miss Buckley had said something to the old man that she would not have said in front of anyone else. The cackling laugh was so horrible that it provided a test of Mr. Greene's fondness for Mr. Wilbur.

The Taproom closed at midnight, and in the more than half empty Inn all was quiet by a quarter past twelve. Mr. Greene made his final rounds of the Taproom, the lobby and the other rooms on the main floor. Walter Downs, the night watchman, was on his patrol. No one else was to be seen. Ordinarily it would have been the time of day Mr. Greene liked best, when his work was finished and his guests all safe for the night. But now his job was not enjoyable and his immediate task was unpleasant, as unpleasant as the inferences he had drawn from that laugh of Mr. Wilbur's. He was certain now that Mr. Wilbur, under the influence of Miss Buckley, had turned into a nasty old man.

"Everything in order, Walter?" said Mr. Greene.

"Everything," said Walter Downs.

"You might have a look around out back, make sure the painter didn't leave any ladders lying around," said Mr. Greene.

"I will. I'll do that after I eat my lunch," said Walter.

"No hurry," said Mr. Greene. He wanted to make sure that Walter would be out of the way for a while. "They're forgetful sometimes. They leave those ladders any place. Person could stumble on them in the dark and we'd have a lawsuit."

"Want me to do it now?"

"No, you go eat your lunch and then do it," said Mr. Greene. "I'll say goodnight to you."

"Goodnight," said Walter Downs, heading for the kitchen.

Mr. Greene took the elevator to the third floor, got out, and walked down to the second floor. It was possible to hear the elevator from Twelve and Fourteen, to judge where it was stopping. He walked down the hall past Twelve and Fourteen, the sound of his steps deadened by the carpeting. The light was on in Fourteen, Miss Buckley's room. It showed in the transom. Twelve was dark. He listened outside Fourteen; Miss Buckley had the radio going softly. Mr. Greene decided that if there was any funny business between Mr. Wilbur and Miss Buckley, it had already been finished for the night. He was somewhat relieved, although he was only postponing the moment when he would catch them together.

He now walked to the end of the hall and pushed the button for the elevator. He heard the machinery go into operation and was waiting for the elevator's slow descent when Miss Buckley's door was opened. He only chanced to see the light from her room suddenly falling like a square on the carpet. Miss Buckley came out of her room in a hurry and went quickly to Mr. Wilbur's door and opened it with a key. She went inside, closing his door behind her. She had never once looked in Mr. Greene's direction.

Mr. Greene in his anger nearly lost control of himself, but he waited a full minute, then went back to Twelve, inserted his passkey, and flung open the door. Miss Buckley was sitting on the bed, holding Mr. Wilbur and rocking from side to side, muttering to him. Mr. Wilbur was babbling words that Mr. Greene could not make out, staring at the foot of the bed.

Miss Buckley looked at Mr. Greene and went on holding Mr. Wilbur in her arms. "He gets these nightmares," she said.

THE MADELINE WHERRY CASE

Mrs. Wherry got off the train and waited on the platform until the train went on its way. There were offers of a lift, which she declined. "Thank you," she said. "I have my car. Just waiting in case Bud was on this train." She became the last person to leave the platform, and she made her way slowly to her sedan, parked on the outermost edge of the lot. She had to pass her husband's VW, which was much nearer to the platform, and if she could have remembered where he hid the key she would have taken his car and left him hers. Her feet hurt.

She got in her sedan and kicked off her shoes and put on a pair of loafers that lay on the floor. She took off her hat and ruffled her hair and lowered the windows in the front doors. She lit a cigarette and had a few long drags on it before tossing it away. Now she started the car and headed for home.

The cool draft she had created by opening the car windows mussed her hair, but she no longer cared. There was a smudge on the fingers of her white glove, where she had grasped the handrail in getting off the train. That didn't matter. She caught a glimpse of her face in the too honest rear-view mirror, and she saw individual grains of face powder and little splits in the texture of her lip rouge that looked like a row of wrinkles. She saw the real wrinkles and the crow's-feet, and she wondered how much worse they would be if she had not always, all her life, been so religious about her cold cream and her facials. "Never soap," her mother had told her. "Not even the mildest soap on your face. I haven't used soap on my face since I was sixteen years old, and if I'm proud of one thing I'm proud of my skin." That was when she was fourteen and leaving for boarding-school, and her mother was giving her parting instructions. That was more than thirty years ago. Thirty-three, to be exact. Thirty-*four*. That whole conversation came back to her now, and she recalled her confusion when she tried to pay attention to her mother's advice. Some of the advice was obvious stuff, but some of it had given her a new look at her mother. How had her conventional, rather prim mother acquired the information to give? "Make it a rule never to lend things," her mother had said. "Things, or money. If the other girls find they can take advantage of you, they will, so you start right out by making it a *rule*. They'll respect you more in the long run." Her mother had not been to a boarding-school; how did she know all that? What's more, her mother was a generous woman, with a reputation for large and small kindnesses. Madeline Wherry wondered now what else her mother could have told her. "You'll let boys kiss you—if you haven't already," she had said. "But you mustn't believe a word they say when they're kissing you. It isn't that they're lying to you. They believe what they say at such times. But how is a young boy to know anything? How are *you* to know anything unless I tell you? And don't trust your instincts, Madeline. They'll play you false."

That was the one she should have remembered.

She put her car in the garage and lowered the door. With her town shoes in one hand she entered the house at the back porch. Theodora was sitting at the kitchen table, doing a crossword puzzle, the radio going full blast. "Oh, you're home early," said Theodora.

"No. This is the train I said I'd be on. Would you mind turning that down just a little?"

Theodora got up and lowered the volume of the radio. "Mrs.

Farr called. Mrs. Eubank. Mrs. Farr said she'd call again this evening, nothing important. Mrs. Eubank wanted me to make sure and tell you about the change in plans. You and Mister were supposed to go there at seven o'clock, but now she don't want you till ha' past. You were supposed to have dinner at her house, but their cook's mother took sick and she had to leave hurriedly for Wilmington, so you're all having dinner out. Was a person-to-person call for you, but the party didn't leave no name. I told them you were expected about now. You know it rained here around lunchtime? Did it rain in New York?"

"No. It looked as though it might, but it didn't."

"Rained steady for about a half an hour. You just can't go by the radio. They said fair, partly cloudy toward evening. I was giving some of those blankets an airing and they got soaked. Me too, I got soaked bringing them in. The shower came so quick I wasn't ready for it. I was busy on the phone talking to my sister and I didn't notice when it started to come down. You'd think they'd know on the radio. Don't they get those reports from the government?"

"I imagine so. What station are you listening to?"

"That? Ain't that Trenton?"

"I don't know. I thought *you'd* know."

"Oh, I don't always keep track of what station."

"Well, I'm going to have a bath, if anyone should call. Tell them to call again in an hour."

"What about your person-to-person?"

"I'm still going to have my bath."

"Uh-huh."

"Did you hang the wet blankets in the cellar?"

"Yes ma'am, I did."

"Good. They should dry out there overnight, and we can hang them outdoors again in the morning."

"There! It *was* Trenton. He just gave the station identification. I can usually tell if it's Trenton. You get to know their voices. There's one I always get mixed up with—"

"Is the mail on the hall table?"

"The mail? Oh, a letter from your daughter. The rest is all ads. It's in there on the hall table, you'll see it."

"Yes."

"Can I have the stamp off of your daughter's letter? I got my nephew is starting a stamp collection. I don't know whether he got an Italy one or not."

"Of course," said Madeline Wherry.

She was half out of her clothes when the telephone rang. It was the person-to-person call. "I'll take it, Theodora. You can hang up, please," said Madeline. "Hello?"

"Are you all right?" he said.

There was no need for him to identify himself. "What a strange question," she said. "Why yes, I'm all right. Why?"

"I was wondering. Have you had your talk with Bud?"

"He's not home yet. But I'll be all right. And please don't call me again, will you? Please?"

"All right, I won't," he said.

"Then why did you call now? You're not making it any easier for anybody. For me or for you. Now don't call again, please. It's over and settled and done with."

"I know that, but I had to call you this once."

"No you didn't. There won't be any trouble with Bud, and even if there was I wouldn't tell you about it. He's got what he wanted, and he can't make any trouble."

"Yes, he's got what he wanted, all right," he said. "Well, I'm sorry to've bothered you."

"We've said it all, including goodbye," she said.

"Right," he said, and hung up.

His anticlimactic call was a minor annoyance, and she tried to think of T. S. Eliot's line about ending in a whimper. The call was almost a whimper. Two hours ago, less than two hours ago, there had been pain, tears, strong feeling. He should have left it at that. Strong feeling had given her strength; now all she wanted to do was sink into her tub, to complete the lethargy that the call had produced.

She was still in the tub when she heard the VW in the driveway, and the routine sounds of her husband's return from his day in town that could not have been a routine day. Then, "Are you taking a bath?"

"Yes," she said.

"Do you want a drink?"

"No, I don't want a drink," she said.

"Well, did you *see* him?" he said.

"Yes, I saw him. I'll be out in a minute. Get yourself a drink if you want one."

"I have one," he said.

She dried herself and ran a comb through her hair and put on her dressing-gown. He was sitting uncomfortably on her daybed, highball glass in hand, smoking a cigarette.

"I saw you in Penn Station," he said.

"Oh, you did?"

"Yes. *I* was in time for the five-eleven, too. I was having a drink and I saw you waiting for the gate to open."

"But you didn't take the five-eleven."

"No, I certainly didn't," he said. "I didn't feel like discussing what we had to discuss on a railroad train."

"Probably very wise," she said. "Well, we're here, and here we can discuss anything."

"All right. You start."

"Well, I telephoned him around ten o'clock and asked him to meet me for lunch."

"Where?"

"Georgetti's. It's on Lexington Avenue, near Thirty-eighth Street."

"Is that where you usually met him?"

"Yes."

"From the beginning?"

"Almost. At first we never went to the same place twice, but then he discovered Georgetti's. Out of the way, off the beaten path, but actually quite convenient, especially for me. Only three blocks from Fifth Avenue, the stores."

"And not too bad for him, either," said her husband.

"No. He could walk from his office."

"Did he have any inkling of what you wanted to see him about? Or did he think you just wanted to have a cozy afternoon?"

"The latter, I think," she said. "He was totally unprepared for what I had to say."

"Too damn bad. What *did* you say?"

"What you told me to say. That I had to stop seeing him. That I was never to see him again. That you've known about it now for three or four months."

"Oh, come on. You didn't hit him one-two-three with three sentences. What did you say?"

"If you think I'm going to try to repeat the whole conversation word for word, you're wrong. I refuse to."

"Did you tell him that you love me?"

"Yes. I told him that you had been unfaithful to me, and that was why you were willing to forgive me. *If* I stopped seeing him."

"What did he say to that?"

"I won't tell you. I'm not going to tell you any of what he said. That was said to me, not to you. Maybe you're entitled to know what I said to him, but not what he said to me."

"You must have told him that you loved him. Didn't you?"

"I have."

"Did you today?"

She hesitated. "No," she said.

"You're lying to me, Madeline. You told him that you'd always love him."

"No, I didn't."

"Didn't he ask you?"

"Yes."

"Oh, I see. He asked you, but you refused to say yes or no. It was going to be all over between you, so you were starting by refusing to say you did or didn't love him. Am I right?"

"Yes," she said.

"Now, the big question. Does he think you do love him?"

"It's such a big question that I'm not going to answer it," she said.

"I'm not getting much out of you, am I?"

"You got what you wanted. I told him I'm not going to see him any more, and he knows I mean that."

"And where did you go from this Georgetti's?"

"Nowhere. We were there till it was time for me to catch my train."

"Do you swear to that?"

"I won't swear to anything. I said what you wanted me to say, and he knows I'm never going to see him again."

"Why are you so sure that he knows it?"

"Because I convinced him of it. And *I* know I'm not going to see him again."

"No, you and I aren't the kind of people that are very good at that." He stood up. "I'm glad it's over, aren't you?"

"What do you expect me to say?"

"That you're glad it's over—if you are."

"I am, only I wish I had made the decision, not you."

"I didn't hold a gun at your head."

"No, not a gun," she said. "Oh, it wouldn't have lasted much longer. Only last week he said he was getting tired of Georgetti's. The food, the menu, the waiters."

"Where did you usually go after Georgetti's?"

She shook her head. "No, Bud. If you want it to be over, it has to be over for you, too. I didn't put *you* through a cross-examination, and I didn't make you stop seeing Marcia Eubank."

"I've told you a hundred times. Marcia and I were never a real affair. She means absolutely nothing to me, and never did mean very much."

"No, but she meant something to me. And so did you. My best friend and my husband."

"It's this damn life we lead," he said. "But maybe some good'll come of it. If I didn't believe we love each other, you and I, I wouldn't have been so tough."

"I know," she said.

"Theodora said you had a letter from Nan."

"Yes, I haven't read it."

"Do you mind if I take it with me? I'll bring it down to dinner."

"All right," she said.

With his empty glass in one hand, and the letter in the other he went out, leaving her with nothing. The telephone was there, and that man could be summoned back into her life, but so easily that he was useless to her. The scene at Georgetti's had been confusing. For her it had begun with the moment in the morning when she decided that this was the day she would obey

Bud's order. This was the day she would give up her lover, and she knew that there would be tears, but she had not expected the tears to be his. Angry protest, angry refusal, yes, but not tears. He was not a man who was given to any such emotional display. He was not a man whom anyone would pick out as any woman's lover. She, yes, she might be picked out as a woman who might be some man's mistress. She spent money on her clothes, she prided herself on her *chic*, she took care of her hair and her skin, she kept up with things to talk about, she made the effort to be pleasing to men and women. And then when she was at last ready to take a lover—partly out of pique, partly out of fear, partly out of boredom—the man she chose was Morton DeKalb. Morton DeKalb, whose work she never quite understood. "No, I'm not a draughtsman," he had said on their first meeting.

"But I understood you to say you were," she said.

"No. I said I was working on some blueprints. That's where you got that impression. I'm an industrial engineer." It turned out that he was over-modest; that he had quite a good job, made between twenty-five and thirty thousand a year, but on their first meeting she was ready to picture him as a man who worked over a draughting board, with his shirt sleeves rolled up and a pencil in his mouth like a horse's bit. The occasion was a Sigma Chi cocktail party at the University Club. Her husband was somewhere around, and her meeting with Morton DeKalb was prolonged only because Bud Wherry was on the cocktail party committee. "I never met your husband," said DeKalb. "But I know him by name. He's a Dartmouth man."

"Yes."

"I'm from Penn State," said DeKalb. "I don't get to many of these things. They usually want to put the chew on you for something. But I more or less had to come to this one. The guest of honor is a member of my chapter, although considerably after my time. Even so he's pretty old to be a major, considering how important he is to the Air Force. I guess they don't hand out those stars the way they used to."

Their conversation was as impersonal as that, and it terminated when Bud beckoned to her to join him. She excused herself, and forgot all about Morton DeKalb, from Penn State.

One week later she was sitting next to him in a restaurant, only vaguely conscious of him as a man who kept trying to compel her to recognize him, leaning forward and looking into her face. Finally he spoke. "Been trying to get you to say hello," he said. "I'm Morton DeKalb. I met you at the Sigma Chi party."

"Oh, yes, I'm sorry," she said. "This is Mr. DeKalb, Mrs. Durbin."

"This is Mr. Overton, Mrs. Wherry, and Mrs. Durber," said Morton DeKalb. "Overton's a Sigma Chi."

"So is *my* husband," said Margaret Durbin.

"Oh, where from?" said DeKalb.

"Oh, all the way from Southern California. S. C. Sigma Chi, Southern Cal."

"Perhaps you ladies would like to have a drink on that," said Overton.

Madeline Wherry saw that Overton was ready to move in, and she thought she sensed some annoyance on the part of DeKalb. She was right. "No, I heard the ladies say they didn't want a cocktail," said DeKalb. "Nice to've seen you again, Mrs. Wherry. Nice to've met you, Mrs. Durber." He was obviously in a position to make decisions for Overton that Overton would have to accept, and he saw to it that Overton's threat to become a nuisance was averted. Luncheon proceeded with no further communication between the two tables, and Madeline Wherry heard DeKalb say, "Well, you go downtown and talk to McCann and tell him what I said. I'll be at the office till six o'clock, or even later. I'll wait there for you." Overton left, and DeKalb ordered a demitasse, lit a cigarette, and stared straight ahead.

"Have your coffee with us," said Madeline Wherry.

"Well, I was hoping you'd ask me," said DeKalb.

"Not me, Maddie. I have to run," said Margaret Durbin. "Goodness! Five of two."

"Run, Margaret. It's my turn to pay," said Madeline Wherry.

Now they were alone, he at his table, she at hers. "Shall we join forces?" he said.

"It can't be for long. I have to go, too. But yes, you sit here, or I'll sit there. You slide over," said Madeline Wherry.

"Funny I never saw you before, and then we meet twice in the same week," said DeKalb. "I guess that's not a very original thing to say. But it's true. You don't come here often."

"No, my friend does, but I have another place I usually go to when I'm in New York."

"You don't live in the city?"

"High Ridge, New Jersey," said Madeline Wherry.

"Oh, yes, I know where it is. We looked at a house there several years ago, but my kids like sailing, so we bought in Rye."

"They decide everything for us, don't they?"

"I guess they do, more or less. What have you got?"

"One, a daugher. Just got married and she's gone to live abroad. Her husband has a Fulbright, and she just graduated from Wellesley. I don't suppose they'll ever come home, they both love Europe so."

"Make it kind of lonely for you, won't it?"

"At first, I guess. But I'll have to get used to it. How many have you got?"

"We have three boys. Two at Deerfield and one a freshman at Wesleyan.

"Then they're all away, too."

"Yes, for most of the year. House is really quiet now, with all three of them away. But they make up for it in the summer. They all have their own friends, and they call our place the DeKalb Yacht Club. We never know how many will show up for breakfast."

"That must be fun."

"It has its disadvantages, but for the most part it's enjoyable."

"I was an only child and my daughter's an only child. I always envied those that had a large family."

"Well, there again," he said. "I had two brothers and two sisters. My father was a schoolteacher, and he educated us all on what it costs me to send one boy to Deerfield. I don't suppose he could have managed *that* if my grandfather hadn't left my mother some money. Student loans got me through State, and one of my sisters came down with polio. We never seemed to be able to get ahead, always scratching for a dollar. But I guess we turned out all right, considering. Both of my brothers went into teaching and they're full professors, one at Cornell, the other at Pitt. And the sister that didn't get polio married a classmate of mine that's doing very well in Pittsburgh Plate Glass. One of their coming men. So between us we've been able to take care of our parents in their senior-citizen years. At least moneywise."

"What happened to the other sister?"

"Oh, she died. That was long before any vaccines like the Salk vaccine."

"I'm still terrified of polio," said Madeline Wherry. "Especially with my daughter planning to live abroad. What would I do? I'd have nobody."

"You'd have your husband," he said.

"Yes, of course." She looked at him quickly, and saw that he was really looking at her for the first time. "I didn't mean that the way it may have sounded. I mean that we'd have nobody, if anything happened to her. Don't look at me that way, Mr. DeKalb."

"What way? I was just surprised at the way you suddenly sounded—at the way you *sounded*. Afraid. Or desperate. You mustn't worry about your daughter. They get shots for this and shots for that. It isn't like the old days."

"That had nothing to do with the way you were looking at me," she said.

"All right, it didn't," he said.

"Then would you mind telling me *why* you thought I was desperate, or what I was afraid of?"

"Well, you'll probably walk out on me, but I'd say that all was not well between you and Mr. Wherry. That remark of yours just slipped out, but you think you *would* have nobody if something happened to your daughter. You're wrong, though. You'd have yourself, and a woman like you, it wouldn't be long before you'd have someone else."

"I've never had anyone else," she said.

"No, but you could have. I imagine that's been proven a hundred times. A woman like you, you didn't have to wait around for a guy like me to tell you you're attractive. Look around this room. Who was the most attractive woman here today? I considered myself lucky just to get the seat next to yours."

"You're very nice to give me this build-up. I need it."

"I know you do, and it's a pleasure to be able to give it. I never expected anything as good as this to come out of a lunch date with Charley Overton. Jesus! But I hope you noticed, Overton's a guy that gets around, and he spotted you right away."

"And you protected me."

"Oh, you caught that? Yes. I was to get Mrs. Durber, and he was to get you. You didn't overhear that part of the conversation, I hope."

"No, but I knew something was going on in his mind."

"In his mind that's the kind of thing that's going on all the time. It's amazing how many women there are that fall for it."

"Did he think I was in a receptive mood? You can be honest."

"Well, yes, I guess he did, more or less."

"But I've never been in a less receptive mood," she said. "So there he's wrong."

"Can I still be honest?"

"Yes, why?"

"Because I think you *are* in a receptive mood, but you don't like to admit it, even to yourself. Especially to yourself."

"Well now, what about you, Mr. DeKalb? You've never so much as mentioned your wife. Your boys, your father and mother, sisters and brothers, and various in-laws. But not a word about Mrs. DeKalb. I assume there is one, and that she's home in Rye, in that quiet house."

"Yes, and she's the quietest thing in it."

"Maybe that's because she's used to being a lone woman in an all-male household."

"Yes, and maybe it's because we have nothing more to say to each other. I don't know."

"How old is she?"

"Forty-six. I guess that has something to do with it," he said. "She won't talk about it, but I guess that's what it is. I was never very smart when it came to women."

"Men that *think* they are, are usually anything but," she said.

"Listen, can I talk to you again? I have to get back to my office. There's a man waiting for me that came all the way from South America. But I can talk to you, I know I can. Will you do that, as a Christian act of kindness?"

"Do you mean, meet you for lunch?"

"Anything you say. Lunch. Cocktails. Anything."

"Give me your phone number, and the next time I'm coming to town I'll call you."

"Would you do that? I'm not a pass-maker, Mrs. Wherry. But I am a guy in a hell of a lot of trouble and with nobody to talk to about it. And I wouldn't be the only one you'd be helping, although you don't owe her a damn thing or me either, for that matter."

She smiled. "You gave me a little build-up. That can be very important at the right time."

"I have to fly out to Seattle the week after next. You couldn't make it next week sometime?"

"I probably can," she said.

She went home that day with a new sense of being not entirely defenseless against Marcia Eubank. If Bud was being no more to Marcia than any of the other men who liked to have her put her hand on their shoulders when she talked to them, he was making an ass of himself. If he was more than that, Madeline Wherry was defenseless—short of an accusation that might be unsupportable. There was no question in her own mind that she would see Mr. DeKalb. At certain moments, when he was intense with his thoughts of the people he loved, he had a habit of clenching his fist that she found very attractive. She always noticed men's hands, when the men themselves were worth noticing.

In the next four years it was usually she who did the telephoning. Theodora, and Theodora's predecessors, were not to be trusted. In a situation like this, no one was to be trusted. But there was more to her precautions than that: always, between one meeting and the next, there was her shameful, disloyal fear that someone like Marcia Eubank would discover that her lover was a man like Morton DeKalb. Her lover should have been someone irresistible to all women, the kind of man who had a terrible reputation, who married women for their money and went through life undismayed by his unpopularity with other men. Once or twice a year Madeline Wherry would buy a hat at a Fifty-seventh Street shop which was patronized by a woman who had been victimized by two such cads. Madeline Wherry would study this woman, watch her trying on hats, eavesdrop on her conversations with the manager and the saleswoman. Josephine Carling, heiress to an automobile fortune. Ex-wife of a Georgian prince and a South American. Some of the indignities Josephine Carling had endured had appeared in the newspapers. Locked out of her own house in Palm Beach without a stitch of clothes on (the Georgian prince). Punched in the face at El Morocco (the South American). No one envied Josephine Carling her sordid notoriety. And yet when Madeline Wherry would see her at the hat store Josephine Carling was always cheerful, profanely witty, quite genuinely liked by the people who waited on her, and unmistakably enjoying life. Madeline Wherry was never introduced to Josephine Carling, but one day when Madeline was sitting at the triple mirrors, hesitating about a hat, Josephine Carling called to her, "Take it! It's perfect for you. I wish I could wear it." Madeline bought the hat and wore it that day to her rendezvous with Morton DeKalb. "Do you know who almost bought this hat?" she said. "Josephine Carling."

"Don't tell me she's a pal of yours," said Morton DeKalb. "Her old man was a production genius, T. T. Carling, and when you think of where all that money's gone to. Her kind will bring on communism quicker than anything I can think of." He could spoil a hat for her. What kind of a lover was it that could spoil the fun of a hat? The answer was, a safe lover, who would return her to her husband unbruised and unsuspected.

But lover he was, with love to give that he gave without stint. His wife had been the only other woman he had been to bed with, and Madeline fell heir to the passion and fidelity that he had bestowed on her. "Where I would be without you," he said to Madeline, "I hate to think. Beth and I came from the same kind of people. Her father owned a drug store, but the big thing in his life aside from his family was church work. I guess he had the record for being reelected president of the inter-church council. Something like fourteen years, I think it was. If he was alive today I know he'd be trying to get one of my boys to enter the ministry. Sure of it. He wouldn't have a prayer, but all the same our boys had a religious upbringing."

"It's a good thing they don't know about me."

"I don't know, Madeline. They are a little young to know about us, and they never will. And yet when you think of how I might have gone haywire. And I could have. I'm just the kind of a guy that does go haywire when he gets to be around my age, and the wife is having her own problems in that department. One of our best men, Stu Knapp, in charge of our Atlanta office, we had to give him a six months' leave of absence. Ill health, we announced it as, but the fact of the matter was it all stemmed from his wife. Same problem as Beth, and Stu got himself involved with a girl that used to be a stenographer in the Atlanta office. She came back to help out during the summer vacations, and the first thing you know she and Stu are going off on trips together and her husband came in one day waving a revolver at everybody, demanding to know where Stu was. We only have sixteen people in our Atlanta office, and of course everybody knew what was going on. But the point is, Stu Knapp was one of the last fellows you'd ever think of as liable to go haywire. Phi Beta Kappa from the University of Georgia, man that never smoked or drank in all the years I've known him."

"Well, my husband isn't likely to come into your office waving a pistol. There's a man in High Ridge that could wave one at him."

"Yes, you told me. That hurts, doesn't it?"

"It did. It doesn't so much any more, except when they think they're pulling the wool over everyone's eyes."

"I don't know what a fellow like Bud Wherry wants to fool around for, when he had someone like you. I guess the same thing could be said about me, but it's a different situation. But then I guess every situation is different. No two alike."

"No."

"For me you're perfect," he said. "You're beautiful, and you're the type woman that I guess every dull bastard like me wants secretly. Only we know we're dull bastards, so we don't make a try for a woman like you. Then something happens, like we run into each other twice in the same week, and out of niceness you listen to my troubles, and then there we are. How I ever got the nerve to come out and say it, 'Will you go to the hotel with me?' God knows I was thinking it, morning, noon and night."

"I must have been, too."

"Just don't ever be sorry, Madeline. I'd kill myself before I ever gave you any cause to be sorry. I'd hate to do anything to disgrace the boys, and Beth. But you come first, now. I can tell you something now that I couldn't have told you three years ago."

"What's that?"

"At first, you know, I didn't love you. I was—dizzy, you might say. Thinking, Good Lord, me in bed with her? I couldn't believe it. And I thought what the hell have I got that she wants? Suspicious. Unsure of myself, was the reason. But you see you didn't make it very difficult—"

"I didn't make it difficult at all," she said. "I just went."

"Yes, that's what I mean. But why me? All right, I'm clean, and I always kept myself in good physical condition. But my own mother wouldn't call me handsome or even good-looking. I'm not rich. I don't get around in café society circles, and outside of a few people in my own profession nobody ever heard of me. I guess love is like lightning. You don't know where it's going to hit, and when it hits it hits quick." At his most profound he was never hard to follow, and since the making of love was a part of their every meeting—lunch, the hotel room that his company kept on a yearly basis, the taxi ride to the Penn Station—the little time before and after their lovemaking partook of the excitement and relaxation of the act itself, and his utterances on the subject of love were not isolated from passion. In four years he had almost no chance to prove that he was the dull bastard he said he was, and she did not want to risk giving him the chance. She was not even very apprehensive about being come upon accidentally in Georgetti's by a woman like Marcia Eubank. The wrong clothes that he constantly wore, his plain and uninteresting face, and the things he would say if he had to be introduced to a Marcia Eubank would convince a Marcia Eubank that he was a nothing. That would be how Marcia would express it, too:

a nothing. Marcia Eubank might even suspect that Morton DeKalb was a cover-up for the real lover, a man at least as interesting as Bud Wherry. Madeline could practically hear Marcia Eubank: "Yes, Madeline Wherry, having lunch with a man at some little hole-in-the-wall on Lexington Avenue. The man was a nothing, strictly Dullsville, but I'll just bet you our little Madeline has *some*body. She doesn't waste all that haute couture on High Ridge, New Jersey." Madeline never did run into Marcia Eubank, but it was odd how often it was Marcia, even more so than Bud, whom she saw in her imagined encounters at Georgetti's, in the hotel lobby, in a taxi with Morton DeKalb during a traffic delay.

One dreadful morning she inexplicably had a need of Morton that transcended any she had ever had before. She sat near her telephone, touching it, taking her hand away from it, then lifting the phone from its cradle and spinning the dial as fast as she could. The voice at the other end of the line said only, "Hello," but Madeline instantly hung up. Accidentally she had dialed Marcia's number.

That was the most terrible day of her life. Without letting Morton know she was coming—she could not touch her telephone again—she drove to New York because there would be an hour's wait before the next train. A policeman stopped her on the Turnpike, and though he let her off with a warning, she was angry with herself for the kittenish coquetry she used to talk him out of giving her a ticket. His look as much as told her to act her age. In New York the garage she and Bud patronized was full up, and she was forced to drive from avenue to avenue, street to street, before she found a parking lot that had room for her car. When she finally got to a pay telephone Morton was in a conference and could not be disturbed until half past twelve. "Then please tell him to meet his cousin at Georgetti's at one o'clock," she said to the switchboard operator.

"I put two and two together," Morton said. "I don't have any cousins, at least none I ever see, but Georgetti's was the tipoff. Is something wrong?"

"I had to see you. Let's get out of here."

"We can't have the room," said Morton. "It's being used by

the manager of our Omaha branch. That's who I was in conference with, and was *supposed* to have lunch with."

"Can't you get another room?"

"I don't know if that's such a good idea, dear," said Morton. "McGaffney may want to go there and wash up, change his shirt or something."

"Try another hotel."

"I could do that, I guess. Excuse me," he said, and went to Georgetti's telephone booth. He came back in a few minutes. "All set. But I'll have to go in first and register and you come up later."

"What hotel is it?"

"It's the Kingston," he said. "It's a kind of a small place on East Forty-eighth Street. The company has an account there but we don't use it very often."

"I never heard of it," she said.

"Well, it isn't the best, but it isn't the worst," he said.

She had to wait in a drug store to give him time to register and get to his room. She telephoned Morton and learned the room number. The lobby was small and nearly deserted, and her unfamiliarity with the layout caused her to go to the right while the elevators were to the left.

"I feel like one of those call girls," she said.

"I'm worried about you," said Morton. "Tell me what's the matter?"

"I wish I knew myself," she said. "I think I must be going off my rocker. I got *that* expression from *you*."

He was in his shirt sleeves. He put his arms around her and held her to him. "You'll be all right. Smoke a cigarette."

"No. I think I got you here under false pretenses," she said. "I'm sorry."

"Oh," he said. "Well, *I'll* smoke a cigarette."

She began to cry. "I don't know what's the *matter* with me. Maybe I *am* going off my rocker."

"Listen, we all get funny moods. We wouldn't be human if we didn't."

"Oh, God, Morton, you only make it worse feeling sorry for me."

"I'll tell you what," he said. "I really have to get back to the office. I'm up to here in work, conferences and all. You take a bath and lie down a while. Maybe get a nap. Then when you're ready to leave, give me a ring. I'll leave word that I'm expecting a call. This morning the boss told everybody that nobody was to be interrupted by outside calls, that's how that happened. But you get a little rest and phone me."

"No. I'll leave now and I'll call you tomorrow. You're very sweet, and I'm sorry. I *am* sorry, but I'll make it up to you." She squeezed his hand and rubbed her cheek against his, and left.

She took a taxi to Penn Station and caught a local train. Not until she got off the train at High Ridge did she remember that she had left her car in New York.

It was easy enough to cook up a story for Bud, and she had a plausible one ready when he got home. She did not need it. He came into the sitting-room, tossed his newspaper and hat on a chair and stood and stared at her with his hands folded behind his back. "What the hell were you doing at the Kingston Hotel? And don't try to lie out of it. You didn't have a room there, because I called up and asked."

"What makes you think I *was* at the Kingston Hotel?"

"Because I saw you coming out. Who's the guy, Madeline?"

"Why does it have to be a guy?"

"Because the reputation the Kingston has, I doubt if you know many of the women that live there. Hundred-dollar girls and kept women."

"It sounds like a good place for Marcia to stay."

"You can talk your silly head off, but I'm going to find out who the guy was. If I don't find out one way, I'll find out another. If I have to beat it out of you, I will. And if that fails, I'll get a copy of the register. You can't win, so you might as well tell me."

"Keep your voice down, and close the door," she said. "If you ever hit me, I'd kill you. I've taken quite enough from you the last few years, making a fool of me with Marcia Eubank. Stupid, both of you. You haven't fooled anyone, not a soul. Yes, I met somebody at the Kingston."

"Who?"

"A man named Morton DeKalb."

"Who?"

"Morton DeKalb."

"Who's he? I know that name. Morton Cobb. They always give his middle initial. Morton D. Cobb. Who the hell is Morton D. Cobb?"

"DeKalb. He's a fraternity brother of yours, and that's how I met him."

"That's the son of a bitch. Now I know who he is. He's with some engineering company. And that's who you're having an affair with. Well, I'll be a son of a bitch. When did this start?"

"A few months ago. When I was sure about you and Marcia. I always suspected you and Marcia, but I was never sure till a few months ago."

"What made you so sure?"

"You and Marcia. What's the use of talking about it? I wouldn't believe anything you told me, and I don't really care."

"What do you mean, you don't care? You cared enough to have an affair with this DeKalb. Well, I'll have a little talk with him tomorrow."

"You do, and I'll divorce you and name Marcia. If you make the slightest effort to embarrass him in any way, by phone or letter or any other way, or go to see him, I'll make it so unpleasant for you and Marcia that you'll both have to move out of High Ridge. You're the only one knows anything about Morton DeKalb, but everybody's seen you and Marcia jitterbugging and twisting and going off by yourselves. People will be on my side, Bud."

"Not when I get through with you," he said.

"You are through with me. Or I'm through with you, either one, it doesn't matter."

"No, it doesn't matter a damn bit."

"I'll tell you what does matter, and that was your threatening to beat it out of me. You remember what happened the time you did slap me."

"That was twenty years ago. One slap."

"And one dead baby."

"The doctor said the slap had nothing to do with the dead baby."

"The baby was inside of me, not inside of the doctor."

"Madeline, we don't have to go through all that again. And don't trot out that old argument that the doctor lied to save my self-respect. Medically, two doctors, not one, said that one slap in the face wasn't responsible. I know, I made sure. And *you* believed them at the time, but the older you get, the easier it is for you to forget what the doctors said, and blame me. I never blamed you, but I could have. You weren't taking proper care of yourself. Oh, God, I know every word you can say and I go on repeating the same words myself. And any time it suits you, you blame me for that. Jesus Christ! Don't you think I wish my son'd been born alive?"

They fell silent, he busy with his resentment, she with hers, until the silence became a sizable thing that they could not ignore. Ceasing to ignore the silence, they could no longer ignore each other, but they had exhausted themselves.

"Well, who's going to do what?" said Bud Wherry.

"I don't know," she said.

"You have to stop seeing this fellow," he said.

"Why?"

"*Why?* All right, you don't. Go on seeing him, but move out of here."

"Tonight?"

"Preferably. If not tonight, if you have no place to go, find some place. But don't be here tomorrow night. I don't want you here, and I don't see why you'd want to be here."

"You could stay in New York. You're there every day," she said. "Oh, yes, but Marcia's here. I didn't think of that."

"Marcia is nothing to me, and I'm nothing to her," he said. "There was never a time when it couldn't have stopped, and it did stop."

"And started again when it was convenient for her."

"Yes."

"And that's the way it will be, all over again. Whenever it's convenient for her. All right, it'll take me a few days to find someplace in New York. I'll have to look for a furnished apartment, temporarily."

"That means, of course, that you're going on seeing this De-Kalb fellow."

"Is there any reason why not?"

"Are you planning to marry him?"

"I don't know. Are you planning to marry Marcia?"

"Certainly not."

"Don't say certainly not. You may have to. This may be a pretty big house, but High Ridge isn't very big. Marcia always liked this house. Or what I did with it. Copied my clothes, copied my house, the way I brought up my daughter. No wonder she appropriated my husband. Well, you have her, or she has you. And she can have the house. It's too bad I was never interested in her husband, then we could have arranged one of those swaps. I just read about another one the other day."

"Stop talking like that. We were never those kind of people."

"We are now. Or would be if I liked Greg Eubank. Maybe you'd like Mrs. DeKalb. I can't help you on that, because I've never seen her. But she has sons, three of them. That didn't keep her husband from falling in love with me, but she has them. Three of them."

"I only wanted our son," he said.

"Yes," she said. "Well, the facts of everyday living. Do you want your dinner at the usual time? Theodora goes home at half past eight no matter whether you and I are separating or not. What do you want me to tell her?"

"About dinner?"

"About dinner. The future plans, arrangements, you'll have to make them yourself. You can't expect me to ask Theodora and Emily to stand by while you and Marcia work things out."

"Suddenly this is all so ridiculous."

"Well, laugh then."

"I didn't say it was funny. I said ridiculous."

"So you did. But you still haven't told me what to tell Theodora, and any minute now she's going to come in and ask."

"Tell her to go home. I don't want any dinner."

"You can have it alone. I'm not going to have any."

"No, if I want anything later I'll go over to the diner. I'm not hungry now."

"You could take potluck at Marcia's," said Madeline. "You might as well start having your serious talks with her."

"Just tell Theodora to go home, will you please?"

"Very well." She went to the kitchen. "Mr. Wherry and I won't be ready for dinner till nine o'clock, so you might as well go home, Theodora," she said. When she returned to the sitting-room Bud was fixing a drink.

"I think she'd like to stay around a while for the fireworks," said Madeline. "At least I got the impression that she knew something was up. However, there goes the back door. She's having a little trouble at home, too. Oddly enough, her husband is carrying on with a neighbor's wife."

"Is she carrying on to get even?"

"Oh, Theodora would never tell me a thing like that."

"Do you want a drink?"

"No."

"Do you mind if I have one?"

"Heavens, why should I? You put it off as long as you could. I never knew you to postpone it this long. This is really an important occasion."

"Yes it is, Madeline," he said. "At least it is to me. From your attitude anybody'd think it was some minor Mister-and-Missus over what TV program to watch."

"Oh, that can be terribly important. Didn't I read about a wife shooting her husband on account of that? Something like that. He wanted to watch one thing, and—"

"Cut it out, will you? Let's see if we can make some sense out of this."

"I thought everything was settled. None of the details, but the major decision. I'm to leave, and you're to stay. The rest will take time, but let's do it through the lawyers. That's what they're paid for."

"If you agree not to see DeKalb again, I say let's give it a six-months' try, or three months, or whatever. A cooling-off period."

"Why?"

"Well, I just got finished doing that with a strike at the factory. I don't know if it's going to work out there, but if we can do it with a labor union, it ought to be worth a try for you and me. Unless you're determined to marry DeKalb. Then, of course—"

"I'm not determined to marry DeKalb."

"Do you love him?"

"Oh—I can't answer that, because I don't know. I can't say I *don't* love him."

"He loves you?"

"Yes, I'm sure of that. Right now it's the only thing in the world I am sure of."

"That may pass away, Madeline. You haven't given it much time."

She refused to correct her earlier lie, to yield her ethical advantage. "I've given it time enough," she said.

"You see, in my case, this thing with Marcia's been going on long enough for both of us to know that it isn't love. And it was never as much as you may have imagined. I swear that to you. There was a time there that for two years I didn't even kiss her. You hate Marcia, but if she was all you say, she could have wrecked our marriage. I admit it. Three years ago, the time you went to Italy, I was with her every night for almost a month. Greg was away, too, if you remember."

"In this house?"

"No."

"You're lying to me."

"All right, twice in this house."

"In my room?"

"Not in your room."

"In yours?"

"Yes, in mine. But that's not the point. The point is, when you came back from Italy that time, it was all over between Marcia and I, and it stayed that way for just about two years. Since then—well, it couldn't have been more casual. A couple of times in New York, twice or maybe three times here."

"She simply had to come to this house, didn't she? Once I thought Marcia Eubank was my best friend. I used to feel flattered when she imitated me, copied everything of mine. 'Oh, Madeline, you have such *chic!*' And where did I get this, where did I get that? I don't see how *you* could do it, though—bring her to this house. Wouldn't it remind you too much of me? I don't see how the two of you could keep from talking about me —but then I suppose you did."

"Madeline, I'm not responsible for her being jealous of you. She is, and she admits it. But that goes way back to when you were young girls, long before I came into the picture. Maybe that's how I got into the picture. Probably was. But only once was she ever any threat to our marriage, and that was when you visited Nan in Italy. I'm sorry for what I did, but I can honestly promise you that I'll never be alone with her again if you give me your word that you'll put an end to it with DeKalb. Now."

"What do you mean by now?"

"Well, tomorrow. Or the next few days. You can't put it off too long. Sometime in the next few days you write him a letter—"

"No, no letter."

"Well, see him, if you have to. But make it final. I don't want him to have any doubt in his mind. None whatsoever. I don't know him, not sure I'd know him if I saw him, but from what I know *of* him, he doesn't sound to me like the kind of a guy that would like all this kind of thing. I know the firm he's with, and they're a very serious-minded outfit. This isn't one of your Madison Avenue advertising huckster setups. Troutman, Von Hurzburg and Muldowney. They made it big during the war, and they've expanded since. We thought of them for the San Diego plant, when we were having that trouble with Campellini and Johnson. I had several talks with Karl Troutman, and he's just not the kind of a man that would tolerate hanky-panky in his organization, believe me. He's the old-time high laced boots and Stetson hat type of engineer."

"If you're trying to show me that you're on good terms with Morton DeKalb's boss, all right. You've shown me," she said. "Another way of saying I didn't make a very good choice."

"I thought we were past that. I thought we were talking a

cooling-off period, giving our marriage a second chance. Do you want to give it a second chance? If you don't, say so. If you do, I've told you how."

"I don't know what I want."

"I wish your mother were still alive. I could make better sense with her than I seem to be making with you."

"You always think Mother would have been on your side. She wouldn't have been, you know."

"Not a question of being on my side, Madeline. Just a matter of making *sense*, making the best of a bad situation, saving the pieces and maybe putting them together again."

"I've decided," she said.

"You have? What?"

"I'm not going to see Morton any more. That is, I'll see him once more and tell him it's the last time. What you and I do after that will have to be a separate decision."

"When will you tell him?"

"Soon. A few days, a week."

"All right," he said.

It took three days and nights for her to make up her mind to telephone Morton, and when she called him he was gentle and reassuring, painfully so in his belief that she was ready to make amends for her frenetic behavior at their last meeting, more painfully so in his ignorance of the purpose of her call. "We don't have to go to Georgetti's," he said. "Let's have a change of scenery? Name some snappy restaurant and I'll take you there."

"No, I'd rather go to Georgetti's," she said.

"Are you sure?"

"Yes, I'm sure," she said.

He was at their usual table when she got there. "You look as if you'd just stepped out of a bandbox," he said.

"Do I? I've often wondered how anybody'd look that just stepped out of a bandbox. Rather crumpled, I should think. I'd like a vodka martini."

He picked up her hand and looked at her. "I missed you," he said. "I almost made some excuse to drive down to High Ridge to see you."

"It's a good thing you didn't."

"Well, I knew that when you were ready to see me, you'd phone."

The waiter served their drinks and went away. She had a long sip of hers and lit a cigarette. "I don't know where to start," she said.

"Yes, there's something on your mind. That I can tell," he said. "But if it has anything to do with our visit to the Kingston, that was my fault. I realized later that I didn't want to make love that day either. We ought to see each other oftener when we aren't going to make love."

"Strange you should say that. Because that's the way it's going to be, that's why I wanted to see you today."

"Oh, don't take me too seriously on that. I'm not suggesting that we turn Platonic."

"Oh, Morton. It isn't even going to be that. It isn't going to be anything. This is the last time I'm ever going to see you, at all."

"Bud?"

"Yes. He saw me coming out of the Kingston. He knew there was something wrong anyway. Oh, God, that whole day was so awful. I could have faked some lie about the Kingston, but I was all the way back to High Ridge before I remembered that I'd driven in and left the car in New York. You'll never know what I went through that day. I started the day with such a surge for you that I had to see you. Then they wouldn't let me talk to you, and I came here not knowing whether you'd got my message, or would understand it. And, oh, everything. So that when Bud got home and accused me of meeting someone, it was anticlimactic. Then the long scene with him."

"Does he know it was me?"

"Yes. I told him. But you're not going to be dragged into it. I don't know why I say dragged in. There isn't going to be a divorce, or at least I don't think so. But you have nothing to worry about. I told him I'd been having an affair with you for three months only."

"Nothing to worry about? How can you say that? I have you to worry about. Haven't I convinced you that I love you, that I've never loved anyone else? Madeline, I'm a man that never knew what love was till four years ago, and that's pretty late in life. Everything before that was—mechanical. Flavorless. I never had any beauty in my life before. I didn't know what it was. To find myself singing little songs when I thought of a person, you. Holy God, girl, this isn't going to stop because—whatever reason Bud Wherry wants it to stop."

"It isn't only Bud. I want it to stop, too."

"Why?"

"Because it has to. It always had to, sometime, and this is the time. I want another vodka martini."

"No. You're not used to them."

"Don't be ridiculous. I *want* another *drink*."

"Well, we're not going to fight over that," he said, and pointed to her glass and nodded to the waiter. "What have I done, or not done, that you can just suddenly like this put me out of your life, and take yourself out of mine?"

"Nothing you've done, nothing I've done. Except every damn thing we ever did with other people before we fell in love. You married a girl called Beth, and I married a man called Bud. And you had three sons and I had a daughter and a son born dead."

"A son born dead? You never told me that."

"No, and you see, there are so many big and little things we kept from each other because we had to. There are some things I told you that I never told Bud, but there are some things he *knows* that I never told you. It's the same with you and Beth."

"Nonsense. I want to know why you decide all this now. You aren't afraid of Bud Wherry. You know I'd marry you if you'd say the word, you've always known that. We'd have financial problems, but the boys are all educated except the youngest, and I've had good offers that I turned down because they'd have meant moving away from New York. Why are you deciding to get rid of me?"

The waiter set her drink on the table.

"I don't know," she said.

"Yes you do," he said.

"Oh, all right, then I do! It's because I'm sick and tired of the whole thing."

"Of me?"

"Yes, of you as part of the whole thing. Of myself, too, don't forget. And of other people, too. Of Bud. Of Marcia Eubank. Of Greg Eubank. Of wanting to go to bed with you and coming to New York, but only seeing you when I had that need. Every time I saw you it was that. I didn't have to say it, but every time I telephoned you you thought it. She wants to go to bed with me, she wants me to make love to her. Four years of that doesn't make it any less humiliating."

"You knew I wanted you all the time."

"You didn't the last time, and neither did I. I thought I did, but as soon as I got here I wanted to leave, and the last straw was that awful hotel. The Kingston. Morton, I don't want to start hating you, but I will. I'll hate you just as I do all the others."

He did not speak. At first the silence was more noticeable in his eyes than in the absence of speech, and the normal plainness of his face was an appropriate setting for his unhappiness. He had spoken the truth, that all his life had been lacking in beauty as he had come to know it four years ago, and the eyes and the mouth were once again as she had first seen them. But there was nothing she would do to end the suffering that had begun for him, his contemplation of the bleak future and the old bleak past.

"*I'll* have a vodka martini," he said.

"Not on top of rye," she said.

"Oh, yes. I can handle rye." He gave the order and waited in silence until the waiter brought the drink. "My friend Charley Overton would know what to do in a situation like this," he said. "Do you remember Charley Overton?"

"Yes. What ever happened to him?"

"I told you. He got the sack, couple of years ago. His days were numbered from the start. The big boss was bound to find out about Charley sooner or later. Always more lenient about booze than about women. And all of a sudden I'm beginning to understand why."

"Why?"

"Well, because at this moment, having had only one drink since yesterday, I have no desire to go back to the office, or go home this afternoon. I've been put in charge of all the basic planning for a fully automated plant that's going to be built near Schenectady. The biggest thing they ever handed me. And I'll tell you something—I couldn't care less."

"And for that you blame me," she said.

"Yes, I guess I do. Inside myself I gave you the credit for the good work I've been doing the last three or four years."

"Be patient. In a little while you'll hate me."

"How can I? I never did as much for you as you did for me," he said.

He had much more to drink, and they went through two cycles of anger and pleading, anger and refusal, until it was time for her to catch her train. In the taxi he was quite drunk, and she had never seen him drunk. His attempts to kiss her were so clumsy that when she got out of the cab it was just like getting away from any pest. He did not leave her with much to weep over.

She was in her room, and she was not sure how long she had been there, sitting on the daybed, staring at her feet, not staring at her feet; hearing the downstairs sounds, not hearing the downstairs sounds. Then there was the undeniable sound of Bud's footsteps on the stairs, and the undeniable presence of Bud in her room. "Say, I was just talking to Theodora. She said we're going out for dinner. I thought it was tomorrow night," he said.

"Tonight," said Madeline Wherry.

"Are we supposed to dress?"

"Yes."

"Well, isn't it time you got a move on?" He took off his jacket and started undoing his necktie. "I'll take a quick shower, if you wouldn't mind putting the studs in my shirt. You know where they are."

"Yes."

"Now come on, Madeline. Don't be late just because it's Marcia. I'm going to prove to you that Marcia doesn't mean a God damn thing and I'm going to prove it tonight."

"Go take your shower," she said.

"Well, you start stirring your stumps, too," he said.

She waited until she heard the water running in his shower bath. She got up and went to his room and got an evening shirt out of his bureau and hung it over her arm. She opened the top drawer of the bureau, where he kept his studs. The little leather box was there, but she never saw it. All she saw, all she focused on, was his revolver, and she took it in her hand without hesitation. With his evening shirt still hanging over her arm she stood with her back to the bureau. The glass door of the shower bath swung open and he came out and reached for a towel.

" 'Dyou find the studs? Put that thing away, Madeline," he said.

"No, I *won't*," she said. She raised it and fired the first shot, which tore away part of his throat. The second shot broke the glass door of the shower bath, the third and fourth entered his chest, the fifth went into his belly, the sixth, which she aimed carefully, entered the region of his heart. He quivered a couple of times, then lay still, and she tossed the revolver on his bed.

She looked down at him once, then returned to her room and sat on the daybed. She looked at the shirt on her arm. "Now don't tell me you didn't deserve it, because you did," she said. "You know damn well you did, Bud Wherry." Then she put her hands to her face and sobbed. "You did, you did, you did, you did," she said.

THE BONFIRE

Kitty Bull said the final goodnights to the children, the final "no, no more stories" to the older two and paid a silent visit to the baby's room (for she firmly believed that a one-year-old can sense a break in his routine even when he is asleep). The cook and the maid were at the early movie in Southampton. The Bannings and their guests—a noisy cocktail party—had taken off for a dinner party in Wainscott, leaving all the lights on in the house next door but leaving, too, a merciful silence. The ocean was reasonably subdued, pounding the beach at long intervals and with only enough force to keep you from forgetting that it was there, that it had been angry most of the day and could be angry again.

She kicked off her Belgian slippers and went out and stood on the top of the dune. There was still enough light for a visibility of five miles, three miles, six miles. Make it three miles. It was about three miles to the Inlet, and she could see two white dots that would be fishing boats heading for the Inlet in a race against the coming darkness. The sand squishing through her toes made her wish she could run down and go for a brief swim, but she could not leave the house so soon. This was the first half hour, when Jeanie might be naughty and find some excuse to call her. She would pay no attention to the first call, and Jeanie might give up; but sometimes Jeanie would be insistent and repeat her call, louder and often, and disturb the other children.

She thanked God for the children. She thanked God . . .

Now she could not see the white dots and she would have to suppose that the fishing boats had got inside the Inlet. The visibility, whatever it had been, was now to be estimated in yards, not miles, and far far out, where the horizon had been, there were three twinkling lights, the riding lights of three other fishing boats that she had not seen before. They would be out there all night and if she got up early enough—five o'clock in the morning—they would still be there, but at six o'clock they would be gone. They were professional fishing boats, bunker boats that filled their nets, loaded up, and returned to Islip or to Baltimore with catches that would be converted into some kind of fertilizer. That, at least, was what Jerry had told her years ago. Five years ago. Six years ago. *Seven* years ago, when they had first come to this house. Could it be seven years? Almost a fifth of her life? One wave, heavier than all the others had been, struck the beach like thunder and she picked up her slippers and went inside.

In her bare feet she went upstairs and stood outside the children's rooms and listened. There was not a sound from them. She opened the door of the baby's room. She could not see him, but when she caught the rhythm of his breathing she closed the door and went downstairs again. The first half hour was more than gone, and for a moment she thought of going for a swim; but that was something she had promised Jerry never to do. Never go in that ocean alone, but especially at night. He had never permitted her to go in alone at night even when he was there in the house, watching a ball game on the TV. It isn't a question of how good a swimmer you are, or of keeping your head, he had told her. Naturally you would have sense enough to conserve your energy, and try to keep the lights of the beach cottages in front of you. But who could see *you* in the dark? Never go in alone at night, he had said; and then one night a year ago, a little tight and just arrived from the hot city, he had broken all his own rules. He had stopped for dinner at Rothman's on the way down, and you did not stop at Rothman's if you were alone, but she guessed whom he had dined with. It was not a clever guess. It was not a guess at all. It was an assumption based as much on instinct as on the things she had heard. "I feel as if I'd been dipped in oatmeal," he had said.

"You've been dipping in something stronger than oatmeal," she said.

"A few. Not enough to do any damage. I'm going for a swim."

"I can't go for a swim. Dr. Mando said not to for a while."

"That's all right. I just want to dunk."

"Why don't you just take a shower?"

"Because I want to go in the ocean! My God, Kitty."

"Well, you're always the one that says—"

"I'm *not* planning to swim to *Brazil*. If you're going to make a federal case of it, I won't go in. But my God, Kitty."

"Oh, go ahead," she said.

She could have stopped him. For a year she had told herself that she could have stopped him, and many times during the second half of that year she had wondered why she had not stopped him. She had given in to him and to his irritability and his stubbornness, but had there not been some irritability, some jealousy, on her part? Four days later they found his body near the Inlet, confirming his identity through his dental history, an X-ray photograph of a shoulder he had broken in college, and physical measurements that matched his in the Navy files. It was he, all right, beyond any reasonable doubt, and it was not necessary for her to look at him. His mother and father had been perfectly wonderful, and so had his brother. The only unpleasantness had been created by his sister, when he had been dead six months.

"You don't mind talking about Jerry, do you, Kitty?" said Edna.

"Not a bit. Why?"

"Well, because he was always against going in the ocean at night. It was so *unlike* him."

"Your father brought that up. Your mother did too."

"I know they did, and you tried to stop him. I know that, too. But can you think of any reason why Jerry would do such a complete about-face? I mean, he was my brother and we were very close."

"I know."

"I adored him. I really did."

"I know you did, Edna."

"But I wasn't blinded to his imperfections," said Edna.

"He had a few. Who hasn't?"

"Yes, who hasn't? Francine Barrow, for instance. You know what she's saying, of course."

"Yes, I do. But I didn't expect you to repeat anything Francine Barrow said. Jerry didn't commit suicide over Francine Barrow. He didn't commit suicide over anyone or anything. He was quite tight that night."

"You might have thought the cold water would have sobered him up."

"It doesn't always work that way. In fact, almost never. Haven't you ever been to a beach party where there was a lot of drinking? I haven't noticed that going in the ocean sobered them up. Quite the contrary, in some cases. I remember one night when you were tight and you went in and came out without your bikini."

"I've never been allowed to forget that," said Edna.

"Well, I only bring it up now to show that cold salt water doesn't necessarily sober you up. Jerry himself said you were really bagged that night. And you were."

"I'm perfectly willing to change the subject, if that's what you want to do, Kitty."

"No, I'd rather have this out. I knew about Francine. It started the last few months I was having the baby, and it continued for the same reason after the baby was born."

"Did you quarrel with him about it?"

"We had some minor quarrels, not over Francine. Although I suppose that was at the bottom of it. I didn't like it. You wouldn't like it if Mike slept with someone else while you were in the midst of having a baby. My first two pregnancies were fairly simple, but not this one. I was having a hard time, and

Jerry wasn't much help to my morale. I've always thought Francine was one of the worst tramps on Long Island anyway."

"So do I, for that matter."

"Well then why do you help her spread that story? Jerry did not commit suicide. I would have known if he'd had any such intentions. The only reason he came down that night was because he was playing in a tournament at the National the next day. That was on his mind, not committing suicide."

"All right, Kitty. I'm sorry I had to bring this up, but I had to."

"Yes, I suppose you did," said Kitty, and the weariness in her voice surprised her. Acute grief had gone and now there was weariness that she had not suspected, and it remained with her for many months. It was much worse than the acute grief. The doctor had told her that she need not worry about having the strength to recover from her pregnancy and take care of the children. Nature is very reliable, he had said; when something like that happened to you, a shock, a dramatic episode, Nature responded. But when the acute grief began to wear off and the postponed weariness set in, that was the time to be careful. She went to see him, and because he was a good man she told him about her sister-in-law's conversation.

"I was afraid there'd be something like that," he said. "She hit you with it at just the wrong time. I'm going to send you up to the hospital for a G.I. series."

"Is that the barium thing? I haven't got an ulcer."

"Let's make sure," said the doctor.

She saw him again in a few days. "Now you can be glad I made you swallow all that barium," he said. "There's no sign of an ulcer."

"I knew there wouldn't be," she said.

"Did you indeed?" he said. He smiled.

"Well, I was right, wasn't I?" she said.

"Gloating, hey?" He had a pencil in his hand and he began sketching on a prescription blank.

"Now what, Dr. Mando? I always know there's something when you start drawing those little pictures. Are they my insides that you're drawing, or just anyone's?"

"You're pretty fresh. I think you're greatly relieved at my good news."

"Well, why shouldn't I be? I'd *hate* to have an ulcer. But come on, Doctor, what's on your mind?"

"*You* are, Mrs. Bull. Four cigarettes just since you've been here. I'm sure your internist has spoken to you about them. I *know* he has, because we had a conversation this morning. He had the first look at your X-ray pictures, you know."

"Yes, you two keep me up in the air like a shuttlecock."

"Badminton," said the doctor.

"Don't tell me I'm not going to be able to play games."

"No, that isn't what's on my mind. You can start swimming any time you feel like it, and golf or tennis, if you're planning to go South."

"I'm staying in New York, but there are places where I can swim and play squash."

"Exercise will be good for you. Dr. Randolph will tell you that, too."

"Fine, and now you tell me what's got you drawing those pictures."

He put down his pencil and sat back in his chair, his hands folded across his chest and reminding her of a spiritual adviser. "Is there any chance that you might be getting married fairly soon?"

"No," she said. "Is there any reason why I shouldn't?"

"On the contrary, there is every reason why you should, from my point of view."

"I haven't thought about it, at least not very much. And there's no man in the offing. Some day I suppose I will. Some day my prince will come." Suddenly, inexplicably, the sound of her words made her burst into tears. The doctor bent forward and gave her one of his large, hand-rolled handkerchiefs.

"Good Lord," she said. She dried her eyes and blew her nose.

"Mm-hmm," the doctor muttered.

"May I keep the handkerchief? I'll send it back to you," she said.

"Of course," said the doctor. He opened his desk drawer and

took out a silver cigarette box. "I keep these out of sight nowadays. Have one?"

"Thanks," she said. He lit it for her. "I remember that lighter," she said.

"Yes, it's quite a beautiful piece of workmanship," he said. He looked at it and put it back in his pocket, and resumed his clerical attitude.

"It was the words of that song," she said.

"Yes, but it wasn't only the words of the song, Mrs. Bull. You know that."

"I do now. I hadn't realized that I was in any such state. But I guess I am, aren't I?"

"Be very strange if you weren't. I've known you pretty well these last six or seven years."

"Well, what do you suggest?" she said.

"I suggest that you start going out a little bit."

"In the hope of meeting some man," she said.

"Naturally."

"And having an affair with him, even if I don't fall in love with him?"

"You may have to wait a long time before you'll admit that you're in love with anyone."

"Yes, you're right," she said.

"In fact, you could conceivably go through the rest of your life without falling in love again."

"Yes," she said.

"Your husband left you three children, and the circumstances of his death. No other man will be able to make that deep an impression on you. On your life. On your memories. So don't expect anyone to."

"You didn't like my husband, did you, Dr. Mando?"

"That's not a very nice question to ask me, young woman. And I'm not going to answer it. But if he were my own son I'd still give you the same advice. You're in your early thirties and most of your life lies ahead of you. That includes having children, if you want any more. And you should, or these nice children you have now will become something that they shouldn't."

"What's that?"

"Walking reminder of your husband, of course. Making it impossible for you to start your new life. I hope you'll meet an interesting man and marry him and have children right away."

"I don't think that's going to happen," she said.

"It won't if you don't give it a chance," said the doctor. "Well, when do you want to see me again?"

"When do *you* want to see *me?*"

"In about three months. Miss Murphy will give you an appointment."

"Not till then? That's the longest I've ever gone without seeing you. Aren't you going to miss me?"

He smiled. "Yes, as a matter of fact I will. But it'll do you good to stay out of here for a while. Save you money too."

"You're such a lovely man, Dr. Mando. You really are," she said.

"Of course I am," he said. "My patients are nice, too. Some of them."

"Me?"

"Go on, young woman. There are women waiting," he said. "And I have to clean out this ash tray."

There was no "interesting" man at any of the small dinner parties she went to. Among the new men there were the pitiers, depressing fellows who acted as though Jerry had died last week; there were the others who were so determinedly cheerful that they seemed to deny that Jerry had ever lived at all. Among the men she had known in the past there were the instant patriarchs, contemporaries of Jerry's who took it upon themselves to plan her life for her; and, not surprisingly, there were two who were ready to move into her life. One of them was a dirty talker, who had never talked dirty to her while Jerry was alive; and the other was Edna's husband, Mike, who had always looked at her from the edges of groups with a dumb lechery that he now expressed in terms of love. "I think you've always known how I felt about you, Kitty," he said.

"Not exactly," she said. It was malicious, drawing him out, but she had not forgiven Edna for her inquisition.

"Maybe not exactly, but you must have had some idea," said Mike.

"Some idea, more or less," she said.

"Invite me to dinner some night. Just me."

"Without Edna?"

"That's the general idea," he said. "I suppose you're going to say that's impossible, but it isn't."

"But it is. If I invited you alone, there could only be one interpretation of that. There isn't any other interpretation."

"Oh, I see. You mean that you'd be the aggressor?"

"Not only the aggressor, but—well, yes, the aggressor. The troublemaker."

"Would you go away with me? If we went in my car, I'd be the aggressor, if that's what you object to. What I'm trying to tell you is—we've gotten sidetracked with this aggressor talk. I want you to see me without Edna, without anyone. To get used to me. And if I can convince you—to marry me."

"Oh."

"I know you're not all that anxious to get married again so soon. But it would take time in any case. Unfortunately people don't just say 'I've had it' and end a marriage that way. But I've been in love with you for a long time. We would have had this conversation sooner or later, even if Jerry had lived."

"I wonder," she said.

"You needn't. He kept you pregnant most of the time or I'd have spoken up sooner."

"That was very considerate of you, Mike."

"Is that sarcasm?"

"Not at all," she said.

"The week after next I'm going to Pinehurst. Come with me. I'm taking my car because it's more convenient. I'm making stops on the way down and then circling back through West Virginia, Ohio, and Pennsylvania. I'll be in Pinehurst for three days, a business convention, and you probably wouldn't want to do that, but you could join me when the convention's over, and we could have the better part of a week together. The most I'd have to spend with my business acquaintances would be two or three hours a day, and you like to read. What do you say?"

"Oh, you know what I'm going to say, Mike. How could I nip off for a week, leaving three small children and telling the nurse that I'd be at such-and-such a motel?"

"You're so practical," he said. "What if I sent Edna away, that is, gave her a trip abroad?"

"I don't know. Yes, I do know. I think that when I'm ready to do anything in that department, I *am* going to have to be the aggressor. I'm the only one that will know when I'm ready—and I'm not ready now."

"That Jerry. He's still got a tight grip on you, hasn't he?"

"Or I have a tight grip on myself. One or the other, or maybe both."

"When you loosen up a little, will you let me know? I'm serious. You can trust me, you know."

"You mean if I just wanted to have sex?"

"Yes. Don't you ever want sex? You've had a lot of it. With Jerry, I mean."

"And for seven years with no one else. So, when the time comes—I'm awfully tired of the word—but I'll be the aggressor. I much prefer 'on the make.'"

"You'll never go on the make, Kitty."

"Except that I did with Jerry. I wanted him, I went after him, and I got him. And I've lost him."

She would have been more abrupt and far more cruel with Mike if she had not realized, midway in the conversation, that the conversation was useful to the clarification of her problems. Mike was in no sense a stimulating man, but he had helped her to see that the next man in her life would have to be one she chose. Whimsically she told herself that she owed something to Mike for his collaboration, and in that mood she thought of inviting him to spend a night with her. But he was a clod and he would be around again and again, believing himself to be in love with her and upsetting the lives of too many people. Nevertheless she felt better for having come even that remotely close. Very tentatively, a toe in the water, she was back in life once more.

It was enough to go on for a while, and there were other things to keep her busy. At home there were the children, uncomprehending of the mystery of death or, in the case of the baby, petulantly demanding that she keep him alive. The older two were forgetting about their father. Kitty put a cabinet-size photograph of Jerry in a silver frame and set it on a table in the livingroom of the New York apartment. It was two days before Jeanie noticed it. She stood in front of the picture for a moment, and Kitty waited for her comment.

"That's Daddy," said Jeanie.

"Yes. It's my favorite picture of him. Do you like it?"

"I guess so."

"But not very much," said Kitty. "What is there that you don't like about it?"

"He's so serious, Mum."

"And that's not the way you remember him? Well, that's because when he was with you and your little brothers he *wasn't* very serious. Nearly always laughing. Little jokes and so forth."

"Didn't he have jokes with you too?"

"Oh, yes. Lots of them."

"Tell me one," said the child.

"A joke that he told me? Well, let me think. A joke that he told me. There was one that Grandfather Bull told him. About an oyster?"

"Tell it to me."

"It's sort of a riddle. What kind of a noise annoys an oyster? Do you know the answer?"

"What?"

"A *noisy* noise annoys an oyster."

"Oh, that's old."

"It sure is. See if I can think of another. Most of his jokes with me were about people. I'll think of some and write them down so I won't forget them. And I'll see if I can find a picture of him smiling. Where shall we put it, if I find one?"

"I don't know. Over there, I guess. Mummy, can I watch TV after supper?"

"Nope. Before supper, yes. After supper, off it goes."

The older boy, Timothy, was only three, cheerful and strong

and increasingly able to take his own part when his sister bullied him. The Irish nurse would say to him, "You're the man of the house, Timothy."

"I yam not a man. I'm a boy, silly."

"You'll be a man soon enough, then."

"You're silly, Margaret. You're silly, silly, silly. You think a boy is a man. You're a man. You have a moustache."

"For that somebody gets no pudding this supper."

"It isn't pudding, it's junket, and I hate junket. So yah!"

And there was the baby, now old enough to follow her with his eyes when he was serene and to scream for her and only for her when he was not.

There was more money than she had expected, and many more lawyers to see. There were certain financial advantages to be gained by a delay in settling Jerry's estate. "This could drag on for another year at least," said her lawyer. "But we want it to. Now for instance, Mrs. Bull, there's the matter of your husband's insurance. He carried a lot of insurance, much more than young men usually do nowadays. But he could afford it, so he did. The interesting thing here is that we've been arguing with the insurance company about the circumstances of your husband's death. We feel that accidental drowning may change the picture to your advantage. On the other hand *they* feel—I have to say this—that the possibility of suicide alters the picture in their favor. The medical examiner's report said accidental death by drowning, but the insurance company is trying to inject the element of suicide, not because they think they can get away with it, but maybe in the hope that we won't collect anything extra, like double indemnity. Give and take, you know. That's their position. But they know perfectly well that we're prepared to go to court. And by prepared I mean that you have enough money without insurance to not have to make a quick settlement. By the way, who is a Mrs. Barrow? Francine Barrow? She wasn't at your house the night your husband lost his life, was she?"

"No. She was a friend of his. And mine, I suppose. My husband had dinner with her early that evening, over on the North Shore. But she wasn't in our house. She's never been in our house."

"No, I shouldn't think so. In a very roundabout way we found out that the insurance company is basing its whole argument on some story of hers."

"Well, she's a congenital liar, among other things."

"That's a good thing to know," said Mr. Hastings. "You understand, Mrs. Bull, that if we collect a large amount of insurance, it'll go a long way toward paying your inheritance taxes. In fact we may come out a little ahead of the game. You'd have no objection to suing the insurance company, I hope?"

"None whatever," said Kitty. "Especially if Mrs. Barrow is on their side."

"When Mrs. Barrow understands a little better what could happen to her in court, she may not want to testify. I know if I were her lawyer I'd tell her to think twice."

"She doesn't embarrass very easily, Mr. Hastings. In plain language, she's a tramp."

"It's a curious thing, though, Mrs. Bull. There's something about a courtroom. The austerity of the furniture. The flag. The judge's robe. The strange language. It produces an atmosphere that's the next thing to a church, and it's intended to. And a woman like this Mrs. Barrow, although she may be shameless in her everyday life, when she gets in court a remarkable change comes over her. They fight like the devil to stay respectable. The insurance companies have very good lawyers. None better. And I seriously doubt that they'd want her to testify. In short, Mrs. Bull, her lawyer will advise her to shut up, and the insurance lawyers won't want her. But I have to give you the whole picture, to explain why we're moving so slowly."

"I'm in no hurry," said Kitty.

"That's good, that's fine. I'm sorry you have to come down here so often. I could save you some of these trips. There's probably a notary public in your neighborhood."

"I like coming down here. It's almost that same atmosphere you just described, the courtroom. And it makes me feel useful, as though I were doing it for my children. Although I'm not."

"Yes you are," said Mr. Hastings.

"Well, maybe I am," she said. "But doing things for them is the same as doing them for myself. It's what I like."

She put on a sweater and went out again and sat on the top of a dune. There were stars but no moon and down the beach at someone's cottage—she was not sure whose—there was a sizable bonfire and moving about it, like comical figures in some pagan rite, were the members of a beach picnic. They were too far away to be recognizable, even to be distinguishable as to sex. It seemed to be a fairly good-sized party and she was glad that the noise they would make was no closer to her house. It was a party of the young, that much she could determine by their frenetic activity. A great deal of running about, chasing, and, as she watched, two of the figures picked up a third figure by the hands and feet and carried it to the ocean and dropped it in. This might go on all night. It was at the McDades', the only cottage in that section that would be having that kind of party for the young.

The young. *She* was young. She had been a young wife, she was a young widow, and people like Dr. Mando continually called her "young woman." She would still be young, really, when those children now asleep in her cottage would be having beach picnics like the McDades'. She was old to them now, as a parent is old to all young children; but to Jerry's father and mother she was so young that they had worried about her ability to cope. She was too young to have been invited to any of the Bannings' noisy parties. She was only four or five years older than some of the members of the McDade picnic. Angus McDade was twenty-six, George Lasswell was twenty-six or seven. Harry Stephenson had been one of Jerry's favorite golfing companions. They would all be at the McDades' picnic.

Something got her to her feet, and she knew what it was. She denied it angrily, then admitted it so that she could dismiss it. It was a word that had first come up in her conversation with Mike, and the word had stayed with her. Aggressor. Well, she was not quite being an aggressor if she was being drawn to the beach bonfire like a moth to a flame. They would be nice to her, they would offer her food and drink, and they would admire her in the ways that she was used to being admired. She would sit with them and drink beer out of a can and smoke a cigarette and in a little while they would start singing and she would sing with them. She would only stay a little while.

She kicked off her slippers. It would make her seem more like one of them if she arrived in her bare feet. She walked down to where the sand was hardest, at the dry edge of the beach that was not being licked by the tide. She turned and headed toward the bonfire, and she was almost very sure of herself, and her step was light. She did not feel that she was leaving footprints on the hard sand.

It was a long way, and she could make out the figures before she could hear them. She was so close to the ocean that its sounds were all she could hear for the first fifty yards, the first seventy-five yards, the first hundred. And then the voices began to penetrate the sounds of the ocean. She walked on and the voices grew more distinct, the voices of young women and young men, a harsh and frightening chorus of people who did not want her. She stopped to listen. Now she could hear baritone derision and alto contempt and soprano coquetry answered by the baritone derision, and though they were ignorant of her existence they were commanding her to stay away.

She turned and for a terrifying second her eyes, so long focused on the bonfire, looked into blackness. She could not move. Then she looked up at the sky until she could see a star, and then there were more stars and to her left were the lights of the cottages on the dunes. She ran all the way home.

THE HARDWARE MAN

Lou Mauser had not always had money, and yet it would be hard to imagine him without it. He had owned the store—with, of course, some help from the bank—since he was in his middle twenties, and that was twenty years ago as of 1928. Twenty years is a pretty long time for a man to go without a notable financial failure, but Lou Mauser had done it, and when it has been that long, a man's worst enemies cannot say that it was all luck. They said it about Lou, but they said it in such a way as to make it sound disparaging to him while not making themselves appear foolish. It would have been very foolish to deny that Lou had worked hard or that he had been a clever business man. "You can't say it was all luck," said Tom Esterly, who was a competitor of Lou's. "You might just as well say he sold his soul to the devil. Not that he wouldn't have, mind you. But he didn't have to. Lou always seemed to be there with the cash at the right moment, and that's one of the great secrets of success. Be there with the cash when the right proposition comes along."

Lou had the cash, or got hold of it—which is the same thing—when Ada Bowler wanted to sell her late husband's hardware store. Lou was in his middle twenties then, and he had already been working in the store at least ten years, starting as a stock boy at five dollars a week. By the time he was eighteen he was a walking inventory of Bowler's stock; he knew where everything was, everything, and he knew how much everything was worth; wholesale, retail, special prices to certain contractors, the different mark-ups for different customers. A farmer came in to buy a harness snap, charge him a dime; but if another farmer, one who bought his barn paint at Bowler's, wanted a harness snap, you let him have it for a nickel. You didn't have to tell Sam Bowler what you were doing. Sam Bowler relied on your good sense to do things like that. If a boy was buying a catcher's mitt, you threw in a nickel Rocket, and sure as hell when that boy was ready to buy an Iver Johnson bicycle he would come to Bowler's instead of sending away to a mail-order house. And Lou Mauser at eighteen had discovered something that had never occurred to Sam Bowler: the rich people who lived on Lantenengo Street were even more appreciative when you gave them a little something for nothing—an oil can for a kid's bike, an ice pick for the kitchen—than people who had to think twice about spending a quarter. Well, maybe they weren't *more* appreciative, but they had the money to show their appreciation. Give a Lantenengo Street boy a nickel Rocket, and his father or his uncle would buy him a dollar-and-a-quarter ball. Give a rich woman an ice pick and you'd sell her fifty foot of garden hose and a sprinkler and a lawn mower. It was all a question of knowing which ones to give things to, and Lou knew so well that when he needed the cash to buy out Sam Bowler's widow, he actually had two banks to choose from instead of just having to accept one bank's terms.

Practically overnight he became the employer of men twice his age, and he knew which ones to keep and which to fire. As soon as the papers were signed that made him the owner, he went to the store and summoned Dora Minzer, the bookkeeper, and Arthur Davis, the warehouse man. He closed his office door so that no one outside could hear what he had to say, although the other employees could see through the glass partitions.

"Give me your keys, Arthur," said Lou.

"My keys? Sure," said Arthur.

"Dora, you give me your keys, too," said Lou.

"They're in my desk drawer," said Dora Minzer.

"Get them."

Dora left the office.

"I don't understand this, Lou," said Arthur.

"If you don't, you will, as soon as Dora's back."

Dora returned and laid her keys on Lou's desk. "There," she said.

"Arthur says he doesn't understand why I want your keys. You do, don't you, Dora?"

"Well—maybe I do, maybe I don't." She shrugged.

"You two are the only ones that I'm asking for their keys," said Lou.

Arthur took a quick look at Dora Minzer, who did not look at him. "Yeah, what's the meaning of it, Lou?"

"The meaning of it is, you both put on your coat and hat and get out."

"Fired?" said Arthur.

"Fired is right," said Lou.

"No notice? I been here twenty-two years. Dora was here pretty near that long."

"Uh-huh. And I been here ten. Five of those ten the two of you been robbing Sam Bowler that I know of. That I know of. I'm pretty sure you didn't only start robbing him five years ago."

"I'll sue you for slander," said Arthur.

"Go ahead," said Lou.

"Oh, shut up, Arthur," said Dora. "He knows. I told you he was too smart."

"He'd have a hard time proving anything," said Arthur.

"Yeah, but when I did you know where you'd be. You and Dora, and two purchasing agents, and two building contractors. All in it together. Maybe there's more than them, but those I could prove. The contractors, I'm licked. The purchasing agents, I want their companies' business, so all I'm doing there is get them fired. What are you gonna tell them in Sunday School next Sunday, Arthur?"

"*She* thought of it," said Arthur Davis, looking at Dora Minzer.

316

"That I don't doubt. It took brains to fool Sam Bowler all those years. What'd you do with your share, Dora?"

"My nephew. I educated him and started him up in business. He owns a drug store in Elmira, New York."

"Then he ought to take care of you. Where did yours go, Arthur?"

"Huh. With five kids on my salary, putting them through High, clothes and doctor bills, the wife and her doctor bills. Music lessons. A piano. Jesus Christ, I wonder Sam didn't catch on. How did *you* catch on?"

"You just answered that yourself. I used to see all those kids of yours, going to Sunday School, all dolled up."

"Well, they're all married or got jobs," said Arthur Davis. "I guess I'll find something. Who are you gonna tell about this? If I say I quit."

"What the hell do you expect me to do? You're a couple of thieves, both of you. Sam Bowler treated everybody right. There's eight other people working here that raised families and didn't steal. I don't feel any pity for you. As soon as you get caught you try to blame it all on Dora. And don't forget this, Arthur." He leaned forward. *"You were gonna steal from me.* The two of you. This morning a shipment came in. Two hundred rolls of tarpaper. An hour later, fifty rolls went out on the wagon, but show me where we got any record of that sale of fifty rolls. That was this morning, Arthur. You didn't even wait one day, you or Dora."

"That was him, did that," said Dora. "I told him to wait. Stupid."

"They're all looking at us, out on the floor," said Arthur.

"Yes, and probably guessing," said Lou. "I got no more to say to either one of you. Just get out."

They rose, and Dora went to the outer office and put on her coat and hat and walked to the street door without speaking to anyone. Arthur went to the back stairs that led to the warehouse. There he unpacked a crate of brand-new Smith & Wesson revolvers and broke open a case of ammunition. He then put a bullet through his skull, and Lou Mauser entered a new phase of his business career.

□

He had a rather slow first year. People thought of him as a cold-blooded young man who had driven a Sunday School superintendent to suicide. But as the scandal was absorbed into local history, the unfavorable judgment was gradually amended until it more closely conformed with the early opinion of the business men, which was sympathetic to Lou. Dora Minzer, after all, had gone away, presumably to Elmira, New York; and though there were rumors about the purchasing agents of two independent mining companies, Lou did not publicly implicate them. The adjusted public opinion of Lou Mauser had it that he had behaved very well indeed, and that he had proven himself to be a better business man than Sam Bowler. Only a few people chose to keep alive the story of the Arthur Davis suicide, and those few probably would have found some other reason to be critical of Lou if Arthur had lived.

Lou, of course, did not blame himself, and during the first year of his ownership of the store, while he was under attack, he allowed his resentment to harden him until he became in fact the ruthless creature they said he was. He engaged in price-cutting against the other hardware stores, and one of the newer stores was driven out of business because of its inability to compete with Lou Mauser and Tom Esterly.

"All right, Mr. Esterly," said Lou. "There's one less of us. Do you want to call it quits?"

"You started it, young fellow," said Tom Esterly. "And I can last as long as you can and maybe a *little* bit longer. If you want to start making a profit again, that's up to you. But I don't intend to enter into any agreement with you, now or any other time."

"You cut your prices when I did," said Lou.

"You bet I did."

"Then you're just as much to blame as I am, for what happened to McDonald. You helped put him out of business, and you'll get your share of what's left."

"Yes, and maybe I'll get your share, too," said Tom Esterly. "The Esterlys were in business before the Civil War."

"I know that. I would have bought your store if I could have. Maybe I will yet."

"Don't bank on it, young fellow. Don't bank on it. Let's see how good your credit is when you need it. Let's see how long the jobbers and the manufacturers will carry you. I *know* how far they'll carry Esterly Brothers. We gave some of those manufacturers their first orders, thirty, forty years ago. My father was dealing with some of them when Sam Bowler was in diapers. Mauser, you have a lot to learn."

"Esterly and Mauser. That's the sign I'd like to put up some day."

"It'll be over my dead body. I'd go out of business first. Put up the shutters."

"Oh, I didn't want you as a partner. I'd just continue the name."

"Will you please get out of my store?"

Tom Esterly was a gentleman, a graduate of Gibbsville High and Gettysburg College, prominent in Masonic circles, and on the boards of the older charities. The word upstart was not in his working vocabulary and he had no epithet for Lou Mauser, but he disliked the fellow so thoroughly that he issued one of his rare executive orders to his clerks: hereafter, when Esterly Brothers were out of an article, whether it was a five-cent article or a fifty-dollar one, the clerks were not to suggest that the customer try Bowler's. For Tom Esterly this was a serious change of policy, and represented an attitude that refused to admit the existence of Mauser's competition. On the street he inclined his head when Mauser spoke to him, but he did not actually speak to Mauser.

Lou Mauser's next offense was to advertise. Sam Bowler had never advertised, and Esterly Brothers' advertising consisted solely of complimentary cards in the high school annual and the program of the yearly concert of the Lutheran church choir. These cards read, "Esterly Bros., Est. 1859, 211 N. Main St.," and that was all. No mention of the hardware business. Tom Esterly was shocked and repelled to see a full-page ad in each of the town newspapers, announcing a giant spring sale at Bowler's

Hardware Store, Lou Mauser, Owner & Proprietor. It was the first hardware store ad in Gibbsville history and, worse, it was the first time Mauser had put his name on Sam Bowler's store. Tom Esterly went and had a look, and, yes, Mauser not only had put his name in the ad; he had his name painted on the store windows in lettering almost as large as Bowler's. The sale was, of course, a revival of Mauser's price-cutting tactic, even though it was advertised to last only three days. And Mauser offered legitimate bargains; some items, Tom knew, were going at cost. While the sale was on there were almost no customers in Esterly Brothers. "They're all down at Mauser's," said Jake Potts, Tom's head clerk.

"You mean Bowler's," said Tom.

"Well, yes, but I bet you he takes Sam's name off inside of another year," said Jake.

"Where is he getting the money, Jake?"

"Volume. What they call volume. He got two fellows with horse and buggy calling on the farmers."

"Salesmen?"

"Two of them. They talk Pennsylvania Dutch and they go around to the farms. Give the woman a little present the first time, and they drive their buggies right up in the field and talk to the farmers. Give the farmers a pack of chewing tobacco and maybe a tie-strap for the team. My brother-in-law down the Valley told me. They don't try to sell nothing the first visit, but the farmer remembers that chewing tobacco. Next time the farmer comes to market, if he needs anything he goes to Bowler's."

"Well, farmers are slow pay. We never catered much to farmers."

"All the same, Tom, it takes a lot of paint to cover a barn, and they're buying their paint off of Mauser. My brother-in-law told me Mauser's allowing credit all over the place. Any farmer with a cow and a mule can get credit."

"There'll be a day of reckoning, with that kind of foolishness. And it's wrong, *wrong*, to get those farmers in debt. You know how they are, some of them. They come in here to buy one thing, and before they know it they run up a bill for things they don't need."

"Yes, I know it. So does Mauser. But he's getting the volume, Tom. Small profit, big volume."

"Wait till he has to send a bill collector around to the farmers. His chewing tobacco won't do him any good then," said Tom Esterly.

"No, I guess not," said Jake Potts.

"The cash. I still don't see where he gets his cash. You say volume, but volume on credit sales won't supply him with cash."

"Well, I guess if you show the bank a lot of accounts receivable. And he has a lot of them, Tom. A lot. You get everybody owing you money, most of them are going to pay you some day. Most people around here pay their bills."

"You criticizing our policy, Jake?"

"Well, times change, Tom, and you gotta fight fire with fire."

"Would you want to work for a man like Mauser?"

"No, and I told him so," said Jake Potts.

"He wanted to hire you away from me?"

"A couple months ago, but I said no. I been here too long, and I might as well stay till I retire. But look down there, Tom. Down there between the counters. One lady customer. All the others are at Mauser's sale."

"He tried to steal you away from me. That's going too far," said Tom Esterly. "Would you mind telling me what he offered you?"

"Thirty a week and a percentage on new business."

"Thinking you'd get our customers to follow you there. Well, I guess I have to raise you to thirty. But the way it looks now, I can't offer you a percentage on new business. It's all going in the opposite direction."

"I didn't ask for no raise, Tom."

"You get it anyway, starting this week. If you quit, I'd just about have to go out of business. I don't have anybody to take your place. And I keep putting off the decision, who'll be head clerk when you retire. Paul Schlitzer's next in line, but he's getting forgetful. I guess it'll be Norman Johnson. Younger."

"Don't count on Norm, Tom."

"Mauser been making him offers?"

"I don't know for sure, but that's my guess. When a fellow starts acting independent, he has some good reason behind it. Norm's been getting in late in the morning and when ha' past five comes he don't wait for me to tell him to pull down the shades."

"Have you said anything to him?"

"Not so far. But we better start looking for somebody else. It don't have to be a hardware man. Any bright young fellow with experience working behind a counter. I can show him the ropes, before I retire."

"All right, I'll leave that up to you," said Tom Esterly. On his next encounter with Lou Mauser he stopped him.

"Like to talk to you a minute," said Tom Esterly.

"Fine and dandy," said Mauser. "Let's move over to the curb, out of people's way."

"I don't have much to say," said Tom Esterly. "I just want to tell you you're going too far, trying to hire my people away from me."

"It's a free country, Mr. Esterly. If a man wants to better himself. And I guess Jakes Potts bettered himself. Did you meet my offer?"

"Jake Potts wouldn't have worked for you, offer or no offer."

"But he's better off now than he was before. He ought to be thankful to me. Mister, I'll make an offer to anybody I want to hire, in your store or anybody else's. I don't have to ask your permission. Any more than I asked your permission to run a big sale. I had new customers in my store that I never saw before, even when Sam Bowler was the owner. I made *you* an offer, so why shouldn't I make an offer to fellows that work for you?"

"Good day, sir," said Tom Esterly.

"Good day to you," said Lou Mauser.

Tom Esterly was prepared for the loss of Norman Johnson, but when Johnson revealed a hidden talent for window decorating, he felt cheated. The window that attracted so much attention that it was written up in both newspapers was an autumnal camping scene that occupied all the space in Mauser's window. Two dummies, dressed in gunning costume, were seated at a campfire outside a tent. An incandescent lamp simulated the glow of the fire, and real pine and spruce branches and fake grass were used to provide a woodland effect. Every kind of weapon, from shotgun to automatic pistol, was on display, leaning against logs or lying on the fake grass. There were hunting knives and compasses, Marble match cases and canteens, cots and blankets, shell boxes of canvas and leather, fireless cookers, fishing tackle, carbide and kerosene lamps, an Old Towne canoe, gun cases and revolver holsters, duck calls and decoys and flasks and first-aid kits. Wherever there was space between the merchandise items, Norman Johnson had put stuffed chipmunk and quail, and peering out from the pine and spruce were the mounted heads of a cinnamon bear, a moose, an elk, a deer, and high above it all was a stuffed wildcat, permanently snarling.

All day long men would stop and stare, and after school small boys would shout and point and argue and wish. There had never been anything like it in Bowler's or Esterly Brothers' windows, and when the display was removed at Thanksgiving time there were expressions of regret. The small boys had to find some place else to go. But Norman Johnson's hunting-camp window became an annual event, a highly profitable one for Lou Mauser.

"Maybe we should never of let Norm go," said Jake Potts.

"He's right where he belongs," said Tom Esterly. "Right exactly where he belongs. That's the way those medicine shows do business. Honest value, good merchandise, that's what we were founded on and no tricks."

"We only sold two shotguns and not any rifles this season, Tom. The next thing we know we'll lose the rifle franchise."

"Well, we never did sell many rifles. This is mostly shotgun country."

"I don't know," said Jake. "We used to do a nice business in .22's. We must of sold pretty close to three hundred of the .22 pump gun, and there's a nice steady profit in the cartridges."

"I'll grant you we used to sell the .22 rifle, other years. But they're talking about a law prohibiting them in the borough limits. Ever since the Leeds boy put the Kerry boy's eye out."

"Tom, you won't face facts," said Jake. "We're losing business to this fellow, and it ain't only in the sporting goods line or any one line. It's every which way. Kitchen utensils. Household tools. Paints and varnishes. There's never the people in the store there used to be. When you's first in charge, after your Pa passed on, just about the only thing we didn't sell was something to eat. If you can eat it, we don't sell it, was our motto."

"That was never our motto. That was just a funny saying," said Tom Esterly.

"Well, yes. But we used to have funny sayings like that. My clerks used to all have their regular customers. Man'd come in and buy everything from the same clerk. Had to be waited on by the same clerk no matter what they come in to buy. Why, I can remember old Mrs. Stokes one day she come in to borrow my umbrella, and I was off that day and she wouldn't take anybody else's umbrella. That's the kind of customers we used to have. But where are those people today? They're down at Lou Mauser's. Why? Because for instance when school opened in September every boy and girl in the public and the Catholic school got a foot-rule from Lou Mauser. They maybe cost him a half a cent apiece, and say there's a thousand children in school. Five dollars."

"Jake, you're always telling me those kind of things. You make me wonder if you wouldn't rather be working for Mauser."

"I'll tell you anything if it's for your own good. You don't have your Pa or your Uncle Ed to tell you no more. It's for my own good too, I'll admit. I retire next year, and I won't get my fifty a month if you have to close down."

"Close down? You mean run out of business by Mauser?"

"Unless you do something to meet the competition. Once before you said Mauser would have trouble with the jobbers and the manufacturers. Instead of which the shoe is on the other foot now. Don't fool yourself, Tom. Those manufacturers go by the orders we send in, and some articles we're overstocked from last year."

"I'll tell you this. I'd sooner go out of business than do things his way. Don't worry. You'll get your pension. I have other sources of income besides the store."

"If you have to close the store I'll go without my pension. I won't take charity. I'll get other work."

"With Mauser."

"No, I won't work for Mauser. That's one thing I never will do. He as good as put the gun to Arthur Davis's head, and Arthur was a friend of mine, crook or no crook. I don't know what Mauser said to Arthur that day, but whatever it was, Arthur didn't see no other way out. That kind of a man I wouldn't work for. He has blood on his hands, to my way of thinking. When I meet Arthur Davis in the after life I don't want him looking at me and saying I wasn't a true friend."

"Arthur would never say that about you, Jake."

"He might. You didn't know Arthur Davis as good as I did. There was a man that was all worries. I used to walk home from work with him sometimes. First it was worr'ing because Minnie wasn't sure she was gonna marry him. Then all them children, and Minnie sick half the time, but the children had to look just so. Music lessons. A little money to get them started when they got married. They say it was Dora Minzer showed him how they could knock down off of Sam Bowler, and I believe that. But I didn't believe what they said about something going on between him and Dora. No. Them two, they both had a weakness for money and that was all there was between them. How much they stole off of Sam Bowler we'll never know, but Arthur's share was put to good use, and Sam never missed it. Neither did Ada Bowler. Arthur wouldn't of stole that money if Sam and Ada had children."

"Now you're going too far. You don't know that, and I don't believe it. Arthur did what Dora told him to. And what about the disgrace? Wouldn't Arthur's children rather be brought up poor than have their father die a thief?"

"I don't know," said Jake. "Some of it was honest money. Nobody knows how much was stolen money. The children didn't know any of it was stolen money till the end. By that time they all had a good bringing-up. All a credit to their parents and their church and the town. A nicer family you couldn't hope to see. And they were brought up honest. Decent respectable youngsters, all of them. You can't blame them if they didn't ask their father where the money was coming from. Sam Bowler didn't get suspicious, did he? The only one got suspicious was Lou Mauser. And they say he kept his mouth shut for six or seven years, so he was kind of in on it. If I ever saw one of our fellows look like he was knocking down off of you, I'd report it. But Lou Mauser never let a peep out of him till he was the owner. I sometimes wonder maybe he was hoping they'd steal so much they'd bankrupt Sam, and then he could buy the store cheaper."

"Well, now that's interesting," said Tom Esterly. "I wouldn't put it past him for a minute."

"I don't say it's true, but it'd be like him," said Jake. "No, I'd never go to work for that fellow. Even at my age I'd rather dig ditches."

"You'll never have to dig ditches as long as I'm alive, and don't say you won't take charity You'll take your pension from Esterly Brothers regardless of whether we're still in business or not. So don't let me hear any more of that kind of talk. In fact, go on back to work. There's a customer down there."

"Wants the loan of my umbrella, most likely," said Jake. "Raining, out."

Esterly Brothers lasted longer than Jake Potts expected, and longer than Jake Potts himself. There were some bad years, easy to explain, but there were years in which the store showed a profit, and it was difficult to explain that. Lou Mauser expanded; he bought the store property adjoining his. He opened branch stores in two other towns in the county. He dropped the Bowler name completely. Esterly Brothers stayed put and as is, the middle of the store as dark as usual, so that the electric lights had to burn all day. The heavy hardware store fragrance—something between the pungency of a blacksmith's shop and the sweetness of the apothecary's—was missing from Lou Mauser's well-ventilated buildings, and he staffed his business with young go-getters. But some of the old Esterly Brothers' customers returned after temporarily defecting to Mauser's, and at Esterly's they found two or three of the aging clerks whom they had last seen at Mauser's, veterans of the Bowler days. Although he kept it to himself, Tom Esterly had obviously decided to meet the go-getter's competition with an atmosphere that was twenty years behind the times. Cash customers had to wait while their money was sent to the back of the store on an overhead trolley, change made, and the change returned in the wooden cup that was screwed to the trolley wire. Tom never did put in an electric cash register, and the only special sale he held was when he offered a fifty percent reduction on his entire stock on the occasion of his going out of business. Three successive bad years, the only time it had happened since the founding of the store, were unarguable, and he put an ad in both papers to announce his decision. His announcement was simple:

50% Off
Entire Stock
Going Out of Business
Sale Commences Aug. 1, 1922
ESTERLY BROTHERS
Est. 1859
Open 8 A.M.—9 P.M. During Sale
All Sales Cash Only—All Sales Final

On the morning after the advertisements appeared, Tom Esterly went to his office and found, not to his surprise, Lou Mauser awaiting his appearance.

"Well, what can I do for *you?*" said Tom.

"I saw your ad. I didn't know it was that bad," said Lou. "I'm honestly sorry."

"I don't see why," said Tom. "It's what you've been aiming at. Why did you come here? If you want to buy anything, my clerks will wait on you."

"I'll buy your entire stock, twenty cents on the dollar."

"I think I'll do better this way, selling to the public."

"There'll be a lot left over."

"I'll give that away," said Tom Esterly.

"Twenty cents on the dollar, Mr. Esterly, and you won't have to give none of it away."

"You'd want me to throw in the good will and fixtures," said Esterly.

"Well, yes."

"I might be tempted to sell to you. The stock and the fixtures. But the good will would have to be separate."

"How much for the good will?" said Lou Mauser.

"A million dollars cash. Oh, I know it isn't worth it, Mauser, but I wouldn't sell it to you for any less. In other words, it isn't for sale to you. A week from Saturday night at nine o'clock, this store goes out of business forever. But no part of it belongs to you."

"The last couple years you been running this store like a hobby. You lost money hand over fist."

"I had it to lose, and those three years gave me more pleasure than all the rest put together. When this store closes a lot of people are going to miss it. Not because it was a store. *You* have a *store*. But we had something better. We never had to give away foot-rules to schoolchildren, or undercut our competitors. We never did any of those things, and before we *would* do them we decided to close up shop. But first we gave some of the people something to remember. Our kind of store, not yours, Mauser."

"Are you one of those that held it against me because of Arthur Davis?"

"No."

"Then what did you hold against me?"

"Sam Bowler gave you your first job, promoted you regularly, gave you raises, encouraged you. How did you repay him? By looking the other way all the time that you knew Arthur Davis and Dora Minzer were robbing him. Some say you did it because you hoped Sam would go bankrupt and you could buy the business cheap. Maybe yes, maybe no. That part isn't what I hold against you. It was you looking the other way, never telling Sam what they were doing to him. *That* was when you killed Arthur Davis, Mauser. Sam Bowler was the kind of man that if you'd told him about Arthur and Dora, he would have kept it quiet and given them both another chance. You never gave them another chance. You didn't even give them the chance to make restitution. I don't know about Dora Minzer, but Arthur Davis had a conscience, and a man that has a conscience is entitled to put it to work. Arthur Davis would have spent the rest of his life trying to pay Sam back, and he'd be alive today, still paying Ada Bowler, no doubt. Having a hard time, no doubt. But alive and with his conscience satisfied. You didn't kill Arthur by firing him that day. You killed him a long time before that by looking the other way. And I'm sure you don't understand a word I'm saying."

"No wonder you're going out of business. You should of been a preacher."

"I thought about it," said Tom Esterly. "But I didn't have the call."

ANDREA

Nearly everything she said was truthful, but because she laughed so much her friends often believed she was joking and remained her friends. She had beautiful teeth, even and strong all the way back, and some of her friends had been known to remark that it was such a pleasure to look at her teeth that it actually did not matter much what she said. There were, of course, a few people who were not deceived by her laughter or diverted by the display of her teeth, and those people hated her. "How can you hate someone like Andrea Cooper?" her more constant friends would say. "There's no one around that brightens up a room the way she does." But Andrea had left many wounded souls along her merry way, and there were men among them as well as women.

Throughout her lifetime Andrea's popularity had always been more immediate and durable with boys and with men. It was said of her that her frankness, her honesty, appealed to the males. It was certainly true that if she had ever been ill at ease with the opposite sex, it did not show. One of the first things I noticed about her when I began to notice her at all was her quick decision, at a party or on the club verandah, to join the young men in preference to the girls. If there were two or three young men standing together she would go up to one of them and tug his sleeve. "Andrea's here," she would say, and she would be sure of her welcome. In those days a lot of girls were borrowing a line from a movie called *Young Man of Manhattan,* in which Ginger Rogers (or maybe it was Toby Wing) said, "Cigarette me, big boy." I never heard Andrea say just those words, but then I did not often hear Andrea use a line that was not her own.

She was then about sixteen years old, maybe fifteen but not seventeen. Her mother and father had come to town the year before, leaving Andrea and her brother in school in California while Mr. and Mrs. Cooper found a suitable place to live. Mrs. Cooper had inherited the second largest department store from her grandmother, and Mr. Cooper, who had been working in a bank in Santa Barbara, was going to try his hand at managing the store. Everyone agreed that King's needed new blood and that Mr. Cooper could not do any worse than the previous managers. With his banking experience he might even put King's back on its feet again. Much to everyone's surprise he did just that, although the results were slow in coming. Mr. and Mrs. Cooper were young, still in their thirties, and young for their age. He possessed a California affability that could have affected people either way, but in his case it worked favorably on the other business men. Mrs. Cooper, a native Pennsylvanian who had grown up on the West Coast, was a rather diffident woman who let her husband do most of the talking. She was obviously devoted to him, had no designs on other women's husbands, and the Coopers fitted in much more quickly than most newcomers to the town. In their first year in town they won the mixed doubles in the club tennis tournament, knocking off a much younger couple who had two legs on the cup and were believed to be invincible.

They had Andrea finish out the year in a Santa Barbara school before transferring her to one in New England, and what with one thing and another, I did not get a good look at Andrea until after her mother and father had been living in town for the better part of two years. "*Who* is *that?*" I said, when I first saw her. She was obviously too young for me; I was already halfway through law school and had been having an affair with a married woman in West Philadelphia. Nevertheless my first reaction on seeing Andrea, with a golden band in her pale blond hair, those teeth, her breasts as firm as fists under her sequined white dress, was of civic pride. This radiant creature had come to live in my home town, and I had seen nothing like her at the Philadelphia parties. It may have been that she was overdressed for her age, but as someone said, she would have looked good in a sweatshirt.

I cut in on her at that first dance, and she flattered me by knowing who I was. "Hello, Judge," she said. "Thanks for rescuing me."

"What do you mean, *judge?*" I said.

"Isn't that what you're going to be?"

"It's a long way off if I am," I said. "But how did you know?"

"I made a point of knowing," she said.

"You mean it was love at first sight?"

"No, I didn't say that. I just said I make a point of knowing *if* they're at all attractive," she said.

"Score one for the common people," I said. "You build me up and then knock me down."

"Didn't knock you down," she said. "How could I? You saved my life. That horny man you cut in on, he's older than my father."

"Peter Hofman," I said.

"He didn't want to dance, he wanted to wrestle."

"That's the price you pay," I said. "You're the belle of the ball. Peter Hofman is always out to show us young fellows that he's the best dancer, the greatest lover."

"I've seen his wife, *and* his children. He ought to keep them in hiding. They're not much of an ad for him."

The music stopped. "Are you thirsty?" I said.

"No, but if you are, go ahead. You want to go out to the smoking-room."

"Not necessarily."

"I'm not supposed to go there," she said. "My parents issued strict orders."

"Do you always obey your parents?"

"Of course, especially when they're in the same room and keeping an eye on me."

"Oh, I haven't seen them," I said. "They're here?"

"They're probably in the smoking-room. Daddy probably having a ginger ale and Mother the same. But I'm sure that's where they are. You go on, I won't mind."

"No, I can get a drink any time."

"Then how would you like to take me out on the porch and give me a cigarette? I've also been told not to smoke, although they know I do smoke. But it's unbecoming, very unbecoming for a young girl to smoke."

"They're pretty strict with you," I said, as we moved toward the verandah.

"They have to be," she said. "Otherwise there's no telling what I'd do. I might be out in the car, wrestling with Mr. Hofman."

"Would you wrestle very hard?"

"If it was Mr. Hofman I'd kick him, you know where," she said.

"Where it would do the most good, but not for old Peter," I said. "I have a car out there."

"Then we won't have to freeze on the porch," she said.

"I've even got a pint of prescription liquor."

"You think of everything, don't you? Unfortunately, they'll smell it on my breath when I kiss them goodnight. Then they won't let me go to the other dances. I'm not supposed to drink till I'm eighteen."

We got in my car, an Essex speedster in which you practically sat on the floor, and I lit her cigarette. "I'll never get used to the weather in the East," she said. "Maybe I'll never get used to the East, period."

"Did you have a heavy beau in California?"

"About your weight, I guess," she said.

"A hundred and seventy-four," I said.

"No, it isn't just him. There's something different about Easterners. Even Mother, brought up in California, she's different

333

than Daddy, the way they look at things. She was born here, but she left when she was a little girl. Do you know who's like us? The Swedes. So it isn't just the climate."

"How are you like the Swedes?" I said. "Have you known many Swedes?"

"My heavy beau was from a Swedish family. They all moved to Southern California from Minnesota. His father and his uncles and aunts, and cousins. I must know a hundred or more. And they're always picked out as typical Southern Californians. People used to think I was one of them, when I went to their parties. But my mother's family were from the North of Ireland, and Daddy's people came from Iowa."

"Aren't there a lot of Swedes in Iowa? They spilled over from Minnesota."

"I didn't know that. Then I may *be* part Swedish. I've never been to Iowa."

"You do look rather Swedish," I said. "I've been there, on the North Cape cruise. You could be taken for a Swede."

"They like to have a good time, and so do I," she said. "I'd give anything for a drink."

"No, you don't want to miss the other parties."

She looked at me, frowning and studying me as though I were some strange specimen that she was having trouble identifying.

"What?" I said.

"I'm not sure," she said, still studying me.

"About what?"

"You. Do you care whether I miss the other parties?"

"I don't, but you do," I said. "I won't even *be* here, but two of the parties are bound to be good, and there's the Assembly."

"I can't go to the Assembly. I'm too young."

"Well, there are the other two. You wouldn't want to miss them. Markel's for one, and Sherbo for the other."

"I suppose they're orchestras," she said.

"You'll soon find out," I said.

"We have Arnheim's. I don't know the Eastern orchestras unless they're on records. It's nice of you to care whether I miss the parties, it really is. Is it because you like me, or what? I mean —me especially?"

"Yes. And I think you'd be a great addition to the parties. You're what we call new talent."

"Thank you," she said. She was thinking. "You're not at all what I expected."

"No?"

"Maybe because you're older. Maybe because you're so Eastern-ish. Both, I guess. Why do you wear those pumps? I thought you only wore them with tails."

"I always wear them. I always have."

"And that kind of a collar. Daddy always wears those collars that open at the neck. Wings?"

"I'll wear a wing collar with tails, but not with a Tuck."

"Daddy says Tux. You Tuck. I'll have to tell my brother these things. He's not here for Christmas, but next year he's entered in Andover. What do you think of Andover?"

"Good."

"Where did you go?"

"I went to a small church school called St. Bartholomew's."

"Oh, come on. A small church school. I've heard about St. Bartholomew's. Then where did you go? Yale?"

"Williams," I said.

"And now you're at the U. of Penn," she said.

"Jesus, don't call it the U. of Penn. Penn, or the U. of P., but not the U. of Penn. Ugh."

"So sorry. When my brother comes here next summer, will you help him out? Show him things?"

"I'm afraid I won't be here next summer," I said. "I have a job in Philadelphia. Anyway, the kind of things you're thinking of, he'll learn them at Andover."

"I'd like him to know them before he goes to Andover."

"How old is this boy?"

"Fourteen."

"Hell, he has plenty of time," I said. "And he might resent my telling him things."

"No he wouldn't. I'd see to that. He listens to me. He adores me, he really does."

"Well, you are rather adorable."

"If you think I am now, wait'll you see me in a bathing suit."

"I can hardly wait," I said.

"You *should* be making passes at me," she said.

"Oh, I don't know."

"Mr. Hofman would be making passes at me," she said.

"Not after you kicked him."

"But you're not afraid I'd kick you."

"No. But you couldn't kick anybody in this car."

"Then why haven't you made a pass at me?"

"Do you really want to know?"

"Yes," she said.

"Because you're a virgin."

"That's never stopped anyone else from making passes at me."

"It stops me."

"Oh, you have to go all the way?" she said. "How do you know I wouldn't go all the way?"

"It would be almost physically impossible in this car."

"You don't approve of necking? Heavy necking?"

"Do you?"

"Morally, I don't. But I've done it."

"But you've managed to stay a virgin. You must have given that Swedish boy a bad time."

"He didn't think so," she said. "He didn't expect me to go all the way. The night before I came East I would have, but he didn't know that."

"Then you were lucky," I said.

"Yes, but I didn't think so at the time. Now I do, but then. I was sure he didn't love me."

"And now you're sure he did?"

"No, and I don't love him any more. We don't even write to each other. I was really glad to get out of California. Not so much glad to get out of California as to be moving back East. Everything is new and different here."

"Maybe not as different as you think," I said.

"Have you ever been there?"

"No," I said.

"Then how can you tell?"

"There are differences, but I don't think they matter so much when you come right down to it," I said.

"Oh, are *you* ever wrong!" she said. "If you went to California you'd find out. I wish I could fall in love here, but I feel like such a stranger."

"That's not why you haven't fallen in love. Use your head. When you're ready to fall in love, the geography isn't going to make any difference. It's the person, not the location."

"It must be the location. I've been ready to fall in love ever since I got here, but the people are so different."

"Don't rush things."

"Why not? I want to rush things."

"Then you probably will, and you won't be a virgin much longer."

"That would suit me," she said.

"Even if you weren't in love?"

"I've thought about that. And I've come to the conclusion that I am not going to wait till I'm in love."

"You're just going to give the fair white body to some guy with a dimple in his chin?"

"Oh, no. I hate dimples in chins."

"Well, then one of us lucky guys without a dimple in our chins."

"You're razzing me, but I'm serious."

"You'd better be, about this. You might have a little accident."

"Not me. I'm not that naïve," she said. "You know, I haven't even called you by your first name. I know it's Philip. But do you know why I'm so relaxed with you? Telling you so much?"

"No, why?"

"Because when you said I oughtn't to take a drink and miss those parties, that was the first time since I came East that anyone was really human. And the funny thing is, you didn't seem very human. You and that collar and those pumps. Studying to be a lawyer. Cold as an icicle. And you're not really."

"No, I'm not."

"Where do you live in Philadelphia? At a fraternity house?"

"No, I share an apartment with two friends of mine. Why, were you thinking of paying me a visit?"

"Naturally. Why else would I ask?"

"We have a thing in the Commonwealth of Pennsylvania called statutory rape."

"It wouldn't be rape if I went there of my own accord," she said.

"Yes, I'm afraid it would. Your father and mother aren't the kind of people that would have me arrested, but frankly you're a bit young for me."

"Look, is this young?" She pulled down the straps of her evening dress and bared her breasts.

"Cut that out," I said.

"Kiss them," she said.

"God damn it, I said cut that out."

"You're a son of a *bitch*," she said. She replaced the straps, and began to weep. I said nothing for a while, then passed her my handkerchief. She took a deep breath and said, "I guess we ought to be going back."

"All right with me," I said.

"You have every right to be cross with me," she said.

"Well, God damn it."

"I *want* somebody."

"I want *you*," I said. "But for God's sake."

"I know, I know."

"No, you don't know, Andrea. You really don't."

"Yes I do. I honestly do, Philip. Honestly and truly, I know everything you could say to me."

"I doubt that but let's forget about it."

She shook her head. "I won't and you won't. Is your number in the telephone book, in Philadelphia?"

"Yes. I could say no, but if you looked you'd find it."

"Right," she said. "What's a good time to call you?"

"After four o'clock, and any evening."

"Next week?"

"Yes," I said.

"You'd be better for me than some guy with a dimple in his chin," she said. She was smiling now, and I put my arms around her and kissed her.

"That's better," she said. "You could love me, you know. I know it, if you don't."

"Oh, I know it now," I said.

We went back to the clubhouse, and several of my friends looked at me in mock disapproval and said things about robbing the cradle. But I told them to grow up, and I think I deceived them by not dancing again with Andrea. I had never been much of a parked-car Romeo, and my reputation for good conduct was paying off. The next week, on a Tuesday afternoon, Andrea came to our apartment on Walnut Street, and I committed statutory rape. Six years later, the week before she was to be married, she came to another apartment I had on Spring Garden Street; and ten years after that, when she had been divorced a second time, she was still the only woman I could not do without.

She had a way of turning up just as I was beginning to convince myself that I ought to put an end to my bachelorhood. Two or three times as much as a year would pass without my hearing from her except for a message scribbled on a Christmas card. In Philadelphia, and I suppose in any other city, a busy man who likes his work is not uncomfortably conscious of the passage of time. I had all the legal practice I could handle, and I was making a good deal of money. From my office on South Broad Street I would alternate between clubs for lunch on working days, and on Sundays I would join a group of men who foregathered to eat and drink and play shuffleboard. My evenings were as socially active or filled with work as I wished to make them, and it did not matter to me that I was sometimes called a selfish pig and a stuffed shirt. Some of the wives who called me a selfish pig for not marrying a suitable divorcée or widow were also pleased to have me as an extra man. And as for my being a stuffed shirt, the epithet was most often conferred upon me by other lawyers who had not done their homework as thoroughly as I. I was an upstate carpetbagger as well, but some of the men who called me that were also known to have remarked that it was too bad I was single and could not run for high public office. There were moments when bachelorhood seemed less desirable than matrimony, but I found that such spells of weakening usually coincided with the end of a long period of silence on the part of Andrea. Days would come when I became so obsessed with the need of her presence that only habit and routine kept me from chucking my practice and seeking her out. But then I would hear from her, remarkably soon and even on the very same day, and we would be together for a while. Only once did we discuss marriage. I proposed to her, and she said, "No, never to you, Phil. It would be pure hell for both of us. I'd rather keep coming back to you than keep running away from you every few months. That's the difference. I actually consider myself faithful to you all these years. And as far as that goes, I consider you faithful to me." There was no more to be said, unless I cared to admit that my fine legal mind had not summarized our situation as precisely as hers.

We had good times together. Between us there were no sexual inhibitions, and almost no twinge of jealousy. She would tell me about the problems she was having in breaking in a new man and she would talk freely and coolly about her husbands and lovers, one after another doomed to failure. "It makes me so cross when you say they call you a selfish pig," she once said. "You were never that with me, never for an instant. But they weren't with us back in that little car of yours. Oh, I love you, Phil. Andrea Cooper Et Cetera loves you."

"And I love Andrea Cooper—without the et cetera," I said.

"Yes," she said. "We have a love. Love, love, love, love, love. Now tell me something about your latest. How is she peculiar?"

"Not very peculiar," I said.

"You're holding out on me," she said.

"Well, one peculiarity," I said. "She likes to drive around with nothing on under her fur coat."

"Oh, yes, I've heard of that. That's fairly common. What does she do in the summertime? A raincoat?"

"I should imagine so," I said.

"My theory is that they want to be raped, but don't want to be, if you know what I mean. They're teasers, I think."

"Yes, that fits in. She's a teaser."

"Is she good at it?"

"Yes, I must say she is. She can be very aggravating."

"But satisfactory?"

"Eventually," I said.

"Is she living with her husband? I assume she's married."

"Oh, yes."

"Does he know about the fur coat business?" she said.

"He doesn't know anything about anything, from what I gather."

"You know what we are, you and I?"

"Among other things, what?" I said.

"What do they call those things? Safety valves. I wonder how many people there are that owe their sanity to us."

"Well, yes, but I owe my sanity to you."

"Oh, that goes without saying, you and I. But I was thinking of the other people."

"But what happens to them when you ditch them? In my case I don't think it matters too much. The women's peculiarities are rather minor things. Some like the phonograph playing, some don't. Some like to be hurt, others don't. But with men, there's the danger of violence."

"Yes," she said. "There is with women, too, but not as much as with men." She was silent.

"What?" I said.

"I was thinking of Stanley Broman. He's a man I had an affair with two years ago, until I broke it off. He's been calling me up late at night. If the Gibbsville operators ever listen in on those calls they must have a lovely opinion of me."

"Get an unlisted number, or turn off your phone," I said.

"I've done both. But what happens next? I'm afraid he may turn up some night."

"Tell him you're getting married again."

"I did, and that was a mistake. He said he was going to do everything to stop it."

"But you're not getting married again, are you?" I said.

"No. At least I have no plans to," she said.

"Then how can he stop what you have no intention of doing?" I said.

"I'm not worried about that. I just don't want to have him come near me again."

"What do you want me to do?" I said.

"I don't know. I was hoping you'd think of something," she said.

"Well, give me all the details and I'll bring in a private detective."

"I don't want to get you mixed up in anything," she said.

"I won't have to be," I said. "My man isn't a movie private eye. He's a member of the bar, a full-fledged attorney-at-law. Name is John MacIlreddy. Actually he was once a cop and studied law at night school. We use him for all sorts of things. Tell me about Mr. Broman."

"Well, he's a promoter. He has an office on Fifth Avenue and a house in Great Neck, Long Island. In his late forties. Married. Two or three children."

"What does he promote?"

"Various things. Sporting events, like prizefighting. Automobile races. I met him one night in the Stork Club, when he came to the table where I was having supper with some characters. You wouldn't know them, but Stanley did. 'The hell with the rest of you,' he said. 'I'm smitten by this lady,' meaning me. 'Well, I'm not smitten by you,' I said, 'so why don't you go back to your table.' But the others were amused, or impressed, or as I later found out, somewhat terrified by Stanley, and he stayed."

"Why were they terrified?" I said.

"Not really terrified, but afraid of him. Apparently he got into fights, and made scenes, and he certainly was mixed up with some very shady characters. In any event, he believed in the direct approach. He pulled a chair up beside me and began talking very dirty and invited me to go to his hotel with him. I stood as much of it as I could, then I excused myself to go to the ladies' room and never went back to the table. When I got outside on Fifty-whatever-it-is Street, he was waiting for me. Sitting in the first taxi. I was actually halfway in the taxi before I realized he was there. He grabbed my hand and pulled me in the rest of the way. Obviously the taxi driver knew him. In fact, he was part owner of a fleet of taxicabs. He's in all sorts of things. Loads of money. Spends a lot on clothes, and was probably a very handsome Jew when he was younger. Oh, let's face it, he had sex appeal. 'I'm gonna take you to your hotel and I'm gonna leave you there,' he said. 'But I just didn't want you to think you were outsmarting me.' And that's exactly what he did. He dropped me at the Barclay, where I was staying, and went on his way.

"The next morning, when they brought my breakfast, there were two dozen yellow roses. How he found that out, I don't know. But they're my favorites, as you know. I opened the envelope to look at the card, and there was this thin little diamond bracelet. No big diamonds, but it was narrow and beautiful. On the card was written, 'Think it over,' and it was signed with his initials. I looked him up in the phone book to know where to return the bracelet, but no Stanley Broman. Then I called up one of the people I'd been to the Stork Club with and found out that he was at the Waldorf. So I sent the bracelet back by messenger. Within half an hour he was on the phone. 'All I wanted you to do was think it over,' he said. 'That didn't take long,' I said. Oh, what's the use of telling you inch by inch? He was waiting for me in the Barclay lobby when I came down to go out for lunch. 'Lady, I told you I was smitten and I am,' he said. 'If necessary I'll move to Gibbsville PA.' I couldn't have dinner with him that night, but I did the next. He took me to the Colony and the theater and El Morocco, behaved like his idea of the perfect gentleman, and left me at the Barclay."

"And then you had an affair with him," I said. "How long did that last?"

"Oh, maybe six months. He never came to Gibbsville. I was firm about that. But he used to send a private plane to take me to New York, and sometimes I'd stay a week at a time. His friends were unbelievable. The women were almost worse than the men. They all looked like whores that had struck it rich, and did they ever hate me! Where did I get this, where did I get that? If it wasn't a personal question, but how much did this cost? What infuriated them most was knowing that Stanley wasn't keeping me. He paid for the plane and I stayed in his suite at the Waldorf, but my clothes were my own and I refused his expensive presents. After all, I have some very nice things I got from you and other people."

"The affair lasted six months, then what? Why did you give him the air?" I said.

"Because my bloomers got warm for someone else, to put it delicately," she said.

"But you don't get rid of people like him that easily," I said.

"I found that out. 'Who is this guy? I'll kill him,' he said. And I said I'd like to see him try. The new man was half a head taller and—and Stanley isn't small—and does boxing every day to keep in shape. Doesn't drink, doesn't smoke. He played football at Holy Cross University, and he could probably go out and play now. He's a lawyer, too, although actually he's a politician."

"Where?"

"In Brooklyn. Not really Brooklyn. Queens, sort of a part of Brooklyn, but closer to Great Neck, where Stanley lives when he goes home. Stanley knew right away who he was, and stopped making threats or trying to see me."

"You told him about Stanley?" I said

"No. I didn't have to, and the affair with Jack Spellacy didn't last long enough to get to the exchange-of-confidences stage. However, it did last long enough to get rid of Stanley. Till about two months ago, when the phone calls began. He called up one night and said he was sending the plane next day. They called me from the airport, and I sent the plane back to New York."

"And the calls have persisted. It's odd that a man like that hasn't showed up in Gibbsville. I'll have to look into that," I said. "In fact, I'll do it right now."

"At this hour? All the offices are closed," she said.

"Watch me spring into action," I said. I telephoned the office of the Philadelphia *Bulletin* and was put through to George Taylor, the financial vice-president, with whom I occasionally had lunch. "George, I'd like to know what you have on a man named Stanley Broman. He's a New Yorker. A promoter. Will you see if you have any clippings on him?" George Taylor promised to call me back or to have someone in the *Bulletin* "morgue" give me the information. I hung up and waited.

"You're marvelous," said Andrea.

"I impress you, do I?" I said.

"This is the first time I've ever seen you in action. That kind of action."

"I know a lot of people," I said. "You never know when they'll come in handy. I have no friends, but I never have had."

"That's your fault. You could have. Or maybe you couldn't.

No, I think you've learned to get along without them. I have no *women* friends. That's why you and I have love, love, love."

The telephone rang. It was a man in the *Bulletin* office. He said he had quite a batch of clippings on Stanley Broman. Did I want him to read them all? It was against the rules to take them out of the building, although in my case they might make an exception. "Just read the headlines and I'll tell you which ones interest me," I said.

He read a dozen or so before he came to one in particular. "Hold it," I said. "Read the whole article, please." He did so, and I asked him to read several others pertaining to the same topic. I thanked him and we hung up. "As I suspected," I said.

"I have never in my life seen you look so smug," she said. "What is it?"

"Good news for you," I said. "Your Mr. Broman will never bother you in Gibbsville. At least that's a reasonable assumption. He faces a lawsuit if he sets foot in our glorious Commonwealth. Under the statute of limitations, as it applies to this case, you're safe for four more years. Apparently he owes a lot of people a lot of money. I know the lawyer who represented him here, and I could find out all there is to know, but that won't be necessary, or desirable, from your point of view."

"You're absolutely clever," she said. "You spotted that right away."

"There had to be some very good reason why a man like that stayed away from Gibbsville. I suggest you say nothing to him about this. What he doesn't know won't hurt us. You'll have to put up with the telephone calls, but at least you can rest easy about his appearing in person. He'll get over you in four years. His kind of ego can't endure defeat, and pretty soon he'll be able to convince himself that you're not worth bothering about. However, I'm glad we found out about the lawsuit. If it weren't for that I might have recommended your taking out a pistol license."

"How can I thank you?" she said.

"In various ways. And you do."

"We just won't say that we love each other."

"We say it all the time," I said. "But we have sense enough to know that our way is the best way for us. When I'm eighty and you're seventy I'll propose to you again."

"And I'll accept your proposal. I would now, but you don't want that hanging over you."

"It would be interesting to announce our engagement now, and say that the wedding will take place in the spring of 1986. I can just see it in the Evening Chat column in the *Bulletin*. Actually, you know, in my business I project myself into the future every day. Bond issues maturing at such and such a date. Wills. Trust funds. Ninety-nine-year leases. Then on the other hand, we're always having title searches that go back to 1681. In case you've forgotten, that was the year William Penn was granted his charter."

"Oh, I knew that all along," she said.

"In a pig's ass you did," I said.

"You can be so *vulgar*," she said. "Thank God."

That was shortly after the end of World War II. She vanished again and I did not see or hear from her until about a year later. My secretary said that Mrs. Andrea Cooper—she had adopted her maiden name—wished to speak to me. Ruth, of course, knew that any call from Andrea had top priority.

"Have you been listening to the radio?" said Andrea.

"Naturally," I said. "I come to the office every day to listen to the radio. We get such good reception here. Why are you so breathless?"

"I just heard over the radio that Stanley Broman's been murdered. Is there anything I ought to do?"

"Well, obviously you didn't do it, so if I were you I'd open a small bottle of champagne. Who gets the medal for this public-spirited act?"

"They don't know. They found him in his car, in the meadows near Newark, New Jersey. The car was on fire, and he was shot and stabbed. Shot *and* stabbed."

"They really wanted to get rid of him, didn't they?"

"Is there anything I ought to do? Am I liable to get mixed up in it? I don't *want* to get mixed up in it, especially now."

"Romance in the air?"

"Very much so. I'm on the verge of marrying my doctor."

"With what *he* must know about you, it must be true love," I said. "No, you have nothing to worry about. You didn't write the late Mr. Broman any letters, did you? You've never been much for letters."

"No, he never put anything in writing if he could help it, either."

"Then I would say that the New Jersey gangsters have given you a very nice wedding present. I'll admit now that I was always a trifle apprehensive about Broman. Just a trifle."

"Don't think *I* wasn't."

"Are you coming to see me before you go to the altar with your doctor?"

"I will if you want me to," she said.

"I always want you to," I said.

"Then I'll come down this afternoon. He's dead, but he frightens me, that man. I have to be back here tomorrow. Is that all right?"

"Of course it's all right," I said.

She was remarkable. She was thirty-three years old, give or take a few months, yet when she arrived at my apartment she was fresh and unstained and—radiant. I always went back to that word to describe her to myself. She almost never wore a hat and she was not wearing one now. Her hair was cut in a longish page-boy style, and I said to her, "Tell me something. Do you dye your hair?"

"I have it touched," she said. "But I'm a light blonde and you damn well know it. What kind of a greeting is that? *Do I dye my hair?*"

"We're very hostile today. I was only curious," I said.

"I drove a hundred miles to see you. I expect a nicer welcome than that. Would it be too much to offer me a drink?"

"You can have anything but a Martini. I won't give you a Martini when you're in this mood."

"I don't want a Martini. Give me a bourbon with ice, no water. Please."

"My question about your hair was in the nature of a compliment. I have a favorite word for you. Radiant. In addition, I was thinking that you had driven ninety-four miles—not a hundred, by the way—and not a hair was out of place."

"I ran a comb through it in the elevator."

I handed her the drink. "Which doctor is it you're going to marry? One of the newer ones?"

"Not so new," she said. "He came there after you left, but he's been there about ten years. Sam Young."

"I know the name, but I've never met him. You know how often I get back there. Maybe once in five years, since Mother died."

"Yes, people have been known to say that the old town isn't good enough for you," she said.

"They're right. It isn't," I said. "The last time anything interesting happened there was when you arrived."

"Are you trying to get me back in a good mood?"

"Trying as hard as I can," I said. "We only have tonight, and then it may be years before we see each other again."

"Oh, I want to sleep with you. You needn't worry about that," she said.

"Well, I was worrying about it," I said.

"I'll always sleep with you," she said. "You were my first, and maybe you'll be my last. Who knows?"

"Why are you marrying Dr. Young?"

"First of all, because he's nice, and if you're going to live in Gibbsville it's better to be married."

"But why go on living in Gibbsville?"

She stretched out on the sofa. "Yes, why? It's home, with Mother and Daddy there, and my kid brother married and raising a family. I've lost all contact with my friends in California. I've been married and divorced twice, and I don't think those marriages did me any great harm, but I can't go on getting married and divorced. Stability. I need some stability, and I'd never get it if I moved away from Gibbsville. Look at what happened to me in New York. I fell in love with a gangster."

"You're dramatizing that," I said. "You didn't fall in love with him, and he wasn't a real gangster."

"Yes he was. I saw enough of him to find that out. He was a

gangster. Maybe he didn't go around with a machine-gun in his hand, but they don't do that any more."

"Someone did, or he wouldn't be lying in the Jersey meadows," I said.

"He was a modern gangster. He made his money in the black market during the war. Not nylons and things like that. He used to call himself a steel executive. Rubber. Steel. Building materials."

"You knew a lot more than I thought you did."

"He thought I was a dizzy blonde that didn't know what was going on. And maybe I was. But I couldn't help but overhear some of his conversations."

"Now I see why you were so worried. You're afraid you might be called on to testify. That's doubtful. If he lived, and there was some kind of Congressional investigation, they'd have the F.B.I. visit you. It's still a possibility, but very remote."

"That's what I want to know," she said. "What do I do if they come and start asking me a lot of questions?"

"The first thing you do is ask for their credentials. I mean that. The F.B.I. men have a kind of wallet with their picture in it. Take your time about examining it. If you have any reason to be doubtful, tell the man that you're going to call their office to check. If he's a phony, he'll give you an argument. If not, and if you're satisfied that he's the real thing, give him all the information he asks for. Sometimes there are two of them. Make them both identify themselves. One man can put on a convincing act, but when there are two of them it's not so easy. Your instinct will warn you. But once you're satisfied, tell them everything. You can trust them. Above all, don't lie to them. You may just happen to lie about something they know all about, in which case you make everything you say suspect."

"Can't I simply say I don't want to talk to them?" she said.

"Yes. But if you do, be sure and call me right away," I said. "By the way, does Dr. Young know about me, you and me?"

"Nobody knows about you and me," she said.

"Still?" I said.

"I've never told anyone. Maybe you have, but I haven't. They all want to know who my first was, and I tell them it was a boy in

California. For some reason they don't seem to mind that. California is so far away. So is my virginity."

"You're feeling a little better now," I said.

"Well, for Christ's sake, starting out with 'Do you dye your hair?' What did you expect? By the way, *you're* getting a bit grey."

"I'm getting grey in your service," I said.

"Yes, I guess that's true," she said. "What I said about Gibbsville and stability—as long as I have you, I have *some* stability. I wouldn't want to live any place that was too far from you."

"I'll never be farther away than the telephone and the airplane. You're announcing your impending nuptials. Well, I have an announcement of my own, just for you. I am never going to get married."

"When you're eighty and I'm seventy?"

"Then, yes, but not before. When I was still in my thirties, I could have adjusted to marriage. But now I'm only seven years from fifty, and my habits are frozen. The first time I ever danced with you, you called me Judge. I was in law school."

"The night I did my strip tease," she said.

I nodded. "And they're even better now than they were then."

"By an inch and a half," she said.

"I wish I could say the same for my own measurements," I said. "Anyway, I remember telling you that a judgeship was a long way off for me. Now it isn't, and that's my ambition, my goal. It always has been. By the time I'm fifty I'll have enough money for one man."

"Don't forget us when we're married," she said.

"I won't. There'll be enough for the two of us," I said. "Do you want to hear about my ambition, or don't you?"

"Yes, dear. I promise not to interrupt any more."

"There are two things I can't discuss with anyone but you. My sex life and my ambition. Naturally I'd like to be an associate justice of the U.S. Supreme Court, but that's out of the question. They don't appoint my kind of lawyer to the Supreme Court any more. I've handled too many cases for large corporations. But I've been sounded out on running for a state job, which I won't do. Before they sound you out they study your qualifications, so mine must be all right. I'm being over-modest. They're damn good. Too good for the job they want me for. However, they did come to me, spontaneously, and they'll come again. And again. Then I'll tell them that I'll run if unopposed."

"You mean if nobody runs against you?"

"Yes. You can't be permanently appointed, you have to be elected. But you can be unopposed. I'm a hell of a good lawyer, you know, with a hell of a good record. The public doesn't know much about me, but the other lawyers do. I've never lost a case in the U.S. Supreme Court, and only two in the state court. And I'm not getting any dumber."

"Just think of you sitting up there in those black robes. I'll go and make faces at you."

"I'll have you held in contempt," I said.

"You do, and I'll tell your guilty secret. What kind of rape was that?"

"Statutory," I said.

"I knew it wasn't statuary. I was anything but statuary. Well, I'll be proud of you. I really will. I am anyway. I can't tell people I've been your girl all these years, but I'm secretly proud. And you're getting grey hairs. And I also notice you're wearing your Phi Beta Kappa key. I never knew you were one."

"I was wearing the key the first night I danced with you," I said.

"Maybe you were, but I didn't know what it was. I never knew what it was till my brother made it. But you must have stopped wearing it."

"Vests are coming back," I said.

"That's not why you're wearing it. You're running for judge. Don't try to fool me, Phil."

"That would be a great mistake, I guess. Besides, I never wanted to fool you."

"We must never try to fool each other," she said. "Let there be two people in the world that don't."

"How about your mother and father?" I said. "You've always had great admiration for them."

"Have I? Not in recent years. Not since I've been able to think for myself, instead of being a yes-man to them. He's cruel, my father. He dominates her in every little thing. For instance, she never wanted to leave California, but he did. He didn't want to be stuck in the bank in Santa Barbara. He wanted to be the manager of King's department store."

"He's done very well, though," I said.

"The store has, I have to admit that. But Mother has aged terribly. She hates the climate, she doesn't like the people. Consequently, she comes to see me every day, not because she wants to see me but because she knows where I keep the vodka. 'Oh, I think I'll have a little cocktail,' she says. Then you ought to see what she pours herself. Right up to the top. One cube of ice, the rest straight vodka. Her little cocktail. Then she has another little cocktail. I tried watering the vodka, but she noticed it right away. Insisted that I get a different brand and offered to pay for it. My mother has become a quiet lush. My brother's no help. He says he's very sorry, but he doesn't want Mother coming to his house and criticizing the way his wife is bringing up their kids. Mother knows she's not welcome there, so I get her every afternoon."

"What if you and the doctor have children?"

"We won't. He's sterile. I didn't say impotent. He can get it up all right, but he's sterile. And I doubt if I could have children now. Three abortions since I was nineteen."

"Beginning with mine," I said.

"Yes, and each of my husbands. The last one the doctor didn't want to do it, but I told him if he didn't do it I'd have to go to some butcher. That was Sam Young. So you see he knew me pretty well before he knew me at all, so to speak."

"A moment ago you spoke of stability," I said. "You said you stayed in Gibbsville because it offered stability, and you mentioned your parents. Then a bit later you gave me a quite unhappy picture of them. He's cruel, she's an alcoholic. What kind of stability do you call that?"

"It's stability. It isn't happiness, but it's stability. What kind of a lawyer's trick is this, going back to things I said before?"

"It's a lawyer's trick, all right," I said. "I'm doing it for a reason. I want to find out why you're marrying your doctor. Does he represent stability?"

"Yes," she said.

"You don't love him."

"No."

"What do you like about him, besides the dream of stability?"

"Are you going to try to argue me out of marrying him?" she said.

"I know better than that," I said.

"Then what are you trying to do?" she said. "You can't make me a better offer."

"No, I can't. But I've always seemed to take the role of uncle, or big brother, with you. You don't remember this, but that first night we sat in my car together—"

"You told me not to take a drink or my parents wouldn't let me go to the other dances."

"You do remember," I said.

"I ought to. That's what got us in the hay together. But I don't see what you're trying to do now."

"It would help if you answered my question, what do you like about the doctor?"

"Well, he's a man. All man. He was married before and his wife died of leukemia, the year he went into private practice. Then he went into the Navy for three years, and after that he came back to Gibbsville, reopened his practice. When I got the flu I sent for him, having already been his patient once before. The abortion. He annoyed me by throwing in a piece of advice that I hadn't asked for. It was part medical and part moral. He said that a woman with my record of abortions ought to have periodic checkups for T.B., and I told him to mind his own business. We became friends, and lovers. He had other women, but I was it, he said."

"What makes either of you think you'll make a good doctor's wife?"

"You *are* trying to talk me out of it," she said.

"All right, maybe I am. Three abortions aren't good for you, but neither are four marriages."

"This will be my third marriage!"

"Which will last two years, then there'll be a fourth. And quite possibly a fifth."

"You're jealous! You pretend you're not, but you are. You don't show it because I go away. You want me to go away so I won't see how jealous you are!"

I waited, and went on. "And there might even be a sixth."

She threw her glass at me, a heavy piece of Steuben. It missed me and broke against the paneling of the wall behind me. The dent in the woodwork was half an inch deep. I got up and stood over the largest piece of glass, which lay on the carpet. I was being dramatic while trying to think of the right thing to say. I was also frightened. Retroactively I could hear the thud of the glass on the woodwork, and imagine what it would have done to my skull. Looking down at the broken glass I was avoiding looking at her, and I did not see her coming toward me. When she touched me I reacted out of fear; I sprang away from her.

"Phil! Phil! I could have killed you!" She put her arms around my waist and held on to me, and then for only the second time in our life together she began to cry. I put my arms around her and held on to her, and she kissed me time after time, on the lips, on my neck, my hands, passionately but without passion. Now, having retroactively heard the glass smashing against the wall, I could retroactively see it passing over my shoulder, and though I was safe I was impotent with the effects of fear. I could feel impotence in my genitals and age in my soul. She stopped kissing me and looked at me. The tears streaked down her cheeks but she had stopped crying. "Are you all right?" she said.

"I want to sit down," I said.

"You're pale," she said.

"Odd," I said.

She held my hand on her bosom and drew me to the sofa, and I sat down. She sat on the edge of the sofa, waiting for whatever was next, act or words. "Think I'll have a cigarette," I said. I was recovering rapidly, but I had to know what to do. It had to be right, or I had lost her forever; that much I knew. It was like that moment in a jury trial when you are addressing the twelve good men and true, and something tells you to stop, or to go on, you're not sure which but you are sure that in two seconds you will have them or have lost them, regardless of whatever else you do or have done, say or have said.

I hesitated, and I guess she read into my hesitation some other emotion than the vestige of fear. Deep disappointment, disillusionment perhaps. She got the cigarette for me and put it in my mouth and lit it. "I would rather die than hurt you," she said. "Than hurt you in any way. If that glass had hit you I'd have jumped out your window. See my hand?" Her hands were shaking. She got up and used the letter-opener and pencil tray from my desk to sweep up the broken glass fragments. She took them and the larger pieces of glass to the kitchen. "I put them in the garbage pail," she said. She was standing in the middle of the room. "Do you want me to go?"

"No," I said.

"What do you want me to do? Shall I fix you a drink?"

"No thanks," I said.

"Please tell me what to do. I can't think," she said.

"Why don't you just come here and sit down?" I said.

She sat beside me and gently put her head on my shoulder and I put my arm around her. We stayed that way for a full two minutes, which can be a long time of silence for two such people as she and I; I suddenly older, she as suddenly younger. "I feel as though I'd thrown something at God," she said.

"I'm not God. I'm not even a very minor god," I said. "I'm not even a good first baseman or I'd have caught the damn thing. Would you mind if we just stayed here and didn't go out for dinner?"

"Oh, I don't *want* to go out for dinner. I'd be almost sure to burst into tears, and embarrass you. Would you like me to show you what a good cook I am?"

"I know what a good cook you are. Let's sit here a while and later on you can make one of your omelettes. Do you want to listen to some records?"

"No thanks," she said. "When you're ready, we'll talk. You have something you want to say, and so have I."

"I haven't much to say, but what there is is fairly important," I said. "I'm all right now but I have to tell you, I'm a different man from five or ten minutes ago. I never thought so before, but I'm a middle-aged man. I don't want to exaggerate anything, but there it is. And you know it. That's why you somehow got me confused with God, because I happen to know you don't believe in God."

"No, I don't. I stopped believing in God when I changed my mind about my father."

"And I suppose I took their place. Father. God. And perennial lover."

"I guess that's right," she said.

"An all-purpose man in your life," I said.

"And what have I been to you? Perennial mistress and what else? Not your mother, or the Virgin Mary."

"Well, there've been hundreds of times when I was a child at your breast."

"You're feeling better now, aren't you?"

"I told you, I'm all right," I said. "But you have to know that when that glass went whizzing by me, my reflexes were slow and one of the slow reflexes was fear. I wasn't afraid till after it was over. A young man's reflexes protect him. I didn't move. I played first base when I was in school but tonight I was rigid. With a kind of anticipatory fear, I guess."

"I threw the glass without any warning," she said.

"A prep school pitcher does the same thing, trying to pick a runner off first base. No signal. No warning. Or a first baseman misses the signal that the pitcher's going to throw to him."

"What has all this stuff about baseball got to do with us?"

"I'm trying to explain what's happened to me. I'll be brief, if you like. In a word, I got old."

"All right, if you insist. You're forty-three years old. I never have any trouble remembering your age."

"But let me go on, Andrea. This is important. I'm forty-three, but *you* suddenly *lost* a batch of years. Your reaction was very young, and you practically said so when you said it was like throwing something at God."

"I'll agree with that, too. It was childish."

"Young-girlish, not childish," I said.

"I've decided not to marry Sam Young," she said.

Her statement was so out of order that in a courtroom I would have requested a recess. For the truth was I had been leading up to a repudiation of my earlier opposition to her marriage. It was frustrating and confusing to have her brush aside my speech before it was made.

"You've decided *not* to marry him?" I said.

"It wouldn't work out. Not even for two years," she said. "It would be very bad for both of us. For him and me, that is."

"What convinced you of that?" I said.

"Something you said, of course," she said. "You asked me why either of us, Sam or I, thought I'd make a good doctor's wife. Actually, we never talked about that. I mean about the doctor's-wife part of it. We've always talked about ourselves and each other, but being a doctor's wife is something special. He must have thought about it, but he avoided bringing it up. I'd make a terrible doctor's wife. He'd lose every patient he has."

"Would he? Why?"

"Because he would, that's why. I'm not cut out for that kind of a life. My mother could have done it, but not me."

"What about all that business of living in Gibbsville and stability and so on?"

"I can always find good reasons for doing something I want to do," she said. "Even now I can think of a good reason for throwing a glass at you. You taunted me, you went too far. You should know better than to make me angry. I'm a very impulsive girl. If I'd hit you, I *would* have jumped out the window. That would have been great, you with your head bashed in, and me lying on the sidewalk in Rittenhouse Square. And all because you needled me when I was tired from a long drive."

"Yes, of course, of course," I said. "Is this final, your decision not to marry Young?"

"Absolutely," she said. "Just as final as my decision not to marry you."

"I was coming to that," I said. "Just thinking out loud, as the advertising people say. Just as a trial balloon, how would it be if you and I got married and kept it secret—don't interrupt me, please—and thereby prevented you from a hasty marriage to someone else?"

"We're not married now, and I prevented myself from a hasty marriage, as you call it."

"So you did. But you're quite liable to find yourself in the same situation again, and marry the man."

"You're quite liable to get another glass thrown at you," she said.

"Not so soon," I said. "Let's speculate as to the advantages for you. I don't know how close you ever came to marrying that gangster. Not very close, I guess. He had that wife in Great Neck or wherever it was, and Jews generally, even gangster Jews, don't go rushing to the divorce courts. But you're impulsive, by your own admission, and the record speaks for itself. Two marriages, two divorces. Both of your ex-husbands married again and I believe they've stayed married?"

"Yes," she said.

"And you were about to marry a widower until you suddenly, impulsively changed your mind. Doesn't all this seem to indicate that it'd be to your advantage to have a legal husband to protect you from your own impulses? Don't start throwing things. I'm asking you to consider the matter."

"I'm considering it. What's the advantage for you?"

"For me? Well, I could say that I was looking ahead to the time when I become a judge. Stability and all that. I'll never marry anyone but you, that's a certainty. But I'd like to be sure of having you, when that time comes."

"You're just so God damn jealous."

"You've probably put your finger on it. Our hidden motives we won't admit to, even to ourselves sometimes."

"The answer is no," she said. "I'm not giving up Sam Young to marry you."

"There would be financial advantages, too," I said. "What do you live on now? It's mostly your stock in King's store, isn't it?"

"Mostly," she said. "I had alimony from my first husband, but that stopped when I married again. I got no alimony from my second husband. I was the guilty party there. Yes, my income is from the store."

"I happen to know something about economic conditions in the coal region. They're not getting any better. I don't know much about King's, but how long do you think they can compete against Stewart's, which is bigger and older, and the new Sears?

King's is in the middle there. And no matter how efficient your father may be, the economic facts of life are running against him. Sears has the big buying power and lower prices. Stewart's has four other stores besides Gibbsville, and third-generation charge accounts. They make money with their charge accounts, because they're not the old-time charge accounts. Stewart's is really in the same business as a loan company. Selling on the installment plan, and collecting their pound of flesh by financing the retail purchases."

"I've heard Daddy talk about that, but it's too deep for me," she said.

"You ought to try to understand it, because it's going to affect you. I don't want to frighten you, but if King's had two or three bad years they'd have to go out of business. I assume that Dr. Young makes pretty good money."

"About twenty thousand a year. He told me."

"And you?"

"Last year, around ten."

"Is that all?" I said.

She nodded. "Daddy told me to expect less this year."

"You spend it all, of course," I said.

"Oh, do I! I'm continually overdrawn. But I work, you know."

"I didn't know," I said.

"Before Easter I help out in ladies' ready-to-wear. Four weeks. And before Christmas in the toy department or wherever they send me. I get a hundred dollars a week, which just about covers what I owe Daddy."

"I'll *bet* it does," I said.

"Not entirely. He gives me the rest as a Christmas present."

"Encouraging bad habits," I said.

"That's exactly what he says."

"Does he worry about you?"

"Not about me. He'd wet his drawers if he knew his little daughter's ex-boy friend was killed by gangsters, but he wouldn't be worrying for me. For himself and Bud, my brother, Bud. I love Bud, but I hate what my father's doing to him. When Bud graduated from Colgate my father gave him a present of a trip abroad, and Bud came back thinking he'd get a job on a newspa-

359

per, in hopes of becoming a foreign correspondent. My father talked him into taking a quote temporary unquote job in the store. It was a job anyone could have done, not a Phi Beta Kappa with a knack for languages. What Daddy really wanted was a doubles partner, and Bud had been captain of the Colgate tennis team. So Bud gave in, and got himself married, and then the war came and he quit his job to go to O.C.S. and they sent him to England with the O.S.S. because he knew German. After the war he wanted to live over there, but he already had one child and his wife was producing another. Well, Daddy began working on him again, a year at a time. You can imagine what happened. Bud could have lived abroad with a wife and one child, on his income. But with a wife and three he had to have more than that. Kids are expensive, so are young American wives. The sad thing, but funny, ironical, is that now Daddy plays golf, and Bud doesn't even get to the semi-finals in the singles any more."

"Let's hope your father doesn't turn the store over to him just before it folds up," I said.

"He would if he thought of it."

"You don't want to marry me for my money?" I said.

"No."

"Or to keep yourself out of trouble?" I said.

"No."

"Or to possibly be of some help to your brother if the store goes out of business?" I said.

"No."

"Or because you know that eventually you will marry me," I said.

"You're more sure of that than I am," she said.

"Only if we both live long enough. I'm not talking about when I'm eighty. I honestly believe we'll be married before that, and unless I'm very wrong, you believe it too."

"You don't know what it's like to be married, Phil. I do. It takes a long time to get used to living with someone, and we both like our privacy. We both like to come and go as we please. You can't do that, and you can't have your privacy, when you're someone's wife. Maybe I was cut out to be an old maid. Not the usual kind of old maid that looks under beds. But an old maid with plenty of memories. I'm not going to marry you just so you'll have a wife in reserve for when you're a judge."

"All right," I said.

"I'm going to get you some supper. Do you mind if I unpack first?"

"Did you bring a bag?"

She laughed. "No, I'm kidding. I didn't even bring a toothbrush. I know you always have extras, and I count on wearing your pajamas. You have your bath and I'll have your supper ready by the time you're out of the shower. Then we can have a quiet evening at home. The kind that makes you think you'd like to be married to me."

I took a shower and put on pajamas and dressing-gown. She had set the table and lighted the candles in my small dining-room. We had the omelette and toast and a bottle of Rhine wine that she found in the refrigerator. "Do you still get your own breakfast every morning?" she said.

"Coffee," I said. "I usually stop at the drug store at Broad and Locust and have bacon and eggs."

"And lunch at your club. When you're having dinner alone what do you do?"

"One of the other clubs, or I can have it sent in from the hotel across the way. But usually at the Racquet Club. Why?"

"That's the life you like, you see? You could afford a much larger apartment and a full-time servant, but you prefer this. I do too, really. The difference being that I do my own cooking, make my own bed and so on. Once a week I have a woman come in to give the place a good cleaning. Are you simply dying to give me a present?"

"Yes."

"They're going to raise my rent from seventy-five to a hundred dollars a month. I could get a cheaper apartment but I don't want to, and so I've been wondering where I could economize, to make up the difference. I figured out that I could save ten dollars a month by going to the hairdresser twice a month instead of once a week. But then what? I went over all my bills and I was amazed to discover that I spend about fifty cents a day on perfume. It comes to that, about fifty cents a day. Fifteen dollars a month. Now if you would like to leave a standing order with your drug store to send me a bottle of perfume once a month, I could go on staying in my apartment and smelling nice, too."

"Write down the name of the perfume or I'll forget it," I said.

"It's a hundred and eighty dollars a year," she said.

"I'll be able to swing it," I said.

"In case I should happen to impulsively marry someone else, I'll tell the drug store to stop sending it to me."

"It would be a waste of time to offer you money, wouldn't it?" I said.

"Don't try *too* hard," she said. "Actually, the way I feel about it is, if I really need more money, I can get a job. Me, that never wears a hat, I have a standing offer to work in a millinery shop. There's a new little fairy on Market Street near the Y.M.C.A. who thinks I'm just *per*fectly a*dor*able, and he'll pay me two hundred dollars a month, five days from ten to four. He calls me Butch, or did till I told him I knew what it meant in fairy talk."

"What does it mean?"

"It means a bull-dike."

"Well, you're certainly not that," I said.

"No, that's the least of my problems. I've had my palm scratched by several women, but that's as far as they ever got. Actually, you know, I think I'm under-sexed. I can go awfully long without it, and the man always has to be somewhat unusual. I know a girl at home that gets tight and she frankly admitted to me that it might just as well be a broom-handle, for all the difference it makes. She doesn't give a damn about the preliminaries, or giving the man any pleasure."

"Do you call me somewhat unusual?"

"I should say I do. Anybody that's put up with me all these years. I'm sure I know you better than anyone else does, but how well is that? Sometimes when I leave you after spending the night with you, I say to myself, 'What does he really think of me? Or does he think of me at all?' I know that we have love, love, love, but sometimes I think I'm just a lay, lay, lay, although I know better. I don't think I could live without knowing that you were somewhere on the same earth."

"How are you going to break it to the doctor?" I said.

"I don't know," she said. "We hadn't set an actual date. Vaguely sometime in the next few months. What I'll probably do is wait till he says something about a definite date, and then I'll put him off. Then the next time he brings it up again, I'll put him off again. On the other hand, I might just tell him tomorrow. I don't know."

"The fair thing to do would be to tell him tomorrow," I said.

"Yes, that would be the fair thing. So I may. On the other hand, what has fairness got to do with it?"

"That's entirely up to you and how you feel about him."

"If I went out with someone else a few times, he might get the message."

"I should think so," I said. "As a doctor's wife in Gibbsville you'd be expected to give up dates with other men."

"If I were going to marry him, I wouldn't have dates with other men, but since I'm not going to marry him, I think I'll have a few dates and let him tell me that that has to stop. Then I'll say I'm sorry, but it isn't going to stop, and that will give him a good out. Result—no wedding bells, but no hard feelings. I like him, and I don't want to lose him as a friend. Also, I want him to go on being my doctor."

"It sounds to me as though Dr. Young might turn into a Gibbsville version of me," I said.

"No, but he might turn into a Gibbsville version of Dr. Young. You see, I can tell you about him but I could never tell him about you. It always comes down to that. I never tell them about you. You're private and personal to me. There's probably some very good psychological reason for that, but offhand I wouldn't know what it is."

"If I were just a little older I might say that you were ashamed of me," I said.

"I see what you mean, yes, but not a woman that's had two husbands and liable to have six," she said. "I wonder, Phil, if we saw each other oftener, would we always spend so much time talking about what's kept us together?"

"No, not if we saw each other oftener."

"We meet, and we're like a child studying its own belly-button," she said. "I was twelve years old before I understood that, either. I still don't understand why men have nipples, but they *would* look very strange without them, now that I've got used to them. Have you got a lot of work to do?"

"It doesn't have to be done tonight," I said.

"If I weren't here, it would be, though."

"Yes," I said.

"Well, let me do the dishes and put things away, and I'll have a bath and get into a pair of your pajamas. Then we can go to bed early and get a good night's sleep and I'll get your breakfast in the morning. You won't have to go to the drug store."

"That seems like a very sensible program," I said. We even made sensible love that night, and at seven-thirty in the morning she brought me a cup of coffee. She was already dressed in a sweater and the skirt of her Glen plaid suit. "Couldn't you sleep?" I said.

"As if I'd been pole-axed, till about six o'clock," she said.

I put my hand under her skirt and felt her leg. She stood still. "Do you think that's wise?" she said.

"What do you think?" I said.

"Whatever you want. All this can come off in no time," she said.

"Are you trying to spare me because I suddenly got old?"

"Well, something like that," she said. "But if you keep doing that, I'm not going to give a damn how old you are."

"Let's see how quickly you can take that stuff off," I said.

"Before you can change your mind, that's how quickly," she said.

"Remember a tune by Vincent Youmans? 'Day will break and you'll awake'?"

"No singing before breakfast," she said. "Supposed to be very bad luck."

"If you don't believe in God you can't believe in foolish superstitions," I said.

She lay on top of me. "Stop being so bossy so early in the morning. If there's anything I hate it's a bossy old man."

"If there's anything I love it's you," I said.

"I know," she said. "That—I know."

I remembered to place the order for her perfume, and for

seven or eight months the only communication I had with her—if it could be called that—was the monthly bill from the drug store. Then my firm took a case involving some mineral rights near Gibbsville and I volunteered to confer with one of the principals, a boyhood chum of mine. We were not at all sure that we wanted to go into court with the case, and someone had to explain the delay. Accordingly, I drove up to Gibbsville and spent the day with my friend. "It was damn nice of you to come," he said. "But I wish they'd told me it was going to be you. Mary and I could have had some of the old crowd in for dinner."

"That's just what I didn't want," I said. "I'll have a little look around, and I may even drive back tonight."

My look around consisted of finding Andrea's telephone number and a visit, on foot, to her apartment. She was pleased but not overjoyed to see me. "Am I wrong, or am I getting a cool reception?" I said.

"No, you're right," she said.

"Did I louse up other plans?"

"I had to get out of something else," she said.

"Dr. Young?"

"Oh, no. Not that kind of thing. It's my brother. If it isn't my brother it's my mother, and in between it's my father. The store is in trouble, and my mother is hitting the bottle and Bud's had a fight with Daddy. The last time I saw you you told me some things about the store. I wish you'd told me more."

"I didn't know more. I was only conjecturing," I said.

"My father is turning out to be a crook. At least that's what Bud thinks."

"Whose money is he stealing?" I said.

"Ours. Mother's and Bud's and mine, among others. I don't want to talk about it," she said.

"I do. It's obviously what's uppermost in your mind, and as long as it is, there's no use talking about anything else."

"All right," she said. "It's complicated, and it's nothing he can be arrested for. But it's crooked. As I understand it, from Bud, Daddy is deliberately letting the store go to hell. They've had an offer to sell it to a chain of stores, with Daddy to be manager if they sold. But Daddy hasn't got any stock in the company. It's all Mother's and Bud's and mine and some cousins'. Bud is our advisor. Before that we always did exactly what Daddy said, but Bud found out that the chain people had offered some ridiculously low price for King's, and Daddy was trying to persuade us to accept it. He had Mother all but talked into it."

"I begin to get the picture," I said.

"Oh, there's a lot more, but that's the gist of it. Bud wants us to fire Daddy, but Daddy has a contract with the company that we all voted for without reading it. Twenty-five thousand dollars a year for life, a share in the profits, et cetera. Can you imagine anybody being such a son of a bitch? According to Bud, Daddy gets some kind of a bonus if the chain stores buy King's. That's why he's so eager to have us sell. That, and an agreement that he'll be the new manager. Daddy has cut down the inventory so that the chain stores won't have to pay for goods on the shelves, and there *are* no goods on the shelves. Customers ask for things, and we're out of them. The chain store of course can buy everything cheaper than we can."

"You're learning something about business," I said.

"I wish I had earlier. I'm working. I have a job in a hat store on Market Street."

"The new little fairy?" I said.

"Oh, did I tell you about that? I guess I did."

"You probably have a case against your father if you wanted to sue him."

"Bud would, but Mother won't, and she can outvote everybody else. Such a hypocrite, my father. He'd never allow us to take a discount at the store unless we were actually on the payroll. Things like that. But he has a Cadillac that the company paid for and his expense account is something you wouldn't believe, according to Bud. He never spends a cent of his own money if he can help it. Mother paid all of Bud's expenses through college, and their house is in his name, although she paid for it. That's enough. Who are you suing? Anybody I know?"

"This isn't that kind of case. It has to do with mineral rights. Mighty dull stuff at this stage of the game," I said.

"How long are you going to be in town?" she said.

"That depends on you. I may go back tonight," I said.

"You can stay, but you have to be out of here before daylight. You can't be seen leaving at eight or nine o'clock in the morning. And you'd be recognized. This building is full of people you used to know. In fact, you may have made a mistake coming here in the first place, but I wasn't thinking very clearly when you phoned."

"I take it you've had your dinner," I said.

"Yes, I was just putting the dishes away when you arrived," she said.

She took a cigarette out of a box and tapped it, a gesture which was not habitual with her. "Listen, are you sore at me?" I said. "And if so, what for?"

"No, I'm not sore at you, but if you stay here tonight I'm going to be more careful. The last time, you knocked me up. That morning when I was all dressed and ready to give you your breakfast. I was unprepared, but I took a chance. Bingo! That's twice you've got me pregnant."

"Why didn't you let me know?" I said.

"What for? You couldn't come and hold my hand."

"Don't tell me Dr. Young performed the abortion," I said.

"Well, he did, and that solved the problem of whether to tell him I wasn't going to marry him. Neatly. 'By the way, Doctor, I'm not going to marry you, and while I'm here will you take care of this little problem?'"

"You didn't say that," I said.

"No, it wasn't as easy as that. He took it rather big. It wasn't any fun at all for either of us. And right about then Bud began telling me what was going on at the store. So you see I'm not sore at just you. I'm sour on the world, and have been for months. The only person I can let down my hair with is my boss. The little fairy. He's the most sympathetic man, woman, or child I've ever known."

"You told him about your abortion?"

"After it was all over and I went to work for him, he asked me one day if I was having love-trouble, and he was so kind that I burst into tears and told him everything but names. He's like a mother hen. Makes me sit down and rest between customers. Takes me to the movies, and dinner at the hotel. Next month we're going to New York together on a buying trip. He's the only bright spot in these last few months, I must say."

"What's his name?"

"His real name is John W. Metz, from Swedish Haven. But he calls himself Jacques. The name of the shop is Jacques, no last name. He studied to be a schoolteacher, but they expelled him in his second year in spite of having good marks and everything. He had a very hard time getting a job. In fact, at one time he worked as a stock-boy at King's, and that was how he got interested in millinery. His father wouldn't have anything to do with him, but he had a sister that helped him get started in business. He's a very good businessman, too. That's the Pennsylvania Dutch, I guess. He reads everything. Books. *The New Yorker. Time. The Wall Street Journal!* You should see his apartment. There's nothing else like it in Gibbsville. It's on the third floor of the building the shop's in, and when you get inside you can't believe you're not in New York or Paris. Très moderne, ness pa? I *love* him."

"Why, I think you do," I said.

She shook her head. "He has boy friends. One's a politician, a really quite horrible man, looks as if he ought to be a priest. He's not, though. He even has the nerve to bring his wife to the shop and sit there while she tries on hats. The only good thing is he can keep Jack out of the clutches of the law. Once in a while they have parties on Saturday night that get a bit raucous. Not that it's a residential neighborhood any more, but they do get noisy."

"I'm very sorry about the pregnancy," I said.

"It was worse on Sam than on anyone else. The blow to his pride, to start with. As I said, he took it big. But just as bad was the fact that he didn't want to do the abortion. He'd warned me once before, and this time he asked me please to go to someone else. He recommended two other doctors. But I said I was frightened. He even tried to get me to have the baby. Even if the father was a married man, I ought to have the baby. And he said frankly he was just as frightened as I was. I said that if anything happened to me, they'd never be able to trace it to him. *I'd* never tell on him. So, there in his office, without a nurse or anyone to assist him, he did it. Nothing went wrong then, but he'd warned me about these fits of depression, and he was certainly right. On top of which, came all this business about the store."

"I feel left out," I said.

"My troubles aren't your troubles," she said.

"I have no troubles to compare with yours," I said. "And besides, you're wrong. Your troubles are my troubles, as far as my wanting to share them is concerned. Apart from the fact that I'm not married and would gladly have married you. Dr. Young was right, there."

"Don't *you* start telling me I should have had the baby. It's a little late for that," she said. "It's easy to say now."

"There's never been a moment in the last fifteen years when I wouldn't have married you if you'd said the word."

"Oh, that's a lie, Phil. That's such a lie that it should have stuck in your throat."

"There were times when I was more ready than others, but I *don't* lie to you. What it comes down to is that you preferred dying to marrying me."

"That's something you just thought up to put me in the wrong. You love to argue, and twist what I say," she said.

"Half true. I love to argue with you, and I suppose I enjoy the give-and-take. But I play fair, and I don't reinforce my arguments with untruths. From force of habit a lawyer is probably more aware of truth and untruth than anyone else."

"Oh, lawyers are not more honest than other people," she said.

"I didn't say anything about honesty. I only said we were more aware, from force of habit, of the truth. We can distort it, in various ways, but we're accustomed to speaking for the record and extremely conscious of such things as perjured testimony, and disbarment proceedings, and so on. Honesty, ethics—that's another matter."

"Oh, shut up," she said.

"Very well," I said. "We're also pretty good at controlling our tempers."

"I said, shut up."

"If we're not going to talk, there's no point in my staying here."

"There's no point anyway," she said. "What you really came here for you're not going to get."

"You haven't even got a very high opinion of yourself, have you? I came here to see you. Sex isn't the only thing that's kept us together all these years." I stood up. "I'll leave you with this thought, my girl. What if I'd come to Gibbsville and not telephoned you? Sex or no sex. Goodnight, and I'm very sorry."

Never in a mllion years would she have called me back after I closed the door, and knowing that, I took my time in making my departure. But she let me go, and the walk back to the hotel was a dreary one. There were not many people on the street; it was just after the dinner hour for most of them. But at one time I had known the ownership of every house in the ten blocks to the hotel, and I had been inside a good many of them, played in their back yards. In a couple of days all my old friends would know that I had been in town on business, and some of them would be hurt or annoyed because I had not looked them up. But I had reconciled myself to that before leaving Philadelphia; what I did not like was this furtive walk from Andrea's apartment to the hotel. I wanted to drive back to the city, but I was too tired physically and my visit to Andrea had not revived me. At the hotel I asked to have dinner in my room and was told that room service was not available after eight o'clock, and so I had to throw my weight around with the manager, whom I did not know but who knew who I was. He assured me that *of course* in my case I could have dinner in my room. When it arrived the soup was tepid and the chicken and vegetables were not even as warm as that. "Be sure and put the tray out in the hall, will you?" said the waiter. No "please" and no "thank-you" for the tip. And no "goodnight." I got out some transcripts of testimony in old mineral rights cases, and wished I was back in Rittenhouse Square. At six o'clock in the morning—I must say I slept well—I asked the telephone operator if I could have a cup of coffee in my room. He, probably a bellboy, said the kitchen wasn't open yet but if a cup of coffee was all I wanted, he himself would bring me that and a cinnamon bun. In five minutes he was at my door, with a thermos of hot coffee and a bun. I gave him five dollars, but I almost kissed him too. "You know this is a five?" he said.

"I know it's a five," I said.

He laughed. "This don't even go on your bill," he said. "They got no way to charge you till the checker comes on in the kitchen. But thanks."

"Not at all. Virtue must not go unrewarded," I said.

"Didn't you used to be here in town?" he said.

"I was born here," I said.

"You's smart to get out. There's nothin' here no more. Nothin'. You used to have the house out Lantenengo, between Fifteenth and Sixteenth?"

"That's right," I said.

"Delivered groceries there, many a time," he said. "I remember that kitchen. A big coal stove, you could of put a thirty-pound turkey in that oven. You had a colored woman for a cook. I used to sit there and get warm."

"You must have worked for Frank Snodgrass."

"For Frank Snodgrass is right. Christ, all them old stores went out of business. The out-of-town chains. I tell you, there's nothin' here. Nothin'."

"I'm afraid you're right," I said.

"Well, I gotta start wakin' them up. Thanks for the fin."

I had no idea who he was, I don't think I had ever seen him before. He probably had been the Snodgrass delivery man during my years at prep school and college. But he remembered Rhoda Hume, our cook, and our Buckeye range, and as far as I was concerned he was right about Gibbsville. For him and for me there was nothin' there, nothin'.

I wrote a note to Andrea. "It is now 7:30 A.M. and I am about to leave. Too early to telephone you. I have finished my business here and will not be coming back. If you need me, or if I can do anything for you, you know where to reach me. I am going abroad next month for about seven weeks, but will leave word with my secretary to forward any messages from you. Love, Phil." I posted the note on my way out of the hotel.

For almost twenty years, now, our love affair had consisted of brief meetings and absences that varied in length. On my part, and I am sure on hers, there had been no deceitfulness; no broken promises of fidelity since there had been no promises. A certain amount, probably a great deal, of honesty ensued as an accompaniment of the freedom we granted ourselves. I was able, for instance, to admit to myself without shame that it was very pleasant to have a love affair with a stunning young woman who came and went and did nothing to disarrange my comfortable bachelorhood. If I occasionally accused myself of selfishness, I defended myself on the ground that she had more than once refused to marry me. Equally true, I could defensively argue, was the fact that I was a convenience for her. In her somewhat raffish life I was the one consistently dependable man to give her the emotional security that she seemed to reject by her conduct with the others. So much so that morally I was probably bad for her. She could always turn to steadfast me, and she always did.

But it was her nature to pass herself around among men, and she would have done so whether I was in her background or not. It was therefore a spurious twinge of conscience that I sometimes allowed myself. Long ago she had told me the complete details of her love affair with the boy in California, and though I was the first male with whom she experienced true copulation, she and the boy had gone from fellatio to coitus interruptus, which she was pleased to call heavy necking. It also pleased her (and my masculinity) to regard me as the taker of her virginity, but the distinction was to at least some extent honorary. We had something besides the sexual relationship, and had had it from the start. But, circumstances permitting, we had always had intercourse at some point during our sporadic reunions. It was customary, and we had always taken it for granted. As usual, I had taken it for granted when I visited her in her apartment, and my dissatisfaction with our meeting was two-fold: I had not gone to bed with her, as I had been looking forward to doing, and our conversation had not brought out a physical reason, meaning the after-effects of her latest abortion, for her coolness. I was inclined to believe that she had not been to bed with anyone since the abortion, and I tended to substantiate my belief with her account of her fondness for her pansy employer. I had known a Philadelphia girl who, after a bad abortion, took up with a band of homosexuals and became one herself, never to return to heterosexuality. At the moment I had no such fears for Andrea, but I did not give the matter much thought. I was more deeply concerned with my overall relationship with her, and disturbed by the appearance of a coolness that was without precedent. We had had quarrels aplenty, but coolness never. As I drove back to Philadelphia I tried to correlate the new coolness with the angry outburst in which she had thrown the glass at me. It was possible that a deep-seated resentment of me had existed that far back, despite the fact that we went on that night to make love with tenderness and consideration. Although I cared for no one else in the world, I realized that I did not know her, and in self-preservation I began to make preparations for the contingency of life without her.

That, however, was not easy. I said I began to make preparations, but no specific preparations occurred to me. How do you go about making plans to live without something you never really had? If she had been really my mistress, I most likely would have had some possessions of hers in my apartment, to put in a box and send back to her. But I did not have so much as a douche bag, a toothbrush, to get rid of. The only thing of that sort that I could do would be to tell the drug store to stop sending her that monthly bottle of perfume, and I briefly considered that move to remind her that she had banished me. But in addition to its being ridiculously petty, such a move would have been effective as a reminder just once. Oddly enough, though, I had hit upon a most significant detail. A couple of days after I got back from the Gibbsville fiasco, the drug store, one of the last of the old-time ethical pharmacies, sent me a letter to notify me that at the request of Mrs. Cooper, they were discontinuing monthly delivery of the perfume. So she had put me out of her life.

Fortunately for my state of mind, I had made my plans for the trip abroad, which was to combine pleasure and business. My passage had been booked in both directions, my hotel reservations made, and the exact time of my business appointments in London, Paris, Brussels, and Berlin was set. On the social side, I had accepted invitations for the two weekends I would be in

England, as well as for the weekend that I would be in France, and it was a safe guess that my overseas acquaintances would wish to entertain for me as the representative of clients. My schedule was tight, but for once I welcomed the restrictions on my free time. I would not have to brood about that little bitch.

I began brooding about her the moment the *Queen Mary* sounded its horn and backed into the channel in the North River. The sound of the horn went right to my guts and standing alone on the boat deck I ignored the Manhattan skyline and stared out toward the Jersey meadows, where her lover had been done in, and I tried to guess the precise direction of a straight line to Gibbsville, Pennsylvania, where at this moment she would be in all likelihood having lunch at the Y.M.C.A. cafeteria. People like her, in jobs like hers, all had lunch at the "Y" cafeteria. I would be having mine shortly in the Verandah Grill of the *Queen Mary*, with a Boston lawyer and his wife who were on their way to a world convention of breeders of Dandie Dinmonts at Edinburgh. I had a feeling that I was going to see a lot of Mr. and Mrs. Wallen, and I was right. She introduced me to her sister, another Dandie Dinmont fancier, and the four of us played bridge all the way to Southampton. By skill, luck, and intense concentration on the cards, I won sixty-five dollars.

The whole trip was like that, more or less. In Brussels, where my business acquaintance was a fat bachelor, I was provided with a tall young blonde who could have worn any item of Andrea's clothes. She was very pleasing to the eye and to the senses, and was under strict orders to accept no money from me. But I gave her fifty dollars anyhow so that she would not think the less kindly of gentlemen from Philadelphia. She knew of Philadelphia as the hometown of Grace Kelly, of the cinema, and of Eddie Fisher, a singer. No, I had never met Miss Kelly or Fisher, and I had to assure the young woman that it was not so much because I was a *snopp* as that Philadelphia was a large city, about twice as many people as Brussels, which she manifestly did not believe. She was a very competent professional, kept busy by the delegates to the Benelux Customs Union, and was moderately pleased when I told her that she reminded me very much of a young woman I knew in the United States. "Your mistress?" she said, and I said yes, and let it go at that. She had guessed immediately that I was not married, and could not explain her guess other than to say that she had never yet been wrong. Intuition. I could not reasonably argue with that; intuitively I had guessed that she was a high-class whore.

She was my only physical contact with her sex throughout my trip, and just what I wanted. I wanted no involvement with a non-professional, no polite wooing for the privilege of the bed. Twice I had conversations with my secretary on the overseas telephone, and she would not have failed to report a message from Andrea. The distance and the time that had intervened since my Gibbsville fiasco now seemed very great indeed. I attributed that notion to my realizing, retroactively, that Andrea intended the rupture to be permanent. If that were the case, three weeks and three thousand miles were only the beginning, and if so, I would do well to make a more serious effort to dismiss her from my thoughts. That I had never done, neither on this trip nor in the past, when she had stayed away from me for a year at a time.

Going home, in the *Queen Elizabeth*, I played bridge with other men for higher stakes than I had played for with the Wallens. I hate to lose at anything, particularly at bridge, and I suggested the ten-cents-a-point game because it was the only way I knew to divert me from the excitement I had begun to feel as soon as I boarded the ship. I drank a little more than I usually do; not enough to have a noticeable effect on my bridge game, but enough to make me ready for sleep when our nightly game was over. There was nothing—meaning no one, meaning Andrea —waiting for me at home, and yet the excitement demanded some attention. Several nights I went to bed quite sozzled, the result of nightcaps following the bridge games. On totting up the score on the night before we were to land, I was delighted to find that I had won more than a thousand tax-free dollars, and I was gratified to discover that the bridge and the whiskey had had the desired palliative effect. One disturbing note: as he paid up, one of my bridge-game companions said, "For a man that put away as much Scotch as you did, you played awfully good bridge." He was a New Yorker, a member of my New York club, and I was glad he was not Philadelphian. At home no one had ever had occasion to comment on my intake of whiskey. I had actually never been a heavy drinker by the standards of the men whom I saw every day. Yet the bridge companion had seen fit to comment on the quantity of my drinking and not on the effect on me.

The next day one of our clients sent a company limousine to meet me at the pier and transport me to Philadelphia, and I was home in time for lunch at the club. Lunch at a club was the antithesis of the kind of excitement that I had been subduing on the ship. I took my seat at the large, common table, and the man next to me said, "I missed you the last couple days," and the man on the other side of me asked me if I had had a good trip. That was par for the course, and I was home again, back in the old routine. From the club I walked to my office, spent an hour with my secretary and another hour with my partners. By quitting time it was hard to believe that I had been in New York that morning, and the most surprising thing of all was that as I slipped back into my routine, I almost believed that Andrea was where she had always been as a sort of offstage character in the comedy-drama of my life. Everything else was the same; why not she? But she refused to stay put in the customary role.

The next few weeks were busy ones for me. After all, I had spent about $7,000 of other people's money, and they were entitled to their conferences and my reports and opinions. I found that it was taking as long to report on the trip as the trip itself had taken, and one day I happened to notice on my calendar that four months had passed since my visit to Gibbsville. It did not seem possible. Meanwhile the mineral rights case had been turned over to Whitman, one of our junior partners, and it was trudging along as such cases tend to do. It could and might go on for years. Two teams of accountants were working on the basically same set of figures and coming out with wildly disparate results, a normal condition when the accountants are on opposite sides of the fence. At a senior partners' weekly meeting, during which we regularly go through the list of our cases, I said, "What about Southern Anthracite? Any progress there?"

Joe Sloan, one of the senior partners, said, "Slow as molasses, Phil. You wouldn't like to have another go at it?"

"Isn't Whitman doing all he can?" I said.

"No criticism of Whitman, but he's young. If we want to goose them, one of us will have to go. It must be six months since you went up to Gibbsville—"

"It's four," I said.

"Well, do you want to wait another two months and then go up? This thing may drag along and drag along till nobody gets any money out of it but the accountants. I was thinking that we could have our accountants do a pressure job, work overtime if necessary, and finish up well ahead of their accountants. Then if you went up to Gibbsville with the final figures you could get both litigants together and say, 'Here it is, let's sit down and work this out.' They won't take our figures as gospel, but they'll have a basis to work on. And I'm afraid you're elected, Phil. You're the only one they'll all listen to. I'd like to get this case finalized. I hate to see all that money going to the accountants, and not to us."

"Joe, you're just greedy," I said.

"I know I am. My one besetting sin," he said.

"I'll think it over and let you know tomorrow," I said.

If Joe Sloan's one besetting sin was greed—which it was not—mine was curiosity. I agreed to go to Gibbsville, and arranged to have a little article printed in the Gibbsville papers to the effect that the Southern Anthracite mineral rights dispute might be reaching its final stages ("Settlement Looms," the paper said) with the arrival of the noted Philadelphia attorney, meaning me, for several days of conferences. The dispute was of sufficient local interest to warrant its being printed on the front page, where Andrea would not miss it. This time everybody in town would know I was coming.

Before departing I received hasty invitations from the Lantenengo Bar Association, the Gibbsville Chamber of Commerce, and the Gibbsville Rotary Club to say a few words. With my judicial ambition in mind, I accepted the Bar Association invitation. They promised that their meeting would be informal, one of their regular monthly dinners, and that they were not asking me to prepare a speech. Anything I cared to say. Off the record. Intra-professional. No questions relating to the Southern Anthracite case or the subject of mineral rights. Just a hastily planned get-together in tribute to one of the county's most distinguished sons.

In theory, I was only the attorney for one party to the mineral rights dispute, but obviously during the first all-day conference I was in command. Whenever anyone was speaking, he would address me, and I slowly assumed the position of arbiter. I had Whitman with me to dig the appropriate papers out of his attaché case, and until late afternoon I did not say a word. Then, shortly after five o'clock, I said, "Gentlemen, this thing has gone on long enough. Here we are, eight men who are reasonable men, men of good will and personal integrity, here to serve the best interests of the people we represent. If that were not the case, I would not do what I am about to do." I paused and looked at each man, excluding Whitman. Across the table was a shyster who should have been disbarred years ago; a johnny-come-lately to the coal industry who had once been a bootlegger; a weak sister of a fellow whose family name was as old as the mining of hard coal; a man from Wilkes-Barre who had been in a lot of trouble for violations of the safety regulations. On our side of the table, besides Whitman and me, were our clients. I reached in my inside coat pocket and drew out a sheet of paper. "This is a memorandum that we prepared in my office. It is confidential, but I am going to read it to you." I then recited, or intoned, an almost day-to-day list of the expenses of the dispute between the two parties: accountants' fees, accountants' expenses, our disbursements, and so on and so on. I gave them five minutes of $125 for this, $54 for that, and finished up by saying, "That comes to sixty-two thousand, nine hundred and twelve dollars and twenty-seven cents. Sixty-two thousand, nine hundred and twelve dollars and twenty-seven cents. That's a lot of coal, gentlemen. A lot of coal. But you haven't even heard the half of it. You may have noticed that I did not mention legal fees. I don't know what our fee will be, but I doubt if it will be less than the accountants' fees. Let's say it will be the same. Sixty-three thousand dollars. That comes to, in round numbers, one hundred and twenty-six thousand dollars. That's *our* side of it. Let's say that your side of it matches that figure. That means that two hundred and fifty-two thousand dollars has been spent by both sides so far. *So far!* At the rate we're going, we could go well over the half-a-million-dollar mark. A half a million dollars is a lot of coal, a lot of coal. You could build a breaker for that kind of money. You could buy fifty trucks. But that's not all. If we go into court, the legal expenses on both sides will be staggering. Staggering. And even *that* isn't all, because I assure you gentlemen, if our side loses, we are going to appeal, and if our side wins, your side will probably appeal." I paused, to let the financial points sink in, and then I continued: "We have all had a tough day. I suggest we adjourn until ten o'clock tomorrow morning." I then, in my capacity as unofficial arbiter, stood up to give the signal for the others to stand up. They did so. If they had not done so, my argument would have been futile, but I had been silent all day and studying the opposition's shyster. They all got up automatically, and the meeting broke up then and there.

"That was masterful," Whitman whispered to me as he was putting his papers back in the attaché case.

"Maybe it was, but I hope you don't think it was the argument that did it. It was the timing and the psychology. Let's get out of here quick," I said.

I had won the case and I knew it. The details would be worked out later. I felt like one of those football players who, having scored a touchdown, leave the ball on the ground for the umpire to pick up. "Tomorrow you take over," I said to Whitman.

"You're not going to be there?" said Whitman.

"That's part of the psychology," I said. "I'll be at the hotel if you need me, but I have no intention of facing that shyster Spockman. He'll spend the night thinking up arguments against me, but they're not going to be any good if I'm not there. You go to the meeting as though we'd agreed to behave sensibly, and I think you'll find that Spockman will be the only hold-out. Care to join me for a drink?"

"No sir, I have to call Mr. Sloan, but thanks."

"I'll be at the Gibbsville Club, then there's a Bar Association dinner that I'm going to. Look in if you feel like it," I said. "It's at the hotel."

I saw some old friends at the Gibbsville Club, where I had retained my non-resident membership. I stayed there until it was time to go to the Bar Association dinner, at which I arrived in a very very cheerful mood. Somehow the rumor had spread that I had conducted a highly successful meeting in the mineral rights case, and I was compelled several times to say that congratulations were premature; but I was a lawyer among lawyers, and they were aware, and pleased, that I had outsmarted Mr. Spockman. He, of course, stayed away from the dinner.

When it came my turn to speak, I played it safe. I was not drunk, but I had had a lot to drink, and this seemed to be a good opportunity to dispel the notion that I was a stuffed shirt. I therefore confined my remarks to professional jokes and anecdotes about old-time members of the county bench and bar. I turned the meeting into a social evening, and when it was over I was told repeatedly that it was the liveliest session they had had in years. About a dozen of us repaired to the taproom to reminisce. At midnight I grew weary of their adulation and obsequiousness, and said goodnight.

There were two identical telephone messages under my door. I checked the number in the telephone book, and it was Andrea, who had not left her name. "Please call 625-1181," and the calls had been received during the time I was at the Gibbsville Club. I called her, and I woke her up. Her speech was slow, heavy with sleep, and I had trouble making her understand that it was I who was calling. "I took a sleeping pill," she said, obviously with an effort.

"Go back to sleep," I said.

"All right," she said, and hung up. She was no good to me that night, and I took a bottle of Scotch out of my bag and poured a nightcap. She was no damn good to me, full of sleeping pills and dead to the world.

In a way, to be perfectly truthful, I was relieved. I had come to Gibbsville on the early morning train, had gone almost immediately to the morning meeting, lunched with Whitman and our clients, returned to the afternoon meeting, and built up to the climax of the meeting which was my speech to Spockman and the others. Then instead of slowing down, I had kept going at the Gibbsville Club and the Bar Association dinner. More than eighteen hours of more or less intense effort. I was annoyed but at the same time grateful that for that night there would be no more demands on my physical and mental resources. I got to bed without finishing my nightcap, and fell asleep with the light on.

From another world came the ringing of my telephone. It rang several times, stopped, and then was rung again with renewed vigor. "For Christ's sake," I said, and answered it. It was my old friend the night man who had delivered groceries for Snodgrass. "There's a lady to see you, sir."

"To *see* me? You mean downstairs?"

"Yes sir, she says you sent for her and she won't go away," he said. In a lower tone, barely audible, he added: "It's somebody you know."

"All right, send her up," I said.

I had time to splash some cold water on my face and run a comb through my hair, but I was unsteady and drowsy when the rap came on the fireproof door. Behind her stood the night man, waiting to see if I was going to let her in. "Hello, come in," I said, and the door closed behind her.

"You did send for me, didn't you?" she said.

"No, I didn't, but you're here," I said.

"Did I imagine it? You did call me, didn't you?"

"Yes, but you were full of sleeping pills, you said."

"One. Not pills, just one."

"I might as well be," I said. "My sleeping pill was Scotch."

"So I see," she said, looking at the unfinished nightcap.

"Do you want some?" I said. "Did I hear three o'clock strike?"

"You could have. It's after four, now."

"Then I didn't hear three o'clock strike. I was really pounding away. Do you want a drink of Scotch? And tap water? It's all I can offer you at this hour."

"And you're not offering that very graciously. No thanks," she said. "Go on back to bed," she said. "I woke up thinking you'd sent for me, but if you didn't—the hell with it."

"How'd you get here?"

"On my Flexible-Flyer," she said. "What do you mean, how did I get here? I have a car. It sits out in front of my apartment all night, case some traveling salesman gets horny. *How* did I *get* here!"

I was coming to, and I knew it by the fact that desire for her was growing in me. I closed the windows, and put on my dressing-gown. "I'm not going to pull a knife on you," I said. "There's no use watching me that way."

"*I'm* not going to pull a knife on *you*, either."

"Well, why don't you take off your coat?"

"Because it's still cold in here," she said.

I turned up the thermostat. "Take off your coat," I said.

"Are we going to go to bed?" she said.

"That's always up to you," I said.

"No, it isn't," she said. "That's what I came here for, but that was when I thought you'd sent for me. However, you deny that. You *didn't* send for me, and I was laboring under a misapprehension."

"If I ask you now, politely and unequivocally, will you go to bed with me?"

"Are either one of us going to get any pleasure out of it?" she said. "I don't think I'll be any good."

"Well, then let's talk," I said. "Frankly, I thought I was never going to see you again."

"I thought I was going to have to struggle along without you, too," she said.

"And you seem to have," I said. "Are you still working at the hat store?"

"Thank *God* I am. Otherwise I would be waiting for horny salesmen to call me at night," she said. "You heard about King's?"

"No."

"Bankruptcy, or receivership. Anyway, it's going out of business. Daddy flew the coop, taking all the cash with him. Mother is living with Bud, my brother. She rented her house, furnished, and that's all she has to live on. Fortunately, she doesn't have to spend much money on food. Just give her a bottle of vodka every day and she's happy and contented."

"That must be pretty tough on your brother. What is he living on?"

"He's a substitute teacher in the high school, and his wife's family are giving them something. There are so many people around here having financial difficulties, it's becoming quite the thing. I hate this hotel. It's always filled up with people from out-of-town, squeezing the last dollar out of Gibbsville."

"What about the hat store?"

"It's amazing. Women can always scrape up twelve-ninety-five for a hat."

"And your fairy friend, your boss?"

"One of the few prosperous men in town," she said.

"And you still love him dearly?" I said.

"Of course I do," she said. "If he was a man, I'd marry him. And he says the same thing about me."

"What about the doctor?"

"He comes to see me once in a while. We go out to dinner together."

"And?"

"Oh, sure," she said.

"Then you might marry him after all," I said.

"No. We don't even discuss marriage any more. We have dinner together. Sex. And he goes home. He's seriously considering going back in the Navy again. If they'll take him back as a lieutenant commander, and let him take a two-year course in urology, he'll go. He's in the reserve, and apparently they need doctors."

"He's willing to give up twenty thousand a year?"

"It's less than that now, and he wouldn't have to pay rent and a secretary and all that. It makes a lot of sense."

She stood up and took off her coat and folded it on the back of a chair. Then she kicked off her shoes and lay beside me on the bed. "Rather crowded in here," she said. She put her arms around me and kissed me on the mouth. "We're getting there," she said.

"I missed you," I said.

She nodded. "Yes," she said. She got up and took off her clothes and got back into bed with me. "Don't you think it'd be polite if you took yours off too?"

"It wouldn't be polite, exactly. I'm getting a paunch. But it'd be more comfortable."

"Well, then be comfortable," she said. She watched me. "You're not *getting* a paunch, you have one. What is it? The booze?"

"It's the booze," I said.

"Is that my fault?"

"If I want to put the blame on someone else, yes," I said.

"Don't become a drunkard on account of me," she said.

"I don't intend to become a drunkard," I said.

"You'd better be careful, then," she said.

"I'm careful," I said.

"No," she said. "You got drunk tonight, didn't you?"

"How did you know?"

"You didn't even finish your last drink," she said. She began to make love to me, startlingly like the Belgian girl, the girl in Brussels who had made me think of her. "Maybe if we went to sleep for a little while," she said.

"No," I said. "Unless you want to."

"Suddenly you lost interest," she said.

"It'll come back," I said.

"Oh, I know that," she said. She sat up. "There's something on your mind. Either that, or you're too tired. Which is it?"

I could not lie to her, so I told her about the Belgian girl.

"Well, it almost had to be something like that," she said. "Now we can forget about her—or, if you want to think about her, turn out the light."

"I don't want to think about her," I said.

"That's good. Don't think about me, either. The hell with thinking. It's me, Phil. Your girl." She nestled down, and slowly we returned to our old selves and now everything was all right.

"That was good," she said. "It's still good. With you it's never over so soon. There's always something left. Something nice. I don't know. Something nice. You have it for me, and I guess I have it for you."

"It'd be too obvious to call it love," I said.

"It obviously isn't love, either," she said. "Love quits on you. At least it always has on me. I guess you're my steady. How many years is it?"

"Oh—twenty."

"Then it certainly isn't love," she said. "Although it certainly is."

"We don't have to have a name for it," I said.

"Phil and Andrea, Incorporated," she said.

"Or as the French say, Société Anonyme," I said.

"I don't quite get it," she said.

"Americans say incorporated, the British say limited. The French say société anonyme, using the initials s.a. You probably thought they stood for sex appeal."

"You've lost me," she said.

"Well, the next time you look at a bottle of perfume—speaking of which, you sorehead."

She smiled. "Yes, that was sorehead. Now you can tell them to start sending it again. What was that horrid noise?"

"It sounded like a bus."

"That's exactly what it was. It's getting daylight," she said. "You have time for a few hours' sleep. And I have time to get out of here before everybody in Gibbsville sees me. Will you take me to dinner tonight, or come to my apartment?"

"Whatever you like."

"Come to my apartment. Société anonyme."

"All right, fine," I said.

I lay in bed and watched her get dressed, an operation that was almost as fascinating as watching her undress. "Shall I open the windows?" she said.

"If you don't mind," I said.

"Of course I don't mind. We have to have a clear head," she said. She kissed me on the forehead and went to the window and opened it. Then she went to the other window and opened it, and I don't know what happened because I was not watching. But when I did look she was not there, and I did not believe that until I heard a most awful scream. Then I believed it, and it is all I have left to believe.

FLIGHT

For the longest fraction of a second, while both feet were off the icy road, Charles Kinsmith was exhilarated. Then he hit the ground with a jolting, humiliating abruptness and for a full minute he remained in a sitting position. Physically and spiritually he was so shocked that he could not get up. But he was so anxious not to be seen in his plight that he summoned all his resources and slowly, cautiously, tentatively got to a kneeling and to a standing position, and walking flatfooted he made his way home.

"That you, Charles?" his wife called from the sitting-room.

"It's me," he said, and muttered to himself, "somewhat the worse for wear." He hung up his coat and hat and put away his stick.

"Wasn't it slippery out there?" she said, without looking up from her darning.

"Very," he said.

"How far did you go?" she said.

"About a half a mile, horizontally, and four feet perpendicularly."

She put her darning in her lap and took off her glasses. "Now let me figure that out. Horizontally is this way, and perpendicularly is up. Did you take a spill?"

"I took a spill. I went up in the air, both feet out from under me, and came down *bang!* on my coccyx bone."

"You poor *thing*," she said. "Did it shake you up? Why don't you have a drink?"

"I'm thinking of having a drink," he said.

"You didn't hit your head or anything, I hope?"

"No need to be alarmed. I'm suffering excruciating pain but nothing's broken."

"You *are* in pain?"

"Of course I'm in pain, woman. Most men would be making a big thing of this, but I happen to be brave."

"Yes, I think you're brave. I really do think so," she said. "At least you don't complain as much as most men. I'll get you a drink. What do you want?"

"A straight bourbon, with a water chaser," he said.

"You weren't wearing any rubbers, were you?" she said.

"The only thing that would have kept me from taking a spill was if I'd been wearing my creepers. Those ice creepers. But inasmuch as I don't know where I put them, I didn't have them on. I haven't had them on for four or five years. Nor have I taken a spill in that time."

"We're getting on," she said. She placed the water tumbler on the table beside him and handed him the glass of bourbon.

"We're not getting on. We're there," he said. "Thanks."

"I believe I'll have one myself."

"It's too early for you to start drinking now," he said.

"It is a littly early, but I just thought you wouldn't want to drink alone."

"This is a medicinal drink."

"Well, I've had a bit of a shock, too," she said.

"Oh? What happened to you?"

"Nothing happened to me, but I don't like to think of you slipping on the ice."

"Then in that case, have a drink."

"No, I guess not. It is too early," she said. "Have your drink and then go upstairs and take a real hot tub. With some Epsom salts in it, if we have any. If we haven't, I know we have some ordinary table salt. Does it hurt now?"

"Yes. It's going to hurt for two or three days. I probably won't be able to get out of bed tomorrow."

"It might be a good idea to call Dr. Gray," she said.

"I'll see how I feel after I've had my bath. If I can't go on enduring this excruciating agony, we can send for Jimmy Gray. He'll surely respond with his usual promptness, along about half past eleven."

"Not if I tell him you're in pain," she said. "He'll come right away, if he possibly can, or he'll send someone else."

"The bourbon is having a good effect."

"That's good," she said. "It may be the best thing for you."

"Four or five of these and I'll be feeling no pain," he said.

"If you're planning to have four or five, have them in the bedroom, because I couldn't possibly get you upstairs."

"Let's take the bottle upstairs and forget about dinner, forget about everything," he said.

"You sure you didn't strike your head?" she said.

"I know the difference between my head and my coccyx bone," he said.

"I'll give you another bourbon and you can take it upstairs with you. Do you want me to run your tub?"

"All right," he said.

She refilled his glass and handed it to him, and he took a sip and started to get to his feet. It was not easy, and he grunted, but he stood full height.

"Shall I assist you?" she said.

"You make it sound like a Boy Scout with an old lady crossing the street. No thanks, I'll make it. You carry my drink and run my tub while I get undressed."

"I can't be sure whether you're serious or not," she said.

"I'm not sure myself, if the truth be known," he said. "Actually I'm not in any great pain, but I got shaken up."

"Yes, that can be as bad as a real injury," she said.

"It *is* a real injury. What are you talking about? What's worse at our age than getting bounced around and unable to get to your feet? I went through positive hell out there."

"You did? How long were you there?" she said.

"Lying there? I must have been lying there—at least a hundred and twenty seconds, every second seeming like a small eternity. But then I finally struggled manfully to my feet, risking another fall, another outrage to my dignity, and not to mention the peril to my fragile bones. But I drew myself up to my full height and marched bravely, triumphantly home. The indomitable spirit of Charles David Kinsmith. Then with scarcely a mention of the whole episode, so's not to disturb the composure of his excitable, loving spouse, he partakes of a small whiskey and a small sip of another, and is now about to mount the stairs to the second-story bedchamber, divest himself of raiment, and gingerly lower himself into the soothing waters of a hot bath."

"What I like about you is your stoical courage."

"That's right. The stiff upper lip, we call it. Never let on when disaster strikes. Suffer in silence."

"Suffer in silence, that's it," she said. "All right, let's go upstairs. You go first and I'll follow."

"In case I shouldn't be too steady on my pins?" he said. "You'll be there to catch me?"

"Yes, my dear," she said.

In the hallway, as they passed the umbrella stand, he pointed a finger at his walking stick. "A hell of a lot of help *you* were," he said. "When the chips are down, a wife is more dependable than a walking stick any day."

"Thank you, dear," she said.

"You are, you know. I'd much rather have you than a cane."

"Would you?"

"I really would," he said.

"Keep moving, don't stop," she said.

"Do you ever think of me as an old stick?"

"No, not so far," she said.

"I should hope not," he said. "After all, I rescued you from those humble surroundings—not humble, but prosaic. And introduced you into the fascinating world of the theater. If you'd married the man your parents chose for you, would you ever have met Freddie Lonsdale? Ina Claire? Arthur Hopkins? Miriam Hopkins? Peggy Hopkins Joyce? Robert Benchley?"

"I don't think I ever met Peggy Hopkins Joyce," she said.

"You always say that, but you did. She was at Antibes in 1925."

"She was, but I wasn't. We didn't go there till 1926."

"The year that we were there, she was there. You took an instant dislike to her."

"That wasn't Peggy Hopkins Joyce. That was Geraldine St. John."

"The English girl. Are you sure?"

"You'll never get it out of your head that it wasn't Peggy Joyce, but it wasn't. It was Geraldine St. John."

"She wasn't even an actress," he said.

"I'll look and see if there's any Epsom salts," she said. "She had been an actress, though."

"No, she *wanted* to be an actress. She was thinking of becoming one."

"Well, whichever it was, she had some reason for buttering you up."

"She wasn't buttering me up," he said. "She was doing her best to seduce me. I was so darned attractive in those days, you must have gone through hell. But fortunately I was a man of strong character, and very much in love with you. I think of all the women that went on the make for me, and how resolutely I spurned them."

"There's only a half a boxful of Epsom salts. Do you think that'll be enough?"

"Oh, sure. Five pounds to a box. Two and a half pounds ought to be enough. The important thing is to have the water hot. The Epsom salts don't make that much difference. It's the heat of the water." He was naked.

"Turn around," she said. "Where did you hit yourself?"

"Isn't there a bruise?"

"Not on the coccyx bone. There's a red mark here, on the left hip, but the skin isn't broken. Do you want me to put something on it? Why don't I wait till you've had your tub, and then I'll use some rubbing alcohol on it. Your clothing protected you, softened the impact."

"If I don't get in the tub you'll be a quivering mass of frustrated passion."

"I know," she said. "Shall I bring your drink in the bathroom?"

"Trying to get me drunk, too. That's what Geraldine St. John tried to do, but it got her nowhere. Absolutely nowhere."

"I'm relieved to know it, after all these years," she said.

He put a foot in the water, and took it out immediately.

"Too hot?" she said.

"Just put your hand in and see," he said.

"I'll take your word for it. Turn on the cold."

"Is that the way it's done?" he said.

"You wanted it hot."

"It's a good thing I didn't put both feet in."

She turned on the cold water, knelt on the floor and made a whirlpool with a scrubbing brush. "Don't catch cold," she said. "Put something on."

"You don't have to look."

"I know, but put on your bathrobe anyway," she said.

"Don't get it too cold."

"I'm going to make it medium temperature and then you can change it to suit yourself, once you get in. It really isn't terribly hot, you know. Your feet were cold, but I think you can stand it now."

"How do you know my feet were cold?"

"Because they're always cold, and you've been out in the snow into the bargain," she said.

Now he put one foot, then the other, in the water and lowered himself into the tub.

"How is it?" she said.

"It'll be all right. Thanks."

"I'm going to fill the hot-water bottle. I suggest you go right to bed after your bath. It's been a shock and sleep is the best thing for it. I'll leave your drink in the bedroom."

"Where are you going?"

"I think I'll go down and put the meat back in the deep-freeze.

I want you to soak in the hot tub for at least a half an hour, and then go right to bed. We'll wait and see how you feel around nine o'clock. If you're still asleep, fine. If not, we can have dinner then."

"All right," he said.

As he lay in the tub, changing the water from time to time, he could hear her moving about in the small house. She came in once at the end of fifteen minutes. "You all right?" she said.

"Completely relaxed," he said.

"Take another fifteen minutes. I've got the heating pad in your bed. I'll turn it on when you've finished your soak. I don't want to put it on too soon."

"It's automatic," he said.

"I know, but I don't trust those things," she said, and went out again.

This time he noticed no thoughts, and though he did not close his eyes, he could not account for a period of five or six minutes and there was no doubt that he had in effect been asleep.

"Are you done to a crisp?" he heard her say.

"Do you realize that it's twenty years for Rex?"

"On the ninth of March," she said.

"The hardest thing to believe is that if he'd lived, we'd have a middle-aged son. He'd be forty-three years old. I'll never be able to stretch my imagination that far, that you and I would have a son forty-three. Forty-three. There's no use kidding ourselves, forty-three isn't young."

"I don't think we kid ourselves very much," she said. "I think you've had enough warm water. How does your back feel?"

"I'll know when I get up," he said.

"Here, I'll give you a hand."

"No, I want to get up normally, use the usual muscles. That's the only way to tell." He got out of the tub, and she held up a bath towel for him. "Feel all right."

"Dry yourself and I'll turn on the heating pad," she said.

"Don't you want to talk about Rex?" he said.

"Not at the moment, no. I want to get you into a warm bed and let you have at least an hour's sleep. Some shut-eye."

"Some what?" he said.

"Some shut-eye," she said.

"I wonder if you realize who the first person was that we ever heard use that expression," he said.

"Shut-eye? Was it Rex?"

"No, it wasn't Rex. It was someone very different from Rex. It was Paul Vincent."

"How can you be so sure of that?"

"Because I'm a playwright, and I listen to what people say."

"But that far back?"

"It was one of the first things I ever heard him say, and he was the first one I ever heard say it," he said. He buttoned up his pajamas.

"I don't think I'll open the window," she said. "I'll come up in an hour or so and open it if you're asleep."

"You don't want to talk about either one of them, Rex or Paul Vincent," he said.

"Do you?" she said.

"I have no objection to talking about Rex," he said. "We don't much, any more. Actually we never did. I think we've always hoped that he might still be alive."

"I never had any such hope. Two of his friends saw his plane go down in smoke, and one of them saw it fall into the ocean. There was no reason to hope. You only tortured yourself by hoping. How did you get started thinking about him now?"

"Some of my best ideas come to me in the bathtub. Just like Archimedes. Remember, 'Eureka!'?"

"Vaguely," she said. "So vaguely that I would have said it was Socrates."

"It was Archimedes. Archimedes," he said.

"He discovered something while taking a bath, but I don't remember what. And I certainly don't know what it had to do with Rex."

"It had nothing to do with Rex, but I made a discovery. Two discoveries, actually. One, that I can think of him without pain. And two, that it's much better to remember him as we do than as a middle-aged man of forty-three."

"Assuming he'd die at forty-three, which I don't assume."

"No, assuming that we'll die whenever we do, and that he'd

have gone on living, to forty-five, or fifty, or whatever we are when we die. When I die, just before I die, one of my last thoughts will be of my son as he was the last time we saw him. Young, strong, brave, gay. And handsome. He was just old enough to be truly handsome. Nobody looks like that when they're forty-three. It's gone at thirty, at the latest. We never saw him when he had to wear reading glasses, or starting to get thick through the middle. I wouldn't want Rex to wear arch supports, or have a receding hair-line. Would you?"

"Yes."

"I wonder. You'd want him alive. But he might have bored you, you know. He would have married a nice girl, in all likelihood. They'd have produced three or four children, the way most of his generation have done, and you and I wouldn't count for much. I gave very little thought to my father and mother after you and I were married."

"Rex never would have bored me," she said. "Are you all tucked in?"

"All tucked in, and all tuckered out," he said. "I think I'll sleep."

"I won't wake you. I'll let you sleep as long as you can. Shall I leave the drink?"

"No, you might as well take it with you," he said. The bedclothes were all the way up to his chin; only his head showed. "Emily, I want to ask you a question."

"Yes, and I'm sure I know what it is," she said.

"Well, did you?"

"Did I what?" she said.

"If you know what the question is, why don't you answer it?"

"Because I could be wrong," she said.

"Did you sleep with Paul Vincent?" he said.

"That's what I thought you were going to ask me. The answer is no."

"The answer has always been no," he said.

"Are you hoping that some day I'll change no to yes?"

"No, but yes would be easier to believe than no."

"Well, I didn't, so go to sleep," she said.

"Why didn't you? You were sore as hell at me about the St. John girl."

"Yes I was, but I wasn't going to make a fool of myself just because you were making a fool of yourself."

"How did I make a fool of myself? She was the one that was acting foolish."

"You were as bad as she was, in a different way. Talking with an English accent."

"My God, you should have heard yourself, parroting Paul Vincent and that lingo of his. He couldn't say sleep, he had to say shut-eye. What were some of the other quaint expressions he used? He never said hands. He said lunch-hooks."

"I don't remember that at all," she said.

"You and the rest of you, you with your gentle upbringing. You all thought he was fascinating because he talked that way. Lunch-hooks. Shut-eye. Puddle-jumper. And none of it was original, although you all thought it was. It all came from cartoonists and the theatrical publications."

"Next time you go for a walk in the snow, wear your creepers," she said. "You seem to have shaken up a lot of old memories."

"I seem to have," he said.

"Do you want this light on?" she said.

"No thanks."

"I'll be in to see how you're getting along," she said . . .

Twice in the next three hours she visited the room, and on the second visit she opened the windows. Both times he was asleep, helpless against an attacker, and the captive of his unwanted dreams, which were seldom nightmarish but always full of complicated problems and dilemmas. Sometimes he would wake up in the night and turn the light on and scribble a few words that were the key to involved plots for plays. In the morning, when he was having his coffee, he would study his notes to himself and be unable to make any sense out of them. "Beautifully logical plot, a well-constructed, logical three-act play," he would say. But he had not written a play in at least ten years. They did not need the money. Back in the Twenties and Thirties he had had two big hits and two moderate successes that together had made him close to a million dollars. Bob Abercrombie had invested the money for him, and his capital was now past the million mark. She, Emily Kinsmith, had an income of her own. "A good thing, too," he would say. "I could never make a living in the theater today. Actually I shouldn't even call myself a playwright any more. I'd have just as much right to call myself a wrestler. I wrestled in college and got a minor letter. But it's almost as long since I've written a play as it is since I helped beat M.I.T. on the mat."

"Except that I have a feeling you were better known as a playwright than as a wrestler."

"You tell that to one of the new managers," he said.

They lived the year round in the house that had once been their summer cottage, out beyond East Hampton on Long Island. A drama critic on *Newsweek* once referred to him as the late Charles Kinsmith, and he spent a day composing several letters of correction, none of which he mailed. "After all, how can I be sure he isn't right?" said Charles. Someone at the Dramatists Guild, an associate professor at the University of Michigan, and a woman at the Pasadena Playhouse wrote to the magazine to set it straight. Excerpts of their letters were printed. Several East Hampton friends said they too had written, but their letters were not published. "Probably because they never actually got written," said Charles.

"Well, you know how people are," said Emily.

"Oh, yes. I know how people are," said Charles.

Just before Christmas they would go to New York on a Monday and stay until Thursday afternoon. "That gives us a chance to see four plays, including one matinee. But last year we were driven to going to a musical comedy. There just weren't four plays I wanted to see. I don't want to see a play in which a man kisses a man. I know it happens. It happens not far from here, every weekend all summer long. It happened when I was in college. I don't even mind plays about homosexuals. But you can do a play about homosexuals without having one character kiss the other on the mouth. The minute you succumb to that temptation, you admit you haven't got much of a play. You have a little shocker, and that's all. I've had adultery in four or five of my plays, but there's never been a bed on the set. *That* would have been quite a temptation to some of my actors and actresses, and I may have been unconsciously guided by prudence. Think of the magnetic attraction a bed would have had for Lita Pastorius, for instance. If we'd had a bed on the set she wouldn't have been able to take her eyes off it. But knowing that there was an imaginary bed offstage, she gave a very convincing performance. The actors have to imagine things as well as the audience, you know. One time we had George Fleming's glass filled with a real Martini and he just drank it down without any enjoyment. It was an experiment. He said himself he preferred plain water onstage. With plain water, he could act. But he was so used to real Martinis in real life that when we gave him one in the play, he didn't react. He was supposed to say, 'This is a fine cocktail,' and it was. I mixed it. But he read the line so unconvincingly that we went back to plain water, and I want to tell you that when an actor turns down a free drink it's something to think about," he said.

East Hampton was far enough away from New York to provide excuses for Charles to stay in the country. To take the morning train he would have to rise at five o'clock; by motor the trip was tiresome and long, through the business sections of the Suffolk County villages and the monotonous parkways of Nassau. In emergencies—which were rare—he could charter an airplane, an expense that he could justify only in rather extreme cases. "What constitutes an extreme case?" he would say. "Well, an actor's funeral, if the actor was in one of my plays and I was still speaking to him, or her, at the end of the run. Or a favorite waiter, if I hear about his funeral in time. The trouble there, of course, is that I seldom knew their last names and I don't always hear about their dying. I go to a restaurant and find out months later. I used to go to critics' funerals, but the critics that reviewed my plays are no longer around. Benchley. Hammond. Mantle. Anderson. Gabriel. Woollcott. I didn't feel I had to go to Nathan's funeral. He was never really a critic. Some funerals mean staying in town overnight. Personal friends. But I find that I haven't nearly as many personal friends as I once had. One of my ushers died last year in Chicago and I didn't know about it till I read it in the alumni magazine. Nothing in the New York papers. On the other hand, when my tailor died there was quite a lengthy obit in both papers, in which I was mentioned as one of his customers. I didn't go to his funeral. He'd been overcharging me for years because he knew damn well I was too lazy to break in someone else. A lot of men my age have stopped having things custom-made. We buy off the rack when we buy at all. It's too depressing to be reminded that a really good suit or pair of shoes will outlast you. My present dinner jacket is thirty-two years old, and I guess that tells as well as anything else could how much we go out in the evening. Every four or five years I buy one of those white linen dinner jackets for the summer festivities. The summer festivities consist of sixteen dinner parties and four appearances at the John Drew Theater. I'm quite accurate about the dinner parties. I counted up by checking through old appointment books of Emily's. It comes out to exactly sixteen a summer, as guest and host. At that it's too many, but between Thanksgiving and Memorial Day there are hardly any. Since the War there's been a tendency for people to keep their houses open all winter, and come down for long weekends. But the entertaining then isn't as elaborate. You don't have to see people unless you really want to. Emily can always pretend I'm working—and I am. I'm writing the libretto of an opera. As soon as you tell people you're writing the libretto of an *opera* they think twice about disturbing you. But it has to be an opera. An opera takes years. Sometimes they ask me if it was commissioned, and I tell them it was certainly not commissioned by the Met, and look wise. Implying that it's a secret project. If they ask me the name of the composer I tell them that *is* a secret. They ask me if it's going to be modern and I make a little joke. 'Not by the time it's finished,' I tell them. It'll never be finished, because it's never been started, but it's been very useful to me for ten years or more, and I've had a great many letters about it. If I were a little more unscrupulous I could have made some money on it. One of the television companies wanted to pay me $10,000 for an option on it. That put me momentarily in a spot, but I wriggled out of it. I said if they were willing to pay me $50,000, I'd listen. I heard no more from them. It was somehow reassuring to learn that they wouldn't go to fifty. I wouldn't like to think that things have gotten so out of hand that a television company would pay me $50,000 for an *option* on an unwritten opera. I sold one of my plays to the movies for $50,000 in 1930, and I thought they must be out of their minds. They weren't though. I see it on television now and then, sometimes the first cast. Not to mention an entirely different story, but it always has to say, 'Based on the play by Charles Kinsmith.' I want to say, '*What* play by Charles Kinsmith,' but Emily's never gotten used to my habit of talking to the radio set or the television. She pretends to think I'm batty. She doesn't mind my talking out loud when I'm actually writing dialog. She could see a reason for that. But muttering things at the TV set shows a lack of restraint that she pretends not to understand. She comes of a tight-lipped Yankee family. Ethan Frome-Calvin Coolidge types. My family were so poor that talk was practically our only form of entertainment. Nobody paid much attention to what anyone else said, but we jawed away from morning to night. It was really like talking to yourself in our house. Two brothers and two sisters and my father and mother, all gabbing at once. Bedlam. And yet we somehow managed to maintain communications. It took me about two years to learn that Emily's family weren't being so taciturn because I was a stranger. It was their way. They came to the table to eat, and they ate everything that was put on their plates, by the old man. He never asked anyone if they *wanted* cauliflower, or turnips. If that's what there was, that's what you got, and you damn well ate it. In silence, preferably. When I finally caught on, and didn't try to make conversation, everybody was more relaxed. Emily's mother said one day, 'Charles, didn't you like your turnips?' and I said, 'Nope.' That was all. But from then on whenever I had a meal at their house they didn't serve turnips. Emily hated turnips, too, but she'd never been asked. She was very well brought up, from a future husband's point of view. Her family never asked her what she wanted, never asked her what she thought. Consequently she was very appreciative of common politeness on the part of outsiders, and if anyone was actually kind to her, or treated her with uncommon respect, or *loved* her —she was extremely appreciative. When I first met her I didn't know any of these things about her family life. She was a classmate of one of my sisters at Wellesley. Not a particularly close friend, but a classmate, and I was introduced to her at their commencement, along with a dozen other girls. As far as I was concerned, Emily was all there was. Dark and shy in her long white dress, then later when she was wearing her mortarboard it wasn't on quite straight. It gave her accidentally a *dash*, although it was unintentional. Is there anything more unfeminine than a girl in a riding habit, with a stiff white stock and her hat on the top of her head? And yet is there anything more feminine? Yes, there is. It's a girl in cap and gown. If she's strongly feminine, it'll come through in spite of the attire, in both cases. Emily and my sister and I rode together on the New York train. I wasn't getting much out of her conversationally, but I knew she liked me, and I was determined to see more of her. Then when we got back to New York we were met by her grandmother's chauffeur, Emile, in black leather puttees and breeches and a tunic that buttoned up to the throat. That was totally unexpected. I'd somehow got the impression that Emily was in better circumstances than we were, but not much better. I'd pictured her father as the insurance man in a small town in Connecticut, because I knew she lived in a small town in Connecticut and that her father was in the insurance business. She'd told me that much. But when I saw that chauffeur I began to wonder. She offered to give us a lift to my aunt's house in Brooklyn, and before my sister could refuse, I accepted. I wanted to find out all I could. Her grandmother's car removed any doubt I had about Emily's financial status. It was a big Renault limousine, with the radiator in the middle of the hood. Ugly as could be, but the effect was overwhelming. It wasn't a new car, even then, but it'd been well taken care of, and I'd never been inside a limousine before. We weren't sure how to get to Brooklyn by car, but Emile knew. In those days a lot of people like Emily's grandmother lived in Brooklyn, and he'd been there oftener than we had. My uncle was a clergyman, pastor of a Dutch Reformed church on Brooklyn Heights, and Emile had actually taken people to weddings there. Emily insisted on going with us—she was postponing her meeting with her grandmother, she told me later. She was terrified of her grandmother, who was her mother's mother. Old Mrs. Van Rhyne disliked Yankees and had never altogether approved of her daughter's marriage to Emily's father. The fact that he had made a big success in the insurance business didn't cut much ice with her. This was all to come out much later, but apparently Mrs. Van Rhyne felt that Mr. Williams had all the Yankee virtues and none of the vices. He was shrewd and thrifty and dependable, but he wouldn't take a drink or look at another woman. Your true Yankee does both. I know. I went to Dartmouth for four years, and all my preconceived notions of Puritan New Englanders went up the flue. Those Green Mountain Boys and State-of-Mainers are very fond of liquor and pussy, no matter what you hear to the contrary. Mrs. Van Rhyne didn't *advocate* adultery and boozing, but she was a handsome woman herself and accustomed to flattering attentions by the male sex. She also liked her little nip. And remember that car, that big green French monster, and that dapper French chauffeur. Most of her contemporaries had Pierce-Arrows and ex-coachmen, usually Irish or English. She had style, and she didn't want her daughter to go through life as a frump. Unfortunately, Mrs. Williams *was* a frump, and Mr. Williams was just what she wanted. A reaction, obviously to the pleasure-loving Mrs. Van Rhyne. I never knew Mr. Van Rhyne. He had passed out of the picture by the time I came along, but I gathered from bits and pieces that I was able to pick up that he was as much in favor of ease and elegance as she was. He never did a tap of work. He went to Columbia for two years and then to Oxford, but Mrs. Van Rhyne was always rather evasive about his Oxford career. I was curious, and I thought of writing to Oxford to try to find out if he ever actually became a member of that university. Then I decided that would be spying, so I never wrote. The Van Rhyne money was in real estate. They owned solid blocks of it in the West Seventies and Eighties, and all they had to do was sit there and watch it triple in value. Theodore Van Rhyne died before he was forty, but people remembered him as a real sybarite. Whenever his name came up they'd always get that look, that tolerant smile that they had when anybody'd mention Edward VII. If you lead a completely useless life, but do it with style and die young enough, you're quite likely to be remembered with more affection than the man who has a record of accomplishment. But the secret is to die young enough. If you think you're going to live to a ripe old age, it's better to pile up a record of accomplishment of some sort. It may be bridge-building, or money-making, or butterfly-collecting, but it has to be something. People don't like to see longevity wasted on a do-nothing. And as a rule, it isn't. Do-nothings don't usually last very long. The first twenty years of a man's life are a struggle, getting through the childhood diseases and accidents, and the sex revolution that begins around eleven or twelve in most boys, and the constant readjustments in relations with your parents. Those first twenty years are anything but do-nothing years. It's the next twenty that determine whether a man is a do-nothing or an accomplisher. He knows what he wants to do, even if it's nothing, and he sets a timer in himself that will go off when his energy is used up. I'm convinced that most people really know just about how long they're going to last, and they guide their lives and expend their resources accordingly. Emily's grandfather, for instance, told Mrs. Van Rhyne that when their daughter got married he wanted his brother Curtis and not his brother William to give her away. Clearly indicating that he didn't expect to be there, and he wasn't. But Emily's mother was only about ten years old at the time. He knew. If you ask a man when he's going to die, he won't be able to tell you, but he knows. I know when I'm going to die, but it isn't going to be from this fall."

"*Charles! Charles!* Wake up, darling," said Emily Kinsmith.

He opened his eyes. She was sitting on the edge of the bed and holding his hand in her two. "You were groaning," she said. "I think it was a nightmare."

"No, I don't remember any nightmare," he said.

"Does your back hurt?" she said. "Maybe that was it."

He pulled himself up to a sitting position. "My back does hurt a little," he said. "But not while I'm lying still. Only when I move."

"You must have been turning in your sleep."

"Maybe," he said. "How long have I been asleep?"

"Oh, about an hour and a half. I came in a couple of times to see how you were."

"How was I?"

"Dead to the world," she said.

"I've been that for a long time. *Newsweek* said so."

"Was it *Newsweek?* I thought it was *Time.*"

"You thought it was time what?"

"I thought it was *Time* that had you in the obituary column."

"Oh, I thought you meant it was time I woke up," he said.

"No, you sleep as long as you like."

"I don't want to sleep any more."

"You want to have dinner?" she said.

"I want to talk," he said.

"All right," she said. She fixed the pillows behind him. "Shall I get you a glass of water?"

"Yes, my mouth is dry."

She got him a tumbler of water and handed it to him. He sipped it slowly. "Do you know how it feels to be a bird? I don't think birds appreciate what they have. For just a fraction of a second, the tiniest fraction of a fraction of a second, I knew how it felt to be a bird today."

"When you had your fall," she said.

"Yes. When my feet left the ground, both feet, and before I came down on my behind. It wasn't like jumping. I've jumped from the top of a barn into a pile of straw and enjoyed it. But that was voluntary. This was something over which I had no control. Suddenly I was given the gift of flight. But being a member of the human species, a descendant of Pithecanthropus erectus, I couldn't adapt myself to the new situation. Nevertheless I had the experience of being air-borne today, and I'm thinking of trying it again. The question is, how? I can't go up on the roof and jump off. I have to wait until Nature gives me the gift again. But I must say it was exhilarating."

"Is that what you were dreaming about?" she said.

"I wasn't dreaming about anything, Emily," he said.

"You most certainly were," she said. "You were groaning and muttering—"

"But I wasn't dreaming. I was talking to somebody."

404

"But you were sound asleep, talking to somebody or not talking to somebody. Who *was* it you were talking to?"

"I have no idea. Nobody in particular," he said.

"Me?"

"No. Nobody I ever knew. Nobody that I could identify in any way. I mean I don't know whether it was a man or a woman, young or old, white or black. I haven't the faintest idea who I was talking to, but that's what I was doing."

"Another form of nightmare," she said. "Can you remember what you were telling this person?"

"Yes, I was telling him about us. About you, and your grandmother and grandfather. The Van Rhynes, I mean. I told him about Emile."

"Emile who?"

"Your grandmother's chauffeur," he said.

"Emile Blanc. What else did you tell him—and I notice you say *him*, so it must have been a man you were talking to."

"I think it probably was a man, but not anyone I know. There's a possibility that it was someone that never existed, a combination of two people. Paul Vincent and Geraldine St. John. They were the last people I thought of before falling asleep."

"No, we were talking about Rex."

"That's true, we were. Do you suppose I could have been talking to Rex? Yes, that's quite possible. Not our Rex, not our boy as we knew him, but a Rex Kinsmith in his forties. A stranger to you and me. Yes, I could have been telling this Rex Kinsmith all about you and me. Mostly about you. Very little about me. Hardly anything about me."

"It might be a good idea if you got out of bed and had something to eat. You could watch television for a while and then go back to bed and you won't have the same dream."

"I'm not sure I don't want the same dream. But now that I know who I was talking to—I think it *was* this Rex Kinsmith—I doubt if I'll pick up the dream where it left off. Then I didn't know who I was talking to, but now I would know."

"Yes, that would change it. You probably will never have the dream again, now that you've figured out who it was."

"Oh, I'm not so sure about that," he said. "I can very easily imagine going to sleep again and starting right out by thinking of this Rex Kinsmith, and addressing him directly."

"That's just the opposite of what you said before," she said.

"No, not quite. This time I'd be starting a new dream, not the old one, and I wouldn't have any doubts as to who I was talking to."

"Oh, well now we're getting into a different thing. Communication with the dead. Did this person ever answer you while you were talking to him?"

"No. Never said anything at all," he said.

"I wish you'd put on your flannel bathrobe and come downstairs and have something to eat. I don't like this conversation very much. You know I don't believe in an after-life. This idea that you were talking to Rex after he'd been dead all these years, but according to your recollection he went on living and is now in his forties."

"I think so, yes," he said.

"Well, you see that's where I part company with you right away. He was killed when he was twenty-three, and I don't know *anybody* that believes you go on growing after you die. Even the most religious people believe that a baby that dies is a baby through all eternity, and a man that lives to be eighty stays eighty."

"You have a point," he said. "Nevertheless I could have created a Rex Kinsmith, like a character in one of my plays, and made him seem so real to my subconscious mind that he becomes a figure that I could talk to."

"Here, put this on," she said, handing him his bathrobe. "And you'd better put on some socks or you'll catch cold."

He held out his hand for the robe, took hold of it, and let it fall on the bedclothes. "I can't, Emily," he said.

"I'll help you."

"You can't either. I can't move."

"What do you mean, you can't move?"

"Just what I say. I think I'm paralyzed."

"No, Charles. You're not paralyzed. You were able to pull yourself up on your pillow."

"Have you got a pin? Stick a pin in my leg. I want to see if I can feel it."

"I don't have to stick you with a pin. I'll pinch you."

"All right," he said.

She put her hand under the bedclothes, and held it there.

"See? I didn't feel anything," he said.

"No, because I haven't touched you," she said.

"Well, touch me," he said. "Are you afraid?"

They looked at each other, eye to eye.

"Have you touched me yet?" he said.

"No."

"Then touch me now, please. I have to know," he said.

She took her hand out from under the bedclothes.

"What?" he said.

She nodded. "I pinched your calf, I even bent your toe back."

"I am paralyzed?" he said.

"Yes," she said.

"It's probably temporary," he said. "I knew I hurt myself taking that spill. You'd better call Jimmy Gray. Call him at home, he'll be having dinner. *And don't worry*. It's only temporary. One of those pinched-nerve things."

"Of course it is," she said.

"I'm just glad I didn't break my hip. That's what happens so often to people our age. That can be real hell, they say. Call Jimmy, and I'll talk to him."

She looked in the directory and dialed the bedside telephone. "This is Mrs. Charles Kinsmith on Jagger Lane. Could I speak to Dr. Gray, please? It's urgent."

"Let me talk to him," said Charles.

She shook her head. "I see. Well, will you please tell him to call me right away? Mrs. Charles Kinsmith, Amagansett 8-5564." She replaced the telephone. "The answering service. I wonder if I ought to try another doctor."

"No," he said.

"Are you in pain?" she said.

"Not really," he said. "More than before, across my back, but none in my legs."

"Is it all right if I lie on the bed beside you?"

"I wish you would," he said.

"I'd give you something to stop the pain, but I don't know what would be the right thing. I don't want to give you the wrong thing."

"Well, you never have," he said. She smiled at him. "Haven't I, dear?"

"Never," he said.

"Are you falling asleep?"

"Hmm?"

"I think you're falling asleep," she said.

He did not answer, and she stared at him. He quivered, shuddered, and expired. She got on the bed and lay beside him. "Take me with you," she said. "Can you hear me, boy? Please take me with you?"

Until Jimmy Gray called there was nothing to be done; no right thing, no wrong thing, and life is divided between the right things and the wrong things. "Isn't it, Charles?" she said. "You know it is. You knew it a minute ago." Now the telephone rang and she reached for it.

"Hello? Yes, is this you, Jimmy? It's Charles. He just went down in flames. He was flying like a bird, and he went down in flames. No, you can't talk to him. He's right here, but he's dead," she said. She hung up. "I wonder what's next," she said. "You know, Charles. What's next?"

THE GENERAL

Their house, be it noted, was in the old part of town, in a section
that had ceased to be fashionable but that at one time had been
not just one but the *only* neighborhood for the very rich to live
in. It was two blocks long, this section, on both sides of the
street. There was no uniformity to the design of the houses, and
yet they all looked the same because they were all built of brick
or brownstone and presented a solid, substantial front of planned
severity. The houses of plaster-covered brick were even more
forbidding than the houses built of cut stone. Stone, being stone,
retained the marks of its ancient porosity and therefore had that
much more life than the bland, grey-brown artificiality of the
plaster. Not until the rich began to desert the neighborhood and
the plaster cracks were neglected did any of the houses begin to
look human. Thereafter the houses and the people in them
commenced to look very human indeed. The residential character of the neighborhood changed completely between 1915 and
1920. Nearly every house was drastically altered to accommodate
commerce. There was a beauty parlor, a tire shop, a bakery, a
grocery store, a motorcycle-bicycle agency, two automobile show-

rooms, an army and navy surplus outfit, a paperhanger-painter's establishment, a shoe repair and hat cleaning establishment, an electrical supply store with a crazy assortment of lighting fixtures hanging like stalactites from the ceiling. The upstairs rooms were used for storage, for the offices of painless dentists, and for apartments. By the time Mr. Coolidge was inaugurated President, the only house in the neighborhood that was strictly a private residence was Number 444, the home of General Dixon L. Hightower and his wife. It surprised no one that they went on living there. It would have amazed their friends if the Hightowers had moved.

The feeling that the Hightowers *belonged* in 444 was not so much due to the fact that Sophronia Hightower had been born in that house as to the widely held belief, among the young and uninformed, that it was General Hightower's lifetime residence. Actually the Stokes family had built 444 and Dick Hightower did not occupy it until his marriage to Sophie Stokes. Thereafter, however, he never left it for any considerable length of time except for his army service during the Spanish-American War, and the annual encampments of the National Guard at Mount Gretna. The coal millionaires of the neighborhood guarded their privacy and the comparative anonymity of their houses, but 444 was the home of the town's only general and in many ways he gave it its character. A workingman who lived to the south of Number 444 would often explain that he came from "down past General Hightower's," and people would know what section of town he lived in. There was not much town left beyond General Hightower's house. Tourists passing through the town without leaving Main Street would get the impression that there was only one really nice house in the community. Unquestionably, in the post-war years Number 444 and the Hightowers belonged together to a degree that house and owner too rarely achieve. Dick Hightower, the general, had added a few touches of his own to the original boxlike structure: two bay windows that could be mistaken for turrets, a crenelated cornice, a stone heraldic eagle clutching arrows over the front door. It was a corner property and the Hightowers had a side yard as well as a back yard, which were protected from trespassers by an iron fence consisting of simulated spears. In the geometric center of the side yard was, of course, a flagstaff topped by a screaming gilt eagle. Every five years or so someone would reinvent the name Fort Hightower for the place, but it never caught on. The joke was always short-lived because in the milder seasons Sophie Hightower was to be seen in the yard, tending her rose bushes and peonies and entertaining her friends in the summer house in the back yard.

Dixon Hightower was a military man, fully qualified by Regular Army experience until he resigned his commission to marry Sophronia Stokes, and entitled to his brigadier's star by virtue of his subsequent promotions in the National Guard of Pennsylvania. At West Point he had remained in the bottom half of his class and therefore upon graduation was assigned to the infantry instead of to the cavalry. Nevertheless he had been under fire in the Indian Territory and had spent ten years at army posts. He knew the difference between a buttonstick and a Gatling gun, although the young and uninformed were inclined to be skeptical of their elders' somewhat vague assurances that the general had once been a warrior. He had five or six medals that he wore to military funerals of former officers of the Guard. The younger crowd, those who were reaching maturity after the 1918 Armistice, had stopped calling him a toy soldier, but they did not seriously believe that he could ever have been in battle. In his blues, wearing his medals and his sword, he would go to funerals and review the local militia, but when the troops went off to the Mexican border in 1916, he marched with them only as far as the railroad station, remounted his horse and rode back to Fort Hightower. It was the same in 1917, when the Guard and the conscripts went away to war, with the difference that now he no longer wore a uniform or rode a horse. He marched with the leaders of the community who were members of the Patriotic League, and instead of a sword he carried a malacca stick. He was past the age when he could be useful except as a member of the draft board, and he was not even in command of that.

"If I'd stayed in the army," he said to Sophie, "I'd have my own division."

"Well, are you sorry you didn't stay in?" she said.

"Oh, please don't misunderstand me," he said, "*You* know I've never regretted that decision. You *must* know, Sophie. Don't you?"

"Well, that's what I've always thought," she said.

"What I meant, all I meant was that there are men my age, or just a few classes behind me, that are divisional commanders today. Joe Westman has a division. Ted Maguire is a major general on Pershing's staff. And other fellows I used to know have two stars and two of them have three stars. Lieutenant generals, they are. Peyton March, and Jack Pershing, not much younger than I, with four stars. My goodness, but the time flies. But I suppose I'm well out of it. I was never very good at army politics, and now I hear that there's no love lost between March and Pershing, and Leonard Wood and Pershing have had a tussle."

"You told me before we were married that you weren't very tactful."

"Well, you've found that out for yourself," he said.

"Yes, I have. But I was thinking of army politics. I wonder how I'd have been as an army wife."

"You'd have managed, for a while," he said. "But if I know you, my girl, some captain's wife would go just a little too far and you'd give her a piece of your mind. As my old friend Sam Bannister used to say, an army officer wears the insignia of his rank but an army wife doesn't have to."

"No, I don't think I'd have made a very good army wife," said Sophie.

"Mind you, you'd have gotten through it if you'd *had* to. I am not saying *that*, Sophie. But I never could have asked you to put up with the discomforts and inconveniences. Not to mention the snubs and the discipline. That kind of a life would have broken your spirit."

"Oh, do you think so?"

"Might have. It very nearly did mine, and I was used to it. It's a very contradictory thing, army life. I remember having a long talk with a British officer I got to know in Washington. He was a career man, then about forty, and a major. I was a good deal younger, but we hit it off well together, and used to see a lot of each other. Charles Willing-Lloyd, hyphenated. Haven't thought of him in years. Welsh, I suppose he was, with the name Lloyd."

"You had a long talk with him?"

"Many. But one I remember particularly. I'd just come up from Brownsville and he and I were comparing notes. The rigors of army life and so on. He'd been in Africa and India and all over, and he was a very interesting conversationalist. There was a small group of us that used to meet for dinner once a month. Army and navy officers, attachés, and we'd play cards for not very high stakes, or some of us would just sit and chat. One evening Charles and I were comparing notes, and he made to me what was a very profound observation. He'd been in action, mentioned in dispatches and so on, but he insisted that it takes a different sort of man to be a good career officer. A war, he said, doesn't demand as much of a man as the day-to-day army routine. When the bugles sound, and the shooting begins, the amateurs rush in. Ready to die, ready to shed their blood, it's true. But they're amateurs. And they will die and they will shed their blood needlessly if we haven't done our jobs between wars. That fact is never understood by the civilian mind. All they see of us in peacetime is parades, gold braid, unloaded weaponry. Military funerals, military balls, the governor's inauguration. And a few weeks of camp in the summer in neat rows of tents with canvas flies over them and flooring underneath. But we've been living under discipline and our men have been too. So that when the amateurs get into it, the professionals can show them that orders are there to be obeyed."

"You wrote me all this in a letter one time," said Sophie.

"Did I? Well, that doesn't surprise me," he said. "I was very full of it at the time, when I was hesitating about whether to resign my commission."

"Your friend nearly persuaded you to jilt me," said Sophie.

"Oh, Sophie, he did no such thing!"

"I know he didn't, Dickie. I'm only joking."

"But you mustn't joke about such things," he said. "There've only been two things in my life I've ever cared deeply for. Our marriage, and the army. And I'd never joke about our marriage. I wish I could feel as deeply about religion, especially now that we're both getting on in years."

"You've always been a good Christian, dear. I don't think the good Lord above will punish you for your doubts. We all have them."

"Not you," he said. "Every year in June, when you take such pride in your roses, all your doubts disappear. You always say the same thing. There has to be a God to create such beauty."

"I haven't said that in years," she said.

"Maybe not in so many words, but it's what you feel."

"There are many times when you haven't the slightest notion what I feel."

"So you say. But that's what you'd like me to think. You're a woman and you like to be mysterious. Perfectly all right, of course. No harm done, as long as it doesn't get out of hand. It's like my saying that I could have my own division. Yes, I'd have my own division, *if*. And you'd be very mysterious, *if*."

"If what?"

"If I'd stayed in the army," he said.

"No, I meant, I'd be very mysterious if what?" said Sophie.

"Well, if you'd been an altogether different kind of a person. And if you'd been an altogether different kind of person I assure you I'd never have resigned my commission to marry you. What's more, if I'd been the kind of man who refused to resign his commission, you never would have married *me*. If, if, if. My goodness, but we waste our time with our ifs. Haven't we got something better to do than that?"

"Well, I have, thank heavens," she said. She rose, put on her wide-brimmed Panama, and picked up her gardening pouch. The Panama had once been his, the pouch was an old musette bag.

"Mysterious? You and I mysterious?" he said.

"I didn't say *you* were," she said.

He smiled and went to his desk, where there were always a great many letters to be answered. She had her flowers, he had his correspondence.

Four times during the winter months they asked friends in for dinner. Once there had been little jokes about the neighborhood to tease the dinner guests who had moved to the west end of town. "Welcome back to The Bowery," Dixon Hightower would say, but the jokes wore a bit thin. Their elderly friend Mrs. McMasters, who had never liked jokes of any kind, put a stop to them. "Since you bring up the subject, Dick Hightower," said Mrs. McMasters. "I don't see why you stay down here. It may be all right for you, but it's no place for Sophie."

"Why not? She's in her old homestead."

"I was in my old homestead, too, but I had sense enough to get out. The smoke from the locomotives—*you* don't know what it is to keep things clean, let alone breathe decent air."

"Get rid of your Reading Company stock," said Hightower.

"I will not get rid of my Reading Company stock. I didn't say the smoke wasn't necessary, but I had sense enough to get out of the thick of it. I own stock in the steel mill, too, but I don't have to listen to the noise. This is no place for Sophie to live. It isn't safe to walk the streets at night."

"Then I'll see that she doesn't. She never has, but I promise not to let her start any bad habits."

"Bad habits?" said Mrs. McMasters.

"Such as walking the streets at night," said Hightower.

"Dixon Hightower, sometimes you go too far with your attempts to be humorous. I prefer to talk about something else, if you don't mind."

The mortality rate among their friends reduced the Hightowers' social obligations. The death of Elsie McMasters not only struck her from their list but made it inconvenient for George and Laura Cromer, who had been dependent on Elsie and her gigantic Locomobile limousine, to get to Number 444. The Cromers had to watch every penny, and taxicabs were out of the question. The Hood McGowens could afford taxis, but when Minnie McGowen discovered a naughty word scratched in the varnish of their Pierce-Arrow outside the Hightowers' house, she resolved that they had paid their final visit to the neighborhood. She did not blame Tom Duffy, the McGowen chauffeur, who was keeping warm in the Hightower kitchen. She was somewhat inclined to blame Dick Hightower for his stubbornness in remaining in that section of town. Daniel Wynkoop, their bachelor friend, showed up on the wrong night, twenty-four hours early, and took pot-luck with Dick and Sophie. Unfortunately he finished off most of a bottle of pre-Prohibition rye before going home, and was beaten and robbed of $25 and a gold watch less than a block away from the Hightowers'. He was unable to give the police an accurate description of his assailants. The Hightowers' surviving friends went on inviting them to their houses, but the balance of social exchange was too one-sided. More and more people were finding excuses not to accept invitations to 444, and even in the dinner season there would be periods two months long in which Dick and Sophie dined alone. Those evenings were not unpleasant for him; he had more time for his correspondence, and the World War had produced a whole new library of military histories, battle reports, and even a crop of novels that viewed war with a jaundiced eye. Dick Hightower disliked the novels and some of the histories, but it amused him to find so many authors who were discovering for the first time an obvious truth that Sherman had stated profanely nearly seventy years before them. His correspondence—at least his part of it—expanded as a result of his reading of the new books. He was in fact quite busy.

Sophie, however, was not much of a reader. She read the local paper in the evening and the Philadelphia *Public Ledger* in the morning; the *Delineator*, *The Ladies' Home Journal* and *Life*. If a friend strongly recommended a novel by Booth Tarkington, Edna Ferber, or John Galsworthy she would read it, and get all through it no matter how long it took. She had a Philadelphia friend who was related to Joseph Hergesheimer, and that was Sophie's nearest connection with a living author. In their evenings at home after dinner she sometimes envied Dick and his absorption in his books and letters. He would laugh aloud at something he had written and triumphantly read it to her. He would exclaim, "Bully!" when he came upon a telling passage in a book, but he would often have to read back over ten or twenty pages of a military campaign to explain why a single line had met with his enthusiastic approval. It was seldom worth it; Ludendorff's right flank was too hard to follow. "I know it doesn't mean the way it sounds to me," she said. "But when any general exposes his right flank, you can imagine what I think."

"Not Ludendorff, though. *He* was never caught with *his* pants down."

"Then why don't they find some other way of saying it?" she said.

After dinner they would have coffee and a thimbleful of a liqueur from their dwindling stock. He was perfectly willing to let her have his share of such things as Benedictine, but the tiny drink was more ceremonial than gustatorial and they agreed that it was the ritual and not the drink that they would miss when their supply was gone. Already they had begun to substitute applejack for their good gin and whiskey in cocktails when guests were not present. Applejack, they had discovered, made an acceptable "whiskey sour," if you limited yourself to two. They had not yet found it necessary to patronize a town bootlegger. When that time came, Dick was going to have to wrestle with his conscience. "Everybody breaks the law, and it's a law that I'm opposed to," he said. "However, I'm not going to feel right about it. I don't like the thought of having some bootlegger say he has General Hightower for a customer. Then there'd be the question of delivering it here. I wouldn't like that at all, and I'm most certainly not going to their place and bring it home with me. I don't keep any at the club, so when someone offers me a cocktail, I just say no, because I can't return the favor. If I knew everybody at the club it might be a different matter, but they have a lot of lawyers from out of town come there for lunch. As long as people call me General I don't think I ought to flout the law of the land. Do you, Sophie? Am I being inconsistent, or hypocritical"?

"Not you, Dick. The law is hypocritical."

"No, I wouldn't say that. It was a constitutional amendment, had to be approved by two thirds of the states, and the law itself isn't hypocritical. Very well meaning. But it doesn't work. The people have tried it, and they don't want it, and those that do want it should step out of the way. Take defeat gracefully. I'll vote in favor of repeal of the law and I know I will. Therefore I think I'm being consistent. But I'd hate to think I was being hypocritical about it, drinking at home and not at the club."

"Where do we get our applejack?" she said.

"You think I'm being inconsistent because I won't deal with the bootleggers?"

"Well, I just thought of it."

"Schertzinger, the farmer, delivers it. He leaves it in the stable, in one of the old box stalls. I leave the cash in an envelope, behind that picture of Dan Patch. A gallon every two weeks."

"Do we drink that much?"

"Just about. Four ounces apiece, every day. That's twenty-eight ounces a week. In four weeks we dispose of 112 ounces, or seven quarts. There are four quarts in a gallon. We never run out of it, because we keep that much ahead of our supply. But I don't consider Adam Schertzinger in the same category with those bootleggers. We've always bought our sweet cider from him and his father, since time immemorial. Nearly all our vegetables. Your mother dealt with the Schertzinger family when you were a little girl."

"Yes, they came to market every Friday."

"I know. Didn't I help them get one of their sons into West Point? Or at least I tried. If he could have overcome that Pennsylvania Dutch accent they'd have taken him."

"He turned out all right," said Sophie.

"Actually much better than if he'd tried to be an army officer. The accent is no handicap to a country doctor, but it would have been at The Point. They're used to southern accents, but they'd have laughed at young Schertzinger. Just imagine how they'd ridicule him. It rains a lot at West Point, and they wouldn't know what he was talking about when he said, 'It makes down uckly.' "

"And 'The pie is all.' "

"Hmm. He wouldn't have much occasion to say that. We saw damn little pie when I was there. Mince pie at Christmas, my plebe year."

Their conversations had a way of drifting toward army life no matter how they started, but it could hardly have been otherwise with Dick Hightower. Other husbands, Sophie had found, did the same thing in conversation with their wives. Doctors digressed to medicine, lawyers to law, bankers to finance. Unlike other husbands, Dick Hightower was a chatterbox, and though his topics might be sandwiched between one army reminiscence and another, he did hold forth on other things. In fact—and she said this about once a year—if other people could know Dick Hightower as she knew him, they would realize that he was one of the most fascinating men you could ever hope to meet. In his youth he had traveled a great deal throughout the United States and territories, he had acquired a knowledge of history and could read French and German without much difficulty, he read the New York and Philadelphia papers at the club every day, he subscribed to magazines like *The Literary Digest*, the *Review of Reviews*, the *Army & Navy Journal*, the *National Geographic*, and *Foreign Affairs*. She did not see where he got the time to read them all, but he could quote from them and did so. Once a year, on Memorial Day, he would give the principal address at the ceremonies at the Soldiers & Sailors Monument, and he would begin the preparation of this speech right after the Christmas holidays. It was such a thorough, painstaking piece of work that both newspapers printed the speech *in toto*, from the copies given them in advance. This was in the nature of a precaution against being misquoted and for the purpose of providing the full text to history students in the public and Catholic high schools. The General Dixon L. Hightower Prize of ten dollars cash and a certificate suitable for framing was awarded annually to the student in each high school who had the best marks in American history. Dick's attendance at the commencement exercises was only one source of the kind of pleasurable experience that animated his conversations with Sophie. ("A little Italian girl won the prize at the Catholic school. Her father and mother can barely speak English.")

But his interests were not all on the intellectual side. He would return from a walk to the post office with ever so many things to tell her, little things that he had noticed that would escape the attention of a less observant man. Every morning, Monday through Friday, he would leave the house at ten o'clock, beautifully dressed in fine weather, with one of his walking sticks and bowler, Homburg, or Panama; grey spats and never the same suit two days running. On cold days he had his fur-lined black broadcloth or his long tweed ulster, and on rainy days inevitably his trench coat. He was so punctual that the motormen on the trolley lines had their own little custom of saluting him with taps on the floor bell, which he would acknowledge with a semi-military wave of the hand. As there were ten-o'clock trolleys for several out-of-town points the general's progress northward to the center of town was, as he said, tintinnabulated. ("You knew that Edgar Allan Poe went to West Point, briefly.")

His first stop was Joseph Ostertag's cigar store. Joseph Ostertag dealt only in cigars, pipes, pipe tobacco, and snuff. He had never sold a cigarette or a box of candy, and he stocked only Piper Heidsieck chewing tobacco for a few special customers (two county judges and a few Catholic priests). Back of his store, invisible from it, was his small cigar factory, in which three men and an apprentice were kept busy hand-rolling the two grades of Ostertag cigars: the twenty-five-cent straight Perfecto, and the two-for-a-quarter Special. Joseph was a dour man who owned the building in which he sold and made his cigars, the adjoining building, which contained a shoe store and three stories of offices, and a large storage warehouse in the North End of town. There were men in a position to know who said they would like to have what Joe Ostertag had *over* a million dollars. Nevertheless he was his own store clerk and did his own sweeping and cleaning. In his store he had a single bentwood chair, not for sociability but because one of his steady customers had once had a heart attack and was compelled to lie on the floor. No one—wife, friend, or customer—was permitted to call him Joe.

Dick Hightower had been a regular customer of Joseph Ostertag's for twenty years, but their opening exchange had not changed.

"Good morning, Joseph."

"Good morning to you, sir."

"Two Perfectoes, please."

Ostertag would raise the lid of the box and allow Dick Hightower to choose, although the cigars were individually foil-wrapped.

"Will you put that on my account, please?"

Ostertag would write in a ledger. "Two . . . Per . . . fec . . . toes . . . D . . . L . . . High . . . tower . . . 4 . . . 4 . . . 4 . . . South . . . Main." It was not necessary to record the price; it had not changed either. As for the quality of the leaf, it had if anything got better, but that was a matter not to be discussed with Ostertag. That was *his* business. In recent years, however, Ostertag and Hightower, having completed their transaction, permitted themselves some additional conversation. It usually concerned the stock market, which, since it was not the cigar business, was not a closed topic. Ostertag, surprisingly enough, traded on margins. But he made up for this uncharacteristically risky practice by getting out of a stock the moment it showed a three-point rise. Weeks would go by in which he did not trade at all, then one of the five stocks in which he specialized would be offered at an attractive price and he would again buy for the three-point profit.

Hightower, using Ostertag's information, would stay in for a five-point rise, but he never bought on margin, and his profits were smaller. He was content with small profits. His speculation was satisfactory if it made him pocket money, two to three thousand dollars a year. Sophie's fortune was administered by a Philadelphia trust company and he never interfered. She gave him $6,000 a year, paid all the household bills and reinvested the surplus income of her trust funds. The surplus had accumulated to more than $100,000, which would be his in the event of her death. The trust funds were not hers to dispose of, but he would never require more than the income from $100,000. And as she pointed out, the $100,000 rightfully belonged to him, inasmuch as she would have given him $7500 a year or $10,000 a year if he had wanted it. But he did not want it. He wanted no more than he had, no difference in the scale of their living, no change in his way of life that would take the fun out of careful spending. He did not wish to wear ready-made clothes, but he made his tailor-made suits and handmade shoes last, so that the arrival of a new suit or a pair of Oxfords was an event, not merely a purchase. "The small pleasures," he would say. The motormen's salute. The conversations with Joseph Ostertag. The reasonable profits in the stock market. The twenty-five-cent-straight cigars.

From Ostertag's he would go to the railroad station newsstand and pay a nickel for his New York paper, if the New York papers had made the train connections. If not, he would buy a Philadelphia *North American* because there was nothing else he cared to buy, and he had to buy something. He would exchange greetings with the station agent, the baggagemaster, and the telegraph operator, and return to Main Street. The traffic policeman operating the semaphore would salute him, and he would raise his hand in a return salute that was a trifle more military than the gesture he accorded the trolley motormen. The policeman, after all, bore arms, and Dick Hightower happened to know he was a former member of the National Guard.

For the next hour or so he would occupy a chair in the board room of the local branch of Westmore & Company, stock brokers. He would leave his overcoat on a hanger but keep his hat on or in his lap. All the customers kept their hats on unless they were seated next to one of the women customers. (Their patronage was invited, but they did detract from the once all-male atmosphere.) Dick Hightower's hour in the Westmore board room was a high point of his day. He would trim the first of his two Ostertag Perfectoes with his gold cutter, and take his place in the front row of chairs. All the customers knew each other, and they felt free to make running comments as the board boys chalked up the quotations coming in on the stock ticker. The regular customers, the daily visitors, were not only acquainted with each other but they also knew which men were trading in which securities. It was a motley crowd of retired business men, merchants, bootleggers, insurance salesmen, lawyers, two old maids and a madam. It was not considered good form for a bank employe to be seen in the board room, a restriction that did not apply to bank directors. Notwithstanding the presence of the women, the board room atmosphere was that of a sporting event, an uninterrupted race meeting five hours long. The chairs were comfortable, the temperature was kept under control, there were plenty of ash trays, and there was a customers' toilet with two urinals. Dick Hightower was a light trader, whose commissions covered only his share of the firm's overhead, but he added tone to the place and Westmore & Company knew it and he knew it.

No other firm in town could claim the simultaneous patronage of the general and the madam, and his manner of saying "Good morning," to her, without ever uttering her name, was precisely correct and an example which the other men followed. One word from him and the firm would have discouraged the madam's visits; but he did not speak that word, and the firm was tacitly grateful for his tolerance.

"You see that woman every day?" Sophie once said.

"Every single day," said Dick Hightower.

"What do you say to her?" said Sophie.

"I say good morning."

"You speak to her? How did you ever get to know her?"

"We were never formally introduced."

"Who does she sit with?"

"Oh, she knows some of the men."

"Do the other women speak to her?"

"Do the other women speak to her? No, I don't believe they do. They never sit with her, I know that."

"She just talks to the men?"

"Well, she's rather used to that," he said.

"What if you had to sit next to her? What would you say to her?"

"It's very doubtful that I'd ever find myself in that predicament. After all, I know how to maneuver myself."

"What if she maneuvered herself next to you?"

"That will never happen. If you didn't know who she was, you'd never take her for a prostitute. She's quite ugly. She wears a sealskin coat, but no jewelry except a wedding ring."

"A wedding ring?"

"Most of them do," he said.

"*Most* of them?"

"When I was a young officer we were often entertained by them. Every good-sized town has at least one madam that young officers know about."

"You never told me that. Did you patronize them?"

"I did."

"Oh, Dick, you didn't."

"Sorry to disillusion you, but I did."

"I suppose I knew that, really."

"You could have found out any time you asked me. Remember, I was past thirty when I met you."

"So was I."

He smiled. "I'd never have known if you hadn't told me."

"That was about all I had to tell," she said. "Think of the difference between that woman and me. I mean in what she knows about life."

"Life? Whatever she knows about life, it hasn't done her much good. If you could see her you'd understand that. It's all written in her face. Women of your sort tend to think of them as tarnished beauties. They're tarnished, all right, but very few of them were ever beauties. You know the expression, as ugly as sin."

"Then why would a nice young man want to have anything to do with them?"

"Because nice young women have to stay nice or they aren't nice any more, if I make myself clear."

"Perfectly," she said.

Unless there were unusually active trading in the market, Dick left Westmore & Company before noon, to be a little ahead of the midday rush at the post office. He had a large mailbox to receive his books and periodicals. He would open it with his key and take out what he wanted and leave the rest for a dull day. He did not wish to be overburdened on his walk to the club, in the course of which he often had to stop and chat with ladies; and while he could manage his cane and a book or two and the removal of his hat, as an officer he had been trained not to carry small parcels while in uniform. Early habits were hard to break. Later habits were easily formed. At the club he would go to the cloakroom and put away his things, wash his hands as in a ceremonial ablution that symbolized his withdrawal from the contacts of commerce and common folk, and his return to the world of the gentleman. Not all the members of the club met his standards, but every gentleman in town was a member of the club. He would rub his soap-softened hands and enter the billiard room, where even at half past eleven in the morning at least one game would be in progress. "I'm up," he would say, and write his initials on a blackboard to signify his intention of challenging the first winner. A wooden plaque, listing the club billiards champions of other years, had D. L. Hightower as champion for 1911 and 1912 and runner-up in 1913, 1914, and 1917. He would never reign again; the younger men were too good for him; but no member could beat him every time they played. He could still run out a string of twenty-one points. He was a slow player, which gave him a psychological advantage over the younger men, and he would play more slowly than usual against those who showed impatience. This strategy delighted his contemporaries, the members of the Old Guard who occupied the same luncheon table every day. "Dick, you old fox, you had young Choate half out of his mind," they would say.

"Don't call me an old fox. Call me an old tortoise," he would say. "The race is not always to the swift." He managed to win enough money to cover his house charges. The seventy-five-cent table d'hôte came to six dollars a week, and he had usually won that amount by the Wednesday. In weeks that he had fallen behind he could count on making a comeback on the Saturday, when he could play all afternoon until he made six dollars. The players were more apt to imbibe on Saturdays.

As a rule there was a lull in the billiard room after lunch on weekdays, but there was likely to be some activity in the card room. Dick Hightower tried to stay out of the post-luncheon auction bridge. He had found that his contemporaries got sleepy after the meal, especially on Monday, Wednesday, and Friday when the club specialty, deep-dish apple pie, was on the menu. The stakes were never high, but it was no fun to see one's partner's eyelids begin to droop, to hear the heavy, regular breathing that portended a nap at the table. "Whitfield is in the land of Nod," someone would say. "Shall we leave him there?"

"What? What? Is it my lead?" the sleepy one would say.

"Not quite. Your partner just said two no trump, and I passed."

"Two no trump? Let's see now, can we review the bidding?"

"All right. I opened with a heart, you said a spade, my partner raised my hearts to two, and Dick said two no trump. I passed."

"And you were the original heart bidder, eh? Oh, yes, now it's coming back to me. I'll have to say three spades."

"And you do say three spades?"

"Yes. Three spades. I *said*, three *spades*. Oh, wait just a second. Two no trump would have given us game. However, I said three spades and three spades it is. Yes, three spades."

Yet even on days when the deep-dish apple pie was not having a toxic effect Dick Hightower would have preferred to be elsewhere. The club notepaper, of stiff stock and nicely embossed, was just right for certain items of his correspondence. At the writing desks, moreover, were sticks of sealing-wax and birthday-cake candles, and envelopes bearing the imprint of Dick's signet ring went out almost daily to sick friends, the lately bereaved, classmates who had achieved honors or grandparenthood, recent hostesses, and the beneficiaries of his spontaneous acts of charity, to whom he did not wish to give his home address. Foremost among these were non-commissioned officers and their families whom he would read about in the newspapers, men whom he had never known and who frequently were residents of distant communities, who had met with misfortune that a five-dollar bill, a ten-dollar bill, might help to alleviate. These gifts, and the acknowledgments of them, were a secret from Sophie and from everyone else. They never amounted to $100 a year, and on several occasions they had invited requests for larger donations, but he refused to be disillusioned by the greedy or the suspicious. Over the years the practice gave him much satisfaction.

"You know, General, a lot of people must think you live here," said Walter Beers, the paid secretary. "You get more mail than the club, outside of bills."

"Well, I do live here, about a quarter of my waking hours, Walter," said Dick Hightower.

"Yes, I guess that's right, when you stop to think of it. You eat one-third of your meals here, leaving out Sunday."

"That's correct, and I get most of my exercise here."

Beers laughed. "Exercise? Here?"

"At the billiard table. Someone, I believe, calculated that an hour at the billiard table is the equivalent of a three-mile walk. I

have my doubts, but we must find out if one of the members has
a pedometer. You don't happen to know of any?"

"To be truthful, General, I don't know what one is. A what
did you call it?"

"A pedometer. Measures how far you walk."

"What do you do, attach it to your foot? I never heard of
one."

"You attach them to your belt, but between us I don't consider them very reliable."

"I wouldn't, either, I don't trust the one I got on my car."

"Is that so? Walter, will you put stamps on these and see that
they go out this afternoon?"

"I'll drop them by the post office on my way home."

An incredibly dull man, Walter Beers, but he had come home
with a wound chevron from Château-Thierry, and Dick Hightower first had known him as company clerk and bugler in old
Company B. A dull, unmilitary man, who nevertheless had battle
stars on his Victory Medal and a *fourragère* on his now tight-fit-
ting uniform. He would be club secretary as long as Dick Hightower had anything to say about it. "Walter, can you still sound
pay-call?"

Walter laughed. "You mean on the bugle, General? Now what
ever made you think of that? My goodness. Pay-call. I can't even
remember how it went, let alone play it. I got my youngest boy,
he's a second-class Scout, and they decided to make him a bugler
on account of me. But they don't have pay-call in the Scouts.
One less he has to learn than me. The neighbors ought to be glad
of that. Pay-call. My goodness, General. I wasn't a bugler overseas. We just used the whistle over there, but I still got the same
original old horn I had in B-Company."

"Hold on to it, Walter. It's government property, but I think
you're entitled to it."

"They'd have a hard time getting it away from me," said
Walter.

Four-thirty or five, time to return to 444, and timed carefully.
The outpouring of the children from the schools was over, the
departure of people who worked in shops and offices had not yet
begun. At home there was tea (after a careful scrubbing of his

hands). Because it was still daylight, Sophie would often have a visitor or two, and Dick was always the only male present. He would be at his courtly best; the head of the house, the host, the man in women's territory like a boy visiting his sister's boarding-school. All that, and The General, the highest-ranking military man in town. His hands were clean, his thin grey hair smoothed down, his necktie in place, the smudges on his shoes rubbed away. There would be a mechanical, innocuous flirtatiousness in his manner, put there as soon as he entered the sitting room, so that Sophie's guests would envy her her life with him. "Haven't you ladies got any gossip for me? There's nothing new at the club, I can assure you," he would say.

Although they might have been exchanging information on the town's latest scandal, they offered none of it to him. He would not have welcomed it if they had. But the pretense of curiosity added a sparkle to the ritual of tea. Any real gossip Sophie had picked up would be duly passed on to him when they were alone, in language of the utmost purity but with illustrative gestures, and as completely descriptive as a police report. He had never asked her how her women friends were able to communicate details without using the language of the gutter or of the physician; they would not repeat naughty words, and they were ignorant of medical terminology. Nevertheless Sophie and her friends made their stories graphically real, and there was nothing in the calendar of sin that she had not at some time been able to convey to him in the telling of an episode. A day or two later—or a day or two earlier—the same story would be told at the club without the language restraints, but the women left nothing out.

Sophie was an accomplished gossip, a talent that compensated for her inability to concentrate on the printed word. As she was childless she was not compelled to protect her own son and daughter from reprisals. As she was beyond reproach in her conduct, she was invulnerable to gossip about herself. And as her husband led a blameless life, she had nothing to fear from misconduct on his part. Not even her chambermaid could find any evidence of the methods by which they took pleasure in each other, and it was assumed that if there had ever been erotic excitement in their marriage, that time had long since passed.

In the early days of their marriage, when Dick was a newcomer to the town, the obvious comment had been made that Sophie was a fortunate young woman to have captured such a handsome young man. She herself was plain, and though a good-sized fortune went with her, the eligible young men of the town had failed to be attracted by it. It was not unusual for a young army officer to marry for money, but when Sophie's husband resigned his commission and took up residence at 444, with no apparent inclination to enter the world of business, he came in for some harsh, if guarded, criticism as a fortune-hunter. The criticism was not entirely fair. Investigation revealed that Dixon Hightower was not a nobody. The Hightower family were old Chester County stock who had scattered over the southeastern section of the Commonwealth, and who numbered among their living members a college president, several clergymen, some successful farmers, and a Philadelphia banker. Sophie's bridegroom was the only son of a weekly newspaper publisher and job printer in Montgomery County, a first cousin of the Philadelphia banker. William Hightower's business brought in little cash, but he accepted goods and services in lieu of it, and he always had a roof over his head and enough to eat. He was a graduate of a Friends Seminary, and had hoped to send his son to the new college at Swarthmore, but the opportunity to educate the boy at govern-ment expense was not to be denied. The rich cousin in Philadel-phia offered no financial assistance, and as William Hightower had not been raised a Quaker, the cousin's scruples against a West Point education were considered to be all foam and no beer.

Dixon Hightower's army experience, beginning with West Point, taught him frugality and at the same time helped him acquire expensive tastes. The frugality was, of course, a refine-ment of the manner in which he had been brought up at home; the expensive tastes were new, but he took to them readily. Throughout his army career he needed financial assistance from his parents. As an army officer his credit was good, but sooner or later his boots had to be paid for, and he could not safely rely on his carefully hoarded winnings at cards for the expenses of the mess and visits to the cities. His father therefore practiced small economies; he smoked a cheap grade of Lancaster County tobacco, wore homemade carpet slippers in his shop and at home. His mother competed with her neighbors in fancywork and dressmaking. Together they were able to contribute as much as $500 a year to the maintenance of their son's standards, and it was worth it to them when he came home on leave, dressed in his blues and bringing them presents that they had paid for. He would be invited to hunt the fox with the nearby gentry and he was popular with its younger members. Their parents, however, knew to the penny what Dixon Hightower's financial expectations must be, and they were vigilant in keeping him at an unromantic distance from their daughters. It did not matter to them when Sophie Stokes, daughter of an upstate coal fortune, determinedly and unabashedly threw herself at the impecunious young lieutenant. Indeed, the mothers were all in favor of a union that would get Sophie a husband and young Hightower safely married. Dixon was well behaved, but not all the young wives were completely happy with their husbands.

Sophie Stokes was already courtesy aunt to the children of her friends, a readily available companion to the young wives during their confinements. She had acquired all the essential information about the young army officer, and knew from her friends that his mother earned pin-money by such work as letting out dresses for the expectant young matrons. She paid a visit to his father's newspaper-printing shop and saw him in his carpet slippers. As a Stokes she was a realist, a member of a family that demanded good value and had been remarkably successful in getting it. There was no doubt in her mind that Dixon Hightower represented good value for her, but he had never visited her part of the Commonwealth and could not be expected to know that she might also represent good value for him. He had been polite to her without displaying any of that extra politeness or cordiality that indicated an attraction. He still called her Miss Stokes.

Toward the end of his leave, before returning to his army duties at Fort Niagara, he was seated next to her at a dinner party, and this, she knew, might be her last chance. "Where is

Fort Niagara?" she said. "I suppose it's somewhere near Niagara Falls."

"Quite near. It's on Lake Ontario. They call it the Niagara Frontier. It's a very pleasant place to be after the heat of Texas."

"And the city of Buffalo is somewhere near, is it not?" she said. "I have friends in Buffalo. The Watsons."

"I've been to their house. Colonel Watson, on Delaware Avenue? Is that the same one?"

"He made his money in railroads. It's the same one. I went to school with his daughter Jessica. Now Mrs. John Fisher."

"Yes, I know Jessica. The Watsons and the Fishers entertain on the grand scale."

"So I'm told," she said. "Is that the sort of life you care for? The entertaining on the grand scale?"

"Yes, I confess I do."

"But you can't do much of it on army pay."

"No, and if I were married I couldn't do it at all."

"Unless you had a rich wife," she said. "Why haven't you got a rich wife?"

He smiled. "Because no rich young lady has ever proposed to me."

"Very well. I do."

"Be careful, I might accept," he said.

"If you knew me better you'd know that I want you to accept."

"Here? Now?"

"Yes," she said.

"Assuming for the moment that you're not pulling my leg, I couldn't accept. Right now, I'm in debt, in no position to marry."

"How much in debt?"

"A little over eight hundred dollars."

"I have it in my purse, upstairs. You may consider it yours."

"It's very unwise to carry that much cash about with you," he said. "Why do you?"

"Because I like to. And if I'm robbed, I have more. Do you know who my father was? The name Stokes doesn't mean anything to you people down here, but I assure you, Lieutenant

Hightower, eight hundred dollars wouldn't make a very large dent in my inheritance."

"Really? Are you a millionairess?"

"Yes."

"As well-to-do as our host," he said.

"Oh, I rather think so."

"In other words, you rather think you are richer than he is."

"I shouldn't be at all surprised. On the other hand, I'm not as rich as the Watsons."

"They're almost too rich, aren't they? I can imagine myself the owner of four horses, but not fourteen. And I don't think I'd care to live in that house on Delaware Avenue. I have a batman, an orderly, in the army. He has the duties of a servant, a valet. But Colonel Watson has a butler, valet, footman, coachman, groom, and I don't know what else. He must have many more at the farm in Batavia. Have you been there?"

"Yes."

"Then you know their scale of living. It's too grand for me. If I should leave the army, I'd share bachelor quarters with another officer, and one man would do for the two of us."

"But you're not going to share bachelor quarters. You're going to marry me. You would love my house. I have Patrick, who was my father's butler and coachman, and we have Rex and Ray, a pair of sorrels. I sold the farm to a cousin of mine, but I could buy it back if you were to insist. My cousin would extract his pound of flesh, but he's entitled to something. What are you thinking?"

"What am I thinking? I was thinking about this conversation. It sounds like a storybook conversation, in a novel, yet it's actually taking place. Nothing surprises me any more, except the commonplace. That's not quite what I'm trying to say. Let's put it this way. The first time I was ever under fire, it didn't seem possible that two hundred yards away, those men were actually firing shots at me. There they were, partly concealed by a rock formation, rocks that had been there since the beginning of time. Men that had been on earth—oh, twenty or thirty or forty years. They were members of an Indian tribe and not many of them live beyond forty. In between them and me was sand and sagebrush. All very commonplace, don't you know? And even the sound of their rifles was nothing new to me. But it all changed in the fraction of a second, when one of my men was picked off, in the middle of a sentence. He'd never been under fire, either, and he was in the midst of saying something to me. Before he could complete the sentence he was dead. I don't mean to shock you with this grisly story, Miss Stokes, but you asked me what I was thinking and that was it. The unpredictability of things."

"Such as having a proposal of marriage from your dinner partner."

"Yes."

"I could have predicted it, though. As soon as I heard you were leaving on Saturday afternoon. I asked to be put next to you at table."

"Did you? Then I believe you are quite serious."

"Oh, yes," she said.

"In that case, I accept. But I'm so accustomed to rules and regulations that I must insist on one thing."

"What is that?"

"That I propose to you. Miss Stokes, will you do me the honor of becoming my wife?"

"Yes, Lieutenant Hightower, I accept with great pleasure."

"Shall I rise and startle the guests with our announcement?"

"No, let's wait. But some of them wouldn't be as startled as you might think," she said.

Even the Philadelphia banking Hightower came to the wedding when he learned that his cousin was marrying a Stokes. Dixon Hightower, no longer in the army, wore a Prince Albert, but his six ushers were in uniform and provided the arch of swords. The bride was given in marriage by the cousin who had purchased her farm, and Jessica Watson Fisher was matron of honor. The groom's father, at the reception, could not resist saying to his banker cousin, "Well, Howard, the boy turned out a lot better than you expected."

"So it would seem, Cousin William," said Howard Hightower. "Are you planning to retire?"

"No. Just not going to worry quite as much," said William Hightower.

"You won't have to. We take care of her money, or some of it."

"Isn't that congenial?" said William Hightower.

The maladjustments between the bride and groom continued after their wedding night until well into the first year of their marriage, and were prevented from becoming disastrous only by their being treated as incidents of the night, not to be discussed in the daytime and never discussed at any great length when they occurred. "It hurts," she would say. "It always hurts."

"It won't always," he said.

"Do you think we'll ever have any children?"

"Do you want children that badly?"

"No. Do you?"

"I'm in no hurry," he said.

"That means you really don't," she said. "But if I'm ever going to, I ought to start now."

"Not everybody has them. And you're an only child and so am I. Do you honestly *want* to have a child, Sophie?"

"I don't think I do. And I'm getting afraid. They say you should have your first before you're thirty, and I'm past that."

"Well, there's only one way to have them, and we can't seem to do that. But we mustn't let it worry us. Our life is very pleasant as it is, don't you agree?"

"Oh, yes. I'm happy. I hope you are."

"Of course I am, Sophie. And I'm not at all sure if I'm cut out for fatherhood. Children don't like me."

"They don't like me, either," she said.

"Then we needn't lose any sleep over that," he said.

By concentrating their sensual ministrations in the first hour of retirement, by ignoring their failure to achieve conventional coitus, they reached a tacit agreement on the relative unimportance of that side of their married life. They were in no frenetic haste to produce offspring; Sophie had never experienced heterosexual or homosexual orgasm; and Dick, who had experienced both, showed her the ways by which she could produce orgasm in him, and for her there was enough excitement to give her pleasure. In the beginning she had been fearful that her failure might drive him away from her, and when it did not, when he turned out to be both patient and understanding, she accepted their modus vivendi as the solution to a problem that existed as a problem only because other women had told her of other experiences. She refused to see a doctor, and Dick supported her in her wish to preserve the secret of her failure. Thus their days contained neither frustration nor the torments of it. Other things mattered more and occupied their thoughts. For her there was the running of the household, her gardening, her friends, her gossip; for him there was the constant contrast between his new regimen (in which he was in full, supreme command) and the years of military restrictions. He was getting used to doing exactly what he wanted to do, without being required to supply explanation or excuse to anyone. For this he was learning to love Sophie, whose money had made his freedom possible, and he now loved the army for the preparation it had given him for this new life.

He was easily persuaded to accept a captain's commission on the governor's staff, was promoted to major at the outbreak of the war with Spain, and returned from Tampa, Florida, a full colonel. He had been out of the Commonwealth a total of three months, quite long enough to convince him that his decision to resign from the Regular Army had been the right one. Sophie had convinced herself that his decision to resign had been a sacrifice on his part, and he allowed her to continue to believe it, since it was something she wanted, but what he wanted now was to keep what he had.

A series of welcoming ceremonies, large and small, public, semi-public, and private, restored him to civilian life once more. Nearly half a century had passed since the town had been able to demonstrate its pride and gratitude to its military men, and the short duration of the hostilities with Spain and the absence of gunshot casualties was additional cause for rejoicing. Colonel Dixon L. Hightower was the man of the hour. There was even talk of running him for Congress. Not many outsiders had so quickly been adopted by the citizens of the town.

In the name of the borough a group of men of substance presented to Dixon Hightower a dress sword from Bailey, Banks & Biddle, at a subscription banquet in Odd Fellows Hall. But he

435

had already, a week earlier, on the night of his return to 444, received a welcome from Sophie that surprised her as much as him: in the course of their first embrace, with neither of them expecting more than there had ever been for them, they were possessed by an intensity, a drive, that was wholly instinctive and that carried them forward into complete copulation. "How did it happen?" he said.

"I was going to ask you," she said.

"Was it because we missed each other?"

"I guess so. It must have been," she said.

"And it didn't hurt?"

"Not really. I didn't notice it. Did it hurt you?"

"Pinched a little, but only a little. Nothing would have stopped me."

"Or me either," she said.

"You haven't been going to see a doctor or anything like that?"

"Nothing. But I missed you. Oh, I wanted you so much. Just to have you in the house with me. Every night I took something of yours to bed with me, held it to my bosom."

"And elsewhere?"

She nodded. "Yes, and elsewhere."

"What sort of thing?"

"Different things. A cravat. A riding crop. A muffler. Whatever I happened to see in your wardrobe. I very nearly sent you something of mine, but how could I tell you that in a letter?"

"I wish you had sent me something of yours," he said.

"Oh, dear. What would you have liked?"

"Oh—some intimate something. Something feminine."

"Something I'd worn?" she said.

"Oh, yes. Lacy, satiny." He got out of bed and turned up the burner.

"What are you going to do?" she said.

"You mustn't look. Close your eyes, or turn away till I tell you to look."

She turned away. "What on earth are you doing?" she said.

"Just be patient, and don't look till I tell you," he said.

"You're getting something of mine, I know that."

"Just be patient," he said.

"How much longer?"

"Count to fifty, slowly," he said.

She commenced to count. When she reached the forties he said, "All right, now you can look."

He stood at the foot of their bed, and he was wearing an evening dress of hers and a pearl necklace, and on his head he had a silken scarf.

"Dixon!" she said.

"Are you surprised?"

"You could almost be a woman," she said.

"I thought you'd laugh," he said.

"I would have, but you even stand like a woman. A *pretty* Madge Prestock."

"Well, that's a compliment. Madge is a handsome woman," he said. "Do you like me this way?"

"I don't know, I'm not sure. It's such a surprise. How can you suddenly transform yourself? Do you like to dress up like a woman?"

"I never have before," he said. He stood in front of her full-length mirror. "If my feet were smaller I could wear your shoes. The next time you go shopping, buy me a pair of high-heeled shoes."

"Do you mean it?"

"Yes. And a wig. You might have to go to Philadelphia for a wig. That place where you rent masquerade costumes. You know the place I mean, down on Chestnut Street. Van Something."

"What color wig?"

"Get two. Blond and brunette. Nobody else has to know," he said. "They could be all your things, and don't you think it would be fun?"

"I don't know. I suppose so," she said.

"I've always wanted to do this," he said.

"What about me? Would you want me to dress up as a man?"

"Haven't you ever wanted to?"

"Oh—when I was little."

"Only when you were little? Didn't you ever go to a fancy dress party in a man's costume?"

"We were never allowed to."

"What would you have gone as if you'd been allowed to?"

"A cowboy, with those white furry trousers."

"Chaparejos. Chaps. I have an old pair of leather ones in the attic. How would you like to put on my blues? Not the breeches, but the trousers and short coat."

"Now?"

"Unfortunately they're at the tailor's, but you could put on one of my civilian suits if you'd like."

"I'd feel very strange," she said.

"We'll do it some other time."

"You really want me to?"

"Yes, I do," he said.

"All right, I will. But I won't make as good a man as you do a woman."

"Oh, what difference does that make? It's just for the fun of it, you and I. Neither one of us would ever think of telling anyone else."

"All right, now please come back to bed."

"I will if you undress me," he said.

"You mean as if I were a man?"

"There's nothing wrong in it, Sophie. I don't see anything wrong. We're husband and wife."

"Yes," she said.

It became so that when she wanted him she would retire early and lay out lingerie, a dress, silk stockings and shoes on the chaise-longue in their bedroom. Without this preliminary, he could not be stimulated. He very soon tired of her awkward efforts to pose as a man. "I'm afraid you'll never learn to tie a four-in-hand," he said. But he never grew weary of his own part in the game, and for the sake of its consummation she played it with him. "I bought you a nice present today," she would say. "Don't ask me what it is. You'll see it sometime this evening." It would be an inexpensive necklace, a bracelet, an article of lingerie. In the mornings before breakfast she would put everything away, out of sight of her chambermaid, and he would shave and dress with no word, no look, no conspiratorial smile that referred to the rites of the night before. At breakfast he would read his newspaper and make his comments on the events of the outside world. He was the same man, because she knew him to be, and as she said about once a year, if other people knew him as she did they would realize that he was one of the most fascinating men you could ever hope to meet.

AFTERNOON WALTZ

In many American towns it often happened that on the main residential street there would be one or two blocks that for one reason or another gave an impression of retiring. Sometimes it was because the leafage of the trees in those blocks darkened the sidewalks. Sometimes the character of the dwellings was uniformly conservative, as if an early house or two had set a style that succeeding builders felt compelled to follow. Whatever the reasons, it was certainly true that when such a block had remained intact for a full generation, it attracted (or held) the kind of people who belonged in that particular neighborhood. The block, the houses, seemed to be occupied by grandparents and the unmarried sisters and brothers of grandparents.

Between Tenth and Eleventh on Lantenengo Street all the houses on the north side were porchless and none was set back from the building line. Most of them had vestibules. A few were constructed to have the front parlor half a story above the street level, so that not even a very tall passer-by could see in the parlor windows. Where the front parlor was on street level, the passer-by's curiosity was frustrated by curtains of heavy lace and lowered window-shades. But the residents of the ten-hundred block were their own best protection against causal peering-in on the part of men on their way to work and women on their way to market. What was there to see in the front parlor or anywhere else in the John Wesley Evans house at 1008?

In point of fact, if an accurate count had been kept of the persons who had set foot in the Evans house since its construction in the 1890's, the total number would not have exceeded a thousand, and that would have included invited visitors, physicians, clergymen, tradesmen and craftsmen. Wesley John Evans, the father of John Wesley Evans, had built to stay, and as there never had been any small children or careless servants in the house, the wear and tear had been kept at a minimum. Wesley Evans and his wife got sick and died, but only in their terminal illnesses had they required doctors and nurses. Their social life was so severely restricted that they had never served a meal to a non-relative on a purely social occasion. When John Wesley Evans entered the house for the first time, he was a college senior on Christmas vacation, and it would never have occurred to him to invite a friend to be his house guest.

As the only child of his parents to reach maturity, John Wesley Evans was brought up in an atmosphere that was compounded of desperate affection and conscientious discipline. He rebelled against neither. He was, in fact, a good boy; obedient, honest, and clean. When in senior year he told his father and mother that he was not yet ready to study for the ministry, they deferred to his wish. It was just as well, since his father died the next summer and his mother would have passed the remaining two years of her life alone in the house at 1008. In the thirty years of her marriage to Wesley John Evans she had never been separated from him for more than three days at a time, and the continual presence of her son was her only comfort against pain and terror. She could not have stood her last ordeal without him. Then too, if he had gone to a seminary and become more imbued with religious doctrine, he might have refused to place within her reach the medicine that enabled her to put an end to her agony. "An accidental overdose," said Dr. Phillips. "But she didn't have long anyway, so if you don't say anything about it, I won't say anything about it."

"I won't say anything about it, Dr. Phillips," said John Wesley Evans.

"No, I was sure you wouldn't," said Dr. Phillips. "If you're ever asked what your mother died of, tell them it was a complication of diseases."

"Is that what my father died of, too? A complication of diseases?"

"Oh, no. He died of quinsy. I was *here* when *he* died," said the doctor. "Nobody was here when your mother died."

"I was in the next room," said John Wesley Evans.

"Yes, I know," said the doctor. "Best we don't carry on any more conversation now, John. We'll just let her rest in peace, as they say." The doctor smiled. "I hope my son'll be as considerate when my time comes. Maybe I might have to send for you."

"If you send for me, I'll come," said John Wesley Evans.

"Well, it'd be only fair. I brought you into the world," said the doctor. "But now let's stop talking. I'll most likely see you at the service."

Thus at age twenty-five John Wesley Evans found himself virtually alone in the world, with capital amounting to $160,000 and a rather large, comfortable house to live in. It surprised him to discover that the freedom he now enjoyed could so quickly become so much of his life that it was all of it. He had not been conscious of being contained by his mother and father, but now that they were no longer there to say or do anything, anything at all, he began to understand that what he wanted most was the release that had come to him through their deaths.

Every morning almost his first thought, which carried through breakfast and beyond, was of a new day in which he could do as he pleased. The small things of major importance gave him opportunities to indulge himself. He never, for instance, had been permitted to lie abed past the hour of eight; now he sometimes appeared in the diningroom at nine. Like all children of his day, he ate what was put before him, a habit which he continued during his four years in college. Now, at twenty-five, he broke the habit, broke it and abandoned it. Sarah Lundy, who did the cooking and general housework, never knew what he was going to want for breakfast. She would bring him his first cup of tea and stand in the doorway while he considered the meal that was to follow. "Today I'll have liver and bacon. Corn bread. Apple butter," he would say. Whatever he ordered, it was never quite like the breakfast that other people ate, and there had to be a lot of it. Breakfast was his big meal. Everybody else ate a big dinner at noon and a light supper, but John Wesley Evans would often eat nothing but fruit, cheese, and bread for the noon meal; then in the evening, at six o'clock, he liked a thick soup and hot apple pie with heavy cream. Throughout the day he might eat a bunch of grapes, some Seckel pears, or whatever else Sarah Lundy had put on the sideboard. Where all the food went she did not know; he remained, as he had always been, all skin and bones; the kind of child and young man that parents feared would die of consumption. Also, he was unusually tall, six foot one, and tall, thin people were often said to have a tapeworm. But if John Wesley Evans had a tapeworm it did not affect his disposition, and people with a tapeworm were generally cranky. John Wesley Evans was generally cheerful, so that Sarah Lundy did not mind much if he put her to a lot of extra work with his unpredictable menus. Until her final illness his mother had done the cooking in the Evans household, and Sarah Lundy was agreeably shocked when John Wesley Evans told her that she was a much better cook than his mother had been. It was the kind of thing he often said to her, the unexpected kind of thing that he had never said while his parents were alive. Sarah Lundy was the first person to realize that John Wesley Evans was an altogether different person from the shy young scarecrow who had always come straight home from school every afternoon and done his sums on the diningroom table. In those days you would hardly know he was in the house. Many times she had entered a room to do her dusting and would be startled to discover him, lying on the floor and reading a book. Thick books, they were, from the glassed-in bookcase in the front parlor, which had a key in the lock. The boy's father and mother did not read the books, and Sarah Lundy was not at all sure that the boy had permission to remove the books from the case. The books, which did not fill all the shelves, were for show, and had been there throughout Sarah Lundy's employment in the Evans household—at the old house on Second Street and the house at 1008 Lantenengo. Sixteen years she had put in with the Evans family; watched two Evans children pass on before either of them reached the age of seven; helped carry W. J. Evans to his bedroom when he had his second stroke; been kept awake at night by Mrs. Evan's moaning and groaning; and now she was being witness to changes in the household that she would have liked better if she understood them better.

There was no doubt about it; her own lot had improved. She did not have to be washed and dressed and downstairs by six-thirty in the morning. As long as the house looked neat and clean she could do her chores on her own schedule. She was practically her own boss, and once John had had his breakfast and his bedroom tended to, she could leave the house to do the marketing three or four days a week, which gave her an opportunity to chat with outsiders and gossip with friends along the way. The walk back up the Tenth Street hill was a little tiring, but the exercise of authority at the grocer's and butcher's and the pleasant conversations made it worth it. Before Mrs. took sick Sarah Lundy had never done the marketing; now she made decisions. "How is your lamb chops today? . . . Do you have any turnips fresh? . . . Let me have a basket of them peaches . . . What are your sweet potatoes selling at?" She had not yet been designated housekeeper by John, but she so considered herself. She could not quite get up the nerve to enter the house by the front door, but that would come. John had voluntarily raised her pay to $35 a month, which was a good sign, especially as he had not raised the pay of the woman who came in on Monday and Tuesday to do the washing and ironing. The week's wash was not as big as it had been, and there were plenty of women only too glad to work for a dollar a day and dinner. (You had to keep an eye on them or they'd walk home with a pound of sugar under their cloaks.) No doubt about it; for both occupants of 1008 Lantenengo Street an era of ease and comfort had begun with the passing of John Wesley Evan's mother.

On the other hand Sarah Lundy, who was Irish and a Roman Catholic, had never been *un*comfortable in a household that was Welsh and Methodist. There were no blacker Protestants than

the Welsh Methodists, and they were actively and deeply hated
by Sarah Lundy's Irish Catholic friends, particularly those whose
menfolk worked in the coal mines. Of very recent memory was
the execution of the Mollie Maguires, and the feeling persisted
that the Mollies had been hanged because they were less powerful than the Welsh bosses. In theory the Mollie Maguire organization had been broken up by the hangings, by the threats of
excommunication by the higher clergy, and by the public indig-
nation over the Mollies' crimes. In fact the organization continued to meet in greater secrecy, necessarily in smaller numbers,
keeping their hatred alive and making absurd plans for the
future. For the time being murder was ruled out, and violence
took the form of beatings administered to non-Mollies by Mollies. No one had to distinguish between one and the other; all
the Irish knew which was which. In spite of the division, the
non-Mollies were loosely united with the Mollies by the common
enemy, the Welsh Protestants, and when Sarah Lundy first went
to work for the Evans family neither party could guess how
the arrangement would turn out. Sarah, with her distrust of
Welsh Protestants, correspondingly was distrusted by Wesley and
Gladys Evans. Sarah had come highly recommended by her
previous employers, but as it happened she was the first servant
ever employed by the Evanses, who had just begun to make
money. Gladys Evans was not a lady, and her treatment of Sarah
Lundy was unsure, varying from unreasonable demands to spurts
of kindness, until Sarah Lundy subtly and patiently established a
reasonable relationship. Thereafter she fitted into the household.
The Evanses were not a family to inspire affection, but their
Methodist morality matched in many ways the aversion to sin
that had been drummed into Sarah Lundy by her own people.
Liquor, beer, tobacco, snuff, card-playing, dancing, breaking the
Sabbath, and free intermingling of the sexes were forbidden in
the Evans household. So had they been at the Lundys'. When
Patrick Lundy came home drunk, he had the choice of sleeping
in the woodshed or the privy, but not in the house, and Rose
Lundy was a strong enough woman to enforce her rule. Life as
the Evanses' hired girl was thus not much different from Sarah's
life at home, except that she got paid and the food was better

and there was more of it. Gladys Evans did not like Sarah's having a crucifix over her bed and holy pictures on her bureau, but as it was unlikely that Wesley Evans would ever enter Sarah's bedroom, the tokens of Sarah's papist affiliation were allowed to remain. It was well known, of course, that churchgoing Catholics never stole, and Gladys Evans never refused Sarah permission to go to church.

Sarah Lundy was not critical of John Wesley Evans and his ways. Compared to other women in her position in the ten-hundred block she had it soft, and she knew it. Nevertheless she was bothered by a superstitious feeling that things were going too well. Life was not that easy. For a little while a person might go along unplagued by trouble and sorrow and pain, but Sarah had been taught that God had not intended that the life here below was to be anything but preparation for the life hereafter. The godless, the sinful, who took their pleasures on earth, would all too soon learn that they had paid for them at the price of eternal bliss. God had given man a free will, and he could make his choice between earthly satisfactions and heavenly salvation. Sarah Lundy believed that Wesley and Gladys Evans, who presumably had been baptized Christians, were quite possibly in purgatory, expiating their venial sins. That was what could happen to Protestants if they lived good lives. The worst that could happen to them would be to spend eternity in limbo because they had not been baptized. The important thing about Wesley and Gladys Evans was that they had served God as well as they knew how, avoiding sin and the occasions of sin, and God would take into consideration the circumstances that kept them from becoming Catholics. Sarah Lundy did not for one minute forget that bad Catholics could be condemned to eternal damnation. God would be more severe in His judgment of Catholics, because they were supposed to know better. It was a very complicated subject if you got into it too deeply, and it was not a subject to discuss with non-Catholics, who asked ignorant questions. But it was a subject that Sarah Lundy occupied her mind with much of the time, and most of the time she was thinking not of just anyone but of John Wesley Evans.

There was no harm in him, no evil. True, he did not have a

job, he did not work. Indeed, he seldom went out of the house. But she could not judge him guilty of sloth, one of the seven deadly sins. Some men were meant to work with their hands, some were meant to work with their brains. John Wesley Evans escaped the charge of sloth because he was doing something with his brains. Bit by bit he was converting the sitting-room back of the parlor into a workroom. "It sounds a little fancy, Sarah, but from now on we'll call this the library," he announced one day.

"The liberry," she said. "All right. I'll get used to it."

"I'm going to build some bookshelves, and some day both these walls will be lined with books from top to bottom."

"Covering the wallpaper?"

"Covering the wallpaper. You'll be able to say you remember this room when it didn't have a single book in it."

"What would I want to say that for?"

"Well, if you don't want to say it there's no reason why you should. But the time will come when you'll be *able* to say it. And the time may not be too far off. This was always the room I liked best. Not the way Papa and Mama had it, but my way. The nicest thing about it is the bay window."

"Where the Mrs. would sit and do her sewing."

"It has the north light. I may take up painting as my hobby."

"Picture-painting?" said Sarah Lundy.

"Oh, I have no such intention, but if I had, this would be a very suitable room for a studio," he said. He paused. "I wonder if I have any talent in that direction. You never know till you try."

"You was always drawing pictures when you was little," said Sarah Lundy.

"When I was little,'" he said. "The trouble is, I wouldn't know how to start. I never knew anyone that painted pictures. No, it won't be painting I'll do here."

"What will it be?"

"Reading. Thinking."

"Just reading and thinking? What's that for a young man to be doing? You ought to be out on these nice days, making friends with people. Enjoying the sunshine. Here you're only twenty-five years of age and a body'd think you were up in your fifties. Reading and thinking. You'll be an old man soon enough, John

Evans. The years go by before you know it, I can say that knows."

"Then you should be told that I intend to spend the rest of my life in this house and the greater part of it in this room," he said. "Reading, and thinking."

"Then you'll never live to your father's age, cooped up like that. Your father never would of seen sixty-two if he didn't move around and get the fresh air in his lungs."

"They went to a great deal of trouble to protect me from the fresh air."

"Only because they were terrified you'd get the consumption."

"Well, I didn't, so they must have been right. And since they seem to've been right, I'll continue their methods. Take a miner out of the mines and he dies in a year."

"Little do you know. And that's not saying how many die of the miner's asthma before they're forty."

"Sarah, I'm properly grateful for your concern, but I've made up my mind. I've already sent away for over a hundred books. At least a hundred."

"A—hundred—books?"

"Before I'm through there'll be at least a thousand in this room, and I'll be able to tell you what's in them."

"I wouldn't listen," said Sarah Lundy. "Nor neither would anyone else in their right senses."

"That I'm sure is true," said John Wesley Evans.

"There! Then what do you want to read a thousand books for? You say yourself nobody's going to listen to you tell what's in them. So what's the good of stuffing your brain with what's in them? I ask you that. Your brain won't hold all that. A thousand books. My Lord and Savior, that's a terrible, terrible thing, John. A terrible thing. I could read and write when I was seven years of age, not saying how long ago that was, and I read me prayerbook and the newspaper, and the leaflets we get after Mass. I could read more if I had to. But a thousand books!"

"I may go to two thousand."

"Your eyesight'll give out before that. There's another thing to worry about. Your eyesight."

"Yes," he said.

She had frightened him and she was sorry. "Not that your eyesight won't last forever if you don't strain it too hard. You understand that. It's the same as anything else. Too much of a good thing's as bad as none at all, and that goes for reading and thinking and fresh air and all."

Sarah Lundy's discovery that John was fearful of damage to his eyesight came as a surprise to her, with a surprising effect. For not only was it news that he worried about his eyes; it was news that he ever worried about anything. Until now she had thought of him as a skinny, bloodless individual; a vegetable of a boy, who lay on the floor and read books when he ought to be out climbing trees. She could not remember his ever crying at night, or coming home with a bloody nose, or threatening to run away, or being punished for sins with his own or the opposite sex. If he had been a pretty or a handsome child, or a remarkably ugly one, a troublesome or happy one, she would have been better prepared for the unmistakable admission contained in the single word "yes" and the way he uttered it. After saying it he left the room, and her female instinct, flabby from disuse, returned to life in a surge of compassion. This aging virgin now knew that he could use her pity. He was afraid of something.

2

Two doors to the west of 1008 lived Mr. and Mrs. Percy B. Shields, and theirs was the first house in the block to have striped awnings over the front windows, upstairs and down. There was not much practical use for awnings in that block. The trees that stood on the edge of the brick sidewalk kept the sun from being too bothersome, and the other residents of the block found curtains and roller-shades and inside shutters very satisfactory. But Mrs. Percy Shields wanted striped awnings, upstairs and down, and it did not bother her that some of her neighbors said the awnings made her house look like a circus. In the first place, they did not make the house look like a circus or like anything else but a house with striped awnings. In the second place, they made the house cooler. She could open her windows, which her neighbors could not do if they insisted on keeping their shades lowered. In the third place, it was her house and as long as she was not breaking any law she could have striped awnings or blue awnings or yellow awnings or any other kind she wished. What her neighbors objected to, if they would only come out and say it, was any bright touch, anything unusual. They might object to her striped awnings, but it might interest them to learn that the most disgraceful houses on Railroad Avenue had exactly the same kind of lace curtains that her neighbors had in their windows. And no awnings. How did Mrs. Percy Shields know about houses on Railroad Avenue? Never mind, she knew. She had it on good authority.

Never for a moment was it suspected that the authority might be Percy Shields. For one thing, he was much too old. Age had kept him from going to the defense of the national capital in 1861, and he was now forty years older. It took him a good twenty minutes to go from his house to the Gibbsville Club, a seven-block downhill walk all the way, and in recent years he had had to depend on his carriage to bring him home. It was true, as they said, that on the way home he had to carry in his belly a quantity of Old Overholt, but he never could have got home if he relied on his legs. Even the downhill walk to the club took some courage; at his time of life a tumble could result in a broken hip, and he had never known any of his contemporaries to recover from that. He therefore walked with care; slowly, and never raising his feet higher than was necessary to keep them from scraping the ground. During the winter months, when there was ice and snow, he was compelled to suspend his walks. Arthur Hawkins, who was hostler, gardener and man-of-all-work for the Shieldses, would help Percy into the swan-type cutter, cover him up with a buffalo robe, and take him to the club. Percy would spend the same amount of time at the club as he did in kinder weather, but he would miss the exercise. Percy's need of Arthur and the horse also interfered with his wife's morning schedule, as it postponed her marketing. Consequently the wintry weather inconvenienced both Harriet and Percy Shields, and on the afternoons of extremely inclement days they could hardly bear to be in the same room with each other.

Harriet Shields observed the custom of afternoon tea, which was made possible by the fact that they had no children and could have their evening meal at a later hour than most households. Harriet served tea six days a week to a different woman friend every day. The amount of information she thus acquired was considerable and of a large variety. Her guests had been chosen for that purpose, and they represented the well-to-do, the genteel poor, the witty, the vicious, and ages from forty to sixty-five. Women past sixty-five, Harriet had found, did not hear much gossip, possibly for the reason that they had difficulty hearing anything at all, and worthwhile gossip could not be shouted to a deaf person. For one maiden lady and one widow Harriet's teas were an ample substitute for the evening meal; the four other regulars came because Harriet Shields had invited them to come, and no one wished to incur her displeasure. They all were, in a word, afraid of her. They had all heard her comments on other women and some men, and the faithful six preferred to remain on her good side. In the course of their weekly conversations with Harriet Shields they had entrusted her with personal confidences, which were safe only so long as her visitors were in good standing with her.

But if they were afraid of her, they also were addicted to the opportunity she provided for a free expression of their own observations and opinions. From week to week they saved up items of confidential and unprintable news for Harriet. Since there were never more than two women present, Harriet and her guest, it was possible to repeat intimate and slanderous details without reckoning with a third person. And while Harriet was duly appreciative of interesting items, she was never shocked and seldom surprised by anything. Another good thing about Harriet was that she did not interrupt; a friend who was emboldened to tell a lurid story did not lose her courage halfway through. If Harriet had heard the story before—as often she had—she would hear the new version all the way out, and then, but not until then, supply corrections and additions. It could be said of Harriet that she practiced scandalmongering as an art.

She, of course, was invulnerable. Such displays of eccentricity as her striped awnings and her taste in millinery were irritating, but not such stuff as gossip is made on. Harriet Shields was still pretty, healthy, and vigorous, but she was not in the least flirtatious or concupiscent. A glass of wine was all she ever drank. She had never taken laudanum. She paid her bills promptly. She did not lose her temper in public or have hysterics. She had a personal fortune, inherited from her father, which gave her a social and financial background that was very nearly the equal of any in the town, and made her immune to the charge that she married Percy Shields for his money. Indeed, it was the other way around: if anyone was vulnerable in that respect it was Percy, who had married a woman with much more money than he and who was a great deal younger. But Percy Shields had always been an affable mediocrity; everyone wished him well, and when Harriet consented to marry him there was universal sanction of the union. No one would have to worry about Percy any longer, and Harriet Stokes's share of the Stokes wealth would remain in Gibbsville. It was also said at the time that it was a real love match. Later this was amended to "ideal marriage." At sixty Percy Shields retired from the practice of the law, a formality which consisted only of his giving up his office in the second-floor rear of the Keystone Trust Company building and moving his law books to a hallway bookcase at 1012 Lantenengo Street. He never looked at them again. Not even once. Not even to notice that a couple of them had been put in upside down.

Harriet Shields's house had somewhat more grandeur inside than the other houses in the ten-hundred block. At the foot of the front stairway was a bronze statuette, mounted on the newel post, of a knight in dull armor holding a spear which supported a gas lamp. The gas line went through the hollow spear. One day Harriet detected a strong odor of gas leaking from the burner. Someone somehow had turned the valve half on. She immediately sent for the plumbers and had the pipeline sealed permanently. The statuette remained on the newel post for decorative purposes, but as a lighting fixture it was useless. "Why don't we get that lamp fixed?" Percy would say once or twice a year.

"Yes, I must remember to do that," Harriet would say. But she had developed a theory that Percy, after one of his long days at the club, had reached out for support on his way upstairs and inadvertently turned the key of the gas valve. Right or wrong, the theory covered a possibility, and the bronze knight provided no more light until he was electrified.

In her front parlor Harriet Shields had a crystal chandelier that was the largest in a private house in all Lantenengo County. Twice a year her maids unhooked each of the thousand and more bits of glass, washed and dried each one and replaced them. The task always took two days, and the entire operation was supervised by Harriet. It was not as simple as Percy Shields made it out to be, for not only was there the job of unhooking the bits of crystal and washing away the six months' collection of grime, but there was also the polishing with ammonia. Harriet and the maids would have to interrupt their work to get away from the smell of the ammonia. On the second day Harriet was at her efficient best, directing the rechanging of the bits of crystal, like stringing pearls. This she accomplished with the help of a detailed sketch of the chandelier, and when the task was completed and the gas turned on, even Percy admitted that there was beauty in the sparkling, subtle changes of color. "Louis Quatorze," he would say. "We must give a ball."

"You always say that, Percy," Harriet would say. "And you'd sooner die than have a ball."

"I'd rather die than arrange for one, is what you mean. But if you did all the work I'd enjoy it."

"We could never have a ball without inviting our neighbors, and who'd want to have *them*?"

"Not me, I'm sure. Consider the subject closed." It would be closed until it was reopened after the next cleaning of the chandelier.

Elegance, luxury, modern conveniences were not put in for the pleasure of Harriet's neighbors. When she added something to the interior of her house she did not even feel compelled to display it to her daily visitors. "Harriet, is it true that you've put in a laundry chute?" said Ellen Walker one day.

"Now where did you hear that?" said Harriet.

"I forget who told me, but I understand you have a new laundry chute that's lined with tin, all the way from the third floor to the basement."

"We have one, but it's been there for over a year. Think of attaching so much importance to a laundry chute."

"There aren't very many in town, you know," said Ellen.

"I'm sure I have no idea how many there are, Ellen. By the way, it's lined with copper, not tin. If I'd thought you'd be interested in a *laundry* chute, I'd have shown it to you a year ago. But good heavens, I'd never think of boring my friends with things like that."

"It would surprise you to know how curious people are, especially about your house."

"It wouldn't surprise me in the least. Not in the least."

"So many people have asked me if I've ever seen your wall safe. A wall safe with a combination lock?"

"Are you asking me if I have one? At least that's more interesting than a laundry chute. Yes, we've had one for a long time."

"Is it because you don't trust banks? That's the rumor I heard."

"Well, all I can say is it wasn't a rumor that started at the Keystone Trust Company. That's where I keep my money and Percy keeps his, and my father kept his and my brother Harry keeps his. That kind of a rumor could do a lot of harm. It *could* have been started by one of the other banks."

Ellen Walker's husband Louis was cashier of the Coal City Trust Company. Momentarily Ellen was on dangerous ground and having difficulty composing a suitable comment.

"I'm sure Louis'd scotch that rumor," said Harriet, who was positive that Ellen was repeating Louis Walker's very words. "Yes, we have a wall safe to keep our things in. My jewelry. Percy's good studs. Things I got from Mother. We're not worried about things being stolen, but the safe is fireproof. Fireproof, Ellen."

"Of course. I never thought of that."

"Well, I had to, you know," said Harriet Shields. "Some day all my things will go to my nieces and my nephews' wives. I can't expect to last forever."

454

"Looking at it that way, it's a responsibility," said Ellen.

"There's no other way to look at it. Those things increase in value every year. Mother's solitaire—well, it isn't polite to talk about such things, but it's worth three times what Papa paid for it. Tripled in twenty years, mind you."

"It's the largest diamond in town, I know that," said Ellen.

"No, there's one larger. But mine is better cut. It isn't only the size of a diamond, Ellen. For instance, yours I imagine is worth more than some I've seen, because it's newer, and the cutting methods are constantly improving."

That was another thing about Harriet Shields. She *knew* so many things. She never went away; a spring trip to Philadelphia to see the new styles, and another in November to do her Christmas shopping. But she did not like to leave Percy, and he could not travel in comfort. Nevertheless Harriet kept up to date on everything in the outside world as well as on matters pertaining to her own circle of acquaintances. She was the only woman on Lantenengo Street who had taken the trouble to find out all the reasons for the war with Spain, which she had done by writing to the district member of the House of Representatives. The name Harriet *Stokes* Shields and the Lantenengo Street, Gibbsville, address carried weight. She knew about Spain, and diamond-cutting, and the superiority of copper over tin, and how to rehang strands of crystal on a chandelier. She spoke French and had once taken lessons on the flute. There seemed to be no end to the variety of subjects that could claim her interest. Imagine writing to a Congressman for information on a war that only lasted a few months!

One day she came out of her house and saw her neighbor, young John Evans, standing in front of his own house but staring at her striped awnings. "Well, Mr. John Wesley Evans. Are you trying to stare a hole through them?"

He removed his hat. "Good morning, Mrs. Shields. I didn't hear what you said."

"I *asked* you if you were trying to stare a hole through my awnings. They've been there, this is the third year. No, next year will be the third. But haven't you ever noticed them before?"

"I noticed them, but I never took a good look at them."

"I'd heard you didn't leave your house much, but even so."

"Well, I was thinking of getting some. I didn't know so much for the front of my house, but my bay window in the back. If it wouldn't be prying, would you mind telling me about how much they ask for an awning?"

"I couldn't say exactly, but if you want to come in I'll look it up. Come on," she said, and turned about, fully expecting that he would obey. He did.

It was his first visit to the Shields house, and he was the first Evans to visit the house. "I've never been in here before," he said.

"Is that so? Well, just sit down a minute and I know right where to find the receipt. Hillyard and Son. Hall. Hill. Hillyard. Here it is. Goodness, I'd forgotten about that."

"What?" said John.

"How much they overcharged me. Eight windows. Two, three, and three. I thought it was going to be forty dollars for the whole thing, but he charged me three dollars extra for the windows on the top floor. He said he had to rent ladders from somebody. His ladders wouldn't go that high. Here, you can see on one receipt, 'Received $40 and no cents, part payment.' Then here's the second receipt, balance due on awnings, paid in full. That was Bert Hillyard. His father was a man of his word. If he said forty dollars, he meant forty dollars. No charging extra because his ladders wouldn't reach. Unfortunately, there's no one else in town that does that kind of work, so you'll have to go to Hillyards'. But if you deal with young Bert, get it all down in black and white first. Now that you're here, would you care for a glass of root beer? We have it on ice, so it should be nice and cool on such a warm day."

"Well, if it wouldn't be going to too much trouble," he said.

"Amy! Two glasses of root beer, and a plate of salty pretzels. Now, John, tell me what you do with yourself all day. I heard that you were writing a book. Is that *true?*"

"No, I'm not writing anything."

"That's what I said. I know you graduated from college, but I was sure they didn't teach you to write. What was the name of your college?"

"Wesleyan. Middletown, Connecticut."

"How far is that from New Haven?"

"Uh, let me think."

"Never mind. I only asked because you knew my brother went to Yale. Harry."

"Yes, I guess everybody in town knows that Mr. Stokes went to Yale."

"What was that again?"

He smiled, and said nothing.

She glared at him, but her glare changed to a smile. "Well, it *is* true that my brother's very proud of having gone to Yale."

"He spoke to my father about sending me there, but Yale was too stylish for us. That was when I was thinking of becoming a preacher."

"I take it you've given that up," said Harriet Shields.

"Yes, I've given it up."

"What do you plan to do instead?"

"Nothing. At least, not take a job, or learn a profession."

"Why, everybody does something in Gibbsville. At least till they're old enough to retire. But you're not old enough to retire."

"I don't have to retire. I never did anything to retire from."

"Then it's not going to be easy for you to find a wife. A man that sits around the house all day isn't what the modern girl is looking for."

"Probably not, but there are two sides to that question, too."

"Meaning, I suppose, that you're going to remain a bachelor."

"I guess that's what I am. A bachelor. I never thought of myself as a bachelor. Just a fellow that wasn't planning to get married. But after you reach a certain age I guess they call you a bachelor."

"You're not a woman-hater, are you?"

"No, I like some. I never got to know many girls."

"What kind of girls do you like?"

"What kind do I like? My goodness, that's another thing I never thought of. I'd have to think."

"I should imagine that a girl would have to show how much she appreciated you before you'd take a fancy to her."

"Then I have a long while to wait."

457

"Not necessarily. If you gave them a chance. Girls are intelligent, too, you know. But you'll never meet the intelligent ones just sitting at home all the time. You have to get out once in a while. Otherwise you'll be an old bachelor before you know it. There are so many different ways to meet girls. Do you play cards?"

"In *our* house?"

"That's true. You're Methodist. They don't allow dancing, either, do they? Well, here's our root beer. I thought you were going to take all day, Amy."

"No ma'am," said the maid. "I had to move a big cake of ice. The iceman pushed everything in back of the box so there was fifty pounds of ice in front of the soft drinks. I told him a hundred times—"

"Thank you. We'll talk about it later," said Harriet. She sipped her root beer. "Yum! Go ahead, drink it while it's nice and cool."

"I was enjoying the smell of your cologne. Is that what you call it? Cologne?"

"Roger and Gallet's Eau de Cologne. Thank you, I'm glad you like it. You see, you're not a woman-hater at all, if you appreciate scent."

"I never said I was a woman-hater. I just don't know any, or hardly any."

"And those you've known haven't been the right kind. Would you like to join the Assembly, now that your parents are gone?"

"What for? You know I don't dance."

"The Assembly isn't only a ball, John. Mr. Shields doesn't dance any more, but we'd never miss an Assembly. Why, for some people in town it's the only opportunity they get all year to put on their best bib-and-tucker, display their party manners. It's a very nice occasion."

"I guess the women would enjoy it, but do the men?"

"Ah, indeed they do. As much as the ladies. I think there's a meeting in a week or two. Suppose I ask Mr. Shields to put your name up? If *he* puts you up, you'll get in, then you'll be a member for life. As long as you pay your ten dollars a year."

"Ten dollars?"

"Oh, now ten dollars won't send you to the almshouse, and some day you may be very glad you joined."

"I can't dance, I don't have a full-dress, and I hardly know any of those people."

"It's time you rectified all those things. A young bachelor who lives on Lantenengo Street has certain obligations. If you don't agree, then you ought to move to the other side of town, where such things don't matter."

"My father was never in the Assembly."

"No, and if he had wanted to be, he couldn't have been."

"Then why should I want to join it? What was the matter with my father?"

"Morally, or financially, nothing, I suppose. But socially, everything."

"I'm no better, socially."

"Oh, yes you are. You have more finish."

"Not so's you could notice it."

"You're wrong. I *have* noticed it. You haven't got *la politesse,* as the French say, but you have a manner. I don't quite know how to describe it, but it's there. Now I suggest that you arrange to take dancing lessons—privately, of course. Then by the time New Year's Eve is here, you'll be able to trip the light fantastic as well as any of them. And you have a great advantage over most of the men—you're tall."

"Dancing lessons?"

"Professor Long and his wife. They give private instruction in Union Hall, you know."

"I couldn't do that, Mrs. Shields. I'd feel foolish."

"Very well, then *I'll* teach you. Tomorrow afternoon you come here at two o'clock, and we'll start our lessons."

"Here?"

"Of course, here. Look at this floor. It was meant for dancing. Take up a few rugs, move a few chairs, and this is really a ballroom. From two o'clock to three. If you haven't got the proper shoes, go down to Schoffstal's and buy a pair. That's where Mr. Shields buys his and most of the other gentlemen. And don't let Bert Hillyard overcharge you the way he did me."

She rose. "I'm sorry there isn't room for you in my buggy, or you could ride down to Schoffstal's with me. But the walk'll do you good."

He walked with her to her carriage, and even in the open air her perfume was inescapable.

3

During the rest of that summer and into the months of autumn John Wesley Evans was seen going in and out of the Shields house twice or three times a week, always early in the afternoon. At that time of day Percy Shields was invariably at the club, and his absence from home during John Evans's visits was duly noted, as was the fact that young Evans had departed before the tea-time arrival of Harriet Shields's daily callers. When the visits had occurred frequently enough and regularly enough, the curious advanced beyond mere speculation: they questioned Sarah Lundy when they encountered her at the meat-market, the grocery store, and on the slow climb up Tenth Street. Even a less subtle woman than Sarah Lundy could not have failed to notice the new friendliness of housewives who in the past had ignored her entirely or had thought nothing of preempting her place in the customers' lines. "Good morning, Sarah. No, you go right ahead, you were here first," they would say. Then they would manage to engage her in conversation which unfailingly included a reference to her young employer. "Busy as ever, with his French lessons," said one woman.

"What French lessons?" said Sarah Lundy.

"I understood he was taking French lessons from Mrs. Shields," said the woman.

"First I heard of it," said Sarah Lundy.

"Oh, yes. Three or four days a week he has a lesson. At least that's what I understood. Well, it's nice for him that he has someone so near."

"First I knew about any French lessons. He goes over there, but I didn't know that's what it was for."

"In connection with a book he's writing," said the woman.

"Ah, that I knew about. He's forever talking about books," said Sarah Lundy.

It was as exasperating to Sarah Lundy as to the curious that she had so little information to give. John Wesley Evans had never so much as told her that he was going to call on Mrs. Shields. At five minutes to two in the afternoon, three afternoons a week, he would leave the house, destination unannounced, and be gone till five or ten after three. Sarah Lundy soon knew that he went to call on Mrs. Percy Shields, but did not know why. When he got home he would close the door of his library, but she could hear him muttering, "*One* two-three, *one* two-three, *one* two-three," over and over again, and once when she made some excuse to enter the library he was doing some kind of exercise.

"You know I don't like to be disturbed when I'm working," he said. "What *is* it?"

"I thought I heard you call me," she said.

"You didn't think any such thing. Go on about your business."

"Either you called me or you're getting the habit of talking to yourself. Is that from one of your French lessons?"

"What French lessons?"

"The ones you're taking off of Mrs. Shields."

"*French* lessons? I see. Is that something you figured out for yourself, or someone else figured out for you? I hazard a guess that it was someone else. Well, you're both wrong. And I'm going to keep you in the dark as long as possible. Forever, if I can."

"I'm sure I care little enough what goes on with you and the old lady. Although she isn't that old that a young man's company—"

"Go on about your business, I said."

He weighed the matter, and after eating a banana and a whole bunch of grapes he came to the conclusion that he must report the conversation to Mrs. Shields.

"Well, I do declare," she said, when he had finished.

"You're not angry?" he said.

"Of course I'm angry," she said.

461

"Not at me, I hope," he said.

"Good gracious, no. Nor at your clumsy Sarah. But I am angry with whoever tried to pump her. I'll find out who that was, and make her pay for it. I love gossip, but I believe in certain rules."

"Certain rules about gossip?"

"Well, yes, in a way," she said. "A lady doesn't descend to gossip with a servant. It's mean and disloyal. They gossip about us, every chance they get, and that's to be expected. But when a woman of our station in life tries to extract juicy morsels from a servant, that's treacherous. Servants find out enough without any help from one of us. I'm going to punish that woman, whoever she was."

"How will you find out who she was?"

"I don't know, but I'll set a trap for her. It could be one of my own little toadies. I rather suspect it is."

"Your own little toadies? One of your servants?"

"Don't you pay attention to what I say? *Not* one of my servants. One of the ladies I have in for tea every day. Those are my toadies."

"Oh, I thought they were your friends," he said.

"I have no friends. If I had any, I lost them when I married Percy Shields. It was perfectly all right for him to marry me, but it was all wrong for me to marry him. You probably won't see the difference, but there was one."

"Why *did* you marry him?"

"Because he was ardent. You're too young to know about such things, but when you're thirty years older you'll know that a man in his fifties *can* be ardent. And he can seem especially so to an ignorant, inexperienced young woman. I adored him."

"But you don't any more?" he said.

"That doesn't last very long, even with two people of the same age. They have children, and that's what makes the marriage last."

"But you had no children, and your marriage has lasted."

"I had a child. A man in his sixties. A toothless baby that had to learn how to walk. Yes, and even had to have his bottle every day. Haven't you ever noticed that my husband walks as if he were afraid he was going to fall, like a little child?"

"I never thought of it that way," he said.

"That's why I love to dance with you, John. When I was a young girl I loved to dance. Not just round-dancing, but any kind. My mother used to tell me that I was getting too big to skip on my way home from school. But I wasn't skipping. I was dancing. Well, let's get to our lesson."

"I don't think you feel like it today," he said.

She looked at him and frowned. "No, I don't," she said. "But how did you know?"

"Oh—mental telepathy. Something like that," he said.

"Call it that, I suppose. It's not a term that has any sweetness, tenderness. But you're afraid of tenderness, aren't you?"

"I don't know," he said.

"You are. And so am I," she said. "I could show you what it can be, but then you'd never come back. Don't look at my neck, my chin, John. The rest of me is very nice."

"I want to see the rest of you," he said.

"Sometime I'll let you, but now you must go."

"Why not now? The door is closed," he said.

"Please go. But if you want to, you can come back tonight."

"How can I? Your husband will be here."

"Come at eleven o'clock. The front door will be unlocked, and I'll be here."

"Where will your husband be?"

"My baby will be sound asleep, snoring, and dead drunk. And nothing will wake him before five o'clock tomorrow morning. At eleven o'clock there won't be anyone on the street, and most of the leaves are still on the trees. I'll be waiting for you, I promise. And if you decide not to come, don't ever come again."

4

The great doctor in Philadelphia said there was nothing to be done. "This is a thing that started in your left eye, most likely when you were no more than ten or twelve years old," said the doctor. "That was when you started wearing glasses."

"Yes sir," said John Wesley Evans. "Fifth grade. I'm going by the teacher I had the first time I put them on."

"Your parents took you to a man in a jewelry store, and he gave you your first pair of glasses. But Dr. Phillips tells me there was a good eye-ear-nose-and-throat man in your town. I don't understand it. Your family weren't poor."

"My mother bought my glasses at the same place where she bought hers," said John. "I guess she didn't know any better."

"That was it, I suppose," said the doctor. He studied his patient. "I can't say now how much difference it would have made, Mr. Evans. But a good eye-doctor would have looked at your left eye and noticed things that needed attention. By that time your right eye had started to go."

"Yes, I had to get new glasses every two years."

"Always from the man in the jewelry store?" said the doctor.

"Yes sir. He let me try on different glasses till I found the ones that were the most comfortable."

"And you'd wear them for two years?"

"Just about. Maybe a little longer. When I went away to college I got thicker ones. Stronger lenses."

"You used your eyes a lot, studying."

"I always did, not only studying but reading. I like to read."

"You haven't spent much time outdoors, have you?"

"No, I liked to read," said John.

"The sunlight bothered you?"

"Yes, I guess it did, thinking back."

"Dr. Phillips tells me you thought of studying for the ministry."

"I gave that up a long time ago. Why?" said John.

"I was thinking of your future," said the doctor. "You ought to plan for it, have something to do."

"It won't be the ministry. I don't believe in God, and I believe in Him less now than I ever did."

"That's understandable, but in the times I've seen you you impressed me as having quite a lot of courage."

"That's bluff," said John.

"Bluffing takes courage under the circumstances, Mr. Evans," said the doctor. "Now I'll be frank with you, because I've found out that I can be. There are probably some doctors who would

464

perform an operation on your eyes. I won't put you through that, because in my opinion the operation would not be successful. However, if you feel that you owe it to yourself to have the operation, Dr. Phillips knows the names of other doctors in my field."

"That isn't giving me much choice, is it?"

"No, and that's why I put it that way. I'm usually the doctor that they come to as a last resort."

"Dr. Phillips said you were the best," said John.

"Well, I don't believe in false modesty, especially in a surgeon. If I knew of a better man, I'd send you to him myself. In about six years I'm going to have to stop doing surgery, and by that time we'll know more and there'll be new men coming along. But not in time to do you any good."

"How long is it going to be before I go completely blind?"

"You'll be able to see, to get around, for another eighteen months, I should say. But you're not going to be able to read more than four or five months. Reading is going to be more and more difficult for you. It is already. Have you done much traveling?"

"None at all," said John.

"Would you like to see the Parthenon? The Eiffel Tower? In other words, I'm suggesting that since you can afford it, now is the time to travel, to see things. And people. If *I* were in your position I'd spend part of that time looking at beautiful women, preferably in bed, and all sizes and colors. But my morals have never been my strong point, as anyone in Philadelphia will tell you."

"I have no morals, either," said John Wesley Evans, more to himself than to the doctor.

"I find that hard to believe," said the doctor.

"Oh, I've never disgraced my parents or anything like that, but *inside* I have no morals. I've never wanted to be a good man. I just wanted to be left alone. You go your way, and I'll go mine. That was my philosophy of life. You find it hard to believe that I have no morals, but I once killed a person."

"You did? How?"

"I didn't shoot them or anything like that. But I helped this person to commit suicide. The person could not have committed suicide without my help."

"Well, legally I suppose you could be held responsible for manslaughter. Not knowing the circumstances, I can't say. But right here on Walnut Street there are dozens of men of the medical profession who face that problem every day. Religious men, too. As an eye doctor I don't have to face the problem as much as a man who does abdominal surgery, for instance. But here on Walnut Street, and all over the country, all over the civilized world, surgeons operate on men and women, make the incision, and discover an absolutely hopeless condition. The patient is asleep, under chloroform. Why not let the poor man, or woman, stay asleep?"

"Why not?"

"Ah, but it's not that easy. There may be another doctor there, and there are always surgical nurses. Some of them know as much about surgical techniques as some doctors. That's the practical side, the chance of being reported and ruined professionally. On the ethical side, it's as bad or worse. Doctors discuss ethics while they're medical students, but after medical school you don't hear as much of that talk. We doctors tend to keep those thoughts to ourselves, the older we get and the more set in our ways. We confine our ethical discussions to something we call ethics, but is really no more than professional courtesy."

"What if I see a woman naked and fall in love with her? Isn't it going to be worse when I can't look at her any more?"

"I was wondering what you were thinking during my speech about ethics," said the doctor.

"Why did you think you had to make a speech?"

"That leaves two questions unanswered," said the doctor. "Well, I mentioned the Parthenon. I was in Athens a great many years ago, and I've never gone back. But I remember the beauty of the Parthenon, and always will. I'm very glad I saw it when I could. That should answer your first question, especially since you're not going to lose your sense of touch. I have often touched women in the dark, and so will you. As for your second question, I make these speeches to get you to talk. I want you to be stimulated to ask me questions. Remember, Mr. Evans, this has been my lifework, and I've had to tell other patients the same thing I've told you. If I can't help you in one way, I may be able to help you in others."

"Now I understand," said John Wesley Evans. "Will I ever stop being afraid?"

"You've already begun to stop," said the doctor. "But that's not saying you aren't going to have a difficult time later on. The fear will pass, but getting reconciled to your blindness may take time. Have you got a friend, a very close friend?"

"One, yes," said John.

"You're lucky," said the doctor. "Man, or woman?"

"A woman."

"She's older, and she's married. Am I right?"

"Yes."

"Does she know you've been to see me?"

"Yes."

"Could you ask her to come and see me?"

"What for?"

"To answer the questions she wants to ask me," said the doctor.

"You certainly do know a lot, Doctor," said John. "She's here in Philadelphia. She's staying at the Bellevue-Stratford Hotel."

"You might as well tell me her name. I'm very close-mouthed. I've had to be."

"Her name is Mrs. Percy B. Shields."

"I could ring up the hotel on the telephone."

"You don't have to. She's waiting outside in a hansom cab."

"Will you go out and ask her to come in?" said the doctor.

John Wesley Evans smiled. "She wanted to come in with me, but I wouldn't let her. She's always right."

5

There is nothing more that need be added to this small story. The reader can fill in for himself the assumption that the news of John Wesley Evans's blindness created genuine dismay. The devotion of Harriet Shields to her young neighbor was soon of a piece with her devotion to her aged husband. When Percy Shields died, the townsfolk were prepared to be tolerant of a marriage between Harriet and John Wesley Evans, but it did not take place. In a little while John Wesley Evans became truly if prematurely a typical resident of the ten-hundred block, one of the sequestered men and women who gave a character to the neighborhood that was as solemn as brownstone and brick. But sometimes on a summer afternoon, on a favorable day in May, a warm day in September, there would be the sound of a waltz coming from Harriet Shields's talking-machine. It was not loud enough to disturb anyone.

FATIMAS AND KISSES

Around the corner from where I used to live there was a little store run by a family named Lintz. If you wanted ice cream, by the quart or by the cone, you could get it at Lintzie's; you could buy cigarettes and the less expensive cigars, a loaf of bread, canned goods, meats that did not require the services of a butcher, penny candy and boxed bon-bons, writing tablets and pencils, and literally hundreds of articles on display-cards that novelty salesmen had persuaded Lintzie to put on his shelves, and which he never seemed to reorder. I doubt if there are many stores like Lintzie's around any more, but his place was a great convenience for the people in the neighborhood. When a house-wife ran short of something she would tell her child to go down to Lintzie's for the bottle of milk or the half pound of butter or the twenty cents' worth of sliced ham. And Lintzie would charge it. He well knew that the housewives in the neighborhood pre-ferred to deal with the downtown meat markets and grocery stores, and that his trade was at least partly on a semi-emergency basis. That, and the fact that he allowed people to charge things, gave him the excuse to maintain a mark-up on most of his stock, and the housewives called him a highway robber. They called him that to his face. But they were careful how they said it. O'Donnell's meat market was the best, and Gottlieb had the best grocery store, but they were downtown and they would not open up for you if you needed a can of soup or a quart of milk at half past eight in the evening. Lintzie and his wife and two children lived upstairs over the store, and someone would always come down and open up for a customer.

Lintzie was a thin man with a Charlie Chaplin moustache and hollow cheeks that were made hollower still by his habit of leaving out his upper plate. He was young to have false teeth; in his late twenties. He had been in the Marine Corps, although he had not gone overseas, and all his worldliness, all his travels, were by benefit of his having been a Gott damn chyrene. He was a Pennsylvania Dutch farm boy, from somewhere east of Reading, and it wondered me, as the Dutch say, how he had ever heard of the marines. So, being in my teens and curious, I asked him. "How I heart abaht the Marine Corps? I didn't never hear about them till once I seen one of them there posters in the post office. I seen a picture of a marine, all dressed up in his plues, his rifle at right shoulder arms, his bayonet in a white scabbard. He looked handsome to me, so I went home and said to my old man I was going to enlist. I won't tell you what the old man said. He said to go ahead, only he said other things besides. Glad to get rid of me. Him and my brother could run the farm without me. My brother was glad to get rid of me too. That way the old man would leave him the farm and me nothing. So I went to where it said on the poster and signed the papers. By Jesus if I knew what it was like them first three months I would of never enlisted. Son of a bitch sergeant with a swagger stick. Drill. Bivouac. Snakes. By Jesus nights I was too tired to cut my throat. That's no joke. But I guess it all done me good. I come out stronger than I went in, but minus the most of my teeth."

"How did that happen?"

"Oh, I got in a fight with a sailor, me and another Gott damn chyrene we were on duty in the Lackawanna Railroad Station in Hoboken, New Chersey. We took him in custody, he was drunk.

But then all of a sudden from all over come them sailors. I had a .45 in my holster but it done me no good. They must of been ten of them chumped us all at once, and one of them hit me across the mouth with my own billy club. That was all the fighting I ever done in the Gott damn chyrenes. The Lackawanna Railroad Station in Hoboken, New Chersey. I got a discharge in October 1918, two weeks before the armistice. But I used to raise a lot of hell in Philly and New York City and Boston, Mass. I could tell *you* some stories if you was older. I was a pretty good-looking fellow till them sailors chumped me. But the son of a bitch that started it, he got something like thirty years' hard labor."

"You identified him?"

"I sure did. I picked him out of twenty of the bastards. I hope he rots. I would of got corporal if it wasn't for him. Maybe I would of stayed in and got gunnery sergeant. But they let me go and now I can't even chew a steak, not with the teeth I got now."

Lintzie's wife was a placid, rather slovenly woman whose hair was never in place. She had an extraordinarily lovely complexion and white little teeth and large breasts that swayed unencumbered by a brassiere. When he addressed her by name, which was seldom, he called her Lonnie. She called him Donald or Lintzie; Lintzie, if she was shouting to him from the back of the store or upstairs, and Donald if she was standing near him. He hardly ever looked at her unless her back was turned. In front of people my age and younger he would say to her, "Go fix yourself up decent, for Christ's sake."

"Aah, shut up," she would say.

But when older people were present they hid their animosity by paying no attention to each other. One day when I went to buy cigarettes, which he was not supposed to sell to me, I waited for Lintzie or Lonnie to appear and wait on me, but neither came. I went back and reopened and closed the door so that the bell would ring again, and she came running downstairs. "Oh, it's you," she said.

"Will you give me a pack of Camels and a pack of Fatimas," I said.

"Charge or pay?"

"*Pay*," I said.

"Who are the Fatimas for? Some girl?"

"For my uncle," I said.

"Yeah, your uncle standing out there with the bicycle. You better watch out, Malloy. Her old lady catches her smoking cigarettes, they'll tell your old man and you'll get hail-Columbia. Give me thirty-five cents."

"Where's Lintzie?" I said.

"To Reading. Why?"

"Just wondered," I said.

"Why?"

"Just wondered," I said. I looked out toward the sidewalk and at the half-ton panel truck parked at the curb, driverless. She put two packs of Camels and two packs of Fatimas on the counter.

"I'll treat you to the butts," she said. "Okay?"

"Thanks," I said.

"The next time her old lady comes in, I won't say anything about you buying her kid Fatimas. Okay?"

"All right," I said.

They never knew—older people—at just what age you started to notice things like a driverless truck and a husband's absence and a delayed appearance, and put them all together. But now Lonnie knew that I had put them all together, and I knew that I had put them together accurately. My discovery was too momentous and mature to confide in the girl who was waiting with her bike. It was too much the kind of thing that I wanted to protect her from, and was indeed eager to protect her from all her life. Those were things I already knew too much about, along with the sight of death and the ugliness of things I had seen in my father's office and in ambulances, hospitals, the homes of the poor, when my father was still trying to make a doctor of me. I could barely endure to see those things myself, but I was a boy. She was a girl, and in ten years or maybe less she was going to be my wife. *Then* I might tell her some of those things, but now Fatimas and kisses were as much as she was ready for.

The bell tinkled as I opened Lintzie's door and tinkled again as I closed it. I guess it was the sound of the bell as much as the Fatimas I flashed that made her giggle. "You got them?" she said. It was a throaty whisper.

"Sure," I said. "Fat-Emmas for you, humps for me. Where do you want to go?"

"Have you got matches?"

"We don't need them. I have my magnifying glass." Matches in a boy's pockets were prima facie evidence of the cigarette habit, like nicotine stains on the fingers. A magnifying glass only created the suspicion that he had been seeing too much of Craig Kennedy, the scientific detective, in his struggles to outwit The Clutching Hand.

I went away to school around that time, and during vacations my hangout was a downtown drug store. Lintzie's was not that kind of place; the neighborhood kids congregated on the sidewalk, drawn to the store by the candy and ice cream, but Lintzie and Lonnie discouraged them from remaining inside. "Get your fingers off them Easter eggs," Lonnie would say. "Stop fooling around with them searchlights. Do you want to wear out the battery?" Lintzie and Lonnie would threaten to put items on the kids' family bills, and sometimes they made good on the threats. Sometimes they billed the wrong family; a fair amount of pilfering went on in spite of the Lintzies' vigilance, and you would see a kid who had just been driven out of the store furtively but proudly displaying a mechanical pencil or a put-and-take top or a carton of fig newtons that he had stolen. One of my younger brothers never came out of Lintzie's empty-handed, even if all he got was a cucumber. I did once see him steal a cucumber. The custom was known locally as the five-finger-grab, and it contributed to the Lintzies' pedophobia, which did not exclude their own messy children. "Go on up and wipe your nose," Lintzie would say. "Tell your mother to sew them buttons on." As a young buck who had danced with Constance Bennett and visited the Pre Cat, I stayed away from Lintzie's as much as possible during that period.

But then my father died and I had to get a job as cub reporter on one of the town papers. Temporarily—and I never considered it anything but temporary—my sphere of activity was limited to my own county. We had almost no income, and my mother kept us going by converting her bonds to cash, a desperation measure that obviously could not last forever. It did not make economic sense—nothing did—but very soon we were steady customers at Lintzie's instead of at the cash-and-carry a block away, where everything was much cheaper. My mother ceased to be a customer at O'Donnell's and Gottlieb's; lamb chops and asparagus seldom appeared on our dinner table. We bought a loaf of bread at a time, a jar of peanut butter, a half dozen eggs, a quarter pound of butter, a half-pint of cream, because at Lintzie's prices nothing must go to waste, to turn stale or sour. "On your way home, stop in at Lintzes' and get a can of tomato soup," my mother would say. She had never referred to it as Lintzie's and she was not going to start now. I had always been able to tell that she did not like Lintzie or his wife, and she liked them less when she owed them money twenty-nine days out of every month. They were not overly fond of her, either; she was a better bookkeeper than they, and never hesitated to prove it.

I had become, among other things, quite a drinker, although I was not yet twenty years old. How I managed to drink so much on no money is still somewhat of a mystery to me, but cheap booze was cheap, and politicians and "members of the sporting fraternity" were expected to buy drinks for newspaper men. "Why not?" an old-timer said to me. "It's small recompense for the dubious pleasure of their company." Lintzie was neither politician nor prizefight promoter, but one afternoon, when I stopped in for a last-minute purchase, he invited me to have a drink with him at Schmelinger's, a neighborhood saloon that had never bothered to pretend to be a speakeasy. "I'm broke," I said.

"I'll buy," said Lintzie.

"That's a different story," I said.

Schmelinger had been a patient of my father's, and I therefore had never been a patron of Schmelinger's, but Lintzie was greeted with the gruff politeness of the barkeep toward the good customer. We sat at a table and had three or four whiskeys—straight, with water chasers—and spent a most enjoyable hour together. In that neighborhood nearly all the men were at work all day, and Lintzie had no men friends. I gathered that he would run over to Schmelinger's for a shot in the middle of the morning and along about three or four in the afternoon, before the housewives' and schoolkids' rush. That was on a Lincoln's birthday, a school holiday. I was rather sorry that I could not count on being fitted into Lintzie's schedule, but I need not have worried. He changed his schedule to fit mine.

At that stage of my life I took my charm for granted; I did not inquire into the possible reasons why a man who was ten years older than I would want to buy me four dollars' worth of expertly cut rye whiskey once or twice a week. But slowly I began to understand first that he had somehow become indifferent to the difference in our ages. From our conversation it appeared that during my time away at school I had somehow added ten, not four, years to my age. Secondly, like everyone else, he needed someone to talk to. And he talked. He had certain recollections of his Marine Corps days that he liked to dwell on repetitiously: practical jokes on comrades-in-arms, small revenges on young officers, standing two feet away from Woodrow Wilson, visits to a whorehouse on Race Street, Philadelphia. From his whorehouse reminiscences he would often proceed, with unconscious logic, to some revelations concerning Lonnie. Her people had intended her to be the wife of his brother, but when Lintzie came home on his first furlough he threw her on the ground and gave her what she'd been asking for. On his next furlough he married her despite the fact that his brother had meanwhile thrown her on the ground and given her what she'd been asking for. But Lintzie had been first, and the baby was almost surely his. Now that the kid was old enough to look like somebody, he did look more like Lintzie than like his brother, so Lintzie guessed he had not made any mistake in that respect. He was not so sure about the second kid, the daughter. She didn't look like anybody, like a Lintz or a Moyer (Lonnie having been a Moyer). But by the law of averages it was probably Lintzie's kid, and he had never been able to prove anything. Lonnie hardly ever went out of the house. Most of the time she waited on customers in her carpet slippers. When she had to go back home for her brother's funeral her shoes did not fit her, so she had to stop on the way to the station and buy a new pair. Two months later, when she was taking the kids to their first day at Sunday School, the new shoes were too small for her. It was hard to believe that she had ever been pretty, but when she was seventeen or eighteen she was as pretty as any girl in the Valley. Some girls didn't care what they looked like after they got married, and Lonnie was one of them. Well, which was worse: the ones who didn't care, or the ones who cared about nothing else and flirted with every son of a bitch with pants on? In another year or two you'd be able to leave her at a hose company picnic and she'd be as safe as if she stayed home. Lintzie had told her as much, and all she said was, "Aah, shut up." That was her answer for everything. Shut up. To Lintzie, to the kids, to her mother, but most of all to Lintzie, and she had said it so often that it sunk in, finally sunk in, and he *did* shut up.

After a while it sunk in on *her* that he had practically stopped talking to her, and she complained about it. He told her he was only doing what she had been telling him to do: she had been telling him for years to shut up, and that's what he did. If she didn't want to listen to anything he had to say, he would talk to her only when it was positively necessary. And her automatic reply to that statement was to tell him to shut up. He realized that she used the expression the way some people say "Go to hell" or "Aw, nuts" but "Aah, shut up" was actually what she said, and he took her at her word. To some extent it made life livable, not to have to talk to her. She was not very much of a talker, not what you'd call a chatterbox, a windbag, but half of what she said was complaints, bellyaching. If it wasn't about money, it was about her feet getting bigger, and if it wasn't about her feet it was why didn't he do more about raising the kids instead of sneaking off to Schmelinger's morning, noon, and night? The funny thing about her complaining was that it was never twice about the same thing. It was probably better than if she harped on the same thing all the time, which would soon drive a man crazy, but on the other hand, she would complain about something and if you paid enough attention to go and do something about the complaint, you damn soon found out that she didn't even remember complaining about it. Like the time he went out and paid $185 for a new Stromberg-Carlson and she asked what the hell did he want to have two radios for, entirely forgetting that she had complained about the old radio and had specifically mentioned the Stromberg-Carlson as the one she wanted next. One day, out of a blue sky, she said to him, "Why didn't you stay in the marines? If you stayed in the marines we'd be living in Hawaii instead of a dump like this." It was such an infuriatingly unreasonable complaint that he hauled off and gave her a kick in the behind. "What'd you kick me for?" she said. Sometimes he thought she didn't have any brains in her head, but she was no dumbbell. In some things she was pretty smart. He let her do the ordering when some of the salesmen came around. She didn't know that seven eights was fifty-six, but she never took the first price on anything, and every time she ordered something, say a gross of pencils, she made the salesman fork over something for nothing. Before she would even begin talking about a sale she would demand free samples—candy, chewing gum, novelties—and use them later to reward kids who went on errands for her.

In the strictest confidence and after more than the usual ration of rye and water, Lintzie told me one day that Lonnie had discovered that most housewives did not bother to keep tabs on what they bought. My mother did not let her get away with it, he said, but other women in the neighborhood did not seem to notice when Lonnie added items to the monthly bills. She was pretty good at it, too. It was hardly ever more than a dollar's worth of stuff per account, but if you added a dollar to every bill it came to around a hundred a month clear profit. At Christmas it was even more. Anyway, it was well over a thousand dollars a year, which was Gott damn good for a woman that couldn't multiply seven eights. Like picking it up off the floor. Thereafter I did not mind taking Lintzie's free drinks. I was, so to speak, the guest of the neighborhood housewives, among whom were a few who had failed to settle accounts with my father's estate.

It also occurred to me that I was receiving a bribe from Lonnie that supplemented the original four packs of cigarettes. It probably would have done her no good to complain, but she could have protested when Lintzie rang up a No Sale on the cash register and helped himself to the money to pay for his hospitality to me. No doubt she was glad to get him out of her sight. Nevertheless I became convinced that Lonnie was appreciative of my early silence, if possibly a little apprehensive that I might break it now that Lintzie and I were drinking companions. Ethically I was not standing on firm ground, but my ethics and my morals and my conscience were taking a continual beating in other areas as well. I was giving myself trouble over girls and women and love and theology and national politics and my uncontrollable temper. Not the easiest of my problems was my willingness to spend as much time with a man whom I regarded as a moron. It was true that I was the victim of circumstances back beyond my control, but I was unable thereby to justify my association with this loquacious lout. Since I could not justify it, I gave up trying to.

Downtown, in back of a second-rate commercial hotel, was another saloon that was as wide open as Schmelinger's and served the same grade of whiskey. Unlike Schmelinger's it catered to a considerable transient trade, principally the traveling salesmen who stopped at the hotel. It was a busy joint, and often half filled with strangers. I went there one night, alone, and sat at a table to drink beer, eat pretzels, and read the out-of-town papers. At the next table were two strangers drinking rye and ginger ale. Salesmen, most likely, and getting drunk. They did not bother me, but I began to pick up some of their conversation. One was telling the other about a customer of his, nothing much for looks, but a positive, guaranteed lay. Nothing novel about that conversation between salesmen, but the speaker gave his companion directions on how to find the accommodating customer, and the address was Lintzie's store. "I got put on to her a couple years ago," he said. "Don't look for any great beauty. This is for a quick jazz when you don't have a date. No money. You give her a dozen samples or shave your prices a little. And you gotta watch out for the husband. He's in and out of the place all day. A boozer. My last time in this town, I was upstairs with the broad and the husband came back from the saloon. I had to hide in a closet till he went out again. All he had to do was open that closet door and I'm cooked, but I been taking off her for a couple years and that's the first time we ever had a close one. Don't tell her I sent you. The first time, you gotta make it on your own, but I want to tell you something, that—ain't—hard. And buddy, she likes it."

I could easily have struck up a conversation with the traveling man and learned more about Lonnie's behavior, but a friend of mine joined me and we were town people against strangers. The salesman had confirmed my suspicions about Lonnie, dormant suspicions because I had not realized that Lonnie was quite so adventurous or quite so careless. Oddly enough, my immediate impulse was to warn Lonnie to use some caution, and my second, contradictory to the first, was no more than a feeling of pity for Lintzie. The practical effect of what I had overheard was to give up my pleasant enough drinking sessions with Lintzie. There was going to be trouble there, I knew it, and I had a very positive wish to stay away from it. I did not want to be drinking with Lintzie while Lonnie was using his absence to entertain a gabby salesman.

In later years I came to believe that Lintzie's first suspicions of Lonnie dated from my withdrawal from our sessions at Schmelinger's. My excuse to him was flimsy, although based partly on fact: that the paper had promoted me to columnist, an extra job that had to be done on my own time. It was flimsy because Lintzie did not believe me. Whenever I saw him he gave me the special look of small dignity offended, the look of small people who do not feel entitled to anger. My subsequent theory about Lintzie's suspicions of Lonnie was that without me (or anyone else) to talk to, he was left entirely with his thoughts, and his world was very small. He had a wife, two kids who gave him no pleasure, and the clientele of his store for whom he had no respect. And of course he had the memories of his ten months as a private in the Marine Corps, patrolling railway stations and piers and being sneered at by sailors and petty officers; occasional visits to whorehouses along the Eastern Seaboard; the time he stood frozen at attention when the President of the whole Gott damn United States passed within two feet of him at the Union Depot in Washington. His brother had never been as far as New York, his father had never been as far as Philadelphia, his mother had never even been to Reading before she was thirty. For a Berks County farm boy Lintzie had seen a lot of the world, but he had not been seeing much of it lately. Schmelinger ran a very sober saloon; the only decoration in the place was a pre-Prohibition framed brewery advertisement, depicting a goat in Bavarian costume raising a beer stein. Schmelinger himself was a strict Roman Catholic who had a daughter a nun and a son studying for priesthood. It was in these surroundings that Lintzie was spending a great deal of his time, probably as much of it as in his own store.

A full year and a little more passed during which I did not have a drink with Lintzie and actually did not set foot in his store. (My mother could send one of my brothers for those last-minute quarts of milk.) I was getting twenty dollars a week on the paper, and the owner, in his benevolence, allowed me to fill the tank of my four-cylinder Buick at the paper's expense. So I was coming up in the world, and I loved my column, which was one of the numerous imitations of F.P.A.'s Coming Tower. One afternoon, after the paper had gone to press and the other reporters had gone home, the phone rang on the city editor's desk and I went to answer it. "Malloy speaking," I said.

"Oh, it's you, Malloy. This is Christine Fultz."

"Hello, Chris, what have you got?" I said. She was a "correspondent" who picked up a few dollars a week for news tips and unreadable (and usually outdated) accounts of church suppers.

"Well, I'll tell you, there's something very funny going on out here."

"Is it funny enough to go in my column?"

"What column is that?" said Chris.

"Never mind. What have you got? Spill it."

"I want the credit for the tip, mind you."

"I'll see that you get the credit for the tip, but first you have to tell me what tip on what," I said.

"It's at Lintzie's. There's a whole crowd of people standing outside there."

"Maybe they're having a bargain sale."

"Be *serious*. Sombody said he shot her."

"Lintzie shot Lonnie?"

"That's what I said, didn't I? But I don't know if it's true or not. I couldn't get very near, there's such a crowd. There was another story circulating that he shot her and the two children, but I don't know that either."

"Are the police there?" I said.

"If they are, they're inside. I didn't see no police."

"When did this happen, do you know?"

"Well, it couldn't of happened very long ago, because I went past Lintzie's an hour ago and there was nobody there. But when I came back you should of seen the crowd. So it must of happened between the time I went past there an hour ago and when I was on my way home."

"Now you're using the old noodle, Chris. What else?"

"*Somebody* said he shot a *man*."

"Lintzie shot a man?"

"Don't go blaming me if that's just a rumor, but that's what one person told me. There's supposed to be a dead man in there, and Lonnie and the two kids."

"But Lintzie? Where is Lintzie?"

"I don't know. He's either inside or he got away. Or maybe he's dead too."

"That's the old noodle again, Chris. Well, thanks very much. You'll get credit for the tip."

"Are you coming out?"

"Try and stop me," I said.

In less than ten minutes I parked my car across the street from Lintzie's. It was my neighborhood, and everyone knew that I was working on the paper, so they made way for me. A cop, the newest on the force, got between me and the door. "No newspaper reporters," he said.

481

"Who said so? You, for Christ's sake? Get out of my way. If you'll turn your thick head around you'll see your boss waving to me to come in." Inside the store Joe Dorelli, a sergeant and detective—all detectives were sergeants—was signaling to me. "You see?" I said to the rookie cop. "I was covering murders when you were playing high school football." It was a lie, but rookie cops were our natural enemies. I went inside.

"What the hell is this, Joe?"

"Lintzie, the Dutch bastard. He come home and caught her in bed with a guy and he shot them. Then the kids come running in from the yard and he shot them too. You want to see the gun? Here's the gun." On the counter was a holster stamped USMC and in it was a Colt .45 automatic pistol.

"Where is Lintzie?" I said.

"Back in the kitchen, talking to the chief. You'd think he just got elected mayor, honest. He phoned in. Me and the chief come right out and the first thing he done was offer us a cigar. Then he took us upstairs and showed us the wife and the boy friend. Wait'll you see them. We're waiting for the fellow to come and take their pictures. Then Lintzie took us down in the cellar and showed us the two kids."

"He shot them down in the cellar?"

"No, on the stairway, between this floor and the bedroom. Then he carried them down in the cellar. I don't know why, and he doesn't either. I said to him why didn't he shoot himself while he was at it? That's what they often do. But he was surprised at such a question. Why should he shoot himself? He looked at me like I wasn't all there."

"Is he drunk?"

"You can smell it on him, but he don't act it. He asked were you here."

"He did?"

"By name," said Dorelli. "That's what I wanted to talk to you. Did you know this was gonna happen? Nobody knows who the guy is. Well, we know his name and he was some kind of a salesman. His wallet was in his pants pocket, hanging on the back of a chair. From Wilkes-Barre, he is, but working for a company over in Allentown. Sidney M. Pollock, thirty-two years of age. But did you know about him and the Lintz woman?"

"No, but I might recognize him."

"We'll get him identified all right."

"I'd like to take a look at him."

"From the front you would. You know what a .45 slug'll do. The right-hand cheekbone it went in. She got it in the heart. Two. He gave her one for good measure. The kids he gave one apiece. Five shots, four dead. But he was a marine, and they teach them to shoot in the marines. I took notice there was a picture of him in the bedroom. Marksman and expert rifleman. Well, do you want to take a look at them?"

I only wanted to see the dead man, and I did recognize him. He was the companion of the traveling salesman who had talked so seductively of Lonnie Lintz. Even after a year there was no mistaking that nose and that hairless skull. I could not have recognized the big-mouth salesman; he had been sitting on my right; but Pollock had been facing him, and me. It was perhaps too much to say that if I had struck up a conversation with them that night, Pollock would not now be lying dead in his underwear on a messy bed in a strange town, in disgrace. I thought of Pollock's wife, if any, and his probably orthodox mother and father in Wilkes-Barre.

"Now you got another treat in store for you," said Dorelli. "Down in the cellar."

"No thanks," I said.

"Me either," said Dorelli. "I had to, but if I didn't have to I wouldn't have. Two kids, for Christ's sake, around the same age as two of mine. This guy is crazy, but don't you write that. That's what he'll claim—and maybe he had a right to kill her and the Jew, but not the kids. He can't pull that unwritten law on the kids. For that he deserves to fry."

"I didn't know you were such a family man, Joe."

"Listen, what you don't know about me would fill a book," he said. "You had enough, we'll go down and see if the chief'll let you talk to Lintz."

I waited in the store while Joe conferred with the chief. A cop named Lundy came in while I was there. "That's something you don't often hear in this town," he said.

"What's that?" I said.

"Them women out there, they want to lynch him."

"We've never had a lynching in this town," I said.

"We never will. It's just talk, but you don't often hear that kind of talk in Lantenengo County. Just talk, but all the same I'm gonna tell the chief to get him outa here."

"You mean you're thinking of *suggesting* to the chief," I said.

"Aah, smart guy," said Lundy. "I hear Lintz and you was great buddies."

"Doing some detective work at Schmelinger's, eh, Lundy? Do you think you'll solve this case?"

"I'll solve you one right in the puss, Malloy," said Lundy.

"Then you'll be right back on the garbage truck. We supported *this* mayor," I said.

Dorelli, at the rear of the store, beckoned to me.

"Any message you wish me to convey to the chief, Lundy?" I said.

"No, you wouldn't get it right, just like that rag you work for," said Lundy. He laughed and I laughed. Lundy was a good cop and he knew I thought so.

"I'll put in a good word for you, then," I said.

"Jesus, don't do that. That'd be the ruination of me, a good word from you."

I joined Dorelli. "You can talk to him, but one of us has to be there."

"Oh, come on, Joe. There's no mystery about this case. Let me talk to him alone."

"We'll do it our way or not at all," said Dorelli.

"Then we'll do it your way," I said.

Dorelli led me to the kitchen. A uniformed cop was standing outside the kitchen door; the chief was sitting across the table from Lintzie, his chin on his chest, staring at him in silence. Obviously the chief had momentarily run out of questions to ask Lintzie. Lintzie turned when I entered. "Oh, there's my buddy. Hyuh, Malloy."

"Hello, Lintzie," I said.

"Say, Chief, let me send over to Schmelinger's for a pint," said Lintzie. "I'll pay for it."

"Pay for it? You got a lot to pay for, you son of a bitch," said the chief.

"I'll be down in the cellar," said Dorelli, and left.

"Well, I guess I went and done it," said Lintzie.

"How did you happen to pick today?" I said.

"I don't know," said Lintzie. "I was over at Schmelinger's and I guess I started to thinking to myself. There was a whole truckload of stuff piled up on the kitchen porch, waiting to be unpacked. I knowed Gott damn well Lonnie wouldn't start unpacking it. It had to be unpacked and put down in the cellar out of the way. So I said to myself if I got it all unpacked I could make the kids take it down in the cellar when they got home. It was a truckload of stuff from the wholesaler. Canned goods. Heavy. In wooden boxes. All I needed was my claw-hammer and I could unpack the stuff and the kids could take it down the cellar a couple cans at a time. Ten or fifteen minutes' work for me and I could be back at Schmelinger's. So I said to Guss I'd see him later and I come home."

"What time was that, Lintzie?" I said.

"Search me. I lost track of time," said Lintzie.

"About quarter of three," said the chief. "Between half past two and three, according to Schmelinger."

"I come in the store door, and I took notice to the salesman's car outside. But I went inside and no Lonnie, and no salesman. The chief don't believe me, but I caught her once before with a salesman, only it wasn't the same one."

"Why don't you believe him, Chief?"

"Because this was a deliberate murder. All this stuff about the packages on the back porch, that's the bunk."

"Look outside, the boxes are there right now in plain sight," said Lintzie.

"He pretended he was going to spend a couple hours at Schmelinger's, the way he usually did. But he only went there long enough to give his wife and the salesman time to go upstairs," said the chief. "He admitted himself he usually kept the .45 upstairs but today he had it hanging on a peg in the cellar stairway. This was a planned first-degree murder."

"How about that, Lintzie?" I said.

"The chief don't have to be right all the time."

"But why was the gun hanging in the stairway?"

"To get it out of the way of the kids. Lonnie said she caught the boy playing with it and I was to get it out of the way. So I took and hung it on a peg in the cellar stairway, where he couldn't reach it. That was two-three days ago. Lonnie could—I was just gonna say Lonnie could back me up on that, but I guess not now."

"No," I said. "So then what?"

"Yes, listen to this part, Malloy," said the chief.

"Then what? Then I went upstairs and caught them in bed."

"Wait a minute, Lintzie. You're skipping a lot. Did you get the gun and then go upstairs?" I said.

"Me? No. I went upstairs and caught them and then I got the gun."

"Did you, before you went upstairs, did you call Lonnie to see where she was? Upstairs or down-cellar?"

"Well, she could hear the bell when I come in the store."

"But you could have been a customer. You didn't call her, or did you?"

"He didn't call her, and he *didn't* come in the front door," said the chief. "He told Dorelli one story and me another, and now he's an altogether different one. He told Dorelli he went around the back way and got his claw-hammer and started opening the boxes. There's no mark of a claw-hammer on any of the boxes, and anyway you make a certain amount of noise opening a wooden box with a claw-hammer. You know, you put the claws under the slats and you start using leverage and it makes a peculiar kind of a noise. But that would have warned the people upstairs. No, he came in the back door, where there is no bell, and he got the .45 and sneaked upstairs and took careful aim and killed the salesman. One shot. Then he let her have two slugs right in the heart. I had a look at the .45 and I'll tell you this much, Malloy. If all my men kept their guns in as good a condition I'd be satisfied. I know something about guns. If you leave a gun in a holster for any length of time, the oil gets gummy, but not this gun. This gun was cleaned and oiled I'd say in the last twenty-four, forty-eight hours."

"I always kept my gun in good condition," said Lintzie.

"Yes. For just such an occasion," said the chief.

"Tell me what you did, Lintzie," I said.

"I shot them, for Christ's sake. And then the Gott damn kids come yelling and screaming and I shot them, too. I ain't denying it. Go ahead and arrest me."

"Oh, we'll arrest you, Mr. Lintz," said the chief. "You *were* arrested, nearly an hour ago. Sergeant Dorelli placed you under arrest, but you don't have a very good memory."

"You shot the kids on the stairway, and then you told Dorelli that you carried them down to the cellar."

"That's what I done. Yeah."

"But I understand that a bullet from a .45 has a terrific impact, that it'll knock a grown man back several feet. So I was wondering, maybe when you shot the kids the impact knocked them down the stairs, and then you picked them up and carried them to the cellar. Is that about right, Lintzie?"

"No," he said.

"What did happen?"

"I held the kids, one at a time, and shot them," said Lintzie.

"Jesus," I said, and looked at the chief.

"They wouldn't hold still," he said.

"Jesus Christ," I said.

"Oh, this is quite a fellow," said the chief. "It takes a real man to grab hold of a kid with one hand and shoot him with the other. And do the same thing all over again with another kid."

"Which did you shoot first, Lintzie? The girl or the boy?"

"Her. Then he come at me. I don't remember holding him."

"The boy tried to defend his sister," said the chief.

"He didn't try to defend nobody, that kid. He was getting ready to shoot me. Him and Lonnie."

"But I thought Lonnie told you to hide the gun," I said.

487

"Till he got older, that's all. She was gonna wait a couple years till we had more money saved up."

"Oh, and then she was going to let him shoot you?" I said.

"You got the idea," said Lintzie. He grinned at me and sneered at the chief. "She thought I was dumb, but I wasn't so dumb."

"You said something about catching her with another man once before," I said. "You never told me about that."

"Yes, I did. Didn't I?"

"No, you never told me that. When did you catch her? Was it like today, you came home and found her with another man?"

"Night," he said.

"Oh, you came home one night and found her?"

"No! I was home. Upstairs. The night bell rang and she went down to see who it was."

"You thought it was a late customer," I said.

"I thought it was, but it was a foreigner. He had whiskers and he wore those funny clothes. You know. He had whiskers on his chin, all the girls were stuck on him."

"Oh, yes. Once I had a billygoat, he was old enough to vote. He had whiskers on his chin. I remember the song."

"This was *him*, though. Not a song."

"Oh, really? And he came in the store and made passes at Lonnie?"

"*She* made passes at *him*. She made passes at everybody except you. She didn't like you, or your mother, or any of you. Boy, oh, boy, the things she used to say about your old man."

"She never knew my old man, but what did she say about him?"

"How he used to operate on people when they didn't have nothing wrong with them. Any time your old lady wanted a new dress, your old man would operate on somebody."

"Oh, well that was true, of course," I said.

"Stop humoring him," said the chief.

"And that's why Lonnie never made passes at me, because she didn't like us. But what about this foreigner with the beard, Lintzie? Did you ever see him any place else? Did you ever see him at Schmelinger's?"

"He used to come in there but I never talked to him."

"He did come in there, though?"

"I seen him there," said Lintzie.

"He had whiskers. Did he wear a kind of a coat with little straps across the front?"

"Such a coat, yes," said Lintzie. "But I never seen him when you were there."

"No, but I think I knew the fellow you mean."

The chief looked at his gold hunting-case watch. "You had long enough, Malloy. I'm taking this fellow down to the squire's office."

"Charging him with first-degree murder?" I said.

"We sure are. An open-and-shut case, like this watch."

"I'll make you a small bet he never goes to Bellefonte," I said.

"I wouldn't take your money," said the chief.

"Bellefonte? Where the electric chair is?" said Lintzie. "Huh. Not me."

"See? He doesn't think so either," I said.

"Who did I used to guard during the war? Tell him, Malloy," said Lintzie.

"Woodrow Wilson, the President of the whole Gott damn United States," I said.

"Can I go upstairs a minute, Chief?" said Lintzie.

"No. You mean you want to go to the toilet?"

"No, I want to get something for Malloy."

"Call Lundy, tell him what it is and he'll get it," said the chief.

"My picture of me, upstairs on the bureau," said Lintzie.

"Oh, for Christ's sake. All right," said the chief.

Lundy went upstairs and brought down the photograph, which I had never seen before, of Private Donald Lintz, U.S.M.C., in his greens and the old-style cap that sat squarely on the top of his head, two badges for shooting pinned to the blouse.

"Put that in the paper, Malloy," said Lintzie.

"That I promise you," I said. "And how about pictures of Lonnie and the kids?"

"You want them too?" said Lintzie. "What do you want them for? I don't want them in the paper."

"Are there any more up there, Lundy?" I said.

"Sure," said Lundy. "Plenty. Her before she got fat, and the two kids."

"No, you can't have them," said Lintzie.

"Get them, Lundy," said the chief.

"You son of a bitch, Malloy," said Lintzie. "You want to make people feel sorry for them."

"Maybe he doesn't, but I do," said the chief. "Malloy, why do you think this fellow has a Chinaman's chance? You can tell me. The D.A. prosecutes, I don't."

"Can you spare five minutes?" I said.

"What for?"

"Will you come with me? It'll only take five minutes at the most," I said.

The chief called Dorelli, told him to keep an eye on Lintzie, and accompanied me to Schmelinger's. I pointed to the old-time beer ad on the wall. "There's Lonnie's other boy friend," I said. "Any fifty-dollar alienist will keep Lintzie out of the chair."

"Maybe you're right," said the chief.

"Something on the house, gentlemen?" said Schmelinger.

"Maybe you're right," said the chief.

"You, Malloy?"

"Not on the house," I said. "You've just lost your best cash customer."

"I won't miss him," said Schmelinger.

"He was good for fifty bucks a week and he never gave you any trouble," I said.

"I won't miss him," said Schmelinger. He ignored me and addressed the chief. "After this fellow stopped coming in with him he just sat there and stared at the Bock beer picture. And I bet you he don't even know it was there."

"Is that so? Well, thanks, Gus. Next time I'm out this way I'll have one with you," said the chief.

We walked in silence halfway to Lintzie's, then the chief spoke. "I thought a great deal of your father. What's a young fellow with your education throwing it all away when you could be doing some good in the world?"

"What education? I had four years of high school," I said.

"You were away to college," he said.

"Away, but not to college."

"Oh, then you're not much better than the rest of us," he said.

"I never said I was, Chief."

"You never said it, but you act it. Your father *was* better than most of us, but he didn't act it."

"No, he didn't have to," I said.

ROGER
TORY
PETERSON

JAYS, THRUSHES, AND TANAGERS

A FIELD GUIDE TO

WESTERN BIRDS

BY

R O G E R   T O R Y   P E T E R S O N

of the National Audubon Society

SPONSORED BY

NATIONAL AUDUBON SOCIETY

AND

NATIONAL WILDLIFE FEDERATION

BOSTON

HOUGHTON MIFFLIN COMPANY

The Riverside Press Cambridge

TO
MY WIFE

THIRTEENTH PRINTING

The Riverside Press
CAMBRIDGE · MASSACHUSETTS
PRINTED IN THE U.S.A.

PREFACE

IT WAS that pioneer, Ernest Thompson Seton, who first tried the idea of pattern diagrams as a method of teaching bird identification. Years ago he published some diagrammatic plates in *The Auk*, showing how Hawks and Owls look in flight overhead.

Those of us who have read Seton's *Two Little Savages* remember how the young hero, Yan, discovered some mounted Ducks in a dusty showcase. This lad had a book which showed him how to tell Ducks when they were in the hand, but since he only saw the live Ducks at a distance, he was frequently at a loss for their names. He noticed that all the Ducks in the showcase were different — all had blotches or streaks that were their labels or identification tags. He decided that if he could put their labels or 'uniforms' down on paper, he would know these same Ducks as soon as he saw them at a distance on the water.

It was on this idea that my *Field Guide to the Birds*, the Eastern counterpart of this volume, was based. It is a handbook designed to complement the standard ornithological works — a guide to the *field-marks* of Eastern birds, wherein live birds may be run down by impressions, patterns, and distinctive marks rather than by the differences of measurements and anatomy that the collector finds useful. The success of this publication prompted Mr. Clinton G. Abbott, Director of the Natural History Museum at San Diego, to ask why I didn't do a similar guide for the West. I dismissed the idea, at first, thinking that although the plan worked out well for eastern North America, it would be almost impossible to do the same thing for the West, where the situation was, it seemed to me, much more confusing. However, after constant prompting and encouragement by Guy Emerson, President of the National Audubon Society, who has had wide field experience in all parts of the country, I decided to give it a try. After tussling with a few of the problems, I came to the conclusion that field identification was no more difficult in the West than in the East, and that most publications made things look more difficult than they were. There was already one excellent handbook in use — Hoffmann's *Birds of the Pacific States* — but this only covered the States of Washington, Oregon, and California, whereas there was hardly a thing that was adequate for most other parts of the West. This guide does not intend to replace Hoffmann's handbook; rather, it could be most effectively used as a companion piece to it. The approach of the two books is quite different. Hoffmann's is especially thorough on the voices and habitats of birds, much more complete than is possible in a book of this size.

The entire manuscript of this book was read and criticized by Guy Emerson and also by Frank Watson and Laidlaw Williams, two of California's most enthusiastic field students. Mr. Ludlow Griscom of Cambridge, Massachusetts, who has as wide a field knowledge of all the birds of North America as any ornithologist, and who has brought the science of field identification to its greatest perfection, also examined the complete manuscript and has given me the benefit of his valuable experience. Mr. Francis H. Allen of West Roxbury, Massachusetts, veteran editor of many widely known ornithological works, has given the text a complete perusal and editorial polishing. Portions of the manuscript were also sent to the following experts for their critical opinions: Irby Davis (Texas and Mexican species), Charles W. Lockerbie (Rocky Mountain birds), Dr. Alden Miller (Owls, Flycatchers, Thrashers, Juncos, etc.), James Moffitt (Ducks and Geese), Dr. Robert Cushman Murphy (oceanic birds), Robert J. Niedrach (Rocky Mountain and Great Plains species), Dr. Robert T. Orr (shore-birds), and Dr. George Miksch Sutton (Mexican and Southwestern birds).

During my trips West which carried me into all the States covered by this book, I have received constant co-operation from numerous well-known bird students who unselfishly put their time and knowledge at my disposal, often spending days driving me around to see the things I wished most to see. I am especially indebted to Edward Chalif of Short Hills, New Jersey; Garrett Eddy and H. W. Higman of Seattle, Washington; Walter Hagenstein of Medina, Washington; H. M. Dubois, Harold S. Gilbert, and other members of the Oregon Audubon Society; Mr. and Mrs. Charles Lockerbie and Dr. A. M. Woodbury of Salt Lake City, Utah; Mrs. Junea Kelly of Alameda, California; Mrs. Amèlia Allen, Mrs. Dorothy Dean Sheldon, and Frank Watson of Berkeley, California; Commander Henry E. Parmenter of San Francisco; Laidlaw Williams of Carmel, California; Miss Helen S. Pratt of Eagle Rock, California; James Murdock of Glendale, California; Frank Gander, Lawrence M. Huey, and Lewis Wayne Walker of San Diego, California; Mr. C. A. Harwell, California representative of the National Audubon Society, and his former associates at Yosemite National Park, Vincent Mowbray and Charles Michael; Randolph Jenks and Dr. Charles T. Vorhies of Tucson, Arizona; Mr. and Mrs. Irby Davis of Harlingen, Texas; James Stevenson of Austwell, Texas; and Thomas Waddell of Eagle Lake, Texas.

Dr. Arthur A. Allen and Charles Brand of Cornell University spent an entire week-end with me in their sound laboratory playing off all the sound recordings of birds which were made on their recent trips West. In this way I was able to make a final check on some of the more puzzling bird voices and compare them with my field descriptions. This was especially helpful in analyzing the voice differences in closely related species that could not always be compared conveniently in the field. In interpreting a few of the more difficult bird songs I have resorted to a system of symbols similar to that developed so successfully by Aretas A. Saunders, to whom I offer my apologies.

As for the drawings, Dr. William Sargent helped me immeasurably on the flight patterns of Hawks by his detailed criticism and the loan of his sketches and notes.

In addition to the foregoing, I am also indebted to the following for notes, suggestions, and other aid: Robert P. Allen, Harold H. Axtell, John H. Baker, H. C. Blanchard, Paul Brooks, Margaret Brooks, Brighton Cain, Dr. Clarence Cottam, David Lloyd Garrison, Dr. William T. Helmuth, Joseph J. Hickey, Richard Johnson, John O. Larson, Sigred Lee, Daniel Lehrmann, J. Norman McDonald, L. Nelson Nichols, Dr. H. C. Oberholser, Charles O'Brien, Richard H. Pough, Charles Shell, Alexander Sprunt, Jr., Mrs. Albert H. Stephens, Wendell Taber, Lovell Thompson, Mrs. Whiting Washington, Dr. Alexander Wetmore, Dr. J. T. Zimmer, and especially my wife who assisted with much of the research and detail work.

For the use of its extensive collections, I wish to thank the American Museum of Natural History in New York City.

References were made to the following works: *Fourth A.O.U. Check-List of North American Birds*, Alexander's *Birds of the Ocean*, Bailey's *Handbook of Birds of the Western United States*, Bailey's *Birds of New Mexico*, Bent's *Life Histories of North American Birds*, Bond's *Birds of the West Indies*, Chapman's *Handbook of Birds of Eastern North America*, Chapman's *The Warblers of North America*, Dawson's *Birds of California*, Dawson and Bowles's *The Birds of Washington*, Eliot's *Birds of the Pacific Coast*, Forbush's *Birds of Massachusetts and other New England States*, Gabrielson and Jewett's *Birds of Oregon*, Grinnell and Storer's *Animal Life in the Yosemite*, Grinnell, Bryant, and Storer's *The Game Birds of California*, Hoffmann's *Guide to the Birds*, Hoffmann's *Birds of the Pacific States*, Howell's *Florida Bird Life*, Kitchin's *Distributional Check-List of the Birds of the State of Washington*, Linsdale's *Birds of Nevada*, May's *The Hawks of North America*, McCreary's *Wyoming Bird Life*, Murphy's *Oceanic Birds of South America*, Myers's *Western Birds*, Niedrach and Rockwell's *The Birds of Denver and Mountain Parks*, Peterson's *A Field Guide to the Birds*, Phillips's *Natural History of the Ducks*, Roberts's *Birds of Minnesota*, Saunders's *A Distributional List of the Birds of Montana*, Saunders's *A Guide to Bird Songs*, Sclater's *A History of the Birds of Colorado*, Simmons's *Birds of the Austin Region*, Sturgis's *Field Book of Birds of the Panama Canal Zone*,

Swarth's *A Distributional List of the Birds of Arizona*, Taverner's *Birds of Canada*, Van Tyne and Sutton's *Birds of Brewster County, Texas*, Witherby's *The Handbook of British Birds*, Wyman and Burnell's *Field Book of Birds of the Southwestern United States*. In addition to the above, numerous local lists and mimeographed publications were consulted, also the files of *The Auk, Bird-Lore, The Condor*, and *The Wilson Bulletin*.

More than to any others, I owe the completion of this guide to Guy Emerson, who constantly urged me on, and to my wife, who spent altogether too many lonely nights at home during the last three years while I burned the midnight oil in my study.

CONTENTS

CONTENTS

ILLUSTRATIONS

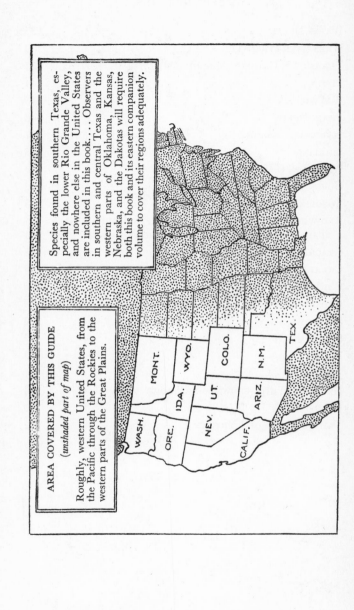

AREA COVERED BY THIS GUIDE
(unshaded part of map)

Roughly, western United States, from the Pacific through the Rockies to the western parts of the Great Plains.

Species found in southern Texas, especially the lower Rio Grande Valley, and nowhere else in the United States are included in this book.... Observers in southern and central Texas and the western parts of Oklahoma, Kansas, Nebraska, and the Dakotas will require both this book and its eastern companion volume to cover their regions adequately.

HOW TO USE THIS BOOK

VETERANS who have watched birds for years will need no suggestions as to ways of using this book. Beginners, however, will do well to bear in mind a few comments that will point to short cuts. A few moments should be spent in familiarizing one's self, in a general way, with the illustrations; the briefest examination of the plates will be sufficient to give the beginner an idea of the shapes of our birds and the groups to which they belong. Ducks, it will be seen, do not resemble Loons; and the Gulls will be readily separable from the Terns. The needle-like bills of the Warblers will immediately distinguish them from the seed-cracking bills of the Sparrows. Birds of a kind — that is, birds that could be confused — are grouped together where easy comparison is possible. Thus, when a bird has been seen in the field, the observer can immediately turn to the picture most resembling it and feel confident that he has reduced the possibilities to the few species in its own group.

In many instances the pictures tell the story without help from the letter-press. This is true of such plates as those illustrating the Swallows, Vireos, Wrens, the diving birds, etc. In every case, however, it is well to check identifications from the drawings by referring to the text. The plates give visual field-marks that may be used in comparing and sorting out species seen in life. The text gives field-marks, size (in inches), manner of flight, voice, range, etc., that could not be pictured, and, in addition, mentions the birds that might, in any instance, be confused with a given species.

In cases where the plates, without the text, do not give definitive identifications, the observer should select the picture that most resembles the bird he saw, and then consult the text. We may, for example, be puzzled by a bird that is certainly a female Merganser. A consultation of the brief descriptions of those birds eliminates the Hooded Merganser because the bird sought had a reddish head — not a dark one. It was seen on the coast, which, so the text tells us, increases the *probability* that it was a Red-breast. And finally, we learn that in the Red-breasted Merganser 'the rufous of the head *blends* into the white of the throat and neck instead of being sharply defined' as in the American Merganser. This characteristic, which accurately describes the bird we have seen, makes the identification certain. This soft merging of color is clearly shown in the plate, but because we had not known what to look for, we failed to notice it.

Far from helping only the beginner who can scarcely tell a Gull from a Duck, it is hoped that the advanced student will find this guide comprehensive enough to be of service in recognizing those accidentals or rarities that sometimes appear in the territory he knows so thoroughly.

Some of the assertions herein contained, of the ease with which certain birds may be distinguished, will possibly be questioned on the ground that older works have stated that they are 'very difficult' or 'impossible' to identify except in the hand.

Doubting Thomases need but take a few trips afield with some of our present-day experts in field identifications to realize the possibility of quickly identifying almost any bird, with amazing certainty, at the snap of a finger. It is but a matter of seeing a bird often enough and knowing exactly what to look for, to be able to distinguish, with a very few exceptions, even the most confusing forms.

Most of the 'rare finds' are made by people who are alive to the possibilities and know what to look for, should they detect anything unusual. It is
the discovery of rarities that puts real zest into the sport of birding, a zest
that many of us would like to interpret as 'scientific zeal' rather than the
quickening of our sporting blood.

Field birding, as many of us engage in it, is a game — a most absorbing
game. As we become more proficient, we attempt to list as many birds as we
can in a day. The May 'big day' or 'Christmas Census' is the apogee of this
sort of thing. Some ornithologists minimize the scientific value of this type
of bird work. Truly, it has but little. Recognition is not the end and aim of
ornithology, but is certainly a most fascinating diversion, and a tool which
the person who desires to contribute to our knowledge of ornithology might
profitably learn to master.

The illustrations. The plates and cuts scattered throughout the text are
intended as diagrams, arranged so that quick, easy comparison can be made
of the species that most resemble one another. As they are not intended to
be pictures or portraits, all modeling of form and feathering is eliminated
where it can be managed, so that simple contour and pattern remain. Even
color is often an unnecessary, if not, indeed, a confusing, factor. In many of
the waterfowl, which we seldom see at close range, this is especially true; so
most of the diagrams are carried out in black and white. With many of the
small birds, however, since color is quite essential to identification, a departure from the monochrome in the illustrations is necessarily made.

Area. The area covered by this book is roughly the United States west of
the one hundred and third meridian. This includes the entire States of Washington, Oregon, California, Nevada, Idaho, Utah, Montana, Wyoming,
Colorado, Arizona, and New Mexico, and the western part of Texas. In addition, those species which are found in southern Texas, especially in the lower
Rio Grande Valley, but nowhere else in the United States, are included in
this book. Typical Eastern species or races thereof which occur in the same
part of southern Texas will be found in the Eastern counterpart of this volume, *A Field Guide to the Birds.*

Along the western edge of the Great Plains in eastern New Mexico, Colorado, Wyoming, and Montana, a number of strictly Eastern birds have been
recorded as stragglers anywhere from one to a dozen times or more. As it is
theoretically possible to see almost any Eastern species sooner or later along
the western edge of the Great Plains, these are not described here. For
eventualities of this sort, bird watchers living east of the mountains should
use both books. Following is a list of Eastern strays compiled from publish d
sources:

> Broad-winged Hawk (Colo.)
> Piping Plover (Colo., Wyo.)
> Woodcock (Colo., Wyo.)
> Buff-breasted Sandpiper (Colo., Mont.)
> Hudsonian Godwit (Wyo., Mont.)
> Barred Owl (Colo., Wyo., Mont.)
> Red-bellied Woodpecker (Colo.)
> Crested Flycatcher (Wyo.)
> Carolina Wren (Mont.)
> Short-billed Marsh Wren (Colo. and Wyo.; bred in Ut.)
> Wood Thrush (Colo.)
> Gray-cheeked Thrush (Mont.)

Prothonotary Warbler (Colo. and Wyo.)
Parula Warbler (Colo. and Wyo.)
Magnolia Warbler (w. Tex., Colo., Wyo.)
Black-throated Blue Warbler (N.M., Colo., Wyo.)
Black-throated Green Warbler (Colo. and Mont.)
Cerulean Warbler (N.M. and Colo.)
Blackburnian Warbler (N.M. and Wyo.)
Chestnut-sided Warbler (Colo. and Wyo.)
Bay-breasted Warbler (Mont.)
Palm Warbler (Colo., Wyo., and Mont.)
Connecticut Warbler (Colo.)
Hooded Warbler (Colo.)
Canada Warbler (Colo.)
Scarlet Tanager (Colo. and Wyo.)
Rose-breasted Grosbeak (N.M., Colo., Wyo., and Mont.)
Indigo Bunting (Colo.)
Leconte's Sparrow (Colo.)
Field Sparrow (Colo.; bred in se. Mont.)
Swamp Sparrow (Mont.)

Others will undoubtedly be added to this list. Some of them have even reached the Pacific Coast, where their occurrence is far more accidental. Eastern species, such as the Black-poll Warbler, Tennessee Warbler, and others that migrate *regularly* through eastern Colorado, eastern Wyoming, and eastern Montana, or breed there, are described in the pages of this book.

Although the *A.O.U. Check-List* includes all of Lower California, western Canada, and Alaska, the author found that by sticking strictly to the western United States, he was able to eliminate between two hundred and two hundred and fifty species and subspecies, thereby whittling the book down to practical field-guide proportions. A few of the accidentals, especially sea-birds, that have been recorded but once or so and might never be recorded again, are excluded. Others, especially Canadian and Mexican accidentals which have been recorded only two or three times, but might reasonably be looked for in the future, are included.

Range. A thorough acquaintance with any existing State or local list should properly be made by the beginner. The importance of these lists can hardly be stressed too much. The writer has only given an abbreviated account of the ranges of each species; an account of the exact range and seasonal distribution would have more than doubled the size of this handbook. Only the range in the western United States is given. Many species have a much wider distribution. The Mallard, as an example, is found over a large part of the globe.

Subspecies. It is a challenge to the field student to be able to identify some of the more well-marked subspecies, but in this book subspecies are merely listed by name under each species, unless field distinctions are fairly obvious. I have used the words 'no apparent field differences' when identification is very difficult or impossible. Advanced students, referring to skins in their local museums, might work out ways of telling some of these, but a too thorough treatment in these pages might only make the beginner overconfident, and would lead to many errors. A more complete discussion of the subspecies problem will be found in the back of this book. Be sure to read it.

Voice. We make our first identification of a species, as a rule, by sight. Then we become familiar with its song or notes. A 'sizzling trill' or a 'bubbling warble' conveys but a wretched idea of the real effect produced by the voice of any particular bird; they are descriptions and help chiefly to fix in our minds a note or song we have already identified. Voice syllabifications in most standard bird works vary greatly, each author giving his own interpretation. There are a few species whose voices we often hear long before we become acquainted with the bird in life — such birds as the Poor-will and the Owls. Then there are those few, such as the small Flycatchers, that are far more easily recognized by voice than by appearance.

Many birds have a variety of call-notes, and often more than one distinct song. Many Warblers, for example, have two songs. These pages will not attempt to treat the voices of birds more than briefly. In a few difficult cases, in analyzing songs, I have resorted to a system of symbols similar to that used by Aretas Saunders in his Eastern classic *A Guide to Bird Songs*. The serious student should secure a copy of *Birds of the Pacific States* by Ralph Hoffmann. This book, which makes an excellent companion volume to this guide, goes into more detail about voice and notes than I have been able to do in this limited space. Hoffmann's interpretations are much clearer than those of most other writers.

Identification by elimination. Identification by elimination plays an important part in field work. For example, there are six similar species of Junco in the Western States. Only one, the Oregon Junco, occurs normally in the Pacific States, so the student in that area, knowing this, does not usually bother about the other five, once having ascertained the bird in question to be a Junco. If he is on the lookout for rarities (the Gray-headed Junco or the Slate-colored Junco, both of which occur occasionally or rarely in the Pacific States), he looks for Juncos with *gray* sides. Any Junco with *buffy* or *rusty* sides is at once eliminated as being the ordinary species.

Then, of course, there is *elimination by habitat.* One would not expect to find a Rosy Finch in the desert or a House Finch above timber line. Habitats and 'life zones' are very distinct in the West. A visitor coming from the East, where life zones are more uniform, is constantly astonished when told he should look for the Blue Grosbeak only in the willow bottoms, the Plain Titmouse in the oaks or pinyons in the foothills, and not to expect the Steller's Jay below the pines. These altitudinal life zones are very well marked, and each has its own bird life. The beginner should learn what to expect in each one of his local zones. Although this book indicates habitat preferences, it makes little formal mention of zones (other than high mountains, foothills, deserts, valleys, etc.), as the distribution of many species varies somewhat in different parts of the West and at different seasons.

Caution in sight records. One should always use a certain amount of caution in making identifications, especially where rarities are concerned. The ornithologist of the old school seldom accepted a sight record unless it was made along the barrel of a shotgun. Today it is difficult for the average person to secure collecting privileges; moreover, a large proportion of the real rarities show up in parks, preserves, sanctuaries, or on municipal property where collecting is out of the question. There is no reason why we should not trust our eyes — at least after we have acquired a good basic knowledge of the commoner species. Caution should be the keynote. A quick field observer who does not temper his snap judgment with a bit of caution is like a fast car without brakes.

A FIELD GUIDE
TO WESTERN BIRDS

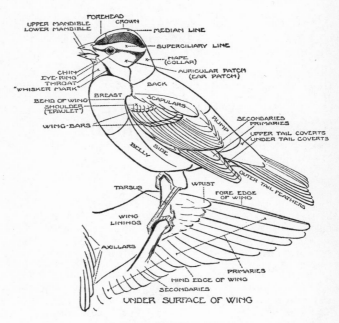

TOPOGRAPHY OF A BIRD
Showing terms used in this volume

LOONS: GAVIIDÆ

LARGE swimming birds, larger than most Ducks and with shorter necks than Geese. The sharp-pointed bill is a characteristic feature. Like the Grebes, they are expert divers. In flight the outline is gangly, with a slight downward sweep to the neck and the big feet projecting beyond the tail.

COMMON LOON. *Gavia immer.* Subsp. (Illus., pp. 2, 12.)
Descr. 28–36. Size of small Goose. *Breeding plumage:*— Head and neck glossy black with white collar; back checkered with black and white; under parts white. Adult in this plumage unmistakable. (Pacific Loon has back of head pale gray.) *Winter plumage:* — Mostly grayish; top of head, back of neck, and back dark gray; cheek, throat, and under parts white. In this plumage the bird resembles closely both the Pacific and the Red-throated Loons, but may be recognized by its large size and stouter bill. Its profile is also less snaky. In spite of its name it is no commoner coastwise than the other two species. (See Pacific and Red-throated Loons.) In flight Loons appear like big Mergansers with legs trailing out behind, but with much slower wing-beats than any Duck. On the water, they appear to be long-bodied, low-lying birds. Sometimes they swim with only the head and neck above water. Cormorants resemble Loons but are much blacker, especially in winter, and in flight the longer neck and tail and faster wing-beats are quite evident. Cormorants swim with the bill pointed slightly upward at an angle.
Voice: — On breeding grounds, loud laughing and yodeling calls; at night or before a storm, a rapid ringing *a-oo-oo.*
Range: — Breeds on fresh-water lakes from Can. s. to Wyo., e. Ore., and ne. Calif. (formerly); migrates throughout w. U.S.; winters along Pacific Coast.
Subsp. (No apparent field differences): (1) Common Loon, *G. i. immer*; (2) Lesser Loon, *G. i. elasson.*

PACIFIC LOON. *Gavia arctica pacifica.* (Illus. pp. 2, 12.)
Descr. 23–24. Similar in size to Red-throated Loon. *Breeding plumage:* — The *gray* hind-neck and black throat make good field-marks. *Winter plumage:* — Very similar to the other Loons at this season. About the size of the Red-throated Loon, but with more contrast between dark crown and light cheek and lacking the *speckled* back of that species. Instead, the markings of the back often have a scaly effect. The bill is quite as slender as that of the Red-throat, but is straight, not slightly upturned.

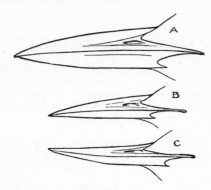

BILLS OF LOONS
A. Common   B. Pacific   C. Red-throated

The Common Loon, which it resembles at a distance in pattern, is a larger bird with a much thicker bill.

Range: — Pacific Coast in migration and winter, occasional at other seasons; accidental inland.

RED-THROATED LOON. *Gavia stellata.* (Illus. pp. 2, 12.)
Descr. 24–27. Smaller than Common Loon; nearer size of Merganser. *Breeding plumage:* — Gray head and *rufous-red* throat-patch unmistakable. *Winter plumage:* — Mainly *grayish* and white in color, like the Pacific Loon, but back speckled with white, giving a paler appearance at long range. In many individuals, the gray on the head and hind-neck is pale, merging into the white and offering none of the black-and-white contrast of the Pacific and Common Loons. The bill of this bird is one of the best field-marks. It seems to be slightly *upturned*, a character that is apparent at a considerable distance. The bills of the Pacific and Common Loons are quite straight.

Range: — Migrant and winter visitant along coast; occasional inland.

GREBES: COLYMBIDÆ

THE Grebes are Duck-like swimming water-birds; poor fliers but expert divers. They may be distinguished from the Ducks by the pointed bill, narrow head and neck, and tailless appearance. The Grebes normally hold their necks quite erect; Loons and Ducks do so mostly when alarmed.

HOLBOELL'S GREBE. *Colymbus grisegena holboelli.* (Illus. p. 12.)
Descr. 18–20. Much larger than any other Grebe, except the Western Grebe; large as a fair-sized Duck. *Breeding plumage:* — Body of bird gray, shading to white below; neck rufous-red; cheeks white; crown black; bill yellowish. *Winter plumage:* — The most familiar plumage. Generally grayish in color; top of head darker; often with a *conspicuous white crescent-shaped mark* on side of head (absent in first-year birds). In flight the bird shows two white patches on each wing. There are several species of birds found in the same waters as this species during the colder months with which it might be confused. The Holboell's Grebe may be distinguished from the Horned and Eared Grebes by its larger size, much heavier head and neck, large dull *yellow* bill, and more uniform gray coloration. (The two smaller Grebes have contrasting white cheeks, white necks, and dark bills.) It can be distinguished from the Loons at long range by its grayer face and neck and dull yellow bill. Loons, on the water, at a distance, appear as long-bodied birds with proportionately shorter necks, whereas the Grebe is a shorter-bodied bird that seems to be all head and neck. In flight, at a distance, this Grebe resembles the female Red-breasted Merganser, but it beats its wings more slowly, has two white patches on each wing instead of one, and holds its neck bent slightly downward — this last a very good field character. The Merganser flies with its neck and body held perfectly horizontal.
Range: — Breeds from n. Wash. and Mont. n.; winters along coast; a rare migrant inland.

HORNED GREBE. *Colymbus auritus.* (Illus. p. 12.)
Descr. 13–15. A small Grebe, typical of lakes, bays, and large bodies of water. *Breeding plumage:* — Head black, with conspicuous buff-colored ear-tufts; neck and flanks rufous-red; back gray; under parts white. *Winter plumage:* — Contrastingly patterned with dark gray and white. Top of head, line down back of neck, and back dark gray; under parts, neck, and cheeks clear white and sharply defined. (See Eared Grebe.)
Range: — Breeds from n. Mont. n.; winters along coast; a few migrate on inland lakes.

EARED GREBE. *Colymbus nigricollis californicus.* (Illus. p. 12.)
Descr. 12–14. *Breeding plumage:* — Smaller than Horned Grebe. Also has buffy facial tufts, but neck *black* instead of chestnut as in that species, and black feathers of crown crestlike instead of flat. *Winter plumage:* — Very similar to that of Horned Grebe. Dark gray and white but dark of head and neck *broader and less clearly defined*, giving a 'dirtier' look. There is

almost invariably a suffused whitish patch in the gray on each
side of the head just back of the ear (see diagram). Neck is
more slender; bill is slimmer and appears slightly upturned. On
the water, the rear parts of the Eared Grebe seem to ride higher.
Range: — Breeds locally, chiefly e. of Cascades and Sierras,
from Can. to e. Calif., n. Ariz., and N.M.; winters along entire
coast and inland from s. Calif. and N.M. s.

MEXICAN GREBE (LEAST GREBE). *Colymbus dominicus
brachypterus.* (Illus. p. 12.)
Descr. 10. A very small dark Grebe, much smaller than the
similarly shaped Pied-billed Grebe, with a slender *black* pointed
bill instead of a thick pale or pied bill.
Range: — Fresh ponds, marshes, and resacas of s. Tex.

WESTERN GREBE. *Æchmophorus occidentalis.* (Illus. p. 12.)
Descr. 22–29. A large Grebe, with an extremely long, slender
neck. In any plumage it is an all *black-and-white* bird. Top
of head, line on back of neck, and back, black; cheeks, neck, and
under parts white. Bill light yellow. The contrasting black-
and-white coloration and single white wing-patch distinguish it
from the winter Holboell's Grebe, which has two white patches
on each wing. The winter Holboell's Grebe is a gray-looking,
instead of a black-and-white, bird.
Range: — Breeds e. of Cascades and Sierras from Can. to n.
Calif., Ut., and Colo.; winters along coast; some migrate inland,
chiefly w. of Rockies.

PIED-BILLED GREBE. *Podilymbus podiceps podiceps.* (Illus.
p. 12.)
Descr. 12–15. A common Grebe of the ponds, creeks, and
marshes. *Breeding plumage:* — Gray-brown, darkest on top of
head and back; throat-patch and spot across bill black. *Winter
plumage:* — Browner, without throat-patch and bill-mark. The
thick, *rounded* bill of the Pied-bill will distinguish it in profile at
a distance, in any plumage, from the Horned or Eared Grebes
with their slender, pointed bills. The Pied-bill has no well-
marked white *patches* in the wing as have all the other Grebes.
Voice: — A Cuckoo-like *cow-cow-cow-cow-cow-cow-cowk-cowk-
cowk* or *kum-kum-kum,* etc.
Range: — Breeds on fresh-water ponds and marshes throughout
w. U.S.; winters in Pacific States and from Ariz. s.

ALBATROSSES: DIOMEDEIDÆ

BLACK-FOOTED ALBATROSS. *Diomedea nigripes.* (Illus.
p. 16.)
Descr. 29–36. Wing-spread 7 ft. Albatrosses are birds of the

open ocean, much larger than any Gulls and with wings which are proportionately far longer. These tremendously long saber-like wings and the rigid Shearwater-like gliding and banking identify this species, the only Albatross now found regularly along the Pacific Coast. It is seldom seen from shore. The plumage is dusky above and below, but at close range a whitish face and pale areas toward the tips of the wings can be seen. Some birds, presumably adults, show white patches at the base of the tail; these are usually not seen as often as dark-rumped birds.

Range: — Pacific Ocean, usually offshore.

SHORT-TAILED ALBATROSS. *Diomedea albatrus.*
Descr. 33–37. Wing-spread 7 ft. A white Albatross, with blackish primaries and tip of tail. Formerly regular along Pacific Coast, but thought to have ceased coming during the last generation. However, as individuals are still recorded in Alaskan waters, it should be looked for off the coast of the Pacific States. Its white body will readily distinguish it from the all-dark Black-footed Albatross. The Laysan Albatross, *D. immutabilis,* another white-bodied species, is a remote possibility but has a *black* instead of a white back. The immature Short-tailed Albatross is dark brown and resembles the Black-footed Albatross, but the bill and feet are *pink or flesh-colored.*

SHEARWATERS AND FULMARS: PROCELLARIIDÆ

SHEARWATERS are Gull-like sea-birds, usually found well off-shore; uniform dusky, or dark above and white below. Their flight, several flaps and a sail, banking on stiff wings in the wave-troughs, is distinctive. A Shearwater's wings are proportionately narrower than a Gull's and the tail is not so fanlike. Six species occur off the Pacific Coast. Three are of the black-breasted type, three are white-breasted. For convenience, the following table is given to show their proportionate probability of occurrence.

Black-breasted Shearwaters
1. Sooty Shearwater — abundant
2. Slender-billed Shearwater — common
3. Pale-footed Shearwater — very rare

White-breasted Shearwaters
1. Pink-footed Shearwater — common
2. Black-vented Shearwater — common
3. New Zealand Shearwater — rare

Fulmars are Gull-like birds similar to, but more robust than, Shearwaters.

SLENDER-BILLED SHEARWATER. *Puffinus tenuirostris.*
Descr. 14. A dark-bellied Shearwater; looks all black at a distance; can best be told from the Sooty Shearwater by its
smaller size and somewhat darker wing-linings. (Sooty has
pale grayish-white linings.) The best time to look for this
species offshore is in the late fall and early winter after the
Sooty Shearwater has decreased in numbers.
Range: — Pacific Coast, chiefly offshore.

SOOTY SHEARWATER. *Puffinus griseus.* (Illus. p. 13.)
Descr. 16–18. Smaller than the California Gull. Uniform dusky
brown; under surface of the wings pale or whitish. A Gull-like
sea-bird that looks all black at a distance (dark Jaegers always
show white at the base of the primaries). This is the commonest
Shearwater, great numbers often being seen offshore, especially
in late spring, in summer, and in fall. It is the only one frequently seen in abundance from the land.
Range: — Pacific Ocean, along coast and offshore.

BLACK-VENTED SHEARWATER. *Puffinus opisthomelas.*
Descr. 12½–15. A white-breasted Shearwater similar in appearance to the Pink-footed Shearwater but much smaller and with
a more rapid wing-motion. It can further be distinguished from
the Pink-footed species by white wing-linings and blackish bill
(Pink-foot usually has grayer wing-linings and a pale flesh-
colored bill). This species is commonest in fall and early winter.
Range: — Chiefly coast of Calif.; occasional in Wash.

PALE-FOOTED SHEARWATER. *Puffinus carneipes.*
Descr. 19½. Very rare. Over a dozen have been taken off Point
Pinos, Calif. A dark-bellied Shearwater, a trifle *larger* than the
abundant Sooty Shearwater, from which it can be distinguished
by its pale *whitish bill, flesh-colored feet,* and lack of pale wing-
linings.

PINK-FOOTED SHEARWATER. *Puffinus creatopus.* (Illus.
p. 13.)
Descr. 19. Four Shearwaters occur *commonly* off the Pacific
Coast. Two appear all black at a distance, and two are two-
toned — dark above and white below. The two white-bellied
species, the Pink-footed and Black-vented, are frequently associated with the abundant Sooty Shearwaters and can easily be
distinguished by size. The Pink-foot is a bit *larger* than the
Sooty Shearwater, the Black-vent is much smaller. The present
species is an easier and more graceful flier than the Sooty, making fewer wing-strokes. It occurs chiefly in summer and fall.
The Pink-foot occurs along most of the coast, the Black-vent
chiefly off Calif. (See Black-vented Shearwater.)
Range: — Pacific Coast, offshore.

NEW ZEALAND SHEARWATER. *Thyellodroma bulleri.*
Descr. 16½. This rare Shearwater might be looked for in fall or winter off the coast of Calif. It is a white-bellied Shearwater, and might be told from the two other white-bellied species by the *gray back*, which contrasts conspicuously with the blackish color of the head and tail and wings. The black areas on the primaries and lesser wing-coverts are said to form a wide inverted W when the bird is on the wing. This should be a good mark. At close range the feet are *yellowish* instead of flesh-colored as in the two similar species. It is said to have a different and more airy style of flight.
Range: — Occasional fall or winter visitor to coast of Calif. (most records off Point Pinos). Also recorded in Ore. and Wash.

PACIFIC FULMAR. *Fulmarus glacialis rodgersi.* (Illus. p. 16.)
Descr. 17–19. Slightly smaller than the California Gull. *Light phase:* — Head and under parts white; back and wings gray; wings darker toward tip, but with *no black markings* as in most Gulls; bill yellow. Resembles a California Gull in this phase, but appearance in the air is different. The wings are held quite stiff and the bird glides and scales in the manner of a Shearwater, or even more like an Albatross. *Dark phase:* — Uniform smoky gray; wing-tips darker, bill yellow. In this plumage the bird remotely resembles the Sooty Shearwater but is much paler. The Fulmar's bill is stubbier than a Gull's or Shearwater's, giving a Dove-like appearance to the head. Some Fulmars are mottled with white on the wings. These formerly went under the obsolete name of Rodgers's Fulmar.
Range: — Pacific Coast, offshore, in migration and winter.

STORM PETRELS: HYDROBATIDÆ

THESE Petrels are the little dark birds that flit over the surface of the sea, usually well offshore, in the wake of fishing boats and ocean-going vessels. Three of the five Pacific species are all black in general appearance, and are difficult to tell apart in the field.

FORK-TAILED PETREL. *Oceanodroma furcata.* (Illus. p. 13.)
Descr. 8. A *pearly-gray* Petrel, absolutely unlike all the other Petrels, which are blackish.
Range: — Breeds on ids. off n. Calif. and Ore.; migrates and winters along entire coast, offshore.

BEAL'S PETREL. *Oceanodroma leucorhoa.* Subsp. (Illus. p. 13.)

Descr. 8. A black Petrel with a *conspicuous white rump*. The three other black Petrels have *dark* rumps. The Leach's Petrel of the Atlantic is a race of this species.

Range: — Breeds on ocean ids. from Alaska to Farallon Ids., Calif.; winters offshore from Wash. to s. Calif.

Subsp. (No apparent field differences): (1) Beal's Petrel, *O. l. beali*; (2) Kaeding's Petrel, *O. l. kaedingi.*

BLACK PETREL. *Oceanodroma melania.* (Illus. p. 13.)

Descr. 9. Of the three all-black Petrels found off the coast of southern California in summer, this is the largest and probably the most common. It nests on the Coronados Ids. off San Diego, in company with the less common Socorro Petrel. (See Socorro and Ashy Petrels.) It can be told from those two birds by its larger size, longer wings, and more languid flight (suggestive of Black Tern).

Range: — Calif.; breeds on Coronados Ids. off San Diego; wanders n. to Marin Co.

ASHY PETREL. *Oceanodroma homochroa.* (Illus. p. 13.)

Descr. 7½. The smallest of the three all-black Petrels. At times it can be seen together with the Black Petrel off the coast of central Calif. When such comparison is possible it can be told without much trouble by its decidedly smaller size, shorter wings, and more fluttery flight. At very close range it shows a certain amount of white on the under side of the wings, and it has shorter legs.

Range: — Coast of Calif.; breeds on Farallon Ids. and Santa Cruz Id.

SOCORRO PETREL. *Oceanodroma socorroënsis.*

Descr. 7¾. One of the three all-black Petrels. Breeds in company with the Black Petrel on the Coronados Ids. and is difficult to distinguish from that species. When it can be compared, it will be seen to be smaller and to have a grayer rump. A small percentage of Socorros have a touch of white on the sides of the rump but seldom forming a conspicuous unbroken patch as in the Beal's Petrel. Some authorities consider it but a race of the Beal's Petrel. Its flight is almost exactly like that of that species and consequently quite different from the other two all-black Petrels. Like the Beal's Petrel it leaps about like a Nighthawk; the Black Petrel has a much lazier movement, and the Ashy Petrel a more fluttery flight (R. C. Murphy).

Range: — Coast of s. Calif.; breeds on Coronados Ids. off San Diego.

TROPIC–BIRDS: PHAËTHONTIDÆ

RED-BILLED TROPIC-BIRD. *Phaëthon æthereus.* (Illus. p. 16.)
Descr. 24–40; tail 7½–26. A slender white sea-bird, nearly size of a California Gull, with a *heavy red bill*, black patch through each side of face, and two extremely long *central tail-feathers* — so long and streaming that they could be more easily compared (in length) to those of the Scissor-tailed Flycatcher than to the needle-pointed outer tail-feathers of the Terns. The rapid Pigeon-like flight (steady wing-beats) and the long tail are distinctive. When the bird sits on the water, it rides with its tail cocked like a Wren's.
Range: — Occasional off s. Calif., well offshore.

PELICANS: PELECANIDÆ

EXTREMELY large water-birds with long flat bills and tremendous throat-pouches. Pelicans fly in orderly lines, alternating several flaps with a short sail, each bird in the flock playing follow-my-leader, flapping and sailing in rhythm, apparently taking the cue from the bird in front. In flight they draw their heads back on their shoulders.

WHITE PELICAN. *Pelecanus erythrorhynchos.* (Illus. p. 16.)
Descr. 55–70. Wing-spread 9 ft. A huge white bird with black primaries in the wing and a great yellow throat-pouch. Flies with head hunched back on shoulders, and long flat bill resting on curved neck. Often flies at a great height. Swans have no black wing-tips; the Wood Ibis has black primaries, but flies with neck extended and long legs trailing. The Snow Goose has a similar pattern but is much smaller, flies with neck extended, and has a small bill.
Range: — Breeds locally on inland lakes from Can. s. to s. Calif., w. Nev., n. Ut., and Wyo. (Yellowstone); migrates through interior to Mex.; winters from Calif. s.

CALIFORNIA BROWN PELICAN. *Pelecanus occidentalis californicus.* (Illus. p. 16.)
Descr. 50–54. Wing-spread 6½ ft. A ponderous, dark water-bird with more or less white about the head and neck (in adults). Immatures have dark heads. Flies with its head hunched back on its shoulders and its long flat bill resting comfortably on its curved neck. Its size and flight, a few flaps and a sail, proclaim it a Pelican; its dusky color at once eliminates its white relative.

Range: — Coastal; breeds along coast of s. Calif.; wanders n. after breeding season to Ore. and Wash.; casual in Ariz.

CORMORANTS: PHALACROCORACIDÆ

LARGE dark water-birds, as large as, or larger than, any of the Ducks. To be confused chiefly with the Loons, or Geese, but the tail is longer and wing-action more rapid. In flight, the neck is held slightly above the horizontal (Loon's neck droops slightly). Of course, in winter, when Loons are paler, Cormorants can be told by their very blackness, especially the adults, which are black beneath as well as above. Loons are always clear white below. Flocks of Cormorants usually fly in line or wedge formation very much like Geese and are sometimes called 'Nigger Geese.' A large dark bird perched in an *upright position* on some rock or buoy over the water can hardly be anything else. Swimming, they lie low like Loons, but with necks more erect and snake-like, and bills pointed upward *at an angle*.

DOUBLE-CRESTED CORMORANT. *Phalacrocorax auritus.* Subsp. (Illus. pp. 11, 16.)
Descr. 30–36. Any Cormorant found inland on large bodies of water in w. U.S. can quite safely be called this species. Along the coast it may be told from the other two Cormorants by its bright *orange-yellow* throat-pouch. (See Brandt's Cormorant.)
Range: — Pacific Coast and locally on large bodies of water inland in Calif., Ore., Ut., Ariz., and w. Nev., and along Great Plains.
Subsp. (No apparent field differences): (1) Double-crested Cormorant, *P. a. auritus*; (2) Farallon Cormorant, *P. a. albociliatus*; (3) White-crested Cormorant, *P. a. cincinatus*.

BRANDT'S CORMORANT. *Phalacrocorax penicillatus.* (Illus. pp. 11, 16.)
Descr. 33. About the size of the Double-crested (Farallon) Cormorant but does not have the yellow throat-pouch. Instead it has a *buffy-brown band across the throat* and in the breeding season a *blue* throat-pouch. Young birds are brownish, with paler under parts. Young Double-crested Cormorants are similar in size but usually *whiter* on the under parts, and show the yellow pouch. (If a young Cormorant has a decidedly whitish breast it is a Double-crest; if the breast is buffy or pale brown, it might be a Double-crest but more likely a Brandt's. If the under parts are deep rich brown, the bird is a Brandt's.)
Range: — Pacific Coast.

HEADS OF CORMORANTS

A. Baird's   B. Double-crested   C. Brandt's

BAIRD'S CORMORANT. *Phalacrocorax pelagicus resplendens.*
(Illus. pp. 11, 16.)
Descr. 25½. Noticeably smaller than the other two Cormorants,
a good mark when comparison is possible. Much more iridescent and glossy at close range in good light. It can also be
told by its more slender neck, small head, and much *thinner
bill.* In the breeding season (February to June) it has a *white
patch* on each flank near the tail. This is especially conspicuous
in flight. The throat-pouch is dull red, but this can be seen only
at very close range.
Range: — Pacific Coast.

DARTERS: ANHINGIDÆ

WATER-TURKEY. *Anhinga anhinga.*
Descr. 34. Similar to a Cormorant but much slimmer; mainly
blackish with *large silvery patches* on the fore part of the wings,
and with a long white-tipped tail and a *long serpentine neck*;
it perches like a Cormorant, in upright posture, on some tree
or snag, but the neck is much snakier. In flight it progresses
with alternate flapping and sailing, the slender neck extended in
front, the long tail spread fanwise. Females have pale buffy
breasts, males blackish. Immature birds are largely brownish
instead of blackish.
Range: — Occurs on lower Colo. R. near Yuma; casual in N.M.
and Colo.

MAN–O'–WAR BIRDS: FREGATIDÆ

MAN-O'-WAR BIRD. *Fregata magnificens.* (Illus. p. 16.)
Descr. 40. Wing-spread 7½ ft. Voyagers in warmer seas often
see long-winged black birds, with forked Barn-Swallow-like
tails, soaring with great ease. These are the Man-o'-Wars, or
Frigate-birds. Their wings are longer in proportion to the body-
bulk than those of any other sea-bird. *Male:* — Black, with
orange throat-patch. *Female:* — White breast. *Immature:* —
Whole head and under parts white.
Range: — Occasional along coast of s. Calif.

HERONS AND BITTERNS: ARDEIDÆ

LONG-LEGGED, long-necked wading birds with long sharp-
pointed bills. In sustained flight their heads are drawn back to
their shoulders. Cranes and Ibises, which are otherwise quite
Heron-like, fly with necks outstretched.

HERONS AND CRANES IN FLIGHT
A. Sandhill Crane   B. Great Blue Heron

HORNED GREBE
SUMMER   WINTER

EARED GREBE
SUMMER   WINTER

MEXICAN GREBE

PIED-BILLED GREBE
SUMMER

WESTERN GREBE

HOLBOELL'S GREBE
SUMMER   WINTER

RED-THROATED LOON
SUMMER   WINTER

PACIFIC LOON
SUMMER   WINTER

COMMON LOON
SUMMER   WINTER

WHITE BREAST
DARK BREAST

PINK-
FOOTED
SHEAR-
WATER

SOOTY SHEAR-
WATER

WHITE
PATCHES

SKUA

SQUARE-CUT
TAIL

FORK-
TAILED PETREL

PEARLY GRAY

BLACK
PETREL

ALL DARK

WHITE
RUMP

LIGHT PHASE

ASHY
PETREL

BEAL'S
PETREL

POINTED
CENTRAL
TAIL-FEATHERS

DARK
PHASE

PARASITIC
JAEGER

BLUNT
CENTRAL
TAIL-FEATHER

LONG-
TAILED
JAEGER

LONG CENTRAL
TAIL-FEATHERS

POMARINE
JAEGER

SHEARWATERS
PETRELS
AND
JAEGERS

GREAT BLUE HERON. *Ardea herodias.* Subsp. (Illus. pp. 12, 17.)
Descr. 42–52. This great bird, often called 'crane' by country people, stands about four feet tall, and is, next to the Sandhill Crane, the largest wading bird common in the Western States. Its long legs, long neck, and sharp-pointed bill, and, in flight, its drawn-in neck, mark the bird as a Heron. The great size and blue-gray coloration, whiter about the head and neck, identify it as this species.
Voice: — A series of three or four low, hoarse croaks.
Range: — Shores, marshes, lakes, and streams from Can. to Mex.; tends to migrate from colder sections in winter.
Subsp. (No apparent field differences): (1) Great Blue Heron, *A. h. herodias*; (2) Treganza's Heron, *A. h. treganzai*; (3) Northwestern Coast Heron, *A. h. fannini*; (4) California Heron, *A. h. hyperonca.*

AMERICAN EGRET. *Casmerodius albus egretta.* (Illus. p. 17.)
Descr. 37–42. A large Heron of snowy-white plumage, with black legs and feet and a *yellow bill.* The Brewster's Snowy Egret is also white, but is much smaller and has a black or blackish bill instead of yellow.
Range: — Breeds in Ore. and Calif.; wandering birds may be seen along Rio Grande and perhaps elsewhere in w. U.S.

BREWSTER'S SNOWY EGRET. *Egretta thula brewsteri.* (Illus. p. 17.)
Descr. 20–27. The western race of the Snowy Egret. A medium-sized White Heron with a *black bill*, black legs, and *yellow feet.* The American Egret is much larger and has a yellow bill and black feet, almost the reverse in color of those parts in the Snowy.
Range: — Breeds in Calif., Colo., and Ut.; migrates or summers in Wyo., Nev., Ariz., N.M., and w. Tex.

REDDISH EGRET. *Dichromanassa rufescens.* (Illus. p. 17.)
Descr. 29. A medium-sized, shaggy-necked, loose-feathered Heron, larger than a Snowy Egret, smaller than an American Egret. *Dark phase:* — Blue-gray with a pale maroon or buffy brown head and neck, and a *flesh-colored, black-tipped bill. White phase:* — Scarcer; appears like American Egret, but shorter and stouter, legs *bluish.* When it is feeding, the quickest way to pick it out is by its clowning actions. The only *necessary* recognition mark to be remembered for either plumage is the flesh-colored, black-tipped bill.
Range: — Gulf Coast of Tex.; occasional in s. Calif. (San Diego).

LOUISIANA HERON. *Hydranassa tricolor ruficollis.*

Descr. 26. Occasional in southern Calif. A slender, medium-sized Heron, dark in color, with a clear white belly. The contrasting white belly is the key-mark in any plumage.

LITTLE BLUE HERON. *Florida cærulea cærulea.*
Descr. 20–29. *Adult:* — A medium-sized, slender Heron, slaty blue, with a maroon head and neck; legs dark. The adult, like the Green Heron, appears quite blackish at a distance, but the latter bird is smaller with much shorter, more yellow legs. *Immature:* — Snowy white, often with a tinge of blue in the primaries; legs dull *greenish*; bill *bluish* tipped with black. Some Snowy Egrets, especially young birds, are frequently suspected of being Little Blues because of greenish leg coloration. Many Snowys show a stripe of yellow or greenish up the posterior side of the legs as the bird walks away from the observer. The thicker bill, with its bluish base, and the lack of the shuffling foot-motions which are so characteristic of the Snowy, will identify this Eastern species.
Range: — E. U.S.; occasional or accidental in Calif.

ANTHONY'S GREEN HERON. *Butorides virescens anthonyi.*
Descr. 16–18½. A small dark Heron with comparatively short greenish-yellow legs. Elevates a shaggy crest when alarmed. Looks quite black and Crow-like at a distance, but flies with slower, more arched, wing-beats. At close range neck and face are rich chestnut.
Voice: — A series of *kucks* or a loud *skyow.*
Range: — Breeds from Portland, Ore., and s. Ariz. s.; winters from s. Calif. s.

BLACK-CROWNED NIGHT HERON. *Nycticorax nycticorax hoactli.* (Illus. p. 17.)
Descr. 23–28. A chunky, rather short-legged Heron. *Adult:* — The only Heron that is black-backed and pale gray or white below; wings gray. *Immature:* — Brown, spotted and streaked with white. Resembles American Bittern, but gray-brown, rather than rich, warm brown. It beats its wings more slowly and lacks the broad black wing-tips of the Bittern.
Voice: — Call, a flat *quok,* is unmistakable.
Range: — Breeds from e. Wash. and s. Wyo. s. to Mex.; winters n. to Ore. and Ut. (a few).

AMERICAN BITTERN. *Botaurus lentiginosus.* (Illus. p. 17.)
Descr. 23–34. In crossing a marsh we frequently flush this large, stocky brown bird. It is rarely seen perching like the other Herons. The dark wing-tips, contrasting with the warm brown of the rest of the bird, distinguish it from the brown young Night Heron. When silhouetted in flight, the faster wing-beats

and the less curved wings are the Bittern's marks. Contrary to many a person's preconceived idea, the Least Bittern resembles it but little. The latter bird is much less than half the size and is contrastingly patterned with buff and black.

Voice: — The pumping, the 'song' of the Bittern, which we hear in the swamps in the spring might be rendered thus: *oong-ka-choonk* — *oong-ka-choonk* — *oong-ka-choonk*, etc. Distorted by distance, the *ka* is often the only audible syllable and sounds like the driving of a stake into the mud. Flushing note, a rapid throaty *kok-kok-kok*.

Range: — Breeds from Can. s. to s. Calif., cent. Ariz., and n. N.M. (probably). Winters chiefly from Calif. s. and occasionally as far n. as Ore. and Wash.

LEAST BITTERN. *Ixobrychus exilis.* Subsp. (Illus. p. 17.)
Descr. 12–14. By far the smallest of the Heron family, nearer size of a Rail. When discovered, it usually flushes close at hand from its hiding-place in the marsh, flies weakly for a short distance, and drops in again. The *large buff wing-patches* and black back distinguish it from any of the Rails, which are quite uniform in coloration. Beginners sometimes call Green Herons Least Bitterns.

Voice: — The call, a soft *coo-coo-coo* coming from the marsh, is often the best indication of the bird's presence.

Range: — Breeds in Calif. and e. Ore.; occurs occasionally in Rocky Mt. States and on Great Plains in e. Wyo. and e. Colo.

Subsp. (No apparent field differences): (1) Western Least Bittern, *I. e. hesperis*; (2) Eastern Least Bittern, *I. e. exilis*.

WOOD IBISES: CICONIIDÆ

WOOD IBIS. *Mycteria americana.* (Illus. p. 17.)
Descr. 35–47. A very large white Heron-like bird with a dark, naked head and large black wing-tips; bill long, stout, and *decurved*. Distinguished in flight, at a distance, from the White Herons by the outstretched neck and the black in the wings and by the alternate flapping and sailing; from the White Pelican by its totally different proportions. Young birds are dark gray with a downy covering on the head and neck.

Range: — Summer visitor to lower Colo. R. in Ariz. and Calif.; occasional elsewhere in s. Calif. and in other W. States.

IBISES AND SPOONBILLS: THRESKIORNITHIDÆ

WHITE-FACED GLOSSY IBIS. *Plegadis guarauna.* (Illus. p. 17.)
Descr. 22–25. A medium-sized Heron-like bird with a long, *decurved* bill; largely bronzy-chestnut, but at a distance appears quite black, like a large black Curlew. At close range it shows a white border about the base of the bill. It flies with neck outstretched, with quicker wing-beats than a Heron, alternating flapping and sailing.
Range: — Breeds or summers from e. Ore., n. Ut., and Wyo. s. to Mex.; winters n. to s. Calif.

ROSEATE SPOONBILL. *Ajaia ajaja.*
Descr. 32. Occasional or accidental in southern California. A *bright-pink* Heron-like bird with a flat spoon-shaped bill. When feeding in the mud the flat bill is swung from side to side. In flight it extends its neck as does an Ibis, but the bird does not sail between wing-strokes so habitually. Immature birds are paler and whiter than adults.

SWANS: CYGNINÆ

VERY large white water-birds, larger and with much longer necks than Geese. Like some of the Geese, they migrate in stringy lines or V-shaped flocks. Their extremely long, slender necks which are fully extended in flight, and the lack of black wing-tips distinguish them from all other large white swimming birds (Snow Goose, White Pelican, etc.). Young birds are tinged with brown.

WHISTLING SWAN. *Cygnus columbianus.* (Illus. p. 24.)
Descr. 48–55. The only wild Swan in most of the West. Usually heard long before the wavering wedge-shaped flock can be detected high in the blue. The much more stream-lined necks, larger size, and lack of black wing-tips eliminate the Snow Goose. Young birds are dingy-looking, not white.
Voice: — High-pitched cooing notes, less harsh than 'honking' of Canada Goose. 'A musical, loud *woo-ho, woo-woo, woo-ho*' (J. Moffitt).
Range: — Winters in Calif., Ore., Ut., and Wyo. (Yellowstone); a migrant in Wash., Mont., and occasionally elsewhere.

TRUMPETER SWAN. *Cygnus buccinator.* (Illus. p. 24.)
Descr. 65. Very rare and local. Larger than Whistling Swan.

BROWN PELICAN
ADULT

WHITE PELICAN

MAN·O'·WAR·BIRD

MALE

IMMATURE

ADULT

DOUBLE·CRESTED CORMORANT

RED·BILLED TROPIC·BIRD

BAIRD'S CORMORANT
ADULT IN BREEDING PLUMAGE
(ABOVE)

BLACK·FOOTED ALBATROSS

LIGHT

DARK

FULMAR

BRANDT'S CORMORANT
ADULT

WHITE·FACED
GLOSSY IBIS

LEAST
BITTERN

WOOD IBIS

AMERICAN BITTERN

ADULT

GREEN
HERON

SANDHILL
CRANE

IMMATURE

BLACK·CROWNED
NIGHT·HERON

SNOWY EGRET

ADULT

BLACK·CROWNED
NIGHT·HERON

AMERICAN EGRET

GREAT BLUE
HERON

DARK
PHASE

REDDISH EGRET

LONG·LEGGED WADERS

Adults can usually be distinguished from the Whistling Swan at close range by the *all-black bill* without the yellow basal spot, but this is not infallible, as some Whistlers lack this spot. Perhaps it is best distinguished from transient Whistlers by its deeper voice in the localities where it is resident.

Voice: — Much louder, lower-pitched, and more bugle-like than that of Whistling Swan.

Range: — Breeds in Yellowstone Park, Wyo., Red Rock Lake, Mont., and neighboring lakes; also a migrant and winter resident in this area. Formerly more widely distributed.

GEESE: ANSERINÆ

LARGE waterfowl; larger, heavier-bodied, and with longer necks than Ducks. In flight some species assemble in V-formation. As is not the case with most Ducks, sexes are alike at all seasons. They are more terrestrial than Ducks and feed mainly on land (except Brant); are to be looked for in grass or grain or stubble fields.

CANADA GOOSE. *Branta canadensis.* Subsp. (Illus. p. 24.)
Descr. The most widespread Goose in the West and the only one that breeds there; a brownish bird with black head and neck that contrast strikingly with the light-colored breast. The most characteristic mark is the white patch that runs from under the chin on to the side of the head. Few people are unfamiliar with the long strings of Geese passing high overhead in V-formation. Their musical honking or barking often heralds the approach of a flock long before it can be seen.

Voice: — A deep double-syllabled 'honking' note, *ka-ronk* or *ha-lunk, ha-lunk.*

Subsp. COMMON CANADA GOOSE. *B. c. canadensis.*
35–42. Much larger than the White-fronted or the Snow Goose. The best-known race and the only one that breeds in w. U.S. Breeds from ne. Calif., n. Nev., n. Ut., and Wyo. n. into Can.; winters from Wash. and Yellowstone Park s. into Mex.

WHITE-CHEEKED GOOSE. *B. c. occidentalis.*
35. Slightly smaller than Canada Goose, with dark, chocolate-colored under parts. Winters along the coast from Puget Sound to n. Calif. (Del Norte and Humboldt Cos.). 'Voice higher-pitched than Common Canada, intermediate in tone between this form and Lesser Canada Goose' (J. Moffitt). The coastal habitat, dark under parts, and higher voice will identify this race.

LESSER CANADA GOOSE. *B. c. leucopareia.*

25–34. A medium-sized Goose, much smaller than the Canada Goose or about the size of the Snow and White-fronted Geese, with which it often associates. Some birds are dark, some quite light. Under parts usually lighter than Cackling Goose. Winters from Wash. to Mex., very abundant in interior valleys of Calif. Voice considerably higher pitched than Common Canada but lower than Cackling Goose: *lo-ank, lo-ank, a-lank, a-lank* (J. Moffitt).

CACKLING GOOSE. *B. c. minima.*
23–25. Hardly larger than a Mallard, slightly smaller, stubbier-necked, and with darker under parts than the Lesser Canada Goose, with which it often associates. In some Cackling Geese there is another partial white collar near the base of the black neck, but this is not a good subspecific character, as individuals of other races sometimes show this. The flight notes are an extremely high-pitched yelping *yelk, yelk, a-lick, a-lick,* or *lick, lick, lick* (J. Moffitt). Winters mainly in Sacramento and San Joaquin Valleys of California.

AMERICAN BRANT. *Branta bernicla hrota.*
Descr. Accidental in w. U.S. Similar to Black Brant but under parts *light*. In the common species the dark of the under parts extends clear to the vent. Both species have light flanks. On the water the two would be almost indistinguishable.

BLACK BRANT. *Branta nigricans.* (Illus. p. 24.)
Descr. 23–29. A small Goose, much smaller than the Common Canada; size of the Cackling Goose. It is strictly coastal, bunching in large, irregular flocks rather than in the strings or V-formation of most other Geese. The Brant resembles the Canada Goose somewhat, but has a black head, neck, and under parts instead of a black head and neck contrasting with a light breast. In other words, the fore parts of a Brant are black to the waterline; a Goose's breast flashes white above the water. The Brant has a small white patch on the neck instead of a large white patch on the face. Then, too, as with all smaller birds, its wing-beats are less slow and labored.
Voice: — A throaty *krrr-onk, krrr-onk* (J. Moffitt).
Range: — Winters in the larger bays and lagoons along the Pacific Coast; casual inland.

EMPEROR GOOSE. *Philacte canagica.* (Illus. p. 24.)
Descr. 26. Size of a White-fronted Goose. A rare visitor to the Pacific States. *Adult:* — A small blue-gray Goose handsomely scaled with black and white; identified by its *white head and hind-neck;* distinguished from the even rarer Blue Goose, which

also has a white head and neck, by its *black throat*, and, at very close range, by the yellow or orange legs (the Blue Goose has pink legs). Immature birds are not so distinctly marked and have the head and neck dusky, speckled with white. In flight this species is very characteristic with its short neck, short wings, and quick, stiff wing-beats.

Range: — A regular straggler in winter s. to Ore., and occasionally Calif.

WHITE-FRONTED GOOSE. *Anser albifrons.* Subsp. (Illus. p. 24.)

Descr. 27–30. Smaller than Common Canada Goose; similar in size to Lesser Snow and Lesser Canada. The commonest Goose in the Pacific States. *Adult:* — At a distance gray-brown, showing no contrast of black neck and light breast as in the Canada. When flying overhead the more uniform color below is at once apparent. At closer range it shows a pink bill, a clear white patch *on the front of the face*, black marks on the belly, and yellow or orange feet. *Immature:* — Dusky, with *yellow* feet, but otherwise without the distinctive marks of the adult. No other common Goose has yellow feet.

Voice: — Flight note, *kah-lah-a-luck*, high-pitched 'tootling,' usually uttered from one to three times; various other notes (J. Moffitt).

Subsp. WHITE-FRONTED GOOSE. *A. a. albifrons.*
Migrates chiefly through Pacific States, rare in Rocky Mt. region; winters in Calif.
TULE GOOSE. *A. a. gambeli.*
A large dark race that winters in the Sacramento Valley, Calif. Can be told in flight by large size, longer neck, and slower wing-beats. Voice harsher and deeper than above race.

LESSER SNOW GOOSE. *Chen hyperborea hyperborea.* (Illus. p. 24.)

Descr. 23–30. A *white* Goose, smaller than the Canada, with *black wing-tips*. Young birds are duskier, but still pale enough to be recognizable as Snow Geese.

Voice: — Notes similar to White-front but single-noted, not 'tootling.' 'Flight notes: loud, nasal, resonant *whouk-whouk, houck*, uttered singly, twice, or rarely three times' (J. Moffitt).

Range: — Occurs in migration in most of W. States. Winters in Pacific States, chiefly Calif.

BLUE GOOSE. *Chen cærulescens.*

Descr. Would be most apt to occur in company with Snow or White-fronted Geese. *Adult:* — A dusky Goose with a white

head and neck (see Emperor Goose). *Immature:* — Dusky in color, much darker than young Snow Goose; very similar to immature White-front, but has *pink* legs instead of yellow, and paler bluish wings.
Voice: — Exactly like Snow Goose.
Range: — Very rare or accidental in w. U.S.

ROSS'S GOOSE. *Chen rossi.* (Illus. p. 24.)
Descr. 23. Two sizes of white Geese are often found together in winter in the interior valleys of Calif. The Ross's Goose can be told from the Lesser Snow Goose by its *smaller size* (near size of Mallard) and *decidedly smaller bill,* which at very close range is seen to lack the black 'lips' of the larger bird. Young birds are somewhat paler than young Snow Geese.
Voice: — 'No loud notes like Snow Goose; a simple grunt-like *kug,* or weak *kek, kek* or *ke-gak, ke-gak,* usually uttered twice. No other California Goose utters a similar note' (J. Moffitt).
Range: — Winters in Calif. (Sacramento and San Joaquin Valleys); migrates ne. through Mont. (Great Falls).

TREE DUCKS: DENDROCYGNINÆ

BLACK-BELLIED TREE DUCK. *Dendrocygna autumnalis autumnalis.* (Illus. pp. 33, 40.)
Descr. 22. A large Duck with a short tail and long heavy legs; largely rusty with a black belly, black wings with *great white patches,* and a bright *coral-pink* bill. No other Duck resembles it. It has a slightly Goose-like aspect.
Voice: — A squealing whistle.
Range: — S. Tex.; accidental in Ariz. and s. Calif.

FULVOUS TREE DUCK. *Dendrocygna bicolor helva.* (Illus. pp. 33, 40.)
Descr. 20–21. A long-legged, Goose-like Duck, blackish above, pale cinnamon below; does not ordinarily frequent trees. In flight, long legs extending beyond tail, slightly drooped neck, and slow wing-beats (for a duck) are distinctive. On the wing the bird looks dark, with blackish wing-linings and a white ring at the base of the tail. The Cinnamon Teal is smaller, not Goose-like in shape, and of a deeper reddish color.
Voice: — A squealing double-noted whistle.
Range: — Cent. and s. Calif., cent. Nev., sw. Ariz., and s. Tex.

SURFACE–FEEDING DUCKS: ANATINÆ

DUCKS of this group, although not always confined to small bodies of water, are most characteristic of creeks, ponds, and marshes. They obtain their food by dabbling and tipping up rather than by diving. When frightened, they spring directly into the air instead of pattering before getting under way. They swim as a rule with the tail held quite clear of the water. Most birds of this group have a metallic *speculum*, or '*mirror*,' a rectangular patch situated at the hind edge of the wing.

MALLARD. *Anas platyrhynchos platyrhynchos.* (Illus. pp. 25, 28.)
Descr. 20–28. *Male:* — Similar to, but smaller than, domesticated Mallard of barnyard; grayish with green head, narrow white ring around neck, ruddy breast, and white tail. A few other Ducks have heads glossed with greenish and are, because of that, frequently mistaken for Mallards, but the white ring around the neck and the dark ruddy breast are diagnostic. *Female:* — A mottled brown Duck with whitish tail and conspicuous white borders *on each side* of metallic wing-patch. Female Pintails appear more stream-lined and have a white border on only one side of the wing-patch or speculum. The bill of the Mallard is *yellowish*. In sustained flight Mallards have a characteristic wing-stroke; it is slower than in most Ducks, and the downward sweep does not carry the wings much below the level of the body. The 'silvery' appearance of the under wings in flight is also a good field-mark.
Voice: — Female quacks like a barnyard Duck (so does female Gadwall). Male, a reedy *yeeb-yeeb*.
Range: — Breeds from Can. s. to Calif. and N.M.; winters n. to n. border of U.S.

NEW MEXICAN DUCK. *Anas diazi novimexicana.* (Illus. p. 25.)
Descr. 22. Like a very dark female Mallard, but male's bill greenish rather than yellow (female's bill indistinguishable); resembles closely the Black Duck and the Mottled Duck, but with a narrow white stripe on each side of the metallic speculum in the wing. (Black and Mottled Ducks do not occur in N.M.) Sexes alike.
Range: — N.M., chiefly along Rio Grande from El Paso to Albuquerque.

BLACK DUCK. *Anas rubripes.* (Illus. p. 28.)
Descr. 20–24. *Both sexes:* — Dark sooty brown with lighter

yellowish-brown head; feet brown or red; bill dull greenish or yellowish; metallic blue speculum on wing; under surface of wing silvery white. The Black Duck in flight, with its uniform dark coloration and flashing white wing-linings, is unmistakable. It resembles a very dark female Mallard but lacks the whitish tail and the white borders on the speculum.

Range: — E. U.S., w. rarely to e. Colo. and e. Wyo. Examples occasionally seen in Calif. might be liberated stock.

GADWALL. *Chaulelasmus streperus.* (Illus. pp. 25, 28.)
Descr. 19–21. *Male:* — A slender *gray* Duck with a white belly and a white patch on the *hind* edge of the wing. This white speculum is diagnostic. On the water the gray feathers of the flanks often conceal the white wing-patch; then the best mark is the black tail-coverts, which contrast sharply with the pale gray of the wing-coverts (see plate). *Female:* — Similar to male but browner; resembles in shape and general color female Pintail, but has white speculum. On the water it is likely to be confused with the female Baldpate, but that bird is more ruddy-colored, with a blue bill. The location of the white wing-patch is the best mark; that of the Baldpate is on the *fore* edge of the wing. Some females and young Baldpates in the fall show so little white in the wing that they might be easily confused with the Gadwall. Female Mallards and female Gadwalls are somewhat similar. Both have yellow in the bill, but the square white speculum and white belly identify the Gadwall.
Voice: — Female quacks similarly to female Mallard.
Range: — Breeds from e. Wash. and Mont. s. to ne. Calif., n. Nev., n. Ut., and Colo.; winters from Wash. and Colo. s. to Mex.

EUROPEAN WIDGEON. *Mareca penelope.* (Illus. p. 28.)
Descr. 18–20. This European bird is not so scarce in North America as was formerly supposed. *Male:* — Similar to following species, but is a *gray* Widgeon with *reddish-brown head* and buffy crown, instead of a brown Widgeon with gray head and white crown. It suggests, upon first acquaintance, a Redhead Duck. In bad light, or when too distant to show color, head appears much darker than rest of bird, quite unlike Baldpate, and sides are much lighter, with less contrast with rear white patch. *Female:* — Very similar to female Baldpate, but in very typical individuals under favorable light conditions head is distinctly tinged with reddish, whereas that of Baldpate is gray. The surest point, but one that can be noted only when the bird is in the hand, or very rarely in the field when the bird flaps its wings, is the appearance of the axillars — dusky in this species, white in the Baldpate.
Range: — Occasional visitor to Calif., Ore., Wash., and perhaps other W. States.

BALDPATE. *Mareca americana.* (Illus. pp. 25, 28.)
Descr. 18–22. The shining white crown of the male, which gives it its name, is the character by which most beginners learn this bird. *Male:* — Mainly brownish with gray head and white crown; patch on side of head glossy green, visible only in good light; patch on fore part of wing white; bill blue with a black tip. *Female:* — Ruddy brown with gray head and neck; belly and fore part of wing white. The Baldpate in flight can be recognized at a good distance by the large white patch on the *fore edge* of the wing; in other Ducks possessing white patches they are placed on the hind edge. The similarly placed blue wing-patches of the Blue-winged Teal, Cinnamon Teal, and Shoveller often appear whitish at a distance, however. Immature birds that have not acquired the white wing-patch are nondescript brownish Ducks with a paler gray head and neck, and a white belly which contrasts sharply with the brown breast.
Voice: — A whistled *whee whee whew* (male). A hoarse growl *grurrr* or *urrrr* (female).
Range: — Breeds from e. Wash. and Mont. s. to ne. Calif., n. Ut., and n. Colo.; winters along Pacific Coast and from s. Nev., cent. Ut., and ne. Colo. s. into Mex.

PINTAIL. *Dafila acuta tzitzihoa.* (Illus. pp. 25, 28.)
Descr. 26–30. Male Pintails in flight are white-bellied Ducks with long, slim necks and long, *pointed* tails, quite different in cut and appearance from the other surface-feeding Ducks. *Male:* — A slender white-breasted Duck, with long, pointed central tail-feathers and conspicuous white line running up side of neck and head. *Female:* — A slender, streaked brown Duck, similar to female Mallard, but more slender and without white-bordered blue speculum in wing. The bill is blue-gray. In flight the light border on the rear of the wings is a good character.
Voice: — Male utters a characteristic double-toned whistle, often in flight; female a hoarse quack.
Range: — Breeds from Can. s. to n.-cent. Calif., w. Nev., n. Ut., and n. Colo. Winters in Pacific States and from ne. Colo. s. to Mex.

GREEN-WINGED TEAL. *Nettion carolinense.* (Illus. pp. 25, 28.)
Descr. 13–15½. *Male:* — Small gray Duck with brown head and conspicuous *white mark* in front of wing. In sunlight, shows an iridescent green speculum in wing and green patch on side of head. *Female:* — A little speckled Duck with an iridescent green speculum. When Ducks fly up from the marsh, Teal are conspicuous by their half-size proportions. If they show no large light-colored patches on the wings, they are this species.

Voice: — Male utters a very characteristic single-noted whistle, sometimes repeated two or three times; female, a crisp quack.
Range: — Breeds from Can. s. to e. Ore., cent. Calif. (formerly), n. Nev., n. Ut., and n. N.M.; winters from Wash. and Mont. s. to Mex.

BLUE-WINGED TEAL. *Querquedula discors.* (Illus. pp. 25, 28.)
Descr. 15–16. *Male:* — Small, dull-colored, with large *white crescent in front of eye,* and large *chalky-blue patch on fore edge of wing.* The blue, at a distance in some lights, looks whitish. *Female:* — Mottled, with large blue patch on fore part of wing. Little half-sized marsh Ducks with large light-colored patches on the front of the wing are either Cinnamon Teal or this species. The white facial crescent identifies the male Blue-wing. It is rare in the Pacific States; the Cinnamon Teal is common. Farther east, the Blue-wing becomes more common. The somewhat larger Shoveller has pale-blue wing-patches, too, but can immediately be recognized by its tremendous bill.
Range: — Breeds from e. Wash. and Mont. s. to ne. Calif., Nev., n. Ut., and N.M.; migrates into Mex.; rare in Pacific States w. of Cascades and Sierras; winters rarely in Calif.

CINNAMON TEAL. *Querquedula cyanoptera.* (Illus. pp. 25, 28.)
Descr. 15½–17. *Male:* — Small, dark *cinnamon-red* Duck with large chalky-blue patches on front edges of wings. *Female:* — Almost identical with female Blue-winged Teal, but a bit rustier and more coarsely marked (see Blue-winged Teal).
Range: — Breeds from Wash. and Mont. s. to n. Calif., Nev., Ut., and N.M.; winters from Calif., Ariz., and N.M. s.

SHOVELLER. *Spatula clypeata.* (Illus. pp. 25, 28.)
Descr. 17–20. *Male:* — Largely black and white; belly and sides rufous-red; head blackish glossed with green; breast white; pale blue patch on fore edge of wing. *Female:* — Mottled brownish, with large blue wing-patch as in male. The Shoveller is a small Duck, somewhat larger than a Teal; best identified by its tremendous long and flattened bill, which in flight gives the bird a long appearance to the fore of the wings. On the water the bird sits very squatty and low, with the bill pointed downward, presenting a distinctive appearance. Broadside on the water, or flying overhead, the pattern of the Drake is totally unlike that of any other Duck. It consists of five alternating areas of light and dark, thus: dark, white, dark, white, dark.
Voice: — Male utters a low musical quack; female, a Mallard-like quack.
Range: — Breeds from e. Wash. and Mont. s. to s. Calif., nw. Nev., Ut., and N.M.; winters in Pacific States and from Ariz. and N.M. s.

CACKLING, LESSER CANADA and COMMON CANADA GEESE

SNOW GOOSE

ROSS'S GOOSE

WHITE-FRONTED GOOSE

ADULT

IMMATURE

BLACK BRANT

EMPEROR GOOSE

TRUMPETER SWAN

WHISTLING SWAN

CINNAMON TEAL ♂

BLUE-WINGED TEAL

GREEN-WINGED TEAL

SHOVELLER

WOOD DUCK

PINTAIL

MALLARD

NEW MEXICAN DUCK

BALDPATE

GADWALL ♂

AMERICAN MERGANSER

RED-BREASTED MERGANSER

HOODED MERGANSER

WOOD DUCK. *Aix sponsa.* (Illus. pp. 25, 40.)
Descr. 17–20. Chiefly a bird of woodland ponds and streams. The male is the most highly colored North American Duck. *Male in winter and spring plumage:* — Highly iridescent; descriptive words fail; the pattern diagram explains it much better. *Female:* — Dark brown with lighter flanks, white belly, dark crested head, and white area about eye. *Male in eclipse plumage (summer):* — Similar to female, but with the white face-markings and red-and-white bill of the spring male. On the wing, the white belly of the Wood Duck contrasts very strikingly with the dark back. This, and the short neck, the fairly long tail, and the angle at which the bill is pointed downward are all good aids to identification.
Voice: — A shrill raucous *whoo-eek* (female) or a wheezy *jeee* (male).
Range: — Breeds in n. Calif., e. Ore., and e. Wash., and, locally or formerly, elsewhere in Pacific States, Ida., Mont., and Wyo.; winters in Pacific States; occasional elsewhere in migration.

DIVING DUCKS: NYROCINÆ

ALTHOUGH birds of this group are often called 'Sea Ducks' or 'Bay Ducks' for convenience, many are found more commonly on the lakes and rivers of the interior; primarily, they are birds of the more open bodies of water, although they breed in marshes. They all dive for food, whereas the Surface-feeding Ducks rarely dive. In taking wing, they do not spring directly upward from the water, but find it necessary to patter along the surface while getting under way.

REDHEAD. *Nyroca americana.* (Illus. pp. 29, 33.)
Descr. 18–23. *Male:* — Mostly gray, with black upper and under tail-coverts, black neck and breast, red-brown head, and blue bill. The male resembles the Canvas-back, but is much grayer; the Canvas-back is very white. The Redhead has a high, abrupt forehead and a blue bill, in contrast to the Canvas-back's long sloping forehead and blackish bill. Redheads flock in much the same formation as Canvas-backs, but are apt to shift about more in the flock. They are shorter and chunkier than the latter, much more like the Scaup in general contour. In flight, at a distance, the gray wing-stripe distinguishes the more uniformly colored Redhead from the contrastingly patterned Scaup. *Female:* — A brownish Duck with a broad gray wing-stripe and a blue bill. The female differs from the female Scaup in having a gray wing-stripe and an indistinct buffy area about the base of the bill, instead of a white wing-stripe and a well-defined

white face-patch. The only other female Ducks with broad gray wing-stripes are the Canvas-back and the Ring-neck. The Canvas-back is larger and paler, with the long profile; the Ring-neck is smaller, darker, and has a conspicuous white eye-ring and a ring on the bill.

Range: — Breeds from e. Wash. and Mont. s. to ne. Calif., Nev., nw. N.M., and s. Colo.; winters in Pacific States, chiefly Calif., and from ne. Colo. s.

RING-NECKED DUCK. *Nyroca collaris.* (Illus. pp. 29, 33.)
Descr. 16–18. *Male:* — A black-backed Scaup. Head, fore parts, and back, black; sides, light gray with conspicuous white mark in front of wing; bill crossed by two white rings. In flight, the only black-backed Duck having a broad *gray* wing-stripe. The name Ring-billed Duck would be much more appropriate, as an examination at very close range is necessary to be aware of the dull chestnut ring that encircles the neck. The rather triangular head-shape is distinctive in both sexes. *Female:* — Brown, darkest on crown of head and back; wing-stripe gray; whitish area about base of bill; white eye-ring, and ring on bill; belly, white. Differs from female Scaup in possessing a *gray* wing-stripe, white eye-ring, and a ring on the bill; from female Redhead in its smaller size, darker back, and the conspicuous rings about the eye and on the bill. Females are a little difficult to tell from the Scaup which they so often associate with, but the males can be picked out at a great distance, as no other species of this distinctive genus has a black back.

Range: — Breeds chiefly in Canada, but occasionally in W. States ('colonies' in sw. Mont. and White Mts. of e. Ariz.); migrates s. to Mex.; winters in Pacific States.

CANVAS-BACK. *Nyroca valisineria.* (Illus. pp. 29, 33.)
Descr. 20–24. *Male:* — White, with rusty-red head and neck, black breast and tail, and blackish bill. *Female:* — Grayish, with a suggestion of the male's general pattern. The long, sloping profile will distinguish either sex from any of the other species which they superficially resemble. In flight, Canvas-backs string out in lines or in V-formation. The long head, neck, and bill give the bird a front-heavy appearance, as if the wings were set far back.

Range: — Breeds chiefly in Can., and locally or occasionally s. to e. Ore., n. Ut., and Colo.; winters along Pacific Coast and from nw. Mont. and n. Colo. s.

GREATER SCAUP DUCK. *Nyroca marila.* (Illus. pp. 27, 29, 33.)
Descr. 17–20½. *Male:* — The two Scaups are the Ducks that at a distance on the water appear to be 'black at both ends and white in the middle.' The flanks and back are finely barred with

WINGS OF SCAUP DUCKS

A. Greater Scaup; long white wing-stripe
B. Lesser Scaup; short white wing-stripe

gray, but at any distance those parts appear quite white. The bill is blue; hence the gunner's nickname, 'Blue-bill.' Close at hand, in sunlight, the black head of the male Greater Scaup is glossed with green; that of the Lesser with dull purple. At a great distance, on the water, drake Golden-eyes and Scaup look somewhat alike, but where the Golden-eye has only a black head, the Scaup is black to the waterline. *Female:* — Brown, with broad white wing-stripe and a well-defined white area at the base of the bill. The two Scaups are our only Ducks possessing a broad white wing-stripe. The white in the Lesser extends about halfway along the hind edge of the wing, while in the present species this stripe extends considerably farther toward the wing-tip (see diagram). This character does not always hold, as the birds sometimes seem to intergrade, but typical individuals can be told in this way.

Range: — Winters along Pacific Coast; chiefly a migrant elsewhere. Much scarcer inland than Lesser Scaup.

LESSER SCAUP DUCK. *Nyroca affinis.* (Illus. pp. 27, 29.)
Descr. 15–18. *Male:* — Similar to Scaup, but slightly smaller, comparatively large-headed, and grayer on flanks; head glossed with dark purple instead of green. These differences are slight

and can be made out only when the bird is near-by in good light. The length of the wing-stripe is the easiest way to separate typical individuals in the field (see Greater Scaup Duck). The Greater is the winter Scaup of deep, open salt-water bays along the Pacific Coast, while the Lesser prefers more sheltered waters, and is much more often found on fresh water than is the Greater. It is the commonest species of the genus and should be used as a standard of comparison for the others.

Range: — A few breed locally in e. Ore., Ida., Mont., Wyo., and n. Colo. Winters in Pacific States and from ne. Colo. s.; a migrant elsewhere. The commonest Scaup in inland localities.

AMERICAN GOLDEN-EYE. *Glaucionetta clangula americana.* (Illus. pp. 29, 33.)
Descr. 17–23. *Male:* — Largely white, with a black back and a black green-glossed head. A large round white spot between the eye and the bill is the best identification mark. In flight the wings show large white patches. The *male*, at a distance, bears a superficial resemblance to the male Merganser, but is stocky and short-necked, with a large, round head, quite unlike the 'long-geared' Merganser. *Female:* — Gray with a white collar and a dark-brown head; wings with large square white patches. The immature male resembles the female but lacks the white collar. The whistling sound produced by the Golden-eye's wings, which has earned for the bird the name 'Whistler,' is often useful in identification.
Range: — Breeds from Can. s. to nw. Mont.; winters along Pacific Coast and irregularly from Mont. to Nev. and Colo., rarely farther.

BARROW'S GOLDEN-EYE. *Glaucionetta islandica.* (Illus. p. 29.)
Descr. 20–23. *Male:* — Similar to drake Golden-eye, but with a greater amount of black on sides of body, a row of *white* spots on black scapulars, black of head glossed with purple instead of green, and a *crescent-shaped* white patch in front of eye, instead of a round white spot. *Female:* — Very difficult to tell in field from female Golden-eye, but bill more yellow, shorter, and deeper. Forehead more abrupt.
Range: — Breeds from Can. s. in mts. to Ore. and Colo.; winters along coast s. to cent. Calif. (rarely) and inland irregularly to s. Colo.

BUFFLE-HEAD. *Charitonetta albeola.* (Illus. pp. 33, 40.)
Descr. 13–15. One of the smallest Ducks. *Male:* — Mostly white, with black back and large, puffy head marked with great white patch that extends from eye around back of head; large white wing-patches in flight. Because of the large triangular

BLACK DUCK GADWALL ♂

♂ MALLARD ♀

♂ PINTAIL ♀

EUROPEAN WIDGEON ♂ ♀ BALDPATE ♂

♀ SHOVELLER ♂ ♀ BLUE WINGED TEAL ♂

GREEN·WINGED TEAL ♂ CINNAMON TEAL ♂

♂ CANVASBACK ♀

♂ REDHEAD ♀

♂ RING-NECKED DUCK ♀

♂ LESSER SCAUP ♀

GREATER SCAUP ♂   BARROW'S GOLDEN-EYE ♂

♂ AMERICAN GOLDEN-EYE ♀

white area on the head, it is sometimes mistaken for the scarcer Hooded Merganser, which is very dark instead of very white.
Female: — Dark little Duck with large head, white cheek-spot, and white wing-patch.
Range: — Breeds in n. Mont. and Can.; migrates s. to Mex.; winters along Pacific Coast and on open bodies of water inland.

OLD-SQUAW. *Clangula hyemalis.* (Illus. pp. 32, 33.)
Descr. ♂ 21, ♀ 17. *Male in winter:* — Patchily patterned with dark brown and white. Head, neck, belly, and scapulars white; breast, back, and wings dusky brown; dark patch on side of head; bill banded with black and pink. The long, pointed central tail-feathers of the male Old-Squaw are different from those of any other Duck except the Pintail, which is a Duck of the marshes, ponds, and rivers, rather than a bird of the ocean. *Male in summer:* — Mostly dark with white flanks and belly, and white patch surrounding eye. *Female in winter:* — Lacks long, pointed tail-feathers of male. Dark above and white below; head white with black crown and cheek-spot. *Female in summer:* — Similar but darker. The Old-Squaw is the only Sea Duck combining white on the body and unpatterned dark wings. In flight it presents a pied appearance with dark, pointed wings that dip low with each beat. The Old-Squaws bunch in irregular flocks ʳather than in long, stringy lines like the Scoters.
Voice: — Noisy musical cries, *onk-a-lik.*
Range: — Winters along Pacific Coast; rare inland.

(WESTERN) HARLEQUIN DUCK. *Histrionicus histrionicus pacificus.* (Illus. pp. 32, 33.)
Descr. 15–17½. *Male:* — A rather small dark blue-gray Duck (blackish at a distance) with reddish-brown sides and odd white patches and spots. A glance at the diagram best explains the bird's appearance. In flight it has the shape, short neck, and manner of a Golden-eye but at a great distance stands out as a uniformly dark bird. Often cocks tail like Ruddy Duck. *Female:* — Dusky brown with two or three round white spots on side of head; may be distinguished from female Buffle-head — which has only one white face-spot — by absence of white in wing; from female Scoters, which it also resembles by its smaller size and shorter bill. In brief, it is a Duck with the pattern of a female Surf Scoter and the shape of a Buffle-head.
Range: — Breeds from Can. s. in mts. to Calif. (occasional in Sierras) and Colo.; winters mostly along rocky shores on coast s. to cent. Calif.

KING EIDER. *Somateria spectabilis.*
Descr. 21–24. *Male:* — A large, heavy Duck; back and belly black; wings black with large white patches; breast and fore

parts whitish; top of head pearl-gray; cheeks tinged with greenish; bill and large frontal processes orange. At a distance the fore parts appear white, the rear parts black. No other Duck gives this effect. *Female:* — A large, chunky brown Duck, heavily barred with black. The heavy barrings and lack of light spots on face distinguish her from female Scoters. *Immature male:* — A dusky, Scoter-like bird with light breast and dark chocolate-brown head. Shows no square white wing-patch, as does the female Golden-eye Duck, a bird with which it might be confused. The amount of white varies in birds changing to adult plumage.

Range: — Casual on coast of Calif.

WHITE-WINGED SCOTER. *Melanitta deglandi.* (Illus. pp. 32, 33.)

Descr. 20–23. The Scoters are the large, chunky, blackish Ducks commonly seen coastwise, flying in stringy formation low over the waves. The White-wing is the largest of the three species. *Male:* — Black with white wing-patches. *Female:* — Dusky-brown with white wing-patch and two white patches on side of head.

Range: — Breeds in Can.; winters along Pacific Coast; rare inland. Non-breeding birds found along coast in summer.

SURF SCOTER. *Melanitta perspicillata.* (Illus. pp. 32, 33.)

Descr. 18–22. *Male:* — Black, with one or two white patches on crown of head — hence nickname 'Skunk-head.' *Female:* — Dusky-brown with two white patches on side of head. The smaller size and lack of white wing-patches distinguish it from similarly marked female White-wing. This species is the only Duck that invariably holds its wings elevated upon alighting, a fine field character.

Range: — Winters along Pacific Coast; non-breeders found all summer. Very rare inland.

AMERICAN SCOTER. *Oidemia americana.* (Illus. pp. 32, 33.)

Descr. 17–21. *Male:* — The only American Duck with *entirely* black plumage. This, and the bright yellow-orange base of the bill, are diagnostic. *Female:* — Dusky brown, with light cheeks contrasting with a darker crown. Females of the other two Scoters have two distinct white patches on each side of the head. At a distance in flight, the female American Scoter shows more light color on the under parts than the females of the other two species of Scoters.

Range: — Winters along Pacific Coast; a few non-breeders summer. Very rare inland.

RUDDY AND MASKED DUCKS: ERISMATURINÆ

RUDDY DUCK. *Erismatura jamaicensis rubida.* (Illus. pp. 32, 33.)
Descr. 14–17. *Male in breeding plumage:* — Largely rusty-red with *white cheeks*, black crown, and large blue bill. *Male in winter:* — Gray with white cheeks, blackish crown, and bluish bill. *Female:* — Similar to winter male, but with light cheeks crossed by dark line. In the air, in any plumage, the Ruddy appears as a small, chunky Duck, quite dark, and unpatterned in color except for the conspicuous white cheeks. On the water it often cocks its tail vertically, like a Wren. It is possible to misidentify a female American Scoter as a winter Ruddy Duck — both are unpatterned except for light cheeks. Occasionally, the Scoter even cocks its tail. The Ruddy Duck is very much smaller, with a definitely shovel-shaped blue bill. The flight of the Ruddy is close to the water, and is extremely fast and buzzy, the short small wings beating very rapidly.
Range: — Breeds locally from Can. s. to s. Calif., n. Ariz., and N.M.; winters in Pacific States and from Ariz. and N.M. s.

MASKED DUCK. *Nomonyx dominicus.* (Illus. p. 32.)
Descr. 12–14. Smaller than any other Duck; somewhat like Ruddy Duck. *Male:* — Rusty with blackish stripes on back, white wing-patches, and black mask on front of face. *Female:* — Like a small female Ruddy, but with *two* black stripes crossing each cheek instead of one.
Range: — Occasional near Brownsville, Tex.

MERGANSERS: MERGINÆ

OUR three Mergansers, or fish-eating Ducks, lack the broad and flattened bills so characteristic of most Ducks; the mandibles are slender, equipped with toothed edges, well adapted for seizing their slippery prey. Most species have crests and are long-geared, slender-bodied birds. In flight, the bill, head, neck, and body are held perfectly horizontal; at a distance, this gives them an unmistakable long-drawn appearance, quite unlike other Ducks.

HOODED MERGANSER. *Lophodytes cucullatus.* (Illus. pp. 25, 40.)
Descr. 16–19. *Male:* — Black and white, with *fan-shaped white* crest on head; breast white with two black bars in front of wing; wing dark with white patch; flanks brownish. The male, distinctive as it is, is often confused with the male Buffle-head.

The Buffle-head is smaller, chubbier, and whiter with white flanks; the flanks of the Hooded Merganser are dark. The white head-patch of the Merganser is outlined with a narrow dark border. *Female:* — Recognized as a Merganser when close at hand by the narrow, spike-like bill, and in flight by the long-drawn appearance, with bill, head, neck, and body held in a horizontal line. Differentiated from the other two female Mergansers by the small size, dark coloration, *dark head and neck,* and buffy crest. The female Wood Duck is also dark and has a crest, but the square white wing-patch and different flight will identify the Merganser. Like the Wood Duck it often frequents woodland pools.

Range: — Breeds locally from Can. s. to Ore. and Wyo.; winters in B.C. and Pacific States and from Ut. and Colo. s.

AMERICAN MERGANSER. *Mergus merganser americanus.* (Illus. pp. 25, 40.)

Descr. 22–27. In line formation, low over the water, the American Mergansers follow the winding course of the creeks and rivers which they frequent. Like the others of the group, they are rakish, long-bodied birds. The large, white, black-headed males are unmistakable. *Male:* — White, with a black back and a green-black head; bill and feet orange; breast tinged with a delicate peach-colored bloom. The whiteness of the bird and the Merganser shape, with bill, head, neck, and body all held horizontal, will identify it in flight a long way off. The Merganser and Golden-eye resemble each other at a distance, but the Golden-eye, aside from having the conspicuous white spot in front of the eye, is smaller, chubbier, shorter-necked, and rounder-headed. *Female:* — Largely gray with a *crested* rufous-red head, red bill, orange feet, and a large square white patch on the wing (see female Red-breasted Merganser).

Range: — Breeds from Can. s. to cent. Calif., n. Ariz., and n. N.M. (rarely); winters along most of coast and on open water inland.

RED-BREASTED MERGANSER. *Mergus serrator.* (Illus. pp. 25, 40.)

Descr. 20–25. *Male:* — Not so white as American Merganser; black head glossed with green and *conspicuously crested*; area on breast at waterline brownish, whereas same area in American Merganser appears white; bill red, feet orange. *Female:* — Largely gray, with crested rufous-red head and large square white patch on wing; bill and feet orange-red. Very similar to female American Merganser, but head less bushy, with rufous blending into white of throat and neck instead of being sharply defined as in that bird. Both sexes are smaller and slimmer in build than the American Merganser. The Red-breasted Mer-

♂ AMERICAN SCOTER ♀

♂ WHITE-WINGED SCOTER ♀

♂ SURF SCOTER ♀

♂ HARLEQUIN DUCK ♀

♂ SUMMER ♂ WINTER ♀ WINTER

OLD-SQUAW

♂ RUDDY DUCK ♀

♂ MASKED DUCK ♀

REDHEAD

GREATER
SCAUP

RING-
NECKED
DUCK

CANVAS-
BACK

BUFFLEHEAD

AMERICAN
GOLDEN-EYE

HARLEQUIN
DUCK

OLD-SQUAW
WINTER

RUDDY
DUCK

BLACK-BELLIED TREE-DUCK

FULVOUS
TREE-DUCK

AMERICAN
SCOTER

SURF SCOTER

WHITE-WINGED
SCOTER

ganser is more characteristic of the ocean than is the American, which is chiefly a fresh-water species Both birds may, at times, be found on the same bodies of water.

Range: — Winters on Pacific Coast; local or rare in Great Basin and Rocky Mt. region.

VULTURES: CATHARTIDÆ

VULTURES are great blackish Eagle-like birds, usually seen soaring in wide circles high in the heavens. Their naked heads are so small for the size of the bird that at a great distance they sometimes appear to be almost headless. Hawks and Eagles have large, well-proportioned heads.

TURKEY VULTURE. *Cathartes aura.* (Illus. p. 41.)
Descr. 30. Wing-spread 6 ft. This species, the only Vulture found in most parts of w. U.S., is nearly Eagle-size with great 'two-toned' blackish wings (the flight feathers are noticeably lighter than the rest of the bird). It is usually to be seen high in the air, soaring on motionless wings in wide circles. The diminutive head and slimmer tail at once distinguish it from the Eagles. At close range the red color of the head can be seen. A Turkey Vulture soars with its wings held perceptibly above the horizontal and rocks unsteadily as it floats along. Eagles and Ravens soar with wings perfectly horizontal. Where all three are common this comparison helps.
Range: — Throughout most of w. U.S.; winters from Calif. and s. Ariz. s. The Turkey Vulture of the West has recently been described as the Western Turkey Vulture (*C. a. teter*), but the name has not yet been adopted.

BLACK VULTURE. *Coragyps atratus atratus.* (Illus. p. 41.)
Descr. 24. Wing-spread under 5 ft. One of the best points of difference between this black-headed species and the Turkey Vulture is the comparatively short tail which barely projects from the hind edge of the wings. The tail of the Turkey Vulture is longer and slimmer. A whitish patch on the under surface of the Black Vulture's wing is also a sure mark. The wings are shorter than the Turkey Vulture's, and the bird flaps more frequently and soars less. Young Turkey Vultures have black heads and are sometimes mistaken for Black Vultures.
Range: — W. Tex. and s. Ariz. (a few).

CALIFORNIA CONDOR. *Gymnogyps californianus.* (Illus. p. 34.)
Descr. 45–55. Wing-spread 8½–10½ ft. Much larger than the

CALIFORNIA CONDOR

Turkey Vulture; adults with extensive *pure white wing-linings* toward the front edges of the wings. Head yellow or orange. Young birds are dusky-headed and lack the white linings, but are twice the size of Turkey Vultures and have much broader proportions. Many Golden Eagles have some white under the wing, but it is placed differently and the shape of the bird is somewhat different (see diagram).
Range: — Now very rare, a small number living in mts. of s. Calif.

KITES: ELANINÆ

WHITE-TAILED KITE. *Elanus leucurus majusculus.* (Illus. p. 45.)
Descr. 15½. This rare species is Falcon-shaped, with long, pointed wings and a long tail, but the flight lacks the dash of Falcons. The bird frequently hovers in one spot like a Sparrow Hawk. *Adult:* — Pale gray with white head, *tail*, and under parts, and a *large black patch* toward fore edge of wing. No other Falcon-like bird (except White Gyrfalcon) has a white tail. Beginners often mistake this species for a Gull. *Immature:* — Broad rusty band on breast; tail tipped with gray.

Range: — Calif., chiefly from San Francisco Bay region to Ventura Co.; rather rare. Straggler in Ore. Also occurs around Brownsville, Tex.

ACCIPITERS, OR SHORT–WINGED HAWKS: ACCIPITRINÆ

LONG-TAILED Hawks with short, rounded wings; woodland birds that do not often soar about high in the air as do the Buteos. The typical flight is several short quick beats and a sail. The Goshawk is not properly an Accipiter, but it belongs to the same subfamily.

GOSHAWK. *Astur atricapillus.* Subsp.   (Illus. p. 45.)
Descr. 20–26. A large, long-tailed, short-winged Hawk with a pearly-gray breast and a blue-gray back; of a lighter gray than the Cooper's or Sharp-shin. It is easily told from the Cooper's Hawk, which it resembles in shape, by its much larger size — considerably larger than a Crow; Cooper's is smaller than a Crow. The gray-backed adult Cooper's is reddish below; the Goshawk, pale gray. The white line over the Goshawk's eye is also distinctive. Young accipitrine Hawks are brown above

IMMATURE COOPER'S HAWK

The Hawks shown in overhead flight in the plates are adults. Immature birds have the same shapes, but in many instances are streaked below as in this bird.

and heavily streaked below. They all have much the same pattern. Size, although sometimes deceptive, is a reasonable point of difference between this species and the Cooper's. A well-pronounced light stripe over the eye in the young Goshawk is about the only definite point of distinction. Some immature birds are generally paler throughout and identifiable on this basis.

Range: — Breeds from Can. s. in mts. to cent. Calif., Ariz., and N.M.; wanders to lowlands in winter.

Subsp. (No apparent field differences): (1) Eastern Goshawk, *A. a. atricapillus*; (2) Western Goshawk, *A. a. striatulus*.

SHARP-SHINNED HAWK. *Accipiter velox.* (Illus. pp. 45, 49.)
Descr. 10–14. A small Hawk with a long tail and short, rounded wings. Flies with several quick beats and a sail. Size near that of Sparrow and Pigeon Hawks, but those two species have pointed wings. Large females are often near the size of small male Cooper's. The two are almost identical in pattern, but generally the Cooper's has a rounded tail and the Sharp-shin a *square-tipped* tail (slightly forked when folded).

Range: — Breeds from Can. s. to Calif., Ariz., and N.M.; winters through most of w. U.S.

COOPER'S HAWK. *Accipiter cooperi.* (Illus. pp. 35, 45, 49.)
Descr. 14–20. A short-winged, long-tailed Hawk; not quite so large as a Crow. Keeps to the woods and does not soar high in the open as often as many other Hawks. Can be known from the Sharp-shin by its *rounded tail*, and from the Goshawk by its much smaller size. Immature birds are usually more sharply and narrowly streaked below than immature Sharp-shins

Range: — Breeds from Can. to Mex.; winters from Wash. and Wyo. s.

BUTEOS, OR BUZZARD HAWKS: BUTEONINÆ (IN PART)

LARGE Hawks with *broad wings* and *broad, rounded tails*, which habitually soar in wide circles, high in the air.

Black or melanistic phases occur in most species, and one must indeed be an expert to tell some of them apart. There is considerable variation in individuals within most of the species. This may cause confusion among beginners. The Hawks figured in the pattern-diagrams are in the most characteristic plumages. Young birds are similar to the adults in shape, but in most species are *streaked lengthwise* below.

RED-TAILED HAWK. *Buteo borealis.* Subsp.   (Illus. pp. 41, 44, 49.)

Descr. 19–24. The tyro usually finds it necessary to wait till this large broad-winged, round-tailed Hawk veers in its soaring so that the rufous-red of the upper side of the tail can be seen. From beneath, adults have light-colored tails with little or no apparent banding. Young birds have grayish tails, which might or might not show banding. The under parts of the Red-tail are more or less zoned (light breast, broad band of dark streakings across belly). With much practice one can easily identify the various Buteos by shape alone. The Red-tail is chunkier, with wider wings and a shorter tail than most of others. There is considerable color variation. Some individuals are very dark, almost black, but *black adults usually show red tails,* a point of distinction from black Swainson's or black Rough-legs.

Voice: — A squealing whistle, *keeer-r-r.*

Subsp. WESTERN RED-TAILED HAWK. *B. b. calurus.*
     Resident through most of w. U.S.
     KRIDER'S HAWK. *B. b. krideri.*
     In appearance, a partially albinistic Red-tail with much white mixed in the plumage, especially about the head. The tail may range from pale red to white, and is crossed by a number of narrow bars. Sask. and s. Man. s. to Wyo. and N.D.

RED-BELLIED HAWK. *Buteo lineatus elegans.*   (Illus. pp. 41, 49.)

Descr. 18–24. A race of the Eastern Red-shouldered Hawk; resident of valleys in central and s. Calif. Recognized as a Buteo by the ample tail and broad wings; distinguished in any plumage from the Red-tail, which is chunkier, wider-winged, and shorter-tailed, by the *heavy banding* across both sides of the tail. The Swainson's Hawk has *fine* banding. Adults are marked with rich chestnut shoulders and bright rusty-red under parts and wing-linings. These barred rusty under parts set it apart from any other Western Buteo. The adult Cooper's Hawk also has rusty under parts but has proportionately shorter wings and a longer tail. Immature birds lack the rusty under parts, and are streaked below as are most other young Hawks. They can be best identified by the tail-banding, proportions, and, in flight overhead, by a light-colored patch or 'window' toward the tip of the wings at the base of the primaries. This is a good mark in any plumage.

Voice: — A piercing *kee-yer* (Red-tail's more like a squeal).

Range: — Valleys and lowlands of cent. and s. Calif.

SWAINSON'S HAWK. *Buteo swainsoni.* (Illus. pp. 41, 44, 49.)

Descr. 19½–22. A Buteo similar in size to a Red-tail but with wings longer and more pointed. The wings when soaring are

held somewhat above the horizontal, giving a slightly Vulture-like or Marsh-Hawk-like impression. In typical adults the wide dark breast-band is a good mark. There are confusing lighter individuals where the breast-band nearly disappears and blackish birds which are hard to tell from other melanistic Buteos. Most individuals can be told very readily in flight overhead by the *unmarked light buffy wing-linings which contrast with the darker-toned flight feathers* (see diagram). From above, the tail is gray, often shading to white at the base. (Do not confuse with Rough-leg.) Black Swainson's Hawks lack the rusty tail of the black Red-tail, and lack the snowy-white primaries and secondaries on the under wing-surface which are such a distinctive feature of black Rough-legs. These wing areas are often quite pale, but *clouded*, not clear white. (See diagram.) When perched, facing the observer, the bird's tail is pale, crossed by narrow black bars. This species migrates in flocks, a habit not common in Hawks.
Range: — Breeds and migrates in dry open country through all of West except the coastal belt (w. of Cascades and Calif. coast ranges).

ZONE-TAILED HAWK. *Buteo albonotatus.* (Illus. pp. 44, 49.)
Descr. 18½–21½. A *black* Buteo, with somewhat more slender wings than the others of its genus. Upon first acquaintance is likely to be mistaken for a Turkey Vulture because of the proportions and '*two-toned*' *wing effect* (see diagram), but the Hawk head and *white tail-bands* identify it. The Mexican Black Hawk, which also occurs along the Mexican border of the U.S., is much chunkier, has evenly colored wings and much wider tail-banding. The Mexican Black Hawk prefers cottonwood stream-bottoms; the Zone-tail is often seen in mountainous country.
Range: — Chiefly near Mex. border of Tex., N.M., and Ariz.

SENNETT'S WHITE-TAILED HAWK. *Buteo albicaudatus hypospodius.* (Illus. pp. 41, 44, 49.)
Descr. 23–24. A long-winged, short-tailed Buteo with *clear white under parts* and *white tail* with a black band near its tip. The upper parts are dark (gray, shoulders rusty-red). The white tail is the best mark. The Ferruginous Rough-leg has whitish under parts and a whitish tail, but lacks the well-defined black band near the tip of the tail. (See Ferruginous Rough-leg.) Immature White-tails are quite blackish, and in flight overhead have whitish tails and blackish wing-linings which contrast with light primaries. The black Ferruginous Rough-leg has the under surface of the primaries and secondaries snowy-white (not clouded). The black Swainson's has a noticeably barred tail and is more evenly black below. The immature White-tail is usually somewhat spotted with white on the breast.
Range: — Southern Tex.

AMERICAN ROUGH-LEGGED HAWK. *Buteo lagopus s.-johannis.* (Illus. pp. 41, 44, 49.)
Descr. 20–23½. A Buteo by shape, but with longer wings and a longer, more rounded tail than most of the others. As it usually flies low in open country, it might easily be taken for a Swainson's Hawk, especially because of the white base of the tail, but the Swainson's tail is not so contrasting (gray, often blending with white at base). The best marks by which to distinguish the normal or light phase from below are the *well-defined black belly* and the *conspicuous black patch at the wrist of the wing.* Light-bellied birds sometimes are seen. The black phase does not have the large amount of white at the base of the tail. It can be told from the black Red-tail by the lack of rusty on the tail and from the black Swainson's by the snowy-white primaries and secondaries on the under surface of the wings (see diagram).
Range: — Winters from n. edge of U.S. s. to s. Calif. and s. N.M.

FERRUGINOUS ROUGH-LEG. *Buteo regalis.* (Illus. pp. 41, 44, 49.)
Descr. 23–24. A large Buteo of the plains and prairies, distinguished from the American Rough-leg by its coloration, ruddy above and whitish below, and the lack of a contrasting black terminal band on the whitish tail. Shows two light-colored areas on upper surface of wings. A very good mark in typical light-bellied birds when flying overhead is a dark V formed by the dark chestnut-colored feathers on the legs. First-year birds lack these dark 'leggings' and are pure white below. In the dark phase the Ferruginous Rough-leg resembles the black American Rough-leg but usually is more tinged with rusty. The long tail is paler, often whitish, without any suggestion of a broad black band at the tip, as in the other species. The snowy-white under surface of the primaries and secondaries, and the pale unbanded tail identify the bird in this confusing plumage.
Range: — Breeds in arid country from e. Wash. and Mont. s. to ne. Calif., Nev., and n. N.M.; winters from Mont., e. Ore., and interior Calif., s. to Mex.; occasional on coast.

HARRIS'S HAWK. *Parabuteo unicinctus harrisi.* (Illus. p. 44.)
Descr. 22. A black Buteo with a flashy white rump and a white band at the tip of the tail; like a Marsh Hawk in habits, but looks more dumpy when perched on yucca, etc. The Harris's Hawk perched close to would show chestnut-colored areas on the body and wings — a mark of distinction from the other black or melanistic Buteos. In flight at a distance, from the side, the white on the Harris's Hawk completely encircles the base of the tail, whereas in the female or young Marsh Hawk it is visible only above, on the rump.
Range: — Se. Calif., s. Ariz., s. N.M., and s. Tex.

MEXICAN GOSHAWK. *Asturina plagiata plagiata.* (Illus. p. 41.)
Descr. 16–18. Not a Goshawk at all, but more like a small Buteo. Adults are distinguished by their Buteo proportions, gray back, gray and white barred under parts, and widely banded black-and-white tail. (Tail-banding will remind Easterners of Broad-winged Hawk.)
Range: — Streams locally along Mex. border of Ariz., N.M., and Tex.

MEXICAN BLACK HAWK. *Urubitinga anthracina.* (Illus. p. 44.)
Descr. 20–23. A black Buteonine Hawk with exceptionally broad wings. Identified by its chunky shape and the broad white band crossing the center of the tail. A white spot near the tip of the wing at the base of the primaries can be seen under favorable circumstances, but is inconspicuous at a distance.
Range: — Along streams near Mex. border of Ariz., N.M., and Tex.

EAGLES: BUTEONINÆ (IN PART)

EAGLES are at once recognizable from the 'Buzzard Hawks,' or Buteos, which they somewhat resemble, by their immense size and proportionately longer wings. The powerful bill of an Eagle is nearly as long as the head, a point of distinct difference from the lesser Hawks.

GOLDEN EAGLE. *Aquila chrysaëtos canadensis.* (Illus. p. 48.)
Descr. 30–40. Wing-spread 6½–7½ ft. The Eagle of the mountainous country. *Adult:* — Evenly black below or with white at the base of the tail. When the bird wheels, showing the upper surface, the white tail, with its contrasting dark terminal band, identifies it. The amount of white varies. The light 'gold' on the hind neck is of occasional importance as a field-mark. *Immature:* — From above and below, typical individuals show a *white flash in the wing* at the base of the primaries, and a white tail with a *broad, dark terminal band.* All manner of variation exists between this typical plumage of the immature and the plumage of the adult described above. The Golden Eagle has a more graceful, Vulture-like flight, flapping less and soaring more than the Bald. Even the general contour is different; the wings are shorter and wider, the tail more ample. Perched at a distance the bird appears flat-headed with a much smaller and less massive bill than the Bald Eagle.
Range: — Mountainous regions of w. U.S.

♂ AMERICAN MERGANSER ♀

♂ RED-BREASTED MERGANSER ♀

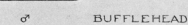

♂ HOODED MERGANSER ♀

♂ BUFFLEHEAD ♀

♂ WOOD DUCK ♀

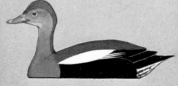

BLACK-BELLIED
TREE-DUCK

FULVOUS
TREE-DUCK

TURKEY VULTURE

BLACK VULTURE

AM. R: LEG

ABOVE

AMERICAN ROUGH·LEGGED HAWK

FERRUGINOUS ROUGH·LEG

SENNETT'S WHITE·TAILED HAWK

RED·TAILED HAWK

RED·BELLIED HAWK

SWAINSON'S HAWK

MEXICAN GOSHAWK

BALD EAGLE. *Haliæetus leucocephalus.* Subsp. (Illus. p. 48.)
Descr. 30–31. Wing-spread 6–7½ ft. The Eagle of the ocean, rivers, and lakes. The adult, with its great size and *snowy-white* head and tail, needs little description. The immature bird is dusky all over. Melanistic Buteos (black Rough-legs, Swainson's, etc.) are much smaller. Immatures are frequently mistaken for Golden Eagles. Although in some individuals there may be some white on the under surface of the wings, it is usually in the linings rather than at the base of the primaries. A young Bald Eagle going into adult plumage may have a tail that is whitish at the base, but never with a contrasting dark band.
Range: — Local from Can. to Mex. chiefly near water; absent in arid sections.
Subsp. (No apparent field differences): (1) Northern Bald Eagle, *H. l. alascanus*; (2) Southern Bald Eagle, *H. l. leucocephalus.*

HARRIERS: CIRCINÆ

MARSH HAWK. *Circus hudsonius.* (Illus. p. 45.)
Descr. 18–24. The *white* rump-patch is the badge of the species. *Adult males* are pale gray; *females*, brown. In ordinary flight, the bird glides low over the ground with the wings held perceptibly above the horizontal, in a manner suggestive of the Vultures. The white rump is always conspicuous. The American Rough-leg and the Swainson's often have white at the base of the tail, but are much more heavily proportioned than the slim Marsh Hawk. When the bird is flying high, the long tail might suggest a Falcon, but the wings are not pointed. The Accipiters have much shorter wings.
Range: — Breeds in marshy country from Can. s. to s. Calif. and N.M. (a few), except in nw. coast belt. Winters from Ore. and Mont. to Mex.

OSPREYS: PANDIONINÆ

OSPREY. *Pandion haliaëtus carolinensis.* (Illus. p. 48.)
Descr. 21–24. Wing-spread 4½–6 ft. A large Eagle-like Hawk — blackish above and *clear white* below; only *large* bird of prey so patterned. Head largely white, suggestive of Bald Eagle. Flies with decided kink or crook in wings. The Eagles and lesser Hawks are all quite straight-winged. The habits of hovering, and of plunging feet first for fish, are characteristic.
Range: — Migrant or summer resident along coast and about large streams and lakes locally from Can. to Mex.

CARACARAS: POLYBORINÆ

AUDUBON'S CARACARA. *Polyborus cheriway auduboni.* (Illus. p. 44.)
Descr. 22. A large, long-legged, long-necked black Hawk. The under surface presents three alternating areas of light and dark — whitish throat and breast, black belly, and white, dark-tipped tail. In flight the *pale-colored patches* at the wing-tips are conspicuous from above or below. These are determinative, especially when seen in conjunction with the white breast area.
Range: — Mexican border of Tex., N.M. (rare), and Ariz. (uncommon).

FALCONS: FALCONINÆ

HAWKS with long, *pointed* wings and comparatively long tails. The wing-strokes are rapid; the slim wings are not built for soaring in the manner of the Buteos.

GYRFALCON. *Falco rusticolus obsoletus.* (Illus. pp. 45, 49.)
Descr. 20–24½. A very large Falcon, usually much larger than the Duck Hawk. It was formerly assumed that three or four races of this bird occur in North America, with a distinction made between black, gray, and white types. Recent studies have led to the conclusion that there is only one Gyrfalcon in North America (Friedmann). White birds are distinguished from the Snowy Owl at a distance by the smaller head, pointed wings, and quicker flight. Black birds are much larger and blacker-breasted than the Duck Hawk. Gray birds are more uniformly colored above and below than the Duck Hawk, without such marked contrast between dark upper parts and light under parts.
Range: — Arctic America; casual in migration, and winter to Mont., Wyo., Wash., and Ore.

PRAIRIE FALCON. *Falco mexicanus.* (Illus. pp. 45, 49.)
Descr. 17. A pointed-winged Hawk, very much like the Duck Hawk in size and appearance, but whereas the back of that bird is slaty-gray, almost blackish, this species is a paler, sandy color. In flight overhead the Prairie Falcon shows blackish patches (formed by the dark flanks and axillars) where the wings join the body. These patches contrast noticeably with the light tone of the rest of the under surface. Female Sparrow Hawks are smaller and darker.
Range: — Chiefly arid sections from Can. to Mex.

DUCK HAWK. *Falco peregrinus.* Subsp. (Illus. pp. 45, 49.)
Descr. 15–20. Recognized as a Falcon by its long, pointed wings
and long, narrow tail, and its *quick*, deep wing-beats that carry
the wings far below the level of the body. Its size, near that of
a Crow, and its dark coloration identify it as this species. (Sparrow and Pigeon Hawks are not much larger than a Robin.) On
perching birds of this species the heavy dark 'moustachios' are
distinctive. (See Prairie Falcon.)
Subsp. DUCK HAWK. *F. p. anatum.*
    Breeds locally, on cliffs, usually near water, from Can.
    to Mex.; winters in Pacific States and from Colo. s.
    PEALE'S FALCON. *F. p. pealei.*
    A dark race, recognizable. Chiefly migrant, and winter
    visitor to coast of Wash. and Ore.

APLOMADO FALCON. *Falco fusco-cœrulescens septentrionalis.* (Illus. pp. 45, 49.)
Descr. 15–18. A handsome medium-sized Falcon of the desert
and dry plains; now very rare in the U.S. Somewhat larger than
the Sparrow Hawk or a little smaller than the Duck Hawk or
Prairie Falcon. Identified readily by its dark wing-linings and
black belly contrasting markedly with its white breast. Thighs
and under tail-coverts orange-brown.
Range: — Formerly deserts along Mex. border of Ariz., N.M.,
and Tex. Now practically gone.

PIGEON HAWK. *Falco columbarius.* Subsp. (Illus. pp. 45, 49.)
Descr. 10–13½. A small Falcon, hardly larger than a Robin.
The male is bluish-gray above, with broad bands on the tail.
Female and young are dusky brown. One subspecies, the Black
Pigeon Hawk, is nearly black above and more heavily marked
below. The long, pointed wings and Falcon-like wing-action
distinguish it from the little Sharp-shinned Hawk, which has
rounded wings. The lack of any rufous-red on the tail or upper
plumage distinguishes it at once from the Sparrow Hawk. In
flight the Pigeon Hawk cuts the air speedily, sailing less between
strokes than the other bird. During migration the Pigeon Hawk
is looked for to best advantage in open country, coastal marshes,
etc.
Subsp. BLACK PIGEON HAWK. *F. c. suckleyi.*
    Decidedly darker than Western Pigeon Hawk, espe-
    cially on the cheeks; belly more heavily marked
    Sometimes recognizable if the student knows the com-
    mon bird well. Winters along coast from Wash. to n.
    Calif.
    RICHARDSON'S PIGEON HAWK. *F. c. richardsoni.*
    Males are often recognizable because they are so pale
    above, especially on the tail and crown (the male West-

ern Pigeon Hawk has a very dark crown).   Breeds in
Great Plains region from Can. s. to n. Mont. Winters s.
through Colo., N.M., and w. Tex.
WESTERN PIGEON HAWK.   *F. c. bendirei.*
Breeds from Can. s. in mts. to n. Calif. and Colo.; win-
ters s. into Mex.

SPARROW HAWK.   *Falco sparverius.*   Subsp.   (Illus. pp. 45,
49.)
Descr. 9–12.   A small Falcon, not much larger than a Robin.
No other *small* Hawk has a rufous-red tail.   At a distance, in
flight, the narrow, pointed wings eliminate the Sharp-shin,
which has short, round wings.   It is the only common *small*
Hawk that habitually hovers, Kingfisher-like, in one spot.   The
Sparrow Hawk almost always pumps its tail on alighting, then
sits fairly erect with an occasional, but characteristic, jerk of
the tail.   (See Pigeon Hawk.)
Voice: — A rapid, high-pitched *killy, killy, killy.*
Range: — Breeds from Can. to Mex.; winters from Wash. and
Wyo. s.
Subsp.   (No apparent field differences): (1) Eastern Sparrow
Hawk, *F. s. sparverius*; (2) Desert Sparrow Hawk, *F. s. phalæna.*

CURASSOWS AND GUANS: CRACIDÆ

CHACHALACA.   *Ortalis vetula vetula.*   (Illus. p. 44.)
Descr. 20–24.   A large brown bird shaped like a half-grown Tur-

CHACHALACA

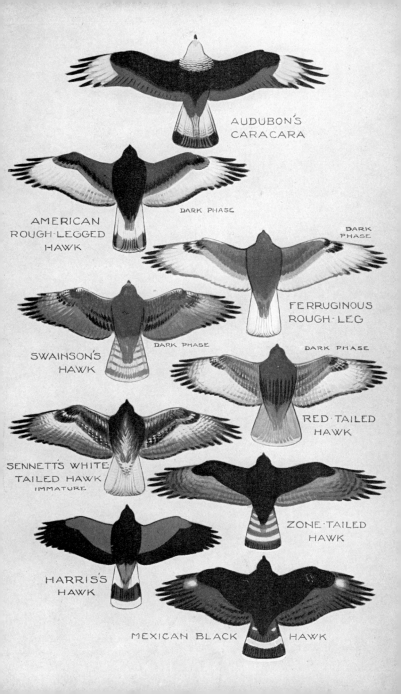

AUDUBON'S
CARACARA

AMERICAN
ROUGH-LEGGED
HAWK

DARK PHASE

DARK
PHASE

FERRUGINOUS
ROUGH-LEG

SWAINSON'S
HAWK

DARK PHASE

DARK PHASE

RED-TAILED
HAWK

SENNETT'S WHITE
TAILED HAWK
IMMATURE

ZONE-TAILED
HAWK

HARRIS'S
HAWK

MEXICAN BLACK   HAWK

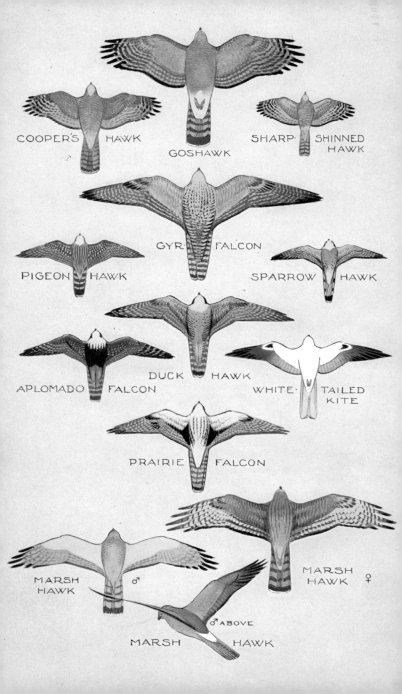

COOPER'S HAWK

GOSHAWK

SHARP-SHINNED HAWK

GYR FALCON

PIGEON HAWK

SPARROW HAWK

APLOMADO FALCON

DUCK HAWK

WHITE-TAILED KITE

PRAIRIE FALCON

MARSH HAWK ♂

MARSH HAWK ♀

MARSH HAWK ♂ ABOVE

key, with a small head and a long rounded tail. Very shy and difficult to observe, a skulking denizen of dense woods and thickets in the lower Rio Grande Valley, where it is best found at daybreak when it calls raucously from the tree-tops.

Voice: — A loud raucous three-syllabled cackling call, *cha'-cha-lac*, repeated in chorus from tree-tops in early morning and evening and sometimes before rain. Dr. Arthur A. Allen describes the harsh chorus of a pair of these birds as *keep'-it-up*, *keep'-it-up*, *keep'-it-up*, etc., answered by a lower-pitched *cut'-it-out*, *cut'-it-out*, *cut'-it-out*, etc.

Range: — Lower Rio Grande Valley, Tex.

GROUSE: TETRAONIDÆ

LARGE Chicken-like birds, larger than Quail. Some are almost restricted to woods; others inhabit prairies and deserts. Peculiar courting antics of males are spectacular and distinctive.

DUSKY GROUSE. *Dendragapus obscurus.* Subsp. (Illus. p. 56.)

Descr. ♂ 21, ♀ 18. Three dusky gray or blackish Grouse occur in the evergreen forests of the West. Two, the Dusky and the Franklin's Grouse, are found in the Rocky Mt. section. The Dusky Grouse is the larger and grayer of the two. The best marks by which to tell the male Franklin's Grouse are the blacker under parts and the *black and white banding on the sides of the rump*. At close range male Franklin's Grouse show *orange-red* or *red* patches over the eyes; Dusky Grouse *yellow or orange*. Female Franklin's Grouse are *blackish* above; female Dusky Grouse, brownish.

Voice: — Male in courtship gives a series of five or six 'hoots' similar to those of the next species but with only fraction of their carrying power.

Subsp. DUSKY GROUSE. *D. o. obscurus.*
　　　　Similar in field to next species. Rockies from n. Ut., se. Ida., and n. Colo. s. to cent. N.M. and cent. Ariz., w. to cent. Nev.
　　　　RICHARDSON'S GROUSE. *D. o. richardsoni.*
　　　　Lacks pale band at tip of tail. N. Rockies from Can. s. to Wyo. and s.-cent. Ida., w. to e. Wash. and e. Ore.

SOOTY GROUSE. *Dendragapus fuliginosus.* Subsp.

Descr. 16–19. A dark gray or blackish Grouse with a light band at the tip of the tail. The only dark gray Grouse found in the fir forests of the Pacific States (except in section east of Cascades in Wash. and Ore.). The range of this species nowhere overlaps those of the Dusky and Franklin's Grouse. Females

are browner than males, but have a gray cast rather than the
rusty-red of the female Oregon Ruffed Grouse.
Voice: — Male in courtship gives a series of six or seven low
muffled booming or hooting notes about one octave lower than
notes of Horned Owl; ventriloquial.
Range: — Evergreen forests in high mts. of Pacific States from
Wash. to s. Calif. (Mt. Pinos), except in section e. of Cascades
in Wash. and Ore.
Subsp. (No apparent field differences): (1) Sooty Grouse, *D. f.
fuliginosus*; (2) Sierra Grouse, *D. f. sierræ*; (3) Mount Pinos
Grouse, *D. f. howardi*.

FRANKLIN'S GROUSE. *Canachites franklini.* (Illus. p. 56.)
Descr. 15–16. Very similar to the Spruce Grouse of e. and n.
Can. See Dusky Grouse for description.
Range: — Mt. regions e. of Cascades from Can. s. to ne. Ore.,
cent. Ida., and w. Mont.

RUFFED GROUSE. *Bonasa umbellus.* Subsp. (Illus. p. 56.)
Descr. 16–19. A large, *red-brown*, or *gray-brown* Chicken-like
bird of brushy woodlands, usually not seen until it springs into
the air with a startling whir. Female Pheasants are somewhat
similar, but have pointed instead of fan-shaped tails, usually
prefer more open country, and they flush with less of a whir, generally croaking as they go. The black band near the tip of the
tail distinguishes this species from the other woodland Grouse.
The Oregon subspecies (coastal belt) is especially distinctive
because of its red-brown color.
Voice: — The drumming of the male might be overlooked as a
distant 'flivver' starting up, or an outboard motor on some far-
distant lake. Their drumming (not a vocal sound, but made by
the wings) starts off slowly, gaining speed until it ends in a
whir: — *bup ... bup ... bup ... bup .. bup . bup . up . r . rrr.* At
a distance the thumping is so hollow that sometimes it hardly
registers as an exterior sound, but seems rather to be a disturbing series of vibrations within the ear itself.
Subsp. OREGON RUFFED GROUSE. *B. u. sabini.*
> Distinguished from next race by rustier color. Coastal
> belt from w. Wash. to nw. Calif.
> GRAY RUFFED GROUSE. *B. u. umbelloides.*
> Like the preceding but with more gray and less rufous
> on the upper parts. E. of Cascades, from Can. s. to n.
> Colo. (formerly), n. Ut., and e. Ore.

WHITE-TAILED PTARMIGAN. *Lagopus leucurus.* Subsp.
(Illus. p. 56.)
Descr. 12–13. Ptarmigan are small Arctic or Alpine Grouse
that change their brown summer plumage for white feathers

when winter sets in. They frequent bleak, barren wastes above timber line on high mountains where few other birds would long survive. This is the only species found in w. U.S. In summer it is brown with a white belly and white wings and tail, conspicuous in flight. In winter the bird is pure white except for black eyes and bill.

Range: — Cascade Mts. of Wash., and Rockies from Mont. to n. N.M.

Subsp. (No apparent field differences): (1) Rainier White-tailed Ptarmigan, *L. l. rainierensis*; (2) Southern White-tailed Ptarmigan, *L. l. altipetens*.

GREATER PRAIRIE CHICKEN. *Tympanuchus cupido americanus.*

Descr. 18. A large brown Hen-like bird of the prairies and brushy grasslands known from the Sharp-tailed Grouse and female Sage Hen by the *short rounded black tail* and, when close, by the heavy transverse barrings on the under parts.

Range: — Great Plains w. to e. Colo. and ne. Mont.; occasional in e. Wyo.

LESSER PRAIRIE CHICKEN. *Tympanuchus pallidicinctus.*

Descr. 16. Similar to Greater Prairie Chicken but much paler.

Range: — Southern Great Plains w. to se. Colo. and e. N.M.

SHARP-TAILED GROUSE. *Pediœcetes phasianellus.* Subsp. (Illus. p. 56.)

Descr. 17½. A *pale* speckled brown Grouse of the prairies with a *short pointed tail.* Female Pheasants have *long* pointed tails; Sage Hens, which also inhabit prairies, are much larger and have black bellies. The various woodland Grouse have wide fanlike tails.

Voice: — In courtship, a hollow 'booming' sound.

Range: — Great Plains w. to foothills in Mont., Wyo., and cent. Colo. Also Great Basin region (e. Wash., e. Ore., Ida., Nev., Ut., w. Mont., sw. Colo., and n. N.M.).

Subsp. (No apparent field differences): (1) Columbian Sharp-tailed Grouse, *P. p. columbianus*; (2) Prairie Sharp-tailed Grouse, *P. p. campestris.*

SAGE HEN. *Centrocercus urophasianus.* (Illus. p. 56.)

Descr. ♂ 28, ♀ 22. Large gray-brown Grouse-like birds of the open sage country, as large as small Turkeys; identified by the contrasting *black belly* and spike-like tail-feathers. Males are considerably larger than females.

Range: — Sagebrush plains e. of Cascades and Sierras from se. Wash. and Mont. s. to e. Calif., Nev., Ut., and n. Colo.

OLD WORLD PARTRIDGES: PERDICINÆ

EUROPEAN PARTRIDGE. *Perdix perdix perdix.*
Descr. 12–14. A grayish Partridge with chestnut-colored markings; smaller than any of the Grouse and larger than a Quail; found locally in farming country where it has been introduced. In flight, the short, chestnut-colored tail is a good mark.
Range: — Has been introduced locally in several W. States.

QUAIL: ODONTOPHORINÆ

SMALL, scratching, Chicken-like birds, smaller than Grouse or Pheasants.

BOB-WHITE. *Colinus virginianus texanus.* (Illus. p. 57.)
Descr. 8½–10½. A small, ruddy, Chicken-like bird, much smaller than a Grouse, or near the size of a Meadowlark. It is distinguished from the Grouse by its smaller size and short round tail; from other Quail by its rusty color; and from the Meadowlark in flight by the lack of white outer tail-feathers. On the ground or perched the male shows a conspicuous white throat and stripe over the eye, the female buffy.
Voice: — A clearly enunciated whistle *Bob-white*, or *Poor Bob-white.*
Range: — Has been introduced locally in several of the W. States.

SCALED QUAIL. *Callipepla squamata.* Subsp. (Illus. p. 57.)
Descr. 10–12. Often called 'Blue Quail.' A pale grayish Quail of open arid country recognized by the scaly markings on the breast and a *bushy white crest* or 'cotton top.'
Voice: — A two-noted, Guinea-hen-like *chek-ah.*
Range: — Arid country in cent. and s. Ariz., s. Colo., N.M., and w., cent., and s. Tex.
Subsp. (No apparent field differences): (1) Arizona Scaled Quail, *C. s. pallida*; (2) Chestnut-bellied Scaled Quail, *C. s. castanogastris.*

CALIFORNIA QUAIL. *Lophortyx californica.* Subsp. (Illus. p. 57.)
Descr. 9½–10½. A small, plump, grayish Chicken-like bird with a *short plume that curves forward* from its crown. Males have an interesting black-and-white face pattern; females are duller. This species frequents open brush country and cultivated areas.
Voice: — Both sexes, a three-syllabled call, *qua-quer-go*, vari-

BALD EAGLE ADULT

BALD EAGLE IMMATURE

GOLDEN EAGLE ADULT

GOLDEN EAGLE IMMATURE

OSPREY

BUTEOS
BROAD WINGS
BROAD ROUNDED TAIL

RED-TAILED HAWK
SWAINSON'S HAWK
AM. ROUGH-LEGGED H.
FERRUGINOUS ROUGH-LEG

Local or Rare Species :
RED-BELLIED HAWK
SENNETT'S WHITE-TAILED H.
ZONE-TAILED HAWK
HARRIS'S HAWK (PARABUTEO)
MEXICAN GOSHAWK (ASTURINA)
MEXICAN BLACK H.(URUBITINGA)

ACCIPITERS
LONG TAIL
SHORT ROUNDED WINGS

GOSHAWK (ASTUR)
COOPER'S HAWK
SHARP-SHINNED HAWK

FALCONS
LONG TAIL
LONG POINTED WINGS

DUCK HAWK
PRAIRIE FALCON
SPARROW HAWK
PIGEON HAWK
Local or Rare Species
GYRFALCON
APLOMADO FALCON

SILHOUETTES OF THREE COMMON TYPES OF HAWKS

ously interpreted as *where are you? you go way, chi-ca-go, tuc-a-hoe*, etc. Note of male on territory a loud *kurk* or *twerk*.

Range: — Native in s. Ore. and Calif. (except in e. parts of Mohave and Colorado deserts, where replaced by Gambel's Quail. Both California Quail and Gambel's Quail occur together in spots on the w. edge of the Colorado and Mohave deserts and sometimes hybridize). Widely introduced elsewhere in W. States.

Subsp. (No apparent field differences): (1) California Quail, *L. c. californica*; (2) Valley Quail, *L. c. vallicola*; (3) Catalina Quail, *L. c. catalinensis*.

GAMBEL'S QUAIL. *Lophortyx gambeli.* Subsp. (Illus. p. 57.)
Descr. 10–11. Replaces the California Quail in the desert regions of the Sw. Similar, but male with a large black patch on a light belly; flanks and top of head more russet, latter giving rise to local name 'Redhead.'
Voice: — A loud *kway-o* and a querulous three-noted call, *chi-quer-go*, somewhat more drawling than California Quail.
Range: — Deserts of s. Calif., s. Nev., sw. Ut., Ariz., cent. and sw. N.M., and extreme w. Tex.; introduced locally elsewhere.
Subsp. (No apparent field differences): (1) Gambel's Quail, *L. g. gambeli*; (2) Olathe Quail, *L. g. sanus*.

MOUNTAIN QUAIL. *Oreortyx picta.* Subsp. (Illus. p. 57.)
Descr. 11. A Quail of the mountains of the Pacific States. Distinguished from the California Quail by the long *straight* head plume and the *chestnut throat*. The flank pattern is also distinctive.
Voice: — A loud mellow cry, *wook?* or *to-wook?* repeated at infrequent intervals by male in breeding season. Both sexes utter rapid, tremulous whistling sounds when alarmed.
Range: — Mts. of sw. Wash., Ore., s. Ida., w. Nev., and Calif. (to s. part).
Subsp. (No apparent field differences): (1) Mountain Quail, *O. p. palmeri*; (2) Plumed Quail, *O. p. picta*.

MEARNS'S QUAIL. *Cyrtonyx montezumæ mearnsi.* (Illus. p. 57.)
Descr. 8. A small Quail of the brushy slopes of desert mountains. The oddly striped face and speckled body of the male are best shown in the drawing. Females are duller without the facial stripings.
Voice: — A soft whinnying or rolling cry.
Range: — Arid regions from cent. Ariz., cent. N.M., and w. Tex. s.

PHEASANTS: PHASIANIDÆ

RING-NECKED PHEASANT. *Phasianus colchicus torquatus.*
(Illus. p. 56.)
Descr. ♂ 33–36, ♀ 20½. A large Chicken-like or Gamecock-like bird with a long, sweeping pointed tail. The male is quite highly colored with a white neck-ring; the female is brown and more Grouse-like. Its pointed tail is much longer than that of the Sharp-tailed Grouse, which lives in grassy country.
Voice: — Males in spring utter a loud double squawk followed by a whir of wings.
Range: — Introduced in many parts of w. U.S.

TURKEYS: MELEAGRIDIDÆ

MERRIAM'S TURKEY. *Meleagris gallopavo merriami.*
Descr. ♂ 48, ♀ 36. Very similar to the familiar Domestic Turkey of the barnyard. Differs from the Eastern Wild Turkey in having whitish tips to the tail-feathers instead of chestnut.
Voice: — Similar to 'gobbling' of Domestic Turkey.
Range: — Mts. of s. Colo., Ariz., N.M., and w. Tex.

CRANES: GRUIDÆ

LONG-LEGGED, long-necked birds, superficially a little like large Herons, but with long feathers on the back, which curl down over the ends of the wings. They also have shorter bills, and bare red skin about the face. Their blaring trumpet-like calls, once heard, dispel any doubt as to their identity. In flight, the wing-motion of Cranes is quite unlike that of either Herons or Ibises. The wings are less bowed and they beat with a very characteristic deft upward flap. Cranes fly with their necks extended (Herons 'tuck' them in). They do not stand as stiff and erect as Herons.

WHOOPING CRANE. *Grus americana.*
Descr. 50. Larger than Sandhill Crane or Great Blue Heron. A large *white* Crane with a red face; neck outstretched in flight, primary wing-feathers black. (See Wood Ibis.)
Range: — Now an extremely rare migrant in Great Plains; w. occasionally to Mont., Wyo., and probably Colo. and N.M. Winters on coastal prairies of s. Tex.

SANDHILL CRANE. *Grus canadensis.* Subsp. (Illus. pp. 12, 17.)
Descr. A long-legged, long-necked, gray bird with a bald red

forehead. The Great Blue Heron is often called a 'Crane,' but the Heron in sustained flight carries its head drawn back to its shoulders, while the Crane flies with neck extended and legs trailing, like a 'flying cross.' The deft upward flap of the wings in flight is typical.

Voice: — A deep, trumpet-like rolling *k-r-r-r-oo* repeated several times.

Subsp. LITTLE BROWN CRANE. *G. c. canadensis.*

34–39. Difficult to distinguish from the Sandhill Crane except when both birds are together, when the smaller size and shorter bill of this race is evident. In California the Little Brown Crane is the commoner race. Breeds in Arctic; migrates through interior of U.S. to Calif., Tex., and Mex.

SANDHILL CRANE. *G. c. tabida.*

40–48. Breeds in ne. Calif., e. Ore., n. Nev., s. Ida., n. Vt., sw. Mont., w. Wyo., and nw. Colo. Winters from Calif. and Tex. s. to Mex.

RAILS, GALLINULES, AND COOTS: RALLIDÆ

RAILS are somewhat Chicken-like marsh-birds of secretive habits, shy rather than wary, and much more often heard than seen. When flushed, they rise from the reeds close at hand, fly feebly with legs dangling for a short distance, and drop back again suddenly into the marsh.

Gallinules and Coots resemble Ducks except for their smaller heads and rather Chicken-like bills.

CALIFORNIA CLAPPER RAIL. *Rallus obsoletus.* Subsp. (Illus. p. 60.)

Descr. 16. A large brown Rail of the *salt marshes*. Its Hen-like appearance, strong legs, long bill, and white patch under the short tail identify it. The only other Western Rail with a long, slender bill, the Virginia, is much smaller (see Virginia Rail).

Voice: — A clattering *kek-kek-kek-kek*, etc.

Range: — Salt marshes from San Diego to San Francisco, Calif. (casually farther n.), also lower Colo. R. from Yuma to Laguna Dam, and Imperial Valley marshes s. of Salton Sea.

Subsp. (No apparent field differences): (1) California Clapper Rail, *R. o. obsoletus*; (2) Light-footed Rail, *R. o. levipes*; (3) Yuma Clapper Rail, *R. o. yumanensis.*

VIRGINIA RAIL. *Rallus limicola limicola.* (Illus. p. 60.)

Descr. 9–10½. A small reddish Rail, less than ten inches in length, with *gray cheeks* and a long, slightly decurved bill, the only small Rail, smaller than a Quail, with a *slender* bill. The only fresh-water Rail with a slender bill. When in salt marshes it might be confused with the California Clapper Rail, which is larger (as large as a small Hen), but the ruddier color and gray cheeks are good marks.

Voice: — *Cut-cutta-cutta*, etc., *wak-wak-wak*, etc., and *kidick-kidick-kidick*, besides various 'kicking' and grunting sounds.

Range: — Breeds from Can. s. to s. Calif., Ut., and Colo.; winters from Mex. n. to n. Calif., Ut., and Colo., casually farther.

SORA. *Porzana carolina.* (Illus. p. 60.)
Descr. 8–9¾. The adult Sora is a small gray-brown Rail with a black patch on its face and throat, and a short, Chicken-like *yellow* bill. This short yellow bill will distinguish the bird readily in any plumage from the only other similar-sized Rail of the fresh-water marshes it inhabits, the reddish Virginia Rail, which has a long, slender bill. The immature bird lacks the black throat-patch, and is buffy-brown below, not gray. It can be confused with the smaller and rarer Yellow Rail.

Voice: — 'Song,' a whinnying series of notes, descending. In the spring, a plaintive whistled *ker-wee*. In the fall, a sharp *keek* is the usual note of response when a stone is tossed into the marsh.

Range: — Breeds from Can. s. to s. Calif., Ut., and n. N.M.; winters from Calif. and Ariz. s.

YELLOW RAIL. *Coturnicops noveboracensis.* (Illus. p. 60.)
Descr. 6–7½. Rare. A small yellowish Rail, showing a conspicuous *white* wing-patch in flight — the only Rail so marked. Yellow Rails are so extremely secretive that it requires the services of a bird dog to hunt for them successfully. They prefer grassy marshes to the reedy swamps frequented by their larger relatives. The immature Sora might be taken for a Yellow Rail but is larger, not so yellow, and lacks the white wing-patch.

Voice: — Clicking or ticking notes, often in long series; usually in this sequence: *tic-tic, tic-tic-tic; tic-tic, tic-tic-tic; tic-tic,* etc. (groups of two and three). Some observers describe another call: *kĭ kĭ kĭ kĭ kĭ kreeah*, the last note with a rolling quality (Francis H. Allen).

Range: — Winters in w.-cent. Calif.; casual in other W. States. Breeds in e.-cent. Calif. (Mono Co.).

CALIFORNIA BLACK RAIL. *Creciscus jamaicensis coturniculus.* (Illus. p. 60.)
Descr. 5–6. A very tiny slaty or blackish Rail with white specks on the back and a black bill; about the size of a young Song Sparrow with a bobbed tail. All young Rails in the downy plum-

age are glossy black, and thus are sometimes called Black Rails by the inexperienced. This species inhabits salt meadows where salicornia grows, and is very difficult to flush, or even get a glimpse of.

Range: — Calif., locally in coastal marshes and occasionally inland.

PURPLE GALLINULE. *Ionornis martinica.*
Descr. 12–14. Accidental in Arizona. Distinguished from the Florida Gallinule by its *deep purple* under parts, *pale blue* frontal shield on bill, and, in flight, the bright *yellow* legs.

FLORIDA GALLINULE. *Gallinula chloropus cachinnans.* (Illus. p. 60.)
Descr. 12–14½. Gallinules are Hen-like birds with stout, rather Chicken-like bills, equally at home swimming like Ducks in the open water or wading like Rails in the shallows and among the reeds, or even perching in the bushes along the margin. This is the only one that ordinarily occurs in the West. A slate-gray Duck-like or Rail-like bird with a *red* bill is certainly this species. A white stripe along the flanks is also distinctive. A Gallinule in the company of Coots is smaller, with a somewhat smaller head.
Voice: — Some notes have whining quality, others Chicken-like.
Range: — Marshes from cent. Calif. and Ariz. s. Casual or accidental elsewhere in West.

COOT. *Fulica americana.* (Illus. p. 60.)
Descr. 13–16. Largely gray with a blackish head and neck, white under tail-coverts, and a whitish Chicken-like bill. In flight a white border shows on the hind edge of the wing. It is the only slate-gray Duck-like bird with a whitish bill. Like the Gallinule, when swimming it pumps its neck and head back and forth to facilitate its progress. The dabbing motion while feeding is also quite characteristic. In deep water it dives expertly. When it takes wing, it patters its feet over the water for a considerable distance.
Voice: — Various cackling and croaking notes.
Range: — Breeds from Can. s. to Mex.; winters in Pacific States and from Colo. s.

JACANAS: JACANIDÆ

MEXICAN JACANA. *Jacana spinosa gymnostoma.* (Illus. p. 60.)
Descr. 8½. Occasional near Brownsville, Tex. Frequents ponds and marshes with dense vegetation where Gallinules are found.

Built somewhat like a shore-bird, with *extremely long toes*. Head and neck blackish, rest of body deep rusty. The best field-marks are the conspicuous yellow *frontal shield* on the forehead and *large pale-yellow wing-patches* (primaries and secondaries). Immature birds which wander north across the Mexican boundary in the fall are entirely unlike adults and slightly suggest Wilson's Phalaropes. They are gray-brown above, with white under parts and a broad white stripe over the eye. The upper breast is tinged with buffy. The extremely long toes, short, rounded wings, and Rail-like flight, notes, and habitat will distinguish them from any shore-bird.

OYSTER–CATCHERS: HÆMATOPODIDÆ

FRAZAR'S OYSTER-CATCHER. *Hæmatopus palliatus frazari.*
Descr. No longer found in Calif. but might occur as a straggler from Mex. Resembles Black Oyster-catcher but has a *white belly* and *white wing-patches*. A race of the American Oyster-catcher of the eastern United States.

BLACK OYSTER-CATCHER. *Hæmatopus bachmani.* (Illus. p. 73.)
Descr. 17. A large heavily built, *all-dark* shore-bird with a heavy *red bill* and pale legs. Unmistakable. Frequents rocky shores along the ocean.
Voice: — A piercing, sharply repeated whistled note.
Range: — Rocky shores and islands along Pacific Coast.

PLOVERS: CHARADRIINÆ

WADING birds, more compactly built, more contrastingly patterned, and with shorter, stouter bills than Sandpipers.

(WESTERN) SNOWY PLOVER. *Charadrius nivosus nivosus.* (Illus. pp. 65, 72.)
Descr. 6. Slightly smaller and very much paler than the Semipalmated Plover, from which it can be distinguished by its slim, black bill, dusky legs, and *incomplete* black neck-ring. The 'ring' is reduced to a black patch on each side of the breast. The Semipalmated Plover is the brown color of wet sand; the Snowy, the color of the sun-bleached dry sand or alkali flats it inhabits.
Voice: — A whistled *too-leep*.
Range: — Breeds along coast and locally inland in Pacific

States, also locally in Ut. and N.M.; winters from cent. Calif. s.

SEMIPALMATED PLOVER. *Charadrius semipalmatus.* (Illus. pp. 65, 72.)
Descr. 6½–8. A small ring-necked shore-bird, brown above and white below; half the size of the Killdeer, from which it may also be distinguished by the short tail and the *single* ring about the neck instead of two. The legs are yellowish and the base of the bill orange (in adults). The Snowy Plover is somewhat similar, but is much paler and whiter, with blackish bill and legs.
Voice: — A plaintive slurred *chi-we*, second note higher.
Range: — Migrates along Pacific Coast; rare inland; winters from cent. Calif. s.

BELDING'S PLOVER. *Pagolla wilsonia beldingi.*
Descr. 7½. A race of the Wilson's Plover, an accidental straggler from Lower Calif. to w. U.S., which might be looked for on s. Calif. beaches. A ring-necked Plover, larger than either the Semipalmated or Snowy Plovers, from which it can be distinguished by its *longer and heavier black bill* and *flesh-colored* legs.
Voice: — A whistled *wheep!*

MOUNTAIN PLOVER. *Eupoda montana.* (Illus. pp. 65, 72.)
Descr. 8–9½. Like a small Killdeer, but with *no breast-rings.* In the breeding season a black mark extends from the bill through the eye. In winter plumage the bird lacks this, but may be told from the winter Black-bellied Plover, which it resembles a little, by its smaller size and the even coloration of its back, *devoid of mottling.* Its habitat is not the shore-line or mud-flat, but prairies, open fields, and alkali-flats.
Voice: — A low whistle; variable.
Range: — Breeds in high plains e. of Continental Divide from Mont. s. to N.M. and w. Tex.; winters from Calif. and s. Ariz. s.

KILLDEER. *Oxyechus vociferus vociferus.* (Illus. pp. 65, 72.)
Descr. 9–11. The Killdeer is the common breeding Plover of the plowed fields, prairies, farm country, lake-shores, and golf-courses. It is larger than the *two* other 'ringed' Plovers, has two breast-bands instead of one, and, in flight, shows an ample, golden-red tail.
Voice: — Noisy; a loud, insistent *kill-deer*, or *kill-dee* or *dee-ee*, oft repeated.
Range: — Breeds from Can. to Mex.; winters in Pacific States and from Colo. s.

GOLDEN PLOVER. *Pluvialis dominica.* Subsp. (Illus. pp. 65, 72.)

Descr. 10–11. A trifle larger than a Killdeer. Spring adults are brown above and black below, with a broad white line extending over the eye down the side of the head. The only other similar bird is the Black-bellied Plover, which is pale gray above, not golden brown, and has a white rump and tail. The Golden Plover has a brown tail. Young birds and winter adults are brown, darker above than below. They are distinguished from the Black-bellied Plover by the lack of white in the wings and tail, and the lack of black axillary feathers beneath the wings (where the wings join the body). In flight, in mixed flocks, they can be picked out by their lack of conspicuous pattern. They prefer prairies, dunes, and burned marshes to the mud-flats.
Voice: — The harsh, whistled *queedle* or *quee* is quite unlike the plaintive *whee-er-ee* of the Black-belly.
Range: — Rare migrant along edge of Great Plains, in Ut., and on Pacific Coast.
Subsp. (No apparent field differences): (1) American Golden Plover, *P. d. dominica*; (2) Pacific Golden Plover, *P. d. fulva*.

BLACK-BELLIED PLOVER. *Squatarola squatarola.* (Illus. pp. 65, 72.)
Descr. 10½–13½. In summer dress the Black-bellied Plover, with its black under parts, resembles no other shore-bird except the rare Golden Plover, which is somewhat smaller and much browner-backed. White-breasted winter birds and immatures are gray-looking and are recognized as Plovers by their stocky proportions and short, stout bills. In any plumage the black axillary feathers under the wing, and the white rump and tail, are determinative.
Voice: — A plaintive slurred whistle, *whee-er-eee*.
Range: — Migrates along Pacific Coast and locally inland; winters along Calif. coast.

SURF–BIRDS: APHRIZINÆ

SURF-BIRD. *Aphriza virgata.* (Illus. pp. 65, 73.)
Descr. 10. A stocky Sandpiper-like shore-bird that inhabits the wave-washed rocks along the ocean where Black Turnstones are found. In flight, it shows a conspicuous *white tail tipped with a broad black band*. It can be told from the Black Turnstone by its somewhat larger size, grayer color, *yellowish* legs, and different flight pattern (see diagram).
Voice: — A sharp *pee-weet* or *key-a-weet*.
Range: — Migrates and winters along Pacific Coast.

RING·NECKED
PHEASANT ♂

RING·NECKED
PHEASANT ♀

SHARP·TAILED
GROUSE

DUSKY
GROUSE ♂

RUFFED
GROUSE ♂

FRANKLIN'S
GROUSE ♂

SAGE
HEN ♂

WHITE·
TAILED
PTARMIGAN   SUMMER

WHITE·
TAILED
PTARMIGAN   WINTER

GROUSE AND
PHEASANTS

MOUNTAIN QUAIL - CALIFORNIA QUAIL - GAMBEL'S QUAIL

SCALED QUAIL - MEARNS'S QUAIL - BOB·WHITE

QUAIL

TURNSTONES: ARENARIINÆ

RUDDY TURNSTONE. *Arenaria interpres morinella.* (Illus. pp. 65, 73.)
Descr. 8–9½. A squat, robust, *orange-legged* shore-bird, larger than a Spotted Sandpiper. In breeding plumage with its *russet-red* back and fantastic black face and breast markings, the bird is handsome enough, but when it flies the real revelation occurs. This harlequin pattern is best explained by the diagram. Young birds and winter adults are more sober in color but easily recognized. The much commoner Black Turnstone has a similar flight pattern but does not have the orange legs, rusty-colored areas, and odd breast-pattern.
Voice: — A rough *chut-a-chut.*
Range: — Migrates along Pacific Coast; very rare inland. Winters from cent. Calif. s.

BLACK TURNSTONE. *Arenaria melanocephala.* (Illus. pp. 65, 73.)
Descr. 9. A squat black shore-bird with blackish breast and white belly. Frequents rocks and ledges along the ocean. Its wing-pattern, shown in the diagram, is very distinctive.
Voice: — A shrill rattling note higher than the Ruddy Turnstone.
Range: — Migrant and winter visitant along coast.

SNIPE, SANDPIPERS, ETC.: SCOLOPACIDÆ

IN GENERAL, small or medium-sized waders with more slender bills than Plovers. Most species are of plain or sober coloration.

WILSON'S SNIPE. *Capella delicata.* (Illus. p. 72.)
Descr. 10½–11½. A striped brown bird, larger than a Spotted Sandpiper, with a short orange tail and an extremely long, slender bill. When flushed, it makes off in a zigzag manner, uttering a sharp, rasping note. Its preferred habitat is wet meadows and the boggy margins of little streams and marshes.
Voice: — Nasal, rasping note when flushed. Nuptial 'song,' uttered in flight, a melodious, winnowing whistle (not vocal).
Range: — Breeds locally from Can. s. to e. Calif., n. Nev., n. Ut., and n. Colo.; winters from w. Wash. and Mont. s. to Mex.

LONG-BILLED CURLEW. *Numenius americanus.* Subsp. (Illus. pp. 58, 73.)
Descr. 20–26, bill 5–7. Curlews are very large brown shore-

HEADS OF CURLEWS

A. Long-billed Curlew   B. Hudsonian Curlew

birds with long *down-curved* bills. The bills of Godwits turn up. In flight they appear as large as some Ducks, and when in flocks often fly in line or wedge formation, with sickle bills extended and legs trailing. Of the two Western species, the Long-bill is the one chiefly encountered in the interior. On the coast, both it and the Hudsonian Curlew occur. The points of distinction are the much larger size of the Long-bill, the more *buffy* coloration, and the lack of contrasting head-striping (i.e., dark line through eye, stripes on crown, etc.). In flight overhead, its *bright cinnamon* wing-linings make a sure means of identification. In many individuals, the bill is seven inches long, or *twice as long* as that of the average Hudsonian, but in a few birds bill-lengths approach each other. Then the other identification marks must be used.

Voice: — A harsh *cur-lee!* with rising inflection. Also a rapid, whistled *kli-li-li-li*.

Range: — Great Basin and Great Plains regions (e. Wash., e. Ore., ne. Calif., s. Ida., Ut., Nev., Mont., Wyo., Colo., and n. N.M.). Winters in cent. and s. Calif. and along coast of Tex.

Subsp. (No apparent field differences): (1) Long-billed Curlew, *N. a. americanus*; (2) Northern Curlew, *N. a. occidentalis*.

HUDSONIAN CURLEW. *Phæopus hudsonicus*. (Illus. pp. 58, 64.)

Descr. 15–18, bill 3–4. (See Long-billed Curlew.)

Voice: — Four or five rapidly repeated short whistles, softer and lower than those of Greater Yellow-legs, *whi-whi-whi-whi-whi*.

Range: — Migrates along Pacific Coast and in interior valleys of Calif.; occasional along Great Plains; winters from s. Calif. s.

UPLAND PLOVER. *Bartramia longicauda.* (Illus. p. 64.)
Descr. 11–12½. A large streaked buffy-brown shore-bird, larger than a Killdeer but with no really distinctive markings; inhabits extensive fields, prairies, burnt meadows, etc. It habitually perches on posts. The general brown coloration, the rather short bill, the comparatively small-headed, long-necked, long-tailed appearance, and the habit of holding the wings elevated upon alighting are all helpful points. It can hardly be confused with any other large brown Sandpiper-like bird in the grass country where it is found. Curlews and Godwits are very much larger and have much longer bills.
Voice: — *Kip-ip-ip-ip.* Also a rolling note in flight. 'Song,' a long-drawn melodious wind-like whistle.
Range: — Breeds sparingly from Can. s. in Plains country to e. Ore. (rare), ne. Ut., Colo. (rare), and N.M. (rare). Casual in migration in ne. Calif. and Ariz.

SPOTTED SANDPIPER. *Actitis macularia.* (Illus. pp. 65, 72.)
Descr. 7–8. The common breeding Sandpiper near lakes and streams through much of the W. It runs along the margin, teetering up and down between steps as if it were a little too delicately balanced on its slim legs. In the breeding plumage the breast is covered with *large round spots*; many Sandpipers are streaked, but this is the only one that is definitely spotted. Juvenile birds and fall and winter adults lack this distinctive spotting. They are olive-brown above and whitish below, with a white line over the eye. A white mark on the shoulder is a good aid. The constant teetering is as good a characteristic as any. The wing-stroke is very short, below the horizontal, the wings maintaining a stiff, bowed appearance, entirely unlike the more deep-sweeping flight of the other small shore-birds. This is the most useful distinction of all when Sandpipers rise from the margin. A white wing-stripe, more broken than that of the other small shore-birds having similar stripes, shows in flight.
Voice: — A well enunciated *peet-weet!* — first note higher. (See Solitary Sandpiper.)
Range: — Breeds from Can. s. to s. Calif., n. Ariz., and N.M.; migrates into Mex.; winters along Pacific Coast.

(WESTERN) SOLITARY SANDPIPER. *Tringa solitaria cin-namomea.* (Illus. pp. 64, 73.)
Descr. 7½–9. A dark Sandpiper, blackish above and whitish below, with a white eye-ring. Resembles a Lesser Yellow-legs, and nods like one, but has a dark rump instead of white, and dark legs instead of yellow. The Spotted Sandpiper *teeters* more than it nods and has a white stripe in the wing, which the Solitary lacks; the Spotted has a narrow wing-arc; the Solitary, deep. Both haunt similar places (margins of pools, lakes,

streams). The Solitary may best be described as a *dark-winged Sandpiper with white sides to the tail, which are very conspicuous in flight.*

Voice: — *Peet-weet weet* (higher-pitched than Spotted).

Range: — Migrates throughout w. U.S.

WANDERING TATTLER. *Heteroscelus incanus.* (Illus. pp. 65, 73.)

Descr. 11. A medium-sized shore-bird of the rocky ocean shores where Black Turnstones and Surf-birds are found. It is solid grayish above, with a white line over the eye; legs yellowish. In breeding plumage, the under parts are white, narrowly barred with black. In fall and winter the under parts are unbarred. It can be told at any time from the three shore-birds that inhabit similar haunts (Black Turnstone, Surf-bird, and Spotted Sandpiper) by its *lack of pattern* in flight (see diagram).

Voice: — A clear *whee-we-we-we*, less sharp than that of Greater Yellow-legs, or *tweet-tweet-tweet*, similar to Spotted Sandpiper's.

Range: — Migrates along Pacific Coast; winters from Calif. s.

(WESTERN) WILLET. *Catoptrophorus semipalmatus inornatus.* (Illus. pp. 64, 73.)

Descr. 14–17. A large gray and white shore-bird, with an unmistakable flashy *black-and-white wing-pattern* (see diagram). At rest, when the banded wings cannot be seen, the bird is of a rather uniform gray appearance and quite nondescript. It is large and slender, smaller than the brown Godwits and Curlews and a little larger and more heavily built than the Yellow-legs, which shows much more contrast between the tones of the upper and under parts. The legs are bluish.

Voice: — In breeding season, an oft-repeated *pill-will-willet*; in migration, a loud *kay-tee* or *kā-eh.*

Range: — Breeds in e.-cent. Ore., ne. Calif., n. Nev. (probably), Ut., e. Mont., Wyo., and Colo. (occasionally); migrates through sw. States; winters along Calif. coast.

GREATER YELLOW-LEGS. *Totanus melanoleucus.* (Illus. p. 64.)

Descr. 13–15. A rather large, slim, gray and white Sandpiper with *bright yellow legs.* Flying, it appears as a dark-winged shore-bird with a whitish rump and tail.

Voice: — The three- or four-syllabled whistle, *whew-whew-whew,* is distinctive. Also in spring, a fast-repeated *whee-oodle, whee-oodle,* etc.

Range: — Migrates through w. U.S.; winters from Ore. and N.M. s.

LESSER YELLOW-LEGS. *Totanus flavipes.* (Illus. p. 73.)

Descr. 9½–11. Exactly like the much commoner Greater Yel-

SHORT,
YELLOW BILLS

MOSTLY
BROWN

GRAY-
BROWN

BLACK
PATCH

SORA
IMMATURE

WHITE
WING·PATCH

YELLOW
BUFF

SORA
ADULT

YELLOW RAIL

SMALL, BLACK

BLACK BILL

BLACK RAIL

LONG BILLS

LARGER,
GRAYER
THAN
VIRGINIA
RAIL

YELLOW
PATCHES

MOSTLY
RED·BROWN

CALIFORNIA
CLAPPER RAIL

VIRGINIA RAIL

ADULT

BLACK NAPE

IMMATURE

LONG TOES

MEXICAN JACANA

RED
BILL

WHITE
BILL

FLORIDA GALLINULE

COOT

RAILS, GALLINULE,
COOT and JACANA

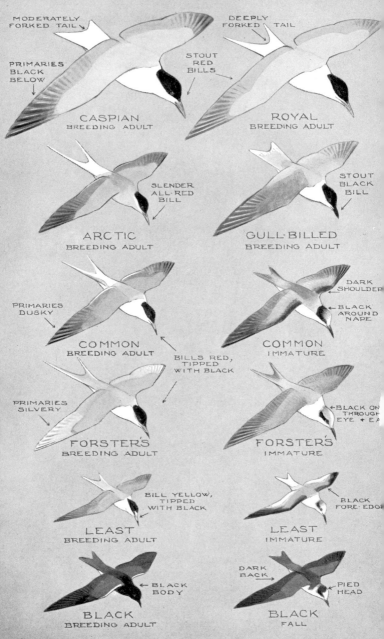

TERNS

low-legs in color, but considerably smaller. The shorter, slim-mer bill of the Lesser is perfectly straight; that of the Greater, *slightly upturned*. The fall Wilson's Phalarope might be mis-taken for this species but is smaller and paler, immaculately white below, has a more needle-like bill, and duller legs (green-ish-yellow or straw-colored).

Voice: — The call most often given by the Greater is a clear, three-syllabled *whew-whew-whew*. That of the Lesser is a flatter, less penetrating cry of one or two notes, *cu* or *cu-cu*. The spring song, corresponding to the *whee-oodle* of the Greater Yellow-legs, is *wheedle-oory*, *wheedle-oory*, etc.

Range: — Migrates through w. U.S.; commonest along edge of Great Plains; uncommon in Pacific States.

KNOT. *Calidris canutus rufus.* (Illus. pp. 64, 72.)
Descr. 10–11. Stout and chunky; larger than a Spotted Sandpiper, or about the size of a Dowitcher. *Spring:* Breast light Robin-red, back mottled gray and black. The short bill, about as long as the head, will distinguish it from the spring Dowitcher, which is also red-breasted. *Fall:* More nondescript, breast whitish. A dumpy light-grayish shore-bird with short legs, a short bill, and a whitish rump. In flight the rump does not show so conspicuously as that of the Yellow-legs, nor does it extend up the back as in the Dowitcher.
Voice: — A soft two-syllabled note.
Range: — Migrates along Pacific Coast; seems to skip Ore.; occasional in Ut.

ALEUTIAN SANDPIPER. *Arquatella ptilocnemis couesi.* (Illus. pp. 64, 73.)
Descr. 8–9. A Sandpiper of irregular occurrence in winter on rocky shores along the Nw. Coast. It is stocky and bluish-gray or slaty colored, resembling somewhat the two other rock-feed-ing species with which it is sometimes found, the Black Turn-stone and the Surf-bird. Both those birds in flight show a broad white band across the base of the tail, *lacking in this species*. It has a white wing-stripe. Very similar to the Purple Sand-piper of the Atlantic Coast.
Voice: — A Flicker-like *clu-clu-clu*.
Range: — Winter visitant to coast of Wash., Ore., and casually Calif.

SHARP-TAILED SANDPIPER. *Pisobia acuminata.*
Descr. 8½. Of rare occurrence along coast of Wash. Like the Pectoral Sandpiper, but in winter plumage, breast rich buffy, *spotted* instead of streaked, with no sharp contrast between white belly and brown of throat and breast (Ludlow Griscom).

PECTORAL SANDPIPER. *Pisobia melanotos.* (Illus. pp. 65, 72.)
Descr. 8–9½. A streaked, brown Sandpiper, larger than a
Spotted; prefers grassy mud-flats and short-grass marshes. The
rusty-brown back is striped with black and lined with white.
The most characteristic thing about the bird is the brownish
streaked breast, which is *defined sharply* against the white belly.
The Least Sandpiper is colored similarly, but is half the size.
The top of the head is darker and the neck longer than that of
the other shore-birds with which it might be confused. Small
individuals might be confused with the less richly marked
Baird's Sandpiper, but the greenish or yellowish legs are a good
mark (Baird's, black).
Voice: — A reedy *krrik, krrik*, heavier than note of Western
Sandpiper.
Range: — Rare coastal migrant; uncommon migrant e. of
Cascades in e. Wash., e. Ore., and Ut.; also along edge of Great
Plains.

WHITE-RUMPED SANDPIPER. *Pisobia fuscicollis.* (Illus.
p. 72.)
Descr. 7½. Somewhat larger than the Western Sandpiper, from
which it is distinguished by its *white rump*, conspicuous in flight.
Other small streaked Sandpipers have only the sides of the
rump white. At rest this species has a more attenuated or
pointed-tailed appearance than other similar shore-birds.
Voice: — A thin, mouse-like *jeet* resembling *jee-jeet* note of
Pipit.
Range: — Migrates through e. U.S.; occurs w. in Great Plains
uncommonly to Mont., Wyo., Colo., and N.M.

BAIRD'S SANDPIPER. *Pisobia bairdi.* (Illus. pp. 65, 72.)
Descr. 7–7½. Resembles a large Least or Western Sandpiper,

TYPICAL BILLS OF 'PEEP'

a. Least Sandpiper   *b.* Semipalmated Sandpiper
c. Western Sandpiper

but paler, with *a very buffy head and breast.* Those two similar species, and the larger Pectoral are more or less *striped* on the back; the Baird's has a more *scaly* appearance, and the predominating color is buff-brown. A 'Peep' Sandpiper, a little larger than a Western, with a buffy wash across the breast, is quite certainly this species.

Voice: — A husky *kree.*

Range: — Migrates along Pacific Coast and through Great Plains and Great Basin.

LEAST SANDPIPER. *Pisobia minutilla.* (Illus. pp. 62, 72.)
Descr. 5–6½. Collectively we call the small Sparrow-sized Sandpipers 'Peep.' These include the Least, Western, and Baird's. All have a characteristic streaked, brown pattern. The Least is the smallest of the three. It may be known at all seasons from the somewhat larger Western Sandpiper by the *yellowish,* or *greenish,* instead of blackish or greenish-black, legs and the *thinner* and shorter bill. In the fall it is browner than the Western and has a more streaked breast.

Voice: — A sharp thin *kree-eet* more drawn out than note of Western.

Range: — Migrates through w. U.S.; winters from cent. Calif. s.

RED-BACKED SANDPIPER. *Pelidna alpina sakhalina.* (Illus. pp. 64, 72.)
Descr. 8–9. Slightly larger than a Spotted Sandpiper. *Spring plumage:* Rusty-red above, with a black patch across the belly and a white breast. No other *Sandpiper* has a black belly. (Black-bellied and Golden Plovers are black below.) *Winter plumage:* Plain, unpatterned gray above, with a gray suffusion across the breast; much darker than a Sanderling. The Western Sandpiper is smaller and shorter-billed. The best mark in the Red-back is the long stout bill for a bird of that size, which has a marked *downward droop* at the tip.

Voice: — A harsh, rasping *cheezp.*

Range: — Migrates through w. U.S., chiefly along coast. Winters along coast.

DOWITCHER. *Limnodromus griseus.* Subsp. (Illus. pp. 64, 72.)
Descr. 11–12½. In any plumage recognized by the very long Snipe-like bill and *white* lower back, rump, and tail. The Wilson's Snipe, the only other bird with similar proportions, is rarely found on the beaches and flats where the Dowitcher commonly feeds, but the two are often found together on grassy 'snipe ground.' In spring plumage the breast is tinged with cinnamon-red; in fall, with light gray.

Voice: — (See Long-billed Dowitcher, below.)

Subsp. EASTERN DOWITCHER. *L. g. griseus.*
Dowitchers of two races migrate through w. U.S. and winter from Calif. s. It was only recently pointed out that the Eastern Dowitcher outnumbers the Long-bill on the West Coast. Formerly it was believed that the Long-bill was the only one that occurred.

LONG-BILLED DOWITCHER. *L. g. scolopaceus.*
The bill measurements of the two Dowitchers overlap, but extreme long-billed birds of this race are easily recognized; the length of the bill, by comparison, dwarfs the head, giving the bird a small-headed appearance. The rusty tinge on the under parts of Long-bills in breeding plumage extends farther down on the belly than in the other bird, often even to the under tail-coverts. The sides of the breast are barred rather than spotted, and the back is darker, with the buffy feather-edgings more restricted. The notes are quite different. That of the Eastern Dowitcher is a trebled *tu-tu-tu* metallic and slightly Yellow-legs-like. The most common note of the Long-bill is a single thin *keek*, occasionally trebled.

STILT SANDPIPER. *Micropalama himantopus.* (Illus. pp. 64, 73.)
Descr. $7\frac{1}{2}$–9. *Fall plumage:* Resembles a Lesser Yellow-legs and has a *similar flight pattern* but is smaller, with a conspicuous white stripe over the eye and *greenish*, not yellow, legs. The bill, which is proportionately longer and heavier, tapering markedly and with a slight droop at the tip, gives the bird a somewhat Dowitcher-like look. Its feeding habits are also similar to that species. *Spring plumage:* Dark gray, heavily marked with *transverse* bars beneath, and having a heavy rusty mark through the eye.
Voice: — A soft *quirt.*
Range: — Migrates through e. U.S., w. uncommonly in Great Plains to Colo. and Wyo.

SEMIPALMATED SANDPIPER. *Ereunetes pusillus.* (Illus. p. 62.)
Descr. $6\frac{1}{3}$. Very similar to the Western Sandpiper and difficult to distinguish in the field. Usually a trifle smaller, and with a noticeably *shorter bill.* Late summer Westerns usually have some rusty on the scapulars, which this species lacks. Least Sandpipers are even smaller, are browner, thinner-billed, and have yellowish legs.
Voice: — Commonest note, a simple *cher* or *cheh.*
Range: — Eastern N.A.; w. uncommonly in migration through Great Plains to Mont., Wyo., and Colo. Occasional in Ut. and Wash.

BLACK-NECKED
STILT

AVOCET

LONG-BILLED
CURLEW

BLACK
OYSTER-CATCHER

MARBLED
GODWIT

SOLITARY
SANDPIPER

WILLET

WANDERING
TATTLER
FALL

RUDDY
TURNSTONE
BREEDING

LESSER
YELLOW-LEGS

SURF-BIRD

STILT
SANDPIPER
FALL

ALEUTIAN
SANDPIPER

BLACK
TURNSTONE

WILSON'S
PHALAROPE
FALL

SHOREBIRDS I

DOWITCHER
FALL

WILSON'S
SNIPE

KNOT
FALL

SANDERLING
FALL

SPOTTED
SANDPIPER
FALL

RED-BACKED
SANDPIPER
FALL

NORTHERN
PHALAROPE
FALL

PECTORAL
SANDPIPER

WHITE-
RUMPED
SANDPIPER
FALL

RED
PHALAROPE
FALL

LEAST
SANDPIPER

BAIRD'S
SANDPIPER

BLACK-BELLIED
PLOVER
FALL

ABOVE

BELOW

KILLDEER

MOUNTAIN
PLOVER

GOLDEN
PLOVER
FALL

SNOWY
PLOVER

SEMI-PALMATED
PLOVER

SHOREBIRDS II

WESTERN SANDPIPER. *Ereunetes mauri.* (Illus. pp. 62, 65.)
Descr. 6–7. This and the Least Sandpiper are the two common streaked Sparrow-sized Sandpipers which are nicknamed 'Peeps.' The Western is larger, has blackish legs (Least, yellow or yellow-green) and a longer, heavier bill. In the fall, the Western lacks the suffusion of dusky across the upper breast which the Least has, and is grayer above, not so brown.
Voice: — A thin *jeet*, shorter and not so drawn out as note of Least Sandpiper.
Range: — Migrates through w. N.A.; winters from cent. Calif. s.

MARBLED GODWIT. *Limosa fedoa.* (Illus. pp. 64, 73.)
Descr. 16–20. A large shore-bird with a long, straight or perceptibly *upturned bill.* The large size and rich *buff-brown* coloration distinguish this species from all other shore-birds except the Curlews, whose bills turn *down.*
Voice: — A harsh *kret, kret.*
Range: — Formerly bred in Ut. Migrates through Calif., Ut., and Great Plains. Rare in Wash. and Ore. Winters from cent. Calif. s.

SANDERLING. *Crocethia alba.* (Illus. pp. 65, 72.)
Descr. 7–8½. A small, plump Sandpiper with a flashing white stripe in the wing. Other small shore-birds have more or less evident wing-stripes, but in none does the stripe contrast so boldly or extend so far along the wing. It is a little larger than a Spotted Sandpiper; usually rusty in the spring; the whitest of the Sandpipers in the fall; bill and legs stout and black; prefers the outer beaches and sand-flats.
Voice: — A short *kip*, distinctive.
Range: — Migrates along coast and Great Plains and through Ut.; winters along coast.

AVOCETS AND STILTS: RECURVIROSTRIDÆ

AVOCET. *Recurvirostra americana.* (Illus. pp. 64, 73.)
Descr. 16–20. A very large shore-bird with a slender *upturned,* somewhat Godwit-like bill. This and the striking coloration, black and white (pinkish head and neck in breeding season), set it quite apart from anything else.
Voice: — A sharp *wheek* or *kleek*, oft-repeated in excited tones.
Range: — Breeds from e. Wash. and Mont. to s. Calif., N.M., and s. Tex.; winters from cent. Calif. and s. Tex. s.

BLACK-NECKED STILT. *Himantopus mexicanus.* (Illus. pp. 64, 73.)

Descr. 13½–15½. A large, slim wader, black above and white below, with *extremely long red legs*. In flight it is white beneath, with black, *unpatterned* wings.

Voice: — A sharp yipping.

Range: — Breeds from s.-cent. Ore., n. Ut., and s. Colo. to s. Calif., s. N.M., and s. Tex.

PHALAROPES: PHALAROPODIDÆ

SMALL Sandpiper-like birds with longer necks than most small waders; equally at home wading or swimming.

Two species, the Northern and the Red Phalarope, are most commonly seen along the coast or out at sea, where, especially in the fall, they much resemble Sanderlings except for their swimming habits. When feeding, they often spin around like tops, rapidly dabbing their thin bills into the roiled water. The females wear the bright colors, the males the dull — a reversal of the usual order of things.

RED PHALAROPE. *Phalaropus fulicarius.* (Illus. pp. 66, 72.)

Descr. 7½–9. The Red Phalarope is the most maritime species of the family in migration, rarely occurring inland. The sea-going habits distinguish it as a Phalarope; in the breeding plumage, the *reddish under parts* (blackish at a distance in poor

PHALAROPES

1. Wilson's Phalarope: *a*, breeding female; *b*, winter
2. Red Phalarope: *a*, breeding female; *b*, winter
3. Northern Phalarope: *a*, breeding female; *b*, winter

light) separate it from the Northern. In fall and winter plumage, it resembles a winter Sanderling, gray and white, but with a characteristic dark *'Phalarope-mark'* through the eye. In this plumage it is very similar to the Northern Phalarope, but is a little larger and paler (more solid 'Gull-gray'). The wing-stripe can, in the Northern, be compared to that of a Sanderling, but in the Red, it does not contrast so much with the gray of the wing. At close range, the *heavier* bill of the Red and the *yellowish* legs will identify it positively (the Northern has *black* legs and a more *needle-like* bill). Another good mark in the gray plumage is the greater amount of gray on the sides of the breast, forming a partial breast-band.

Voice: — Similar to Northern Phalarope.

Range: — Migrates offshore along Pacific Coast; casual inland.

WILSON'S PHALAROPE. *Steganopus tricolor.* (Illus. pp. 66, 73.)

Descr. 8½–10. This is the common Phalarope of lakes and ponds of the interior. In breeding plumage the broad neck-stripes of *cinnamon blending into black* are the most conspicuous mark. In flight the bird bears a striking resemblance to a small Yellow-legs; it is dark-winged (no wing-stripe as in the other Phalaropes) with a white rump. In fall, the Wilson's Phalarope is gray-backed and immaculately white below, and has a thin needle-like bill, and greenish or straw-colored legs. The manner when feeding along the margin is very nervous. The swimming and spinning habit, when indulged in, is quite conclusive.

Voice: — A grunting note, also a nasal *wurk.*

Range: — Breeds from e. Wash. and Mont. s. to cent. Calif., Nev., Ut., and Colo. Migrates to S.A.

NORTHERN PHALAROPE. *Lobipes lobatus.* (Illus. pp. 66, 72.)

Descr. 6½–8. Should a 'Sanderling' be observed at sea, and should it light upon the water, then it is a Phalarope. The present species occurs at times on inland lakes as well as along the coast. In the breeding plumage, it is gray above with a patch of *rufous-red on the side of the neck* (the Red Phalarope is completely rufous below). In winter plumage, the way we often see them (even in late summer), the two are much more similar (see Red Phalarope). The Phalarope has a shorter wing-stripe than the Sanderling, which it resembles in flight, and it flies with a deeper stroke.

Voice: — A sharp *kit,* similar to note of Sanderling.

Range: — Migrates through w. U.S., chiefly off coast, but common locally inland.

JAEGERS: STERCORARIIDÆ

THE Jaegers are dark Hawk-like, or rather Falcon-like, sea-birds that may occasionally be seen chasing and plundering Gulls and Terns. Their plumages vary considerably; so we have light phases, birds with dark backs and light under parts; dark phases, birds of uniform dark coloration; and intermediates. One noticeable field character is the *flash of white* displayed in the wing across the base of the primary feathers. This feature and the two *elongated central tail-feathers* will immediately distinguish these birds as Jaegers. Immature birds of the three species do not show the distinctive differences in the central tail-feathers and are difficult to identify in the field.

The rare Skua belongs to this group, but lacks the long central tail-feathers of the Jaegers. The British call all Jaegers 'Skuas.'

POMARINE JAEGER. *Stercorarius pomarinus.* (Illus. pp. 13, 68.)

Descr. 20–23. Distinguished from the other Jaegers by the shape of the central tail-feathers, which are broad and twisted. It is larger and heavier than the following species (a little smaller

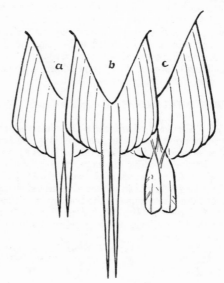

TAILS OF JAEGERS

a. Parasitic   *b.* Long-tailed   *c.* Pomarine

than a California Gull). Immatures lacking the broad central
tail-feathers can be told from immatures of the other two Jaegers
by their larger size and much heavier bill.
Range: — Migrates off Pacific Coast.

PARASITIC JAEGER. *Stercorarius parasiticus.* (Illus. pp. 13,
68.)
Descr. 16–21. The most frequently seen Jaeger of the three.
The pointed central tail-feathers, usually short compared with
those of the other Jaegers, provide the best specific character.
(Immatures of the other two species often have the central tail-
feathers short or lacking, however.)
Range: — Migrates along Pacific Coast.

LONG-TAILED JAEGER. *Stercorarius longicaudus.* (Illus.
pp. 13, 68.)
Descr. 20–23. The Long-tail is much less often seen than the
other two Jaegers. As the central tail-feathers of the Parasitic
Jaeger vary greatly in length, only typical birds with extremely
attenuated central tail-feathers with points extending eight to
ten inches can be safely identified as this species on this character alone. White-bellied Long-tails are usually much whiter on
the breast than the same plumage of the Parasitic, and have a
more clean-cut black cap, sharply defined against a broad white
collar (breast and face of Parasitic are usually somewhat dingy
or clouded).
Range: — Migrates off Pacific Coast, but observed much less
often than other two Jaegers.

SKUA. *Catharacta skua.* (Illus. p. 13.)
Descr. 20–22. A rare sea-bird, about the size of a California
Gull. A large dark-brown Hawk-like bird with a short *square-
cut slightly uptilted tail* and *conspicuous white patches at the base
of the primaries.* Resembles a dark Jaeger, but the wings are
wider and rounded at the tips, not long and pointed. Flight
suggests Hawk (Buteo).
Range: — Casual off coast of Calif. and Wash. These Pacific
Coast Skuas have been designated as the Chilean Skua (*C. s.
chilensis*) in the literature, but Dr. Robert Cushman Murphy
says they are not typical and either represent a little-known
dark-brown phase of the Chilean Skua or an undescribed race.

GULLS: LARINÆ

LONG-WINGED swimming birds with superb powers of flight.
Gulls differ from the Terns in averaging larger, having the bill,
which is proportionately shorter, slightly hooked, and the tail

square-cut or rounded, rarely forked. Gulls are more robust in form and wider of wing than the Terns. In Gull terminology the word *mantle* is frequently used, meaning the upper surface of the wings and the broad strip of back separating them.

The three Gulls most frequently found on inland bodies of water in the West are the California, Ring-billed, and Bonaparte's. The Franklin's Gull occurs exclusively inland but is local (Great Plains and Great Salt Lake).

In identifying adult Gulls the most important marks lie in the feet, bills, and wing-tips. In studying them, notice carefully the following:

   (1) Feet (whether pinkish, yellowish, greenish, red, or black)
   (2) Bills (whether yellowish, greenish, red, or black, and whether distinctively marked)
   (3) Wing-tips (whether solid black, black with white spots or 'mirrors,' gray, or white. The wing-patterns of most species are quite distinctive. See diagram.)

At the end of this brief discussion is a simplified analysis of the above points in the adults of the fourteen species of Gulls known to occur in the West.

Immature birds are more difficult. They are usually darkest in plumage the first year, lighter the second. The leg and bill color of the more confusing species (Glaucous-winged, Western, Herring, California, Ring-bill, and Short-bill) is not helpful, as the majority of individuals of them have *pinkish* legs (at least at first). The bills of first-year Glaucous-wings, Westerns, and Herrings are usually *blackish*, while those of Californias, Ring-bills, and Short-bills are more or less pinkish at the base. The bills of second-year birds of all six species are basically pinkish or flesh-colored. For the most part, plumage and size must be depended upon for the analysis of these six confusing species.

ANALYSIS OF ADULT GULLS

Species	Bill	Legs	Wing-tips
Glaucous	Yellow with red spot on lower mandible	Flesh-colored	White primaries, unmarked
Glaucous-winged	Yellow with red spot on lower mandible	Flesh-colored	Gray spot
Western	Yellow with red spot on lower mandible	Flesh-colored	Black (with small white tips) blending into *dark* mantle

ANALYSIS OF ADULT GULLS (*Cont.*)

Species	Bill	Legs	Wing-tips
Herring	Yellow with red spot on lower mandible	Flesh-colored	Contrasty black tips with white spots or 'mirrors' within the black
California	Yellow with red or red and black spot on lower mandible	Greenish	Contrasty black tips with white spots or 'mirrors' within the black
Ring-billed	Yellow with complete black ring	Yellowish or yellow-green	Contrasty black tips with white spots or 'mirrors' within the black
Short-billed	Yellow-green, unmarked	Yellow-green	Contrasty black tips with white spots or 'mirrors' within the black
Laughing	Dark red or dusky	Dark red or dusky	Blackish, blending into dark mantle
Franklin's	Dark red	Dark red-brown	Irregular black bar crossing white ground
Bonaparte's	Black	Red	Long white triangle, tipped black
Heermann's	Red	Black	Black, unmarked
Kittiwake	Yellow, unmarked	Black	Solid black, cut straight across
Red-legged Kittiwake	Yellow, unmarked	Red	Solid black, cut straight across
Sabine's	Black with yellow tip	Black	Long, clear-cut black triangle

GLAUCOUS GULL. *Larus hyperboreus.* (Illus. pp. 76, 77.)
Descr. 26–32. A large chalky-white Gull *without dark wing-tips*; usually a little larger than the Western or Glaucous-winged Gull. Immature birds in the first winter are pale cream-colored or very pale buffy, but are recognizable as this species by the extremely pale coloration and the 'frosty' primaries or wing-tips, which are even a shade lighter than the rest of the wing. Second-year birds are often extremely white throughout. Adults, which occur less frequently, have a pale-gray mantle, but the unmarked white primaries are still con-

spicuous. The adult Glaucous-winged Gull, which is the only Western species which at all resembles it, always has some dusky gray in the primaries. Immature Glaucous-winged Gulls are much darker than this species and resemble it but little.

Range: — Rare winter visitor along Pacific Coast; straggler to Colo.

GLAUCOUS-WINGED GULL. *Larus glaucescens.* (Illus. pp. 76, 77.)

Descr. 24–27. *Adult:* — A *pink-footed* Gull with a pale-gray mantle and *gray* markings toward the tips of the wings, the only Western Gull so marked. *First year:* Gray-brown throughout; similar to first-year Western Gull but lighter and browner, less dusky, and *primaries the same gray-brown as the rest of the bird,* not darker or black, as in that species or the other Gulls with which it might be confused. *Second year:* Paler and grayer, primaries gray. *Gray wing-tips in any plumage.*

Range: — Breeds along coast of Wash.; found along entire coast in migration and winter.

WESTERN GULL. *Larus occidentalis.* Subsp. (Illus. pp. 76, 77.)

Descr. 24–27. A *pink-footed* Gull with a *very dark mantle.* At a great distance the dark gray of the mantle often stands out as a dark or blackish spot superimposed on the white of the under parts, making identification simple. The northern race of the Western Gull, found from central Calif. to Wash., has a paler mantle, which, however, is still noticeably darker than that of the California Gull. The pink feet are also a helpful point. *First year:* A large dark gray-brown Gull distinguished from the first-year California Gull by the larger size and much heavier and darker bill, and from first-year Glaucous-winged Gull by the blackish primaries. *Second year:* Head and under parts whitish; bird has 'saddlebacked' appearance of adult. The stout bill and black primaries are good aids to identification.

Subsp. WESTERN GULL. *L. o. occidentalis.*
    Paler-backed. Breeds along coast from Wash. to n. Calif. and Farallons; winters s. to s. Calif.
WYMAN'S GULL. *L. o. wymani.*
    Noticeably darker-backed. Easterners will be somewhat reminded of Great Black-backed Gull. Breeds along coast of Calif. from Monterey Co. s.

HERRING GULL. *Larus argentatus.* Subsp. (Illus. p. 76.)

Descr. 23–26. *Adult:* — The only large Gull with a *pearly gray* mantle that combines the characteristics of *black wing-tips* and *flesh-colored legs.* The Western Gull has a much darker mantle and a dark eye (Herring Gull, whitish eye). The California Gull has greenish legs. *First year:* Dusky gray-brown throughout,

UPLAND PLOVER

WILLET
FALL

GREATER
YELLOWLEGS

HUDSONIAN
CURLEW

SOLITARY
SANDPIPER

MARBLED
GODWIT

AVOCET

BLACK-
NECKED
STILT

KNOT
SPRING

DOWITCHER
SPRING

STILT SANDPIPER
SPRING

RED-
BACKED SANDPIPER
SPRING

ALEUTIAN SANDPIPER

SHOREBIRDS III

BLACK-BELLIED
PLOVER

FALL

SPRING

GOLDEN PLOVER
SPRING

KILLDEER

SEMIPALMATED PLOVER

SNOWY PLOVER

MOUNTAIN PLOVER
SPRING

BAIRD'S SANDPIPER

PECTORAL SANDPIPER

WESTERN SANDPIPER

SPOTTED SANDPIPER
SPRING

SANDER-LING
FALL

RUDDY TURNSTONE
SPRING

WANDERING TATTLER
SPRING

SURF-BIRD
FALL

BLACK TURNSTONE
FALL

SHOREBIRDS IV

not easily distinguishable in the field from first-year Western Gull, but bill usually longer without such a deep angle on the lower mandible. The brown coloration is a shade tawnier, not so gray, and the forehead and front of face is much paler, perhaps a good field-mark (first-year Western has much duskier face). *Second year:* Whiter. The tail is broadly tipped with dark which blends into the white of the rump. Easily told from the second-year Western Gull, which has a more 'saddlebacked' appearance. Much more similar to the second-year California Gull, but much larger with larger and heavier bill.

Range: — Migrates and winters along Pacific Coast and Great Plains.

Subsp. (No very apparent field differences): (1) Herring Gull, *L. a. smithsonianus*; (2) Thayer's Gull, *L. a. thayeri.*

CALIFORNIA GULL. *Larus californicus.* (Illus. pp. 76, 77.)
Descr. 20–23. *Adult:* — Several species of Western Gulls have gray 'mantles' and black wing-tips which give them a similar pattern. This is one of the commonest, and might be used as a basis of comparison. It resembles the smaller Ring-billed Gull, which also has greenish legs, but this species has a *red* or *red and black spot* on the lower mandible of bill, not a complete black ring as in adult Ring-bill. It shows more white in wing-tips than Ring-bill. The distribution of the black on the under side of the tip of the wing of the adult will identify it at almost any distance. It is cut straight across 'as if dipped in ink.' The other black-wing-tipped Gulls also have their characteristic under-wing patterns, though they are not quite as useful as that of the California Gull. *First year:* Dusky brown throughout; bill flesh-colored with black end. Most second-year immature Gulls have bills like this, but in no other dusky brown first-year bird is there so much light flesh-color. Distinguished from the first-year Western Gull by its lighter coloration, smaller size, and smaller bill; from young Ring-bills by the darker coloration and lack of a contrasting tail-pattern. *Second year:* Paler; whiter below and with more white at base of tail. The different tail-pattern still distinguishes it from the Ring-bill; the small size, small bill, and lighter back from the second-year Western.

Range: — Breeds locally on inland lakes from Can. s. to Mono Lake, Calif., Great Salt Lake, Ut., and Yellowstone Lake, Wyo. Winters along Pacific Coast and inland in Ut., Ore., and Calif.

RING-BILLED GULL. *Larus delawarensis.* (Illus. pp. 76, 77.)
Descr. 18–20. *Adult:* — Very similar in pattern to the California Gull, but may be distinguished by smaller size, lighter mantle, *complete black ring* on bill, and *more yellowish-green legs. Immature:* — Whitish below, gray-brown above; similar to second-year California Gull, which has semblance of ring on

bill. One of the best distinguishing features, aside from the slightly smaller size, is the pattern of the tail. In the California Gull the tail terminates in a broad dark band that blends into the whitish color of the rump. The band near the tip of the tail of the Ring-bill is narrower (a little over an inch wide) and sharply defined. (See immature Short-billed Gull.)

Range: — Breeds on lakes in interior from Can. s. to s. Ore., Ut., and Colo. Migrates along Pacific Coast and inland (perhaps commonest Gull inland); winters from Ore. and Colo. s.

SHORT-BILLED GULL. *Larus canus brachyrhynchus.* (Illus. pp. 76, 77.)

Descr. 16–18. *Adult:* — Has *greenish legs.* Is smaller than the Ring-billed Gull with a small, *unmarked greenish-yellow bill.* Shows more white in the wing-tips than either the California or the Ring-billed Gull. *Immature:* — First year, uniform sooty grayish-brown, making it look like a half-pint-sized first-year Western or Herring Gull with a tiny bill. Differs from young Ring-billed Gull in having a brownish instead of a whitish belly. The second-year plumage is even more like the young Ring-bill. but the bird is smaller, with a *smaller, more Plover-like bill* and a less contrasting tail-pattern. (The rump is duskier and the blackish of the tail wider, not confined to a clean-cut band.)

Range: — Migrates and winters along Pacific Coast.

LAUGHING GULL. *Larus atricilla.* (Illus. p. 76.)

Descr. 15½–17. A little smaller than a Ring-billed Gull; larger than a Bonaparte's. Distinguished in any plumage from other small Gulls by its *dark mantle* and the conspicuous *white border* that lines the hind edge of the wings. In the breeding season, the head is black; in winter, white with dark markings. The immature bird is a very dark small Gull with a *white rump.* The white border on the rear edge of the wing and the dark breast are also good marks.

Range: — Occurs in w. U.S. only at Salton Sea, Calif., where it has recently bred.

FRANKLIN'S GULL. *Larus pipixcan.* (Illus. pp. 76, 77.)

Descr. 13½–15. A bird of the Great Plains and Great Salt Lake. Bears some resemblance to Bonaparte's Gull. In summer the breast has a pale rosy 'bloom,' and the head is black. In fall and winter, the bloom is gone, and the head is white, with a dark patch extending from the eye around the back of the head. The best mark is the very sharply defined black markings which form an *uneven band across the white tips of the wings.* The diagram explains it. There is a long triangle of white in the front edge of the Bonaparte's wing, giving a very different effect.

The only other small Gull found in the prairies which is apt to be confused with this species is the Ring-bill, which has white spots, or 'mirrors,' in the black wing-tips, and pale legs (Franklin's Gulls are dark reddish). Immatures are quite different from young Bonaparte's or young Ring-bills, *small dark-backed Gulls with conspicuous white rumps.* Young Bonaparte's are pale, with whitish primaries; young Ring-bills are paler, with a narrow tail-band.

Range: — Breeds and migrates in Ut.; migrant along w. edge of Great Plains and in N.M.

BONAPARTE'S GULL. *Larus philadelphia.* (Illus. pp. 76, 77.)
Descr. 12–14. The smallest of the Western Gulls. Can be identified at a great distance by the characteristic wing-pattern created by the *white outer primaries,* which contrast strikingly with the gray of the mantle. In the breeding plumage this species has a black head. In winter adults and immature birds the head is white with a conspicuous black spot behind the eye. Immature birds have a narrow black band on the tip of the tail.
Range: — Migrates and winters along coast; local migrant inland, especially in Pacific States and Ut. and on Great Plains.

HEERMANN'S GULL. *Larus heermanni.* (Illus. pp. 76, 77.)
Descr. 18–21. The easiest of Western Gulls to identify. *Adult:* — Dark gray with a *whitish head, red bill,* and black tail. *Immature.* — Lacks white head; very dark, with bill brown or partly red.
Range: — Summer and fall visitor along Pacific Coast; winters in Calif.

PACIFIC KITTIWAKE. *Rissa tridactyla pollicaris.* (Illus. pp. 76, 77.)
Descr. 16–18. An 'offshore' Gull of the ocean, smaller than either the California or the Ring-billed, which it resembles in coloration. The legs of the Kittiwake are *black.* Another good point is the appearance of the black wing-tips, which are solid black, and cut *straight across* as if they had been dipped in ink. The immature bird is most likely to be confused with the Bonaparte's Gull in the same plumage, but the Kittiwake has a dark bar on the back of the neck, instead of a dark spot behind the eye, and has more black in the outer primaries and the *fore border* of the wing. Belongs to the same species as the Atlantic Kittiwake.
Range: — Migrates and winters along Pacific Coast, offshore.

RED-LEGGED KITTIWAKE. *Rissa brevirostris.*
Descr. 14–15¾. Wing-pattern similar to Kittiwake, but bird

smaller, *legs bright red*. (Bonaparte's Gull also has bright-red legs.)
Range: — Accidental on coast of Ore.

SABINE'S GULL. *Xema sabini.* (Illus. pp. 76, 77.)
Descr. 13–14. An offshore Gull, the only species with a *forked* tail. The jet-black outer primaries and the conspicuous triangular white patch on the hind edge of the wing create a distinctive wing-pattern that renders this little Gull unmistakable. The head is dark only in the breeding plumage.
Range: — Migrates along Pacific Coast, offshore; occasional inland.

TERNS: STERNINÆ

THE Terns are Gull-like water-birds, differing from the Gulls in being more slender in build, narrower of wing, and more graceful in flight. The bill is considerably more slender and sharper-pointed, usually held pointed downward toward the water. The tail is forked. Most Terns are white, or whitish, with black caps. Six species have red or orange bills. In fall and winter the black cap is more or less imperfect or absent, the black of the forehead being largely replaced by white. At this season the red bills of the three similar small species (Forster's, Common, and Arctic) become clouded with dusky, rendering them useless as aids in identification. Immature birds are similar to winter adults but usually are marked with dusky on the upper plumage. A typical Tern habit is to plunge head first into the water Kingfisher-fashion.

GULL-BILLED TERN. *Gelochelidon nilotica aranea.* (Illus. p. 61.)
Descr. 13–14½. Somewhat larger and paler and with tail less forked than the Common or Forster's Terns; feet black. The *stout*, almost Gull-like, *black* bill is, perhaps, the best field-mark.
Voice: — A rasping, three-syllabled *ză-ză-ză* (has Magpie-like quality).
Range: — Breeds at Salton Sea, in s. Calif.; does not occur elsewhere in West.

FORSTER'S TERN. *Sterna forsteri.* (Illus. p. 61.)
Descr. 14–15. This is the small black-capped Gull-like bird with the red bill which is so familiar along the ocean and around other large bodies of water. The Forster's is the commonest of the White Terns in the W. *Adult in breeding plumage:* — White with a light-gray mantle and black cap; bill orange-red with a black tip; feet orange-red; tail deeply forked. *Immature*

GLAUCOUS-WINGED

GLAUCOUS

HERRING

WESTERN

CALIFORNIA

HEERMAN'S

RING-BILLED

LAUGHING

SHORT-BILLED

KITTIWAKE

FRANKLIN'S   SABINE'S   BONAPARTE'S

GULLS - Adults

1ST YR.

GLAUCOUS-WINGED

1ST YR.

GLAUCOUS

1ST YR.

WESTERN

2ND YR.

WESTERN

1ST YR.

CALIFORNIA

2ND YR.

CALIFORNIA

1ST YR.

HEERMAN'S

1ST YR.

RING-BILLED

FRANKLIN'S

1ST YR.

SHORT-BILLED

KITTIWAKE

SABINE'S

BONAPARTE'S

GULLS - IMMATURES

and winter adult: — Similar, without the black cap; instead, a heavy black patch like an ear-cap on the side of the whitish head. (See Common Tern.) Bill largely dusky at this season instead of bright red.

Voice: — A harsh nasal *za-a-ap* or a nasal *keer*, not so drawn out as note of Common Tern.

Range: — Breeds inland from e. Wash. and Wyo. s. to e. Calif., Nev., Ut., and Colo.; migrates and winters along coast of cent. and s. Calif.

COMMON TERN. *Sterna hirundo hirundo.* (Illus. p. 61.)
Descr. 13–16. Very similar to the much commoner Forster's Tern in size and appearance. White, with pale-gray mantle and black cap; bill and feet orange-red; tail deeply forked. *Winter plumage:* — Similar, but without the black cap; instead, a heavy black patch extending from the eye around the back of the head. Red of bill obscured with dusky. This species in adult plumage is generally considered very difficult to identify in the field because of its close resemblance to the Forster's Tern, but with a little practice it actually becomes an easy matter. The tail of the Forster's is of nearly the same tone of gray as the back and wings; that of the Common is a clear white that contrasts strikingly with the gray of the back. Then, too, the primaries of the Forster's are *silvery* (lighter than rest of wing), in direct contrast to those of the Common, which are *dusky* (darker than rest of wing). Immature Forster's Terns have a black patch through the eye and ear, while in the Common Tern this same dark area extends from the eye clear around the back of the head. The dusky patch on the fore part of the wing in the immature Common Tern is absent in the Forster's.

Voice: — A drawling *kee-arr* more drawn out than corresponding note of Forster's.

Range: — Migrant along coast and in Ut. Breeds locally or occasionally in Wash. and Mont.

ARCTIC TERN. *Sterna paradisœa.* (Illus. p. 61.)
Descr. 14–17. *Adult:* — Grayer than Forster's Tern. Very difficult to distinguish from the Common Tern. Grayish-white with a darker gray mantle, black cap, and *blood-red* feet and bill; tail deeply forked. A good mark is the *white streak below the black cap.* In the Common the whole face seems clear white. The Arctic Tern is *grayer* than any of the other species which it closely resembles. In summer plumage the bill is blood-red *to the tip,* whereas those of the Common and Forster's are orange-red, *usually* (but not always) tipped with black. The tarsi of the Arctic Tern are shorter than those of the others, so when the bird is at rest, it stands lower. The tail is longer and more streaming than that of the Common (projecting slightly be-

yond the wing-tips when at rest), and the flight is more willowy. Immature birds, so far as we know, are quite indistinguishable. Fall adults probably are also, as the red bill becomes quite dusky.

Voice: — Note shriller than Common Tern's, often ending in rising inflection.

Range: — In migration along Pacific Coast, usually well offshore; seldom seen on beaches.

LEAST TERN. *Sterna antillarum.* Subsp. (Illus. p. 61.)
Descr. 8½–9½. The smallest of the Terns. *Adult:* — White, with a pale-gray mantle and black cap; white patch cutting into black cap on forehead; bill and feet *yellow.* The extremely small size and the yellowish bill and feet render identification certain. *Immature:* — Bill darker; dark patch from eye around back of head, large dark areas on fore edge of wings. May be mistaken for the fall Black Tern, but is smaller, paler above, and with a *whitish,* instead of dark, tail.

Voice: — A harsh squealing *zeek* or *zree-eek.*

Range: — Breeds on coast n. to cent. Calif.; also along North Platte R. in Wyo.; occasional in Colo.

Subsp. (No apparent field differences): (1) Least Tern, *S. a. antillarum*; (2) Brown's Tern, *S. a. browni.*

ROYAL TERN. *Thalasseus maximus maximus.* (Illus. p. 61.)
Descr. 18–21. A large Tern, slightly smaller than the California Gull or the Caspian Tern, which it closely resembles. The more deeply forked tail and more slender bill are the best field-marks by which to differentiate the bird from the Caspian Tern. At rest, the wing-tips of the Caspian extend well beyond the end of the tail; those of the Royal barely reach the tail-tip. (See Caspian Tern.)

Voice: — A harsh *keer*, higher than note of Caspian.

Range: — Coast of Calif. from San Francisco Bay s.

ELEGANT TERN. *Thalasseus elegans.*
Descr. 16–17. This rare species should be looked for in the early fall along the coast from San Francisco Bay south. It most likely will be with Royal Terns, from which it can be picked out by its smaller size, about halfway between that of the Royal and the Forster's. The student should not attempt to identify this species until he first knows those two commoner species from A to Z.

CASPIAN TERN. *Hydroprogne caspia imperator.* (Illus. p. 61.)
Descr. 19–23. About the size of a California Gull, from which it may be distinguished by its black cap, red bill, and forked

tail. The great size and large red bill will set this species apart from all others of this group except the Royal. The tail of the Caspian is forked for only a quarter of its length; that of the Royal for fully half its length. The Caspian Tern occurs inland on many bodies of water as well as on the coast, but the Royal is confined to the coast from San Francisco south. When both species are together this species may be distinguished readily at long range from the Royal Tern by the greater amount of dark in the primaries, especially below.

Voice: — A deep raucous *ka-arr*, deeper than note of Royal.

Range: — Breeds locally inland from Can. s. to s. Ore., e. Calif., Ut., and Wyo.; migrates through Pacific States.

BLACK TERN. *Chlidonias nigra surinamensis.* (Illus. p. 61.)
Descr. 9–10. *Breeding plumage:* — Head and under parts black; back and wings gray; under tail-coverts white. In this plumage it is the only *black-bodied Tern. Immature and adult in winter:* — Head and under parts white; back and wings gray; dark markings on head, about eye, ear, and back of neck. The winter plumage comes very early; mottled, changing birds appear in midsummer. In this pied plumage the short tail and deeply swooping wing-beats are good points.

Voice: — A sharp *keek* or *klea*.

Range: — Breeds locally inland from Can. s. to Calif., Nev., and Colo. Migrates through interior and on coast from Monterey, Calif., s.

AUKS, MURRES, AND PUFFINS:
ALCIDÆ

BIRDS of this group frequent salt water and are quite accidental elsewhere. Most of them prefer the open ocean or rocky shores. They are Duck-like in appearance, but may be distinguished by their short necks, and pointed, stubby or deep and compressed bills. When flying, they beat their wings very rapidly on account of the narrow wing-arc, and are given to much circling and veering, seldom holding the straight course of a Duck. On the water most species appear chubby and neckless (except California Murre and Pigeon Guillemot).

CALIFORNIA MURRE. *Uria aalge californica.* (Illus. p. 92.)
Descr. 16–17. Size of a small Duck, identified by its black-and-white pattern and slender pointed bill. *Breeding plumage:* Head, neck, back, and wings *dark*; under parts and line on the hind edge of the wing *white*; bill *pointed. Winter plumage:* Similar, but white on the throat and side of face, and a *short black mark extending from eye into white of face.* Larger and with

a longer, more pointed bill than any other Western 'Alcid.' A race of the Common Murre.

Range: — Coastal; breeding chiefly on islands from Wash. to cent. Calif.; winters along coast to s. Calif.

PIGEON GUILLEMOT. *Cepphus columba.* (Illus. p. 92.)
Descr. 12–14. About the size of our smallest Ducks. *Breeding plumage:* A small black Duck-like bird with large *white shoulder patches, red feet,* and a pointed bill. The White-winged Scoter, with which it might be confused, is much larger, with white patches placed on the rear edge of the wing, not on the fore edge, and which show less plainly as the bird rides the water. *Winter plumage:* Pale with white under parts and blackish wings with large white patches as in summer. *No other Western 'Alcid' has white wing-patches* (although others have white linings on the under sides of the wings). Very similar to the Black Guillemot of the Atlantic.

Range: — Coastal, resident along rocky shores and islands from Santa Barbara Ids., Calif., n. to Wash.

MARBLED MURRELET. *Brachyramphus marmoratus.* (Illus. p. 92.)
Descr. 9½–10. Three Murrelets occur more or less commonly in the winter along the Pacific Coast. They are chubby, neckless-looking little sea-birds, dark above and white below, with conspicuous white throats. This species seems to be the commonest, and can be told from others in winter plumage by the *strip of white between the back and wing.* *Breeding plumage:* Dark brown above; heavily *barred* on the under parts. The only Alcid so colored.

Range: — Coastal. Summers along coast of Wash. and Ore.; winters s. to s. Calif.

XANTUS'S MURRELET (SCRIPPS'S MURRELET). *Endomychura hypoleuca.* (Illus. p. 92.)
Descr. 10. Does not show as much white in the sides as the other two Murrelets, and white of under parts does not run so far up on sides of neck (see diagram); upper parts without distinctive pattern (other two species distinctively patterned above). Summer and winter plumages similar. It was pointed out recently that the original Xantus's Murrelet came from Guadalupe Island, Mexico, and that the birds off the California Coast were quite different, so it was proposed that the California bird be designated by the name Scripps's Murrelet and the other one retain the name Xantus.

Range: — Oceanic. Breeds on ids. off s. Calif.; winters n. to cent. Calif.

CRAVERI'S MURRELET. *Endomychura craverii.*
Descr. Probably indistinguishable in the field from Xantus's Murrelet, but identifiable under exceptional circumstances or in the hand by the *clouded wing-linings.* (Wing-linings of Xantus's are usually *immaculate white,* not spotted or clouded.) Thought by some to be just a race of the preceding species.
Range: — Breeds in Gulf of Calif.; occurs after breeding season n. to Monterey, Calif.

ANCIENT MURRELET. *Synthliboramphus antiquus.* (Illus. p. 92.)
Descr. 10. *Winter plumage:* Like the Marbled Murrelet but *without* the white strip on the back. *Back paler, contrasting with the black cap.* Throat often dusky, but white extending up sides of neck as in Marbled Murrelet. *Breeding plumage:* The sharply cut black throat-patch and white stripe over the eye make identification certain.
Range: — Winters along Pacific Coast.

CASSIN'S AUKLET. *Ptychoramphus aleuticus.* (Illus. p. 92.)
Descr. 9. A small chubby neckless sea-bird, the smallest of the Alcidæ; smaller than any of the Murrelets, from which it can be told at any season by its obscure coloration and dusky throat. In winter all the other *small* Alcidæ have white either on the throat or on the sides of the neck.
Range: — Resident offshore along entire coast.

PAROQUET AUKLET. *Cyclorrhynchus psittacula.* (Illus. p. 92.)
Descr. 10. A small 'Alcid' with black upper parts and white under parts, characterized by a *stubby, upturned red bill.* Puffins, the only other 'Alcids' with red bills, have much larger bills.
Range: — Coastal, offshore. Winters s. to cent. Calif.

RHINOCEROS AUKLET. *Cerorhinca monocerata.* (Illus. p. 92.)
Descr. 15. A dark neckless-looking sea-bird, larger than the Murrelets, smaller than a Murre. *Winter plumage:* Resting on the water, the size, *uniform dark coloration,* and lack of a white throat and breast distinguish it from all other Alcids, except the immature Tufted Puffin. The smaller, more slender brownish-yellow bill and the tendency to occur closer inshore identify this Auklet. The Cassin's Auklet is also dusky with a dark throat, but is very much smaller (9 inches). *Breeding plumage:* Acquired in late winter. Characterized by conspicuous *white mustaches* and *white eye plume.*
Range: — Coastal. Breeds on ids. off coast of Wash.; winters s. along entire coast.

HORNED PUFFIN. *Fratercula corniculata.* (Illus. p. 92.)
Descr. 14½. A Puffin with *clear white under parts* and a black band across its breast would be this uncommon species. Immature Tufted Puffins have pale under parts but not clear white.
Range: — Occasional in winter, offshore s. to Calif.

TUFTED PUFFIN. *Lunda cirrhata.* (Illus. p. 92.)
Descr. 15. A chunky sea-bird, with an amazing *triangular* bill. *Breeding plumage:* Blackish with white cheeks, *large triangular red bill,* and *long curved buffy-yellow ear-tufts.* Nothing else like it. *Winter adult:* — White cheeks and yellow ear-tufts gone; a chunky *all-black* bird with a deep-*red bill. Immature:* — Whitish below, bill smaller and dark. Resembles the immature Rhinoceros Auklet, but the bill is considerably stouter.
Range: — Coastal. Resident offshore from Wash. to Santa Barbara Ids., Calif.

PIGEONS AND DOVES: COLUMBIDÆ

Two types of Pigeons occur in N.A.; those with fanlike tails, of which the Domestic Pigeon is the most familiar, and the slimmer, brownish type with rounded or long pointed tails. The Mourning Dove is the most characteristic of the latter group. The notes of the various species are very distinctive, once learned.

BAND-TAILED PIGEON. *Columba fasciata fasciata.* (Illus. p. 120.)
Descr. 15½. A heavily built Pigeon, with a broad rounded tail. Readily distinguished from the Mourning Dove, which has a pointed tail. More easily mistaken for the Domestic Pigeon, except for its woodland or mountain habitat and the tendency to alight in trees. Under favorable circumstances the pale broad tail-band can be seen as the bird flies. At close range, a white crescent is visible on the nape of the neck. The rump is not conspicuously pale as in the domestic species, and the legs are *yellow,* not red.
Voice: — A hollow Owl-like *oo-whoo* or *whoo-oo-whoo,* repeated several times.
Range: — Breeds in Pacific States from Cascades and Sierras to coast; also in se. Ariz., N.M., Colo., and w. Tex.; winters in sw. U.S.

RED-BILLED PIGEON. *Columba flavirostris flavirostris.* (Illus. p. 120.)
Descr. 13. A rather large dark Pigeon, with a broad rounded tail. In favorable light shows much deep maroon on the fore

parts. Distinguished from all other Pigeons in the lower Rio Grande Valley by its size and uniform dark appearance.

Voice: — Cooing similar in quality to that of White-winged Dove but more drawn out: *who who wooooooo*, the long note almost rising to a wail. Dr. G. M. Sutton describes the song of the ardent male as *Ooooooo, up-cup-a-coo, up-cup-a-coo, up-cup-a-coo*.

Range: — Lower Rio Grande Valley, Tex.

ROCK DOVE *or* **DOMESTIC PIGEON.** *Columba livia.*
Descr. This bird has become feral, and in places is as firmly established as a wild species as the House Sparrow. It needs no description. (See Band-tailed Pigeon.)

(WESTERN) MOURNING DOVE. *Zenaidura macroura marginella.* (Illus. p. 120.)
Descr. 11–13. The common Wild Dove of much of the West. A small *brown* Pigeon, smaller and slimmer than a Domestic Dove, with a *pointed*, not fan-shaped, tail, which shows large white spots when the bird flies. This pointed tail distinguishes it from any other Dove.
Voice: — A mournful *coah-cooo-cooo-coo*. At a distance only the last three *coos* are audible.
Range: — Breeds throughout w. U.S.; winters from Ore. and s. Colo. s.

CHINESE SPOTTED DOVE. *Spilopelia chinensis chinensis.* (Illus. p. 120.)
Descr. Larger than Mourning Dove, with a moderately long rounded or square-tipped tail which has much white in the corners. *A broad collar of black and white spots* encircling the back of the neck is the most distinctive mark.
Voice: — A typical Dove-like cooing, *coo-who-coo*; resembles somewhat voice of White-winged Dove.
Range: — Found commonly around Los Angeles, Calif., where it has been introduced.

RINGED TURTLE DOVE. *Streptopelia risoria.*
Descr. Slightly larger than the Mourning Dove with moderately long *rounded* tail which has much white in the corners. Much *paler* than Mourning Dove, with a *narrow black ring encircling the back of the neck*. In flight the dark primaries contrast boldly with the pale coloration of the rest of the bird.
Range: — Has been introduced around Los Angeles, Calif.

WHITE-WINGED DOVE. *Melopelia asiatica.* Subsp. (Illus. p. 120.)
Descr. 11–12½. Like a Mourning Dove but heavier, with a

rounded tail, which is tipped with a broad white band. The best field-mark is a large *white patch* on the wing. No other Dove has this.

Voice: — A harsh cooing, *coo-uh-cuck'-oo* or *who cooks' for you'?* Sounds vaguely like crowing of a young Rooster.

Range: — Se. Calif. (deserts), s. Ariz., sw. N.M., and s. Tex.

Subsp. (No apparent field differences): (1) Eastern White-winged Dove, *M. a. asiatica*; (2) Western White-winged Dove, *M. a. mearnsi.*

MEXICAN GROUND DOVE. *Columbigallina passerina pallescens.* (Illus. p. 120.)

Descr. 6¾. A very small short-tailed Dove, *not much larger than a Sparrow,* with wings that flash rufous-red in flight. (See Inca Dove.)

Voice: — A series of soft coos, sounding double at close range *coo-oo, coo-oo, coo-oo,* etc.

Range: — Se. Calif., s. Ariz., N.M., and w. Tex.

INCA DOVE. *Scardafella inca inca.* (Illus. p. 120.)

Descr. 8. A very small Dove. May be told from the Mexican Ground Dove by the *comparatively long* square-ended tail, which has conspicuous white sides. The Ground Dove's tail is dark and stubby. Like the Ground Dove it shows some rufous in wing in flight. Perched, the back has a scaly appearance.

Voice: — Usually two notes of nearly even emphasis *coh-coo,* or, as heat-hating residents of Arizona interpret it, '*no hope.*'

Range: — Ariz., s. N.M. (rare), and sw. and s. Tex.

WHITE-FRONTED DOVE. *Leptotila fulviventris angelica.* (Illus. p. 120.)

Descr. 12. A dark-winged, ground-inhabiting Dove with a rounded white-tipped tail. Best identified from all other Doves by its whitish under parts. In flight, shows reddish wing-linings.

Voice: — A low, soft, ghostly *oo-whooooooo,* lower in pitch and softer than the notes of any other Dove; at a distance, only the hollow long-drawn *whooooooo* is audible.

Range: — Lower Rio Grande Valley, Tex.

PARROTS: PSITTACIDÆ

THICK-BILLED PARROT. *Rhynchopsitta pachyrhyncha.*

Descr. 16½. A heavily built green Parrot, with a very heavy black bill and red forehead. Young with white bill and less red. The only Parrot that occurs in w. U.S.

Range: — Occasional in mts. of se. Ariz., especially Chiricahua Mts. Has also occurred in sw. N.M.

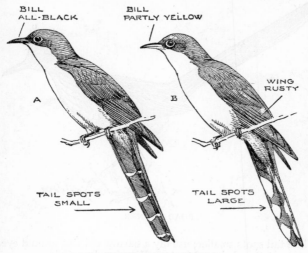

A. BLACK-BILLED CUCKOO

B. YELLOW-BILLED CUCKOO

ANIS, ROAD–RUNNERS, CUCKOOS, ETC.: CUCULIDÆ

YELLOW-BILLED CUCKOO. *Coccyzus americanus.* Subsp. (Illus. p. 85.)
Descr. 11–13½. Known as a Cuckoo by the slim proportions and coloration, dull brown above and whitish below; further distinguished by the presence of *rufous* in the wings, *large* white spots at the tips of the tail-feathers, and, at close range, the *yellow* lower mandible of the bill. In flight the slim look and the flash of rufous in the wings are the best marks.
Voice: — A rapid throaty *ka ka ka ka ka ka ka ka ka ka ka ka ka ka kow kow kowp kowp kowp kowp.*
Range: — Breeds from Wash. and Colo. s. to Mex.
Subsp. (No apparent field differences): (1) Yellow-billed Cuckoo, *C. a. americanus*; (2) California Cuckoo, *C. a. occidentalis.*

BLACK-BILLED CUCKOO. *Coccyzus erythropthalmus.* (Illus. p. 85.)
Descr. 11–12. Brown above, white below; similar to preceding species, but without rufous wings and yellow lower mandible.

ROAD-RUNNER

White tail-spots smaller; usually a narrow red ring around eye.
Range: — Breeds in e. Mont., e. Wyo., and ne. Colo.

ROAD-RUNNER. *Geococcyx californianus.* (Illus. p. 86.)
Descr. 20–24. The 'Chaparral Cock' is quite unique. It is long
and slender, heavily streaked, with a long expressive tail, a
shaggy crest, and strong legs for running. In flight the short,
rounded wing shows a white crescent. The bird is more likely to
run than fly.
Voice: — Song, a series of six or eight Dove-like *coos* descending
in pitch (last note about pitch of Mourning Dove's call). Dr.
George M. Sutton describes the most characteristic note as 'an
incisive note made by rolling mandibles sharply.'
Range: — Chiefly arid or semi-arid regions from n.-cent. Calif.,
Ut., and Colo., s. to Mex.

GROOVE-BILLED ANI. *Crotophaga sulcirostris sulcirostris.*
(Illus. p. 87.)
Descr. 12½. A coal-black Cuckoo-like bird, with loose-jointed
tail, short wings (hence a weak flight), and a deep bill with a
high, curved ridge on the upper mandible. The peculiar bill formation gives the bird a decidedly Parrot-like or Puffin-like profile. Except for the bill, the bird might easily be mistaken on
first acquaintance for a Great-tailed Grackle.
Voice: — A repeated *pee-oh*, or *tee-ho*, the first note higher and
thin, the second guttural; also Cuckoo-like calls and wailing
notes.
Range: — Lower Rio Grande Valley, Tex.; occasional in Ariz.

GROOVE-BILLED ANI

OWLS: TYTONIDÆ AND STRIGIDÆ

NOCTURNAL birds of prey, characterized by the large head, large eyes, *facial disks*, and soft, moth-like, noiseless flight. They seem quite neckless. Some species have conspicuous feather-tufts, or 'horns'; others are round-headed, devoid of such orna-mentation.

BARN OWL. *Tyto alba pratincola.* (Illus. p. 93.)
Descr. 15–20. A long-legged, light-colored Owl with a *white heart-shaped face.* Distinguished in flight at a distance as an Owl by the large head and light, moth-like flight; as this species, by the whitish or pale-cinnamon under parts and buffy or rusty upper plumage (Short-ear does not have such pale under parts).
Voice: — A rasping hiss or 'snore.'
Range: — From Wash. and Colo. s. to Mex.

SCREECH OWL. *Otus asio.* Subsp. (Illus. p. 93.)
Descr. 8–10. A small gray Owl with conspicuous ear-tufts, the only common *small* Western Owl so adorned. Screech Owls in w. U.S. are invariably gray except for two races, the Macfar-lane's Screech Owl (e. Wash., e. Ore., ne. Calif., Ida., and w. Mont.), which has two color-phases, gray and brown, and the

Kennicott's Screech Owl of w. Wash., which is *usually* dark brown.

Voice: — A series of several hollow whistles on the same pitch, distinctly separated at first, and running into a tremolo at the end; often likened to the rhythm of a small ball bouncing faster and faster to a standstill; sometimes preceded by two prolonged opening notes. Usual call very different from descending whinny of eastern Screech Owls.

Range: — Can. to Mex.

Subsp. (No apparent field differences except in Nos. 3 and 4 — see above): (1) Aiken's Screech Owl, *O. a. aikeni*; (2) Rocky Mountain Screech Owl, *O. a. maxwelliæ*; (3) Macfarlane's Screech Owl, *O. a. macfarlanei*; (4) Kennicott's Screech Owl, *O. a. kennicotti*; (5) Brewster's Screech Owl, *O. a. brewsteri*; (6) California Screech Owl, *O. a. bendirei*; (7) Pasadena Screech Owl, *O. a. quercinus*; (8) Mexican Screech Owl, *O. a. cineraceus*; (9) Sahuaro Screech Owl, *O. a. gilmani*.

FLAMMULATED SCREECH OWL. *Otus flammeolus.* (Illus. p. 93.)

Descr. $6\frac{1}{2}$–7. A rare little Owl, much smaller than the Screech Owl, largely gray (and a touch of tawny), with inconspicuous rounded ear-tufts. *The only small Western Owl with brown eyes.*

Voice: — A single soft mellow *hoot*, low in pitch for so small an Owl, repeated steadily at intervals of two or more seconds; sometimes two notes, *hoo-hoot*.

Range: — Locally distributed or rare in high mts. from Mex. to e. Wash. and Ida.

SPOTTED SCREECH OWL. *Otus trichopsis.*

Descr. Often found living in same localities as the Mexican race of the Screech Owl (*Otus asio cineraceus*). U.S. individuals of the Spotted Screech Owl are gray like *Otus asio*, and very similar in appearance, but may be distinguished by the large white spots on the lower hind neck and scapulars, larger black spots on the under parts, and much longer facial bristles. They are more easily identified at night by voice.

Voice: — Four notes given thus: *boobooboo-boo*, *boobooboo-boo*, etc. (three notes, a pause and a fourth note). At times, a repeated four-syllabled *chooyoo-coocoo*, vaguely reminiscent of call of White-winged Dove; also a series of four to seven rapid, evenly spaced notes: *boo boo boo boo boo boo boo*.

Range: — Found chiefly among oaks in canyons between 4000 and 6500 feet in mts. of s. Ariz.

HORNED OWL. *Bubo virginianus.* Subsp. (Illus. p. 93.)

Descr. 18–25. The only *large* Owl (nearly two feet in length) with ear-tufts, or 'horns.' The Long-eared Owl is much smaller (fifteen inches; Crow-sized in flight), with lengthwise streakings, rather than crosswise barrings, beneath. In flight this Owl is larger than our large Buteo Hawks (Red-tail, etc.); is darker, looks neckless, and is larger-headed. The race of this bird known as the Arctic Horned Owl, *B. v. subarcticus*, which occasionally wanders s. to Ida. and Ore., is quite recognizable by its extreme paleness. Some individuals are almost as white as Snowy Owls.

Voice: — A deep resonant hooting of three to eight hoots; males usually four or five, in this rhythm: *hoo, hoo-oo, hoo, hoo*; females six or eight: *hoo, hoo-hoo-hoo, hoo-oo, hoo-oo*.

Range: — Can. to Mex.

Subsp. (No apparent field differences except in No. 1 — see above): (1) Arctic Horned Owl, *B. v. subarcticus*; (2) Montana Horned Owl, *B. v. occidentalis*; (3) Northwestern Horned Owl, *B. v. lagophonus*; (4) Dusky Horned Owl, *B. v. saturatus*; (5) Pacific Horned Owl, *B. v. pacificus*; (6) Western Horned Owl, *B. v. pallescens.*

SNOWY OWL. *Nyctea nyctea.* (Illus. p. 93.)
Descr. 20–26. A large *white* Owl with a round head. More or less flecked or barred with dusky. The Barn Owl is whitish on the under parts only. Young Owls of all species are white or whitish before the feathers replace the down, and are often dubbed 'Snowy' Owls. Even in callow youngsters of this sort, the resemblance to their parents is already visible; stubby ear-tufts adorn the fuzzy heads of baby Horned Owls, while the heart-shaped faces of Barn Owls reflect their parentage.
Range: — Arctic, s. irregularly in winter to Wyo. and Ore., rarely farther (San Francisco Bay, Calif.).

HAWK OWL. *Surnia ulula caparoch.* (Illus. p. 93.)
Descr. 15–17. A medium-sized, diurnal Owl, with a long Falcon-like tail; smaller than a Crow; maintains a more inclined body-posture at rest, not so upright as other Owls; often perches at the tip-top of a tree or in some other exposed situation and bobs its tail in the manner of a Sparrow Hawk.
Range: — Casual in winter in Mont., Wyo., and Wash.

PYGMY OWL. *Glaucidium gnoma.* Subsp. (Illus. p. 93.)
Descr. 7–7½. A very small 'earless' Owl of the woodlands, smaller than a Screech; rusty-brown or gray-brown with a striped breast. The most widely distributed small earless Owl in forested areas of the West. It is frequently heard calling or seen flying in the daytime. Has a proportionately smaller head and longer tail than most other small Owls. When perched, tail is held at a perky angle from body. A black patch on each side of hind neck is a good mark when seen.

Voice: — A rolling series of mellow Owl-like whistled notes ending with two or three slow deliberate notes thus: *too-too-too-too-too-too-too-too — took — took — took.* Commonest note a single *took* uttered every two or three seconds.

Range: — Can. s. to s. Calif., s. Ariz., and N.M.

Subsp. (No apparent field differences): (1) Rocky Mountain Pygmy Owl, *G. g. pinicola;* (2) Coast Pygmy Owl, *G. g. grinnelli;* (3) California Pygmy Owl, *G. g. californicum.*

FERRUGINOUS PYGMY OWL. *Glaucidium brasilianum.*

Descr. 6½. Very similar to the Pygmy Owl, and perhaps best recognized by its habitat, woodlands along low river-bottoms within the range outlined below. The breast streakings are *brownish* rather than black. In southern Arizona the other Pygmy Owl is a bird of the mountains. This little Owl has a habit of jerking or flipping its tail.

Voice: — *Chu, chu, chu,* a number of times repeated (Bendire); *chook* or *took,* sometimes repeated thirty or forty times at rate of about once per second, suggesting exhaust of a small distant engine (Sutton).

Range: — Rio Grande Delta, Tex., and low river valleys of s. Ariz.

ELF OWL. *Micropallas whitneyi whitneyi.* (Illus. p. 93.)

Descr. 6. A very tiny earless Owl about the size of a Sparrow, under parts largely reddish-brown, 'eyebrows' white. Found chiefly in deserts where Sahuaro cactus grows, but also in wooded canyons up to 5000 feet or more. Sits in hole in cactus or tree in daytime, but most frequently heard at night, when it may be seen with a flashlight.

Voice: — A series of rapid high-pitched notes, *whi-whi-whi-whi-whi-whi,* often becoming higher and more excited and chattering in the middle of the series; or *chew-chew-chew-chew-chew* or *teook-teook-teook-teook,* etc., rapidly uttered and descending slightly.

Range: — Se. Calif., s. Ariz., sw. N.M., and sw. Tex. (Chisos Mts.).

(WESTERN) BURROWING OWL. *Speotyto cunicularia hypugœa.* (Illus. p. 91.)

Descr. 9. A small brown *ground* Owl often seen in daytime; about the size of a Screech Owl, earless and with *very long legs* (for an Owl); resident of deserts, prairies, and open barren country.

Voice: — Commonest note, a tremulous chuckling or chattering call; at night a high mellow *coo-co-hoo,* or *coo-hoo,* like Roadrunner or Dove in quality, but higher.

BURROWING OWL

Range: — Open country of most of w. U.S. from Pacific e. through Great Plains; migratory in nw. States.

SPOTTED OWL. *Strix occidentalis.* Subsp. (Illus. p. 93.)
Descr. 19. Large dark-brown earless Owl of the woodlands, with a puffy round head. The large dark eyes (all other large Owls except the Barn Owl have yellow eyes) and the heavily spotted and barred under parts will identify the bird. Rare throughout most of its range.
Voice: — A high-pitched hooting, like barking of a small dog; much higher than that of the Horned Owl. Usually given in groups of three: *hoo, hoo-hoo,* or four: *hoo — whoowhoo — whooo.*
Range: — Mts. from Mex. n. to s. Colo., Ariz., and Cascades of cent. Calif. (Mariposa Co.); also coast belt from Marin Co., Calif., to Wash.
Subsp. (No apparent field differences): (1) California Spotted Owl, *S. o. occidentalis;* (2) Northern Spotted Owl, *S. o. caurina;* (3) Mexican Spotted Owl, *S. o. lucida.*

GREAT GRAY OWL. *Scotiaptex nebulosa nebulosa.* (Illus. p. 93.)
Descr. 24–33. Larger even than the Horned Owl; resembles somewhat the much smaller Spotted Owl; like that bird, it is earless, but *gray,* not brown. The eyes are *yellow,* and the under parts are heavily striped lengthwise. The facial disks are especially large, and come to the top of the head as the bird sits, and are outlined against the sky.

Range: — Rare resident from tree-limit in Can. s. to n. Mont., n. Ida., and probably Yellowstone Park, Wyo.; also in Cascades and Sierras to Yosemite region of Calif. (rarely); occurs more frequently in winter in nw. States.

LONG-EARED OWL. *Asio wilsonianus.* (Illus. p. 93.)
Descr. 13–16. A medium-sized Owl of the woodlands, with long ear-tufts; much smaller than the Horned Owl, streaked lengthwise, rather than barred crosswise, beneath. The 'ears' are situated close together toward the center of the forehead, giving the bird an entirely different aspect. The rusty face distinguishes it from the smaller Screech Owl. In flight the ear-tufts are pressed flat against the head; then the large amount of gray separates it from the much buffier Short-eared Owl.
Voice: — A low mellow Dove-like call of three or four notes: *hoo, hoo, hoo* or *who-hoo, hoo, hoo.* Also 'a cat-like whine, and a high-pitched whistled *whee'-you*' (Ludlow Griscom).
Range: — Breeds from Can. s. nearly to Mexican boundary; winters from Wash. and Wyo. s.

SHORT-EARED OWL. *Asio flammeus flammeus.* (Illus. p. 93.)
Descr. 13–17. Nearly the size of a Crow; a diurnal Owl of the marshes. The buffy-brown color and the irregular flopping flight, suggesting that of a Nighthawk, identify it. It might possibly be mistaken for one of the Hawks, but the Owl has a somewhat slovenly flight, and appears quite big-headed and neckless. Large buffy wing-patches show in flight. (See Barn Owl.)
Voice: — An emphatic sneezy *keee-yow!* 'like a hurt cat' (C. W. Lockerbie).
Range: — Breeds in marshy or open country from Can. s. to Colo. and ne. Calif. (occasionally farther); winters from Wash. and Mont. s. to Mex.

RICHARDSON'S OWL. *Cryptoglaux funerea richardsoni.* (Illus. p. 93.)
Descr. 9–12. Near the size of a Screech Owl, but *earless*. The even smaller Saw-whet is the species that most closely resembles it. The facial disks of the Richardson's Owl are *framed with black*, and the bill is *yellowish* (Saw-whet, black). The forehead is heavily spotted with white. The Pygmy Owl is much smaller and redder, with well-defined *black* breast-streaks.
Range: — Breeds in Can.; casual in winter s. to Ore. and Colo.

SAW-WHET OWL. *Cryptoglaux acadica acadica.* (Illus. p. 93.)
Descr. 7–8½. A very small, ridiculously tame little Owl; smaller than Screech Owl, *without* ear-tufts. It can be told from the Pygmy Owl by the wide *soft-brown stripes* on the under parts,

XANTUS'S MURRELET
(SCRIPPS'S MURRELET)

ANCIENT MURRELET
WINTER   SUMMER

CASSIN'S AUKLET

MARBLED MURRELET
WINTER   SUMMER

PAROQUET AUKLET

WINTER

RHINOCEROS AUKLET
SUMMER

HORNED PUFFIN
WINTER

IMMATURE

TUFTED PUFFIN
SUMMER

PIGEON GUILLEMOT
WINTER   SUMMER

CALIFORNIA MURRE
WINTER   SUMMER
ALCIDAE

SCREECH

GREAT HORNED

LONG-EARED

FLAMMULATED
SCREECH

SNOWY

BARN

SPOTTED

SHORT-
EARED

GREAT GRAY

RICHARDSON'S

HAWK

SAW-WHET

ELF

OWLS

PYGMY

the proportionately larger head and shorter tail (see Pygmy Owl). The young Saw-whet is very different, chocolate-brown with a *blackish* face and conspicuous white patches or 'eyebrows' forming a broad V between the eyes.

Voice: — A mellow whistled note repeated mechanically in endless succession, often between one hundred and one hundred and thirty times per minute, *too, too, too, too, too, too,* etc.; has bell-like quality in distance. Also a rasping double note.

Range: — Breeds from Can. s. in evergreen forests to mts. of N.M., Ariz., and Sierra Nevada of Calif.; in winter s. to s. Calif.

GOATSUCKERS: CAPRIMULGIDÆ

THE Goatsuckers are ample-tailed nocturnal birds with small bills and weak, tiny feet. During the day they rest horizontally on some limb, or on the ground, where their mottled brown pattern blends with the surroundings.

STEPHENS'S WHIP-POOR-WILL. *Antrostomus vociferus arizonæ.* (Illus. p. 93.)

Descr. 9–10. Best known by its call, oft-repeated at night in mountain woodlands. When discovered during the day, the

GOATSUCKERS

A. Merrill's Pauraque   B. Stephens's Whip-poor-will
C. Poor-will

bird springs from its hiding-place and flits away like a large dusky moth. If it is a male, large white tail-patches flash out; if it is a female, it appears largely brown; never does it show the white wing-patches characteristic of the Nighthawk. It is considerably larger and duskier than a Poor-will, and the white tail-patches of the male are much more conspicuous (tipped for 1½ inches). The Poor-will's tail is only tipped with white for ½ inch. The latter bird also shows much more white on the throat. Female Whip-poor-wills have only a small amount of white or buff in the tail, but can be told from the Poor-will by the buffy-brown appearance around the head and breast.

Voice: — At night a loud oft-repeated *prrrip-purr-rill* or *whip-poor-will*, more rolling than cry of Eastern bird.

Range: — Breeds in mts. of s. Ariz., s. N.M., and w. Tex.

POOR-WILL. *Phalænoptilus nuttalli.* Subsp. (Illus. p. 93.)
Descr. 7–8. Best known by its call heard at night. When flushed during the day it flutters up like a large gray-brown moth. It appears smaller than a Nighthawk, has more rounded wings (with no white bars). Its tail is tipped with white. Prefers arid or semi-arid country.

Voice: — At night a loud, oft-repeated *Poor-will* or more exactly, *Poor-jill*; when close, *Poor-jill-ip*.

Range: — Breeds chiefly in arid country from Can. to Mex. (e. of Cascades and Sierras); and from Rogue River Valley in s. Ore. to Lower Calif. (w. of Cascades and Sierras).

Subsp. (No apparent field differences): (1) Nuttall's Poor-will, *P. n. nuttalli*; (2) Dusky Poor-will, *P. n. californicus*; (3) Desert Poor-will, *P. n. hueyi.*

MERRILL'S PAURAQUE. *Nyctidromus albicollis merrilli.* (Illus. p. 93.)
Descr. 12. A large Goatsucker of the Whip-poor-will type, best identified at night by voice. The Whip-poor-will and the Chuck-will's-widow migrate through its range, but it can be told from those species when accidentally discovered in the daytime by the bold black triangular marks on the scapulars, and the *white band across the primary wing-feathers*. It can be told from the Nighthawk, which also has white in the wing, by the *large amount of white in the tail*. Note the tail's shape (see diagram).

Voice: — At night a hoarse whistle, *pur-we'eeeer*, repeated. The accent is in the middle of the call. At a distance only the *we'eeeer*, which is rolled out emphatically, can be heard. By no stretch of the imagination does it seem to say '*Pau-ra-que.*'

Range: — Gulf coast of Tex. and Lower Rio Grande Valley.

NIGHTHAWK. *Chordeiles minor.* Subsp. (Illus. p. 95.)
Descr. 8½–10. The Nighthawk is the slender, slim-winged bird

NIGHTHAWKS

A. Nighthawk   B. Texas, or Lesser, Nighthawk

we see flying erratically about after insects high in the air. In courtship the male occasionally folds his wings and dives earthward, zooming up sharply at the end of the drop. The *broad white patch* across the wing is the Nighthawk's mark.

Voice: — A nasal *peent* or *pee-ik*.

Range: — Breeds from Can. s. to Tex., N.M., Ariz., mts. of s. Calif., and coast of n. Calif.

Subsp. (No apparent field differences): (1) Eastern Nighthawk, *C. m. minor*; (2) Howell's Nighthawk, *C. m. howelli*; (3) Western Nighthawk, *C. m. henryi*; (4) Pacific Nighthawk, *C. m. hesperis*; (5) Sennett's Nighthawk, *C. m. sennetti*.

TEXAS, *or* **LESSER, NIGHTHAWK.** *Chordeiles acutipennis texensis.* (Illus. p. 95.)

Descr. 8–9. Smaller and browner than the other Nighthawks, with *white bar closer to tip of wing.* This species is most easily identified by its odd calls (below) and its manner of flight, *very low over the ground*, never high like other Nighthawks. In the breeding season it is a bird of the lowlands, whereas other Nighthawks, breeding within its range, prefer the mountains.

Voice: — Does not have the characteristic *spee-ik* or *peent* of other Nighthawks; instead a low *chuck chuck* and a soft purring or whinnying sound very like the trilling of a toad.

Range: — Breeds in lowlands of sw. U.S. n. to n.-cent. Calif., s. Nev., s. Ut., and cent. Tex.

SWIFTS: MICROPODIDÆ

SWALLOW-LIKE birds with long, stiff wings, more slender than those of Swallows. Unlike most other birds, they often appear to beat their wings alternately, not in unison; such is often the *illusion*, at least, although slow-motion pictures seem to disprove this. The effect is somewhat bat-like. Their wings fairly twinkle as they fly and they frequently sail between spurts, holding the wings *bowed* in a very characteristic manner.

BLACK SWIFT. *Nephœcetes niger borealis.* (Illus. p. 96.)
Descr. 7¼. Rare. A large *black* Swift with a slightly forked tail which it sometimes fans wide in flight. Known from the Purple Martin, the only other Swallow-like bird of similar size, with black under parts, by its longer, slimmer wings and different flight (see Swifts, above). Has a more leisurely flight than other Swifts. The Vaux's Swift is much smaller, with a paler throat and under parts and a rounded tail. At close range the Black Swift shows a touch of white around the face.
Voice: — A light twitter.
Range: — Migrates and breeds at scattered points along Pacific Coast, and inland in mts.

CHIMNEY SWIFT. *Chætura pelagica.*
Descr. 5–5½. Very similar to Vaux's Swift, but somewhat larger and darker. Probably not easily distinguishable in the field, but any small dark Swift occurring on the Plains in e. Wyo. and e. Mont. would most likely be this species.
Range: — E. U.S., rarely to e. Mont. and e. Wyo.

SWIFTS

A. White-throated   B. Black   C. Vaux's

VAUX'S SWIFT. *Chœtura vauxi.* (Illus. p. 96.)
Descr. 4½. A small dark Swallow-like bird, with no apparent tail (except when tail is spread). A good metaphor that can be applied to it is a 'cigar with wings.' The long slightly curved, stiff wings and twinkling flight mark it as a Swift; the small size and dingy under parts as this species.
Voice: — A feeble chipping call.
Range: — Breeds chiefly near coast from Santa Cruz, Calif., n. to Alaska; casual e. to Mont. and Nev.; migrates through s. Calif. and Ariz.

WHITE-THROATED SWIFT. *Aëronautes saxatalis.* Subsp. (Illus. p. 96.)
Descr. 6½–7. Known as a Swift by its long, narrow, stiff wings and characteristic twinkling and gliding flight; and from other Swifts by the contrasting black-and-white pattern. The Violet Green Swallow, which is often found in the same places, has pure white under parts but lacks the black patches.
Voice: — A shrill, excited *je je je je je je*, etc., in descending scale.
Subsp. WHITE-THROATED SWIFT. *A. s. saxatalis.* Breeds locally from s. Can. s. through W. States to Mex., chiefly in mts.; winters from Santa Barbara, Calif., s.

HUMMINGBIRDS: TROCHILIDÆ

THE smallest of all birds; iridescent, with long needle-like bills for sipping honey from flowers. The wing-motion is so rapid that the wings look like blurry gauze. The brilliant throat feathers or 'gorgets' are the best aid in identifying the males. Females lack these, and are mostly greenish above and whitish below, often presenting a very difficult identification problem. Some females are not safely distinguishable in the field. In a few cases certain sounds made by the males are very distinctive. These are mentioned, but only when they are especially outstanding. It might conceivably be possible to tell nearly every species by the sounds it produces. At certain seasons the countryside is full of young Hummers that are just about impossible for even crack field experts to identify. It is important to realize this and not worry too much about them.

LUCIFER HUMMINGBIRD. *Calothorax lucifer.* (Illus. p. 98.)
Descr. 3½. Very rare or accidental in U.S. Male has purple throat and *rusty* sides. The rusty sides and lack of purple on the forehead would distinguish it from the Costa's. The slightly decurved bill is also a fair field-mark.
Range: — Occasional in s. Ariz. and w. Tex. (Brewster Co.).

BLACK-CHINNED HUMMINGBIRD. *Archilochus alexandri.*
(Illus. p. 98.)
Descr. 3¾. *Male:* — Identified by the *black throat* and the conspicuous white collar below it. The brilliant blue-purple patch on the lower part of the throat shows only in certain lights.
Female: — Greenish above, whitish below. Cannot be told in field from female Costa's. (See Costa's Hummingbird.)
Range: — W. U.S.; breeds from Mex. n. to e. Wash. (rare) and nw. Mont. (rare); commonest in s. parts of Calif., Ariz., and N.M., and in w. Tex.; winters in s. Calif. and to the southward.

COSTA'S HUMMINGBIRD. *Calypte costæ.* (Illus. p. 98.)
Descr. 3¼. *Male:* — Throat and forehead *purple* or *amethyst.* The feathers of the 'gorget' are longer and stand out more from the sides of the throat than in any other Hummer. The male can possibly be confused with the male Anna's, which is larger and has the throat and forehead *rose-red*, not purple. The Black-chin has blue-purple on the throat, but it is very restricted and there is none on the forehead. The sound made by the male Costa's as it dives through the air during its mating performance is distinctive — a high, shrill hissing sound, ventriloquial in effect, growing louder and dying away. This species has a habit of *soaring* from one flower clump to another. *Female:* — Greenish above, whitish below; impossible to distinguish in the field from the female Black-chin, but although the two are often found together, the Costa's usually prefers more arid conditions. Females on the nest might be identified by the difference in nest construction. That of this species is usually thatched on the outside with lichens or bits of dead leaves; that of the Black-chinned is a felt-like or cocoon-like structure, usually made of the yellowish down of the sycamore, devoid of exterior decoration (occasional nests have a few lichens).
Range: — Breeds in low country of sw. U.S. (s. Calif., s. Ut., s. Nev., and Ariz.).

ANNA'S HUMMINGBIRD. *Calypte anna.* (Illus. p. 98.)
Descr. 4. *Male:* — Somewhat larger than other California Hummingbirds, with a red throat and *red forehead.* The male is the only California Hummingbird that seems to 'sing.' From a perch, it utters a long series of squeaking and grating notes. The sound made by the male as it dives through the air in its mating performance or 'pendulum dance' is also distinctive, a *sharp explosive or popping sound* as it reaches the bottom of the dive. *Female:* — Similar to females of other California Hummingbirds, but with practice can be told by its larger size and darker green color above. As a rule it has grayer under parts and a more heavily spotted throat than the female Costa's or Black-chin. There is often a central patch or scattering of red spots.

HUMMINGBIRDS

1. BLACK-CHINNED HUMMINGBIRD, ♂ MALE; ♀ FEMALE
2. BUFF-BELLIED HUMMINGBIRD, ♂ MALE
3. WHITE-EARED HUMMINGBIRD, ♂ MALE; ♀ FEMALE
4. BROAD-BILLED HUMMINGBIRD, ♂ MALE; ♀ FEMALE
5. COSTA'S HUMMINGBIRD, ♂ MALE
6. LUCIFER HUMMINGBIRD, ♂ MALE
7. RIVOLI'S HUMMINGBIRD, ♂ MALE; ♀ FEMALE
8. BLUE-THROATED HUMMINGBIRD, ♂ MALE; ♀ FEMALE
9. ANNA'S HUMMINGBIRD, ♂ MALE; ♀ FEMALE
10. BROAD-TAILED HUMMINGBIRD, ♂ MALE; ♀ FEMALE
11. CALLIOPE HUMMINGBIRD, ♂ MALE; ♀ FEMALE
12. ALLEN'S HUMMINGBIRD, ♂ MALE
13. RUFOUS HUMMINGBIRD, ♂ MALE; ♀ FEMALE

ROGER
TORY
PETERSON

1 ♂
2 ♂
3 ♂
4 ♂

5 ♂
6 ♂
7 ♂
8 ♂

9 ♂
10 ♂
11 ♂
12 ♂
13 ♂

1 ♀
9 ♀
10 ♀
11 ♀
13 ♀

4 ♀
7 ♀
8 ♀
3 ♀

This is the only Hummingbird commonly found in California in midwinter.

Range: — Calif. w. of Sierras; resident at low altitudes n. to San Francisco Bay region and head of Sacramento Valley; in autumn farther north; casual in Ariz.

BROAD-TAILED HUMMINGBIRD. *Selasphorus platycercus platycercus.* (Illus. p. 98.)

Descr. 4½. This Rocky Mt. species can be identified at once by the sound of its wings, a *shrill trilling* as the bird flies from place to place. The female produces scarcely any sound. *Male:* — Back green, throat-patch bright *rose-red*; resembles Ruby-throat of East. The only other Hummer with a solid-red throat-patch normally occurring in its range, the Rufous Hummingbird, has a rufous back. *Female:* — Similar to female Black-chin and Costa's, but sides tinged with buffy, and touch of rufous at sides of tail (near base when tail is spread). Resembles female Calliope even more closely except for its considerably larger size.

Range: — Rocky Mt. region; breeds from Mont. and s. Ida. s. to Mex. and w. to e. Wash. (rare), e. Ore. (rare), and w. Ariz.

RUFOUS HUMMINGBIRD. *Selasphorus rufus.* (Illus. p. 98.)

Descr. 3½. *Male:* — Upper parts bright red-brown in full breeding plumage, throat flame-red. *No other Hummingbird has a rufous back.* The male Allen's Hummingbird has a rufous *rump* and rufous cheeks and, when perched at a distance or overhead, looks very much like a Rufous Hummingbird, but *be sure to see the middle of the back. Female:* — Similar to other female Hummingbirds but has some rufous on the rump or tail-feathers. Cannot be told from the female Allen's Hummingbird in the field (in the hand, female Allen's has narrower tail-feathers). In migration in the Rockies, the female Rufous might be mistaken for the female Broad-tailed Hummingbird, which shows just a touch of rufous at the base of the tail-feathers (but not in the center of the rump).

Range: — Breeds from Ore. and sw. Mont. n. into Can.; migrates through valleys of Pacific States in spring and throughout mts. of entire w. U.S. in autumn.

ALLEN'S HUMMINGBIRD. *Selasphorus alleni.* (Illus. p. 98.)

Descr. 3¼. *Male:* — Green back, *rufous rump*, and red throat. The only similar Hummingbird, the male Rufous, has the entire back rufous. The two species can easily be confused if not scrutinized carefully. (See Rufous Hummingbird.) *Female:* — Not distinguishable in field from female Rufous.

Range: — Calif.; breeds along coast from Ventura Co. n. to Humboldt Co.; migrates farther inland, casually through Ariz.; some winter in Santa Barbara Ids.

CALLIOPE HUMMINGBIRD. *Stellula calliope.* (Illus. p. 98.)
Descr. 3. The smallest U.S. Hummer; seldom found away from mountains. *Male:* — Throat with *red rays on a white ground*, the only Hummingbird with this effect. *Female:* — Can be told from female Rufous, which occurs in high mountains in late summer, by lack of rusty on center of rump (has a touch of rusty at base of all tail-feathers except central pair). Distinguishable from female Broad-tail of Rockies, which closely resembles it, by the smaller size when comparison is possible.
Range: — Breeds in high mts. of w. U.S. from Can. s. to s. Calif. and n. N.M., and from Rockies w. to e. Wash., e. Ore., and Sierras of Calif.

RIVOLI'S HUMMINGBIRD. *Eugenes fulgens.* (Illus. p. 98.)
Descr. 5. *Male:* — A large Hummingbird with *blackish belly*, *bright green throat*, and *purple crown*. Looks all black when seen at distance. Wing-beats discernible, not buzzy as in smaller Hummers; sometimes scales on set wings like a Swift. *Female:* — A large Hummingbird, greenish above, heavily washed with greenish or dusky below. Can be told from female Blue-throated by more mottled under parts, heavily spotted throat, dark greenish tail, and smaller grayish tail-corners (Blue-throated has uniformly gray under parts and a blue-black tail with exceptionally large white spots at corners); wings of Rivoli project back of its tail, noticeable when bird is perched.
Range: — Mts. of se. Ariz. and sw. N.M.

BLUE-THROATED HUMMINGBIRD. *Lampornis clemenciæ.*
Subsp. (Illus. p. 98.)
Descr. 5. *Male:* — A large Hummingbird with black and white streaks through the eye and a *blue throat*. The only Hummer in which the *male* has *white spots* in the tail. *Female:* — A large Hummingbird, with *evenly gray* under parts, white marks on the face, and a large blue-black tail which has *exceptionally large white spots* at the corners. This long, broad tail with its prominent white patches is the best field-mark in all plumages. (See female Rivoli's Hummingbird.)
Range: — Sw. Tex. (Chisos Mts.), sw. N.M. (San Luis Mts.), and mts. of s. Ariz. (s. and e. of Tucson).
Subsp. (No apparent field differences): (1) Texas Blue-throated Hummingbird, *L. c. clemenciæ*; (2) Arizona Blue-throated Hummingbird, *L. c. bessophilus.*

BUFF-BELLIED HUMMINGBIRD. *Amazilia yucatanensis chalconota.* (Illus. p. 98.)
Descr. 4½. *Male:* — Under parts *buffy*, throat *green*, bill coral-red or pink with black tip. The only coral-billed Hummingbird

in the Brownsville region of Tex., and the only one with a green throat. *Female:* — Similar to male.
Range: — Rio Grande Delta, Tex.

WHITE-EARED HUMMINGBIRD. *Hylocharis leucotis leucotis.* (Illus. p. 98.)
Descr. 3¼. *Male:* — Under parts greenish, throat blue and green, forehead purple, bill pink with black tip, *broad white stripe behind eye. Female:* — Lacks the metallic forehead and throat-patches but is easily identified by the pink bill and bold white eye-stripe similar to those of the male.
Range: — Mts. of se. Ariz. (Huachuca, Chiricahua, Santa Rita).

BROAD-BILLED HUMMINGBIRD. *Cynanthus latirostris* (Illus. p. 98.)
Descr. 3¼. *Male:* — Greenish above and below with a metallic *blue throat.* The bill, *bright pink or red* with a black tip, is the best mark. The bird that resembles it most is the White-eared Hummingbird, which also has a pink bill. The White-ear has a broad white head-stripe, while the present species has only a tiny spot of white behind the eye. *Female:* — Identified by pink at base of bill and distinguished from female White-eared Hummingbird, the only other pink-billed species found in its range, by the *lack* of the white eye-stripe. The unmarked pearly-gray throat and under parts furnish a good mark. The females of the White-ear and of most other species have some spotting on the throat.

COPPERY-TAILED TROGON, *male*

Range: — Mts. of s. Ariz. and sw. N.M., also sw. Tex. (Brewster Co. — rare).

TROGONS: TROGONIDÆ

COPPERY-TAILED TROGON. *Trogon ambiguus ambiguus.* (Illus. p. 101.)

Descr. 11½. *Male:* — Head and upper parts dark glossy green (blackish at a distance), *under parts bright rose-red*, separated by a white band from the dark head; tail square-tipped and moderately long; bill stout and pale. The posture as shown in the picture, the slightly Parrot-like profile, and the bright-red under parts identify this unusual bird. *Female:* — Similar, but head and upper parts brown and with much less red on under parts.

Voice: — A rapid series of low, coarse notes, sounding like a Hen Turkey: *kowm kowm kowm kowm kowm kowm kowm* (slightly dissyllabic); Sutton describes it as *cory cory cory*, etc.

Range: — Mts. of s. Ariz.

KINGFISHERS: ALCEDINIDÆ

BELTED KINGFISHER. *Megaceryle alcyon.* Subsp. (Illus. p. 102.)

Descr. 11–14. Hovering above the water in readiness for the plunge, or flying with peculiar uneven wing-beats, rattling as it

A. BELTED KINGFISHER, *male*
B. TEXAS KINGFISHER, *male*

goes, the Kingfisher is easily learned by the novice. Perched, it is big-headed, larger than a Robin, blue-gray above, with a ragged crest and one (male) or two (female) broad breast-bands.
Voice: — A loud rattle.
Range: — Breeds from Can. s. to s. Calif. and N.M.; winters from Mex. n. to Wyo. and n.-cent. Calif., and along coast to Wash.
Subsp. (No apparent field differences): (1) Eastern Belted Kingfisher, *M. a. alcyon*; (2) Western Belted Kingfisher, *M. a. caurina*.

TEXAS KINGFISHER. *Chloroceryle americana septentrionalis.* (Illus. p. 102.)
Descr. 7¼. A very small Kingfisher, not much larger than a large Sparrow; upper parts greenish-black, with white spots; collar and under parts white. The male has a broad rusty breast-band. (In the Belted Kingfisher the female wears the rusty band.) The long bill, large head, and the shape when perched over the water identify it as a Kingfisher; the small size as this species.
Voice: — A clicking note; also a sharp squeak.
Range: — S. Tex. n. to Mason, Kerr, Bexar, and Comal Cos., and westward along Rio Grande Valley to Valverde Co. Casual in s. Ariz.

WOODPECKERS: PICIDÆ

TREE-CLIMBING birds, with stiff, spiny tails which act as props in their upward progress. The flight of most species is undulating, produced by several quick beats and a pause. The males of most species have some amount of red on the head.

NORTHERN, *or* **YELLOW-SHAFTED, FLICKER.** *Colaptes auratus luteus.*
Descr. 12–13. Differs from the following species, which is the common Flicker of the W., by having *yellow* wing- and tail-linings, and a *red crescent* on the back of the head. The male has a black *mustache mark* instead of red. Hybrids or intermediates between the two species are more frequently seen than typical examples of this species in the W. States. Some of these have orange-yellow wing-linings and spotted 'whiskers,' or one whisker black, the other red.
Voice: — Similar to Red-shafted Flicker.
Range: — E. U.S. w. to e. Mont., e. Wyo., and e. Colo.; occasional in Pacific States, especially in Wash.

RED-SHAFTED FLICKER. *Colaptes cafer.* Subsp. (Illus. p. 112.)
Descr. 13–14. Flickers are brown-backed Woodpeckers; flight

HEAD OF PILEATED WOODPECKER, *male*

deeply undulating: overhead this species shows considerable *salmon-red* under the wings and tail. The brown back and conspicuous *white rump*, visible as the bird flies up, is the best field-mark at a distance. Close up, a black crescent shows across the breast.

Voice: — Song, a loud *wick-wick-wick-wick-wick*, etc.; notes, a loud *kew* or *kee-yer* and a *flick-a, flick-a.*

Range: — Breeds throughout w. U.S.; winters throughout most of range.

Subsp. (No apparent field differences): (1) Northwestern Flicker, *C. c. cafer*; (2) Red-shafted Flicker, *C. c. collaris.*

MEARNS'S GILDED FLICKER. *Colaptes chrysoides mearnsi.* (Illus. p. 112.)

Descr. 13. A desert Flicker. Similar to the Red-shafted Flicker but with wing- and tail-linings *yellow* instead of red. Differs from the Northern, or Yellow-shafted, Flicker, which would never occur in the desert, in lacking the red crescent on the back of the head and in having a red mustache mark in the males. In short, this species has the head of the Red-shafted Flicker and the body of the Yellow-shaft.

Voice: — Similar to Flicker's.

Range: — Resident in deserts of se. Calif. and s. Ariz., mainly in Sahuaro belt along Colo. R. and tributaries.

(WESTERN) PILEATED WOODPECKER. *Ceophlœus pileatus picinus.* (Illus. p. 104.)

Descr. 17–18. A very large, *Crow-sized* Woodpecker of the deep woodlands with a conspicuous red *crest.* It is the only Western

Woodpecker with a crest. The great size, bounding flight, and flashing black-and-white coloration identify it at a distance. The diggings, large *oval* or *oblong* holes, are certain evidence of its presence.

Voice: — One common call resembles that of a Flicker, but is louder, and more hesitant — *kuk* — *kuk kukkuk* — *kuk* — *kuk*, etc. Another call is more ringing and hurried than that of a Flicker, and often rises in pitch at the beginning.

Range: — Heavy timber from Wash. s. along coast to Marin Co., Calif., and in Sierra Nevada to Yosemite; e. to Ida. and w. Mont.

GOLDEN-FRONTED WOODPECKER. *Centurus aurifrons.* (Illus. p. 112.)

Descr. 9½. *Male:* — A 'zebra-backed' Woodpecker with drab-colored under parts and a white rump. Shows a small white wing-patch in flight. The head is marked by three separated patches of bright color: yellow on the forehead, red on the crown, and orange on the nape of the neck. The only other common Woodpecker in southern Texas, the Ladder-backed Woodpecker, also has a 'ladder' or 'zebra' back, but is much smaller with a striped black-and-white face. In central Texas this species occurs with the similar Red-bellied Woodpecker. The bright red crown of the latter species is all in one piece, not broken into patches. *Female:* — Similar to male, but lacking the red patch. Has the conspicuous yellow hind-neck patch.

Voice: — A rolling *churr*.

Range: — S. Tex. n. to n.-cent. part and w. to the Big Bend (Brewster Co.).

GILA WOODPECKER. *Centurus uropygialis uropygialis.* (Illus. p. 112.)

Descr. 8–10. *Male:* — A 'zebra-backed' Woodpecker of the desert, showing a white patch in each wing in flight; head and under parts dull gray-brown; round red patch on top of head. *Female:* — Similar, without the red crown. The only other Woodpeckers occurring in the low desert country where this species is found are the Flickers and the Ladder-backed Woodpecker. Flickers are brown, and the Ladder-backed Woodpecker has a striped face. Neither shows a white wing-patch in flight, so characteristic of this species.

Voice: — A rolling *churr* and a sharp *pit*.

Range: — Low desert regions along Colo. R. in se. Calif. and extreme se. Nev.; and e. through s. Ariz. to sw. N.M.

RED-HEADED WOODPECKER. *Melanerpes erythrocephalus.* (Illus. p. 112.)

Descr. 8½–9½ This and the Red-breasted Sapsucker are the

only Woodpeckers with the *entire* head red. Many other species have a *patch* of red somewhere or other on the head. At a distance in flight it appears as a black-and-white Woodpecker with large square white patches on the rear edge of the wing. The immature bird is brown-headed; the large white wing-patches identify it. Perched, these patches make the lower back look white. As the Red-breasted Sapsucker is a bird of the Pacific States, the two species would never occur in the same locality.
Voice: — A loud *chur-chur*.
Range: — E. U.S. w. to cent. Mont., cent. Wyo., cent. Colo., and e. N.M.

CALIFORNIA, *or* ACORN, WOODPECKER. *Balanosphyra formicivora.* Subsp. (Illus. p. 112.)
Descr. 9½. A bird of the oaks and yellow pines. A black-backed Woodpecker with a white rump and a small white patch in each wing in flight. The clownish black, white, and red head-pattern, shown in the diagram, is unmistakable. Both male and female have red crowns.
Voice: — Most characteristic note, *whack-up*, *whack-up*, *whack-up*, or *ja-cob, ja-cob, ja-cob.*
Range: — Sw. Ore., Calif., Ariz., N.M., and w. Tex. (se. to Kerr Co. and Chisos Mts.).
Subsp. (No apparent field differences): (1) California Woodpecker, *B. f. bairdi*; (2) Mearns's Woodpecker, *B. f. aculeata*; (3) Ant-eating Woodpecker, *B. f. formicivora.*

LEWIS'S WOODPECKER. *Asyndesmus lewis.* (Illus. p. 112.)
Descr. 11. A large dark, black-backed Woodpecker, with a rosy-red belly (the only Woodpecker so marked), a wide gray collar around the breast and back of neck. and a red face-patch. The reddish under parts and the flight, somewhat like that of a small Crow, are the best marks. Sexes alike.
Voice: — Usually silent. A harsh *churr* in breeding season.
Range: — Timbered country in transition zone from Can. s. to cent. Calif., Ariz., and N.M.; more widely distributed in winter.

RED-NAPED SAPSUCKER. *Sphyrapicus varius nuchalis.* (Illus. p. 112.)
Descr. 8–8½. Best identified in all plumages by the combination of *red forehead patch* and *longitudinal white patch* on the black wing. Males are the only Western Woodpeckers with both a red forehead and red throat-patch. Females have white throats. Very similar to the Yellow-breasted Sapsucker of the E.
Voice: — A nasal note, *cheerrrr*, slurring downward. On the nesting grounds the drumming of the Sapsucker is very distinctive, several rapid thumps followed by several slow rhythmic ones.

WHITE
BELLY

EASTERN KINGBIRD

STRIPED
YELLOW
BREAST

SULPHUR-BELLIED
FLYCATCHER

WHITE RIM

BLACKISH
TAIL

YELLOWISH
BELLY

WESTERN KINGBIRD

*Two other Kingbirds
are similar to
this species:*

CASSIN'S KINGBIRD
COUCH'S KINGBIRD

YELLOWISH
BELLY

ASH-THROATED
FLYCATCHER

RUSTY
TAIL

*Two other Flycatchers
are similar to
this species:*

MEXICAN CRESTED FLYCATCHER
OLIVACEOUS FLYCATCHER

EASTERN   WESTERN   CASSIN'S   COUCH'S

TAILS of KINGBIRDS

FLYCATCHERS I

RUSTY UNDERPARTS

STREAKED BREAST

PINKISH SIDES

BRIGHT RED AND BLACK

♀

♂

SAY'S PHOEBE

VERMILION FLYCATCHER

BLACK BREAST

BLACK   PHOEBE

EYE·RING

WING· BARS

NO EYE·RING

WING BARS

BROWNISH WING·BARS

SMALL SIZE

WESTERN FLYCATCHER

WESTERN WOOD PEWEE

BEARDLESS FLYCATCHER

Five other Flycatchers are very similar to this species:

TRAILL'S
WRIGHT'S
HAMMOND'S
GRAY
LEAST

GRAY THROAT

WHITE THROAT

WHITE TUFTS (NOT ALWAYS VISIBLE)

WHITE STRIP SEPARATING DARK SIDES

COUES'S FLYCATCHER

OLIVE-SIDED FLYCATCHER

FLYCATCHERS II

Range: — Chiefly mts. e. of Cascades and Sierras from e. Wash. and Mont. s. to ne. Calif., Ariz., cent. N.M., and w. Tex.; winters s. into Mex.

RED-BREASTED SAPSUCKER. *Sphyrapicus varius.* Subsp. (Illus. p. 112.)

Descr. 8½–9. Although the Red-breasted Sapsucker and the Red-naped Sapsucker are considered to be races of the same species, they are so absolutely different in appearance that it is better to describe them under separate headings. In the Red-breasted Sapsucker the *entire head and breast are bright red.* The long white wing-patch and the rest of the markings are somewhat like those of the Red-naped Sapsucker. Immature birds are duller. (See Red-headed Woodpecker.)

Voice: — Similar to Red-naped Sapsucker.

Range: — Breeds in higher mts. of Calif., s. Ore. (Klamath, Jackson, and Josephine Cos.), w. Ore. (w. slope of Cascades), and w. Wash. Winters in adjacent lowlands and s. along Calif. Coast to Monterey.

Subsp. (No apparent field differences): (1) Northern Red-breasted Sapsucker, *S. v. ruber*; (2) Southern Red-breasted Sapsucker, *S. v. daggetti.*

WILLIAMSON'S SAPSUCKER. *Sphyrapicus thyroideus.* Subsp. (Illus. p. 112.)

Descr. 9½. *Male:* — Identified by the black crown, black back, and long white shoulder-patch. The white face-stripes and narrow red throat-patch are also distinctive. The belly is yellow. Flying, the male looks black with a white rump and white wing-patches, the only Woodpecker of the evergreens so patterned. The Red-naped Sapsucker is not so dark. *Female:* — Very different, a *zebra-backed* Woodpecker with a white rump, barred sides, and a *brown head.* No other Woodpecker of the evergreens resembles it.

Voice: — A nasal *cheeer* or *que-yer,* similar to notes of other Sapsuckers or suggestive of squeal of Red-tailed Hawk. Drumming distinctive; broken, several rapid thumps followed by three or four slow, accented ones, usually thus: - - - - - -, -, -, -, -.

Range: — Breeds chiefly in high Cascades, Sierras, and Rockies and adjacent high mt. ranges from Can. s. to s. Calif., cent. Ariz., and N.M. Winters at lower altitudes in Pacific States and from s. N.M. and w. Tex. into Mex.

Subsp. (No apparent field differences): (1) Williamson's Sapsucker, *S. t. thyroideus*; (2) Natalie's Sapsucker, *S. t. nataliæ.*

HAIRY WOODPECKER. *Dryobates villosus.* Subsp. (Illus. p. 112.)

Descr. 8½–10¼. Many other Woodpeckers have white rumps

or white bars or stripes on the back, but the Downy and the Hairy are our only common *white-backed* Woodpeckers. They are almost identical in pattern, checkered and spotted with black and white; the *males* with a small red patch on the back of the head; the *females*, without. The Hairy is like a magnified Downy; it is much larger; the bill is especially large, all out of size-relation to the Downy's little 'bark-sticker.' The Three-toed Woodpecker (*Picoides tridactylus*) of the high mountains often has a white back and resembles the Hairy (see Three-toed Woodpecker). The Hairy Woodpecker of the humid coastal belt in Wash. and Ore. which is known as the Harris's Woodpecker is recognizably different from the other races. There is very little white spotting on the wings, and the under parts are tinged with smoky or brownish.

Voice: — A Kingfisher-like rattle, run together more than call of Downy Woodpecker. Note, a sharp *pleek!*

Range: — Forested regions from Can. s. in mts. to Mex.

Subsp. (No apparent field differences except in No. 2 — see above): (1) Eastern Hairy Woodpecker, *D. v. villosus*; (2) Harris's Woodpecker, *D. v. harrisi*; (3) Cabanis's Woodpecker, *D. v. hyloscopus*; (4) Modoc Woodpecker, *D. v. orius*; (5) Rocky Mountain Hairy Woodpecker, *D. v. monticola*; (6) White-breasted Woodpecker, *D. v. leucothorectis*; (7) Chihuahua Woodpecker, *D. v. icastus*.

DOWNY WOODPECKER. *Dryobates pubescens.* Subsp. (Illus. p. 112.)

Descr. 6½–7. Identified by white back, small size, and small bill. (See Hairy Woodpecker and Nuttall's Woodpecker.) The Downy Woodpecker of the humid coastal belt in Wash. and Ore., which is known as the Gairdner's Woodpecker, is recognizably different from the other races. There is very little white spotting on the wings, and the under parts are tinged with smoky or brownish.

Voice: — A rapid series of notes, descending in pitch at the end of the series, less run together than those of Hairy Woodpecker. Note, a flat *pick*, not as sharp as Hairy's note.

Range: — Forested regions from Can. s. to s. Calif., n. Ariz., and n. N.M.

Subsp. (No apparent field differences except in No. 2 — see above): (1) Batchelder's Woodpecker, *D. p. leucurus*; (2) Gairdner's Woodpecker, *D. p. gairdneri*; (3) Willow Woodpecker, *P. p. turatii.*

LADDER-BACKED WOODPECKER. *Dryobates scalaris.* Subsp. (Illus. p. 112.)

Descr. 7½. A small black-and-white Woodpecker of the desert. Males have red caps. It is the only '*ladder-backed*' Woodpecker *with a striped face* in the range outlined below. The similar Nuttall's Woodpecker is found only in Calif., and never occurs in the desert, so the ranges do not overlap.

Voice: — A rattling series of notes, descending in pitch toward the end (similar to Downy's). Note, a sharp *pick*.

Range: — Arid country in se. Calif., Ariz., N.M., se. Colo., w. Okla., and Tex. (e. to 97th meridian).

Subsp. (No apparent field differences): (1) Texas Woodpecker, *D. s. symplectus*; (2) Cactus Woodpecker, *D. s. cactophilus*.

NUTTALL'S WOODPECKER. *Dryobates nuttalli.* (Illus. p. 112.)

Descr. 7. A small black and white Woodpecker. Males have red caps. It is the only '*ladder-backed*' Woodpecker with a *striped face* found in Calif. w. of the Sierras. (See Ladder-backed Woodpecker.) The only similar Woodpecker found in its range is the Downy, which has a white, *unbarred* back.

Voice: — A high-pitched rattling cry and a loud *prrit*.

Range: — Foothills of Calif. w. of Cascades and Sierras (except along nw. coast belt).

ARIZONA WOODPECKER. *Dryobates arizonæ arizonæ.* (Illus. p. 112.)

Descr. 8. A dark, brown-backed Woodpecker with a *striped face* and heavily barred sides. Males have a red patch on the nape. It is the only brown-backed Woodpecker with the exception of the Flickers.

Voice: — A sharp *spik* or *tseek*, sharper than notes of Downy and Ladder-backed Woodpeckers.

Range: — Oak belt of mts. in se. Ariz. and sw. N.M.

WHITE-HEADED WOODPECKER. *Dryobates albolarvatus.* Subsp. (Illus. p. 112.)

Descr. 9. A black Woodpecker with a *white head.* No other Woodpecker resembles it. A large white wing-patch shows in flight. Males have a red patch on the nape.

Voice: — A sharp *chick*, sometimes rapidly multiplied, *chick-ik-ik-ik*; also a rattle similar to Downy Woodpecker's.

Range: — Cascades and Sierras from Wash. to s.-cent. Calif., also mts. of s. Calif. (San Gabriel, San Bernardino, San Jacinto, Santa Rosa, and Cuyamaca Mts.); e. to Ida. and w. Nev.

Subsp. (No apparent field differences): (1) Northern White-headed Woodpecker, *D. a. albolarvatus*; (2) Southern White-headed Woodpecker, *D. a. gravirostris*.

ARCTIC THREE-TOED WOODPECKER. *Picoides arcticus.* (Illus. p. 112.)

Descr. 9–10. A Woodpecker with a white breast, heavily barred sides, and a *solid black* back. The male has a yellow crown-patch which the female lacks. She can be told by the combination of solid black back and heavily barred sides. The two Three-toed Woodpeckers inhabit the evergreen forests of the higher mts.; there their presence can often be detected by large patches scaled from the trunks of dead conifers.

Voice: — A sharp *chick* or *chuck*.

Range: — High mts. from Can. s. to cent. Calif. (Sierras), Mont., and n. Wyo.

THREE-TOED WOODPECKER. *Picoides tridactylus.* Subsp. (Illus. p. 112.)

Descr. 9–9½. The males of the two Three-toed Woodpeckers are the only species of the family with *yellow* caps. The '*ladder-back*' or *white-back* will separate this species from the black-backed Arctic Three-toed. The female lacks the yellow cap and resembles the Hairy Woodpecker, but the *barred* flanks identify it. (In many specimens the white of the back is crossed by bars, which make an additional mark.) White-backed individuals resemble the Hairy Woodpecker more closely. Occasional male Hairy Woodpeckers have yellow or orange head-patches and are called Three-toed Woodpeckers, but they lack the barring on the flanks.

Voice: — Similar to that of Arctic Three-toed Woodpecker.

Range: — High mts. from Can. s. to Ore., Ariz., and N.M.

Subsp. (No apparent field differences): (1) Alpine Three-toed Woodpecker, *P. t. dorsalis*; (2) Alaska Three-toed Woodpecker, *P. t. fasciatus.*

COTINGAS: COTINGIDÆ

XANTUS'S BECARD. *Platypsaris aglaiæ albiventris.*

Descr. 6½. Accidental in U.S. but to be looked for along Mexican border. *Male:* — A big-headed, thick-billed bird, somewhat resembling a Flycatcher. Gray with blackish *cap and cheeks* and a *lovely rose-colored throat*. *Female:* — Brown with a rusty tail, a *dark gray cap*, and a *light buffy collar* around nape. Under parts whitish washed with buffy.

Range: — Accidental. Recorded from Lower Rio Grande Valley, Tex., and mts. of se. Ariz.

FLYCATCHERS: TYRANNIDÆ

BIRDS of this family usually perch in an upright attitude on exposed twigs or branches, from which, at intervals, they sally forth to snap up passing insects. They are not so restless as most birds, but sit quite motionless save for an occasional jerk of the tail.

EASTERN KINGBIRD. *Tyrannus tyrannus.* (Illus. p. 106.)
Descr. 8½–9. When this large slaty-black and white Flycatcher flies from one perch to another, the white band at the tip of its fanlike tail leaves no doubt as to its identity. The red crownmark, invariably emphasized in color plates, is usually concealed and seldom noticed.
Voice: — A series of high rasping notes.
Range: — Breeds from e. N.A. w. to e. Wash., e. Ore., n. Nev., Ut., and e. N.M.; a straggler in Calif.

COUCH'S KINGBIRD. *Tyrannus melancholicus.* Subsp. (Illus. p. 106.)
Descr. 9½. Back olive, head gray, belly yellowish. Very similar to the Western and Cassin's Kingbirds, but tail more deeply forked, *brownish*, without hint of black, and *without white edgings*. The common Kingbird of the Lower Rio Grande.
Voice: — A high nasal *queer* or *chi-queer*, resembling notes of Cassin's Kingbird but higher; also a scolding series of notes.
Range: — Tex. (Lower Rio Grande Valley) and s. Ariz. (rare and local).
Subsp. (No apparent field differences): (1) Couch's Kingbird, *T. m. couchi*; (2) West Mexican Kingbird, *T. m. occidentalis*.

WESTERN, *or* **ARKANSAS, KINGBIRD.** *Tyrannus verticalis.* (Illus. p. 106.)
Descr. 8–9½. Smaller than a Robin, with a pale-gray head and back, yellowish under parts, and a dark mark through the eye. The best index to the identity of the four Kingbirds is their tails. In this species, the black tail is bordered on each side with white as in a Junco or Vesper Sparrow, but the borders are much narrower. Immature Arkansas Kingbirds do not always have the white on the sides of the tail, and may be mistaken for the Cassin's Kingbird, but the paler and grayer back will identify them.
Voice: — A shrill bickering call; various shrill twittering notes; also a sharp *whit*.
Range: — Breeds at low altitudes throughout W. States except in w. Wash. and along coast of Ore. and n. and cent. Calif. Winters in Mex.

CASSIN'S KINGBIRD. *Tyrannus vociferans.* (Illus. p. 106.)
Descr. 9. Like the Western, or Arkansas, Kingbird but darker, with an *olive-gray* rather than pearly-gray back, and *no white sides on the tail*. Immature Western Kingbirds sometimes lack these white edges, but the paler and grayer backs identify them. This species appears to have a whiter throat than the two simi-

SCISSOR-TAILED FLYCATCHER

lar Kingbirds, owing to the darker chest coloration. Although
in many places this species prefers somewhat higher altitudes,
the Western and Cassin's are often found together. Then their
strikingly different calls are often a help.
Voice: — A low nasal *queer*, or *chi-queer*, or *chi-bew*; also an
excited *ki-dear*, *ki-dear*, *ki-dear*, etc.
Range: — Breeds from cent. Calif., Ut., and s. Wyo. s. to Mex.;
winters from cent. Calif. into Mex.

SCISSOR-TAILED FLYCATCHER. *Muscivora forficata.* (Illus.
p. 112.)
Descr. 11½–15. A beautiful bird, pale pearly-gray, white, and
pink, with an extremely long scissor-like tail. The sides and
wing-linings are salmon-pink. No other land bird in its range
has such streaming tail-feathers. Perched, the 'scissors' are
folded. Immature birds with short tails resemble the Western,
or Arkansas, Kingbird, but have a touch of *pinkish* on the lower
belly instead of yellowish. The breast is whiter, and there is
more white in the sides of the tail.
Voice: — A harsh *keck*, or *kew*; also shrill, excited twitterings
and chatterings.
Range: — S. Great Plains w. to se. N.M. and w. Tex.

WOODPECKERS

1. GILDED FLICKER, MALE
2. RED-SHAFTED FLICKER, MALE
3. ARIZONA WOODPECKER, MALE
4. DOWNY WOODPECKER, MALE
5. GOLDEN-FRONTED WOODPECKER, MALE
6. LADDER-BACKED WOODPECKER, MALE
7. NUTTALL'S WOODPECKER, MALE
8. HAIRY WOODPECKER, MALE
9. GILA WOODPECKER, MALE
10. RED-BREASTED SAPSUCKER, MALE
11. RED-NAPED SAPSUCKER, MALE
12. THREE-TOED WOODPECKER
13. WILLIAMSON'S SAPSUCKER, FEMALE
14. RED-HEADED WOODPECKER, MALE
15. ARCTIC THREE-TOED WOODPECKER, MALE
16. WILLIAMSON'S SAPSUCKER, MALE
17. CALIFORNIA, OR ACORN, WOODPECKER, MALE
18. LEWIS'S WOODPECKER, MALE
19. WHITE-HEADED WOODPECKER, MALE

HEAD OF DERBY FLYCATCHER

DERBY FLYCATCHER. *Pitangus sulphuratus derbianus.*
(Illus. p. 113.)
Descr. 10½. A very large short-tailed Flycatcher, near the size
of the Belted Kingfisher, and somewhat like that bird in actions,
often catching small fish. It has rufous wings and tail, bright
yellow under parts and crown-patch, and a *strikingly patterned
black-and-white face.* The yellow under parts and black and
white face identify it at once.
Voice: — A loud *git-a-hear!* also *wheep!*
Range: — Lower Rio Grande Valley, Tex.

SULPHUR-BELLIED FLYCATCHER. *Myiodynastes luteiven-
tris swarthi.* (Illus. p. 106.)
Descr. 8. A large *streaked* Flycatcher with a rufous tail, white
stripe over the eye, and narrow yellow crown-patch; under parts
yellowish with black streakings, back also streaked. *No other
Flycatcher has a streaked yellow breast.*
Voice: — 'A high penetrating *kee-zee'-ick!* given by both male
and female, often in duet' (G. M. Sutton); has also been likened
to creaking of wheelbarrow.
Range: — Higher mts. of se. Ariz., chiefly where there are syca-
mores.

MEXICAN CRESTED FLYCATCHER. *Myiarchus tyrannulus.* Subsp.
Descr. 9–9½. Like the Ash-throated Flycatcher, but an inch or
more longer, with a proportionately larger bill; breast deeper
yellow and back more olive. These are all differences of degree
only. To tell the two species apart the field student must have
a keen ear or be very sure of size and color differences. The
Crested Flycatcher (*M. crinitus*), which migrates through the

range of the Mexican Crested in s. Tex., can be distinguished by the *brown* lower mandible of the bill and the different call-notes (most characteristic note a loud whistled *wheeeep!* with rising inflection).

Voice: — A sharp *pwit*, and a rolling throaty *purreeet*. Voice much more vigorous and raucous than Ash-throated Flycatcher.

Range: — Lower Rio Grande Valley, Tex., and deserts of s. Ariz. (Sahuaro belt).

Subsp. (No apparent field differences): (1) Mexican Crested Flycatcher, *M. t. nelsoni*; (2) Arizona Crested Flycatcher, *M. t. magister*.

ASH-THROATED FLYCATCHER. *Myiarchus cinerascens cinerascens.* (Illus. p. 106.)

Descr. 8–8½. A medium-sized Flycatcher, smaller than a King-bird, with two white wing-bars, white throat, *pale yellowish belly, and rufous tail.* The Kingbirds have pale yellow bellies, but dusky or *blackish* tails. Except in s. Ariz. and along the lower Rio Grande in Tex., no other Flycatcher in the West has a rufous tail. (See Mexican Crested Flycatcher and Olivaceous Flycatcher.)

Voice: — *Pwit*; also a rolling *prrrit* and *ke-wherr*.

Range: — Breeds from e. Ore., e. Wash., n. Ut. (occasionally), and s. Wyo. (occasionally), s. into Mex.; prefers low altitudes and foothills, especially in arid or semi-arid country.

OLIVACEOUS FLYCATCHER. *Myiarchus tuberculifer oli-vascens.*

Descr. 7¼. Of the same type as the Ash-throated Flycatcher, rufous-tailed and yellow-bellied, but considerably *smaller*, with a gray instead of white throat.

Voice: — A mournful drawling whistle, slurring downward, *peeur*; very characteristic.

Range: — Breeds in mts. of se. Ariz.; casual in sw. Tex. (Chisos Mts.).

EASTERN PHOEBE. *Sayornis phœbe.*

Descr. 6½–7. Similar to the Western Wood Pewee, but with a whiter breast and *without* conspicuous wing-bars. Its lack of wing-bars and persistent tail-wagging habit are good points. The bill is black, those of the Wood Pewee and the other small Flycatchers are pale or yellowish on the lower mandible.

Voice: — A well-enunciated *fee-bee*.

Range: — Breeds locally in se. Colo. and e. N.M.

BLACK PHOEBE. *Sayornis nigricans nigricans.* (Illus. p. 107.)

Descr. 6½. Upper parts, head, and breast *black*; belly *white*. in sharp contrast to black of sides and breast. The only black-breasted Flycatcher.

Voice: — Song, a thin, strident *fi-bee, fi-bee*, the first two notes rising, the last two dropping; note, a sharp *kip*.

Range: — Resident in w. Tex., s. N.M., Ariz., s. Ut., s. Nev., and n. through Calif. (chiefly w. of Sierras).

SAY'S PHOEBE. *Sayornis saya saya.* (Illus. p. 107.)

Descr. 7–8. A Bluebird-sized Flycatcher with pale-*rusty* under parts. The brownish back, black tail, and rusty breast give the bird the look of a small Robin, but its Flycatcher habits identify it. The only Flycatcher that might be confused with it is the female Vermilion Flycatcher.

Voice: — A plaintive *pee-ur*.

Range: — Breeds in open or arid country from Can. s. to Mex. except in humid coastal sections; winters chiefly from N.M., Ariz., and cent. Calif. s.

TRAILL'S FLYCATCHER. *Empidonax trailli.* Subsp.

Descr. 5¼–6. A small Flycatcher with a dark back, and light breast, conspicuous light *eye-ring* and two white *wing-bars*. Four other common Western Flycatchers, the Hammond's, Wright's, Gray, and Western, fit this description exactly. They are all much more easily identified by their breeding habitats and their songs than by the almost imperceptible differences in coloration. This species is the brownest of the genus, and lives in thickets of willow and alder along streams, especially in low country but also in mt. meadows.

Voice: — *Fay-be'-o*, or *weep-a-dee'-ar*, with accent on next to last syllable; some birds contract this into a sneezy *fitz-be'-o* or *fitz-bew*. The other similar Western Empidonaces have songs made up of two or three separate elements, not uttered as a single emphatic phrase as in this species. Note, a low *pit*.

Range: — Breeds from Can. s. to Mex. (from Rockies w.) and to ne. Colo. (e. of Rockies).

Subsp. (No apparent field differences): (1) Alder Flycatcher, *E. t. trailli*; (2) Little Flycatcher, *E. t. brewsteri*.

LEAST FLYCATCHER. *Empidonax minimus.*

Descr. 5–5¾. A small Eastern Empidonax that gets into Wyo. and Mont. in those sections that lie east of the Rockies. Grayer above and whiter below than the other small Flycatchers of this group occurring in those two States. Its voice and the open groves of trees which it inhabits identify it.

Voice: — A sharply snapped *che-bec'* with the accent on the second syllable.

Range: — Breeds in e. N.A., w. to cent. Mont. and e. Wyo.; migrant in e. Colo.

HAMMOND'S FLYCATCHER. *Empidonax hammondi.*
Descr. 5–5½. Of the five similar Western Empidonax Flycatchers, the Wright's and the Hammond's have given field students the most headaches. It is considered a standing joke among Western ornithologists that no one seems to have an infallible way of telling them apart in the field. The Wright's and the Hammond's both breed in the transition and Canadian zones of the mts. higher up than the Western Flycatcher breeds. The habitats of the two hardly overlap, the Hammond's on the whole occurring higher up in the taller firs, while the Wright's prefers the chaparral or a mixture of chaparral and firs. As a rule, this species is more olive above, not so gray; the under parts are more yellowish, contrasting with a grayer chest-band. These points are so intangible and variable as to be of almost no use in the field.
Voice: — Voice descriptions by different writers vary greatly. Personally the author can see no great difference in the songs of the Wright's and the Hammond's. Birds which he was assured were *hammondi* sang a thin colorless song as follows:

Se-lip   twur   tree-ip

This order sometimes varies. Hoffmann ventured the opinion that the low *twur* or '*tsurp*' note is always typical of *hammondi*. The birds which the author was told were Wright's sang similarly, but with perhaps less emphasis. His transcription is as follows:

See-pit   serzel   pee-ee

The arrangement is very similar to that of *hammondi*, especially the first and third elements. The low note, *serzel* or *se-wer*, is double-noted rather than a single *twur* and does not drop quite so much in pitch.
Range: — Breeds in coniferous forests of mts. from Can. s. to

cent. Calif. (Yosemite) and Colo.; usually at higher altitudes than next species.

WRIGHT'S FLYCATCHER. *Empidonax wrighti.*
Descr. 5¼–6. See Hammond's Flycatcher.
Voice: — See Hammond's Flycatcher.
Range: — Breeds in high chaparral or deciduous growths on mts. from Can. s. to s. Calif., n. Ariz., n. N.M., and w. Tex.

GRAY FLYCATCHER. *Empidonax griseus.*
Descr. 5½. Very similar to the Wright's Flycatcher, but slightly larger, and grayer on the back, and with the base of the lower mandible more flesh-colored, points seldom seen in the field. This, like most of the other Empidonax Flycatchers, can hardly be safely identified in the field except on the breeding grounds, when it is identified by its habitat. In e. Ore. this is sagebrush country. In Ut., according to Dr. Woodbury, the bird's habitat is arid pinyon and juniper country ('Pygmy Forest'). In neither habitat would one expect to find the Wright's or Hammond's Flycatcher.
Voice: — Notes said by Swarth to be identical to Wright's Flycatcher. Hoffmann differs with this, stating that the song is less varied than Wright's or Hammond's, with only two elements, a vigorous *chiwip* and a fainter *cheep* in a higher pitch (used in a variety of combinations).
Range: — Breeds in Great Basin from w. Colo. to extreme e. Calif. and e. Ore.; winters from s. Calif. and s. Ariz. s.

WESTERN FLYCATCHER. *Empidonax difficilis difficilis.*
(Illus. p. 107.)
Descr. 5½–6. Upper parts olive-brown, under parts washed with yellowish, wing-bars whitish, eye-ring white. Very similar to the other small Flycatchers of this group, but under parts usually more yellowish, *including the throat.* Some individuals of the other species have a faint wash of yellow on the under parts and closely resemble it, but their throats are white. Its breeding habitat is canyons, and shady groves of trees near streams or around dwellings. It is the most widely distributed Empidonax.
Voice: — A sharp lisping *ps-seet*, with rising inflection. The song, heard chiefly at daybreak, is composed of three thin colorless notes:

Bz-zeek trip Seet!

Range: — Breeds from Can. s. to Mex. border.

BUFF-BREASTED FLYCATCHER. *Empidonax fulvifrons pygmæus.*
Descr. 5. A very small Flycatcher of the Empidonax group with a *white eye-ring* and *white wing-bars*, but easily distinguished from its confusing relatives by its rich *buffy* breast.
Voice: — *Chicky-whew* (Lusk).
Range: — Breeds in mts. of se. Ariz. and sw. N.M.

COUES'S FLYCATCHER. *Myiochanes pertinax pallidiventris.* (Illus. p. 107.)
Descr. 7¾. In the high mts. along the Mexican border of Ariz. and N.M. a large gray Flycatcher is seen which looks like a large Wood Pewee but has a larger head, slight triangular crest, and less conspicuous wing-barring. The lower mandible of the bill is conspicuously yellow. It resembles even more closely the Olive-sided Flycatcher in size and shape, but the under parts are more uniformly gray, the throat is *grayer*, and there is no white strip up the middle of the breast separating the dusky sides.
Voice: — A plaintive whistled *ho-say, re-ah,* or *ho-say, ma-re-ah,* hence the bird's nickname, 'José Maria'; suggests call of Olive-sided Flycatcher. Note, a low *pip.*
Range: — Breeds in mts. of cent. and se. Ariz. and sw. N.M.

WESTERN WOOD PEWEE. *Myiochanes richardsoni richardsoni.* (Illus. p. 107.)
Descr. 6–6½. A Sparrow-sized Flycatcher, dusky gray-brown above and lighter gray on the breast and sides. It has two narrow white wing-bars but no white eye-ring. The slightly larger size, much darker back, grayer under parts, and lack of an eye-ring distinguish it from any of the smaller Flycatchers. When perched, the long wings extend two-thirds to three-fourths the length of the tail instead of one-third the way as in the Empidonax group.
Voice: — A nasal whistle *peeyee* or *peeeer.*
Range: — Breeds from Can. to Mex.

OLIVE-SIDED FLYCATCHER. *Nuttallornis mesoleucus.* (Illus. p. 107.)
Descr. 7¼–8. A rather large, bull-headed Flycatcher, usually seen perched at the extreme tip of a dead tree or exposed branch. It resembles the smaller Wood Pewee but the distinctive points are its large bill, white throat, and *dark chest-patches* separated or nearly separated by a narrow strip of white down the center from the throat to the belly. It also has two tufts of white which sometimes poke out from behind the wings near the back.
Voice: — Note, a trebled *pip-pip-pip.* Song, a spirited whistle,

hip-three'-cheers! or *whip whee' wheer!* the middle note highest, the last slurring down.

Range: — Breeds in coniferous forests from Can. s. to s. Calif., cent. Ariz., N.M., and w. Tex.; also in eucalyptus groves in cent. Calif.; migrates into Mex.

VERMILION FLYCATCHER. *Pyrocephalus rubinus mexicanus.* (Illus. p. 107.)

Descr. 5½–6½. *Male:* — Unmistakable. *Head and under parts, flaming vermilion-red*; tail and upper parts *blackish. Female:* — Much plainer, upper parts dark brown, breast white, belly and under tail-coverts *tinged with pinkish or salmon.* The only other Flycatcher that might be mistaken for the female is the Say's Phoebe, which is longer-tailed and more extensively buffy or 'pinkish' below. The white breast of the female Vermilion is *narrowly streaked* with dusky. Immature females have yellowish bellies.

Voice: — A twittering Phoebe-like *zi-breee* or *p-p-pit-zeee*; note, *zeep.*

Range: — Resident in arid regions of s. and w. Tex., s. N.M., s. and w. Ariz., sw. Ut., s. Nev., and se. Calif.; winters occasionally along coast of sw. Calif.

BEARDLESS FLYCATCHER. *Camptostoma imberbe.* (Illus. p. 107.)

Descr. 4½. A very small, nondescript Flycatcher whose general appearance and behavior suggest a Kinglet, a Vireo, or an immature Verdin. Upper parts olive-gray; under parts dingy white; indistinct wing-bars and eye-ring; bill small and dark. Distinguished from the *Empidonax* Flycatchers by its smaller size, smaller head, different behavior, and very small bill. The Vireo most apt to be confused with it is the Bell's Vireo, which is somewhat larger, with a slightly more yellowish wash on the sides. In many individuals of this Flycatcher the wing-bars are distinctly buffy or even brownish; those of the Vireo are whitish or grayish. The immature Verdin is probably the bird that resembles the Beardless Flycatcher most closely, but the young Verdin's bill is strongly yellow at the base.

Voice: — Call-note a thin *peeee-yuk.* Song a series of fine rather gentle notes, *ee, ee, ee, ee, ee,* increasing in volume toward the middle of the series (G. M. Sutton).

Range: — Low woodlands along streams in se. Ariz. and Rio Grande Delta in Tex.

HORNED LARK

LARKS: ALAUDIDÆ

HORNED LARK. *Otocoris alpestris.* Subsp. (Illus. p. 120.)
Descr. 7–8. A streaked brown terrestrial bird, larger than a
Sparrow, with two small erectile black *horns* (not always noticeable), and a black collar, or ring, below the yellow throat; *walks*,
does not hop; frequents plains, prairies, extensive fields, and
shores; flying overhead, looks light-bellied with a contrasting
black tail. The contrasting face pattern, shown in the diagram,
is distinctive.
Voice: — Song, a long tinkling twitter, irregular and high-
pitched. Note, *tee* or *tee titi.*
Range: — Breeds and winters from Can. to Mex.
Subsp. (No apparent field differences): (1) Pallid Horned Lark,
O. a. arcticola; (2) Desert Horned Lark, *O. a. leucolæma*; (3)
Streaked Horned Lark, *O. a. strigata*; (4) Dusky Horned Lark,
O. a. merrilli; (5) Island Horned Lark, *O. a. insularis*; (6) Cali-
fornia Horned Lark, *O. a. actia*; (7) Ruddy Horned Lark, *O. a.
rubea*; (8) Montezuma Horned Lark, *O. a. occidentalis*; (9)
Scorched Horned Lark, *O. a. adusta*; (10) Mohave Horned Lark,
O. a. ammophila; (11) Sonora Horned Lark, *O. a. leucansiptila.*

SWALLOWS: HIRUNDINIDÆ

SPARROW-SIZED birds with long, slim wings and extremely graceful flight. Although the voices of Swallows are very distinctive,
once learned, they do not adapt themselves well to verbal
description, hence are omitted in the following accounts. (See
Swifts.)

WHITE
WING
PATCHES

WHITE-
WINGED
DOVE

POINTED
TAIL

MOURNING
DOVE

WHITE
CRESCENT

LIGHT
TAIL-BAND

UNIFORMLY
DARK
COLORATION

BAND-TAILED
PIGEON

RED-
BILLED
PIGEON

SPOTTED
NECK

WHITISH
UNDERPARTS

CHINESE
SPOTTED
DOVE

WHITE
FRONTED
DOVE

← REDDISH WINGS →

SLENDER TAIL
WITH WHITE SIDES

SHORT
BLACK TAIL

INCA
DOVE

GROUND
DOVE

PIGEONS and DOVES

BLUE-BLACK BREAST ♂   GRAYISH BREAST ♀

PURPLE MARTIN

DEEPLY-FORKED TAIL

BARN SWALLOW

LIGHT RUMP

CLIFF SWALLOW

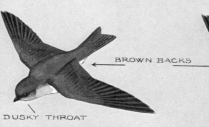

BROWN BACKS

DUSKY THROAT

ROUGH-WINGED SWALLOW

BAND ACROSS BREAST

BANK SWALLOW

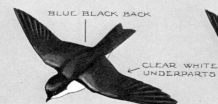

BLUE-BLACK BACK

CLEAR WHITE UNDERPARTS

TREE SWALLOW

WHITE PATCHES

VIOLET-GREEN SWALLOW

SWALLOWS

VIOLET-GREEN SWALLOW. *Tachycineta thalassina lepida.*
(Illus. p. 121.)
Descr. 5½. Dark above, adults glossed with green and purple;
clear white below. Separated from the Tree Swallow, which
also has immaculate white under parts by the greener back
coloration and the *white patches* that almost meet over the base
of the tail. When the bird is perched, it will be seen that the
white of the face is more extensive, *partially encircling the eye.*
Range: — Breeds from Can. s. to Mex., chiefly in mts. s.

TREE SWALLOW. *Iridoprocne bicolor.* (Illus. p. 121.)
Descr. 5–6. Steely blue-black or green-black above and *clear
white* below. The only other Swallow possessing such immaculate white under parts is the Violet Green, which shows conspicuous white rump-patches. (See Rough-winged Swallow.)
Range: — Breeds from Can. s. to s. Calif. and Colo.; winters
from cent. Calif. s.

BANK SWALLOW. *Riparia riparia riparia.* (Illus. p. 121.)
Descr. 5–5½. A small *brown-backed* Swallow with a distinct
dark *band* across the white breast. The only other brown-
backed Swallow, the Rough-wing, lacks this band.
Range: — Breeds from Can. s. to s. Calif., Ariz. and N.M.

ROUGH-WINGED SWALLOW. *Stelgidopteryx ruficollis.*
(Illus. p. 121.)
Descr. 5–5¾. A *brown-backed* Swallow, larger and lighter brown
than the Bank Swallow, with the dark breast-band absent. The
light under parts shade into a dingy color toward the throat.
Immature Tree Swallows in late summer are rather brownish
above and might be mistaken for this species, except for their
white throats and more snowy-white under parts. The breast
of the Rough-wing is dingier; the back browner, not so sooty.
Range: — Breeds from Wash. and Mont. s. to s. Calif., Ariz.,
and n. N.M.; winters occasionally in s. Ariz.

BARN SWALLOW. *Hirundo erythrogaster.* (Illus. p. 121.)
Descr. 6–7½. Pinkish or cinnamon-buff below, with a blue-black
back and a *very deeply forked* tail; the only native Swallow that
is really 'Swallow-tailed.' It is also the only one with white
spots in the tail.
Range: — Breeds from Can. s. to Mex.; a few winter in se. Calif.

CLIFF SWALLOW. *Petrochelidon albifrons.* Subsp. (Illus.
p. 121.)
Descr. 5–6. In flight the pale rusty or *buffy* rump quickly distinguishes the bird; perched overhead with other Swallows, it
appears *square-tailed* with a *dark* throat-patch. Cliff Swallows

nest in gourd-like nests plastered against cliffs, under bridges, or beneath the eaves on the *outside* of barns. Barn Swallows build open nests, *usually* but not always on the *inside* of barns. The race of this bird known as the Mexican Cliff Swallow (s. Ariz., sw. N.M., and Brewster Co., Tex.) can be told from other Cliff Swallows, with which it sometimes associates, by its dark *chestnut* forehead, nearly as dark as the throat. The foreheads of other Cliff Swallows are *pale buff*, the throat dark.

Range: — Breeds from Can. to Mex.; a few winter in se. Calif.
Subsp. (No apparent field differences except in No. 3; see above): (1) Northern Cliff Swallow, *P. a. albifrons*; (2) Lesser Cliff Swallow, *P. a. tachina*; (3) Mexican Cliff Swallow, *P. a. melanogaster*.

COAHUILA CLIFF SWALLOW. *Petrochelidon fulva pallida.*
Descr. Like Cliff Swallow but throat *pale rusty* or *buffy* not dark chestnut. Quite distinctive in field.
Range: — Occurs in s.-cent. Tex. (Kerr Co.).

PURPLE MARTIN. *Progne subis subis.* (Illus. p. 121.)
Descr. 7½–8½. Our largest Swallow. The male is uniformly blue-black *above and below*. No other Swallow is black-bellied. (See Black Swift.) The female is whitish-bellied, often with a pale collar around the back of the neck; she may be known by her size, and from the much smaller Tree Swallow by the dingy grayness of the throat and breast.
Range: — Breeds from Can. s. to Mex.

JAYS, MAGPIES, AND CROWS: CORVIDÆ

CANADA JAY. *Perisoreus canadensis.* Subsp. (See Frontis.)
Descr. 11–13. A large *gray* bird of the cool forests of high mountains; larger than a Robin, with a *dark patch* on back of head, and a *white crown*; suggests a huge, overgrown Chickadee. This species is very similar to the next, but the under parts are grayer, the crown is more extensively white, and the tail is tipped with white. Their ranges do not overlap. Young birds are dark slate-colored, lightening out toward the tail.
Voice: — A soft whistled *whee-ah*; also many other notes, some harsh, some pleasant.
Subsp. ROCKY MOUNTAIN JAY. *P. c. capitalis.*
White of crown much more extensive, going back to nape (dusky collar on nape only about one-half inch wide). High forests of Rocky Mt. region from Can., s. to n. N.M. and cent.-e. Ariz.; w. to e. Wash. and e. Ore.

CANADA JAY. *P. c. canadensis.*
White of crown confined chiefly to forehead, seldom
extending much behind eye (blackish collar on nape
much more conspicuous than in preceding race, 1 to 1½
inches wide). Head-pattern suggests Oregon Jay. Said
to be the race inhabiting the Black Hills in ne. Wyo.

OREGON JAY. *Perisoreus obscurus.* Subsp.
Descr. 9½–11. Similar to the preceding species but smaller and
with whiter under parts (see Canada Jay). Confined to Pacific
States.
Voice: — Similar to Canada Jay.
Range: — Cascades and Pacific slope from Wash. to n. Calif.
(Mendocino Co., Mt. Shasta, and Warner Mts.).
Subsp. (No apparent field differences): (1) Oregon Jay, *P. o.
obscurus*; (2) Gray Jay, *P. o. griseus.*

BLUE JAY. *Cyanocitta cristata.* (See Frontis.)
Descr. 11–12. A *large* blue bird, larger than a Robin; blue above,
whitish below, and *crested*. The Steller's Jay which does not occur so far east, is darker, without the whitish areas on the wings,
tail, and under parts.
Voice: — A harsh slurring *jeeah* or '*jay*'; also many other notes,
some musical.
Range: — E. N.A. w. to e. Colo. and e. Wyo.

STELLER'S JAY. *Cyanocitta stelleri.* Subsp. (See Frontis.)
Descr. 12–13½. *A large dark black and blue bird with a long*
crest. Fore parts blackish or brownish black; wings, tail, and
under parts deep blue. It is the only Jay with a crest and the
only *blue* bird of any sort with a crest found between the Pacific
and the Rockies. East of the Rockies the Blue Jay occurs.
This is the Jay of the pines and other conifers. The California
Jay is the Jay of the oaks and scrub.
Voice: — A loud *shook-shook-shook* or *shack-shack-shack* or
wheck — wek — wek — wek — wek or *kwesh kwesh kwesh*; also
many other notes.
Range: — Coniferous forests from Can. s. to Mex. (in mts.) and
to Monterey Co., Calif. (on coast).
Subsp. (No apparent field differences): (1) Steller's Jay, *C. s.
stelleri*; (2) Coast Jay, *C. s. carbonacea*; (3) Blue-fronted Jay,
C. s. frontalis; (4) Black-headed Jay, *C. s. annectens*; (5) Long-
crested Jay, *C. s. diademata.*

CALIFORNIA JAY. *Aphelocoma californica.* Subsp. (See
Frontis.)
Descr. 11½–12. Larger than a Robin. *A blue Jay without a
crest.* Head, wings, and tail blue; back brownish; under parts

pale gray; dark band across breast. The pale under parts and lack of a crest distinguish it readily from the Steller's Jay. The Steller's Jay prefers pines; this species, oaks.

Voice: — A harsh *check-check-check-check* higher than Steller's Jay; also *kwesh kwesh kwesh kwesh*. One of the commonest calls is a *shreek* with a rising inflection.

Range: — Chiefly oaks from extreme s. Wash., s. Idaho, and s. Wyo. s. to Mex., and from Rockies and cent. Tex. w. to coast.

Subsp. (No apparent field differences): (1) Long-tailed Jay, *A. c. immanis*; (2) Nicasio Jay, *A. c. oöcleptica*; (3) California Jay, *A. c. californica*; (4) Woodhouse's Jay, *A. c. woodhousei*; (5) Texas Jay, *A. c. texana*.

SANTA CRUZ JAY. *Aphelocoma insularis.*
Descr. 12. The Jay found on Santa Cruz Island off the Calif. Coast is regarded as a distinct species. It is almost identical with the California Jay but is somewhat larger and more richly colored.
Range: — Santa Cruz Id. off Santa Barbara, Calif.

ARIZONA JAY. *Aphelocoma sieberi.* Subsp. (See Frontis.)
Descr. 11½–13. A blue Jay without a crest. Resembles somewhat the California (Woodhouse's and Texas) Jay but *under parts more uniform in color*, lacking the whitish throat and the dusky band across the breast. The blue is paler and dustier, the back grayer. The voice is very different.
Voice: — A rough querulous *drenk* or *jenk.*
Range: — Live-oak regions of se. Ariz., sw. N.M., and cent.-w. Tex. (Chisos Mts., Brewster Co.).
Subsp. (No apparent field differences): (1) Arizona Jay, *A. s. arizonæ*; (2) Couch's Jay, *A. s. couchi.*

GREEN JAY. *Xanthoura luxuosa glaucescens.* (See Frontis.)
Descr. 11–12. The only *green* Jay. Throat-patch, *black*; top of head, bright blue; sides of tail, yellow. It is absolutely unmistakable, as the color plate shows.
Voice: — *Cheh cheh cheh cheh*; also a dry throaty rattle like a cricket frog and other calls.
Range: — Lower Rio Grande Valley, Tex.

AMERICAN MAGPIE. *Pica pica hudsonia.* (Illus. p. 125.)
Descr. 17½–21½, tail 9½–12. Larger than Jays, the Magpies are the only large *black-and-white* land birds with *long, sweeping* tails. In flight the iridescent tail streams out behind and large white patches flash in the wing. This species has a black bill.
Voice: — A rapid *cheg cheg cheg cheg*. Also a nasal querulous *maaag* or *maa — maa.*

GRAYISH
BACK

WHITE EYE-BROW STRIPE

CHICKADEES HAVE
BLACK CAPS AND BIBS

BLACK-CAPPED
CHICKADEE

MOUNTAIN CHICKADEE

CHESTNUT BACK

LONG GRAY TAIL

BROWNISH CAP

CHESTNUT-BACKED
CHICKADEE

BUSH-TIT

YELLOW HEAD

GRAYISH CREST

VERDIN

PLAIN TITMOUSE

"BRIDLED" FACE

BLACK CREST

♂

BRIDLED TITMOUSE

BLACK-CRESTED TITMOUSE

CHICKADEES AND TITMICE

CAP DOWN TO EYE.

STRIPE THROUGH EYE

PYGMY NUTHATCH

RED-BREASTED
NUTHATCH

CURVED
BILL

CREEPING
POSTURE

EYE SURROUNDED
BY WHITE

BROWN CREEPER

WHITE-BREASTED
NUTHATCH

STRIPED CROWN

EYE-RING

♀

♀

GOLDEN-CROWNED
KINGLET

RUBY-CROWNED
KINGLET

LONG BLACK AND WHITE TAILS

BLUE-GRAY CROWN

BLACK CAP

EYE-RING

♂

♂

WESTERN GNATCATCHER

PLUMBEOUS GNATCATCHE

NUTHATCHES, CREEPER
KINGLETS AND GNATCATCHERS

AMERICAN MAGPIE

Range: — Rocky Mt. region from Can. s. to n. Ariz. and n. N.M. and w. to e. Wash., e. Ore., and e. Calif. (e. slope of Sierras).

YELLOW-BILLED MAGPIE. *Pica nuttalli.*
Descr. 16–18, tail 9½–10¼. Similar to the American Magpie, but bill *yellow.*
Voice: — Similar to American, or Black-billed, Magpie. Bird quieter.
Range: — Valleys of cent. Calif., chiefly Sacramento and San Joaquin Valleys.

RAVEN. *Corvus corax.* Subsp.
Descr. 21½–26½. Although a Raven is nearly twice the bulk of a Crow, when comparison is not possible this difference does not always help. The flight, however, is distinctive. Hawk-like, the Raven alternates flapping with soaring. It soars on horizontal wings; the Crow and the Turkey Vulture with wings bent upward. The ample tail, seen from below, is distinctly *wedge-shaped.* Perched, at not too great a distance, the shaggy throat feathers are evident. On the whole, the Raven replaces the Crow in arid country or along rocky coasts.
Voice: — A Raven croaks: *cr-r-ruck.* (A Crow caws.)
Range: — Most of w. U.S., especially in arid or dry regions.
Subsp. (No apparent field differences): (1) American **Raven**, *C. c. sinuatus*; (2) Northern Raven, *C. c. principalis.*

WHITE-NECKED RAVEN. *Corvus cryptoleucus.*
Descr. 19–21. A small Raven, nearer the size of the Crow.
The typical Raven of the low desert country from s. Tex. to se.
Ariz. In this range the larger American Raven is most commonly seen in the mts., while the White-neck prefers the yucca
deserts. The Crow does not occur in the range of the White-
neck (except in sw. Oklahoma). The base of the feathers on the
neck and breast of this species are *white*. This often shows when
the bird's feathers are ruffled by the desert wind.
Voice: — A hoarse *kraak*, flatter than croak of American Raven.
Range: — Deserts of se. Ariz., s. N.M., se. Colo., sw. Okla., and
w. and s. Tex.

CROW. *Corvus brachyrhynchos.* Subsp.
Descr. 17–21. Much larger than any of the Blackbirds, and
smaller than the Raven, the Crow needs no description. (See
Raven.)
Voice: — A loud *caw* or *cah*, easily imitated by the human
voice.
Subsp. WESTERN CROW. *C. b. hesperis.*
W. U.S. from Can. s. to s. Calif., cent. Ariz., and cent.
N.M.
NORTHWESTERN CROW. *C. b. caurinus.*
Puget Sound area of w. Wash. Although the A.O.U.
Check-List (1931) calls this bird a race of the Crow,
C. brachyrhynchos, some authorities insist it is more
closely related to the Fish Crow, *C. ossifragus*, of the
Atlantic Coast (Ludlow Griscom). Certainly it is true
that this bird differs from the Western Crow in the
same way that the Fish Crow differs from the Eastern
Crow. Its habitat is the salt water; it is smaller, has a
noticeably quicker wing-beat, and, most important of
all, its voice is more nasal (a short, nasal *car* or *că*, instead of an honest-to-goodness *caw*).

PIÑON JAY. *Cyanocephalus cyanocephalus.* (See Frontis.)
Descr. 10–11½. In appearance and actions like a small *dull blue*
Crow, hardly larger than a Robin, with a long sharp bill. It
can be easily told from the California Jay by its short tail
and uniform coloration, and from the Steller's Jay by lack of a
crest (Steller's Jay depresses crest when flying). It is often seen
in large noisy flocks, especially in arid country where Piñon
pines and junipers grow. Often seen walking about on ground
like Crows.
Voice: — A high nasal cawing, *kaa-eh*, or *karn-eh*, with descending inflection; has mewing effect. Also Jay-like notes and chattering sounds.
Range: — Rocky Mt. area and e. slope of Cascades and Sierras

from Wash., Ida., and cent. Mont., s. to s. Calif., Ariz., s. N.M., and w. Tex.

CLARK'S NUTCRACKER. *Nucifraga columbiana.* (See Frontis.)
Descr. 12–13. Built like a small Crow, with a *light gray body* and conspicuous *white patches* in black wings and tail. Can be confused with no other bird of the high mts. (Canada Jays and Oregon Jays do not have white patches.)
Voice: — A harsh grating caw, *khaaa* or *khraa.*
Range: — High mts. from Can. s. to s. Calif., Ariz., and N.M.

TITMICE, VERDINS, AND BUSH–TITS: PARIDÆ

SMALL birds, smaller than most Sparrows, with proportionately longer tails and small stubby bills; extremely active, hanging upside down as well as right side up in their busy search for insects.

BLACK-CAPPED CHICKADEE. *Penthestes atricapillus.*
Subsp. (Illus. p. 124.)
Descr. 4¾–5½. A small gray, black and white bird, smaller than a Sparrow. Chickadees are the only small birds with the combination of *black cap, black bib,* and *white cheeks.* This species can be told from the Mountain Chickadee by its *solid* black cap, and from the Chestnut-backed Chickadee by its *gray* back.
Voice: — A clearly enunciated *chick-a-dee-dee-dee* or *dee dee dee.* In spring a clear two-noted or three-noted whistle, *fee-bee*; or *fee-bee-ee,* the first note higher.
Range: — Can. s. to nw. Calif. (Siskiyou Co.), e. Ore., ne. Nev., and n. N.M.
Subsp. (No apparent field differences): (1) Long-tailed Chickadee, *P. a. septentrionalis*; (2) Oregon Chickadee, *P. a. occidentalis.*

MEXICAN CHICKADEE. *Penthestes sclateri eidos.*
Descr. 5. Similar to Black-capped Chickadee, but *black of throat more extensive,* spreading across upper breast; sides *dark gray* (other Chickadees have buffy or rusty sides).
Range: — Chiricahua Mts. of se. Ariz. (7000–10,000 ft.), and mts. of extreme sw. N.M.

MOUNTAIN CHICKADEE. *Penthestes gambeli.* Subsp. (Illus. p. 124.)
Descr. 5–5¾. Similar to Black-capped Chickadee but black of cap broken by *white line over each eye.*

Voice: — Song, three high clear whistled notes *fee-bee-bee*, first note highest, second two on same pitch and more distinctly separated than in call of Black-capped Chickadee. Some races utter three or four thin whistled notes going slightly down the scale in half-notes. 'Chickadee' notes huskier than those of Black-capped Chickadee; *chuck-a-zee-zee-zee*.
Range: — Mts. from Can. to w. Tex., N.M., Ariz., and s. Calif. (except along humid coast belt).
Subsp. (No apparent field differences): (1) Grinnell's Chickadee, *P. g. grinnelli*; (2) Short-tailed Chickadee, *P. g. abbreviatus*; (3) Bailey's Chickadee, *P. g. baileyæ*; (4) Mountain Chickadee, *P. g. gambeli*; (5) Inyo Chickadee, *P. g. inyoënsis*.

COLUMBIAN CHICKADEE. *Penthestes hudsonicus columbianus*.

Descr. 5–5½. The small size and black bib proclaim it a Chickadee; the general color of the upper parts is dull *brown* rather than gray or rufous, and the cheeks are duller than those of other Chickadees, and the cap is duller and *browner*. A race of the Hudsonian, or Brown-capped, Chickadee of eastern Canada.
Voice: — The notes are slower and more drawling than those of the Black-cap; instead of a lively *chick-a-dee-dee-dee*, it utters a wheezy *chick—che—day—day*.
Range: — In U.S. only nw. Mont. (rare).

CHESTNUT-BACKED CHICKADEE. *Penthestes rufescens*.
Subsp. (Illus. p. 124.)
Descr. 4½–5. The dusky cap, black bib, and white cheeks identify it as a Chickadee; the *rufous back* as this species. The sides also have some chestnut.
Voice: — Hoarser and more rasping than Black-cap, *tsick-tsick-a-dee-dee*. This species has no whistled call as do most other Chickadees.
Range: — Coast belt from cent. Calif. (n. San Luis Obispo Co.) to Wash., and sparingly to e. Ore. and w. Mont.
Subsp. (No apparent field differences): (1) Chestnut-backed Chickadee, *P. r. rufescens*; (2) Nicasio Chickadee, *P. r. neglectus*; (3) Barlow's Chickadee, *P. r. barlowi*.

BLACK-CRESTED TITMOUSE. *Bæolophus atricristatus*.
Subsp. (Illus. p. 124.)
Descr. 5–6. A small gray bird with a *slender black crest*; under parts white, sides rusty. The Titmice are the only small *gray* birds with conspicuous crests. This is the only Titmouse found in s. Tex. and along the Rio Grande.
Voice: — Chickadee-like notes, also a rapidly whistled *peter peter peter peter* or *hear hear hear hear*.

Range: — Lowlands of Tex. from n. part (Young and Armstrong Cos.) s. to Rio Grande Valley; e. to Brazos R. and w. to Tom Green, Concho, and Brewster Cos.
Subsp. (No apparent field differences): (1) Black-crested Titmouse, *B. a. atricristatus*; (2) Sennett's Titmouse, *B. a. sennetti*.

PLAIN TITMOUSE. *Bæolophus inornatus.* Subsp. (Illus. p. 124.)
Descr. 5–5½. The birds bearing the name Titmouse are the only small gray-backed birds with conspicuous crests. This is the only species found in most of the W., and the only one without distinctive markings, hence its name. Has a preference for oaks or pinyon-juniper association.
Voice: — *Tchick-a-dee-dee*, similar to notes of Chickadee. In spring an accented whistled chant *weet-y weety weety* or *tee-wit tee-wit tee-wit.*
Range: — S. Ore., s. Ida., and sw. Wyo., s. to s. Calif., s. Ariz., se. N.M., and cent.-w. Tex.
Subsp. (No apparent field differences): (1) Oregon Titmouse, *B. i. sequestratus*; (2) Plain Titmouse, *B. i. inornatus*; (3) San Diego Titmouse, *B. i. transpositus*; (4) Gray Titmouse, *B. i. griseus.*

BRIDLED TITMOUSE. *Bæolophus wollweberi annexus.* (Illus. p. 124.)
Descr. 4½–5. The crest and black-and-white 'bridled' face identify this Southwestern species. (See diagram.)
Voice: — Notes similar to those of other Titmice and Chickadees but more rapid (*tsick-a-dee-dee-dee-dee*, etc.).
Range: — Oak regions of mts. of se. and cent. Ariz. and sw. N.M.

VERDIN. *Auriparus flaviceps.* (Illus. p. 124.)
Descr. 4–4½. A very small gray bird with a *yellowish head*; bend of wing *rufous*. Lives in brushy valleys in the low desert country. Immature birds lack the yellow and rusty, and might possibly be mistaken for Bush-Tits, but the latter species is much longer-tailed and does not inhabit the desert valleys, preferring mountain-slopes covered with trees.
Voice: — An insistent *see-lip* or *see*. Song, a whistled *weet.*
Range: — Deserts of se. Calif., s. Nev., sw. Ut., w. and s. Ariz., s. N.M., and s. Tex.

BUSH-TIT. *Psaltriparus minimus.* Subsp. (Illus. p. 124.)
Descr. 4–4¼. Little plain gray-backed birds that travel about in flocks, constantly conversing in high-pitched notes as they investigate the trees for food. The nondescript drab color,

stubby bill, and rather long tail identify them. It is said that light-eyed birds are females, dark-eyed birds males. Birds of the race known as the Lead-colored Bush-Tit (Rocky Mt. and Great Basin regions) can be told from the Bush-Tits of the Pacific States by their *brown* cheeks. Males of the Lloyd's Bush-Tit (mts. between Pecos and Rio Grande in cent.-w. Tex.) have *blackish* cheek-patches.

Voice: — Insistent light *chips* and lisps constantly uttered as flock moves about.

Range: — W. Wash., w. and s. Ore., s. Ida., Ut., and w. Wyo., s. to Mex. and from Rockies and cent.-w. Tex. (Pecos River) w. to coast.

Subsp. (No apparent field differences except in Nos. 3 and 4; see above): (1) Coast Bush-Tit, *P. m. minimus*; (2) California Bush-Tit, *P. m. californicus*; (3) Lead-colored Bush-Tit, *P. m. plumbeus*; (4) Lloyd's Bush-Tit, *P. m. lloydi*.

NUTHATCHES: SITTIDÆ

SMALL, chubby tree-climbers; Sparrow-sized or smaller, with a long bill and a stubby tail that is never braced against the tree Woodpecker-like as an aid in climbing. No other tree-climbers habitually go down tree-trunks *head first*, as these little birds do.

WHITE-BREASTED NUTHATCH. *Sitta carolinensis.* Subsp. (Illus. p. 125.)
Descr. 5-6. Easily identified by the white breast, the blue-gray back, the black cap, and the habit of frequently traversing tree-trunks *upside down.*
Voice: — Spring song, a series of low, slightly nasal, whistled notes all on the same pitch, *whĭ whĭ whĭ whĭ whĭ whĭ whĭ whĭ* or *who who who*, etc. Note, a nasal *yank* or *hank.*
Range: — Wash. and Mont. s. to Mex.
Subsp. (No apparent field differences): (1) Rocky Mountain Nuthatch, *S. c. nelsoni*; (2) Slender-billed Nuthatch, *S. c. aculeata*; (3) Inyo Nuthatch, *S. c. tenuissima.*

RED-BREASTED NUTHATCH. *Sitta canadensis.* (Illus. p. 125.)
Descr. 4¼-4¾. Smaller than the White-breast; buffier below, with a *broad black line* through the eye.
Voice: — The call corresponding to the *yank yank* of the White-breast is higher and more nasal, *henk, henk,* like a 'baby' Nuthatch or a 'tiny tin horn.'
Range: — Mainly evergreen forests from Can. to s. Calif., s. Ariz., and s. N.M. (chiefly a migrant in southernmost parts of range).

PYGMY NUTHATCH. *Sitta pygmæa.* Subsp. (Illus. p. 125.)
Descr. 4½. A very small Nuthatch, usually smaller than either the Red-breasted or the White-breasted with a *gray-brown cap coming down to the eye.* A whitish spot is sometimes visible on the nape of the neck. Inhabits forests of yellow pines and other similar pines. Very similar to Brown-headed Nuthatch of se. U.S.
Voice: — A metallic piping *kit — kit — kit* and a high *ki — dee,* constantly repeated, sometimes becoming an excited twitter or chatter.
Range: — From Wash. and Mont. s. to Mex. and from Rockies w. to Cascades (e. slopes) and Sierras. Also mts. of s. Calif. and coast of middle Calif. (San Luis Obispo Co. to Mendocino Co.).
Subsp. (No apparent field differences): (1) Pygmy Nuthatch, *S. p. pygmæa*; (2) Black-eared Nuthatch, *S. p. melanotis*; (3) White-naped Nuthatch, *S. p. leuconucha.*

CREEPERS: CERTHIIDÆ

CREEPER. *Certhia familiaris.* Subsp. (Illus. p. 125.)
Descr. 5–5¾. Much smaller than a Sparrow; a slim little brown bird with a rather long, stiff tail used as a prop when climbing; sometimes difficult to detect, so well does the bird blend with the bark of the trees. The name Creeper fits.
Voice: — Note, a long thin *seeee,* similar to a note of Golden-crowned Kinglet. Song, several weak, clear notes, *see-ti-wee-tu-wee,* or *see-see-see-ti-ti-see,* the *see* notes resembling the thin call-note.
Range: — Breeds in heavily forested areas from Can. s. to Monterey, Calif. (along coast) and to Mex. (in mt. areas). Spreads to adjacent lowlands in winter.
Subsp. (No apparent field differences): (1) Rocky Mountain Creeper, *C. f. montana*; (2) Mexican Creeper, *C. f. albescens*; (3) Sierra Creeper, *C. f. zelotes*; (4) California Creeper, *C. f. occidentalis.*

WREN–TITS: CHAMÆIDÆ

WREN-TIT. *Chamæa fasciata.* Subsp. (Illus. p. 132.)
Descr. 6½. Far more often heard than seen. A small Sparrow-sized brown bird with a long tail. Back dusky; under parts *cinnamon-brown* with faint dusky streaks; eye *white.* The long, rounded, slightly cocked tail and dull-cinnamon under parts are good marks if the bird can be seen as it slips through the chaparral or shrubbery. The Bush-Tit, which is smaller and

grayer, usually travels about in flocks and does not hide itself so persistently.

Voice: — Song, heard every month in the year, a staccato series of short ringing notes all on the same pitch, usually starting deliberately and running into a rapid trill; sometimes the song is double-noted, and sometimes it drops slightly in pitch.

Range: — Coast belt and interior valleys of Calif. and coast belt of Ore.

Subsp. (No apparent field differences): (1) Coast Wren-Tit, *C. f. phæa*; (2) Ruddy Wren-Tit, *C. f. rufula*; (3) Gambel's Wren-Tit, *C. f. fasciata*; (4) Pallid Wren-Tit, *C. f. henshawi*.

DIPPERS: CINCLIDÆ

DIPPER *or* **WATER OUZEL.** *Cinclus mexicanus unicolor.* (Illus. p. 132.)

Descr. 7–8½. An inhabitant of rushing mountain streams; a dark *slate-colored* bird, shaped like a large chunky Wren (size of a large Thrush) with a short tail. Legs pale; eyelids *white*. Its bobbing motions, slaty coloration, and chunky shape are distinctive.

Voice: — Note, a sharp *zeet* given singly, or rapidly repeated. Song clear and ringing, Mockingbird-like in form (with much triplication and quadruplication of notes), but higher and more Wren-like. Sings throughout year.

Range: — Mt. streams of w. U.S. from Can. s. to s. Calif., n. Ariz., and N.M.

WATER OUZEL

GRAY·BROWN ABOVE

NO FACIAL
STRIPING

HOUSE WREN

DARK
BREAST

HEAVILY·
BARRED
FLANKS

WINTER WREN

WHITE
CORNERS

BEWICK'S WREN

STRIPED
BACK

MARSH WREN

BUFFY
TIPS

FINELY·STREAKED
BREAST

ROCK WREN

WHITE
THROAT

DARK
BELLY

CAÑON WREN

HEAVILY·SPOTTED
BREAST

CACTUS WREN

EYE
WHITE

UNDERPARTS
CINNAMON·BROWN

WREN·TIT

WRENS AND WREN·TIT

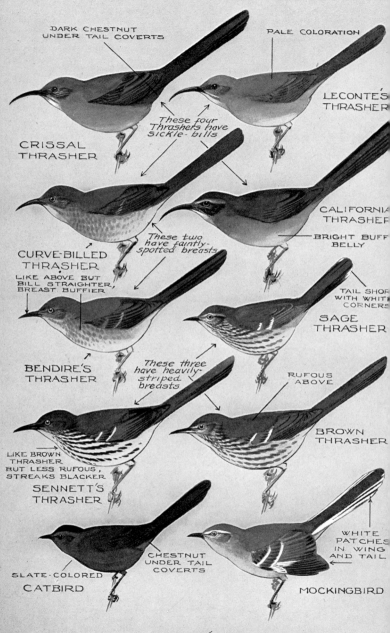

DARK CHESTNUT
UNDER TAIL COVERTS

PALE COLORATION

LECONTE'S
THRASHER

*These four
Thrashers have
sickle-bills*

CRISSAL
THRASHER

CALIFORNIA
THRASHER

BRIGHT BUFF
BELLY

*These two
have faintly-
spotted breasts*

CURVE-BILLED
THRASHER

LIKE ABOVE BUT
BILL STRAIGHTER,
BREAST BUFFIER

TAIL SHOR
WITH WHIT
CORNERS

SAGE
THRASHER

*These three
have heavily-
striped
breasts*

BENDIRE'S
THRASHER

RUFOUS
ABOVE

LIKE BROWN
THRASHER
BUT LESS RUFOUS,
STREAKS BLACKER

BROWN
THRASHER

SENNETT'S
THRASHER

WHITE
PATCHES
IN WING
AND TAIL

SLATE-COLORED
CATBIRD

CHESTNUT
UNDER TAIL
COVERTS

MOCKINGBIRD

THRASHERS ETC. *(Mimic Thrushes)*

WRENS: TROGLODYTIDÆ

SMALL, energetic brown-backed birds, most species smaller than Sparrows, with slender bills; tails often cocked over the back.

(WESTERN) HOUSE WREN. *Troglodytes aëdon parkmani.* (Illus. p. 132.)
Descr. 4½–5¼. A Wren of the forests, gardens, etc.; recognized as a Wren by the small size, brown coloration, energetic actions, and habit of cocking its tail over its back; distinguished from the others by its grayer-brown color, and the lack of any evident facial stripings or white in the tail.
Voice: — A stuttering, gurgling song, rising in a musical burst, then falling at the end.
Range: — Breeds in w. U.S. from Can. s. to Mex. border and cent.-w. Tex.; winters from cent. Calif. and Tex. s. into Mex.

(WESTERN) WINTER WREN. *Nannus hiemalis pacificus.* (Illus. p. 132.)
Descr. 4. A very small dark Wren, smaller than a House Wren; has a much stubbier tail than that species, a light line over the eye, and a *brownish*, heavily barred belly; often bobs its head like Rock Wren; frequents mossy tangles, ravines, brush-piles, etc.
Voice: — Song a high rapid tinkling warble, long sustained and often ending on a high light trill. Note, a hard two-syllabled *kip-kip.*
Range: — Breeds in evergreen forests from Can. s. to cent. Calif. (Monterey Co. and Yosemite) and n. Colo. Winters from Can. s. to s. Calif. (Los Angeles Co.) and N.M. (rarely).

BEWICK'S WREN. *Thryomanes bewicki.* Subsp. (Illus. p. 132.)
Descr. 5–5½. The *white line* over the eye and the *whitish tips* of the outer tail-feathers distinguish this species from the House Wren and all other similar species except the Rock Wren. The Bewick's Wren is much darker and browner above than the Rock Wren, and has a whiter throat and breast. (See Rock Wren.)
Voice: — Song variable. Most races have a song that decidedly resembles that of the Song Sparrow, starting on two or three high notes, dropping lower, and then ending on a thin trill. Another rendering is *swee, swee, cheeeeeeee* (first two notes high, last trilled). The songs of the different subspecies and different individuals vary so much that a blanket description is not adequate.

Range: — W. Wash. and Ore. (w. of Cascades), Calif., w. and s. Nev., s. Ut., sw. Wyo., w. Colo., Ariz., N.M., and Tex.
Subsp. (No apparent field differences): (1) Baird's Wren, *T. b. eremophilus*; (2) Seattle Wren, *T. b. calophonus*; (3) Nicasio Wren, *T. b. marinensis*; (4) Vigors's Wren, *T. b. spilurus*; (5) San Joaquin Wren, *T. b. drymœcus*; (6) San Diego Wren, *T. b. correctus*; (7) Santa Cruz Wren, *T. b. nesophilus*; (8) Catalina Wren, *T. b. catalinæ*; (9) San Clemente Wren, *T. b. leucophrys*.

CACTUS WREN.   *Heleodytes brunneicapillus couesi.*   (Illus. p. 132.)
Descr. 7–8½. A very large Wren of the cactus country. Distinguished from the other Wrens by its much larger size and *heavily spotted* throat and breast. It also shows a white stripe over the eye and white spots in the outer tail-feathers. The only other arid-country bird with which it can be confused is the Sage Thrasher (which also has a spotted breast, white eye-line, and white spots in the tail), but the latter species is more Thrasher-like or Robin-like in appearance, grayer, *without* white stripings on the back.
Voice: — A rapid monotonous *cheh-cheh-cheh-cheh*, etc., or *chug-chug-chug-chug-chug-chug-chug*, on same pitch and gaining rapidity; unbirdlike.
Range: — Desert regions of s. Calif., s. Nev., s. Ut., Ariz., N.M., and s. Tex.

LONG-BILLED MARSH WREN.   *Telmatodytes palustris.*
Subsp. (Illus. p. 132.)
Descr. 4½–5½. The Wren of the Marshes; brown, with a conspicuous white line over the eye; known from the other small Wrens with white eye-stripes by the *black-and-white stripes on the back*.
Voice: — Song, a reedy, gurgling series of notes.
Range: — Breeds or occurs in marshes from Can. s. to N.M. and ne. Calif. and from Great Plains to coast.
Subsp. (No apparent field differences): (1) Western Marsh Wren, *T. p. plesius*; (2) Tule Wren, *T. p. paludicola*; (3) Suisun Marsh Wren, *T. p. œstuarinus*; (4) Prairie Marsh Wren, *T. p. dissaëptus*.

CAÑON WREN.   *Catherpes mexicanus.*   Subsp.   (Illus. p. 132.)
Descr. 5½–5¾. A reddish-brown Wren, with a *dark reddish-brown belly*, contrasted with a *white breast and throat*. The conspicuous white throat is the best field-mark. The deep chestnut belly also distinguishes this species at once from the Rock Wren. Inhabits canyons, rocky slopes, and sometimes buildings.
Voice: — A gushing cadence of clear curved notes tripping down

the scale; sometimes picking up at the end; *te-you, te-you te-you, tew tew tew tew*, etc., or *tee tee tee tee tew tew tew*, etc.

Range: — Resident in w. U.S. from se. Wash., Ida., and Wyo. s. to s. Calif., Mex., and w. Tex.

Subsp. (No apparent field differences): (1) White-throated Cañon Wren, *C. m. albifrons*; (2) Cañon Wren, *C. m. conspersus*.

ROCK WREN. *Salpinctes obsoletus obsoletus.* (Illus. p. 132.)
Descr. 5¼–6¼. A rather *gray* Wren with a finely streaked breast (streaks visible at close range). Shows conspicuous *whitish* or *buffy* patches at the end of the tail. The finely streaked breast and pale back distinguish this species from the Bewick's Wren; the pale belly and gray color from the Cañon Wren. Inhabits rocky slopes and canyons.
Voice: — Song, a harsh mechanical chant, *tew, tew, tew, tew*, or *chr-wee, chr-wee, chr-wee*, or *che-poo che-poo che-poo*; commonest call a loud dry trill all on one pitch; also a clear *ti-keer*.
Range: — Breeds in w. U.S. from Can. s. to Mex. except in nw. coast belt; winters in Calif., Ariz., and N.M.

MOCKINGBIRDS AND THRASHERS: MIMIDÆ

THIS family of birds, sometimes called 'Mimic Thrushes' comprises a group of Robin-sized birds with strong legs and slender, more or less decurved bills. The tail is usually fairly long and expressive.

(WESTERN) MOCKINGBIRD. *Mimus polyglottos leucopterus.* (Illus. p. 133.)
Descr. 10–11. As large as a Robin, but more slender and longer-tailed; gray above and white below, with *large white patches* on the wings and tail, conspicuous in flight. Mockingbirds resemble Shrikes somewhat, but lack the black facial masks and have more white in the wings and tail. (See Townsend's Solitaire.)
Voice: — Song consists of a great variety of phrases, some clear and musical, others harsh. Each phrase is usually repeated *several* times. Note, a loud *tchack*.
Range: — Breeds from cent. Calif., se. Ore. (rare), and s. Wyo. s. to Mex.; winters from cent. Calif., s. Ariz., and s. N.M. s.

CATBIRD. *Dumetella carolinensis.* (Illus. p. 133.)
Descr. 8½–9¼. Smaller and slimmer than a Robin; *slaty gray* above and below, with a black cap and chestnut-red under tail-

coverts (these are seldom noticed in the field). Aside from the very dissimilar Dipper, the only other uniformly grayish song-birds, the female Cowbird and female Brewer's Blackbird, are shorter-tailed, not so slaty, and lack the distinctive black cap and rusty under tail-coverts.

Voice: — Catlike mewing note, distinctive. Song, a series of notes and short phrases, some musical, others harsh. Notes not repeated as in songs of Mockingbird and some Thrashers.

Range: — Breeds chiefly in e. U.S. w. through Rocky Mt. section to e. Wash., ne. Ore., n. Ut., Colo., n. N.M., and e.-cent. Ariz. (White Mts.).

BROWN THRASHER. *Toxostoma rufum.* (Illus. p. 133.)
Descr. 10½–12. Slightly larger and slimmer than a Robin, bright *rufous-red* above, *heavily striped* below. Differs from the Thrushes in possessing a much longer tail and a curved bill, and in being *streaked* rather than spotted below. The eye is yellow. No other Thrasher has a bright *rufous-red* back.

Voice: — Song, a series of deliberate notes and short phrases, resembling the Catbird's song, but each phrase quickly *re-peated*. Note, a harsh *chack*.

Range: — Breeds in e. U.S. w. to base of Rocky Mts. in Mont., Wyo., and Colo.

SENNETT'S THRASHER. *Toxostoma longirostre sennetti.* (Illus. p. 133.)
Descr. 10½–12. Similar to Brown Thrasher but back less rufous and breast-streaks black rather than brown. Easily told from the other resident Thrasher in the region it occupies, the Curve-billed (Brownsville) Thrasher, by its darker color and *bold black breast-stripes*.

Voice: — Song, a series of notes and phrases similar to other Thrashers but phrases not repeated as much. Call-note, *too-ree*.

Range: — S. Tex. (Lower Rio Grande Valley and lower Gulf Coast).

BENDIRE'S THRASHER. *Toxostoma bendirei.* (Illus. p. 133.)
Descr. 9½–10½. Of the several similar species of pale clay-colored Thrashers that inhabit the sw. deserts, this is one of the easiest to identify, because it has a *shorter, straighter, more Robin-like bill* than the others (see plate). The eye is yellow and the breast faintly spotted.

Voice: — Song, a *continuous* musical warble, not broken into phrases as in other Thrashers. Note, *tirup*.

Range: — Deserts of sw. U.S. (se. Calif., Ariz., and rarely sw. N.M.).

CURVE-BILLED THRASHER. *Toxostoma curvirostre.* Subsp. (Illus. p. 133.)
Descr. $10\frac{1}{2}$–$11\frac{1}{2}$. In the sw. deserts there are several very similar Thrashers, slim Robin-sized birds with decurved bills, long tails, dull gray-brown backs, and cinnamon-tinged bellies. This species can be told from the other Thrashers that have deeply curved bills, by the *faintly spotted breast.* The Bendire's Thrasher has similar breast spotting but a short *straight* bill. Some Curve-billed Thrashers have narrow white wing-bars and white spots at the tip of the tail, but in others these are almost obsolete. The eye is pale orange.
Voice: — Note, a sharp liquid *whit-wheet!* like a human whistle of attention. Song, a series of notes and phrases, Mockingbird-like in quality but without so much repetition.
Range: — S. Ariz., N.M., w. Okla., and w. and s. Tex.
Subsp. (No apparent field differences): (1) Palmer's Thrasher, *T. c. palmeri*; (2) Curve-billed Thrasher, *T. c. curvirostre*; (3) Brownsville Thrasher, *T. c. oberholseri*.

CALIFORNIA THRASHER. *Toxostoma redivivum.* Subsp. (Illus. p. 133.)
Descr. $11\frac{1}{2}$–13. A large dull gray-brown bird, with pale-cinnamon belly and under tail-coverts; tail long, bill *sickle-shaped.* This is the only Thrasher of this type in Calif. w. of the se. desert divides except on the w. side of the San Joaquin Valley, where the pale Leconte's Thrasher is found. The eye is dark.
Voice: — Song, a long-sustained Mockingbird-like series of notes and phrases, some musical, some harsh; the phrases are often *repeated*, but not several times as in the Mockingbird's song. The song is also lower-pitched and more leisurely than the Mocker's. Note, a sharp *wheek.*
Range: — Calif., w. of deserts and Sierras, n. along coast through San Francisco Bay region and in interior to Shasta Co. in n. part of state.
Subsp. (No apparent field differences): (1) California Thrasher, *T. r. redivivum*; (2) Sonoma Thrasher, *T. r. sonomæ.*

LECONTE'S THRASHER. *Toxostoma lecontei lecontei.* (Illus. p. 133.)
Descr. $10\frac{1}{2}$–11. A very *pale* Thrasher of the desert, with a dark tail. Separated from the Crissal Thrasher by its much paler coloration, and from the Curve-billed Thrasher by its unspotted breast. Like the immature Crissal Thrasher, young birds have whitish eyes. Adults have dark eyes.
Voice: — Snatches of song infrequent, heard mostly in early morning; similar to songs of other Thrashers but more disjointed and less repetitious.
Range: — Deserts of s. and w. Ariz., extreme sw. Ut., extreme

s. Nev., and se. Calif.; also in s. San Joaquin Valley of Calif. (Kern Co. n. to s. Fresno Co.).

CRISSAL THRASHER. *Toxostoma dorsale dorsale.* (Illus. p. 133.)
Descr. 11½–12½. Distinguished from Curve-billed Thrasher by its unspotted breast and rustier under tail-coverts, from Leconte's Thrasher by its much darker color and darker and rustier under tail-coverts. The rusty under tail-patch, deeper in color than in other Thrashers, is especially characteristic. Immature birds have whitish eyes, adults dark.
Voice: — Song, similar to songs of other Thrashers but not so loud and vigorous.
Range: — Deserts of sw. U.S. (s. Nev., s. Ut., se. Calif., Ariz., s. N.M., and w. Tex.)

SAGE THRASHER. *Oreoscoptes montanus.* (Illus. p. 133.)
Descr. 8–9. Nearly size of Robin, and similar in shape. A gray-backed bird with a straight slender bill, heavily streaked breast, white spots at the tip of the tail, and pale yellow eye. The small size, shorter tail, and striped breast distinguish it from the other Western Thrashers. When perched, it frequently jerks its tail. (See Cactus Wren.)
Voice: — Song, a series of clear ecstatic warbled phrases, sometimes repeated in true Thrasher fashion, but more often continuous, suggestive of Black-headed Grosbeak; more rapid and joyous than songs of most Thrashers.
Range: — Breeds in arid sagebrush country from e. Wash. and Mont. s. to s.-cent. Calif. (chiefly e. of Sierras) and n. N.M., winters in s. Calif., s. Ariz., and s. N.M.

THRUSHES, BLUEBIRDS, AND SOLITAIRES: TURDIDÆ

THREE Western species that bear the name 'Thrush' are brown-backed birds with *spotted* breasts. Robins, Bluebirds, Solitaires, and the Varied Thrush, although entirely unlike the other Thrushes in color, betray definite indications of their relationship to this group through their speckle-breasted young. The family as a whole have rather long legs for songbirds, and moderately slender bills.

ROBIN. *Turdus migratorius.* Subsp.
Descr. 8½–10½. One of the most familiar of all birds; easily recognized by its gray back and *brick-red* breast. In the male, the head and tail are blackish; in the female, paler. The bill is

yellow. Young Robins have speckled breasts, but the gray back and rusty under parts identify them.
Voice: — Song, a clear, whistled caroling, often long continued; made up of short phrases of two or three notes each.
Range: — Breeds in w. U.S. in Canadian and transition zones from Can. s. to Mex. and from Pacific Coast e. to Great Plains. Winters from Wash. and Wyo. s.
Subsp. (No apparent field differences): (1) Northwestern Robin, *T. m. caurinus*; (2) Western Robin, *T. m. propinquus*.

TAMAULIPAS THRUSH. *Turdus grayi tamaulipensis.*
Descr. A Mexican species accidental near Brownsville, Tex. Very much like a Robin in appearance, voice, and actions, but different in color. 'Grayish-brown above with a slight olive wash; below, pale buffy or clay-color. The chin and throat are striped with thin lines of darker color' (Irby Davis).

VARIED THRUSH. *Ixoreus nævius.* Subsp. (See Frontis.)
Descr. 9–10. *Male:* — Similar to Robin but with an *orange eye-stripe, orange wing-bars*, and a *black band* across the rusty breast. *Female:* — Breast-band gray. *Immature:* — Breast-band imperfect or speckled with orange; under parts speckled with dusky. The rusty wing-bars and eye-stripe and shorter tail distinguish them from young Robins.
Voice: — A long, eerie, quavering whistled note, followed, after a pause, by one on a lower or higher pitch.
Range: — Breeds in evergreen forests of nw. Calif. (Humboldt Co.), Ore. (w. and ne. parts), Wash. (w. and se. parts), n. Idaho, and nw. Mont. Winters s. along coast to Monterey, Calif., and in interior Calif.
Subsp. (No apparent field differences): (1) Pacific Varied Thrush, *I. n. nævius*; (2) Northern Varied Thrush, *I. n. meruloides*.

HERMIT THRUSH. *Hylocichla guttata.* Subsp. (See Frontis.)
Descr. 6½–7½. Larger than a Sparrow, smaller than a Robin, a brown-backed bird with a slender bill and spotted breast. The *reddish tail*, conspicuous as the bird flies away, distinguishes the Hermit Thrush from the Russet-backed Thrush and the Willow Thrush. It is the only one of the three that winters in the W. States. At rest the Hermit Thrush has a characteristic trick of *raising* the tail slowly at frequent intervals.
Voice: — Song, clear and flute-like. Four or five phrases in different pitches, each introduced by a long, pure opening note. Each phrase is given in turn after a deliberate pause. Although the phrases themselves are in different pitches, the notes of each phrase roll around on approximately the same pitch. The pure introductory note is diagnostic.

Range: — Breeds from Can. s. along coast to Monterey, Calif., and in mts. throughout w. U.S. to s. Calif., Ariz., and N.M. Migrates throughout w. U.S. and winters from Ore., Ariz., s. N.M., and w. Tex. s.

Subsp. (No apparent field differences): (1) Alaska Hermit Thrush, *H. g. guttata*; (2) Dwarf Hermit Thrush, *H. g. nanus*; (3) Monterey Hermit Thrush, *H. g. slevini*; (4) Sierra Hermit Thrush, *H. g. sequoiensis*; (5) Mono Hermit Thrush, *H. g. polionota*; (6) Audubon's Hermit Thrush, *H. g. auduboni*.

RUSSET-BACKED THRUSH. *Hylocichla ustulata.* Subsp.
(See Frontis.)

Descr. 6½–7½. When we come upon a Thrush that lacks any warmth of color in its plumage and is uniformly gray-brown or olive-brown above, then we can be sure we have found this species. The bird also has a conspicuous *buffy eye-ring.* It has a more heavily spotted breast than the Willow Thrush, and lacks the rusty tail of the Hermit.

Voice: — Song, melodious, breezy flute-like phrases; distinguished from other Thrushes by tendency of each phrase to climb *upwards.*

Range: — Breeds in mts. of w. U.S. from Can. s. to Colo., Ut., Nev., and S. Calif.; also in moist woodlands in lowlands e. of Cascades and Sierras in the Pacific States.

Subsp. (No apparent field differences): (1) Russet-backed Thrush, *H. u. ustulata*; (2) Olive-backed Thrush, *H. u. swainsoni.*

WILLOW THRUSH. *Hylocichla fuscescens salicicola.* (See Frontis.)

Descr. 7–7½. A Thrush uniformly cinnamon-brown or tawny-brown above is quite certainly a Willow Thrush. (Olive-back is dull gray-brown above; Hermit reddish on the tail only.) The breast of this species is the least spotted of the three similar Thrushes; the spots are *indistinct*, not blackish. At a distance the bird sometimes looks quite clear-breasted. Inhabits woodlands along stream-bottoms. It is a race of the Eastern Veery.

Voice: — A liquid, breezy whistle, wheeling *downward*: *vee-ur, vee-ur, veer, veer*. Note, *chew* or *view.*

Range: — Breeds e. of Cascades from e. Wash. and Mont. s. to ne. Ore., Nev., Ut., and Colo. Migrates through Ariz. and N.M., but rarely observed there.

EASTERN BLUEBIRD. *Sialia sialis.* Subsp.
Descr. 6½–7½. Similar to Western Bluebird, but with throat *rusty*, not blue, and back *solid blue*, without a rusty patch (some Western Bluebirds lack this patch, however).

Voice: — Note, a simple *chur-wee* or *wee-chur-wee*. Song, a short soft warble.

Range: — Breeds in e. U.S. w. sparingly to e. Mont., e. Wyo., and e. Colo. Occasional in high mts. of se. Ariz. (Santa Ritas and Huachucas). In these mts. the following species is the common breeding Bluebird.

Subsp. (No apparent field differences): (1) Eastern Bluebird, *S. s. sialis*; (2) Azure Bluebird, *S. s. fulva*.

WESTERN, *or* MEXICAN, BLUEBIRD. *Sialia mexicana.*

Subsp. (See Frontis)

Descr. 6½–7. A little larger than a Sparrow; head, wings, and tail *blue*; breast and back *rusty-red*. (In some individuals the back is partially or wholly blue.) Appears round-shouldered when perched. Female paler and duller than male. Except for the Eastern Bluebird the only other blue bird with a red breast is the male Lazuli Bunting, which can be recognized by its conspicuous wing-bars. The Mountain Bluebird has a *blue* breast.

Voice: — A short *pew* or *mew*. Also a hard chattering note.

Range: — Breeds in foothills and pines throughout Pacific States and in n. Idaho and w. Mont. Also in Rocky Mt. section from Ut. and Colo. s. to Mex. Occasional in Wyo. Winters in Pacific States and in s. Ut., Ariz., N.M., and w. Tex.

Subsp. (No apparent field differences): (1) Western Bluebird, *S. m. occidentalis*; (2) Chestnut-backed Bluebird, *S. m. bairdi*.

MOUNTAIN BLUEBIRD. *Sialia currucoides.* (See Frontis.)

Descr. 6½–7¾. *Male:* — *Azure blue above and below*, belly white. Readily told from the Western Bluebird by its *blue breast*. The only other blue songbird with a blue breast found in the West is the male Blue Grosbeak, which has a short thick bill and brown wing-bars. *Female:* — Dull brownish with bluish rump, tail, and wings. Distinguished from female Western Bluebird by straighter posture, lack of rusty wash on breast, and paler, greener blue color.

Voice: — A low *chur* or *phew*. Song, a beautiful clear short warble, higher-pitched than that of Eastern Bluebird and hardly suggesting it (Francis H. Allen). Suggests caroling of Robin (W. Weydemeyer).

Range: — Breeds chiefly in mt. sections from e. slope of Cascades and Sierras to Great Plains and from Can. s. to s. Calif., cent. Ariz., and N.M. Winters from Ore., Ariz., and Colo. s. into Mex.

TOWNSEND'S SOLITAIRE. *Myadestes townsendi.* (See Frontis.)

Descr. 8–9½. A gray-bodied bird, slimmer than a Robin, with a white *eye-ring*, *white sides* on the tail, and a *buffy patch* in the center of the wing. The beginner is likely to be confused by the bird at first, imagining it to be some sort of a Thrasher, a Flycatcher, or almost anything but a Solitaire. The white in the tail and the light wing-patches give the bird a not too remote resemblance to a Mockingbird in flight. The eye-ring and darker breast at once distinguish it from that species.

Voice: — Song, long and warbled, suggesting Black-headed Grosbeak's, but more rapid.

Range: — Breeds in high mts. from Can. s. through Sierras to San Bernardino Mts. in s. Calif. and through Rockies and adjacent high ranges to cent. Ariz. and N.M. Winters at lower levels from Wash. and Mont. s.

GNATCATCHERS AND KINGLETS: SYLVIIDÆ

WESTERN GNATCATCHER. *Polioptila cœrulea amœnissima.* (Illus. p. 125.)
Descr. 4½–5. Like a miniature Mockingbird in color and shape. Western Gnatcatchers are very tiny, slender mites, smaller even than Chickadees, blue-gray above and whitish below, with a narrow white eye-ring, and a *long, contrastingly colored tail* (black in the center, white on the sides, often cocked like a Wren's tail). A race of the Blue-gray Gnatcatcher of the East. (See Plumbeous Gnatcatcher.)
Voice: — Note, a thin complaining *peeee*; song, a thin squeaky, wheezy series of notes.
Range: — Breeds from Colo., s. Ut., s. Nev., and n. Calif. (Shasta Co.) s. into Mex. Winters in s. Calif. and s. Ariz.

PLUMBEOUS GNATCATCHER. *Polioptila melanura.* Subsp. (Illus. p. 125.)
Descr. 4½. Similar to Western Gnatcatcher but with *black cap* and much less white in tail.
Voice: — Note, a thin *chee* repeated two or three times (Western Gnatcatcher gives single note).
Subsp. PLUMBEOUS GNATCATCHER. *P. m. melanura.*
    Deserts of se. Calif., s. Nev., Ariz., N.M., and Rio Grande Valley of w. Tex.
    BLACK-TAILED GNATCATCHER. *P. m. californica.*
    Under parts *dull gray* instead of whitish as in Plumbeous Gnatcatcher; almost no white in corners of tail. San Diegan district of sw. Calif., n. to Ventura.

(WESTERN) GOLDEN-CROWNED KINGLET. *Regulus satrapa olivaceus.* (Illus. p. 125.)

Descr. 3½–4. Kinglets are tiny mites of birds, smaller than Warblers and hardly more than half the size of Sparrows. Their diminutive proportions and somber olive-gray backs make them difficult to discern among the thick branches of the evergreens through which they forage. The present species, except for summer juveniles, always shows a conspicuous bright crown, yellow in the female, orange in the male. Another point of distinction (if it be needed) is that the Golden-crown has a *white stripe* over the eye, the Ruby-crown a white eye-ring.

Voice: — Call-note, a high wiry *see-see-see* (similar to Creeper's single *seee*). Song, a series of thin notes (like the ordinary call-notes) rising up the scale, then dropping into a chatter.

Range: — Breeds in high mts. from Can. s. to n. N.M., Ariz., and s. Calif. and in evergreen forests along coast s. to cent. Calif. (Marin Co.). Migrates or winters in adjacent country from Can. s. to s. Calif. and Mex.

RUBY-CROWNED KINGLET. *Corthylio calendula.* Subsp. (Illus. p. 125.)

Descr. 3¾–4½. Very tiny and short-tailed; olive-gray above with two pale wing-bars; male with a scarlet crown-patch (usually concealed). The best recognition mark is the conspicuous *white eye-ring* which gives the bird a big-eyed appearance. Any King-let not showing a conspicuous crown-patch is of this species. The stubby tail distinguishes it at once from any of the War-blers. It can very easily be confused with the Hutton's Vireo (see under that species). The race known as the Sitka Kinglet, which winters south along the Pacific Coast to Monterey, Cali-fornia, is said to be distinguishable in the field from the Western Ruby-crowned Kinglet by its smaller size and darker coloration (Grinnell).

Voice: — Note, a husky two-syllabled *ji-dit*. Song, a remark-able performance for so small a bird, starting with three or four high *tees*, then several low *tews* and ending in a repetitious chant, thus: *tee tee tee tew tew tew tew, tee-diddle, tee-diddle, tee-diddle.* Variable.

Range: — Breeds in evergreen forests from Can. s. in high mts. to s. Calif., cent. Ariz., and cent. N.M. Migrates through low-lands, and winters along Pacific Coast and from interior Calif., Ariz., and N.M. s. into Mex.

Subsp. (No apparent field differences except possibly in No. 3 — see above): (1) Eastern Ruby-crowned Kinglet, *C. c. calen-dula*; (2) Western Ruby-crowned Kinglet, *C. c. cineraceus*; (3) Sitka Kinglet, *C. c. grinnelli.*

A. AMERICAN PIPIT   B. SPRAGUE'S PIPIT

PIPITS: MOTACILLIDÆ

AMERICAN PIPIT. *Anthus spinoletta.* (Illus. p. 144.)
Descr. 6–7. Near the size of a Sparrow, but with a *slender* bill;
under parts *buffy* with streakings; *outer tail-feathers white*; frequents open country, plowed fields, shore flats, etc. It may be
known from the Vesper Sparrow, which also shows white outer
tail-feathers, by the buffy under parts and the habits of *constantly bobbing its tail*, of *walking* instead of hopping, and of
dipping up and down when in flight.
Voice: — Note, a thin *jee jeet*, or, by a stretch of the imagination, *pĭ-pit*, thinner than note of Horned Lark.
Range: — Breeds near timber line from Can. in high mts. s. to
Ore. and n. N.M. Migrates through open country of w. U.S.,
and winters in Calif., Ariz., and N.M. and along coast n. to
Wash. The racial identity of this species in the W. is at present
unsettled, as two new races have been described, whereas
formerly they were regarded to be the same as the Eastern bird.

SPRAGUE'S PIPIT. *Anthus spraguei.* (Illus. p. 144.)
Descr. A buffy bird with a striped back, not solid dark upper
parts like American Pipit. The breast-streakings are fine and
sparse, not so heavy as in the American Pipit. The upper parts,
streaked conspicuously with buff and black, make the best
mark. It is the breeding Pipit of the plains region just e. of the
mt.-ranges in Mont. In Mont., the other Pipit breeds in the
barren parts of high mts. in the w. part of the state. The American Pipit is highly social, whereas this species often tends to
occur singly or in pairs. The thin Pipit bill will help distinguish
either species from obscure plumages of the Longspurs.
Range: — Breeds in prairies of Mont. e. of mts. Migrates
through e. Wyo. to Tex.

A. BOHEMIAN WAXWING   B. CEDAR WAXWING

WAXWINGS: BOMBYCILLIDÆ

BOHEMIAN WAXWING. *Bombycilla garrula pallidiceps.*
(Illus. p. 145.)
Descr. 7½–8½. Resembles the Cedar Waxwing closely, but is
larger, has some *white in the wing*, is grayer, and possesses *chestnut-red* under tail-coverts instead of white.
Voice: — A low trill, longer and rougher than lisp of Cedar Waxwing.
Range: — Breeds in w. Can. Winters irregularly s. to n. Calif.
and Colo.

CEDAR WAXWING. *Bombycilla cedrorum.* (Illus. p. 145.)
Descr. 6½–8. Between the size of a Sparrow and a Robin; a
sleek, *crested*, brown bird with a broad *yellow* band at the tip of
the tail. It is the only sleek *brown* bird with a long crest.
Voice: — A high thin lisp or *zee.*
Range: — Breeds from Can. s. to n. Calif. and Colo. Winters
from Wash. and Colo. s. into Mex.

SILKY FLYCATCHERS:
PTILOGONATIDÆ

PHAINOPEPLA. *Phainopepla nitens.* Subsp. (Illus. p. 146.)
Descr. 7–7¾. Size of an Oriole. *Male:* — A slim *glossy black* bird

PHAINOPEPLA, *male*

with a *slender crest* and conspicuous *white patches* in the wing. No other bird resembles it. *Female:* — *Dark gray,* with slender crest, but no white wing-patches. The rather uniform *gray* coloration and lack of a yellow tail-band distinguish the female from the Cedar Waxwing.

Voice: — Note, a soft, low *wurp.* Song, a weak, casual warble, wheezy and disconnected.

Range: — Breeds chiefly in arid lowlands of Calif., s. Nev., s. Ut., Ariz., and sw. N.M. and w. Tex. (Brewster Co.). Winters in s. Calif., s. Ariz., and w. Tex.

Subsp. (No apparent field differences): (1) Northern Phainopepla, *P. n. lepida*; (2) Mexican Phainopepla, *P. n. nitens*.

SHRIKES: LANIIDÆ

NORTHWESTERN SHRIKE. *Lanius borealis invictus.*
Descr. 9–10½. A race of the Northern Shrike. In the colder parts of the W. States during the winter months a Robin-sized bird, sitting quite still, *alone* in the *tip-top* of some tree, is likely to be a Northwestern Shrike. If it is this species, closer inspection shows it to be light gray above and white below, with a *black mask* through the eyes. On taking flight it drops low, and, progressing with a peculiar wing-motion on a bee-line course, rises suddenly to its tree-top perch. This species can be told

from the very similar Loggerhead Shrike by its slightly larger size and *finely barred* breast. Another very good point, at close range, is the bill: those of the other two are solid black; the basal portion of the lower mandible of the present species is *pale-colored*. The other two have a narrow strip of black above the bill. Generally speaking, however, winter Shrikes in the colder parts of the w. U.S. are Northwestern Shrikes. Young birds are browner but still recognizable as this species by the fine vermiculations on the breast, which are even more pronounced than in the adult.

Voice: — Song, a long-continued Thrasher-like succession of phrases, harsher on the whole than the Thrasher's song.

Range: — Breeds in w. Can.; winters irregularly s. to n. Calif., N.M., and n. Tex.

LOGGERHEAD SHRIKE. *Lanius ludovicianus.* Subsp. (Illus. p. 147.)

Descr. 9. Slightly smaller than a Robin; big-headed and slim-tailed; gray above and white below, with a conspicuous *black mask* through the eyes. (See Northwestern Shrike.) The species is most frequently confused with the Mockingbird because of its gray, black, and white coloration and white patches in the wing, but the Mockingbird is slimmer, longer-tailed, has larger wing-patches, and lacks the black mask through the eyes.

Voice: — Song, a few musical notes and phrases, repeated. Somewhat Thrasher-like, but more deliberate, often with long pauses between passages.

Range: — Breeds from Can. s. to Mex.; winters in Calif. and in arid sections of sw. U.S.

Subsp. (No apparent field differences): (1) White-rumped Shrike, *L. l. excubitorides*; (2) California Shrike, *L. l. gambeli*; (3) Island Shrike, *L. l. anthonyi*.

LOGGERHEAD SHRIKE

STARLINGS: STURNIDÆ

STARLING. *Sturnus vulgaris vulgaris.* (Illus. p. 148.)
Descr. 7½–8½. The Starling, introduced from Europe into the
e. U.S., has now reached the Rockies and might eventually penetrate the Far West. It is a *short-tailed* 'Blackbird,' with somewhat the shape of a Meadowlark. In spring the plumage is
glossed with purple and green (visible at close range), and the
bill is *yellow* In winter plumage the Starling is heavily speckled,
and the bill is dark, changing to yellow as spring approaches.
No other 'Blackbird' has a *yellow* bill. Young birds are dark
dusky gray, a little like the female Cowbird, but the tail is
shorter, and the bill longer and more spike-like, not stout and
conical. The flight of Starlings is swift and direct, not rising and
falling as much as that of Blackbirds.
Voice: — Many of the whistled notes are extremely musical;
other sounds are harsh and rasping. Frequently very good imitations of other species are given.
Range: — E. U.S., spreading westward. Has at this date (1940)
reached base of Rockies and Ut. To be looked for on Pacific
Coast.

STARLING, *male in spring*

VIREOS: VIREONIDÆ

SMALL olive- or gray-backed birds, slightly smaller than most
Sparrows; very much like the Warblers, but with somewhat
heavier bills, and less active, slowly searching for insects under
the leaves instead of flitting about. Because of their white wing-

bars and white eye-rings, some species might be confused with the small *Empidonax* Flycatchers, but they do not sit in the typical upright Flycatcher posture, and the eye-rings join a light spot between the eye and bill, giving more the appearance of white spectacles.

BLACK-CAPPED VIREO. *Vireo atricapillus.* (Illus. p. 190.)
Descr. 4½–4¾. The only Vireo with the *top and sides of the head black.* It has conspicuous white wing-bars and white 'spectacles' formed by the eye-ring and loral patch (between the eye and bill).
Voice: — Song, short phrases, similar to other Vireos but somewhat more varied.
Range: — Cent. and cent.-w. Tex. (to Brewster Co.) and parts of sw. Okla. and s. Kans.

HUTTON'S VIREO. *Vireo huttoni.* Subsp. (Illus. p. 190.)
Descr. 4¼–4¾. A small olive-brown Vireo with two broad white wing-bars, a *partial* eye-ring, and a large light loral spot (between eye and bill). The appearance of this large light spot and the incomplete eye-ring *interrupted by a dark spot* above eye (see diagram) distinguish it from the other Vireos with eye-rings or 'spectacles.' It can be mistaken by the beginner for one of the small *Empidonax* Flycatchers, which, however, sit in an upright posture and have complete eye-rings. The bird that most closely resembles it is the Ruby-crowned Kinglet. The Vireo has a heavier bill, is slightly larger, and is much more deliberate in its movements. (Does not flirt wings like Kinglet.) The notes are especially distinctive. In most of its range, the preferred habitat of this species is live-oaks.
Voice: — A hoarse double-noted *zu-weep* with rising inflection, sometimes continuously repeated; Vireo quality. Also 'a hoarse aspirate *Day, de'-de'-de''* (Laidlaw Williams).
Range: — Resident in Pacific States (w. of Cascades and Sierras), and oak belt of mts. of se. Ariz., sw. N.M., and w. Tex.
Subsp. (No apparent field differences): (1) Hutton's Vireo, *V. h. huttoni*; (2) Stephens's Vireo, *V. h. stephensi.*

BELL'S, *or* **LEAST, VIREO.** *Vireo belli.* Subsp. (Illus. p. 190.)
Descr. 4¾–5. A small light-gray-backed Vireo. Perhaps the most nondescript of the Vireos. Distinguished from the Warbling Vireo by the faint wing-bars and narrow light eye-ring. The other similar Vireos have much more conspicuous eye-rings. Its habitat is willows and bushes along low streams.
Voice: — Song, low husky phrases repeated at short intervals; sounds like *cheedle cheedle chee? cheedle cheedle chew!* The latter phrase, which is given the more frequently, has a downward in-

flection at the end and sounds as if the bird were answering its own question.

Range: — Breeds in Calif. (central valleys, coast from Monterey Co. s., and se. portion), s. Ariz., sw. N.M., and w. Tex.; also e. Colo.

Subsp. (No apparent field differences): (1) Bell's Vireo, *V. b. belli*; (2) Texas Vireo, *V. b. medius*; (3) Arizona Vireo, *V. b. arizonæ*; (4) Least Vireo, *V. b. pusillus.*

GRAY VIREO. *Vireo vicinior.* (Illus. p. 190.)
Descr. 5½–5¾. A gray-backed Vireo of the chaparral and juniper on the slopes of arid mts. Has a *narrow white eye-ring* but differs from other Vireos having similar eye-rings by having *no wing-bars* or one faint one. Might be confused with Bell's, or Least, Vireo because of similarity in appearance, but the latter species prefers the willows of stream-bottoms and would not be found on arid slopes. The Gray Vireo, though drab, has much character, flopping its tail like a Gnatcatcher.
Voice: — Very similar to song of Solitary Vireo (Cassin's and Plumbeous) but more rapid and 'patchy.' (Solitary would not be found in the above arid habitat.)
Range· — Breeds from s. Calif., s. Nev., sw. Colo., and extreme w. Okla. s. into Mex.

SOLITARY VIREO. *Vireo solitarius.* Subsp. (Illus. p. 190.)
Descr. 5–6. A Vireo possessing *both* conspicuous white wing-bars and conspicuous white 'spectacles.' The Bell's, or Least, Vireo has these marks indistinct; in the Warbling Vireo they are wanting. The Gray Vireo has only a conspicuous eye-ring. The present species can be told from the Hutton's Vireo by the complete eye-ring and snowy-white throat.
Voice: — A series of short whistled phrases, with a rising or falling inflection, rendered with a short wait between phrases.
Subsp. PLUMBEOUS VIREO. *V. s. plumbeus.*
> Breeds in Rocky Mt. region from n. Nev., n. Ut., s. Mont., and se. Wyo. s. into Mex. Lacks the contrast of *gray* head and *olive* back of next race.
> CASSIN'S VIREO. *V. s. cassini.*
> Breeds in Pacific States. When at close range, in good light, easily distinguished from the Plumbeous or any other Vireo possessing wing-bars by the *gray* head contrasting with an *olive* back; almost identically like the Blue-headed Vireo of the East, which is also a race of this species. The Plumbeous race is uniformly gray above.

YELLOW-GREEN VIREO. *Vireo flavoviridis flavoviridis.*
Descr. 6¼–6¾. Of very rare occurrence near Brownsville, Tex.

WARBLERS

1. Grace's Warbler
2. Audubon's Warbler, *a.* male in spring; *b.* female in autumn
3. Myrtle Warbler, male in spring
4. Virginia's Warbler
5. Black-throated Gray Warbler, male
6. Black and White Warbler, male
7. Black-poll Warbler, *a.* male in spring; *b.* female; *c.* autumn
8. Lucy's Warbler
9. Townsend's Warbler, *a.* male; *b.* female
10. Golden-cheeked Warbler, male
11. Hermit Warbler, *a.* male; *b.* female
12. Tennessee Warbler, male in spring
13. Pileolated Warbler, *a.* male; *b.* female
14. Yellow Warbler, *a.* male; *b.* female
15. Sennett's Warbler, male
16. Calaveras Warbler
17. Macgillivray's Warbler, *a.* male: *b.* female
18. Orange-crowned Warbler
19. Long-tailed Chat
20. Grinnell's Water-Thrush
21. Yellow-throat, *a.* male; *b.* female
22. Olive Warbler, *a.* male: *b.* female
23. Red-faced Warbler
24. Painted Redstart
25. American Redstart, *a.* male; *b.* female

Similar to Red-eyed Vireo, both in behavior and in voice, but with strong yellow tones. Sides bright olive-green and under tail-coverts *yellow* (Red-eye, white). A Vireo similar to a Red-eye during the summer months in the lower Rio Grande Valley would probably be this species. Its preferred habitat is thick-leaved trees near water.

RED-EYED VIREO. *Vireo olivaceus.* (Illus. p. 190.)
Descr. 5½–6½. Olive-green above, white below, *no wing-bars*; best characterized by the *gray cap* and the *black-bordered white stripe* over the eye. The red eye is of little aid. The Warbling Vireo is paler, and more uniformly colored above, without such contrasting facial striping. The songs of these two birds are absolutely unlike.
Voice: — A monotonous series of short phrases of a Robin-like character, repeated sometimes as often as forty times in a minute. Resembles song of Solitary (Plumbeous) Vireo but less musical and with the phrases repeated more frequently.
Range: — Breeds chiefly in e. U.S., w. to e. Colo., e. Wyo., and, in nw., to Portland, Ore., and Seattle, Wash. Accidental in Calif.

(WESTERN) WARBLING VIREO. *Vireo gilvus swainsoni.* (Illus. p. 190.)
Descr. 5–6. Only two species of Vireos found in the W. have *no* wing-bars or eye-rings. If the head is contrastingly striped, it is a Red-eye. If the head is *indistinctly* striped, then it is the present species. Of the two, this has the wider distribution in the W.
Voice: — Song, a rather lengthy languid warble unlike the abrupt phraseology of the other Vireos; resembles slightly the Purple Finch's song, but less spirited. A characteristic call-note in the summer is a wheezy querulous *twee*.
Range: — Breeds from Can. s. to Mex. border.

WOOD WARBLERS:
COMPSOTHLYPIDÆ

THESE are the sprightly 'butterflies' of the bird world — bright-colored mites, smaller than Sparrows, with thin bills. The Vireos are similar in shape, but their colors are duller and their movements when patiently foraging among the leaves and twigs are rather sluggish, unlike the active flittings of the Warblers. The majority of Western Warblers have some yellow on them. Easterners will find that many Eastern Warblers have their Western counterparts, if not in a similar subspecies in a similar species; for example: *Nashville* — Calaveras; *Orange-crowned* — Orange-crowned; *Yellow* — Yellow; *Myrtle* — Audubon's; *Black-throated Green* — Hermit; *Mourning* — Macgillivray's; *Yellow-throated* — Grace's; *Yellow-breasted Chat* — Long-tailed Chat; *Wilson's* — Pileolated; *Yellow-throat* — Yellow-throat. At least fifteen species of purely Eastern Warblers have been recorded occasionally or accidentally in the W., especially along the edge of the Great Plains in e. Mont., e. Wyo., and e. Colo. Descriptions of these waifs will be found in the Eastern counterpart to this volume, *A Field Guide to the Birds*.

BLACK AND WHITE WARBLER. *Mniotilta varia.* (Illus. p. 150.)
Descr. 5–5½. Occasional in w. U.S. *Striped lengthwise with black and white* — the zebra's counterpart among birds; *creeps* along tree-trunks and branches. The Black-throated Gray Warbler is the only one that at all resembles it, but that species has a *solid black cap*, the present species has a *striped* crown.
Voice: — Song, a high thin *tisi tisi tisi tisi tisi tisi tisi tisi*, all on one pitch; resembles Redstart's song but is thinner and longer (*tisi* repeated at least six times).
Range: — E. N.A.; occasional in migration w. to e. Colo., e. Wyo., and e. Mont.; occasional also in Calif.

TENNESSEE WARBLER. *Vermivora peregrina.* (Illus. p. 150.)
Descr. 4½–5. *Adult male in spring:* — Very plain; unmarked save for a *conspicuous white stripe over the eye*; head gray, contrasting with olive-green back; under parts white. The bird in this plumage, with the white eye-stripe, is much like the Red-eyed and the Warbling Vireos, but the smaller size, the Warbler actions, and the thin, fine-pointed bill identify it. *Adult female in spring:* — Similar to the male, but head less gray and under parts slightly yellowish. The eye-line is the best mark. *Adults and immatures in autumn:* — Olive-green above, yellowish below, with no streaks; yellowish line over eye. Resembles the Orange-crowned Warbler, but the under tail-coverts are *white*, not yellow.
Voice: — Song, two-parted, *teet-see, teet-see, teet-see, teet-see, de-de-de-de-de-de-de-de*. The end of the song is like that of the Chipping Sparrow but more emphatic. It is loud and repetitious, one song quickly following the preceding one.
Range: — Migrates through e. Colo., e. Wyo., and e. Mont.; said to breed in mts. of nw. Mont.

ORANGE-CROWNED WARBLER. *Vermivora celata.* Subsp. (Illus. p. 150.)
Descr. 4½–5. A dull-colored Warbler *without wing-bars or other distinctive marks*; olive-green above, *greenish-yellow below*; the

'orange crown' is seldom visible (Calaveras also has a veiled crown-patch); sexes similar. The points to remember are the greenish-yellow under parts and lack of wing-bars. (The Calaveras Warbler has brighter under parts and a white eye-ring; the Hutton's Vireo and Ruby-crowned Kinglet, which might possibly be confused with it, both have light wing-bars.) One race of this species, the Dusky Warbler, is recognizable by its dull coloration, greenish drab throughout, not much paler on the under parts. However, as dull autumn immatures of the other races are so very similar to it, it is not safe to identify this subspecies in the field except on the breeding grounds (Channel Ids., Calif., and coast near San Diego), or along the coast of Calif. during the winter months. The favorite habitat of the Orange-crowned Warbler is brush-covered slopes. In the Pacific States the racial name, Lutescent Warbler, has become quite established through usage, but for the sake of consistency we suggest instead, the use of the species name, Orange-crowned Warbler, as more than one race occurs in migration.

Voice: — Song, a weak, colorless trill, dropping in pitch and energy at the end. Often the song changes pitch twice, rising a little then dropping.

Range: — Breeds from Can. s. to s. Calif., Ariz., and N.M., and from Rockies w. to coast. Migrates throughout. Winters from cent. Calif. and s. Ariz. s. into Mex.

Subsp. (No apparent field differences except in No. 4 — see above): (1) Eastern Orange-crowned Warbler, *V. c. celata*; (2) Rocky Mountain Orange-crowned Warbler, *V. c. orestera*; (3) Lutescent Warbler, *V. c. lutescens*; (4) Dusky Warbler, *V. c. sordida*.

CALAVERAS WARBLER. *Vermivora ruficapilla ridgwayi.* (Illus. p. 150.)

Descr. 4–4¾. A small, rather plain Warbler; throat and under parts bright yellow; *head gray*, contrasting with the olive-green back; eye-ring *white*; sexes similar. The *white eye-ring* in conjunction with the bright *yellow* throat is the best mark. The Macgillivray's Warbler has a white eye-ring, but its throat is dark gray or brownish (autumn female). The Calaveras is a race of the Eastern Nashville Warbler. Preferred habitat: deciduous growth on mountain-slopes.

Voice: — Song, two-parted, *see-bit, see-bit, see-bit, chitititititititi* (first part measured, last part run together).

Range: — Breeds in Pacific States from Can. s. to cent. Sierras in Calif., also e. to Ida. Migrates through Pacific States; occasional in Rockies.

VIRGINIA'S WARBLER. *Vermivora virginiæ.* (Illus. p. 150.)

Descr. 4. A *gray-looking* Warbler with a pale breast and *yellow-*

ish rump and under tail-coverts. At close range a narrow white eye-ring, a rufous spot on top of the head, and a touch of yellow on the breast can be seen. Immature birds lack the coloration on the crown and breast but can be told by their gray color and the touch of yellow at the base of the tail. The Lucy's Warbler resembles this species but has a *chestnut* rump instead of a yellowish one. The habitat is oaks on mountain-sides and foothills.

Voice: — Song, a loose, colorless series of notes on nearly the same pitch; rises ever so slightly at end: *chip-chlip-chlip-chlip-chlip-wick wick.* Resembles song of Audubon's Warbler in quality.

Range: — Breeds in s. Rocky Mt. region from s. Ariz. and ne. N.M. n. to Nev., Ut., and n. Colo.

COLIMA WARBLER. *Vermivora crissalis.*
Descr. Very similar to the Virginia's Warbler, differing chiefly in lacking the yellowish wash on the breast; also darker in general coloration. In the Chisos Mts. in Tex., a deliberate-acting, gray-looking Warbler with yellow near the base of the tail can quite safely be called this little-known species, although the Virginia's Warbler occurs as a migrant in the vicinity.

Voice: — Song, 'a simple trill, much like that of the Chipping Sparrow but rather shorter and more musical and ending in two lower notes' (Van Tyne).

Range: — In U.S. found only in Chisos Mts., Tex. (oaks between 6000 and 7500 ft.).

LUCY'S WARBLER. *Vermivora luciæ.* (Illus. p. 150.)
Descr. 4. A little Warbler of the desert; gray-backed, with a white breast. Its best field-mark is a *chestnut rump-patch.* It also has a small patch of chestnut on the crown. The Warbler that most closely resembles it, the Virginia's Warbler, has a *yellowish* rump-patch. Immature birds are largely gray without distinctive marks.

Voice: — Song, a high and rapid utterance, *weeta weeta weeta che che che che che,* on two pitches (sometimes ending on lower pitch, sometimes on higher). Has quality of Yellow Warbler's song when ending on higher notes. Resembles Calaveras when ending on lower pitch.

Range: — Breeds in deserts of sw. U.S. (from Santa Clara Valley, Ut., s. through Ariz., sw. N.M., and se. Calif.).

SENNETT'S WARBLER. *Compsothlypis pitiayumi nigrilora.* (Illus. p. 150.)
Descr. 4¼–4¾. A *bluish* Warbler with a *yellow* throat and breast. Two white wing-bars are also noticeable. A suffused yellowish patch on the back is a clinching point, if it can be seen. The most noticeable field-character is the yellow throat, sharply sep-

arated from the blue crown by a black line (see color plate).
Female: — Similar; face-pattern not so contrasting. The general blue and yellow color is distinctive. The Parula Warbler, which migrates through the range of this bird, is very similar, but males can be easily distinguished by a dark *band* crossing the yellow of the breast and much longer wing-bars.
Voice: — Commonest song, a buzzy trill which climbs the scale and tips over at the top; also a series of buzzy notes which ascend the scale by short steps. Both these songs are almost identical with those of the Parula Warbler.
Range: — Resident in lower Rio Grande Valley, Tex. Found in woodlands where hanging moss is prevalent.

OLIVE WARBLER. *Peucedramus olivaceus.* (Illus. p. 150.)
Descr. 4½–5. *Male:* — A unique-looking Warbler, easily identified by its *orange-brown head and upper breast* set off by a *black cheek-patch.* The back is dark gray, the belly white, and the wings have much white in them. *Female:* — Less distinctive; crown and nape olive, sides of throat and breast yellowish, back gray, wing-bars white. Has a dusky ear-patch, and might be confused with female Townsend's Warbler, but lacks the dark breast-streakings. Even more like female Hermit Warbler, but with more yellow on breast, less on face; cheek-patch darker and bill much longer.
Voice: — Song, a ringing chant with several variations: *tiddle tiddle tiddle ter,* or *cut-year, cut-year cut-year,* or *peter peter peter peter* (Titmouse-like).
Range: — Pine forests of high mts. of se. Ariz. and sw. N.M.

YELLOW WARBLER. *Dendroica æstiva.* Subsp. (Illus. p. 150.)
Descr. 4–5. The only small bird that in the field appears to be *all yellow.* Many of the other Warblers are yellow below, but none of them is so yellow on the back, wings, and tail. Many Warblers have white spots in the tail; this is the only species with *yellow* spots. At close range the male shows chestnut-red breast-streakings. In the female these are faint or nearly lacking. Has a preference for trees and shrubbery along streams. In some localities the Goldfinch shares the nickname 'Yellowbird,' but it has *black* wings and a *black* tail. The Pileolated Warbler can be mistaken for it but has a darker back and a black spot on the crown. The Alaska Yellow Warbler, *D. a. rubiginosa,* is darker and more greenish than the other races and is often easily recognizable in life. The immature of this race can be confused with the Orange-crowned Warbler by the beginner.
Voice: — A clear bright *tsee-tsee-tsee-tseetsa-wee* or *tsee-tsee-tsee-tsee-tsee-wee-a,* given rapidly.
Range: — Breeds from Can. s. to s. Calif., s. Ariz., s. N.M., and w. Tex.

Subsp. (No apparent field differences except sometimes in No. 2): (1) Eastern Yellow Warbler, *D. a. æstiva*; (2) Alaska Yellow Warbler, *D. a. rubiginosa*; (3) California Yellow Warbler, *D. a. brewsteri*; (4) Sonora Yellow Warbler, *D. a. sonorana*.

MYRTLE WARBLER. *Dendroica coronata.* (Illus. p. 150.)
Descr. 5–6. The Myrtle Warbler is very similar to the Audubon's in pattern, but the throat is pure *white* instead of yellow. Adult males have two narrow white wing-bars instead of a large white wing-patch.
Voice: — Song, very similar to Audubon's Warbler, a Junco-like trill, that either *rises* or *falls* in pitch at the end. Call-note recognizably different in timbre from that of Audubon's Warbler.
Range: — Breeds in Can. and Alaska; migrates through Pacific States and e. of Rockies in e. Mont., e. Wyo., and e. Colo.; also recorded from N.M. and Ariz. Winters in Calif. and Tex.

AUDUBON'S WARBLER. *Dendroica auduboni.* Subsp. (Illus. p. 150.)
Descr. 4¾–5¼. The Audubon's Warbler can be identified in any plumage by its bright *yellow rump*, in connection with its note, a loud *tchip*. *Male in spring:* — Blue-gray above, with a heavy black breast-patch shaped like an inverted U. Throat, crown, and side-patches yellow. The large white wing-patches are very distinctive. *Female in spring:* — Brown instead of gray, but pattern similar except for the conspicuous wing-patch. *Winter adults and young:* — Brownish above, whitish below, streaked with dark; throat and rump yellow. The comparatively rare Myrtle Warbler shows a similar yellow rump as it flies. (See Myrtle Warbler.)
Voice: — Song, loose and Junco-like in quality, but two-parted, either rising or dropping in pitch at the end, *seet-seet-seet-seet-seet, trrrrrrrr.* Note, a loud *tchip*.
Subsp. AUDUBON'S WARBLER. *D. a. auduboni.*
Breeds from Can. s. to mts. of s. Calif., Ariz., and se. N.M.; winters in Pacific States and lower Rio Grande Valley, Tex.
BLACK-FRONTED WARBLER. *D. a. nigrifrons.*
Breeding males often recognizable by the heavier, more extensive black area on the breast and sides, often greatly restricting the white area on the belly. Breeds in mts. of se. Ariz. (Huachuca and Chiricahua Mts., etc.).

BLACK-THROATED GRAY WARBLER. *Dendroica nigrescens.* (Illus. p. 150.)
Descr. 4½–5. Gray above and white below with a *black-and-white striped face.* (See diagram.) Most like the Townsend's

Warbler, which has *yellow* on face and under parts instead of white. The only other birds with *both* black cap and black bib are the Chickadees, which have *white cheeks*. *Females* lack the black throat but retain the black eye- and crown-patches. (See Black and White and Black-poll Warblers.)

Voice: — Song, a buzzy chant, *zeedle zeedle zeedle zeet' che* (next to last note higher than others). Song variable, sometimes ending on the higher note, but always recognizable by its drawly quality, which one observer characterized as 'full of *z*'s.'

Range: — Breeds from Wash., Nev., n. Ut., and w. Colo. s. to s. Calif., s. Ariz., and s. N.M.

TOWNSEND'S WARBLER. *Dendroica townsendi.* (Illus. p. 150.)

Descr. 4¼–5. Easily distinguished by the *black-and-yellow striped head* (see diagram) and striped yellow under parts. The Hermit Warbler has a black throat but lacks the black cheek-and-crown-patches. The Golden-cheeked Warbler, which resembles it even more closely, is found only in central and southern Texas. Female Townsend's Warblers have the throat largely yellow instead of black, but there is still enough of the male's yellow-and-black face and breast pattern to identify them.

Voice: — Song, similar to Black-throated Gray: '*Dzeer Dzeer Dzeer tseetsee.* The first three or four notes similar in pitch with a wheezy buzzy quality, followed by two or more quick higher-pitched sibilant notes' (H. H. Axtell).

Range: — Breeds from Can. s. to w. Ore., w. Mont., and w. Wyo. (occasionally); migrates throughout West; winters along coast from Wash. to Calif.

GOLDEN-CHEEKED WARBLER. *Dendroica chrysoparia.* (Illus. p. 150.)

Descr. 4¾. Found only in cedar-clad hills of cent. Tex. (see range below); the only Warbler with the combination of yellow cheeks and black throat found in this habitat. *Male:* — Similar to Townsend's Warbler (which is never found in cent. Tex.) but with less black on the cheeks, no yellow on the breast, and a *solid black* back. *Female:* — Similar to male but back olive-green (resembles Black-throated Green Warbler, but migrants of the latter species are always in hardwoods and shade trees of lowlands, when in cent. Tex.; Golden-cheeks are always in the cedar ridges).

Voice: — Song, 'a hurried *tweeah, tweeah, twee-sy*, with some individuals introducing an extra note or two' (H. P. Attwater). Has buzzy quality of Black-throated Green.

Range: — Breeds in a section of the Edwards Plateau of cent. Tex. from San Antonio and Austin w. to Kerr, Tom Green, and Concho Cos.

HERMIT WARBLER. *Dendroica occidentalis.* (Illus. p. 150.)
Descr. $4\frac{1}{2}$–$4\frac{3}{4}$. The bright *yellow face* set off by the *black throat* and dark back is the best mark. The Townsend's Warbler has black cheek- and crown-patches. It resembles more closely the Eastern Black-throated Green Warbler. In the female the black of the throat is replaced by grayish or white, but its general resemblance to the male is still evident. It can be told from the female Townsend's by its grayer back and *white* instead of yellow breast.
Voice: — Song, three high lisping two-syllabled notes followed by two abrupt lower ones: *sweety, sweety, sweety, chup'-chup'*, or *seedle, seedle, seedle, chup'-chup'*. The abrupt end notes are very distinctive. Usually heard high in tall evergreens.
Range: — Breeds in Pacific States from w. Wash. s. through Sierras of Calif. to Mt. Whitney. Migrates through s. Calif., Nev., and Ariz.

GRACE'S WARBLER. *Dendroica graciæ graciæ.* (Illus. p. 150.)
Descr. $4\frac{1}{2}$. A *gray-backed Warbler with a yellow throat.* Belly white; two white wing-bars, yellowish line over the eye, and black stripes on the sides. Lives among pines high in sw. mts. Easily distinguished from Audubon's Warbler by lack of black across breast, and absence of yellow rump. Easterners will note its close resemblance to Yellow-throated Warbler.
Voice: — A repetitious *cheedle cheedle che che che che*, ending in a Chippy-like trill.
Range: — Breeds in pine forests on high mts. of sw. Colo., cent. and e. Ariz., and N.M.

BLACK-POLL WARBLER. *Dendroica striata.* (Illus. p. 150.)
Descr. 5–$5\frac{1}{2}$. *Male in spring:* — A striped gray Warbler with *a solid black cap* and *white cheeks*; reminds the beginner of a Chickadee, but lacks the black throat. Might be confused with the female Black-throated Gray Warbler, but the latter species has *black* cheek-patches. The Black and White Warbler, the only other species with which it might be confused, has a *striped* crown, and black cheeks. *Female in spring:* — Less heavily streaked, lacking the black crown-patch; a plain, black-streaked Warbler, greenish-gray above, white below; may be known from the Black and White by the lack of contrasting head-stripings, and from the female Audubon's and Myrtle by the absence of yellow in the plumage. *Autumn birds:* — Olive-green above, with two white wing-bars; dingy yellow below, faintly streaked; a drab greenish-looking Warbler with white wing-bars. (Orange-crown lacks wing-bars.)
Voice: — Song, a high, thin, mechanical *zi — zi — zi — zi — zi — zi — zi — zi — zi*, all on one pitch, becoming louder and more emphatic in the middle of series.

Range: — A spring migrant e. of Rockies in e. Colo., e. Wyo., and e. Mont.

OVEN-BIRD. *Seirus aurocapillus.*

Descr. 5½–6½. A Sparrow-sized ground Warbler of the leafy woodlands; has somewhat the appearance of a small Thrush — olive-brown above, but *striped* rather than spotted beneath. A *light orange patch* on the top of the head is visible at close range. The bird is usually seen *walking* on pale *pinkish* legs over the leaves or along some log.

Voice: — The song is most graphically described as an emphatic *teach'er*, TEACH'ER, TEACH'ER, etc., repeated rapidly, louder and louder, till the air fairly rings with the vibrant accents (to be more exact, the accent is really on the *second* syllable thus: *cherte'a*, CHERTE'A, CHERTE'A, etc.).

Range: — Breeds in Black Hills section of ne. Wyo. and extreme se. Mont. and locally in cent. Colo.; migrates sparingly through se. Wyo. and e. Colo.; casual in Calif.

GRINNELL'S WATER-THRUSH. *Seiurus noveboracensis notabilis.* (Illus. p. 150.)

Descr. 5–6. The Water-Thrush is a brown-backed bird about the size of a Sparrow, with a *conspicuous light stripe over the eye, and heavily striped under parts.* Though a Warbler by anatomical structure, its life along the streams and wooded swamps has made it ridiculously like a little Sandpiper; when not running along the water's edge it is constantly *tettering* up and down in much the manner of the 'Spotty' of the shore. The light under parts are strongly tinged with yellowish or buffy. A race of the Northern Water-Thrush of e. U.S.

Voice: — A vigorous song often dropping in pitch and ending in a diagnostic *chew-chew-chew.*

Range: — Breeds from Can. s. locally to w. Mont.; an uncommon or rare migrant in Mont., Wyo., Colo., N.M., and Ariz. Casual in Calif.

MACGILLIVRAY'S WARBLER. *Oporornis tolmiei.* (Illus. p. 150.)

Descr. 4¾–5½. *Male:* — Olive above, yellow below, with a *slate-gray hood* completely encircling the head and neck, and a white *eye-ring.* The only remotely similar Warbler with a white eye-ring is the Calaveras, which has a *yellow* throat. *Female* similar, but hood much paler, and washed out on throat. Stays near the ground in brushy places.

Voice: — Song, a rolling chant, *chiddle, chiddle, chiddle, turtle-turtle,* the voice dropping on the last two notes; or *chiddle-chiddle-chiddle, wick, wick.* One popular interpretation of the song is *sweeter-sweeter-sweeter, sugar-sugar.* Some observers confuse it with the two-parted song of the Calaveras Warbler, but it lacks the well-measured brightness in the opening notes.

Range: — Breeds from Can. s. to cent. Calif., cent. Ariz., and n. N.M.; migrates into Mex.

YELLOW-THROAT. *Geothlypis trichas.* Subsp. (Illus. p. 150.)
Descr. 4½–5½. The *male*, with its *black mask*, or 'domino,' needs no detailed description. *Females and immature birds* are plain olive-brown with a yellow throat and buffy-yellow breast. The black mask is absent. They may be distinguished from any other similar Warblers (female Yellow, female Pileolated, and Orange-crown) by the *whitish* belly. The others are solid yellow below. The habitat is swamps, stream-beds, and marshes.
Voice: — Song, very distinctive; a rapid, well-enunciated *witchity-witchity-witchity-witchity-witch.* In some individuals this is lengthened to *witchity-ta-witchity-ta-witchity-ta-witch,* or shortened to *witchy-witchy-witchy-witch.* The call-note, a husky *tchep,* is also distinctive.
Range: — Breeds locally from Can. s. to s. Tex., N.M., s. Ariz., and s. Calif.; migrates throughout West. Winters in cent. and s. Calif. and in s. Ariz.
Subsp. (No apparent field differences): (1) Western Yellow-throat, *G. t. occidentalis*; (2) Salt Marsh Yellow-throat, *G. t. sinuosa*; (3) Tule Yellow-throat, *G. t. scirpicola.*

RIO GRANDE YELLOW-THROAT. *Chamæthlypis poliocephala poliocephala.*
Descr. 5½. This Mexican species which has been authentically recorded but a few times in the U.S. should not be confused with the totally different Yellow-throat (*Geothlypis trichas*), a race of which occurs in the lower Rio Grande Valley. It is a different species, considerably larger, with a thicker, more Vireo-like bill. The male can be immediately told by its *restricted black face-patch between the eye and bill.* This is quite different from the extensive mask of *G. trichas.* The female lacks the black, but is larger than the female Yellow-throat and lacks the whitish on the belly.
Voice: — Song, cheerful and Bunting-like, not like that of *G. trichas* (Sutton).
Range: — Occasional (formerly at least) in lower Rio Grande Valley, Tex.

LONG-TAILED CHAT. *Icteria virens longicauda.* (Illus. p. 150.)
Descr. 6½–7½. Except for its color, the Chat seems more like a small Thrasher or a Mocker than a Warbler. Its superior size (considerably larger than a Sparrow), its rather long tail, its eccentric song and actions, and its brushy habitat, all suggest those larger birds. Both sexes are plain olive-brown above, with

white 'spectacles'; the throat and breast are *bright yellow*; the belly white. The long tail and the large size at once eliminate the possibility of its being any other Warbler. Habitat, brushy places along stream-beds, valleys, and canyons. A race of the Yellow-breasted Chat of e. U.S.
Voice: — An odd song made up of various harsh or whistled notes in repetitive series, suggestive of Mockingbird but with long deliberate pauses between series. Characteristic passages are: *chut-chut-chut-chut-chut-chut* (like Bullock's Oriole); *weck-weck-weck-weck-weck-weck*; *kook — kook — kook* (whistled), etc.
Range: — Breeds from Wash. and n. Mont. s. into Mex.

RED-FACED WARBLER. *Cardellina rubrifrons.* (Illus. p. 150.)
Descr. 5¼. A gray-backed Warbler with a *bright-red face and breast*; black patch on head, white nape, and white belly. The only other Western Warbler sporting the same shade of red is the Painted Redstart, which, however, has no red on the face.
Voice: — A clear sweet Warbler song similar to that of Yellow Warbler (Painted Redstart has a more repetitious quality).
Range: — High mts. of se. Ariz. and sw. N.M.

PILEOLATED WARBLER. *Wilsonia pusilla.* Subsp. (Illus. p. 150.)
Descr. 4¼–5. *Male:* — A yellow Warbler with a *round black cap.* *Females and immature* birds may, or may not, show traces of the black cap. If they do not, they appear as small, plain Warblers, olive-green above and bright yellow below, with *no streaks, wing-bars, or marks of any kind.* The aspect of the round, beady black eye superimposed on the yellow face is an aid. The Yellow Warbler is yellower above and shows *yellow* spots in the tail. The Orange-crown is much dingier, not so bright yellow below. The female Yellow-throat has a whitish belly. The preferred habitat is thick shrubbery in woodland openings. The Eastern Wilson's Warbler is a race of this bird.
Voice: — Song, a dry series of notes all on same pitch . . . *chi-chi-chi-chi-chit-Chit-Chit*, becoming louder and faster toward end (poco crescendo). Note, a husky *chip* or *chimp.*
Range: — Breeds from Can. s. in high mts. to w. Tex., n. N.M., n. Ariz., and s. Calif.; also in coast belt of Wash. and Ore. and along coast range s. to San Diego, Calif.; migrates throughout.
Subsp. (No apparent field differences): (1) Northern Pileolated Warbler, *W. p. pileolata*; (2) Golden Pileolated Warbler, *W. p. chryseola.*

AMERICAN REDSTART. *Setophaga ruticilla.* (Illus. p. 150.)
Descr. 4½–5½. The Redstart is one of the most butterfly-like of birds. It is constantly flitting about in sprightly fashion, drooping its wings and spreading fanwise its tail as if to make all who take notice admire. *Male:* — Largely black with *bright orange*

patches on the wings and tail; belly white. No other Warbler found in the W. is colored anything like it. *Female:* — Chiefly olive-brown above, white below, with large *yellow* flash-patches on the wings and tail. *Immature male:* — Considerable variation; much like the female; yellow often perceptibly tinged with orange. The typical Redstart pattern is obvious in any plumage. Habitat, saplings and second-growth deciduous timber.

Voice: — Two commonest songs, *tsee tsee tsee tsee tsee-o* (with drop on last syllable), and *teetsa teetsa teetsa teetsa teet* (double-noted). These two songs are commonly *alternated*, an excellent field aid.

Range: — Breeds in e. U.S. and diagonally nw. through Colo., n. Ut., Wyo., and Mont. to e. Ore. and e. Wash. Casual in migration in Calif., Ariz., and N.M.

PAINTED REDSTART. *Setophaga picta picta.* (Illus. p. 150.) **Descr.** 5. Black with *large white patches* in the wings and tail and a *large bright red patch* on the breast. The only other Warbler marked with the same shade of red is the Red-faced Warbler. The Painted Redstart has no red on the face. Sexes similar.

Voice: — Song, a repetitious *weeta weeta weeta wee* or *weeta weeta, chilp chilp chilp.* The note is a ringing Finch-like *clee-ip* or *che-ilp*, surprising in a Warbler.

Range: — High mts. of cent. and s. Ariz., sw. N.M., and w. Tex. (Chisos Mts.).

HOUSE SPARROW
A. Female   B. Male

WEAVER FINCHES: PLOCEIDÆ

HOUSE, *or* **ENGLISH, SPARROW.** *Passer domesticus domesticus.* (Illus. p. 162.)

1. BOBOLINK: a, *male*; b, *female*
2. LARK BUNTING: a, *male*; b, *female*

Descr. 5–6¼. A species with which everybody is familiar. Males have black throats, females whitish ones (see cut).
Range: — Distributed widely about civilization; about cities, towns, farms, and ranches throughout West.

MEADOWLARKS, BLACKBIRDS, AND ORIOLES: ICTERIDÆ

As MEMBERS of this group are so vastly different, it is difficult to make any generalizations for use in the field, except that they have conical, sharp-pointed bills and rather flat profiles. They are best characterized under their various species.

BOBOLINK. *Dolichonyx oryzivorus.* (Illus. p. 163.)
Descr. 6½–8. *Male in spring:* — A songbird that is *black below and largely white above*, a direct reversal of the normal tone-pattern of other birds, which are almost invariably lighter below. The male Lark Bunting resembles it somewhat but has its white areas *confined to the wings. Female and late summer and autumn male:* — Somewhat larger than Sparrows, largely *yellowish-buff* with *dark stripings* on the crown and upper parts. Frequents meadows and prairies.
Voice: — Song, long, reedy, and bubbling, starting with low melodious notes and rollicking upward in pitch.
Range: — Breeds in e. U.S. and diagonally nw. through Colo. (occasionally), Wyo., Mont., and n. Ut. to nw. Nev., ne. Calif. (rare), e. Ore., and e. Wash.; migrates through e. Colo.

RIO GRANDE MEADOWLARK. *Sturnella magna hoopesi.*
Descr. 8–9. A race of the Eastern Meadowlark. Very similar to

the Western Meadowlark but the yellow of the throat not so extensive; it does not edge into the cheeks. This is a fine point, hardly useful for field recognition. The species is most easily recognized by its song (below).

Voice: — Song, clear slurred whistles, might be rendered *tee-you*, *tee-yair*, very different from bubbly, flute-like song of Western Meadowlark.

Range: — Se. Ariz., s. N.M., and s. Tex., s. into Mex.

WESTERN MEADOWLARK. *Sturnella neglecta.* (Illus. p. 164.)
Descr. 8–10. Our first acquaintance with the Meadowlark usually comes early in our studies. On crossing some extensive field or piece of open country, a rather large, chunky brown bird flushes from the grass, showing a conspicuous patch of *white* on each side of the short, wide tail. Several other ground-dwelling birds, the Pipit, Longspur, Vesper Sparrow, and Junco show similar white outer tail-feathers. All of these are very much smaller, with the slimmer proportions of Sparrows. Should we see a Meadowlark perched on some distant fence post, our glass will reveal a bright yellow breast crossed by a black V, or gorget. (See plate.) The Flicker is similarly sized and brown above, but with a white *rump* instead of white sides of the tail, and it flies in a very different, *bounding* manner. The Meadowlark's flight is distinctive — several short, rapid wing-beats alternated with short periods of sailing.

Voice: — A variable song of seven to ten notes, flute-like, gurgling and double-noted.

Range: — Breeds from Can. s. to Mex.; winters from Wash. and Mont. s.

YELLOW-HEADED BLACKBIRD. *Xanthocephalus xanthocephalus.* (Illus. p. 164.)
Descr. 8–11. *Male:* — A Robin-sized Blackbird with a *yellow* head; shows a conspicuous white patch in the wing in flight. Females are smaller and browner, with most of the yellow confined to the throat and upper breast. Inhabits marshes.

Voice: — Note, a low *krick* or *kack*. Song, low hoarse rasping notes produced with much effort, 'like rusty hinges on the old barn door' (Lockerbie).

Range: — Breeds from Can. s. to s. Calif., n. Ariz., and N.M., and from Great Plains w. to e. Wash., e. Ore., and interior of Calif.; winters from sw. Calif., s. Ariz., and s. N.M. s. into Mex.

COMMON RED-WING. *Agelaius phœniceus.* Subsp. (Illus. p. 164.)
Descr. 7–9½. *Male:* — Black, with *red epaulets* or patches at the bend of the wings. Absolutely unmistakable. Often, when at rest, the scarlet is concealed, only the buffy or yellowish margin

RED-WINGS, MEADOWLARKS, BLACKBIRDS, ORIOLES, GROSBEAKS BUNTINGS, TOWHEES, SPARROWS

1. RED-WING, *a*. MALE; *b*. FEMALE

2. WESTERN MEADOWLARK

3. YELLOW-HEADED BLACKBIRD, *a*. MALE; *b*. FEMALE

4. BULLOCK'S ORIOLE, *a*. MALE; *b*. FEMALE

5. AUDUBON'S ORIOLE

6. SCOTT'S ORIOLE, *a*. MALE; *b*. FEMALE

7. HOODED ORIOLE, *a*. MALE; *b*. FEMALE

8. BLACK-HEADED GROSBEAK, *a*. MALE; *b*. FEMALE

9. BLUE GROSBEAK, *a*. MALE; *b*. FEMALE

10. VARIED BUNTING, *a*. MALE; *b*. FEMALE

11. PAINTED BUNTING, *a*. MALE; *b*. FEMALE

12. LAZULI BUNTING, *a*. MALE; *b*. FEMALE

13. GREEN-TAILED TOWHEE

14. TEXAS SPARROW

15. DICKCISSEL, *a*. MALE; *b*. FEMALE

16. *a*. BROWN TOWHEE; *b*. CAÑON TOWHEE

17. ABERT'S TOWHEE

18. SPOTTED TOWHEE, *a*. MALE; *b*. FEMALE

of the red patch being visible. *Immature male:* — Dusky-brown, but with the scarlet patches of the adult male. *Female and young:* — Brownish; identified by the sharp-pointed bill, Blackbird appearance, and *well-defined stripings below*. No other female Blackbirds (except next species) have these breast-streakings. Inhabits marshes and swampy places. One race, known as the Bicolored Red-wing (San Francisco Bay region and Sacramento and San Joaquin Valleys of Calif.) differs from other Red-wings in having the 'epaulets' *solid red*, without yellow edges.

Voice: — Notes, a loud *check* and a high, slurred *tee-err*. Song, a gurgling *konk-la-reeee* or *o-ka-leee*, the last note trilled or quavered.

Range: — Nearly all parts of W., from Can. to Mex., where there are suitable marshes; winters in varying abundance over a large part of the W., but shows a tendency to migrate out of colder sections.

Subsp. (No apparent field differences except in No. 6 — see above): (1) Giant Red-wing, *A. p. arctolegus*; (2) Thick-billed Red-wing, *A. p. fortis*; (3) Nevada Red-wing, *A. p. nevadensis*; (4) Northwestern Red-wing, *A. p. caurinus*; (5) San Francisco Red-wing, *A. p. mailliardorum*; (6) Bicolored Red-wing, *A. p. californicus*; (7) Kern Red-wing, *A. p. aciculatus*; (8) San Diego Red-wing, *A. p. neutralis*; (9) Sonora Red-wing, *A. p. sonoriensis*.

TRICOLORED RED-WING. *Agelaius tricolor.*

Descr. 7½–9. *Male:* — Similar to Common Red-wing but with *white* edge on red patch instead of yellow. *Female:* — Very similar to female Common Red-wing but under parts darker. This species nests in large densely crowded colonies often numbering many thousands, whereas *A. phœniceus* is territorial.

Voice: — Notes, quite different from Red-wing's; harsher and less musical.

Range: — S. Ore. (Klamath Lake) and valleys of Calif. (w. of Sierras).

ORCHARD ORIOLE. *Icterus spurius.*

Descr. 6–7¼. *Adult male:* — A *chestnut*-and-black Oriole; all other male Orioles are either bright orange or yellow. Females are difficult to tell from other female Orioles but are decidedly *greener*. Young males have the greenish cast, and a black throat-patch.

Range: — E. U.S., breeding w. to w. Tex. (Brewster Co. and Davis Mts.); occasional in e. Colo. and e. Wyo.

AUDUBON'S ORIOLE. *Icterus melanocephalus auduboni.*
(Illus. p. 164.)

Descr. 8–9¼. A *yellow* Oriole with black head, wings, and tail. The *yellowish back* is absolutely distinctive. All other male Orioles have black backs. The sexes are similar. The only other black-headed, *yellow* Oriole, the Scott's, is found farther w., and not in the range of this species in s. Tex.

Voice: — Song, quite different from those of other Orioles; made up of low whistled notes of a human quality, disjointed, with half-tones; suggests a small boy learning to whistle.

Range: — Resident in lower Rio Grande Valley, Tex. (casually to San Antonio).

HOODED ORIOLE. *Icterus cucullatus.* Subsp. (Illus. p. 164.)
Descr. 7–7¾. *Male:* — Orange and black with a black throat and *orange crown* or 'hood.' It is the only Oriole with the top of the head orange. *Female:* — Back olive-gray, head and tail dull yellowish, under parts yellowish, wings with two white bars. Similar to female Bullock's Oriole, but with under parts entirely yellow (Bullock's has whitish belly). The immature male resembles the female but has a *black throat.* The extensively yellow belly will separate it from the corresponding plumage of the Bullock's. The bill of this species is slenderer, more curved than that of Bullock's.

Voice: — Song, a mixture of throaty notes and piping whistles, *chut chut chut whew whew,* the opening notes throaty. Song sometimes more musical. Note, a sharp *eek.*

Range: — Breeds in s. and s.-cent. Calif., s. Ariz., sw. N.M., and lower Rio Grande Valley, Tex.

Subsp. SENNETT'S ORIOLE. *I. c. sennetti.*
　　Breeds in lower Rio Grande Valley, Tex.
　　ARIZONA HOODED ORIOLE. *I. c. nelsoni.*
　　Breeds in s. and s.-cent. Calif., s. Ariz., and sw. N.M.;
　　winters in Mex.

ALTA MIRA ORIOLE. *Icterus gularis tamaulipensis.*
Descr. 8¼–9¼. A Mexican species, accidental near Brownsville, Tex. 'Almost exactly like Sennett's Hooded Oriole, but larger, thicker-billed, and more orange (does not shade off to yellow on rump and belly). The main field-mark is the upper wing-bar, which is *yellow or orange* instead of white. Sexes similar.' (Irby Davis.)

SCOTT'S ORIOLE. *Icterus parisorum.* (Illus. p. 164.)
Descr. 7¼–8¼. *Male:* — A lemon-yellow Oriole with black head, back, wings, and tail. The *solid black head* and the *yellow* instead of orange under parts distinguish it immediately from the two other Orioles which are found in its range, the Bullock's and Hooded. *Female:* — Similar to other female Orioles but of a more greenish-yellow cast beneath. (Female Hooded has more

orange-yellow under parts; female Bullock's, a whitish belly)
The immature male has a black throat similar to that of the
young male Hooded Oriole. The dingier coloration of the under
parts and the *grayish* instead of yellow cheeks will identify it.
The preferred habitat of this species is desert country, especially
where tree yuccas or agaves predominate.
Voice: — Song made up of rich variable whistled notes; suggests
Western Meadowlark.
Range: — Breeds in desert country of s. Calif., s. Nev., sw. Ut.,
Ariz., s. and cent. N.M., and w. Tex.

BALTIMORE ORIOLE. *Icterus galbula.*

Descr. 7–8. *Male:* — Bright orange and black, known from the
male Bullock's Oriole by the *solid black head* and smaller amount
of white in the wing. Along the w. edge of the Great Plains,
where the ranges of these two species overlap, puzzling hybrids
sometimes occur. *Female:* — Similar to female Bullock's, but
much more orange-yellow below, not so whitish on the belly;
back not so gray.
Range: — Summer resident in e. U.S., rarely w. to e. Mont., e.
Wyo., and e. Colo., e. of Rocky Mts. Casual in Ut.

BULLOCK'S ORIOLE. *Icterus bullocki.* (Illus. p. 164.)

Descr. 7½–8½. Smaller than a Robin. The *male* is fiery *orange
and black*, with large *white wing-patches*. Except for the Redstart, the Orioles are the only birds colored with such intense
orange. This is the only Oriole found in most sections of w.
U.S. It can be told from the others by its black crown and
orange cheeks. *Female and young:* — Olive-gray above, yellowish on tail and under parts; two white wing-bars. Female
Orioles resemble female Tanagers somewhat, but Tanagers are
darker above and on the sides of the head, and do not have such
sharp-pointed bills. This species, which looks the least Tanager-
like, resembles the females and young of other Orioles, but is less
extensively yellow below, usually with much *whitish on the belly*.
The back is decidedly grayer. Immature males resemble females but have *black throats*. They can be told from the corresponding plumage of the Hooded Oriole by the whiteness of
the belly.
Voice: — A series of accented double notes with one or two
piping notes thrown in. Call-note, a sharp *skip*; also a chatter.
Range: — Breeds from Can. s. into Mex.; winters in Mex.

RUSTY BLACKBIRD. *Euphagus carolinus.*

Descr. 8½–9½. *Male in spring:* — Very similar to male Brewer's
Blackbird, but at close range will be seen to have dull greenish
instead of purplish head reflections. The iridescence is almost
lacking, not noticeable as in the Brewer's Blackbird or the

A. BRONZED GRACKLE   B. BREWER'S BLACKBIRD, *male*

Bronzed Grackle. *Female in spring:* — Slate-colored; resembles female Brewer's Blackbird but grayer, and with the eyes *yellowish* instead of dark. *Adults and young in autumn and winter:* — Very easy to identify; more or less tinged with *rusty*, closely barred beneath. Female Red-wings are heavily *striped* beneath, not barred. No other Blackbird gives the effect of being washed with rusty or ochre on the body.

Range: — Probably a regular migrant through e. Colo., e. Wyo., and e. Mont., but often overlooked. Casual in Calif.

BREWER'S BLACKBIRD. *Euphagus cyanocephalus.* (Illus. p. 168.)

Descr. 8–9½. *Male:* — A Blackbird with a white eye; shows *purplish* reflections on head and greenish reflections on body in strong light. Looks all black at a distance. Distinguished from Red-wing by lack of red shoulders and from Cowbird by longer tail and longer, more pointed bill. *Female:* — Brownish-gray with dark eyes. Distinguished from female Red-wing by lack of stripings, and from female Cowbird by longer bill.

Voice: — Note, a harsh *check*. Song, a harsh wheezy *que-ee* or *ksh-eee*, like the creaking of a rusty hinge.

Range: — Breeds from Can. s. to Calif., n. Ariz., and N.M.; winters from Wash. and Mont. (occasionally) s. into Mex.

GREAT-TAILED GRACKLE. *Cassidix mexicanus mexicanus.* (Illus. p. 169.)

Descr. ♂ 16–17, ♀ 12–13. The Great-tail, or 'Jackdaw,' is at once recognized by its large size, a Blackbird well over a foot long with a long, wide *keel-shaped* tail. It is smaller than a Crow

GREAT-TAILED GRACKLE

or Raven, considerably larger than a Brewer's Blackbird. The proportionately large, creased tail is the best mark. The only other Grackle, the Bronzed, would not occur in the same range in the area covered by this book. Females are brown, not black, and are *much* smaller than the males.

Voice: — A harsh *check check check*, also a variety of harsh whistles and clucks.

Range: — Occurs locally in s. and w. Tex. and s. N.M., especially along Pecos and Rio Grande; possible in se. Ariz.

BRONZED GRACKLE. *Quiscalus quiscula æneus.* (Illus. p. 168.)
Descr. 11–13. Grackles are large Blackbirds, larger than Robins, with long wedge-shaped tails. A crease in the center often gives the tail a keel-shaped appearance. The line of flight is more even, not as undulating as that of other Blackbirds. Like the male Brewer's Blackbird, this species has a pale eye and iridescent coloring, but the larger size and longer tail, *which is somewhat wedge-shaped*, are good marks. The Brewer's is about the size of a Red-wing; this species, considerably larger.

Voice: — Note, *chack*; 'song,' harsh, squeaky notes.

Range: — Breeds in e. U.S. w. to foothills of Rockies in Mont., e. Wyo., and e. Colo.; casual in Ut.

COMMON COWBIRD. *Molothrus ater.* Subsp. (Illus. p. 170.)
Descr. 7–8. A rather small Blackbird with a short, conical, Sparrow-like bill. The *male* is the only black bird with a *brown* head. The *female* is uniformly gray. She can be told from the female Red-wing by her lack of streakings and from the female

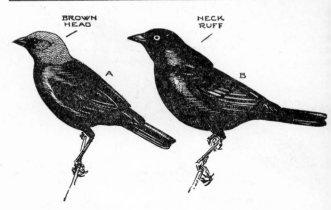

A. COWBIRD, *male*   B. RED-EYED COWBIRD, *male*

Brewer's Blackbird by the shorter bill and smaller size. When mixed in with other Blackbirds, Cowbirds are obviously smaller and walk about with their tails lifted high off the ground. The Finch-like bill is always a good mark.

Voice: — Note, *chuck*. Song, bubbly and creaky, *glug — glug — gleeee*, or *klug-tseeee*, last note high-pitched.

Range: — Breeds e. of Cascades and Sierras from Can. to Mex., and also in cent. and s. Calif. Rare in w. Ore. and w. Wash. Tends to winter in s. part of range.

Subsp. (No apparent field differences): (1) Eastern Cowbird, *M. a. ater*; (2) Nevada Cowbird, *M. a. artemisiæ*; (3) California Cowbird, *M. a. californicus*; (4) Dwarf Cowbird, *M. a. obscurus*.

RED-EYED COWBIRD. *Tangavius æneus*. (Illus. p. 170.)
Descr. 6½–8¾. *Male:* — Larger than the Cowbird and more uniform in coloration (does not have brown head). The red eye can only be seen at close range. The most distinctive field-mark in the breeding season is a conspicuous *ruff* on the back of the neck. Females are smaller, with smaller neck ruffs. They are dull blackish, more like their mates, not gray like females of *M. ater*.
Range: — S. Tex. n. to San Antonio. A race of this bird, the status of which is still unsettled, is occasional in Ariz. (vicinity of Tucson).

TANAGERS: THRAUPIDÆ

THE males of the group are among the most brilliant-colored of birds, the three species occurring in the West possessing more o less bright red. Females are duller, green above and yellow below, a little like large Warblers or Vireos; they are somewhat larger than House Sparrows. Female Tanagers are most likely to be confused with Orioles, but are sluggish, much less active, and do not have such sharp-pointed bills. The dark color of the crown comes down over the cheeks farther — nearly to the throat.

WESTERN TANAGER. *Piranga ludoviciana.* (See Frontis.)

Descr. 6¼–7. *Male:* — Yellow and black, with a *red face.* Totally unlike any other American bird. Males in autumn lose most of the red. *Female:* — Dull greenish above and yellowish below. It is the only female Tanager with conspicuous white or yellowish wing-bars. It resembles the female Bullock's Oriole, but the tail and the sides of the face are darker. The bill is shorter and not so sharply pointed.

Voice: — Song, made up of short phrases, similar to those of Black-headed Grosbeak or Robin in form, but less sustained and hoarser ('like a Grosbeak or Robin with a sore throat'). Note, a dry *pi-tic* or *pit-i-tic.*

Range: — Breeds from Can. s. to mts. of s. Calif., s. Ariz., N.M., and w. Tex.; winters in Mex.

HEPATIC TANAGER. *Piranga flava hepatica.* (See Frontis.)

Descr. 7–7¾. *Male:* — A bright-red Tanager of the sw. mts. Can be told from Cooper's Tanager by darker coloration (orange-red or flame-red), *dark ear-patch,* and *blackish bill.* (Cooper's has yellowish-brown bill.) *Female:* — Dusky above, yellowish below; can be told from female Orioles by shorter bill and lack of wing-bars, and from female Cooper's Tanager by more orange-yellow throat and *blackish* instead of yellow lower mandible. Although the two species can be found together in places, the typical habitat of the Hepatic is mountain woodlands; that of the Cooper's, low stream-bottoms.

Voice: — Song, similar to that of Cooper's Tanager, but call-note quite different, a single *chuck.*

Range: — Breeds in mts. of Ariz., N.M., and w. Tex.

COOPER'S TANAGER. *Piranga rubra cooperi.* (See Frontis.)

Descr. 7–7½. *Male:* — Bright rose-red *all over* (does not have crest like Cardinal). *Female:* — Olive above, deep yellow below. The wings lack the conspicuous white or yellowish wing-bars possessed by the female Western Tanager and the female Orioles, which it otherwise resembles. *Immature males* acquiring the adult plumage may be patched with red and green. This species is a race of the Eastern Summer Tanager. (See Hepatic Tanager.)

Voice: — Song made up of short phrases, Robin-like in form, not as 'burry' as Western Tanager. Has quality similar to that of the Black-headed Grosbeak's song. Note, *chick-tuk*, or *chick-i-tuck*, somewhat similar to Western Tanager.

Range: — Breeds chiefly along river-bottoms in se. Calif. (Colo. R.), s. Nev., s. and cent. Ariz., s. and cent. N.M., and w. Tex.

GROSBEAKS, FINCHES, SPARROWS, AND BUNTINGS: FRINGILLIDÆ

THE best character by which this family can be recognized is the bill, which is short and stout, adapted for seed-cracking. The birds not belonging to this group which are most apt to be mistaken for *Fringillidæ*, because of their stout, conical bills, are the Cowbirds and the Bobolinks. Three types of bills exist within the group: that of the Grosbeak, extremely large, thick, and rounded in outline; the more ordinary Canary-like bill, possessed by most of the Finches, Sparrows, and Buntings; and that of the Crossbill, the mandibles of which are crossed, somewhat like pruning shears, at the tips. Many of the Grosbeaks, Finches, and Buntings are highly colored, in contrast to the Sparrows, which are, for the most part, plain, streaked with brown.

CARDINAL. *Richmondena cardinalis.* Subsp. (Illus. p. 178.)
Descr. 8–9. Smaller than a Robin. *Male:* — All red except for black patch at base of bill; *the only all-red bird with a crest.* (The Pyrrhuloxia is red and gray.) *Female:* — Largely yellowish-brown, with some red; at once recognizable by crest and heavy red bill. The female Pyrrhuloxia is similar but gray-backed and with a yellow bill.
Voice: — Song, a series of clear slurred whistled notes; several variations; note, a short thin chip.
Range: — S. Ariz., sw. N.M., and cent., w., and s. Tex. Cardinals occurring in s. Calif. are supposedly introduced (probably Eastern birds).
Subsp. (No apparent field differences): (1) Gray-tailed Cardinal, *R. c. canicauda*; (2) Arizona Cardinal, *R. c. superba*.

PYRRHULOXIA. *Pyrrhuloxia sinuata.* (Illus. p. 178.)
Descr. 7½–8¼. *Male:* — A slender *gray and red Finch with a crest,* and a small stubby, almost Parrot-like bill. The rose-colored breast and crest suggest the male Cardinal, but the gray back at once sets it apart. Females are gray-backed and yellow-breasted with a touch of red in the wings and crest. They resemble female Cardinals but have yellow bills. The latter birds are brown-backed, and have large red bills. This species prefers arid country with a growth of mesquite and similar chaparral.

Voice: — Song, a clear *quink quink quink quink quink*, all on one note; also a slurred whistled *what-cheer*, *what-cheer*, etc., thinner and shorter than Cardinal's song.
Range: — S. Ariz., s. N.M., and w. and s. Tex.

BLACK-HEADED GROSBEAK. *Hedymeles melanocephalus.* Subsp. (Illus. p. 164.)
Descr. 6½–7¾. *Male:* — The *rusty* breast, *black* head, and boldly marked black-and-white wings make it unmistakable. The only Western birds whose coloration remotely resembles it are the Robin, Varied Thrush, and Spotted Towhee, none of which would be confused with it. *Female:* — Largely brown, but easily recognized by its *rusty-brown* breast, *striped head*, and heavy pale bill.
Voice: — Song made up of rising and falling passages; resembles song of Robin, but more fluent and mellow; note, a sharp *ik* or *eek*. Easterners will note resemblance to Rose-breasted Grosbeak's voice.
Range: — Breeds from Can. s. to Mex.
Subsp. (No apparent field differences): (1) Black-headed Grosbeak, *H. m. melanocephalus*; (2) Rocky Mountain Grosbeak, *H. m. papago.*

BLUE GROSBEAK. *Guiraca cærulea.* Subsp. (Illus. p. 164.)
Descr. 6½–7½. *Male:* — Deep dull blue; appears black at distance, then resembling Cowbird. The only other *all-blue* bird is the Mountain Bluebird. The Grosbeak has a much larger bill than the Bluebird, and shows two broad *chestnut-brown* wing-bars. *Female:* — Larger than House Sparrow, or about size of Cowbird; brown, lighter below, with two *buffy* wing-bars. The female Lazuli Bunting resembles it somewhat, but is smaller (smaller than House Sparrow), with a much smaller bill. The preferred habitat is willows or brush along low stream-bottoms.
Voice: — Song, a Finch-like warble, short phrases rising and falling. Suggests song of Purple Finch but slower in tempo. Note, a sharp *pink* slightly more musical than similar note of Brown Towhee.
Range: — Breeds in river-valleys in s. and cent. Calif., s. Nev., s. Colo., Ariz., N.M., and w. Tex.
Subsp. (No apparent field differences): (1) Western Blue Grosbeak, *G. c. interfusa*; (2) California Blue Grosbeak, *G. c. salicaria.*

LAZULI BUNTING. *Passerina amœna.* (Illus. p. 164.)
Descr. 5–5½. *Male:* — A small bright-blue Finch. Head and upper parts *turquoise blue*; band across breast and sides *cinnamon*; belly and wing-bars white. It is most likely to be mistaken by the beginner for a Western Bluebird, but the small size, short

Finch bill, and *white wing-bars* are the distinctive points. *Female:* — A small nondescript Finch, *brownish* above and below, lightening on throat and belly. It has whitish wing-bars, and at close range just a trace of gray-blue in the wings and tail. The lack of streakings on the back or breast distinguish it from any of the dull Sparrows. It can be told from the female Blue Grosbeak by its smaller size, smaller bill, whiter wing-bars, and darker coloration. Prefers dry brushy canyon-slopes and hillsides.

Voice: — A high and strident Finch song with well-measured phrases at varying pitches. Introductory notes usually paired — *sweet-sweet, chew-chew*, etc. Easterners will note resemblance to Indigo Bunting's song.

Range: — Breeds from Can. s. to s. Calif., n. Ariz. (probably), n. N.M. (a few), and w. Tex.; migrates into Mex.

VARIED BUNTING. *Passerina versicolor.* Subsp. (Illus. p. 164.)

Descr. $4\frac{1}{2}$–$5\frac{1}{2}$. *Male:* — A small dark Finch with a plum-purple body (looks black at distance); crown blue with a *bright red patch on the nape*, 'colored like an Easter egg.' The nearest thing to it is the more brightly colored Painted Bunting, which has a bright red breast. *Female:* — A small plain *gray-brown* Finch with a lighter breast. *No wing-bars, stripes, or distinctive marks of any kind.* Very similar to female Indigo Bunting, but latter species is browner with a trace of wing-bars and faint blurry breast-streakings. Female Seedeater is smaller and browner and has wing-bars. Immature male Varied Buntings are tinged with bluish. This species prefers dry mesquite thickets.

Voice: — Song, a thin bright Finch song, more distinctly phrased and less warbled than Painted Bunting. Notes not so distinctly paired as in song of Lazuli Bunting.

Range: — Breeds in lower Rio Grande Valley, Tex.; local or casual in s. Ariz. and se. Calif.

Subsp. (No apparent field differences): (1) Varied Bunting, *P. v. versicolor*; (2) Beautiful Bunting, *P. v. pulchra.*

PAINTED BUNTING. *Passerina ciris.* (Illus. p. 164.)

Descr. $5\frac{1}{4}$. Of all our birds undoubtedly the most gaudily colored. *Male:* — A little Chippy-sized Finch, a patchwork of *bright red, green, and indigo* — blue-violet on head, green on back, red on rump and under parts. *Female:* — Very plain; greenish above, paling to lemon-green below; no wing-bars. The only other small greenish Finch, the female Arkansas Goldfinch, has whitish wing-bars.

Voice: — Song, a bright, pleasing warble; resembles song of Warbling Vireo but more wiry; note, a sharp chip.

Range: — Breeds in se. U.S. w. to w. Tex. and s. N.M. (Pecos and Rio Grande Valleys); occasional in s. Ariz.

DICKCISSEL. *Spiza americana.* (Illus. p. 164.)
Descr. 6–7. About size of House Sparrow but a bit slimmer. *Male:* — Suggestive of tiny Meadowlark, with yellow breast and black bib. *Female:* — Very much like female House Sparrow, but paler, with much whiter stripe over eye, touch of yellow on breast, and bluish bill. Chestnut bend of wing is also distinctive. The Dickcissel is a frequenter of prairie country. Males in fall have the black of throat obscured or lacking.
Voice: — Song, a staccato, mechanical-sounding rendering of its name — *Dick-ciss-ciss.*
Range: — Breeds in e. Wyo. and e. Colo. (a few); migrates through Tex.; occasional in N.M. and Ariz.

EVENING GROSBEAK. *Hesperiphona vespertina.* Subsp. (Illus. p. 178.)
Descr. 7½–8½. A large, chunky, short-tailed Finch, considerably larger than House Sparrow. The dusky, dull yellowish color, and extremely large, conical whitish bill distinguish it at once. A wing, recognized as a Finch by the characteristic undulating flight and distinguished from Pine Grosbeak, only Conifer Finch of similar size, by shorter tail. The large white wing-patches show at a great distance in flight. Snow Bunting is only other northern or winter Finch showing so much white in wing. *Male:* — Body clouded with dusky around head and breast, dull yellowish toward rear parts; wings black with large white patches, bright yellow patch on forehead. *Female:* — Gray, but with just enough of the yellow and the black and white to be recognizable. The female Pine Grosbeak is slimmer, with a smaller *dark* bill, much less white in the wing, *none in the tail.* The Eastern Evening Grosbeak, which winters s. to e. Wyo. and probably Wash., is easily distinguished from the Western bird by its less dusky coloration. The yellow is much more extensive on the back and under parts.
Voice: — Song, a short uneven warble; note, a ringing Finch-like chirp, *cleer* or *clee-ip.*
Range: — Breeds in high mts. from Can. s. to Sierra Nevada of cent. Calif. and mts. of s. Ariz. and N.M. Winters in adjacent lowlands and s. to s. Calif.
Subsp. (No apparent field differences except in No. 1 — see above): (1) Eastern Evening Grosbeak, *H. v. vespertina*; (2) Western Evening Grosbeak, *H. v. brooksi*; (3) Mexican Evening Grosbeak, *H. v. montana.*

CALIFORNIA PURPLE FINCH. *Carpodacus purpureus californicus.* (Illus. p. 178.)

Descr. 5¼–6. Purple is hardly the word; old rose is more like it. *Male:* — About size of House Sparrow or Linnet, rosy-red, brightest on head and rump ('like a Sparrow dipped in berry juice'). It resembles closely the male House Finch, or Linnet, but *lacks* the sharp dark streakings on the breast and belly. In parts of the Sierras and Cascades, the breeding ranges of the California Purple Finch and the Cassin's Purple Finch overlap. The latter species can be told by its pale breast coloration and the squarish red crown-patch, which contrasts abruptly with the brown of the neck and back. The red of the California Purple Finch blends in more smoothly. (See Pine Grosbeak and Redpoll.) *Female:* — A heavily striped brown Sparrow-like bird with a broad whitish line over the eye. The large stout bill distinguishes it from the streaked Sparrows. The best mark of distinction from the female House Finch is the *dark cheek-patch behind the eye*, bordered above and below by broad pale stripes. Immature birds resemble females. (See Cassin's Purple Finch.) **Voice:** — Song, a fast, lively warble; resembles song of House Finch but is lower in pitch, shorter in length, less disjointed; more rolling and well knit. Note, a dull metallic *tick*, or *pit*, unlike any note of the House Finch.
Range: — Breeds in Transition Zone of Pacific States from Can. to Mex. and e. to Cascades and Sierra Nevadas. Distributed more widely in winter.

CASSIN'S PURPLE FINCH. *Carpodacus cassini.* (Illus. p. 178.)
Descr. 6–6½. The Purple Finch of the Rocky Mt. region. (It occasionally wanders to the Coast.) *Male:* — Similar to the California Purple Finch (which breeds only in Pacific States) but larger, red of breast paler, and tail more deeply notched; *squarish red crown-patch contrasting abruptly with brown of neck and back.* This and the *lack* of sharply defined belly streakings distinguish it from the House Finch. See Pine Grosbeak and Redpoll. *Female:* — A streaked brown Sparrow-like bird; back olive-gray streaked with black; under parts whitish narrowly streaked with dark. The larger size and sharper dark stripings on the back and under parts distinguish it from the female House Finch. The larger size, whiter under parts, and narrow breast-streakings distinguish it from the female California Purple Finch.
Voice: — Song, a lively warble, similar to that of California Purple Finch but not so closely knit; halfway between song of House Finch and Purple Finch.
Range: — Breeds in high mts. from Can. s. to n. Ariz. and n. N.M., and from Rockies w. to Cascades and Sierras, where the California Purple Finch is also found; Cassin's prefers higher altitudes. Wanders to adjacent lowlands in winter.

HOUSE FINCH, *or* **LINNET.** *Carpodacus mexicanus.* Subsp. (Illus. p. 178.)

Descr. 5½. *Male:* — Near size of House Sparrow, brownish with *bright red* breast, forehead, stripe over eye, and rump. It resembles the male of the Purple Finches (which do not nest about buildings) but is brighter red, not so rose-colored. Some individuals are almost orange. The *narrow dark stripes* on the sides and belly are the best mark of distinction. *Female:* — A striped Sparrow-like bird, gray-brown above; under parts whitish streaked with dusky. See female California Purple Finch and female Cassin's Purple Finch.

Voice: — A bright lengthy Finch song, loose and disjointed in structure. Sometimes the song ends in a harsh nasal *wheer* or *che-urr.* Notes, Finch-like, some of them reminiscent of chirping of English Sparrow but more musical.

Range: — Resident in lowlands, deserts, open country, foothills, and towns from se. Wash., Ore., s. Idaho, and s. Wyo. s. into Mex.

Subsp. (No apparent field differences): (1) Common House Finch, *C. m. frontalis*; (2) San Clemente House Finch, *C. m. clementis*; (3) San Luis House Finch, *C. m. potosinus.*

SHARPE'S SEEDEATER. *Sporophila morelleti sharpei.* (Illus. p. 178.)

Descr. 3¾–4¼. *Male:* — A very small Finch with whitish or buffy under parts and blackish upper parts, wings, and tail. Much white in the wing; bill very short, stubby, and swollen. There is often a narrow, indistinct dark breast-band and a light collar around the neck. The Goldfinch (*Spinus tristis*) in winter plumage resembles this species but has a bigger, longer bill. *Female:* — A tiny brown-backed Finch with buffy under parts and light wing-bars. The small size, buffy under parts, and stubby bill are good marks. The amount of white in the wings varies (See female Varied Bunting.)

Voice: — A sweet loud song for so small a bird; begins on several high repeated notes and drops to several notes on a lower pitch; *sweet sweet sweet sweet, cheer cheer cheer cheer* (often only two *cheers*).

Range: — Lower Rio Grande Valley, Tex.

PINE GROSBEAK. *Pinicola enucleator.* Subsp. (Illus. p. 178.)

Descr. 8–9½. The largest of the Conifer Finches; near the size of a Robin. *Male:* — Large size, rosy-red color, and two white wing-bars identify it. (The White-winged Crossbill is rosy-red with white wing-bars, but is smaller, about size of House Sparrow, with slender cross-tipped bill.) *Female:* — Gray with two white wing-bars; head and rump tinged with yellow. *Immature male:* — Similar to female but with touch of red on head and rump. A Robin-sized Finch in the conifer forests of the high mountains is quite surely this species. The Evening Grosbeak is shorter-tailed, with chunkier proportions. All Finches rise and fall in their flight, but this one is a regular 'roller-coaster.'

Voice: — Song, melodious; most characteristic call, a clear three-syllabled whistle, *tee-tee-tew*, remarkably like cry of Greater Yellow-legs.

Range: — Resident in high mts. from Can. s. to n. N.M., cent.-e. Ariz., and cent. Sierra Nevada, Calif.; winters sometimes to lower altitudes, esp. in nw.

Subsp. (No apparent field differences): (1) Alaska Pine Grosbeak, *P. e. alascensis*; (2) Kodiak Pine Grosbeak, *P. e. flammula*; (3) Rocky Mountain Pine Grosbeak, *P. e. montana*; (4) California Pine Grosbeak, *P. e. californica*.

GRAY-CROWNED ROSY FINCH, or LEUCOSTICTE. *Leucosticte tephrocotis.* Subsp. (Illus. p. 178.)

Descr. 5¾–6¾. A Sparrow-sized bird of the snow-fields of nigh mts. above timber line. *Dark brown body* with a *pinkish wash* on the wings and rump. The dark brown breast and *light gray patch* on the back of the head distinguish this species from the other rose-colored Finches (Purple Finches, Redpolls, Crossbills, etc.). Females are duller than males, with the gray crown-patch less conspicuous or almost wanting.

Voice: — High Finch-like chirping notes, suggestive of English Sparrow.

Subsp. HEPBURN'S ROSY FINCH. *L. t. littoralis.*
Distinguished in field from next race by the gray of the crown, which extends *below the eye across the cheeks, often to the throat.* Breeds above timber line on mts. from Alaska s. in Cascades to n. Calif.; winters se. in mts. to e. Calif., Nev., Idaho, Mont., Wyo., Ut., and Colo.

GRAY-CROWNED ROSY FINCH. *L. t. tephrocotis.*
Breeds from nw. Mont. n. into Can. In winter w. to Cascades and s. to Ut. and Colo.

SIERRA NEVADA ROSY FINCH. *L. t. dawsoni.*
Breeds on high peaks of cent. Sierra Nevadas, Calif. Similar to above race but somewhat darker.

BLACK ROSY FINCH. *Leucosticte atrata.* (Illus. p. 178.)

Descr. 6. Similar to Gray-crowned Rosy Finch, but with body *blackish* instead of chestnut-brown.

Voice: — Similar to preceding species; high-pitched chirping notes. 'A rather high-pitched plaintive *cheew* repeated continuously' (C. W. Lockerbie).

Range: — Breeds in Salmon R. Mts. of Idaho, mts. of n. Ut., and mts. of w. Wyo.; winters to Mont., se. Wyo., s. Ut., Colo., and N.M.

GROSBEAKS, FINCHES, SNOW BUNTING, JUNCO

1. PYRRHULOXIA, *a.* MALE; *b.* FEMALE

2. CARDINAL, *a.* MALE; *b.* FEMALE

3. WHITE-WINGED CROSSBILL, *a.* MALE; *b.* FEMALE

4. PINE GROSBEAK, *a.* MALE; *b.* FEMALE

5. RED CROSSBILL, *a.* MALE; *b.* FEMALE

6. CASSIN'S PURPLE FINCH, *a.* MALE; *b.* FEMALE

7. CALIFORNIA PURPLE FINCH, *a.* MALE; *b.* FEMALE

8. HOUSE FINCH OR LINNET, *a.* MALE; *b.* FEMALE

9. REDPOLL, *a.* MALE; *b.* FEMALE

10. BLACK ROSY FINCH, MALE

11. *a.* GRAY-CROWNED ROSY FINCH, MALE; *b.* HEPBURN'S ROSY FINCH, MALE

12. BROWN-CAPPED ROSY FINCH, MALE

13. PINE SISKIN

14. EVENING GROSBEAK, *a.* MALE; *b.* FEMALE

15. SHARPE'S SEEDEATER, *a.* MALE; *b.* FEMALE

16. LAWRENCE'S GOLDFINCH, *a.* MALE; *b.* FEMALE

17. COMMON GOLDFINCH, *a.* MALE; *b.* FEMALE

18. *a.* GREEN-BACKED GOLDFINCH, MALE; *b.* ARKANSAS GOLD-FINCH, MALE

19. SNOW BUNTING, *a.* MALE IN WINTER; *b.* FEMALE

20. OREGON JUNCO, MALE

BROWN-CAPPED ROSY FINCH. *Leucosticte australis.* (Illus. p. 178.)
Descr. 5¾–6¼. Similar to Gray-crowned Rosy Finch, but with brown of body *lighter* and head *without* conspicuous light-gray patch; crown dusky or blackish. Female Gray-crowned Rosy Finches often have very little evidence of a light crown-patch but are duskier in general color, not so light a brown as this species.
Voice: — Similar to other Rosy Finches.
Range: — Breeds in high mts. of Colo. and probably in n. N.M.; winters in valleys of Colo. and s. into N.M.

HOARY REDPOLL. *Acanthis hornemanni exilipes.*
Descr. 4½–5½. Similar to Common Redpoll, but smaller and whiter. The white rump, *devoid of streakings*, is the best mark.
Range: — Subarctic; very rare winter visitor to Mont.

REDPOLL. *Acanthis linaria.* Subsp. (Illus. p. 178.)
Descr. 5–5½. In notes, size, shape, and actions, Redpolls resemble Goldfinches and Siskins; little streaked, gray-brown birds that may be known in any plumage by a *bright-red cap* on the forehead and a *black chin. Males* are pink-breasted. Purple Finches are larger and redder (*entire head* and much of back and under parts are reddish); Siskins are darker with more heavily striped under parts. Prefers open country, and birches.
Voice: — Most characteristic note, *chug* or *chet-chet.*
Subsp. COMMON REDPOLL. *A. l. linaria.*
Subarctic, wandering irregularly s. in winter to e. Ore. and Colo.
GREATER REDPOLL. *A. l. rostrata.*
Somewhat larger (5½–6), darker, and with larger bill than Common Redpoll. Difference can sometimes be made out when the two birds are together in same flock. Winters s. to Mont., casually to Colo.

PINE SISKIN. *Spinus pinus pinus.* (Illus. p. 178.)
Descr. 4½–5. A small *heavily streaked* brown Finch with a *flash of yellow* in wing and tail. In size and actions resembles Goldfinch. All Goldfinches are unstreaked; Redpolls are paler, without the heavy streakings across front of breast; female Purple Finches and House Finches are similar, but larger (size of House Sparrow), with larger bills. None of these (except dissimilar Lawrence's Goldfinch) shows any yellow in either wings or tail. Most Siskins are seen flying high overhead, uttering their characteristic calls.
Voice: — Song, similar to Goldfinch's, but more coarse and wheezy; commonest call, a loud *clee-ip* or *chlee-ip*, also a light

tit-i-tit and a long buzzy *shreeeee* — latter unique among bird-notes.

Range: — Breeds chiefly in evergreen forests of mts. from Can. s. to s. Calif., Ariz., and N.M.; in migration and winter throughout most of w. U.S.

COMMON GOLDFINCH. *Spinus tristis.* Subsp. (Illus. p. 178.)

Descr. 5–5½. Smaller than a House Sparrow. Flight extremely undulating. *Male in summer:* — *A small yellow bird with black wings.* The Yellow Warbler, which shares with this bird the nickname 'Yellow-bird' and 'Wild Canary,' is yellow all over. The bright yellow back distinguishes this species from other Goldfinches. *Female in summer:* — Dull olive-yellow with blackish wings; distinguished from other small olive-yellow birds (Warblers, etc.) by its stout Finch bill. (See female Arkansas Goldfinch.) *Winter males, immatures, etc.:* — Much like the summer female. The two similar small winter Finches, the Redpoll and the Siskin, are *streaked*; the Goldfinch is evenly colored above and below.

Voice: — Song, a clear, long-sustained Canary-like warble. Each dip in flight often punctuated by a simple *ti-tee-di-di*.

Range: — Breeds from Can. s. to Colo., Nev., and s. Calif.; winters from Can. to Mex.

Subsp. (No apparent field differences): (1) Eastern Goldfinch, *S. t. tristis*; (2) Pale Goldfinch, *S. t. pallidus*; (3) Willow Goldfinch, *S. t. salicamans*.

ARKANSAS GREEN-BACKED} GOLDFINCH. *Spinus psaltria.* Subsp. (Illus. p. 178.)

Descr. 4. *Male:* — A very small *yellow-breasted* Finch with a *black cap* and black-and-white wings. It can be easily told in the breeding plumage from the male Common Goldfinch, *S. tristis*, by the absence of the bright-yellow back. In the winter, males of the latter species become brownish and lose their caps. Males of the present species retain the black cap all winter. Males of the two races of this species are quite distinctive. (See *subsp.*, below.) *Female:* — Very similar to female of Common Goldfinch, *S. tristis*, but back more greenish, not so brownish.

Voice: — Sweet plaintive notes very distinctive: *tee-yee* (rising inflection) and *tee-yer* (dropping inflection). Song, Canary-like, more phrased and less sustained than that of Goldfinch (*S. tristis*).

Subsp. ARKANSAS GOLDFINCH. *S. p. psaltria.*
Males have *black* backs. From Colo., N.M., and cent.-n. Tex. s. into Mex.
GREEN-BACKED GOLDFINCH. *S. p. hesperophilus.*

Males have *olive-green* backs. Immature male Arkansas Goldfinches are olive-backed, but have telltale blackish streakings on the back. Breeds from Ore. and Ut. through s. Calif. and s. Ariz.; winters from n. Calif. and s. Ariz. s. into Mex.

LAWRENCE'S GOLDFINCH. *Spinus lawrencei.* (Illus. p. 178.)
Descr. 4–4½. *Male:* — A gray-headed Goldfinch with a touch of yellow on the throat and rump, and *broad yellow wing-bars.* It has a black patch on the forehead and chin. No other male Goldfinch has a *black chin.* There is no seasonal change. *Female:* — Similar to male without black face-patch. The grayer color and *broad yellow wing-bars* distinguish her from other female Goldfinches.
Voice: — Song similar to that of Common Goldfinch (*S. tristis*). Call-note, distinctive; 'can be written *tink-oo*, the syllables emphasized equally. I have almost duplicated it by striking a glass tumbler, then a small plate with a spoon.' (Frank Watson.)
Range: — Breeds in cent. and s. Calif. w. of Sierras; winters in s. Calif. and sw. Ariz. (Colo. R. Valley).

RED CROSSBILL. *Loxia curvirostra.* Subsp. (Illus. p. 178.)
Descr. 5¼–6½. Size near that of House Sparrow. The sound made by the cracking open of the cones of evergreen trees, upon which they mainly feed, often betrays their presence. The crossed, pruning-shear mandibles are distinctive; at a distance, when crossed tips are not visible, the comparative slenderness of the bill is obvious (bills of other Finches are relatively shorter and stouter). *Male:* — *Brick-red*, brighter on the rump; wings and tail dusky. Several other Finches are *rosy-red*, but this is only brick-red bird of group. *Female:* — Dull olive-gray; yellowish on the rump and under parts. The plain dark wings distinguish this species from white-winged Crossbill. Immature birds are heavily striped above and below, and look like large Pine Siskins. The larger, crossed bill and absence of yellow in the wings are the points to look for.
Voice: — Song, Finch-like warbled passages; note, a hard *pip-pip* or *pip-pip-pip.*
Range: — Breeds in evergreens in high mts. from Can. s. to cent.-w. Tex., s. Ariz., s. N.M., and s. Calif., and along coast from Wash. to n. Calif.
Subsp. (No apparent field differences): (1) Sitka Crossbill, *L. c. sitkensis*; (2) Bendire's Crossbill, *L. c. bendirei*; (3) Mexican Crossbill, *L. c. stricklandi.*

WHITE-WINGED CROSSBILL. *Loxia leucoptera.* (Illus. p. 178.)
Descr. 6–6¾. *Male:* — Size of House Sparrow; *rosy-pink* with black wings and tail and *two broad white wing-bars.* The Pine

Grosbeak is rosy, with white wing-bars, but is much larger (near size of Robin). *Female and young:* — Olive-gray with yellowish rump, like Red Crossbill, but with *two broad white wing-bars.* The wing-bars are often quite evident when the birds are in flight and help in picking out individuals of this species from mixed flocks of Crossbills. Both Crossbills are usually found in conifers.

Voice: — A comparison of the notes of the two Crossbills will help. The common notes of the White-wing are a sweet *peet* and a dry *chif-chif.* The note corresponding to the *chif-chif* in the Red Crossbill is a hard *pip* or *pip-pip.* Song of White-winged Crossbill, a succession of loud trills on different pitches.

Range: — Breeds in Can.; winters irregularly s. to Puget Sound, n. Ore. (Cascades), and Colo.

TEXAS SPARROW. *Arremonops rufivirgatus rufivirgatus.* (Illus. p. 164.)

Descr. 5½–6. About size of House Sparrow, a plain *olive-backed* Finch with two broad dull-brown stripes on the crown. Upper parts uniform in coloration, without wing-bars or stripes on the back. Under parts whitish, with buffy wash across breast and along sides. Because of its olive-green back it resembles the Green-tailed Towhee, which sometimes occurs in its range in winter, more than it does any Sparrow. The Green-tailed Towhee is larger, with a gray breast, clear-cut white throat, and solid rufous crown.

Voice: — Song, a series of dry notes all on one pitch, starting off deliberately and trailing off into a Chippy-like rattle. 'Also an insect-like buzz as the birds chase each other through the thickets' (Irby Davis).

Range: — S. Tex. n. to Corpus Christi.

GREEN-TAILED TOWHEE. *Oberholseria chlorura.* (Illus. p. 164.)

Descr. 6¼–7. Slightly larger than House Sparrow, a ground-dwelling Finch with a plain *olive-green back, rufous* crown, and conspicuous *white* throat; breast gray. The rufous cap and white throat are the best marks. Some races of the Brown Towhee have quite a rusty crown, but the throat is always buffy.

Voice: — A mewing note like a kitten, and a *chink* like Brown Towhee; song, somewhat Song-Sparrow-like in quality, opening with one or two sweet notes and ending in long burry notes: *weet-chur — cheeeeeee — churrrr.* Often confused with Fox Sparrow's song but less brilliant and musical. Has more of a dry burr in the long notes.

Range: — Breeds in mts. from cent. Ore. and s.-cent. Mont. s. to s. Calif., se. N.M., and cent.-w. Tex.; w. to Cascades and Sierras; winters from s. Calif., s. Ariz., and w. Tex. s. into Mex.

These three have single breast spots

"WHISKER-MARK"
SOLID

"WHISKER-MARK"
USUALLY
BROKEN OR
RAGGED

CHESTNUT
CHEEK-PATCH

WHITE
CORNERS

BELL'S   SAGE   LARK

FOX

HEAVILY-
SPOTTED

TAIL TINGED
WITH RUSTY

VESPER

WHITE OUTER
TAIL FEATHERS

LARGE
CENTRAL
SPOT

SHORT
BREAST
STRIPES

OCHRE HEAD
STRIPINGS

UFFY
REAST-BAND

LINCOLN'S   SONG   BAIRD'S

LIKE SAVANNAH
BUT BACK-
MARKINGS
WASHED OUT,
CROWN-STRIPE
OBSCURE

RESEMBLES
SONG, BUT
WITH WHITISH
CROWN-STRIPE
AND NOTCHED
TAIL

LIKE SAVANNAH
BUT DARKER,
CROWN-STRIPE
OBSCURE

RGE
ILL

LARGE BILLED   SAVANNAH   BELDING'S

CROWN
STRIPED

BACK PLAINLY
MARKED

CROWN
SOLID

BACK OBSCURELY
MARKED

These two
have clear breasts

GRASSHOPPER   CASSIN'S

SPARROWS I

These three have rufous-red caps

WHITE EYE-STRIPE →

BLACK "WHISKER"

CENTRAL SPOT

TREE

CHIPPING
SPRING

RUFOUS-CROWNED

STRIPED CROWN

BROWN CHEEK-PATCH

CROWN SOLID, FINELY STREAKED

CLAY-

COLORED
SPRING

BREWER'S

BLACK CROWN

← These three have black throats

WHITE STRIPES

GRAY HEAD

HARRIS'S
ADULT

DESERT

BLACK-CHINNED

BUFFY CHEEKS

BLACK AND WHITE CROWNS

GRAY THROAT

WHITE THROAT

BLACK BLOTCH

HARRIS'S
IMM.

WHITE-CROWNED
ADULT

WHITE-THROATED
ADULT

YELLOW CROWN

BROWN AND BUFF HEAD STRIPES

GOLDEN CROWNED
ADULT

WHITE-CROWNED
IMM.

SPARROWS II

SPOTTED TOWHEE. *Pipilo maculatus.* Subsp. (Illus. p. 164.)
Descr. 7–8¼. Smaller and more slender than Robin, which it
remotely resembles; *reddish confined to the sides.* Frequents
brushy places; often detected by noisy rummaging among dead
leaves. *Male:* — Entire head and upper parts black, with rows
of numerous *white spots* on back and wings; *sides Robin-red;* belly
white. In flight, bird looks black, with large white spots showing
toward outer tips of long, ample tail. *Female:* — Similar, but
head dusky brown instead of black.
Voice: — A drawn-out, buzzy trill, *chweeeeeee.* Some races utter
two or three low short introductory notes; *chup chup chup
zeeeeeeeee.*
Range: — Breeds from Can. to Mex. and from Great Plains and
w. Tex. to the Pacific; winters in Pacific States and from Ariz.
and N.M. s.
Subsp. (No apparent field differences): (1) Arctic Towhee,
P. m. arcticus; (2) Spurred Towhee, *P. m. montanus;* (3) Nevada
Towhee, *P. m. curtatus;* (4) Oregon Towhee, *P. m. oregonus;*
(5) Sacramento Towhee, *P. m. falcinellus;* (6) San Francisco
Towhee, *P. m. falcifer;* (7) San Diego Towhee, *P. m. megalonyx;*
(8) San Clemente Towhee, *P. m. clementæ.*

BROWN TOWHEE. *Pipilo fuscus.* Subsp. (Illus. p. 164.)
Descr. 8¼–9½. A rather large dull-gray-brown bird with a moderately long tail; suggests a very plain overgrown Sparrow. The
only distinctive marks on this somber Finch are the pale-*rusty
under tail-coverts* and the streaked buffy throat. It can be told
from the Thrashers, which it somewhat resembles, by its
smaller size and short Sparrow-like bill. Lives on ground and
among brush. The race known as the Cañon Towhee (Ariz.,
N.M., s. Colo., and w. Tex.) can be told from the Brown
Towhees of the Pacific States by its rufous crown and obscure
central breast-spot.
Voice: — Note, a sharp metallic *chink.* Song, a rapid *chink-
chink-ink-ink-ink-ink-ink-ink,* almost like a repetition of the
ordinary call-note. The series often ends in a trill. In some
races the song sounds more like *chilp — chilp — chilp — chilp
— chilp — chilp — chilp.*
Range: — Sw. Ore. (Josephine, Jackson, and Douglas Cos.),
Calif., Ariz., N.M., s. Colo., and w. Tex. The Abert's Towhee,
P. aberti, replaces this species in the Colorado Desert of se.
Calif. and the hot deserts along the Colorado R. and its tributaries in s. and w. Ariz.
Subsp (No apparent field differences except in No. 5 — see
above): (1) Oregon Brown Towhee, *P. f. bullatus;* (2) Sacramento Brown Towhee, *P. f. carolæ;* (3) San Francisco Brown
Towhee, *P. f. petulans;* (4) California Brown Towhee, *P. f.
crissalis;* (5) Cañon Towhee, *P. f. mesoleucus.*

ABERT'S TOWHEE. *Pipilo aberti.* (Illus. p. 164.)
Descr. 8¼–9. A desert species, similar to the Brown Towhee, but browner, the entire under parts buffy-brown. The best mark is a *black patch* around the base of the bill.
Voice: — Similar to Brown Towhee.
Range: — Deserts of se. Calif. (Colo. Desert w. to Palm Springs), s. Nev., sw. Ut., s. Ariz., and sw. N.M.

LARK BUNTING. *Calamospiza melanocorys.* (Illus. p. 163.)
Descr. 5½–7½. *Male in spring:* — Like a small Blackbird (about House Sparrow size) *with large white wing-patches.* (Bobolink has much white *on back* as well as on wings; both are open-country birds.) *Females, young,* and *autumn males* are brown with stripings on breast; they slightly resemble female Purple Finches except for their paler color and open-country habitat. Usually some members of the flock show white or buffy wing-patches.
Voice: — Song, sweet and trilling.
Range: — Breeds in prairie country of Mont., Wyo., Colo., e. N.M., and nw. Tex., chiefly on Great Plains, but also sparingly w. of Continental Divide. Winters in s. Tex., Ariz., and deserts of se. Calif.

SAVANNAH SPARROW. *Passerculus sandwichensis.* Subsp. (Illus. p. 182.)
Descr. 4¾–6. An open-country Sparrow; like a *short-tailed* Song Sparrow with a pale or *yellowish stripe* over the eye, a whitish stripe through the crown, and *pale pink legs.* The tail of a Savannah Sparrow is slightly forked, not rounded like that of the Song Sparrow.
Voice: — Song, a dreamy lisping *tsit-tsit-tsit-tseeee-tseee* (last note dropping). At a distance only the two long notes can be heard.
Range: — Breeds from Can. s. to cent. Calif., Nev., Colo., and n. N.M.; migrates s. into Mex.; and winters in the Pacific States, Ariz., N.M., and Tex.
Subsp. (No apparent field differences): (1) Western Savannah Sparrow, *P. s. alaudinus*; (2) Aleutian Savannah Sparrow, *P. s. sandwichensis*; (3) Nevada Savannah Sparrow, *P. s. nevadensis*; (4) Bryant's Sparrow, *P. s. bryanti.*

BELDING'S SPARROW. *Passerculus beldingi.* (Illus. p. 182.)
Descr. 4½–5½. Similar to the Savannah Sparrow, with which it is often found, but *breast-streakings heavier and blacker* and stripe through crown *indistinct.* The legs are browner, not so pinkish. An inhabitant of salt marshes of s. Calif. (See Large-billed Sparrow.)

Voice: — Song similar to Savannah Sparrow but with more emphatic ending, *tsip tsip tsip tsree, tsick-a-tsee* (Hoffmann).
Range: — Breeds in salt marshes of s. Calif., n. to Santa Barbara.

LARGE-BILLED SPARROW. *Passerculus rostratus.* Subsp. (Illus. p. 182.)

Descr. $4\frac{3}{4}$–$5\frac{3}{4}$. Similar to Belding's and Savannah Sparrows, with which it is often found, but much paler and *browner without the well-defined dark markings on the back and wings*; breast-streakings brownish, not black. One of the best marks is the bill, which is *much heavier* than that of either the Belding's or Savannah. An inhabitant of coastal marshes of s. Calif. Also likes vicinity of buildings. Easterners will be reminded of the Ipswich Sparrow.
Range: — Breeds in Mex. and Lower Calif.; winters along coast of s. Calif. n. to Santa Barbara.
Subsp. (No apparent field differences): (1) Large-billed Sparrow, *P. r. rostratus*; (2) San Lucas Sparrow, *P. r. guttatus*.

(WESTERN) GRASSHOPPER SPARROW. *Ammodramus savannarum bimaculatus.* (Illus. p. 182.)

Descr. $4\frac{1}{4}$–5. A *short-tailed*, flat-headed little Sparrow of the open fields; crown with a pale stripe through the center; back striped with chestnut and black. Differs from the Savannah Sparrow in having an *unstreaked* buffy breast. Its flight is comparatively weak. The conspicuously striped back, very short tail, and unstreaked buffy breast are the best marks.
Voice: — Two songs; well described by Guy Emerson as ' (1) an insect-like tumble of notes, (2) two short introductory notes and a long thin buzz, without change of pitch — *pit-tuck zeeeeeeeeeeee.*' The second song is the more characteristic.
Range: — Breeds locally from e. Wash. and Mont. s. to s. Calif. (w. of Sierras), Colo., and s. Tex.; winters from cent. Calif. and s. Tex. s.; a few migrate through Ariz. and N.M.

BAIRD'S SPARROW. *Ammodramus bairdi.* (Illus. p. 182.)

Descr. 5–$5\frac{1}{2}$. An open-country Sparrow with a light breast crossed by a *narrow band of fine black streaks*. Head yellow-brown streaked with black. The best mark is the *very broad center stripe on the crown*, which is conspicuously *ochre*. The Savannah Sparrow has more extensive streakings on the under parts, not confined to a narrow band. The light stripe through the crown is much narrower. The habitat of the Baird's Sparrow is dry upland prairies where the native grass is long.
Voice: — Song often begins with three or four musical chips and ends in a trill in a lower pitch; more musical than insect-like efforts of Savannah; variable.

Range: — Breeds from Can. to cent. Mont. (rarely); migrates through e. Wyo., Colo., N.M., and se. Ariz.; winters from cent. Tex. s.

VESPER SPARROW. *Poœcetes gramineus.* Subsp. (Illus. p. 182.)
Descr. 5½–6¼. The *white outer tail-feathers* flashing conspicuously as the bird flies make the best mark. Perched, it looks like a grayish Song Sparrow, but seems to have more of an eye-ring. A *chestnut-colored patch* at the bend of the wing, visible at close range, is determinative. Several other common open-country birds have white outer tail-feathers: the Meadowlark, which is very much larger and chunkier; the Juncos, which are slate-gray; the Longspurs; and the Pipit. The last-named bird is the most similar, but close scrutiny reveals that it is thin-billed, *walks* instead of hops, and frequently *wags its tail.* The Lark Sparrow has large white spots in the outer *corners of the tail*, in addition to the white edges.
Voice: — Song throatier and more minor in quality than that of Song Sparrow, and beginning with a pair of low, clear whistled notes (Song Sparrow begins with *three* repetitious notes on a higher pitch).
Range: — Breeds from Can. s. to Ore., ne. Calif. (e. of Sierras), n. Ariz., n. N.M., and Tex.; winters from s. and cent. Calif., s. Ariz., and cent. Tex. s. into Mex.
Subsp. (No apparent field differences): (1) Oregon Vesper Sparrow, *P. g. affinis*; (2) Western Vesper Sparrow, *P. g. confinis.*

(WESTERN) LARK SPARROW. *Chondestes grammacus strigatus.* (Illus. p. 182.)
Descr. 5½–6¼. An open-country Sparrow with *chestnut* ear-patches, striped crown, and white breast with single dark central spot. *The best mark is the rounded tail with much white in the outside corners* (somewhat as in Spotted Towhee — not as in Vesper Sparrow). Young birds are finely streaked on the breast and lack the central spot, but are otherwise quite recognizable.
Voice: — A variable song consisting of clear notes and trills, best characterized by buzzing and churring passages interspersed here and there.
Range: — Breeds from Can. to Mex. except in humid nw. coast belt; winters from n. Calif. and s. Tex. s.

RUFOUS-WINGED SPARROW. *Aimophila carpalis.*
Descr. 5–5¼. A very rare Sparrow within the limits of the U.S. Like a Chipping Sparrow but with a gray line through the rufous of the crown, somewhat as in an immature Chippy in winter.

The best mark is a *bright rufous shoulder on the wing*. The habitat is a mixture of long grass and low mesquite.

Voice: — Song suggests Song Sparrow.

Range: — Se. Ariz. (very rare and local).

RUFOUS-CROWNED SPARROW. *Aimophila ruficeps.*
Subsp. (Illus. p. 183.)
Descr. 5–5¾. A Sparrow with an unstreaked breast and *rufous red cap*. A black 'whisker' mark on each side of the throat is the best field-mark. The only other Sparrow with a solid reddish cap that normally occurs in the range of this species is the Chipping Sparrow, which has a conspicuous black line through the eye and a white line over it (see Chipping Sparrow). The breeding habitat of the present species is distinctive — dry hillsides covered with low bushes and grass.
Voice: — A stuttering and gurgling song, first part ascending slightly, last notes descending; suggestive of House Wren in general effect. Some authors liken it to a weak Lazuli Bunting's song. Most characteristic note, a nasal *chur, chur, chur, chur* or *dear, dear, dear*.
Range: — W. Tex., w. Okla. (Witchita Mts.), s. N.M., Ariz., and s. and cent. Calif. (n. to Sonoma, Solano, Sutter, and Placer Cos.); casual in se. Colo.
Subsp. (No apparent field differences): (1) Rufous-crowned Sparrow, *A. r. ruficeps*; (2) Santa Cruz Sparrow, *A. r. obscura*; (3) Ashy Sparrow, *A. r. canescens*; (4) Rock Sparrow, *A. r. eremœca*; (5) Scott's Sparrow, *A. r. scotti*.

BOTTERI'S SPARROW. *Aimophila botterii botterii.*
Descr. 5¼–6¼. A dingy plain-breasted Sparrow of the coastal prairies near Brownsville, Tex. It is very nondescript, best told by its unstreaked dingy-white or buffy-white breast. The Cassin's, the only other Sparrow breeding in the same habitat, is almost identical, but is grayer and shows more dusky in the tail. The Botteri's has a much browner tail. The simplest way to tell them is by their very different songs (see below). In migration and winter the Grasshopper Sparrow invades the same area, but can be told by the browner coloration, conspicuous light stripes on the back, and conspicuous stripe through the crown. The Botteri's Sparrow is apparently not present during the winter months.
Voice: — Song, a constant tinkling and 'pitting,' sometimes running into a dry rattle. Very different from song of Cassin's Sparrow, with which it is often found.
Range: — Lower Rio Grande Valley, Tex., and formerly se. Ariz.

CASSIN'S SPARROW. *Aimophila cassini.* (Illus. p. 182.)

Descr. 5¼–5¾. A plain grayish Sparrow of open grassy country, under parts dingy-white or buffy-white without any markings, or with a touch of streaking on the lower sides. The lack of distinctive marks makes it difficult to describe. Its dull grayish upper parts obscurely marked with brown and the unmarked breast are the best clue. As for the other obscure, clear-breasted Sparrows of the open country, the Grasshopper is browner, more contrastingly marked on the back, and has a buffier breast and a light stripe through the crown. The Brewer's is smaller-headed, more Chippy-like in appearance, and distinctly striped with buff and black above. The song of the Cassin's is very distinctive.

Voice: — Song, quite sweet; one or two short opening notes, a high sweet trill and two lower notes thus: *ti ti tseeeeeee tay tay*. Oftentimes the bird 'skylarks' or flutters into the air and sings, giving the long high trill as the climax before it drops down. The song is vaguely suggestive in quality of that of the Savannah Sparrow.

Range: — Breeds in se. Nev., se. Colo., Ariz., N.M., w. Okla., and w. and s. Tex.

DESERT SPARROW. *Amphispiza bilineata*. Subsp. (Illus. p. 183.)

Descr. 4¾–5¼. A pretty, gray-backed Sparrow with white under parts, *white face-stripes* and a *jet-black throat-patch*. The face-pattern is distinctive (see diagram). Lives in desert country. Sexes similar. The only other bird with a face-pattern resembling it is the Black-throated Gray Warbler, which has broad white wing-bars.

Voice: — Song, a sweet *cheet cheet cheeeeeee* (two short, clear opening notes and a fine trill on a lower or higher pitch).

Range: — Breeds in desert country of Calif., Nev., Ut., w. Colo., Ariz., N.M., and w. and s. Tex.; winters from se. Calif., s. Ariz., s. N.M., and Tex. s.

Subsp. (No apparent field differences): (1) Black-throated Sparrow, *A. b. bilineata*; (2) Desert Sparrow, *A. b. deserticola*.

BELL'S SPARROW. *Amphispiza belli belli*. (Illus. p. 182.)

Descr. 5–5½. The Bell's Sparrow and the Sage Sparrow are very similar; both are gray birds, identified by the combination of a *single dark breast-spot* and *dark marks on the side of the throat*. The Sage Sparrow is paler, with the 'whisker-stripe' narrower and broken into a disconnected series of black lines on the side of the throat. In the Bell's Sparrow this mark is solid and unbroken. In winter the two species sometimes occur together in s. Calif. The breeding habitats of the two species are quite different — that of the Bell's Sparrow, hillsides covered with low brush; that of the Sage Sparrow, flat desert-like country dotted with sage and similar low bushes. The Lark Sparrow resembles these species a trifle because of the single breast-spot and 'whisker-marks,' but is easily distinguished by its rusty head-stripes and large white patches in the tail.

Voice: — Song, 'four to seven notes forming a jerky but somewhat melodic phrase which is rapidly *repeated* two or three times, the higher notes with a squeaky, sibilant tone, the lower notes tinkling.' (H. H. Axtell.)

Range: — Calif., w. of Sierras; n. in interior to Shasta Co. and on coast to Marin Co.; also on San Clemente and other coastal ids.

SAGE SPARROW. *Amphispiza nevadensis.* Subsp. (Illus. p. 182.)

Descr. 5½–6¼. (See Bell's Sparrow.)

Voice: — A simple song of set pattern, suggestive of Song Sparrow in quality, *tsit-tsoo-tseee-tsay*, third note highest.

Range: — Breeds e. of Cascades and Sierras in e. Wash., e. Ore., e. Calif., cent. and s. Ida., Nev., Ut., sw. Mont., w. Wyo., w. Colo., and nw. N.M.; also w. of Sierras in cent. and s. Calif.; from Fresno s. to Mt. Pinos, Ventura Co., w. to Carrizo Plain, San Luis Obispo Co. Winters from s. edge of breeding range to deserts of se. Calif., s. Ariz., s. N.M., and w. Tex.

Subsp. (No apparent field differences): (1) Northern Sage Sparrow, *A. n. nevadensis*; (2) California Sage Sparrow, *A. n. canescens.*

JUNCOS. *Junco.*

Before describing the various Juncos, a general discussion of the group might be of help. They are unstriped, Sparrow-like birds characterized by *conspicuous white outer tail-feathers* and gray or black heads. Some species show considerable areas of rusty-red on the back or sides. In identifying them in the field, the three points of major importance are the head (whether black or gray), the sides (whether 'pinkish' or gray), and the back (whether rusty or gray). For convenience the following simplified breakdown is given. Females are duller than the males, and somewhat more confusing.

Species with gray sides:
    White-winged (white wing-bars)
    Slate-colored (fairly uniform gray coloration)
    Gray-headed (rusty back, pale upper mandible)
    Red-backed (rusty back, black upper mandible)
Species with rusty or 'pinkish' sides:
    Oregon (rusty back, black head)
    Pink-sided (brownish back, gray head)

WHITE-WINGED JUNCO. *Junco aikeni.* (Illus. p. 191.)

Descr. 6–6¾. A gray Junco with a *gray back.* Resembles Slate-colored Junco, but larger and paler, usually with two *white wing-bars* and a greater amount of white in the tail. All specimens outside the range outlined below should be carefully examined, as sometimes aberrant examples of the Slate-colored Junco show some white in the wing. In specimens of the White-winged Junco the four outer tail-feathers on each side are white.

Voice: — Song, a loose musical trill, similar to the songs of other Juncos.

Range: — Breeds in se. Mont., Black Hills in e. Wyo. and w. S.D., and nw. Neb.; winters from Black Hills to s. Colo. and n. N.M.

SLATE-COLORED JUNCO. *Junco hyemalis hyemalis.* (Illus. p. 191.)

Descr. 6–6½. A gray Junco with a *gray back*. The *uniform coloration* of the upper parts, without red or brown areas, is distinctive. Immatures often have a touch of buff or brownish on the sides, but the color always blends into the color of the hood, and is not sharply separated, as in the Oregon or Pink-sided Juncos. The color of the back also blends into the hood.

Voice: — Song, a simple trill, suggestive of Chipping Sparrow's but more musical. Note, a hard click.

Range: — Breeds in Can. and Alaska; winters s. to Colo. and n. N.M., chiefly e. of Rockies; occasional in Pacific States, s. to s. Calif.

OREGON JUNCO. *Junco oreganus.* Subsp. (Illus. pp. 178, 191.)

Descr. 5–6. *A reddish-backed* Junco easily identified by the *black head*. The yellowish or rusty sides distinguish it from all others except the Pink-sided Junco, which has a paler, *gray head* and a *dull brown* back. (See Pink-sided Junco.) Females have grayer heads, and the rusty of the back is not so sharply defined, but the 'pink' or brownish sides are always sharply separated from the gray of the hood. This is the only common species of Junco in the Pacific States. The Slate-colored Junco is found there occasionally and the Gray-headed Junco rarely. To search for these last two in the Pacific States, look for Juncos with *gray* sides. There are a number of subspecies of the Oregon Junco distinguished by subtle differences in color, but the best authorities conclude that they are not separable except in the hand, so field students should designate them all merely as Oregon Juncos.

Voice: — Song, a loose quavering trill all on same pitch; resembles Chipping Sparrow's song, but slower and more musical. Note, a light smack or click; also twittering notes.

Range: — Breeds in nw. Mont., n. Ida., Wash., Ore., and Calif. (s. to San Diego Co.); winters through Pacific States and over entire Rocky Mt. Tableland to Mex.

BLACK CAP

INCOMPLETE EYE-RING

These three Vireos have conspicuous wing-bars

BLACK-CAPPED

HUTTON'S

CONSPICUOUS "SPECTACLES"

SOLITARY

ONE OR TWO FAINT WING-BARS

ONE FAINT WING-BAR OR NONE

These two Vireos have inconspicuous eye-rings. They are best separated by habitat (see text)

BELL'S (LEAST)

GRAY

INCONSPICUOUS HEAD-STRIPES

UNIFORMLY COLORED ABOVE

CONSPICUOUS HEAD-STRIPES

CROWN GRAY, BACK OLIVE

These two Vireos have no wing-bars

WARBLING

RED-EYED

VIREOS

JUNCOS

Subsp. (No apparent field differences): (1) Oregon Junco, *J. o. oreganus*; (2) Shufeldt's Junco, *J. o. shufeldti*; (3) Montana Junco, *J. o. montanus*; (4) Thurber's Junco, *J. o. thurberi*; (5) Point Pinos Junco, *J. o. pinosus*.

PINK-SIDED JUNCO. *Junco mearnsi.* (Illus. p. 191.)
Descr. 5½–6. Known from the Oregon Junco by the *gray* head, duller back and more extensive 'pinkish' areas on the sides, sometimes extending across the breast. Female and Immature Oregon Juncos, with grayish heads, resemble this species more closely but have the head somewhat washed with brown, and less clearly set off from the back. A Junco with the combination of clear-gray head and bright 'pink' sides is quite certainly a Pink-sided Junco.
Voice: — Similar to notes of other Juncos.
Range: — Breeds from Can. to s. Ida., s.-cent. Mont., and n. Wyo.; winters s. through Wyo. and Colo. to Ariz. and N.M.

GRAY-HEADED JUNCO. *Junco caniceps.* (Illus. p. 191.)
Descr. 5½–6. The combination of *ashy-gray* sides and *bright rufous* back distinguish this species from all others except the Red-backed Junco. The bill of the present species is pale flesh-colored *above and below*. That of the Red-backed has a black upper mandible.
Voice: — Song, a loose Chippy-like trill similar to that of other Juncos.
Range: — Breeds in Rockies in s. Wyo., Colo., Ut., Nev., and n. N.M.; winters s. to Mex.

RED-BACKED JUNCO. *Junco phæonotus.* Subsp. (Illus. p. 191.)
Descr. 5½–6½. The combination of grayish sides and *bright rufous* back distinguish this species from all others except the Gray-headed Junco. The best point of distinction is the bill, which in the Red-back has the entire upper mandible *black*. This species does not occur north of Ariz. and N.M. The two sub-species of this bird are easily distinguished by the color of the eye (see below).
Voice: — Song (Arizona Junco), lively and musical, ending with a Chipping-Sparrow-like rattle as in other Juncos, but usually with a more complicated opening; sometimes thus: *chip chip chip, wheedle wheedle, che che che che che.*
Subsp. RED-BACKED JUNCO. *J. p. dorsalis.*
    Eye *dark*; lower mandible flesh-colored. Breeds in high mts. of N.M. and ne. Ariz.; winters s. to sw. Tex. and Mex.
    ARIZONA JUNCO. *J. p. palliatus.*
    Eye *bright yellow*; lower mandible pale yellow. Resident of mts. of se. Ariz.

(WESTERN) TREE SPARROW. *Spizella arborea ochracea.* (Illus. p. 183.)

Descr. 6–6½. A single *round black spot* in the center of the breast and a bright *red-brown cap* identify the 'Winter Chippy.' Two conspicuous white wing-bars are also characteristic.

Voice: — Song, sweet and variable, beginning with one or two high sweet clear notes; note, a distinct *tseet*; feeding-note, a musical *teeler* or *teelwit.*

Range: — Breeds in Can.; winters s. in Rocky Mt. section to N.M. and w. Tex., and w. to e. Wash., e. Ore., and Ariz. (casually).

(WESTERN) CHIPPING SPARROW. *Spizella passerina arizonæ.* (Illus. p. 183.)

Descr. 5–5½. A very small clear gray-breasted Sparrow with a bright *rufous cap*, a *black line* through the eye, and a *white line* over it. *Young birds* in late summer are finely streaked below, but are recognized by their small size and moderately long forked tail. *Immature birds* in winter look like the adults, but are buffier, with a striped crown. *Winter adults* are browner, not so gray-breasted. (See Rufous-crowned Sparrow and Brewer's Sparrow.)

Voice: — Song, a dry chipping rattle or trill, all on one pitch. Note, a short chip.

Range: — Breeds from Can. to s. Calif., cent. Ariz., and N.M.; winters from s. Calif., s. Ariz., and cent. Tex. s. into Mex.

CLAY-COLORED SPARROW. *Spizella pallida.* (Illus. p. 183.)

Descr. 5–5½. A small open-country Sparrow, clear-breasted like Chippy, but with a *light stripe* through center of crown and a sharply outlined brown *ear-patch.* *Fall immatures* are even more like Chippies of the same age, but the crown is more distinctly striped and without much hint of rufous. The surest point is the rump, which is *buffy-brown*; that of the Chippy is gray. The Brewer's Sparrow is also similar but lacks the well-marked head-pattern.

Voice: — Song, a rasping, insect-like *zi-zi-zi-zi-zi.*

Range: — Breeds in prairies of n.-cent. U.S., w. to e. Mont., e. Wyo., and e. Colo.; winters from s. N.M. and s. Tex. s.

BREWER'S SPARROW. *Spizella breweri.* Subsp. (Illus. p. 183.)

Descr. 5. A small pale Sparrow of the arid sage country and deserts. Clear-breasted; resembles Chipping Sparrow but slimmer, sandier-colored, and with *crown finely streaked*, with no hint of rufous. Young Chipping Sparrow in fall might be confused with it, but the crown of the latter species is browner and often divided by a pale median line.

Voice: — Song, long musical buzzy trills on different pitches; suggests trilling and chopping of Canary, but weaker; sounds like a Chipping Sparrow trying to sing like a Canary.

Range: — Breeds in Great Basin and Rocky Mt. sections from Can. s. to N.M. and Ariz. and w. to e. Wash., e. Ore. (e. of Cascades), and Calif. (e. of Sierras, also local in s. Calif.); winters from s. Calif., s. Ariz., and cent. Tex. s.

Subsp. (No apparent field differences): (1) Brewer's Sparrow, *S. b. breweri*; (2) Timberline Sparrow, *S. b. taverneri*.

WORTHEN'S SPARROW. *Spizella wortheni*.

Descr. 5½. A Mexican species that has once been taken in southern N.M., whence it was first described. Resembles Chipping Sparrow but without the conspicuous eye-stripes, having instead a *conspicuous white eye-ring*; bill *pinkish* or rufous. Resembles very closely the Field Sparrow, which has never occurred in N.M., but rusty of crown less extensive, and eye-ring more conspicuous.

BLACK-CHINNED SPARROW. *Spizella atrogularis*. Subsp. (Illus. p. 183.)

Descr. 5–5½. A uniquely different Sparrow; has a reddish-brown back like many other species, but *head and under parts gray*, with a *black chin-patch*. The *flesh-colored bill* is set off conspicuously by the black patch that encircles it. Immatures lack the black patch, but can be told by the *unmarked gray head and breast*, which contrast with the rusty-brown back. The habitat is dry mountain-slopes covered with sage, chamise, or other low bushes.

Voice: — Song, a series of notes on about same pitch, or descending slightly; starts with several high, thin, clear notes and ends in a rough trill, *sweet, sweet, sweet, weet trrrrrrr*.

Range: — Breeds in s. N.M., Ariz., and locally in s. Calif. (n. to Monterey Co. and Owens Valley; occasionally farther).

Subsp. (No apparent field differences): (1) Mexican Black-chinned Sparrow, *S. a. atrogularis*; (2) California Black-chinned Sparrow, *S. a. cana*.

HARRIS'S SPARROW. *Zonotrichia querula*. (Illus. p. 183.)

Descr. 7–7¾. Larger than House Sparrow, or about size of Fox Sparrow; identified by its boldly marked black-and-gray head. The *black crown- and throat-patches* join to encircle the bright pinkish bill. Sexes similar. The black bib suggests no other species except the male House Sparrow, which, of course, could hardly be confused with it. Young birds are browner about the head and might have the black incomplete or confined to a disconnected blotch across the breast.

WHITE STRIPE STARTS FROM EYE

WHITE STRIPE STARTS FROM BILL

A

B

BILL PINKISH

BILL YELLOWISH

HEADS OF WHITE-CROWNED SPARROWS

A. White-crowned   B. Gambel's   C. Nuttall's

Voice: — Song, plaintive, consisting usually of three notes, *whee whee whee.*
Range: — Breeds in Can.; in migration and winter to Great Plains, w. irregularly to Mont., Wyo., Colo., and casually to other W. States.

WHITE-CROWNED SPARROW. *Zonotrichia leucophrys.* Subsp. (Illus. pp. 183, 194.)
Descr. $5\frac{3}{4}$–7. *Adult:* — Breast clear pearly-gray, crown high and puffy, *broadly striped with black and white.* The conspicuous striped crown makes this abundant and well-known bird one of the handsomest of all the Sparrows. *Immature:* — Buffier, with head-stripings of dark red-brown and light buffy-brown instead of black and white; *bills pinkish or yellowish.* Immatures might be mistaken for the Golden-crowned Sparrow. The different subspecies can, with practice and care, be identified in the field by plumage and song. In the Rocky Mt. section only two races, the Gambel's and White-crowned Sparrows, occur. In the Gambel's, the white eye-stripe *starts from* the bill; in the White-crown, near the eye (see diagram). In s. Calif. ordinarily the Gambel's is the only one found, so there is no problem. In cent. Calif. all four races occur. Of these, the White-crown occurs only in the Sierras. It is chiefly in the San Francisco area that students are concerned with the fine points of separating the various races by appearance and voice. The Nuttall's Sparrow, the resident race, which apparently does not migrate, is known to vary remarkably in song in different localities (see below). The advice of the author is to learn the song-pattern of the local breeding birds thoroughly, and when the migrants with strange songs arrive, see whether they have pink bills (Gambel's) or yellow bills (Puget Sound), then proceed to memorize carefully their respective song-patterns by some such method as suggested below.
Subsp. (Including *descr., voice,* and *range.*)
WHITE-CROWNED SPARROW. *Z l. leucophrys.*

Descr. Differs from the other races in having the white eye-stripe start *from the eye* instead of from the bill.

Voice: — Song, several plaintive whistled notes followed by a husky trilled whistle. As in the other subspecies, the birds sing a bit differently in different localities. Following is a transcription made in Yosemite:

Say See Say Saw Cheeeeeeeeeer
(Clear plaintive whistles) (Husky nasal trill)

Range: — Breeds in high mts. of w. U.S. from Can. s. in Rockies to n. N.M., and in Sierras to cent. Calif.; migrates through Rocky Mt. region s. into Mex.; winters in s. Ariz., N.M., and Tex.

GAMBEL'S SPARROW. *Z. l. gambeli.*

Descr. Adult differs from White-crown by having white eye-stripe *start from bill* instead of from eye. Has cleaner, grayer-appearing neck than the two coastal races. Bill *pinkish* or *flesh-colored.* (Nuttall's and Puget Sound *yellowish.*) Immatures have lighter and rustier head-stripes than immature Nuttall's or Puget Sound Sparrows.

Voice: — Song variable, more formless than Nuttall's or White-crown. Below is one transcription:

Say Chidichi See Say Saw

Range: — Breeds from Can. s. to cent. Mont.; migrates throughout w. U.S. except nw. coast belt; winters from Calif. and Ut. s.

PUGET SOUND SPARROW. *Z. l. pugetensis.*

Descr. A dark race similar to Nuttall's but black head-stripings heavier.

Voice: — Song usually starts with long note, higher-pitched than rest of song. The transcription below is adapted from the notes of Amelia Allen.

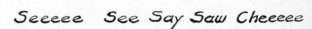

Seeeee   See Say Saw Cheeeee

Range: — Breeds in humid nw. coast belt from Wash. s. to n. Calif. (Mendocino Co.); winters s. along coast to s. Calif.

NUTTALL'S SPARROW. *Z. l. nuttalli.*

Descr. Breast and neck browner than Gambel's Sparrow; bill *yellowish* (Gambel's flesh-colored or orange-brown). Head-stripes wider and blacker than Gambel's.

Voice: — Song varies greatly in different localities, although birds stick to a 'community pattern'; for example, those at Point Reyes in Marin Co., Calif., sing:

Seeeee Chechechecheche Cheer
(whistle) (Metallic warble) (Nasal)

In one part of Berkeley they sing:

See See Chee Chechechechecheer
(Clear) (Burr) (Rattle with overtones)

While at Carmel they sing with a characteristic double note.

Say   See   Chidi Chidi   Cheew
(Clear) (Clear) (Double notes) (Nasal)

Range: — Permanent resident around San Francisco Bay region and along coast of cent. Calif. from Mendocino Co. to Santa Barbara Co.

GOLDEN-CROWNED SPARROW. *Zonotrichia coronata.* (Illus. p. 183.)
Descr. 6–7. *Adult:* — Like a White-crowned Sparrow with *no white line over the eye* and a *golden-yellow,* instead of white, stripe through the center of the crown. Immature White-crowns (Gambel's, etc.) have the center of the crown buffy and resemble the Golden-crown, but have broad buffy lines over the eyes, which the latter species lacks. Immature Golden-crowns look like large female House Sparrows, but are browner and sometimes have a dull yellowish suffusion on the crown. Often they lack this yellow suffusion and are very plain. These birds have little distinctive about them, unless it be the fine streaking on the otherwise unpatterned crown.
Voice: — Song, three high whistled notes of plaintive minor quality, coming down the scale.
Range: — Breeds in Can. and Alaska; winters in Ore. and Calif. w. of Sierras; migrates through Wash.; casual in Nev. and Colo.

WHITE-THROATED SPARROW. *Zonotrichia albicollis.* (Illus. p. 183.)
Descr. 6½–7. *Adult:* — Clear-breasted with *white throat-patch* and *striped black-and-white crown.* The abrupt white throat, and *yellow* on eye-line between bill and eye, distinguish it from any of the White-crowns. *Immature:* — Duller, but with all essential recognition-marks of adults.
Voice: — Song, several clear, pensive whistled notes easily imitated; starts on one or two long clear whistles and changes pitch abruptly. Note, a hard *chink,* also a slurred *tseet.*
Range: — Breeds in Can., migrates through e. U.S. w. rarely to e. Mont., e. Wyo., and e. Colo.; also a rare but regular winter visitor to the Pacific States, especially Calif.

FOX SPARROW. *Passerella iliaca.* Subsp. (Illus. p. 182.)
Descr. 6¼–7¼. Large for a Sparrow; larger than a House Sparrow; dark brown or gray with heavily streaked under parts.

The heavy spottings and streakings often cluster together densely on the upper breast. In some birds the tail has a strong tinge of rusty. This species, which likes ravines, slopes, and brushy places, has many confusing subspecies. They can be roughly divided into two types: gray-headed Fox Sparrows with large grayish bills and brown-headed Fox Sparrows with yellowish bills. It is hopeless and misguided for the field student to try to separate them, for often in migration and winter half a dozen races might be represented in the same flock. The only race that can be identified easily in the field is the Eastern Fox Sparrow, *P. i. iliaca*, which is a rare or casual winter visitor to the Pacific States. It shows much bright rufous, especially the tail- and breast-streakings. There is much gray around the face. No Western Fox Sparrow shows such bright rusty coloration.

Voice: — A brilliant musical song; usually begins with one or two clear notes followed by a sliding note: *sweet sweet cheer chillip chillip*, etc. The arrangement varies greatly, but the song is easy to remember once heard. (See voice of Green-tailed Towhee.)

Range: — Breeds in high mts. from Can. to w. Colo. (rare) and s. Calif. (San Gabriel, San Bernardino, and San Jacinto Mts.), and from Rockies w. to Sierras, Cascades, and ids. off coast of nw. Wash. Migrates and winters in Pacific States. A rare migrant to Ariz. and N.M.

Subsp. (No apparent field differences except in No. 1 — see above): (1) Eastern Fox, *P. i. iliaca*; (2) Alberta Fox, *P. i. altivagans*; (3) Shumagin Fox, *P. i. unalaschensis*; (4) Kodiak Fox, *P. i. insularis*; (5) Valdez Fox, *P. i. sinuosa*; (6) Yakutat Fox, *P. i. annectens*; (7) Townsend's Fox, *P. i. townsendi*; (8) Thick-billed Fox, *P. i. megarhyncha*; (9) Sooty Fox, *P. i. fuliginosa*; (10) Slate-colored Fox, *P. i. schistacea*; (11) Warner Mountains Fox, *P. i. fulva*; (12) Trinity Fox, *P. i. brevicauda*; (13) Inyo Fox, *P. i. canescens*; (14) Mono Fox, *P. i. monoënsis*; (15) Yosemite Fox, *P. i. mariposæ*; (16) Stephens's Fox, *P. i. stephensi*.

LINCOLN'S SPARROW. *Melospiza lincolni.* Subsp. (Illus. p. 182.)

Descr. 5–6. Like Song Sparrow, with shorter tail; streakings on under parts much finer and not aggregated into as large a center spot; best identified by broad band of pale buff across breast. The buffy band and fine breast-streakings distinguish it from all except the immature Song Sparrow. It is grayer-backed, with a more contrastingly striped crown. A narrow *eye-ring* is also quite characteristic. Likes wet brushy places and boggy spots.

Voice: — Song, sweet and gurgling, suggests both House Wren and Purple Finch, starting with low passages, rising abruptly in pitch, then dropping at the end.

Range: — Breeds in high mts. from Can. s. to s. Calif., cent.

Ariz., and N.M.; migrates through lowlands of w. U.S.; winters from cent. Calif., Ariz., and cent. Tex. s. into Mex.
Subsp. (No apparent field differences): (1) Lincoln's Sparrow, *M. l. lincolni*; (2) Forbush's Sparrow, *M. l. gracilis*.

SONG SPARROW. *Melospiza melodia.* Subsp. (Illus. p. 182.)
Descr. 5–6¾. Breast heavily streaked, the streaks confluent into a *large central spot*: pumps its tail as it flies. The Savannah Sparrow, though streaked similarly below, shows yellow over the eye, and has a shorter, *forked* tail. The tail of the Song Sparrow is not so noticeably notched. *Young* birds are more finely streaked, often without the central spot. (See Lincoln's Sparrow.) There are many subspecies in the West, varying in size and general coloration. Those that breed in arid sections are paler; those in humid districts, duskier. In winter different races sometimes intermingle, especially in Calif. The student should not attempt to untangle them in the field.
Voice: — Song, a variable series of notes, some musical, some buzzy, usually starting with three repetitious notes, *sweet sweet sweet*, etc. Call-note, a low nasal *tchack*.
Range: — Breeds from Can. s. to s. Calif., sw. Ariz., and n. N.M.; winters from Wash. and Mont. s. into Mex.
Subsp. (No apparent field differences): (1) Dakota Song Sparrow, *M. m. juddi*; (2) Mountain Song Sparrow, *M. m. fallax*; (3) Modoc Song Sparrow, *M. m. fisherella*; (4) Merrill's Song Sparrow, *M. m. merrilli*; (5) Sooty Song Sparrow, *M. m. rufina*; (6) Rusty Song Sparrow, *M. m. morphna*; (7) Mendocino Song Sparrow, *M. m. cleonensis*; (8) Samuels's Song Sparrow, *M. m. samuelis*; (9) Suisun Song Sparrow, *M. m. maxillaris*; (10) Modesto Song Sparrow, *M. m. mailliardi*; (11) Alameda Song Sparrow, *M. m. pusillula*; (12) Heermann's Song Sparrow, *M. m. heermanni*; (13) San Diego Song Sparrow, *M. m. cooperi*; (14) Santa Cruz Song Sparrow, *M. m. santæcrucis*; (15) Santa Barbara Song Sparrow, *M. m. graminea*; (16) San Clemente Song Sparrow, *M. m. clementæ*; (17) San Miguel Song Sparrow, *M. m. micronyx*; (18) Desert Song Sparrow, *M. m. saltonis*; (19) Yakutat Song Sparrow, *M. m. caurina*.

McCOWN'S LONGSPUR. *Rhynchophanes mccowni.* (Illus. pp. 200, 201.)
Descr. 6. *Spring male:* — Forehead and patch on breast black; tail largely white. The hind-neck is *gray*, not brown or chestnut as in other Longspurs. *Female and winter plumages:* — See Chestnut-collared Longspur.
Voice: — Song, given in flight, a variety of clear sweet warbles, 'much the same character as Lark Bunting' (R. J. Niedrach).
Range: — Breeds in Great Plains, w. to e. Mont., e. Wyo., and ne. Colo.; migrates and winters in e. Colo., e. Ariz., N.M., and w. Tex.

LONGSPURS

1. Alaska: a, *female*; b, *male in spring*
2. Chestnut-collared: a, *female*; b, *male in spring*
3. McCown's: a, *female*; b, *male in spring*

ALASKA LONGSPUR. *Calcarius lapponicus alascensis.* (Illus. pp. 200, 201.)
Descr. 6–7. Longspurs, like Horned Larks and Pipits, are birds of the fields, plains, and barren grounds; like those two they *walk or run*, seldom hop. This species often associates with Horned Larks or Snow Buntings. With Snow Buntings it appears as a smaller, House-Sparrow-like bird, with *dark wings*; when with Horned Larks it can be recognized by the short, Sparrow bill, and the lack of an outlined yellow throat, and on the wing by the *smaller tail* and more undulating flight. Alone, it appears a trifle like a House Sparrow, but *walks or creeps.* Two white wing-bars, some narrow black streakings on the sides, and a varying amount of reddish on the nape of the neck are distinctive points. It has much less white in the tail than the other Longspurs. In the spring both sexes acquire a black throat and breast (breeding Chestnut-collared Longspur has black breast but whitish throat).
Voice: — The note of this Longspur amongst a flock of Larks or Buntings is a dry rattle that can be detected immediately.
Range: — Breeds in n. Alaska; winters s. to e. Ore. (occasionally), Nev., and Colo.; chiefly e. of Rockies. Accidental in Calif.

TAIL-PATTERNS OF LONGSPURS

a. Chestnut-collared   *b*. McCown's   *c*. Alaska

CHESTNUT-COLLARED LONGSPUR. *Calcarius ornatus.*
(Illus. pp. 200, 201.)
Descr. 5½–6½. Smallest of the Longspurs — smaller than a
House Sparrow. *Male in breeding plumage:* — Solid *black* below
except on throat; nape of neck, *chestnut. Female and winter
male:* — Sparrow-like, known from other Longspurs (except
McCown's) by large amount of white on sides of tail. Vesper
Sparrow and Pipit have straight white sides of tail to tip;
Chestnut-collared and McCown's Longspurs have dark band on
end of tail. In Chestnut-collar the dark central tail-feathers
curve into the terminal band, fanwise; in McCown's, the band
is more angular, forming a T with the dark central feathers (see
diagram).
Voice: — Song, short, feeble but musical, 'suggestive of Western
Meadowlark in melody' (R. J. Niedrach).
Range: — Breeds in Great Plains w. to Mont. and e. Wyo.;
migrates and winters in e. Colo., e. Ariz., N.M., and w. Tex.

SNOW BUNTING. *Plectrophenax nivalis nivalis.* (Illus. p. 178.)
Descr. 6–7¼. The great amount of white distinguishes the
Snow Bunting. Some individuals look quite brown as they run
about on the ground, but when they spring into the air the extensive white wing-patches flash forth. As they fly overhead,
they look almost entirely white; Pipits and Horned Larks are
both black-tailed.
Voice: — Note, a clear whistled *teer*; also a musical purring note.
Range: — Breeds in Arctic; winters s. to Ore., Wyo., and Colo.
(a few), chiefly in prairie country.

SUBSPECIES

THE problem of subspecies is a very confusing one, especially in the western United States. When the author first planned his manuscript, he listed under each species all subspecies and their ranges, in much the same manner as in his Eastern *Field Guide*. Dr. Alden Miller, who has done much work on taxonomic problems, and is a leader of ornithological thought in the West, strongly urged that subspecies be left out entirely unless they can actually be identified in the field. There are many good reasons for following such a plan. First and foremost, there still seems to be no clear-cut idea as to what a subspecies is, other than that it is a geographical race that often blends with others of the same species. To explain it simply, the Song Sparrows of the desert differ from those of the mountains in being somewhat paler, so they are called by a different name. These differences are sometimes well marked, but often they can only be determined by experts after very careful examination in the hand. There is a constant dispute raging amongst ornithologists about various local races, and it is often a matter of opinion to which subspecies a bird belongs, or even whether a certain subspecies is worthy of recognition at all.

Even the concept of species is not entirely agreed upon. It was recently stated by Dr. Ernst Mayr that at least ninety-four of the 755 full species of North American birds will be considered by some authors to be merely subspecies of other species. A few Western examples are the Large-billed, Belding's, and Savannah Sparrows; the various Juncos; the Leucostictes; the Myrtle and Audubon's Warblers; etc. However, we need not concern ourselves with this theoretical question, as most of these examples are quite distinguishable in the field.

The *A.O.U. Check-List*, which has initiated the use of vernacular names for subspecies, has got things into a mess by not always indicating in the name to which species a subspecies belongs. All Song Sparrows are called Song Sparrows; i.e., San Diego Song Sparrow, Rusty Song Sparrow, etc. This is fine, but on the other hand, the several races of the Steller's Jay are designated by such totally unrelated names as Black-headed Jay, Long-crested Jay, Blue-fronted Jay, and Coast Jay. There is little in some of these names to indicate whether the bird is a race of the Steller's Jay or the California Jay. The inference might even be drawn that they are all distinct species.

Another angle is that the various races of the Steller's Jay *intergrade* on the borders of their ranges. In the latest revisionary work on this species, it was brought out that the birds around Seattle cannot be called by any currently accepted name, as they are not quite like those on the Coast farther to the south, nor typical of the form found to the north on Vancouver Island, nor yet quite like the birds in the Cascades. They are intermediates with a blend of characters. In other words, there could just as easily be ten races of this bird as five, depending on where the lines are to be drawn or how fine the splitting is to be. The point I am driving at is that if the subject is so indefinite as all this, the problem is not one for a beginner. It is better that he use only the name Steller's Jay, which is the accepted species name. This is far more scientific than using a name that has disputed validity. Subspecies have a real meaning to the student of bird distribution and evolution, but not much to the field amateur. Dr. George Miksch Sutton writes:

'One of the worst problems of present-day field bird study, as I see it, is this desire to use trinomials. Right here, at Cornell, we face the problem. . . . I asked my students to turn in a field notebook last year, and every one of them listed trinomials wherever he possibly could, without bothering himself to discover what specimens had actually been collected and identified, what the characters of certain races were, etc. They all were willing to take someone else's word on the subspecies — to use the name that seemed to fit geographically, to employ what I call *fake* accuracy. In other words, *Turdus migratorius migratorius*, Eastern Robin, looked more thoroughgoing to them than simply *Turdus migratorius*, Robin. The use of the trinomial very often is a sort of four-flushing.'

Junea Kelly, who has taught many bird classes around San Francisco, writes similarly:

'In most cases an observer cannot identify a subspecies in the field, and only uses the subspecific name because the bird is seen in a certain locality. I have never felt that this was a very satisfactory way of making out a "list." It might be approximately accurate for the breeding season, but how about the rest of the year? How is an observer to know exactly when non-breeders have arrived?'

Before taking the plunge and following Dr. Miller's suggestion, I thought it wise to get the opinions of a few other people. After writing to about twenty-five representative Westerners and Easterners about the treatment of subspecies, I finally arrived at a plan that I believe will work for all, yet still do the job Dr. Miller had in mind. Most Westerners were insistent about leaving out subspecies entirely, or at least playing them down. Most Easterners, and a few Westerners, said they would feel cheated if the subspecies were not left in, so I finally worked out the following plan:

When subspecies are readily identifiable in the field they will be treated exactly as they are in my Eastern *Field Guide*, with considerable importance given to each subspecies. A good example of this is the Canada Goose. When there are no apparent field differences, only the range *for the species as a whole* will be given. The advantage of this is that the amateur will not have to wade laboriously through the range of each subspecies to see whether his territory falls within it. If all the subspecies ranges were outlined prominently in the body of the text, the student would be encouraged to use the vernacular subspecific names, which, as has been explained, leads to confusion.

It is necessary to include at least the *names* of subspecies, however, as failure to list them would only be misleading; for example, if a person consulted a local publication and found the name Black-eared Nuthatch (a race of the Pygmy Nuthatch), he would be very much troubled if he did not find this bird in the *Field Guide* An almost identical example is described by Clinton G. Abbott, of the Natural History Museum at San Diego:

'When there was no one else in the office, a woman came in and told my secretary that we failed to include the Pygmy Nuthatch in our identification series of San Diego birds. With no one to explain the situation to her (that the White-naped Nuthatch and the Pygmy Nuthatch are the same thing) she went out feeling very much disturbed. In the plan which you are to follow in your book, if this woman had looked up Pygmy Nuthatch, she would have seen that some of the subspecies have different names, and might then have been induced to look more carefully on the labels in our cases.'

In most cases, it is quite easy to settle on an inclusive species name. To the average Westerner, the *Willow* Woodpecker or *Batchelder's* Woodpecker is still just a Downy. There are, however, a few vernacular names of subspecies that have already gained such a foothold that it would be difficult to eradicate them now; for instance, *Lutescent* Warbler (a race of the Orange-crown) and *Farallon* Cormorant (a race of the Double-crested). Most vernacular subspecies names are of recent manufacture, and have not become well established in popular use. Yet if every bird book that came out gave them full importance, it would not take long before these names were as firmly intrenched in usage as 'Lutescent' Warbler and 'Farallon' Cormorant.

The next edition of the *A.O.U. Check-List* plans to incorporate species headings, so when I have been in doubt, I have referred to the Committee's choice of a name, except in about three instances when I have disregarded it, using instead the Western name which seemed the more appropriate; for example, *Pileolated* Warbler instead of Wilson's Warbler.

This book is primarily for the amateur who merely wishes to

attach a name or a 'handle' to the creature before him. Another group consists of those who are more or less students of the subject. They will range from those who know little to those who have spent years of study and who will wish to use the book in areas unfamiliar to them. It is in deference to some of these, who will feel the book is incomplete if the ranges of subspecies are omitted, that I have decided to include these ranges, but to de-emphasize them, and relegate them to this chapter in the back of the book. For a more extended account of these ranges, the student should refer to the 1931 edition of the *A.O.U. Check-List.*

In the ten years between publication of the last *Check-List* and the publication of this handbook about eighty new subspecies have been described. Probably not half of these will be accepted by the A.O.U. Check-List Committee, so rather than include all of these, many of which are at present of questionable status, I have adhered strictly, or very nearly so, to the last edition of the *Check-List.*

If subspecific names are used at all, it is my advice to call birds by these names only on their breeding-grounds, and not when indistinguishable migrants of other races might be present.

At Mr. Ludlow Griscom's suggestion, I have reversed or altered the treatment of several highly complex migratory species, such as the Fox Sparrow, analyzing them by States or regions. Thus, a person in the Rockies knows he has to deal only with one Fox Sparrow and will not wade through the other sixteen to be sure they do not occur in migration in his area.

COMMON LOON. *Gavia immer:* (1) Lesser Loon, *G. i. elasson;* breeds from Can. s. to Wyo., e. Ore., and ne. Calif. (formerly); migrates through w. U.S.; winters along Pacific Coast. (2) Common Loon, *G. i. immer;* some authorities say it is this race and not the preceding one that occurs in Calif.

BEAL'S PETREL. *Oceanodroma leucorhoa:* (1) Beal's Petrel, *O. l. beali;* breeds from Alaska to Farallon Ids., Calif.; winters offshore from Wash. to s. Calif. (2) Kaeding's Petrel, *O. l. kaedingi;* breeds in Lower Calif.: wanders n. to s. Calif.

DOUBLE-CRESTED CORMORANT. *Phalacrocorax auritus:* (1) Double-crested Cormorant, *P. a. auritus;* Great Plains and, according to some authorities, the breeding bird of Great Salt Lake. (2) Farallon Cormorant, *P. a. albociliatus;* Pacific Coast of Ore. and Calif.; also bodies of water inland in Calif., Ore., Ariz., and w. Nev. (3) White-crested Cormorant, *P. a. cincinatus;* coast of Wash.

GREAT BLUE HERON. *Ardea herodias:* (1) Great Blue Heron, *A. h. herodias;* e. Mont. (2) Treganza's Heron, *A. h. treganzai;* interior from e. Wash., e. Ore., s. Idaho, and Wyo. s. to se. Calif. (Salton Sea) and Mex., and e. to cent. Colo. (edge of Great Plains). (3) Northwestern Coast Heron, *A. h. fannini;* coastal Wash. (4) California Heron, *A. h. hyperonca;* Calif. and Ore. w. of Sierras and Cascades.

LEAST BITTERN. *Ixobrychus exilis:* (1) Western Least Bittern, *I. e. hesperis;* breeds in Calif. and e. Ore.; occurs occasionally in Rocky Mt. States. (2) Eastern Least Bittern, *I. e. exilis;* e. U.S. w. occasionally to e. Wyo. and e. Colo.

CANADA GOOSE. *Branta canadensis:* (1) Common Canada Goose, *B. c. canadensis;* breeds from ne. Calif., n. Nev., n. Ut., and Wyo. n. into Can.; winters from Wash. and Yellowstone Park s. into Mex. (2) White-cheeked Goose, *B. c. occidentalis;* winters along coast from Puget Sound to n. Calif. (Del Norte and Humboldt Cos.). (3) Lesser Canada Goose, *B. c. leucopareia;* winters from Wash. to Mex., especially in interior valleys of Calif. (4) Cackling Goose, *B. c. minima;* winters mainly in Sacramento and San Joaquin Valleys of Calif.

WHITE-FRONTED GOOSE. *Anser albifrons:* (1) White-fronted Goose, *A. a. albifrons;* migrates chiefly through Pacific States, rare in Rocky Mt. region; winters in Calif. (2) Tule Goose, *A. a. gambeli;* winters in Sacramento Valley, Calif.

GOSHAWK. *Astur atricapillus:* (1) Eastern Goshawk, *A. a. atricapillus;* said to be the breeding form in Colo., Wyo., Ut., and probably Mont.; also migrates through Mont. e. of Continental Divide. (2) Western Goshawk, *A. a. striatulus;* breeds from Can. s. in mts. to cent. Calif.; also a few in Ariz. and N.M.; winters more widely in w. U.S.

RED-TAILED HAWK. *Buteo borealis:* (1) Western Red-tailed Hawk, *B. b. calurus;* resident through most of w. U.S. (2) Krider's Hawk, *B. b. krideri;* Sask. and s. Man. s. to Wyo. and N.D.

BALD EAGLE. *Haliæetus leucocephalus:* (1) Northern Bald Eagle, *H. l. atascanus;* winters s. to Wash. and Mont. (2) Southern Bald Eagle, *H. l. leucocephalus;* local resident from Can. to Mex.

DUCK HAWK. *Falco peregrinus:* (1) Duck Hawk, *F. p. anatum;* breeds locally from Can. to Mex.; winters in Pacific States and from Colo. s. (2) Peale's Falcon, *F. p. pealei;* migrant and winter visitor to coast of Wash. and Ore.

PIGEON HAWK. *Falco columbarius:* (1) Black Pigeon Hawk, *F. c. suckleyi;* winters along coast from Wash. to n. Calif. (2) Richardson's Pigeon Hawk, *F. c. richardsoni;* breeds in Great Plains region from Can. s. to n. Mont.; winters s. through Colo., N.M., and w. Tex. (3) Western Pigeon Hawk, *F. c. bendirei;* breeds from Can. s. in mts. to n. Calif. and Colo.; winters s. into Mex.

SPARROW HAWK. *Falco sparverius:* (1) Eastern Sparrow Hawk, *F. s. sparverius;* breeds from Can. s. to Calif. and Colo.; winters from Wash. and Wyo. s. to Mex. (2) Desert Sparrow Hawk, *F. s. phalæna;* resident of s. Calif., Ariz., and N.M.

DUSKY GROUSE. *Dendragapus obscurus:* (1) Dusky Grouse, *D. o. obscurus;* Rocky Mts. from cent. Ariz. and cent. N.M. n. to n. Ut., se. Idaho, and Wyo. (intergrading with next race in Mont.). (2) Richardson's Grouse, *D. o. richardsoni;* mt. regions from Can. s. to cent. Idaho and Mont.

SOOTY GROUSE. *Dendragapus fuliginosus:* (1) Sooty Grouse, *D. f. fuliginosus;* coastal belt from Wash. to nw. Calif. (2) Sierra Grouse, *D. f. sierræ;* extreme s. Ore. (Warner Mts.) and s. in Sierras to Kern Co., Calif., and on inner side of coast range to Mt. Sanhedrin. (3) Mount Pinos Grouse, *D. f. howardi;* s. Calif. from Mt. Pinos to Kern Co.

RUFFED GROUSE. *Bonasa umbellus:* (1) Oregon Ruffed Grouse, *B. u.*

sabini; coastal belt from w. Wash. s. to nw. Calif. (2) Gray Ruffed Grouse, *B. u. umbelloides*; e. of Cascades from Can. s. to n. Colo. (formerly), n. Ut., and e. Ore.

WHITE-TAILED PTARMIGAN. *Lagopus leucurus:* (1) Rainier White-tailed Ptarmigan, *L. l. rainierensis*; Cascade Mts. of Wash. (2) Southern White-tailed Ptarmigan, *L. l. altipetens*; Rocky Mts. from Mont. to n. N.M.

SHARP-TAILED GROUSE. *Pediœcetes phasianellus:* (1) Columbian Sharp-tailed Grouse, *P. p. columbianus*; e. Wash., e. Ore., Idaho, n. Ut., w. Mont., w. Wyo., w. Colo., and n. N.M. (2) Prairie Sharp-tailed Grouse, *P. p. campestris*; Great Plains w. to e. Mont., e. Wyo., and e. Colo.

SCALED QUAIL. *Callipepla squamata:* (1) Arizona Scaled Quail, *C. s. pallida*; from cent. Ariz., s. Colo., and w. Tex. s. (2) Chestnut-bellied Scaled Quail, *C. s. castanogastris*; cent. and s. Tex.

CALIFORNIA QUAIL. *Lophortyx californica:* (1) California Quail, *L. c. californica*; humid coastal belt of n. and cent. Calif.; introduced in Wash. (2) Valley Quail, *L. c. vallicola*; native in s. Ore. and s. through Calif. except in humid coast strip (from cent. Calif. n.). Absent also in Colo. and Mohave Deserts (except w. edge). Widely introduced elsewhere in W. States. (3) Catalina Quail, *L. c. catalinensis*; Catalina Id., Calif.

GAMBEL'S QUAIL. *Lophortyx gambeli:* (1) Gambel's Quail, *L. g. gambeli*; deserts of s. Calif., s. Nev., sw. Ut., Ariz., cent. and sw. N.M., and extreme w. Tex.; introduced locally elsewhere. (2) Olathe Quail, *L. g. sanus*; supposed to have developed in sw. Colo. from birds introduced there years ago.

MOUNTAIN QUAIL. *Oreortyx picta:* (1) Mountain Quail, *O. p. palmeri*; humid mountains near coast from w. Wash. to Monterey Co., Calif. (2) Plumed Quail, *O. p. picta*; e. of Cascades in Ore., s. Idaho, extreme w. Nev., and through Sierras to mts. of s. Calif.

SANDHILL CRANE. *Grus canadensis:* (1) Little Brown Crane, *G. c. canadensis*; breeds in Arctic; migrates through interior of U.S. to Calif., Tex., and Mex. (2) Sandhill Crane, *G. c. tabida*; breeds in ne. Calif., e. Ore., n. Nev., s. Idaho, n. Ut., sw. Mont., w. Wyo., and nw. Colo.; winters from Calif. and Tex. s. to Mex.

CALIFORNIA CLAPPER RAIL. *Rallus obsoletus:* (1) California Clapper Rail, *R. o. obsoletus*; salt marshes of Monterey and San Francisco Bays, Calif.; casual farther n. (2) Light-footed Rail, *R. o. levipes*; salt marshes from San Diego to Santa Barbara, Calif. (3) Yuma Clapper Rail, *R. o. yumanensis*; lower Colo. R. from Yuma to Laguna Dam; also marshes in Imperial Valley s. of Salton Sea.

GOLDEN PLOVER. *Pluvialis dominica:* (1) American Golden Plover, *P. d. dominica*; rare migrant on Pacific Coast, along edge of Great Plains, and in Ut. (2) Pacific Golden Plover, *P. d. fulva*; has been recorded in Calif.

LONG-BILLED CURLEW. *Numenius americanus:* (1) Long-billed Curlew, *N. a. americanus*; breeds in Ut., s. Idaho, e. Nev., Colo., and n. N.M.; winters from cent. Calif. s. (2) Northern Curlew, *N. a. occidentalis*; breeds in e. Wash., e. Ore., ne. Calif., nw. Nev., Mont., Wyo., and ne. Colo.; winters s. to s. Calif ; either this race or the preceding one migrates through s. N.M. to s. Tex.

DOWITCHER. *Limnodromus griseus:* (1) Eastern Dowitcher, *L. g. griseus*; migrates through w. U.S. and winters from Calif. s. (2) Long-billed Dowitcher, *L. g. scolopaceus*; migrates through w. U.S. and winters from Calif. s.

WESTERN GULL. *Larus occidentalis:* (1) Western Gull, *L. o. occidentalis;* breeds along coast from Wash. to n. Calif. and Farallons; winters s. to s. Calif. (2) Wyman's Gull, *L. o. wymani;* breeds along coast of Calif. from Monterey Co. s.

HERRING GULL. *Larus argentatus:* (1) Herring Gull, *L. a. smithsonianus;* migrates and winters along Pacific Coast and Great Plains. (2) Thayer's Gull, *L. a. thayeri;* occurs s. to Calif. and Colo.

LEAST TERN. *Sterna antillarum:* (1) Least Tern, *S. a. antillarum;* breeds along North Platte R. in Wyo.; occasional in Colo. (2) Brown's Tern, *S. a browni;* breeds on coast n. to cent. Calif.

WHITE-WINGED DOVE. *Melopelia asiatica:* (1) Eastern White-winged Dove, *M. a. asiatica;* s. Tex. (2) Western White-winged Dove, *M. a. mearnsi;* se. Calif., s. Ariz., and sw. N.M.

YELLOW-BILLED CUCKOO. *Coccyzus americanus:* (1) Yellow-billed Cuckoo, *C. a. americanus;* e. U.S., breeding w. to e. Colo. (2) California Cuckoo, *C. a. occidentalis;* breeds from Wash. and cent. Colo. s. to Mex.

SCREECH OWL. *Otus asio:* (1) Aiken's Screech Owl, *O. a. aikeni;* se. Colo. and n. N.M. (2) Rocky Mountain Screech Owl, *O. a. maxwelliæ;* foothills and plains adjacent to Rocky Mts. from e. Mont. to n.-cent. Colo. (3) Mac-farlane's Screech Owl, *O. a. macfarlanei;* e. Wash., e. Ore., ne. Calif., Idaho, and w. Mont. (4) Kennicott's Screech Owl, *O. a. kennicotti;* w. Wash. (5) Brewster's Screech Owl, *O. a. brewsteri;* range starting in n.-cent. Wash., turning gradually w. through w. Ore. (6) California Screech Owl, *O. a. bendirei;* coast of Calif. from San Francisco Bay n. to sw. Ore. (s. Klamath, Jackson, Josephine, and Curry Cos.). (7) Pasadena Screech Owl, *O. a. quercinus;* s. Calif. w. of the deserts and n. along w. side of Sierra Nevada to Mt. Shasta. (8) Mexican Screech Owl, *O. a. cineraceus;* mts. of s. Ariz., s. N.M , and w.-cent. Tex. (9) Sahuaro Screech Owl, *O. a. gilmani;* deserts of se. Calif. and s. Ariz. and along Colo. R. to extreme s. Nev.

HORNED OWL. *Bubo virginianus:* (1) Arctic Horned Owl, *B. v. subarcticus;* s. in winter to Idaho and Ore. (casual). (2) Montana Horned Owl, *B. v. occidentalis;* Mont., Wyo., s. Idaho, se. Ore., and ne. Calif. (3) Northwestern Horned Owl, *B. v. lagophonus;* Idaho, ne. Ore., and e. Wash. (4) Dusky Horned Owl, *B. v. saturatus;* Pacific Coast region from nw. Calif. (Humboldt Co.) through w. Wash. (5) Pacific Horned Owl, *B. v. pacificus;* s.-cent. Ore. and Calif. (except Colo. Desert and extreme n. coast). (6) Western Horned Owl, *B. v. pallescens;* se. Calif., Colo., Ut., Ariz., N.M., and w. Tex.

PYGMY OWL. *Glaucidium gnoma:* (1) Rocky Mountain Pygmy Owl, *G. g. pinicola;* Rocky Mt. section from Mont., Idaho, and ne. Ore. s. to N.M. and s. Ariz. (2) Coast Pygmy Owl, *G. g. grinnelli;* coast belt of Pacific States s. to Monterey Co., Calif., and e. to base of Mt. Shasta and Lake Co., Calif. (3) California Pygmy Owl, *G. g. californicum;* Calif. (except range of preceding race, and desert regions of se. Calif.), also Cascade Mts. of Ore. and Wash.

SPOTTED OWL. *Strix occidentalis:* (1) California Spotted Owl, *S. o. occidentalis;* mts. of s. Calif. and along edge of Sierras to Mariposa Co. (2) Northern Spotted Owl, *S. o. caurina;* coast belt from Wash. to Marin Co., Calif. (3) Mexican Spotted Owl, *S. o. lucida;* mts. of s. Colo., Ariz., N.M., and w. Tex.

POOR-WILL. *Phalænoptilus nuttalli:* (1) Nuttall's Poor-will, *P. n. nuttalli;* breeds e. of Cascades from e. Wash. and Mont. s. to e. Calif., s. Ariz., and cent. Tex.; winters from se. Calif. and s. Tex. s. (2) Dusky Poor-will, *P. n. californicus;* Calif., breeds w. of Sierras and Mohave and Colorado

Deserts n. to head of Sacramento Valley; also sw. Ore. (Rogue R. Valley).
(3) Desert Poor-will, *P. n. hueyi*; breeds in deserts of se. Calif. and sw. Ariz.

NIGHTHAWK. *Chordeiles minor:* (1) Eastern Nighthawk, *C. m. minor*;
said to breed in nw. Wash. (2) Howell's Nighthawk, *C. m. howelli*; central
Rocky Mt. region (Wyo., ne. Ut., Colo., and ne. N.M.). (3) Western Nighthawk, *C. m. henryi*; s. Rocky Mt. region (sw. Colo., e. Ariz., and N.M.).
(4) Pacific Nighthawk, *C. m. hesperis*; breeds in Wash., Ore., Idaho, w.
Mont., nw. Wyo., w. and cent. Ut., Nev., coast of n. Calif., and in mts. to s.
Calif. (5) Sennett's Nighthawk, *C. m. sennetti*; breeds in n. Great Plains w.
to e. Mont. and e. Wyo.

BLUE-THROATED HUMMINGBIRD. *Lampornis clemenciæ:* (1) Texas
Blue-throated Hummingbird, *L. c. clemenciæ*; Chisos Mts., Tex. (2) Arizona
Blue-throated Hummingbird, *L. c. bessophilus*; mts. of s. Ariz. (s. and e. of
Tucson) and sw. N.M. (San Luis Mts.).

BELTED KINGFISHER. *Megaceryle alcyon:* (1) Eastern Belted Kingfisher,
M. a. alcyon; e. N.A. w. to base of Rockies. (2) Western Belted Kingfisher,
M. a. caurina; breeds w. of Rockies to Pacific; winters n. to s. Ariz. and n.-
cent. Calif. and along coast to Wash.

RED-SHAFTED FLICKER. *Colaptes cafer:* (1) Northwestern Flicker, *C. c
cafer*; Pacific Coast from n. Calif. (Humboldt Co.) through w. Ore. and Wash.
(w. of Cascades). (2) Red-shafted Flicker, *C. c. collaris*; breeds throughout
w. U.S. except where preceding race is found; winters throughout most of
range.

CALIFORNIA, or ACORN, WOODPECKER. *Balanosphyra formicivora:*
(1) California Woodpecker, *B. f. bairdi*; Calif. and sw. Ore. (2) Mearns's
Woodpecker, *B. f. aculeata*; Ariz., N.M., and w. Tex. (3) Ant-eating Woodpecker, *B. f. formicivora*; s.-cent. Tex. (Kerr Co. and Chisos Mts.).

RED-BREASTED SAPSUCKER. *Sphyrapicus varius:* (1) Northern Red-
breasted Sapsucker, *S. v. ruber*; breeds in w. Wash. and w. Ore. (w. of Cascades); winters s. along Calif. coast to Monterey. (2) Southern Red-breasted
Sapsucker, *S. v. daggetti*; breeds in higher mts. of Calif.; also in s. Ore. (Klamath, Jackson, and Josephine Cos.); winters in adjacent lowlands.

WILLIAMSON'S SAPSUCKER. *Sphyrapicus thyroideus:* (1) Williamson's
Sapsucker, *S. t. thyroideus*; high Cascades and Sierras of Pacific States; winters at lower altitudes. (2) Natalie's Sapsucker, *S. t. nataliæ*; Rocky Mt. section from Mont. to cent. Ariz. and N.M.; winters from s. N.M. and w. Tex.
into Mex.

HAIRY WOODPECKER. *Dryobates villosus:* (1) Eastern Hairy Woodpecker, *D. v. villosus*; pine hills of extreme e. Mont. (2) Harris's Woodpecker,
D. v. harrisi; nw. coast belt from w. Wash. s. to Humboldt Co., Calif. (3)
Cabanis's Woodpecker, *D. v. hyloscopus*; Calif. from Mendocino Co. and cent.
Sierras s. (4) Modoc Woodpecker, *D. v. orius*; Cascades and Sierras from s.-
cent. Wash. to cent. Calif., e. to Nev. (5) Rocky Mountain Hairy Woodpecker, *D. v. monticola*; Rocky Mt. section from e. Wash., ne. Ore., and Mont.
s. to e. Ut. and n. N.M. (6) White-breasted Woodpecker, *D. v. leucothorectis*;
s. Ut., Ariz. (except s. part), N.M. (except cent.-n. and extreme sw. corners).
and cent.-w. Tex. (7) Chihuahua Woodpecker, *D. v. icastus*; s. Ariz. and sw.
N.M.

DOWNY WOODPECKER. *Dryobates pubescens:* (1) Batchelder's Woodpecker, *D. p. leucurus*; Rocky Mt. region from Can. s. to n. N.M. and n.
Ariz.; w. to e. Wash., e. Ore., and extreme ne. Calif. (Warner Mts.). (2)
Gairdner's Woodpecker, *D. p. gairdneri*; coastal belt from w. Wash. to Mendocino Co., Calif. (3) Willow Woodpecker, *D. p. turatii*; Calif. (except nw.
coast and desert ranges) and s. Ore. (Klamath, Jackson, and Josephine Cos.).

LADDER-BACKED WOODPECKER. *Dryobates scalaris:* (1) Texas Woodpecker, *D. s. symplectus*; se. Colo., w. Okla., and Tex. (e. of Pecos River to 97th meridian). (2) Cactus Woodpecker, *D. s. cactophilus*; desert country from w. Tex. (w. of Pecos R.) through N.M. and Ariz. to se. Calif.

WHITE-HEADED WOODPECKER. *Dryobates albolarvatus:* (1) Northern White-headed Woodpecker, *D. a. albolarvatus*; Cascades and Sierras from Wash. s. to s.-cent. Calif. (Kern and Ventura Cos.); e. to Ida. and w. Nev. (2) Southern White-headed Woodpecker, *D. a. gravirostris*; mts. of s. Calif. (San Gabriel, San Bernardino, San Jacinto, Santa Rosa, and Cuyamaca Mts.).

THREE-TOED WOODPECKER. *Picoides tridactylus:* (1) Alpine Three-toed Woodpecker, *P. t. dorsalis*; sw. Mont. and Wyo. s. to Ariz. and N.M. (2) Alaska Three-toed Woodpecker, *P. t. fasciatus*; Wash., Ore., Ida., and nw. Mont.

COUCH'S KINGBIRD. *Tyrannus melancholicus:* (1) Couch's Kingbird, *T. m. couchi*; Tex. (lower Rio Grande Valley). (2) West Mexican Kingbird, *T. m. occidentalis*; s. Ariz. (rare and local).

MEXICAN CRESTED FLYCATCHER. *Myiarchus tyrannulus:* (1) Mexican Crested Flycatcher, *M. t. nelsoni*; lower Rio Grande Valley, Tex. (2) Arizona Crested Flycatcher, *M. t. magister*; deserts of s. Ariz. (Sahuaro belt).

TRAILL'S FLYCATCHER. *Empidonax trailli:* (1) Alder Flycatcher, *E. t. trailli*; breeds in e. N.A., w. presumably to Mont., e. Wyo., and ne. Colo. (2) Little Flycatcher, *E. t. brewsteri*; breeds in w. U.S. from Wash., cent. Ida., and cent. Wyo. s. to s. Calif., s. N.M., and w. Tex.

HORNED LARK. *Otocoris alpestris.* Horned Larks of one race or another breed throughout most of West from Can. s. to Mex. Races that migrate into areas where they do not breed are as follows: Pallid Horned Lark (n. Great Basin and n. Rocky Mt. sections), Dusky Horned Lark (n. and cent. Calif.), Island Horned Lark (coast of s. Calif. adjacent to Santa Barbara Ids.), Desert Horned Lark (se. Calif. and Ariz.). There is probably more or less of an intermingling of other races in certain sections, such as the Great Plains, Arizona, etc., but little is known about this at present. Most races are found all year round in their breeding-ranges, which are as follows: (1) Pallid Horned Lark, *O. a. arcticola*; breeds in mts. of Wash. (Cascades s. to Rainier). (2) Desert Horned Lark, *O .a. leucolæma*; breeds in Rocky Mt., Great Basin, and Great Plain areas from Mont. and s. Ida. s. to extreme e. Calif. (White Mts.), Nev., Ut., n. N.M., and w. Tex. (3) Streaked Horned Lark, *O. a. strigata*; breeds in nw. coast belt w. of Cascades from Wash. s. to nw. Calif. (Siskiyou Co.). (4) Dusky Horned Lark, *O. a. merrilli*; breeds from e. Wash. (e. of Cascades), n. Ida., and nw. Mont. s. to ne. Calif. and nw. Nev. (5) Island Horned Lark, *O. a. insularis*; Santa Barbara Ids., Calif. (6) California Horned Lark, *O. a. actia*; Calif. from San Francisco to San Diego and e. to San Joaquin Valley and desert divide. (7) Ruddy Horned Lark, *O. a. rubea*; Sacramento Valley, Calif. (8) Montezuma Horned Lark, *O. a. occidentalis*; cent. Ariz. and N.M. (9) Scorched Horned Lark, *O. a. adusta*; cent.-s. Ariz. (10) Mohave Horned Lark, *O. a. ammophila*; Mohave Desert to Owens Valley, Calif., and sw. Nev. (11) Sonora Horned Lark, *O. a. leucansiptila*; deserts along Colorado R. in se. Calif. and sw. Ariz.

CLIFF SWALLOW. *Petrochelidon albifrons:* (1) Northern Cliff Swallow, *P. a. albifrons*; breeds from Can. to s. Calif., n. Ariz., n. N.M., and w. Tex. A few winter in se. Calif. (2) Lesser Cliff Swallow, *P. a. tachina*; breeds in w. Tex. and se. along Rio Grande Valley. (3) Mexican Cliff Swallow, *P. a. melanogaster*; breeds in s. Ariz. and sw. N.M., and also in Brewster Co., Tex., in proximity of preceding race.

CANADA JAY. *Perisoreus canadensis:* (1) Rocky Mountain Jay, *P. c. capitalis;* Rocky Mt. region from Can. s. to n. N.M. and cent.-e. Ariz.; w. to e. Wash. and e. Ore. (2) Canada Jay, *P. c. canadensis;* Black Hills in ne. Wyo.

OREGON JAY. *Perisoreus obscurus:* (1) Oregon Jay, *P. o. obscurus;* Pacific slope of Wash., s. through coast mts. of Ore. to nw. Calif. (Mendocino Co.) (2) Gray Jay, *P. o. griseus;* Cascades from Wash., through Ore. to n. Calif. (Mt. Shasta and Warner Mts.).

STELLER'S JAY. *Cyanocitta stelleri:* (1) Steller's Jay, *C. s. stelleri;* coast belt of Wash. (2) Coast Jay, *C. s. carbonacea;* humid coast belt of Calif. from Monterey Co., Calif., to n. Ore. (3) Blue-fronted Jay, *C. s. frontalis;* mts. of Calif. (except humid coast belt n. of Monterey Co.). (4) Black-headed Jay, *C. s. annectens;* n. Rocky Mt. and Great Basin sections from e. Wash. Ida., and Mont. s. to e. Ore. and Wyo. (5) Long-crested Jay, *C. s. diademata* s. Rocky Mt. and Great Basin sections from Ut. and s. Wyo. s. to Mex.

CALIFORNIA JAY. *Aphelocoma californica:* (1) Long-tailed Jay, *A. c. immanis;* extreme e. Wash., Ore. (valleys between Cascades and coast ranges also Klamath and Lake Cos., Ore.), and Calif. (Sacramento and San Joaquin Valleys and adjacent slopes). (2) Nicasio Jay, *A. c. occleptica;* coast of n. Calif. from Humboldt Bay s. to e. side of San Francisco Bay. (3) California Jay, *A. c. californica;* coast of Calif. from San Francisco Bay (s. arm) s. to Mex. (4) Woodhouse's Jay, *A. c. woodhousei;* Rocky Mt. region from se. Ore., s. Ida., and s. Wyo. s. to se. Calif. (e. of Sierras), s. Ariz., s. N.M., and sw. Tex. (5) Texas Jay, *A. c. texana;* cent. and cent.-w. Tex. (Kerr and Edwards Cos. to Davis Mts.).

ARIZONA JAY. *Aphelocoma sieberi:* (1) Arizona Jay, *A. s. arizonæ;* se. Ariz. and sw. N.M. (2) Couch's Jay, *A. s. couchi;* cent.-w. Tex. (Chisos Mts. Brewster Co.).

RAVEN. *Corvus corax:* (1) American Raven, *C. c. sinuatus;* most of w. U.S. (2) Northern Raven, *C. c. principalis;* said to be the race in w. Wash. (*A.O.U. Check-List*), but specimens do not bear this out.

CROW. *Corvus brachyrhynchos:* (1) Western Crow, *C. b. hesperis;* w. U.S. from Can. s. to s. Calif., cent. Ariz., and cent. N.M. (2) Northwestern Crow *C. b. caurinus;* Puget Sound area of w. Wash.

BLACK-CAPPED CHICKADEE. *Penthestes atricapillus:* (1) Long-tailed Chickadee, *P. a. septentrionalis;* Rocky Mt. region from Can. s. to n. N.M. w. to e. Wash. and e. Ore. (2) Oregon Chickadee, *P. a. occidentalis;* nw. coast belt w. of Cascades from w. Wash. s. to nw. Calif. (Siskiyou Co.).

MOUNTAIN CHICKADEE. *Penthestes gambeli:* (1) Grinnell's Chickadee, *P. g. grinnelli;* e. of Cascades in ne. Ore., e. Wash., and n. Ida. (2) Short tailed Chickadee, *P. g. abbreviatus;* Cascade region and Sierras from Ore. s. to Mt. Whitney, Calif., also nw. Nev. (3) Bailey's Chickadee, *P. g. baileyæ* mts. of s. Calif. from s. extremity of Sierras (Tulare Co.) and Santa Lucia Mts. (Monterey Co.) s. to San Diego Co. (4) Mountain Chickadee, *P. g. gambeli;* Rocky Mt. region from Mont. and Wyo. s. to Ariz., N.M., and w. Tex. (5) Inyo Chickadee, *P. g. inyoënsis;* higher mts. of e. Calif. (e. of Sierras in Mono and Inyo Cos.).

CHESTNUT-BACKED CHICKADEE. *Penthestes rufescens:* (1) Chestnut backed Chickadee, *P. r. rufescens;* Pacific Coast from n. Calif. (Sonoma Co. to Wash. and sparingly e. to e. Ore. and w. Mont. (2) Nicasio Chickadee *P. r. neglectus;* coast belt of Marin Co., Calif. (3) Barlow's Chickadee, *P. r. barlowi;* coast of middle Calif. (San Francisco Bay to n. San Luis Obispo Co.).

BLACK-CRESTED TITMOUSE. *Bæolophus atricristatus:* (1) Black-crested Titmouse, *B. a. atricristatus*; Rio Grande Valley of Tex. (2) Sennett's Titmouse, *B. a. sennetti*; lowlands of cent. Tex. from Tom Green and Concho Cos. e. to Brazos R., and from Young Co. s. to Nueces and Bee Cos.

PLAIN TITMOUSE. *Bæolophus inornatus:* (1) Oregon Titmouse, *B. i. sequestratus*; s. Ore. (Jackson and Josephine Cos.) and n. Calif. (Siskiyou Co.) between coast and Cascade ranges. (2) Plain Titmouse, *B. i. inornatus*; n and cent. Calif. (Mendocino and Shasta Cos. s. to San Luis Obispo and Kern Cos.). (3) San Diego Titmouse, *B. i. transpositus*; sw. Calif. (w. of desert divides from San Diego Co. to Santa Barbara Co.). (4) Gray Titmouse, *B. i. griseus*; Rocky Mt. and Great Basin regions from sw. Wyo. and s. Ida. s. to cent.-w. Tex., s. N.M., s. Ariz., and e. Calif. (e. of Sierras).

BUSH-TIT. *Psaltriparus minimus:* (1) Coast Bush-Tit, *P. m. minimus*; coastal belt from Wash. s. to Mex. border. (2) California Bush-Tit, *P. m. californicus*; interior valleys from s.-cent. Calif. (Kern Co.) n. to s. Ore. (Josephine, Jackson, and Klamath Cos.). (3) Lead-colored Bush-Tit, *P. m. plumbeus*; Rocky Mt. region from w. Wyo. and se. Ore. s. to w. Tex., N.M., n. and e. Ariz., and se. Calif. (desert ranges). (4) Lloyd's Bush-Tit, *P. m. lloydi*; cent.-w. Tex. (mts. between Pecos and Rio Grande).

WHITE-BREASTED NUTHATCH. *Sitta carolinensis:* (1) Rocky Mountain Nuthatch, *S. c. nelsoni*; Rocky Mt. region (e. of Cascades and Sierras) from e. Wash. and Mont. to Mex. (2) Slender-billed Nuthatch, *S. c. aculeata*; Pacific States from w. Wash. (rare) to Mex. and from coast e. to Cascades and Sierras. (3) Inyo Nuthatch, *S. c. tenuissima*; Panamint and White Mts. of Calif. (e. of Sierras).

PYGMY NUTHATCH. *Sitta pygmæa:* (1) Pygmy Nuthatch, *S. p. pygmæa*; middle Calif. (pines near coast from San Luis Obispo Co. to Mendocino Co.). (2) Black-eared Nuthatch, *S. p. melanotis*; Cascades (e. slopes) and Rocky Mt. region from Wash. and Mont. s. to Mex.; also Sierra Nevada of Calif. s. to San Bernardino Mts. (3) White-naped Nuthatch, *S. p. leuconucha*; mts. of s. Calif. (Riverside, San Diego, and Imperial Cos.).

CREEPER. *Certhia familiaris:* (1) Rocky Mountain Creeper, *C. f. montana*; Rocky Mt. section from Mont., Ida., and ne. Ore. (Blue Mts.) s. to N.M. and cent. Ariz. (2) Mexican Creeper, *C. f. albescens*; mts. of se. Ariz. and extreme sw. N.M. (3) Sierra Creeper, *C. f. zelotes*; Cascades of Wash. and Ore. (summits and e. slope) and through Sierras to mts. of s. Calif.; spreading to adjacent lowlands in winter. (4) California Creeper, *C. f. occidentalis*; forest regions of coast belt in Pacific States from w. Wash. (including w. slope of Cascades) s. to Monterey, Calif.

WREN-TIT. *Chamæa fasciata:* (1) Coast Wren-Tit, *C. f. phæa*; Pacific Coast belt of Ore. (2) Ruddy Wren-Tit, *C. f. rufula*; Pacific Coast belt of n. Calif. s. to w. shore of San Francisco Bay and n. Santa Cruz Co. (3) Gambel's Wren-Tit, *C. f. fasciata*; cent. Calif. from San Francisco Bay (e. and s. shores) s. through Santa Clara Co. and along coast to San Luis Obispo Co. (4) Pallid Wren-Tit, *C. f. henshawi*; sw. Ore. (Rogue River Valley), interior valleys of Calif., and along coast of s. Calif. from Santa Barbara Co. s.

BEWICK'S WREN. *Thryomanes bewicki:* (1) Baird's Wren, *T. b. eremophilus*; arid regions of sw. U.S. from w. Colo., sw. Wyo., s. Ut., and s. Nev. s. through extreme w. Tex., Ariz., N.M., and se. Calif. (2) Seattle Wren, *T. b. calophonus*; Pacific slope in Wash. and Ore. (w. of Cascades). (3) Nicasio Wren, *T. b. marinensis*; coast of n. Calif. s. to San Francisco Bay. (4) Vigors's Wren, *T. b. spilurus*; coast of cent. Calif. from San Francisco Bay (Golden Gate and Berkeley) s. to n. Monterey Co. (5) San Joaquin Wren, *T. b. drymœcus*; interior Calif. (Sacramento and San Joaquin Valleys, including both slopes of Sierras), also w. Nev. (6) San Diego Wren, *T. b. correctus*;

sw. Calif. from Monterey and San Benito Cos. s. to San Diego. (7) Santa
Cruz Wren, *T. b. nesophilus*; Santa Cruz Id., Calif. (8) Catalina Wren, *T. b.
catalinæ*; Santa Catalina Id., Calif. (9) San Clemente Wren, *T. b. leucophrys*
San Clemente Id., Calif.

MARSH WREN. *Telmatodytes palustris:* (1) Western Marsh Wren, *T. p.
plesius*; marshes in Rocky Mt. region from Can. s. to ne. Calif. and N.M.
and from e. Wash. and e. Ore. e. to edge of Great Plains. Winters from s.
Calif. and Tex. (occasionally farther n.) s. into Mex. (2) Tule Wren, *T. p.
paludicola*; resident along Pacific Coast from w. Wash. to s. Calif. (3)
Suisun Marsh Wren, *T. p. æstuarinus*; interior Calif. (Sacramento and San
Joaquin Valleys from Colusa Co. to Tulare Co.), also s. Nev. (4) Prairie
Marsh Wren, *T. p. dissaëptus*; breeds on Great Plains west probably to e.
Mont. and e. Wyo.

CAÑON WREN. *Catherpes mexicanus:* (1) White-throated Cañon Wren,
C. m. albifrons; cent.-w. Tex. (mouth of Pecos R. to Brewster Co.). (2) Cañon
Wren, *C. m. conspersus*; resident in w. U.S. from se. Wash., Ida., and Wyo.
s. to s. Calif., Mex., and w. Tex.

CURVE-BILLED THRASHER. *Toxostoma curvirostre:* (1) Palmer's
Thrasher, *T. c. palmeri*; s. Ariz. (except extreme se. corner). (2) Curve-billed
Thrasher, *T. c. curvirostre*; w. Tex., N.M., and extreme se. Ariz. (n. to s.
parts of Chiricahua and Huachuca Mts.). (3) Brownsville Thrasher, *T. c.
oberholseri*; lower Rio Grande Valley, s. Tex.

CALIFORNIA THRASHER. *Toxostoma redivivum:* (1) California Thrasher,
T. r. redivivum; s. Calif. (w. of deserts and Sierras) n. to Monterey and Placer
Cos. (2) Sonoma Thrasher, *T. r. sonomæ*; n.-cent. and cent. Calif. (Shasta
Co. s. to Eldorado Co. and through San Francisco Bay region to Santa Cruz)

ROBIN. *Turdus migratorius:* (1) Northwestern Robin, *T. m. caurinus*;
coast belt of Wash. and nw. Ore. (2) Western Robin, *T. m. propinquus*;
breeds in w. U.S. in Canadian and transition zones from Can. s. to Mex.
and from Pacific Coast e. to edge of Great Plains except in w. Wash., where
previous race is found. Winters from Wash. and Wyo. s.

VARIED THRUSH. *Ixoreus nævius:* (1) Pacific Varied Thrush, *I. n. nævius*;
breeds in evergreen forests of w. Wash. and w. Ore. (coast to e. edge of Cascades) and nw. Calif. (Humboldt Co.). Winters s. along coast to Monterey,
Calif. (2) Northern Varied Thrush, *I. n. meruloides*; breeds in Rocky Mt.
region in nw. Mont., n. Ida., se. Wash., and nw. Ore.; winters mainly in interior Calif.

HERMIT THRUSH. *Hylocichla guttata.* Six subspecies of the Hermit
Thrush migrate through w. U.S. or winter from Ore., Ariz., s. N.M., and Tex.
s. Practically all six migrate se. across Sw. States into w. Tex. and Mex.
Two of these races (1) Alaska Hermit Thrush, *H. g. guttata*, and (2) Dwarf
Hermit Thrush, *H. g. nanus*, breed in w. Can. and Alaska and migrate
throughout most of W. States. They are the wintering races of Ore. and Calif.
The breeding ranges of the other four subspecies are: (3) Monterey Hermit
Thrush, *H. g. slevini*; heavy forests of coast belt of Calif. (s. Monterey Co.
n. to Trinity Co.); also sw. Ore. (Siskiyou Mts.). (4) Sierra Hermit Thrush,
H. g. sequoiensis; Cascades and other high mts. in cent. and w. Wash. and
cent. and w. Ore.; also Sierras and other high mts. of Calif. (except humid
coast belt and White Mts.); also w. edge of Nev. (5) Mono Hermit Thrush,
H. g. polionota; White Mts. of e. Calif. and mts. of Great Basin in Nev.
(6) Audubon's Hermit Thrush, *H. g. auduboni*; Rocky Mt. region from Ida.
and Mont. s. to e. Nev., Ariz., and N.M., and w. to se. Wash. and ne. Ore.
(Blue and Wallowa Mts.).

RUSSET-BACKED THRUSH. *Hylocichla ustulata:* (1) Russet-backed

Thrush, *H. u. ustulata*; breeds in moist woodlands of Pacific States from Can. to s. Calif. and from coast to and including Cascades and Sierras. (2) Olive-backed Thrush, *H. u. swainsoni*; breeds in Rocky Mt. region (e. of Cascades and Sierras) from e. Wash. and Mont. s. to e.-cent. Calif., Nev., Ut., and Colo. Migrates s. into Mex.

EASTERN BLUEBIRD. *Sialia sialis:* (1) Eastern Bluebird, *S. s. sialis*; breeds in e. U.S. w. sparingly to e. Mont., e. Wyo., and e. Colo. (2) Azure Bluebird, *S. s. fulva*; occasional in summer in high mts. of s. Ariz. (Santa Ritas and Huachucas).

WESTERN BLUEBIRD. *Sialia mexicana:* (1) Western Bluebird, *S. m. occidentalis*; breeds throughout the Pacific States and in n. Ida. and w. Mont.; winters in Pacific States. (2) Chestnut-backed Bluebird, *S. m. bairdi*; breeds in Rocky Mt. section from Ut. and Colo. s. to Mex.; occasional in Wyo.; winters in s. Ut., Ariz., N.M., and w. Tex.

PLUMBEOUS GNATCATCHER. *Polioptila melanura:* (1) Plumbeous Gnatcatcher, *P. m. melanura*; deserts of se. Calif., s. Nev., Ariz., N.M., and Rio Grande Valley of w. Tex. (2) Black-tailed Gnatcatcher, *P. m. californica*; San Diegan district of sw. Calif. n. to Ventura.

RUBY-CROWNED KINGLET. *Corthylio calendula:* (1) Eastern Ruby-crowned Kinglet, *C. c. calendula*; breeds in Rocky Mt. section from Can. s. to cent. Ariz. and cent. N.M. Migrates through adjacent low country and winters from Ariz. and s. N.M. s. into Mex. (2) Western Ruby-crowned Kinglet, *C. c. cineraceus*; breeds in higher mts. of Calif. and in Ore. and Wash. (chiefly e. of Cascade divide), also n. Ida.; winters in Calif. (3) Sitka Kinglet, *C. c. grinnelli*; winters chiefly along coast s. to Monterey Co., Calif.

PHAINOPEPLA. *Phainopepla nitens:* (1) Northern Phainopepla, *P. n. lepida*; breeds in sw. U.S. (Calif., s. Nev., s. Ut., Ariz., and sw. N.M.); winters in s. Calif., s. Ariz., and w. Tex. (2) Mexican Phainopepla, *P. n. nitens*; breeds in w. Tex. (Brewster Co.).

LOGGERHEAD SHRIKE. *Lanius ludovicianus:* (1) White-rumped Shrike, *L. l. excubitorides*; breeds e. of Cascades and Sierras from Can. s. to se. Calif., Mex., and w. Tex.; winters in sw. U.S. (2) California Shrike, *L. l. gambeli*; breeds in Calif. w. of Cascade-Sierra divide and in e. Wash. and parts of Ore.; winters in Calif. (3) Island Shrike, *L. l. anthonyi*; Santa Barbara Ids., Calif.

HUTTON'S VIREO. *Vireo huttoni:* (1) Hutton's Vireo, *V. h. huttoni*; resident in Pacific States (w. of Sierras and Cascades). (2) Stephens's Vireo, *V. h. stephensi*; oak belt of mts. of se. Ariz., sw. N.M., and w. Tex.

BELL'S, or LEAST, VIREO. *Vireo belli:* (1) Bell's Vireo, *V. b. belli*; breeds in e. Colo. (2) Texas Vireo, *V. b. medius*; breeds in sw. Tex. (Presidio, Brewster, and Kinney Cos.). (3) Arizona Vireo, *V. b. arizonæ*; breeds near streams in deserts of se. Calif., s. Ariz., sw. N.M., and cent.-w. Tex. (4) Least Vireo, *V. b. pusillus*; breeds in Calif. (interior from upper Sacramento Valley s., and coast from Monterey Co. s.).

SOLITARY VIREO. *Vireo solitarius:* (1) Plumbeous Vireo, *V. s. plumbeus*; breeds in Rocky Mt. region from n. Nev., n. Ut., s. Mont., and se. Wyo. s. into Mex. (2) Cassin's Vireo, *V. s. cassini*; breeds in Pacific States.

ORANGE-CROWNED WARBLER. *Vermivora celata:* (1) Eastern Orange-crowned Warbler, *V. c. celata*; breeds in Can. and Alaska; winters in s. Calif.; a migrant elsewhere. (2) Rocky Mountain Orange-crowned Warbler, *V. c. orestera*; breeds in Rocky Mt. region from e. Wash. (e. of Cascades) and Mont. s. to Ariz. and N.M. (3) Lutescent Warbler, *V. c. lutescens*; breeds in Pacific

States w. of Sierras and Cascades; winters in Mex. (4) Dusky Warbler *V. c. sordida*; breeds on Channel Ids., Calif., and on coast near San Diego; winters along coast of Calif., casually n. to San Francisco.

YELLOW WARBLER *Dendroica æstiva:* (1) Eastern Yellow Warbler, *D. a æstiva*; breeds in e. N.A. and in Rocky Mt. region s. to Nev. and n. N.M. (2) Alaska Yellow Warbler, *D. a. rubiginosa*; breeds from Vancouver Id. to Alaska; migrates through Pacific States and N.M. (3) California Yellow Warbler, *D. a. brewsteri*; breeds in Pacific States w. of Cascades and Sierras. In migration also in e. Calif. and Ariz. (4) Sonora Yellow Warbler, *D. a sonorana*; breeds in desert regions of se. U.S. (se. Calif., sw. Ut., s. and w. Ariz., s. N.M., and w. Tex.).

AUDUBON'S WARBLER. *Dendroica auduboni:* (1) Audubon's Warbler, *D. a. auduboni*; breeds from Can. s. to mts. of s. Calif., Ariz., and se. N.M.; winters in Pacific States and lower Rio Grande Valley, Tex. (2) Black-fronted Warbler, *D. a. nigrifrons*; breeds in mts. of se. Ariz. (Huachuca and Chiricahua Mts., etc.).

YELLOW-THROAT. *Geothlypis trichas:* (1) Western Yellow-throat, *G. t. occidentalis*; breeds in w. U.S., Mont., and Wash. s. to w. Tex., N.M., s. Nev., and Calif. (except where following races are found); migrates throughout. (2) Salt Marsh Yellow-throat, *G. t. sinuosa*; resident in salt and fresh marshes in coast belt of Calif. from San Francisco Bay s. to San Luis Obispo Co. (3) Tule Yellow-throat, *G. t. scirpicola*; resident in salt marshes of s. Calif. n. to Santa Barbara and s. fork of Kern R., also along Colo. R. to s. Nev. and extreme sw. Ut., also valleys of extreme s. Ariz.

PILEOLATED WARBLER. *Wilsonia pusilla:* (1) Northern Pileolated Warbler, *W. p. pileolata*; breeds at high altitudes from Can. s. to mts. of s. Ore., ne. Calif., n. Ariz., n. N.M., and w. Tex.; migrates throughout. (2) Golden Pileolated Warbler, *W. p. chryseola*; breeds in Pacific States; w. Wash., w. Ore., and Calif. (coast ranges and Sierras); migrates throughout Calif. and casually in Ariz.

RED-WING. *Agelaius phœniceus.* Red-wings breed in suitable places from Can. to Mex Various races usually winter somewhere within their breeding ranges, but have a tendency to migrate from the colder sections in winter. There is probably some intermingling of the races in winter, but very little is known about this. In the Rocky Mts. and Great Plains sections two races are known to be strongly migratory into the ranges occupied by other Red-wings; there are the Giant Red-wing (s. to Colo. and Tex.) and the Thick-billed Red-wing (s. to Ariz., N.M., and w. Tex.). The Pacific States birds seem to be more stationary. The breeding ranges are as follows: (1) Giant Red-wing, *A. p. arctolegus*; Can. s. to Mont. (2) Thick-billed Red-wing, *A. p. fortis*; central Rocky Mt. region (e. Ida., Wyo., and Colo.). (3) Nevada Red-wing, *A. p. nevadensis*; Great Basin region (Ida., e. Wash., e. Ore., e. Calif. e. of Sierras, Nev., Ut., n. Ariz., and N.M. except sw. corner). (4) Northwestern Red-wing, *A. p. caurinus*; nw. coast belt from w. Wash. to n. Calif. (Mendocino Co.). (5) San Francisco Red-wing, *A. p. mailliardorum*; central coast region of Calif. (Sherwood, Mendocino Co., s. to Monterey Co. and e., incl. Suisun Bay and valleys between inner coast ranges). (6) Bi-colored Red-wing, *A. p. californicus*; Sacramento and San Joaquin Valleys of Calif. and San Francisco Bay area. (7) Kern Red-wing, *A p. aciculatus*; south Fork Valley of Kern R., Kern Co., Calif. (8) San Diego Red-wing, *A. p. neutralis*; s. Calif. (Pacific slope n. to San Luis Obispo Co.). (9) Sonora Red-wing, *A. p. sonoriensis*; se. Calif. (lower Colo. R. Valley), s. Ariz., extreme s. Nev., and sw. N.M.

HOODED ORIOLE. *Icterus cucullatus:* (1) Sennett's Oriole, *I. c. sennetti*; breeds in lower Rio Grande Valley, Tex. (2) Arizona Hooded Oriole, *I. c. nelsoni*; breeds in s. and s.-cent. Calif., s. Ariz., and sw. N.M.; winters in Mex.

COWBIRD. *Molothrus ater:* (1) Eastern Cowbird, *M. a. ater*; breeds in N.M. (except extreme sw. corner) and Colo. (2) Nevada Cowbird, *M. a. artemisiæ*; breeds in Rocky Mt. region from Can. s. to e. Calif., s. Nev., Ut., and Wyo., and from Great Plains w. to e. Wash., e. Ore., and e. Calif. (e. of Sierras); winters s. into Mex. (3) California Cowbird, *M. a. californicus*; San Joaquin Valley of Calif. from Merced Co. s. to Kern Co. (Not considered a good subspecies by some authorities.) (4) Dwarf Cowbird, *M. a. obscurus*; s. Calif. (from Ventura and Inyo Cos. s.), s. Ariz., extreme sw. N.M., and s. Tex.

CARDINAL. *Richmondena cardinalis:* (1) Gray-tailed Cardinal, *R. c. canicauda*; cent. and cent.-w. Tex. (2) Arizona Cardinal, *R. c. superba*; s. Ariz. and sw. N.M.

PYRRHULOXIA. *Pyrrhuloxia sinuata:* (1) Texas Pyrrhuloxia, *P. s. texana*; Tex. (Nueces, Bee, Bexar, Kendall, and Tom Green Cos. s. into Mex.). (2) Arizona Pyrrhuloxia, *P. s. sinuata*; s. Ariz., s. N.M., and cent.-w. Tex.

BLACK-HEADED GROSBEAK. *Hedymeles melanocephalus:* (1) Black-headed Grosbeak, *H. m. melanocephalus*; breeds in Pacific States from Wash. s. throughout Calif.; also w. Nev. (2) Rocky Mountain Grosbeak, *H. m. papago*; breeds in Rocky Mt. States from Can. to Mex.

BLUE GROSBEAK. *Guiraca cærulea:* (1) Western Blue Grosbeak, *G. c. interfusa*; breeds in river valleys in se. Calif. (Colo. R.), s. Nev., s. Colo., Ariz., N.M., and w. Tex. (2) California Blue Grosbeak, *G. c. salicaria*; breeds in s. and cent. Calif.

VARIED BUNTING. *Passerina versicolor:* (1) Varied Bunting, *P. v. versicolor*; breeds in lower Rio Grande Valley, Tex. (2) Beautiful Bunting, *P. v. pulchra*; recorded casually or locally in se. Calif. and s. Ariz.

EVENING GROSBEAK. *Hesperiphona vespertina:* (1) Eastern Evening Grosbeak, *H. v. vespertina*; breeds in Can.; winter visitant s. to e. Wyo. and probably Wash. (2) Western Evening Grosbeak, *H. v. brooksi*; breeds in high mts. from Can. to Sierra Nevada of cent. Calif. and mts. of n. Ariz. and N.M. Winters in adjacent lowlands and s. to s. Calif. (3) Mexican Evening Grosbeak, *H. v. montana*; high mts. of se. Ariz.

HOUSE FINCH or LINNET. *Carpodacus mexicanus:* (1) Common House Finch, *C. m. frontalis*; from se. Wash., Ore., Ida., and Wyo. s. into Mex., and from Great Plains and cent. Tex. to w. coast. (2) San Luis House Finch, *C. m. potosinus*; sw. Tex. (along Rio Grande). (3) San Clemente House Finch, *C. m. clementis*; San Clemente Id., Calif.

PINE GROSBEAK. *Pinicola enucleator:* (1) Alaska Pine Grosbeak, *P. e. alascensis*; breeds in Alaska and w. Can.; winters s. to Wash. and Mont. (2) Kodiak Pine Grosbeak, *P. e. flammula*; breeds in coastal Alaska; winters s. irregularly to Wash. (3) Rocky Mountain Pine Grosbeak, *P. e. montana*; high mts. in Rockies from Ida. and Mont. s. to n. N.M.; also in Cascades in n. Wash. (4) California Pine Grosbeak, *P. e. californica*; high summits of central Sierra Nevada, Calif.

GRAY-CROWNED ROSY FINCH or LEUCOSTICTE. *Leucosticte tephrocotis:* (1) Hepburn's Rosy Finch, *L. t. littoralis*; breeds above timber line on mts. from Alaska s. in Cascades to n. Calif.; winters s. and e. in mts. to e. Calif., Nev., Ida., Mont., Wyo., Ut., and Colo. (2) Gray-crowned Rosy Finch, *L. t. tephrocotis*; breeds from nw. Mont. n. into Can.; in winter w. to Cascades and s. to Ut., Colo. (3) Sierra Nevada Rosy Finch, *L. t. dawsoni*; high peaks of cent. Sierra Nevada, Calif.

REDPOLL. *Acanthis linaria:* (1) Common Redpoll, *A. l. linaria*; subarctic, wandering irregularly s. in winter to e. Ore. and Colo. (2) Greater Redpoll, *A. l. rostrata*; winters s. to Mont., casually to Colo.

COMMON GOLDFINCH. *Spinus tristis:* (1) Eastern Goldfinch, *S. t. tristis*; breeds in e. U.S. w. to e. Mont., e. Wyo., and e. Colo.; sometimes winters in same area. (2) Pale Goldfinch, *S. t. pallidus*; breeds e. of Cascades in Rocky Mt. section from e. Wash. and w. Mont. s. to Nev. and w. Colo.; winters to Mex. (3) Willow Goldfinch, *P. t. salicamans*; resident in Pacific States from w. Wash. through Calif., chiefly w. of Cascades and Sierras.

ARKANSAS GOLDFINCH. *Spinus psaltria:* (1) Arkansas Goldfinch, *S. p. psaltria*; Colo., N.M., and cent.-n. Tex. s. into Mex. (2) Green-backed Goldfinch, *S. p. hesperophilus*; breeds from Ore. and Ut. through s. Calif. and s. Ariz.; winters from n. Calif. and s. Ariz. s. into Mex.

RED CROSSBILL. *Loxia curvirostra:* (1) Sitka Crossbill, *L. c. sitkensis*; along coast from Wash. to n. Calif. (2) Bendire's Crossbill, *L. c. bendirei*; breeds in mts. of w. U.S. from Can. s. in Cascades and Sierras to Calif. and in Rockies to Colo. and n. N.M.; wanders to adjacent lowlands and s. to s. Calif. (3) Mexican Crossbill, *L. c. stricklandi*; higher mts. of s. Calif., Ariz., s. N.M., and cent.-w. Tex.

SPOTTED TOWHEE. *Pipilo maculatus.* The five Pacific Coast races of the Spotted Towhee are apparently non-migratory except for the Oregon Towhee, which has a tendency to move southward, sometimes invading the range of the Sacramento Towhee in s. Ore. and n. Calif. West of the Cascades and Sierras the Nevada Towhee is somewhat migratory, going s. to the lower Colo. R. Valley in se. Calif. and w. Ariz. The two Rocky Mt. races are strongly migratory, the Arctic Towhee migrating through Wyo. and ne. Ut. to Colo. and Tex., and the Spurred Towhee into the southern part of its breeding range and Mex. Breeding ranges are as follows: (1) Arctic Towhee, *P. m. arcticus*; breeds in Mont. and e. Wyo. (2) Spurred Towhee, *P. m. montanus*; Ut., w. Wyo., Colo., w. Tex., N.M., Ariz., s. Nev., and se. Calif. (Panamint Mts.). (3) Nevada Towhee, *P. m. curtatus*; e. Wash., e. Ore., Ida., n. Nev., and ne. Calif. (e. of Sierras). (4) Oregon Towhee, *P. m. oregonus*; w. Wash. and w. Ore. (Cascades to Pacific). (5) Sacramento Towhee, *P. m. falcinellus*; interior Calif. (Sacramento and San Joaquin Valleys and slopes of Sierras); also s. Ore. (Jackson and Josephine Cos.). (6) San Francisco Towhee, *P. m. falcifer*; coast region of Calif. (Monterey Co. to Humboldt Co.). (7) San Diego Towhee, *P. m. megalonyx*; coast of s. Calif. (n. to San Luis Obispo Co. and e. to s. Kern Co.). (8) San Clemente Towhee, *P. m. clementæ*; San Clemente and Santa Catalina Ids., Calif.

BROWN TOWHEE. *Pipilo fuscus:* (1) Oregon Brown Towhee, *P. f. bullatus*; sw. Ore. (Josephine, Jackson, and Douglas Cos.). (2) Sacramento Brown Towhee, *P. f. carolæ*; interior valleys of Calif. w. of Sierras from Kern Co. and n. to Shasta Co. (3) San Francisco Brown Towhee, *P. f. petulana*; coast of n. Calif. (Humboldt Bay s. to Santa Cruz). (4) California Brown Towhee, *P. f. crissalis*; coast of s. Calif. (from Monterey s. to Mex. and e. to w. edge of San Joaquin Valley and deserts). (5) Cañon Towhee, *P. f. mesoleucus*; s. Colo., Ariz., N.M., and w. Tex.

SAVANNAH SPARROW. *Passerculus sandwichensis:* (1) Western Savannah Sparrow, *P. s. alaudinus*; breeds in Can. and Alaska; migrates through Pacific States and w. Great Plains; winters in Calif. and Tex. (2) Aleutian Savannah Sparrow, *P. s. sandwichensis*; breeds in Aleutians, Alaska; winters along coast to cent. Calif. (occasionally). (3) Nevada Savannah Sparrow, *P. s. nevadensis*; breeds in Great Basin (e. Wash., e. Ore., e. Calif., Nev., Ut., Idaho, Mont., Wyo., Colo., and n. N.M.); winters s. into Mex. (4) Bryant's Sparrow, *P. s. bryanti*; San Francisco Bay area and coast of Calif. from San Luis Obispo Co. n. to Humboldt Co.

LARGE-BILLED SPARROW. *Passerculus rostratus:* (1) Large-billed Sparrow, *P. r. rostratus*; breeds in Mex. and ne. Lower Calif.; winters along coast of s. Calif. n. to Santa Barbara. (2) San Lucas Sparrow, *P. r. guttatus*; breeds on San Benito Ids., Lower Calif.; winters occasionally along coast of s. Calif. with preceding race.

VESPER SPARROW. *Poœcetes gramineus:* (1) Oregon Vesper Sparrow, *P. g. affinis*; breeds in Wash. and Ore. w. of Cascades; winters in s. and cent. Calif. (2) Western Vesper Sparrow, *P. g. confinis*; breeds from Can. s. to n. Ariz., n. N.M., and Tex., and from Great Plains w. to e. Wash., e. Ore., ne. Calif., and Nev.; winters from s. Calif. (w. of Sierras), s. Ariz., and cent. Tex. s. into Mex.

RUFOUS-CROWNED SPARROW. *Aimophila ruficeps:* (1) Rufous-crowned Sparrow, *A. r. ruficeps*; Calif. w. of Sierras from Sonoma, Solano, Sutter, and Placer Cos. s. to Kern Co. (2) Santa Cruz Sparrow, *A. r. obscura*; Santa Cruz Id. and probably adjacent ids., Calif. (3) Ashy Sparrow, *A. r. canescens*; s. Calif. (San Diegan district from Ventura Co. to Mex.). (4) Rock Sparrow, *A. r. eremœca*; breeds in Okla. (Wichita Mts.) and Tex. (Cook Co., sw. to Pecos R. and Brewster Co.). (5) Scott's Sparrow, *A. r. scotti*; Ariz., s. N.M., and w. Tex.; casual in se. Colo.

DESERT SPARROW. *Amphispiza bilineata:* (1) Black-throated Sparrow, *A. b. bilineata*; n.-cent. Tex. s. into Mex. (2) Desert Sparrow, *A. b. deserticola*; breeds in desert country of Calif., Nev., Ut., w. Colo., Ariz., N.M., and w. Tex.; winters from se. Calif., s. Ariz., and s. N.M. s.

SAGE SPARROW. *Amphispiza nevadensis:* (1) Northern Sage Sparrow, *A. n. nevadensis*; breeds in Great Basin district (e. Wash., e. Ore., e. Calif. (e. of Sierras), cent. and s. Idaho, Nev., Ut., sw. Mont., w. Wyo., w. Colo., and nw. N.M.); winters from s. edge of breeding range to deserts of s. Calif., Ariz., N.M., and w. Tex. (2) California Sage Sparrow, *A. n. canescens*; breeds in cent. and s. Calif. w. of Sierras from Fresno south to Mt. Pinos, Ventura Co., w. to Carrizo Plain, San Luis Obispo Co., and e. to Owens Valley; winters s. to Mexican border.

OREGON JUNCO. *Junco oreganus.* Races of this species winter throughout the w. U.S. from Can. to Mex. as follows: ROCKY MT. REGION, Shufeldt's Junco and Montana Junco; GREAT BASIN REGION, mostly Shufeldt's Junco, and a few Montana Juncos in n. portion (e. Wash. and e. Ore.); COAST BELT OF WASH. AND ORE., Oregon Junco and Shufeldt's Junco; CALIFORNIA, Oregon Junco (along coast s. to San Francisco), Shufeldt's Junco (n. and cent. Calif.), Thurber's Junco (lower levels throughout State), Point Pinos Junco (winters on breeding grounds, see below). The breeding ranges are as follows: (1) Oregon Junco, *J. o. oreganus*; breeds in w. Can. and Alaska. (2) Shufeldt's Junco, *J. o. shufeldti*; breeds from Can. s. to Ore. (except s. part). (3) Montana Junco, *J. o. montanus*; breeds from Can. s. to Idaho and nw. Mont. (4) Thurber's Junco, *J. o. thurberi*; breeds from s. Ore. s. throughout mts. of Calif. except where next race is found. (5) Point Pinos Junco, *J. o. pinosus*; coast district of cent. Calif. from San Mateo and Alamedo Cos. s. to Monterey Co.

RED-BACKED JUNCO. *Junco phœonotus:* (1) Red-backed Junco, *J. p. dorsalis*; breeds in high mts. of N.M. and ne. Ariz.; winters s. to sw. Tex. and Mex. (2) Arizona Junco, *J. p. palliatus*; resident of mts. of se. Ariz.

BREWER'S SPARROW. *Spizella breweri:* (1) Timberline Sparrow, *S. b. taverneri*; breeds in nw. British Col.; occurs in Mont. and Wash. in migration. (2) Brewer's Sparrow, *S. b. breweri*; breeds chiefly in Rocky Mt. section from Can. s. to N.M. and Ariz., and w. to e. Wash., e. Ore. (e. of Cascades), and Calif. (e. of Sierras, also local in s. Calif.); winters from s. Calif., s. Ariz., and cent. Tex. s.

BLACK-CHINNED SPARROW. *Spizella atrogularis:* (1) Mexican Black-chinned Sparrow, *S. a. atrogularis*; breeds in Ariz. and s. N.M. (2) California

Black-chinned Sparrow, *S. a. cana*; breeds locally in s. Calif. n. to Monterey Co. and Owens Valley; occasionally farther.

WHITE-CROWNED SPARROW. *Zonotrichia leucophrys:* (1) White-crowned Sparrow, *Z. l. leucophrys*; breeds in high mts. of w. U.S. from Can. s. in Rockies to n. N.M. and in Sierras to cent. Calif.; migrates through Rocky Mt. region s. into Mex.; winters in s. Ariz., N.M., and Tex. (2) Gambel's Sparrow, *Z. l. gambeli*; breeds from Can. s. to cent. Mont.; migrates throughout w. U.S. except nw. coast belt; winters from Calif. and Ut. s. (3) Puget Sound Sparrow, *Z. l. pugetensis*; breeds in humid nw. coast belt from Wash. s. to n. Calif. (Mendocino Co.); winters s. along coast to s. Calif. (4) Nuttall's Sparrow, *Z. l. nuttalli*; permanent resident around San Francisco Bay region and along coast of cent. Calif. from Mendocino Co. to Santa Barbara Co.

FOX SPARROW. *Passerella iliaca.* A highly migratory species, with numerous (16) critical subspecies. Many are known as yet from very limited areas in the breeding season, and their migration routes and wintering grounds are scarcely known. Seven subspecies breed north of the U.S. and swarm through the Pacific Coast States on migration and in winter, where they mingle with Fox Sparrows of eight other races which breed in those three States. Those from n. of the U.S. boundary are: (1) Alberta Fox, *P. i. altivagans*; (2) Shumagin Fox, *P. i. unalaschensis*; (3) Kodiak Fox, *P. i. insularis*; (4) Valdez Fox, *P. i. sinuosa*; (5) Yakutat Fox, *P. i. annectens;* (6) Townsend's Fox, *P. i. townsendi*; and (7) Thick-billed Fox, *P. i. mega-rhyncha.* Even the Eastern Fox Sparrow, *P. i. iliaca*, occurs occasionally in the Pacific States. For the sake of clarity the following form of analysis is given: WASHINGTON, the Sooty Fox, *P. i. fuliginosa*, breeds on the coast and ids. in the nw. corner of Wash. and winters s. along the coast. Several other races migrate along the coast, and at least two, Shumagin Fox and Valdez Fox, are to be expected in winter. The Slate-colored Fox, *P. i. schistacea*, breeds in e. Wash. w. to the Cascades. OREGON, three breed: (1) Slate-colored Fox, *P. i. schistacea* (e. Ore.); (2) Warner Mountains Fox, *P. i. fulva* (Steens, Hart, and Warner Mts. and e. slope of Cascades n. to cent. Ore.); (3) Yosemite Fox, *P. i. mariposæ* (Siskiyous and w. slope of Cascades in Jackson and Josephine Cos.). None of these winter. Several other races migrate along the coast from the n., and at least three, Kodiak, Valdez, and Yakutat, are known to winter. CALIFORNIA, six breed: (1) Warner Mountains Fox, *P. i. fulva* (high mts. of ne. |Calif. from Modoc and Lassen Cos. n.); (2) Trinity Fox, *P. i. brevicauda* (inner n. coast ranges of Calif. from Trinity Co. s. to Mendocino Co. and Colusa Co.); (3) Inyo Fox, *P. i. canescens* (White Mts. of Inyo and Mono Cos., also mts. of cent. Nev.); (4) Mono Fox, *P. i. monoënsis* (e. slope of Sierras in vicinity of Mono Lake); (5) Yosemite Fox, *P. i. mariposæ* (n. and cent. Sierras s. to Inyo Co.); (6) Stephens's Fox, *P. i. stephensi* (San Gabriel, San Bernardino, and San Jacinto Mts., Mt. Pinos, and s. Sierras n. to Fresno Co.). These six races winter together westward toward the coast, where they are joined by eight other races. ROCKY MT. REGION, only one race occurs, the Slate-colored Fox, *P. i. schistacea*; breeds in Idaho, Mont., n. Nev., Ut., Wyo., and w. Colo. (rare); migrates sparingly to Ariz. and N.M.

LINCOLN'S SPARROW. *Melospiza lincolni:* (1) Lincoln's Sparrow, *M. l. lincolni*; breeds in high mts. from Can. s. in Cascades, Sierras, and Rockies to s. Calif. and n. N.M.; migrates through lowlands of w. U.S.; winters from cent. Calif., Ariz., and cent. Tex. s. into Mex. (2) Forbush's Sparrow, *M. l. gracilis*; breeds in Alaska; winters in cent. Calif. s. to Monterey, casually to s. Calif.

SONG SPARROW. *Melospiza melodia.* Song Sparrows of seventeen races breed in the West from Can. s. to s. Calif., sw. Ariz., and n. N.M. They winter from Wash. and Mont. s. into Mex. Most of them are permanently resident or partially resident in the areas in which they breed. Races that migrate into areas where they do not breed are as follows: GREAT PLAINS, Dakota Song; SOUTHERN ROCKY MT. REGION, Mountain Song; GREAT BASIN REGION, Merrill's Song; WASHINGTON, Sooty Song (nw. coast), Yakutat Song (coast), and Merrill's Song (e.); OREGON, Yakutat Song (coast), and Merrill's Song (inland); CALIFORNIA, Mountain Song (se.), Yakutat Song (along n. coast), Rusty Song (coast to cent. Calif.), Modoc Song (w. and s. Calif.), Merrill's Song (chiefly e.). Breeding ranges are as follows: (1) Dakota Song Sparrow, *M. m. juddi*; extreme e. Mont. (2) Mountain Song Sparrow, *M. m. fallax*; Rocky Mt. district (ne. Ore., e. Nev., cent. and s. Idaho, w. Mont., Wyo., Colo., Ut., and n. N.M.). (3) Modoc Song Sparrow, *M. m. fisherella*; e. Ore. (except Blue Mt. section), sw. Idaho, nw. Nev., and ne. Calif. (e. of Sierras). (4) Merrill's Song Sparrow, *M. m. merrilli*; e. Wash. (e. of Cascades) and n. Idaho. (5) Rusty Song Sparrow, *M. m. morphna*; w. Wash. and w. Ore. (w. of Cascades). (6) Mendocino Song Sparrow, *M. m. cleonensis*; coast of nw. Calif. (Mendocino Co. to Ore. line; also coast of extreme sw. Ore.). (7) Samuels's Song Sparrow, *M. m. samuelis*; salt marshes of n. side of San Francisco Bay and s. side of San Pablo Bay, Calif. (8) Suisun Song Sparrow, *M. m. maxillaris*; lowlands surrounding Suisun Bay, w.-cent. Calif. (9) Modesto Song Sparrow, *M. m. mailliardi*; interior valleys of Calif. (Sacramento and n. San Joaquin Valleys s. to Stanislaus Co. except vicinity of Suisun Bay). (10) Alameda Song Sparrow, *M. m. pusillula*; salt marshes around s. arm of San Francisco Bay, Calif. (11) Heermann's Song Sparrow, *M. m. heermanni*; s. San Joaquin Valley, Calif. (Merced Co. to Kern Co.). (12) San Diego Song Sparrow, *M. m. cooperi*; coast district of s. Calif. n. to Santa Barbara. (13) Santa Cruz Song Sparrow, *M. m. santæcrucis*; coast district of cent. Calif. s. of San Francisco Bay to San Luis Obispo Co. (14) Santa Barbara Song Sparrow, *M. m. graminea*; Santa Barbara Id., Calif. (15) San Clemente Song Sparrow, *M. m. clementæ*; San Clemente, Santa Cruz, and Santa Rosa Ids., Calif. (16) San Miguel Song Sparrow, *M. m. micronyx*; San Miguel Id., Calif. (17) Desert Song Sparrow, *M. m. saltonis*; deserts of se. Calif., s. Nev., sw. Ut., and sw. Ariz. (18) Sooty Song Sparrow, *M. m. rufina*; se. Alaska.

HOME–REFERENCE SUGGESTIONS

THIS handbook is primarily a field guide. *The Book of Birds,* obtainable from the National Geographic Society, Washington, D.C., is recommended as a companion volume for home use. This contains an almost complete series of color portraits of both Eastern and Western birds. *Birds of the Pacific States,* by Ralph Hoffmann (Houghton Mifflin Company), is an excellent handbook for use in California, Oregon, and Washington. It gives seasonal dates and approximate abundance of different species in the three Pacific States, and also goes into more detail on voice than was possible in this volume. *Birds of New Mexico,* by Florence Merriam Bailey, which is available through the New Mexico Department of Game and Fish, Santa Fe, New Mexico, is a splendid volume for use anywhere in the Southwest. Be sure to consult your nearest museum or bird club about any available local publications or lists.

Following is a list of the most important or recent publications covering different States and major regions: WASHINGTON: *Distributional Check-List of the Birds of the State of Washington,* by E. A. Kitchin (Pacific Northwest Bird and Mammal Society, Seattle, Wash., 1934). OREGON: *Birds of Oregon,* by Gabrielson and Jewett (Oregon State College, Corvallis, Oregon, 1940). CALIFORNIA: (1) *Birds of the Pacific States,* by Ralph Hoffmann (Houghton Mifflin Company, 1927). (2) *Birds of California* (four large volumes), by William Leon Dawson, 1923; out of print. (3) *Animal Life in the Yosemite,* by Grinnell and Storer (University of California Press, 1924; out of print). ARIZONA: *A Distributional List of the Birds of Arizona,* by Harry S. Swarth (Pacific Coast Avifauna No. 10, Cooper Ornithological Club, University of California, 1914). NEVADA: *The Birds of Nevada,* by Jean M. Linsdale (Pacific Coast Avifauna No. 23, Cooper Ornithological Club, University of California, 1936). UTAH: No State publication at present, but one is contemplated. IDAHO: No State publication at present. MONTANA: *A Distributional List of the Birds of Montana,* by Aretas A. Saunders (Pacific Coast Avifauna No. 14, Cooper Ornithological Club, University of California, 1921). WYOMING: *Wyoming Bird Life,* by Otto McCreary (University of Wyoming, Laramie, 1937). COLORADO: (1) *A Guide to the Birds of Colorado,* by W. H. Bergtold (Smith-Brooks Printing Company, Denver, 1928). (2) *The Birds of Denver and Mountain Parks,* by Niedrach and Rockwell (Popular Series No. 5, Colorado Museum of Natural History, 1939). NEW MEXICO: *Birds of New Mexico,* by Florence Merriam Bailey (New Mexico Department of Game and Fish, Santa Fe, 1925).

TEXAS: Dr. H. C. Oberholser is completing a work on the Birds of Texas which should be of extreme value throughout the State. Until this comes out the following local publications, though treating limited areas, will be most useful. (1) *The Birds of Brewster County, Texas,* by Van Tyne and Sutton (Miscellaneous Publications No. 37, Museum of Zoölogy, University of Michigan, 1937). (2) *Birds of the Brownsville Region, Southern Texas,* by Griscom and Crosby (*The Auk* — July, 1925, October, 1925, and January, 1926).

For more complete data on ranges of Western birds, the *A.O.U. Check-List of North American Birds* (American Ornithologists' Union, Rudyerd Boulton, Treasurer, Field Museum of Natural History, Chicago, Ill.) is the standard. For reference in western Canada, use *Birds of Canada,* by P. A. Taverner (The Musson Book Company, Toronto).

INDEX

(Page numbers in italics refer to illustrations.)